D1244782

DRUGS and the LAW

Detection, Recognition & Investigation

by
Gary J. Miller

GOULD PUBLICATIONS, INC.

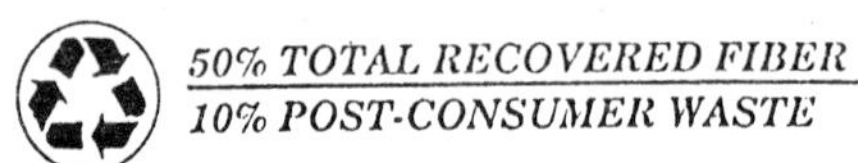

Published by
GOULD PUBLICATIONS, INC.
1333 North U.S. Hwy. 17-92
Longwood, FL 32750-3724
(407) 695-9500

ISBN 0-87526-398-4

PREFACE

One of the most serious problems in the world today is the use and abuse of a wide variety of chemical substances. Most Americans consider illicit drugs and alcohol in particular among the major problems facing our nation today. The concern is not only the high financial cost of enforcement, education and treatment, but the high social cost of American lives and the drug-related street crime that has made our cities increasingly unsafe.

America has been involved in a global war on drugs. Arrests have increased, the prison jail population has increased, drug seizures have gone up, millions of dollars in financial assets have been seized. Yet the problem is still there, and drug cartels continue to flourish. While drug abuse has stabilized somewhat, the problems of drug-related crime and unsafe streets continue to increase.

For the past 25 years, the U.S. strategy has been demand reduction (through education, treatment and rehabilitation) and supply reduction (through crop eradication, arrests, interdiction and seizures, asset forfeitures, etc.). Current efforts involve a comprehensive program to control each phase from the grower to the user. Pressure is being applied at all points in the chain resulting in increased seizures of drugs and financial assets, increased arrests and prosecution of traffickers, intensified investigations into money laundering and through effective education, prevention and treatment, and rehabilitation programs.

Drugs and the Law—Detection, Recognition & Investigation is an attempt to reach law enforcement officers, narcotics enforcement officers, students, counselors, educators, parents, and all the other dedicated people who are concerned with the drug problem. To be effective, it is important to have an accurate understanding of the law and procedures, the identification of drugs, the various ways drugs are packaged, the identification of people under the influence, the recognition of the characteristics of addiction, and all the related topics covered herein.

Officers must recognize and be able to handle many situations including encounters with motorists under the influence of a drug, or citizens under the influence of a drug on the street, in a residence or in a public place. An officer must know when he or she witnesses the buying or selling of controlled substances. The officer must know the elements of the crime and how to safely handle the situation. Knowledge about drugs is important because the officer can only enforce the law if violations of the law are recognized. It is also important because many drugs alter behavior as well as mood, perception and physiology. Some people become violent, combative, and assaultive when under the influence. Early recognition of drug influence could save lives.

In our society, people use drugs to modify how they perceive and feel about themselves and the world about them. Drugs are used to relieve pain, reduce anxiety, counter depression, heighten pleasure, aid in healing and for a

 md

variety of other reasons. The knowledge learned in studying this text will help you to be an effective force in reducing the drug problem and consequently decreasing those criminal offenses which are related to drug abuse.

Included after each chapter is a "REFERENCES" section. These listings will enable the reader to research selected topics in depth. At the end of this volume is a complete and comprehensive index.

Future editions are planned which will incorporate changes and new developments in the field. Please return the "IMPORTANT" subscription card at the front of this publication so that you can be notified of new editions as they are published.

Comments from users of this publication and ways to improve it to facilitate its use would be appreciated by the publisher.

ABOUT THE AUTHOR

Gary Miller first became interested in law enforcement while serving in the United States Navy. After an honorable discharge, Mr. Miller attended Santa Rosa Junior College, receiving an A.A. degree in Police Science. He continued his education at Sacramento State University, earning a B.A. degree. He furthered his educational goals at Washington State University where he received a M.A. degree in Police Science.

Mr. Miller has worked in a variety of jobs in the criminal justice system. He served as a correctional officer with the California Department of Corrections and as a probation officer with the Sonoma County Probation Department. His interest in drug abuse and addiction began while he was employed by the California Department of Justice, Bureau of Narcotics Enforcement, as a narcotics agent. Since that time he has been actively involved in police education and training as an assistant professor in the Administration of Justice Department at San Jose State University, a program specialist at Modesto Junior College Police Academy and instructor and program coordinator at San Jose City College. From 1979-1991, he served as the Director of the Central Coast Counties Police Academy.

Mr. Miller is presently teaching in the Police Academy, the Administration of Justice Degree Program and in-service training program for police officers at Gavilan Community College.

DEDICATION

This book is dedicated to all those who have devoted their lives to making this world a safer place to live.

A special dedication to those who have lost their lives to protect us.

A personal dedication to a friend and partner in fighting the drug war who tragically lost his life. To all that knew him, Lauren Platt, Special Agent with the California Bureau of Narcotic Enforcement, we miss you.

DRUGS and the LAW
Detection, Recognition and Investigation
TABLE OF CONTENTS

 md

This page intentionally left blank.

CHAPTER I

CURRENT CONSUMER PATTERNS OF ILLICIT DRUG USE

PRIMARY STUDIES

Although several studies indicate a downward trend, drug abuse continues to be a serious problem in the 1990s, especially in the United States.

One study by the National Institute on Drug Abuse (NIDA), the High School Senior Survey, reports on the drug use and related attitudes of U.S. high school seniors, college students, and young adults. The survey distinguishes among 11 classes of drugs ranging from marijuana and inhalants to hallucinogens, cocaine, heroin, and alcohol/tobacco. It focuses primarily on higher frequency rather than one-time use.

Over the study period 1975 to 1989, the NIDA survey indicates a considerable decline in the use of illicit drugs by high school seniors. In this age group, usage of crack and other forms of cocaine decreased the most. The report shows an even larger decline in drug use among college students and young adults. In addition to these figures, however, the study indicates that by their mid-twenties, over 80 percent of the young adults in the United States will have tried an illicit drug and that the level of drug use among American high school seniors and young adults is the highest of any industrialized nation.

A second report, begun in 1987 by the Partnership for a Drug-Free America, shows a corresponding reduction in overall drug use each successive year. Like the NIDA report, the Partnership's Attitude & Usage Study indicates a significant decrease in the use of cocaine, with usage among American teenagers dropping by 44 percent in 1986. However, the Partnership's study also revealed that in the 13- to 17-year old age group, overall drug use did not decrease in successive years since 1987, as it did for other age groups.

With respect to cocaine use, another report by the NIDA, the Household Survey, concurs with these two studies. The survey indicates that overall cocaine use dropped by 32 percent in the three-year period from 1985 to 1988.

Each of these studies involved different methodologies, age groups and time frames; yet all three have confirmed the same downward trends, especially in the use of cocaine.

GENERAL ACCOUNTING OFFICE SURVEY

Despite these figures of decreasing drug use, the General Accounting Office contends that Federal government surveys of crack cocaine use in the United States severely underestimate the problem.

Although the NIDA's annual High School Senior and Household surveys have shown overall declines in the use of cocaine, according to the GAO, those surveys do not include populations such as high school dropouts, drug treatment center patients, the homeless, and arrestees. The GAO concludes, "If these populations were considered, the estimate of the extent of the cocaine problem may be much higher."

The GAO's report to Representative Charles Rangel (D-NY), chairman of the House Select Committee on Narcotics Abuse and Control, was made public March 6, 1991. Rangel, who has long been critical of the White House's response to the nation's drug problem, said the GAO report was "finally, a government study that tells the whole story."[1] Considering the exclusion of large populations of drug users from national studies, the reports of a general downward trend may be obscuring a more extended and elusive problem of undetected drug abuse in the United States.

SOCIETAL COSTS

No one has discovered a way to do a completely accurate census of illicit drug use. However, some reliable estimates place the number of drug abusers well into the millions. While predominately poor urban neighborhoods remain the most visible and fertile ground for drug abuse activities, these activities also predominate in widely-varying geographic and demographic locations.

In Connecticut, the State Drug Abuse Commission concluded that 22 percent of the state's 7th- to 12th-grade students are "regular, substantial or extensive drug users." [2]

With statistics like these, the pervasiveness of the drug problem has engendered an overwhelming response by Americans in all economic and social strata. Based to a large degree on the intensive dissemination of information by the government and the media, the public tends to view drug abuse as a real and imminent threat to the home, the schools, the workplace, and the community as a whole. Daily reports and statistics of drug-related homicides, crimes of violence, overdoses, and personal tragedy have focused public opinion and personalized the physical and psychological dangers of illicit drug use.

Public opinion polls reflect this growing concern. Drug use is the number one problem identified by high school students and their parents. In a survey of "young professionals" conducted in 1989 and published by *Rolling Stone* magazine, 26 percent of those surveyed felt someone close to them had a serious drug problem. This increased personalization of the drug problem has helped make people aware of its urgency in the community; yet, despite the growing awareness, there remain to be addressed several extensive societal costs which threaten the livelihood of the nation as a whole.

The social effects of drug abuse are devastating. The most damaging consequence is that illicit drug trafficking impedes national economic productivity. It corrupts individuals with the lure of huge profits; it offers incentives to turn to crime to obtain the money needed to feed drug habits;

---

[1] Report GAO/HRD-91-55 FS, GAO, P.O. Box 6015, Gaithersburg, MD 20877.

[2] "Drug Trafficking: A Report to the President of the United States." U.S. Dept. of Justice, Office of the Attorney General, August 3, 1989, p. 2.

and, most importantly, it creates physical and economic dependencies that impair the ability to perform in school and the workplace.

A more direct economic impact lies in the fact that money spent on illicit drugs represents resources lost to legitimate productive enterprises. Furthermore, the funds laundered by drug dealers inevitably enter the economy and have the capacity to corrupt those who, sometimes unknowingly, assist in the laundering. As drug traffickers buy legitimate businesses, the effect is less to integrate the dealers into society than to draw parts of the economy into the drug trade. In addition to this direct economic impact of drug trafficking, the indirect economic effects of drug abuse carry over into the workplace, whether one considers the accidents caused by employees under the influence of drugs, the resulting decrease in productivity due to drug abuse, or the burden placed on employers when anti-drug-abuse programs must be implemented in their companies.

Another overlooked economic burden of drug abuse lies in the widespread implementation of health care and treatment. The abuse of drugs causes severe medical problems: death from overdoses, addicted mothers and newborns, and the spread of diseases such as AIDS and hepatitis through the sharing of contaminated needles by intravenous drug users. The channeling of scarce resources into health care and treatment (not to mention research) has increased the overall cost of the drug problem for the entire nation.

1. Costs to the Taxpayer

In fiscal year 1981, the Federal government's drug-related expenditures were $1.5 billion. In fiscal year 1990, the estimated cost will have nearly quadrupled to over $5.9 billion. These costs include drug-related law enforcement, prevention, and treatment programs. If additional expenditures are counted, such as state and local costs, assistance to foreign countries for eradication and training programs, and military and intelligence costs, the annual bill to taxpayers would exceed $12 billion.

The cost of Federal drug-related investigations has also advanced from $181.9 million in 1981 to an estimated $760.8 million in 1990. These funds support the domestic investigative efforts of a number of Federal agencies from the Drug Enforcement Administration (DEA) to the U.S. Park Service. A 1987 study from the President's Commission on Organized Crime estimated that 18 percent, or over $5 billion, of state and local law enforcement investigative resources was directed at drug-related investigations.

In addition to these law enforcement expenditures, the cost of drug prosecutions at the Federal level further illustrates the increasing drain on limited tax resources. The U.S. Attorney for the Western District of Tennessee states that the number of Assistant U.S. Attorneys assigned to drug-related cases increased 500 percent in 1987-1988. Similarly, the number of drug cases in the Western District of Wisconsin increased over 1,000 percent in the period from 1984 to 1988. Overall, Federal drug prosecution costs increased from $44.5 million in 1981 to a projected figure of $322 million in 1990. Taxpayers might also bear in mind that the funds necessary to support the Federal drug prosecution effort were often provided at the expense of other prosecutorial efforts such as white collar crime, racketeering, environmental, and antitrust litigation.

As the number of investigations and prosecutions grows, the cost of incarcerating convicted drug dealers also increases. Statistics from the Department of Justice estimate that 44 percent, or nearly half of the 49,925 Federal prisoners incarcerated in 1989 were charged with drug violations. The cost to the Federal government is approximately $12,000 per year per inmate, or over $239 million a year for this category of offender. Moreover, an additional 80,000 to 90,000 inmates are housed in state and local correctional facilities. These figures reveal just a few of the direct costs to taxpayers.

While the expenditure of Federal dollars to combat drug abuse is readily quantifiable, estimates of national revenues lost through the illegal drug trade are difficult to depict with precision. The Internal Revenue Service estimates that the underground economy generated by the illicit drug trade is between $25 and $30 billion a year. Assuming a 28 percent Federal tax bracket, the annual loss to the Federal government in uncollected taxes is $8 billion, conservatively. Loss of revenue from state and local taxes calculated at 10 percent is an additional $3.1 billion, resulting in a total estimated tax loss, per annum, of $11.1 billion.

Federal funds used to support treatment and prevention have also increased in recent years. In fiscal year 1987, $413.4 million was allocated for drug abuse treatment, with $532.9 million allocated for prevention. Estimates for 1990 are $735.3 million and $1.1 billion, respectively.

These burdensome expenditures are directed primarily at treating the estimated 37 million Americans who use illicit drugs and, secondarily, at educating the millions of others who do not understand the physical and psychological consequences of substance abuse.

Illicit drug abuse can lead to serious health complications. According to statistics from the Drug Abuse Warning Network (DAWN), cocaine, heroin, and other illegal drug use was the cause of death for more than 3,000 Americans in 1987, and the number is increasing. Despite the overall downward trend reported by national studies, these and several other state mortality rates underscore the current problem of drug abuse. In 1988, the U.S. Attorneys from North Carolina reported 49 cocaine-related deaths, compared to 28 in 1987. A report from the Vermont State Office of the Chief Medical Examiner also indicated a 400 percent increase in drug-related deaths from 1984 through 1987.

In addition to these mortality rates, hospitals and related health care institutions are reporting dramatic increases in drug-related infant addiction. The New York City Commissioner for Human Services reported a 284 percent increase in newborns testing positive for drugs during the years 1984 to 1988. In Multnomah County, Oregon, of the infants born addicted to drugs, 69 percent were reported affected by cocaine, 29 percent by marijuana, 22 percent by amphetamines, 5 percent by heroin, and 7 percent by other drugs. Crack, the highly addictive cocaine derivative, has also had a devastating effect on infants. In Tallahassee, Florida, a city of approximately 100,000, an estimated 20 crack babies are born each month, a large percentage of whom never survive infancy.

In the last decade, the health aspects of drug abuse have been even more widely publicized due to the relationship between intravenous drug use and

AIDS. New York City, which has more AIDS cases than any other U.S. city, has estimated that intravenous drug use is responsible for 35 percent of the known AIDS cases. Inner-city hospitals are also reporting increasing numbers of infants born with congenital AIDS.

These statistics indicate that drug use clearly exacerbates other medical problems and increases the cost of health care for the entire nation. Drug abuse causes health insurance premiums to rise and public facilities to become overcrowded, especially in economically deprived areas. As a matter of national concern, drug abuse and the health care required to deal with its effects have the potential to severely weaken the U.S. economy. One study suggests that the cost to treat one infant born to a crack cocaine-addicted mother may be as high as $125,000.[3]

One other important consideration in calculating costs to taxpayers is that the health complications caused by drug abuse divert scarce resources that could be employed in treating other high-priority medical problems.

2. Corruption

In addition to the national economic burden caused by the treatment of drug abuse, the lure of huge profits derived from the drug trade also threatens to weaken our drug law enforcement system. The enormous funds generated by illicit drug trade are often used for the corruption of public officials. In southwestern Kentucky's Morgan County, a two-year undercover investigation resulted in the conviction of both the Judge Executive and the Sheriff. Both law enforcement officials were found guilty of accepting $5,000 monthly payments to protect a large cocaine distribution ring within their jurisdiction. The combination of large profits and low pay makes some state and local law enforcement officers susceptible to such corruption by drug dealers. Often, this corruption takes the form of simply ignoring planes landing on remote airstrips or failing to patrol rural highways. In the last few years, Tennessee's Eastern District has witnessed the conviction of seven sitting sheriffs and two former sheriffs for accepting bribes from drug traffickers.

In the Western District of Tennessee, moreover, it was discovered that the county sheriff and his chief investigator were actively assisting the operation of a marijuana and cocaine distribution ring. The organization imported marijuana as well as cultivated it in rural areas of the county. Among other offenses, the sheriff and his assistant acted as accomplices by selling confiscated drugs to members of the distribution ring. These corrupted law enforcement officials effectively squeezed out the drug trade competition by confiscating their drugs and re-selling them to a protected distribution ring. Another example of such corruption can be cited from Pitkin County, Colorado. Reports have concluded that Pitkin County's former sheriff, upon learning of a Federal undercover investigation, placed an advertisement in the local newspaper warning residents of the investiga-

---

[3] "A Report to the President of the United States." U.S. Dept. of Justice, Office of the Attorney General, August 3, 1989.

tion and advising them to leave the area if they had recently sold drugs to strangers.

This ready temptation for fast money extends to Federal officials as well. In a case reported by the Western District of Tennessee, a Drug Enforcement Administration agent was sentenced to five years in prison after pleading guilty to using his position to assist drug smuggling efforts in the Memphis area and to disclosing sensitive and confidential government information to drug organizations. Even a U.S. congressman in the Northern District of Georgia was convicted of lying to a grand jury in a case growing out of a money laundering scheme.

3. The Workplace

On a more local scale, estimates of the extent of drug abuse in the workplace vary, but they all indicate that it is becoming a crisis. A 1984 government study assessed the annual cost of unrealized productivity due to drug use at $33 billion.[4] Furthermore, drugs which were once viewed as a problem primarily among lower-income groups have moved to the boardroom and Wall Street. Drug use in the workplace has effects that reach far beyond the individual user; drug-impaired employees endanger themselves as well as their fellow workers. The results of such drug use include the loss of productivity as well as increases in absenteeism, theft, workers' compensation and health benefit claims, and work-related accidents. Unquantifiable costs include lower employee morale, increased legal liability of employees, and family financial problems.

Drug abuse in the workplace has created an additional cost to the employer that is eventually passed on to the consumer: drug testing. Incidents such as the Amtrak tragedy in 1987, in which 16 people died, and the subsequent discovery that the involved engineers tested positive for drug use, have created the need for extensive and accurate drug testing. A related incident in the Middle District of Pennsylvania in 1988 revealed that three employees of the Peach Bottom nuclear power plant were selling large quantities of methamphetamine to fellow employees. The prosecution of these employees revealed that a number of workers had used drugs on the job, endangering the lives of thousands of citizens. Even among Fortune 500 companies, drug testing of applicants or workers increased from 3 percent in 1982 to an estimated 40 percent in 1989.

4. The Environment

The costs of domestically growing and producing illicit drugs are borne by all Americans. Marijuana farmers and clandestine laboratory operators are responsible for the pollution of numerous waterways and underground streams throughout the United States as well as for creating public safety hazards in national forests and residential communities.

Marijuana cultivators, in particular, are responsible for the careless destruction of foliage and wildlife. Poisons such as Warfarin and Havoc are used in several areas where deer have acquired a taste for the cannabis

---

[4] "Drugs in the Workplace." National Criminal Justice Reference Service, TB010620, No. 47.

plant. As a result, California growers in 1984 were responsible for the deaths of more than 1,600 deer. In some areas, growers have used as much as 300 pounds of rodenticide per acre. Such massive use not only kills the rodents, but also birds and other small wildlife, thus introducing these poisons indirectly into the human food chain.

The carcinogenic and highly toxic chemicals used in the laboratory production of illegal substances also present extreme hazards to the environment. Each year, the DEA pays over $5 million to have these chemicals removed and destroyed. However, when the laboratory operators dump these directly into the ground or local sanitation system, the chemicals cannot be readily removed and threaten to pollute water supplies. These same chemicals present dangers to law enforcement officials as well. In Oregon, for example, state and local regulations require all law enforcement personnel to wear protective clothing when entering laboratory sites. And in the Eastern District of California, it is estimated that 4 percent of all clandestine laboratory raids result in the hospitalization of at least one investigator, making this the largest single source of on-the-job injury incurred by Federal drug agents.

Even the public is put directly at risk by these manufacturers and growers. It is estimated that one in five clandestine laboratories experience a fire or explosion. Unfortunately, the majority of laboratory discoveries are made possible by these accidents. Other public hazards are caused by marijuana growers who protect their plots with armed guards or booby traps. Often pipe bombs, punji pits, animal traps, electric fences, and guard dogs are used by growers to deter confiscation or theft of their crops. These devices can be activated by anyone, including unsuspecting visitors and law enforcement personnel. Thus, the presumption of public access to public lands does not always apply in areas of extensive illegal cultivation. Parks and forests in Hawaii and California have been closed to visitors and employees on several occasions until law enforcement authorities were able to reclaim the land. Not even the animal refuges are safe. In Gelmer County, Georgia, a black bear was found dead from overdosing on a duffel bag of cocaine dropped in a clandestine landing area.

5. Increased Crime

As the increasing use of harmful defense mechanisms by drug cultivators would indicate, the links between drug abuse and crime are real and growing stronger. Several Department of Justice statistics confirm this hypothesis. The Department's National Institute of Justice reports that in fiscal year 1988 more than one-half of the male arrestees in 14 major cities tested positive for drug use, and the Federal prison sentences for drugs between the years 1980 and 1990 increased 274 percent.[5]

---

[5] "Bureau of Justice Statistics, National Update." U.S. Dept. of Justice, Office of Justice Programs, April 1992, Vol. 1, No. 4.

In 1990, the Federal Bureau of Investigation (FBI) reported an estimated 1,089,500 State and local arrests in drug abuse violations in the United States. Compare this with 559,900 arrests in 1981. Over the past 9 years these totals have increased substantially.[6]

Almost half of all Federal offenders sentenced to prison in 1990 were convicted of drug offenses. In some states the percentage is higher.[7]

The links between drug use and criminal behavior are further documented by research. One report from Baltimore, Maryland states that addicts committed four to six times more crime during periods of heavy drug use than in periods when they were relatively drug-free.[8]

A 1985 research project by Johnson, et al., entitled *Taking Care of Business*, in Harlem, N.Y. revealed that daily heroin abusers averaged 1,400 crimes a year, while those who used heroin three times a week averaged 500 crime per year.[9] The message is clear that a decline in drug use will cause a decline in individual crime rates among drug users.

These and other effects of drug abuse inevitably influence our entire nation. From decreased economic viability to environmental damage, the societal costs incurred by drug trafficking and drug abuse make it clear that the current drug problem in the United States is far from a definitive resolution.

PRINCIPAL DRUGS OF ABUSE

COCAINE/CRACK

Cocaine usage illustrates the pervasiveness of drug abuse and drug addiction in the United States. Far from being confined to usage by the "junkie on the street," cocaine is often cited as the drug of choice for the upwardly mobile, affluent drug user. Districts across the country have reported on cocaine's widespread use by people from all social backgrounds and economic strata.

Representative of areas reporting widespread cocaine usage among the affluent is Columbus, Ohio, where the cocaine clientele is characterized as "predominately white collar, upwardly mobile whites." Reports from New Jersey describe an organization of addicts, sellers, and distributors that, among its members, include a number of stock and bond brokers who are simultaneously employed at Wall Street brokerage firms in New York City.

The penetration of cocaine usage into America's heartland can be exemplified by the fact that 86 percent of 1987 drug cases prosecuted in the Western District of Wisconsin involved cocaine. And in the predominately

---

[6] "Drugs & Crime Data, Fact Sheet: Drug Data Summary." U.S. Dept. of Justice, Office of Justice Programs, Bureau of Justice Statistics, November 1991.

[7] "Bureau of Justice Statistics, National Update." U.S. Dept. of Justice, Office of Justice Programs, January 1992, Vol. 1, No. 3.

[8] Ball, Shaffer, Nurco. "Day-to-Day Criminality of Heroin Addicts in Baltimore," 1983.

[9] Reported in a *Manual for Police Chiefs and Sheriffs, Reducing Crime by Reducing Drug Abuse.* U.S. Dept. of Justice, Bureau of Justice Assistance, Washington, D.C., June 1988.

rural Northern District of Iowa, twice as much cocaine was seized in 1988 as in any previous year. District reports in Iowa conclude that "cocaine is readily available in all communities, to all levels of society, from the metropolitan areas to the smallest rural villages." It should be kept in mind that in Iowa the phrase "metropolitan areas" refers to such places as Des Moines, Davenport, Cedar Rapids, and Council Bluffs—not New York, Chicago, Los Angeles, or Miami. In other states, far removed from major metropolitan areas such as New York and Los Angeles, cocaine is also readily available. The Middle District of North Carolina reports being "awash in cocaine", while Kansas reports that "the cocaine abuse problem has risen to an alarming level." [10]

In recent years, variant and even more deadly forms of cocaine have been synthesized in laboratories or produced through techniques that concentrate the cocaine to make it more powerful. The most widely used form of this "altered" cocaine is known as "crack."

Crack, a form of cocaine that has been processed for smoking, has grown enormously in usage and distribution in recent years. Crack is both less expensive and more physically and psychologically destructive than is traditional cocaine. Cocaine HCl is cocaine hydrochloride, which is cocaine in powdered form used for snorting or injecting. It is soluble in water, while crack cocaine is insoluble. Crack cocaine is processed from cocaine HCl by using baking soda, water and heat. The end result is cocaine that can only be heated to vapors and inhaled into the lungs.

Prior to the mid-1980s, most users "snorted" cocaine or injected it subcutaneously. The development of smokeable crack cocaine has greatly altered this usage pattern. Not only is the unit cost of crack lower than that of traditional cocaine HCl, but its effects are more intense and short-lived. Crack also has the advantage of relieving addicts' fears of using needles that have been contaminated by AIDS or other communicable diseases.

With its small dosage units and low cost, crack has opened up an entirely new, lucrative market of low-income users. Indeed, there is evidence to indicate that its development was directly aimed at increasing the cocaine market by providing a low-cost version of the drug. While an ounce of cocaine HCl worth $1,000 converts to 25,000 milligrams of crack with a street price of $2,500, the real profit in crack is generated by its remarkably high sales volume. Crack's profitability, ease of processing, and ease of transportation, combined with the user's need for a more frequent "hit" than with other forms of cocaine, have provided pushers with a new, easily marketable product that creates a heavy, repetitive demand.

Originally, crack was distributed primarily by local dealer networks which would buy the traditional cocaine HCl from wholesalers, convert it to crack, and then sell it to users. This system of local preparation has given way to the involvement of larger organizations in the direct processing,

---

[10] "Drug Trafficking: A Report to the President of the United States." U.S. Dept. of Justice, Office of the Attorney General, August 3, 1989.

distribution, and sale of crack. Intense competition for market share and "turf" has led to violent crack wars in major distribution areas.

Based upon information obtained from intelligence sources, drug treatment clinics, and street studies units, it is fairly clear that, in addition to intravenous cocaine use, the use of crack continues to gain in popularity. Given that national studies indicate an overall decline in cocaine use, this estimate would suggest that the frequency of crack use among dependent individuals is increasing at a far greater rate than the use of traditional cocaine in the general population.

In its 1990 report, "The Crack Cocaine Epidemic: Health Consequences and Treatment," the GAO states that those who smoke crack are as likely as intravenous cocaine users to contract the human immunodeficiency virus (HIV), which causes AIDS. The report cites a study of prostitutes indicating that, since crack users often combine sex with drug use, they more commonly contract such sexually transmitted diseases (STDs) as gonorrhea, trichonomas, chlamydia, genital warts, and syphilis. These STDs, particularly those that cause genital ulcers, have been found to "greatly increase the risk that HIV infection, when present, will be transmitted."

The GAO report concludes that smoking cocaine in crack form has increased in recent years because it provides users with a more rapid and intense drug experience than snorting cocaine. Users also see it as safer than snorting cocaine, which can cause injury to nasal membranes, or injecting the drug, which poses the threat of infections such as HIV.

However, the GAO reveals that there are greater health risks involved in the smoking of crack since it is a more highly addictive substance than traditional cocaine and since extended use increases the possibility of psychiatric disorders, strokes, or even death. Prenatal exposure is also known to result in infant dependency or developmental deficiencies.

Crack is of special concern to law enforcement officials due to the alarming speed with which it has established itself in areas across the country. The crack problems of such coastal cities as New York, Washington, D.C., Miami, and Los Angeles have been well covered in the news media, but reports from other jurisdictions around the country reinforce the severity of crack's growth in use and availability.

The Savannah, Georgia office of the DEA estimates that 80 percent of the cocaine traffic in its jurisdiction involves crack, and the Southern District of Georgia reports that "crack is quickly approaching epidemic proportions in south Georgia." Authorities in neighboring Alabama say that "the major drug problem confronting south Alabama is clearly crack" and report "a crack explosion" in Mobile. In the heart of the Midwest, Fort Wayne, Indiana—whose motto is "City of Churches"—has been given a new motto by drug enforcement authorities, "the crack capital of Indiana." In this city of 182,000, between 60 and 70 "crack houses" (distribution centers for crack) are in operation. This "epidemic of major proportions" developed within the 18-month period from 1988 to 1989.[11]

Crack use appears to be spreading rapidly across the country from large cities to small towns. An undercover operation in the small town of Temple, Texas, revealed that defendants were using stolen food stamps to buy crack.

In the Central District of California, the U.S. Attorney reports that the two major street gangs of Los Angeles, the Crips and the Bloods, have been establishing crack distribution outlets in cities across the country.[12] The Los Angeles Police Department has identified 47 cities, from Seattle to Kansas City to Baltimore, in which Los Angeles street gang traffickers have appeared. Typically, the traffickers transport 5 to 20 shipments of cocaine from Los Angeles into other cities; the cocaine is then converted into crack form. Since Los Angeles is the base of these crack distribution networks, profits from crack sales are returned there.

In New York as well, investigative information continues to show that the crack market is structured and supplied at the street level by large drug organizations capable of providing 100,000 vials of crack per week. One crack organization operated by two brothers from the Dominican Republic was dismantled in 1988. The organization distributed crack under the brand name "Basedballs" and was believed to be responsible for the sale of 10,000 vials per day.[13]

As crack usage becomes more prevalent, the need for treatment also increases. Yet the pyschological and physical effects of crack are different than other illicit drugs. The GAO report[14] states that populations using crack "are both harder to treat and have special needs that many traditional [drug] treatment programs are not designed to meet." The report outlines such traditional methods as detoxification, outpatient programs, therapeutic communities, and short-term residential programs. It also notes that between 1990 and 1991, the NIDA was investigating at least 13 drugs to aid in crack treatment by such means as replacement therapies, blocking the effect of the drug, tempering or eliminating withdrawal, or preventing addiction from occurring.

These representative reports from districts across the nation illustrate the powerful appeal of crack to new markets of users as well as the effect of crack use on diverse locales throughout the country.

HEROIN

There are an estimated one-half to three-quarters of a million heroin addicts in the United States. Of these, over 200,000 are estimated to be in the New York City/Hudson Valley area. Among addictive illicit drugs, this

---

[11] "Drug Trafficking: A Report to the President of the United States." U.S. Dept. of Justice, Office of the Attorney General, 1989.

[12] *Ibid.*

[13] *International Drug Report.* International Narcotic Enforcement Officers Association, Vol. 3, No. 7, July 1990.

[14] Report GAO/HRD-91-55FS, GAO, P.O. Box 6015, Gaithersburg, MD 20877.

makes heroin second only to cocaine in both the extent of its use and its devastating social effects.

The heroin available in the United States originates principally from three sources: Mexico, Southeast Asia (Burma, Thailand, and Laos), and Southwest Asia (Afghanistan, Pakistan, and Iran). "The Golden Triangle," encompassing eastern Burma, northern Thailand and northern Laos, produces more heroin than any other region in the world. The Golden Triangle's 1991 opium crop has been estimated at 2,500 tons, or what will eventually become 250 tons of heroin. Of this opium crop, 2,000 tons were produced in Burma (the world's largest opium producer), some 300 tons in Laos, and 15-20 tons in Thailand.

Although Burma produces the most opium, Thailand, with its entrenched drug network, acts as the most important heroin conduit for Western countries. Thailand's drug network is comprised primarily of couriers, or "mules," who come from a wide range of nationalities. Drug enforcement agents have been successful in apprehending several of these low-level offenders, exemplified by the growing number of African couriers caught in Thailand. In 1990, 116 Nigerians were arrested in Bangkok.

Through its availability, heroin continues to be one of the most problematic addictive drugs. Increasing ease of access threatens to make heroin use even more widespread in the future. In the 1970s, drug dealers made huge profits from the sale of marijuana; in the 1980s, they made fortunes from cocaine. The networks established in the 70s and 80s to ship and market marijuana and cocaine are now ideal for heroin. Colombian exporters predict that, in the 1990s, heroin will be the drug of choice in the United States.

Colombian exporters may well be promoting their own drug trafficking efforts. The climate in Colombia is excellent for cultivation of the poppy plant, from which heroin is derived. Forty-five percent of the gum removed from a Colombian poppy pod contains raw morphine. Compared to a morphine content of 18 to 33 percent in other heroin-producing areas, the cultivation methods used in Colombia produce more morphine base with fewer plants.

Since at least 1984, Colombian farmers have been growing small plots of poppy plants. Colombia's heroin exports were then minuscule. But in January 1992, investigations revealed that poppies are growing on more than 50,000 acres in 12 Colombian departments. Most of the plantations have been discovered southwest of Bogota. According to Colombian officials, guerillas of the Colombian Revolutionary Armed Forces and the National Liberation Army are actively engaged in the heroin trade.

In addition to this military involvement in the heroin trade, it has also been determined through observation of the chemical "signatures" found in Colombian heroin, that chemists from Iran and Thailand are residing in the Colombian and Bolivian opium regions. The main chemical precursor—a necessary chemical in the manufacturing of a particular drug—for heroin production, acetic anhydride, is difficult to acquire in Colombia. By using alternate precursors, or changing the "recipe," Colombian heroin has developed its own signature. From such signatures, DEA chemists have detected the presence of both Southeast Asian (SEA) and Southwest Asian

(SWA) chemists in Colombian-produced heroin. These circumstances enable DEA chemists to monitor the heroin that originates in Colombia. Evidently, another function of these SEA and SWA chemists is to teach Colombian chemists heroin-processing techniques.

The involvement of both armed organizations and international drug manufacturers makes law enforcement against heroin particularly vital in Colombia. The Colombian National Police (CNP) have seized several labs and destroyed approximately 2,500 acres of poppy fields to date. It appears that heroin processors are now having some difficulty obtaining enough morphine base for heroin production; yet, the market for heroin in the United States continues to thwart law enforcement efforts.

Heroin traffickers employ several methods of smuggling the drug from both the Far East and South America to the United States. Seizures made by the DEA/New York show that heroin is often brought first into Canada, then into the New York metropolitan area. Swallowing drug-filled condoms and boarding flights directly to New York or Miami is also a currently-used method of smuggling. Employing such methods on commercial air flights, heroin smugglers have a wide variety of routes from which to choose. If heroin production increases, other methods such as those utilized in cocaine smuggling, are likely to be employed.

New York City is America's most significant heroin importation and distribution center. Each year DEA/New York is responsible for 30 to 60 percent of the DEA's total heroin seizures nationwide. According to intelligence agencies, recent seizure analysis, and investigative information, heroin traffickers operating in New York are currently developing new trafficking routes, expanding distribution, and selling a processed heroin of very high purity. The drug continues to be available at all levels of supply and, at the street level, heroin purities remain higher than throughout the rest of the city. Far exceeding their traditional range, current street purity levels are ranging from 2 to 75 percent, with a citywide average of 41 percent.

According to recent reports, heroin is emerging as a primary drug of abuse. Increasingly, drug users are becoming aware of the physical risks involved in taking crack or cocaine, and they are shifting to heroin which produces a longer high. The purity and potency of the heroin now available also makes it easier to "snort" or inhale, thus eliminating the need for intravenous injection, which has served as a deterrent to the casual heroin user.

Southeast Asian (SEA) heroin is the most available type of heroin in the city, followed by Southwest Asian (SWA) heroin. Mexican black tar heroin and Colombian source heroin occasionally turn up in New York on a sporadic basis but always in small amounts.

Despite the drug's increased availability, purity, and usage, heroin investigations have had a slight impact on heroin trafficking in both New York and California. One of New York's most significant investigations occurred in September 1990 and resulted in the seizure of over eight million dollars, the largest amount of money ever seized in connection with a heroin investigation. After extensive surveillance over a six-month period, search warrants executed at three Brooklyn locations led to four arrests, seizure of one submachine gun, approximately 350 grams of heroin, one heroin press, cylinders, wrapping and cutting material, and the record amount of over eight million dollars in cash. The cash was found inside 20 suitcases and duffel bags.[15]

In what has been termed the nation's largest heroin seizure, U.S. Customs and Drug Enforcement officials netted more than half a ton of heroin in a San Francisco, California area warehouse raid on June 21, 1991. The seizure involved 1,080 pounds of china white heroin. The street value of the heroin was estimated at about $3 billion, according to Bob Bender, Special Agent in Charge of the San Francisco DEA Office. This heroin shipment was first discovered in the middle of May, 1991 during a routine check of imports by Customs Inspectors at the Port of Oakland. The heroin had been shipped from Taiwan aboard the vessel "President Truman." It was then traced to a warehouse in Hayward, California (in the San Francisco area) where four principals of an Asian drug ring were arrested. The shipment originated somewhere in the "Golden Triangle" of Burma, Laos and Thailand.[16]

Although the Federal government is now engaged in international negotiations to reduce the supply of opium and its foreign manufacture into heroin, as well as to increase border surveillance to reduce its importation, we cannot be optimistic about their efforts. Previous attempts by the United States to stop foreign cultivation and manufacture have proved unsuccessful.

HEROIN SUBSTITUTES

In addition to illicit use of heroin, analgesics with accepted medical uses have long been abused by the heroin addict population. Last year saw a continuation in the popularity of hydromorphone (Dilaudid) among intravenous addicts, and oxycodone (Percodan) among oral addicts. Fentanyl (Sublimaze), 80 times more powerful than morphine, was used not only as a heroin substitute but also as a narcotic of choice. Analogs of fentanyl have begun to appear in California as unauthorized chemists have determined how to "design" drugs, or alter their chemical structure, thus circumventing the Controlled Substances Act.

MARIJUANA

Marijuana abuse patterns are beginning to undergo significant changes. Although commercial grades of primarily Colombian-source marijuana remain widely available and abused, more potent grades of marijuana including domestic sinsemilla are increasing in usage, especially among older, more experienced users. Due to the significantly higher potency of sinsemilla and manicured marijuana, as compared to commercial grades, there is some reason to believe that the potency factor, rather than increased incidence of marijuana use among younger persons, is primarily responsible for the increase in marijuana-related emergency room episodes.

Marijuana is the only illicit drug that is domestically cultivated for commercial use in illicit drug trafficking. It is estimated that approximately

---

[15] "Trends in Traffic: Heroin." *International Drug Report*. International Narcotic Enforcement Officers Association.

[16] *The California Narcotic Officer*. CNOA, Vol. 8, No. 4, Oct. 1991, Santa Clarita, CA 91350.

25 percent of the U.S. supply of marijuana in 1988 was domestically produced. Foreign suppliers of marijuana include Mexico, Jamaica, Thailand, Colombia, Laos, and Belize.

In many ways, the most overtly sinister aspects of domestic organizations that deal primarily in marijuana trafficking involve the violence and ruthlessness with which they pursue their cultivation, distribution, and sales activities. Commercial cultivators booby-trap their plots and are often armed with sophisticated weapons and surveillance equipment to protect them.

Some growers, especially in the western United States, insinuate their cultivation activities into national forests and other public lands for the purpose of concealment and to minimize risk should they be caught. By operating on publicly owned property, the grower denies the government the legal remedy of confiscation of the land on which the illegal activity is being perpetrated.

Marijuana cultivation activity in some rural areas is so intense that it distorts entire local economies through the influence of the drug monies it generates. These are often areas in which some of the local inhabitants consider marijuana cultivation to be neither immoral nor undesirable, and in which these residents welcome part-time work in cultivation as a supplemental source of income. In some rural communities, marijuana has even become the primary cash crop, developing an underground economy with fixed prices to benefit everyone involved in the drug's cultivation and distribution.

Domestic marijuana growers are also developing more advanced growing techniques. Most efforts center around the development of techniques to increase the marijuana's level of THC (the active chemical). For example, they cultivate sinsemilla, the potent unpollinated female plant. Growers also use hydroponic techniques (the growth of plants in nutrient-rich water rather than in soil) to increase the crop's yield and concentrate the plant's active ingredients. To decrease the possibility of detection, indoor cultivation is also on the rise.

An investigation in 1988 in Wyoming revealed a case of two men who had indoor hydroponic marijuana operations near Henry, Nebraska, and Guernsey, Wyoming. The two friends exchanged ideas and information on marijuana cultivation but maintained independent operations with independent customers. One of the men developed an automatic watering and fertilization system, and the other developed an automatic, timed track-lighting system. In addition to sharing these ideas, they purchased their growing equipment together to reduce overall costs, producing high-grade sinsemilla with an extremely high THC content. Each organization was capable of producing 100 plants at a time, and the two organizations could have produced over 1,000 pounds of sinsemilla per year, selling for as much as $1,000 per pound on the street. The marijuana produced by these two men was substantially higher in quality than the best quality Mexican marijuana commonly available and, accordingly, commanded a substantially higher price.

Law enforcement agencies have taken note of other changes in cultivation methods. Growers tend to harvest the top 10 to 15 inches of the flower, with the seed still intact in the closed pod. The advantage of this cultivation method is that the top portion, known as the "cola" or tail, has a higher concentration of THC and can fetch a retail price three times higher than the compressed brick variety of marijuana. Furthermore, the advent of "cola" marijuana has overcome one of the major disadvantages of brick marijuana—its bulk. Instead of smuggling multi-ton loads of compressed bricks, traffickers can realize even greater profits with smaller loads of "cola." These developments make domestic marijuana cultivation more difficult to combat.

Nonetheless, a handful of marijuana trafficking organizations have been discovered and dismantled. In one investigation covering the period 1988-1989, the breakup of a high-level smuggling organization led to the discovery and dismantling of a network of more than 15 U.S. and Canadian distributors who had been smuggling 60 to 70 tons of marijuana into the United States annually. Over 90 Canadian money laundering organizations based in Toronto and in West Palm Beach, Florida, were also identified. A total of 51 indictments were returned in the United States and Canada, and $21 million in assets were seized.[17]

PHARMACEUTICALS

Although many "pills" have been found to be counterfeit, pharmaceuticals continue to be used as recreational, experimental illicit drugs. Currently, the bulk of Quaalude tablets available in the United States is primarily counterfeit, containing an alternative depressant or sedative substance such as diazepam or phenobarbital. This development appears to be a result of the increase in laboratory seizures by DEA and other law enforcement agencies. Available information suggests that many abusers are becoming wary of counterfeit Quaaludes due to the frequently poor quality of the product as well as erratic and fluctuating potency. Increasingly, diazepam (Valium) as well as Xanax tablets and capsules are supplanting methaqualone as the "street" depressant of choice.

Diversion Investigators—police officers, detectives and narcotic officers who specialize in the investigation of the diversion of legal pharamceutical chemicals into illegal ones—report that the most commonly abused pharmaceuticals are Doriden, Xanax, Dilaudid, Sidnex and Valium. Unethical doctors continue to contribute to the illicit supply of controlled substances in the United States by writing numerous prescriptions for non-medical use. Cocaine, Valium and Darvon are the most widely abused controlled substances of methadone patients. Also, script forgery rings and physician "shoppers" are active in all areas of the United States and are particularly interested in obtaining Dilaudid, Doriden, Percodan, Demerol and Tuinal.

METHAMPHETAMINE

Methamphetamine is one of the most popular and one of the oldest of the currently used synthetic drugs. In powdered form, it has been used since the 1960s. Methamphetamine is also known as "crank" or "speed." The tradi-

---

[17] "Drug Trafficking: A Report to the President of the United States." U.S. Dept. of Justice, Office of the Attorney General, August 3, 1989.

tional method of administering powdered methamphetamine has been either by injection or orally through pills.

The main active ingredient in methamphetamine is phenylacetone, also known as P2P, phenyl-2-propanone, benzyl methyl ketone, or methyl benzyl ketone—each of these names representing an attempt to describe its chemical structure in something approximating English. Phenylacetone has been a controlled substance since 1979. However, like many controlled substances, it can be manufactured using a combination of non-controlled substances—in this case, phenylacetic acid, sodium acetate, and acetic anhydride.

The principal sources for methamphetamine are clandestine labs in southeastern Texas, southern and northern California and northwestern United States, especially Oregon. In 1989, the California Department of Alcohol and Drug Programs released a study entitled "Amphetamines" which stated that California has the highest abuse of amphetamines in the nation. The California Drug Abuse Data System (CAS-DADS) continues to keep track of drug abuse in the state.[18]

Even though abuse appears to be concentrated in California, the use of methamphetamine is currently spreading eastward throughout the United States. During 1987 to 1989, law enforcement officials seized approximately 140 million dosage units of methamphetamine in New Mexico. Additionally, over 16,000 pounds of precursor chemicals were seized. The Northern District of Texas reports that its methamphetamine problem is as great as its cocaine problem, and the Eastern District of Texas reports that methamphetamine "is perhaps the major narcotics problem in the district." [19] Rural areas in Louisiana, Georgia, Arkansas, and as far east as South Carolina and Massachusetts, have even reported increased crystal methamphetamine trafficking activities.

Although most methamphetamine available to traffickers is produced in illicit domestic laboratories, a new smokeable form of crystal methamphetamine has been introduced into the United States from Asia, originally entering the country through Hawaii. The effects of this smokeable crystal methamphetamine are somewhat comparable to, but not as intense as those of crack. While the average crack "high" lasts approximately 10 minutes, "crystal meth," as it is sometimes called, provides an effect that can last from 2 to 14 hours. Dealers tout it as a "safe" alternative to crack cocaine. Overdoses, however, are often fatal and crystal methamphetamine has the same highly addictive characteristics and relatively low price that have made crack cocaine such a rapidly expanding menace. In Hawaii, use of the new smokeable form of methamphetamine called "ice" has developed into an epidemic. Some drug experts predict that methamphetamine has the potential of becoming the crack problem of the 1990s.

---

[18] Resource Center, Department of Alcohol and Drug Programs, 111 Capital Mall, Sacramento, CA 95814-3279.

[19] "Drug Trafficking: A Report to the President of the United States." U.S. Dept. of Justice, Office of the Attorney General, August 3, 1989.

HALLUCINOGENS

Among hallucinogenic/psychedelic drugs, phencyclidine,[20] known as PCP, continues to dominate. Manufactured in relatively rudimentary clandestine facilities, the drug is generally distributed by small, locally oriented organizations. During the last several years, however, PCP distribution and abuse patterns have undergone several changes. Initially, distribution was concentrated in white, working-class communities; however, PCP has become increasingly available on the streets of several major U.S. cities.

Although abuse fell substantially in 1980-81 due to a bad "street" reputation and law enforcement successes in curtailing its manufacture, PCP use has recently increased, particularly in Los Angeles, Washington D.C, and New York City.

With increased availability in metropolitan areas, PCP has been become a popular drug to use in combination with heroin or other illicit substances. The number of emergency room admissions and medical examiner reports for PCP/heroin combinations increased significantly through the years 1986 to 1989. Likewise, a study done by the National Institute on Drug Abuse (NIDA) in 1989 reported that PCP users frequently used twice as many substances as non-PCP users. The report concluded that these users were probably ingesting other drugs in an effort to mediate the psychic and emotional distress of PCP.[21]

Although PCP is one of the more potent and problematic hallucinogens in use today, other more mild psychedelic drugs, such as mescaline (peyote) and psilocybin (mushrooms), continue to be used. The use of these hallucinogens has remained stable in the last 10 years.

Perhaps the backbone of the lure to hallucinogenic drugs, lysergic acid diethylmide, or LSD, is regaining popularity with those who are too young to remember the 1960s experience. LSD is making a comeback on our high school campuses across the United States.

In Georgia, seizures of as many as 15,000 to 20,000 dosage units have been reported in 1988, and the Southern District reports that LSD is in moderate demand on college campuses, on military installations, and among blue-collar workers. Georgia's Northern District also reports a resurgence in LSD's popularity. An exemplary LSD-related death was reported from Atlanta in 1988 when a 19-year old male leapt from a bridge after ingesting an overdose of the drug.

In the Middle District of North Carolina, it has been reported that most LSD is concentrated on college campuses, while North Carolina's Eastern District reveals that use of the drug is a growing problem on its five military installations. In Louisiana as well, the Eastern District declares that LSD use has recently increased.

---

[20] Technically, PCP is pharmacologically classified in its own classification called phencyclidine.

[21] "PCP (Phencyclidine)." National Institute on Drug Abuse. CAP No. 13, 1986.

Consumer Patterns of Illicit Drug Use

Reports from several other districts around the country indicate that LSD's return to popularity may not be restricted to the southeastern states. In the Northern District of Iowa, for example, LSD seizures have increased over 400 percent in the last two years; and the Western District of Wisconsin is experiencing a significant increase in the number of prosecutions related to LSD.[22] In 1989, the first LSD lab was found in full operation since the early 1970s in Mountain View, California. Law enforcement officers seized 30 grams of crystal LSD, 460,000 doses of microdot and blottered LSD, liquid LSD, blotter papers of LSD, a pill press machine and LSD chemicals and lab equipment.[23]

While these reports do not amount to a strong indication of an LSD epidemic or a return to anything approaching the widespread LSD usage of two decades ago, they do demonstrate that there is new activity in this market and that its development bears watching.

DESIGNER DRUGS

"Designer drugs" are chemical compounds that have been specifically designed as analogs to controlled substances. An analog is a substance that is sufficiently different from a controlled substance (to legally differentiate it from a drug on the controlled substances list) but which is similar in chemical structure and in pharmacological effects to its illicit counterpart. Chemists intent on circumventing drug regulations have become adept at creating such substances, which have effects on users that are nearly indistinguishable from the effects of illicit controlled substances.

Unfortunately, the legal definitions of drugs on the controlled substances list are often very narrow, both in order to enhance the strength of cases brought in the legal system and in order not to unduly inhibit or discourage legitimate chemical and pharmacological research.

One of the more infamous designer drugs is "Ecstasy," a combination of synthetic mescaline and amphetamine that has a hallucinogenic effect. Ecstasy is known by chemists as MDMA for methylene dioxymethamphetamine. Although controlled by the DEA in 1985, this drug has a periodic surge in popularity and is currently in vogue in the club scenes of New York, Texas, and California. Other "chemical cousins" of ecstasy have been nicknamed "Adam" and "Eve" by the traffickers as part of their marketing technique.

The most successful designer drug is the opiate form of fentanyl (discussed above, in the section on heroin). Fentanyl was originally developed as an anesthetic; however, it was modified into opiate form by chemists with the express purpose of creating a heroin analog that would bypass the restrictions of controlled substance laws. Although fentanyl analogs have since been included in the controlled substances list, unethical chemists continue to create new substances which appear on the street faster than government agencies can track them down.

---

[22] "Drug Trafficking: A Report to the President of the United States." U.S. Dept of Justice, Office of the Attorney General, August 3, 1989.

[23] *The California Narcotic Officer.* CNOA, Spring 1989, Santa Clarita, CA 91350.

DRUG LABS

Despite the proliferation of drugs manufactured by chemists, seizures of illicit drug labs remain at an all-time high. Some lab seizures involve PCP, synthetic narcotics, and LSD. However, methamphetamine labs account for over 60 percent of the total labs seized. Nearly half of the methamphetamine labs in the U.S. are located in California, and San Diego County leads the nation in annual lab seizures.

DRUGS USED IN COMBINATION WITHOUT SMOKING

Drugs used in combination are the rule rather than the exception today. Since most combinations involve smoking, they are discussed in a separate section below. Nonetheless, several drug combinations are taken intravenously or by ingestion. For example, the intravenous injection of heroin and cocaine, known as "speedballing," continues to be a popular combination. Some variations on "speedballing" include substitute stimulants in place of the cocaine. One such variation combines heroin and phentermine, known on the streets of Washington, D.C. as "Bam."

Often, drug users who are intimidated by intravenous injection prefer to replace heroin with combinations of illicit narcotics taken by ingestion. Under this category of narcotic, the most popular combinations are pentazocine and tripelenamine (known as "T's and Blues"), and a combination of hydromorphone (Dilaudid) and codeine, known as "Hits" and "Loads." Available data suggests that users of these narcotics comprise a distinct addict sub-population whose abuse patterns and demographic characteristics are markedly different from the heroin addict population. It is likely that, even if heroin becomes less available, the abuse of pharmaceutical narcotics and narcotic analogs will continue.

PATTERNS OF DRUG ABUSE THAT INVOLVE SMOKING

For many people, smoking is an acceptable method of drug use, including many for whom injection of street drugs would not be acceptable. Familiarity with smoking is an important factor in the spread of drug abuse. Due to extensive tobacco and marijuana smoking in this culture, most people (especially teenagers) are familiar with drug use by smoking, and they do not perceive smoking to be as culturally deviant as self-administration of drugs by intravenous injection. Most people associate intravenous injection with "hardcore drug abusers," but do not perceive that smoking drugs is often just as harmful as injecting them.

It is true that smoking does not produce many of the medical complications that frequently occur with intravenous drug abuse, such as infection with the human immunodeficiency virus (HIV), infectious endocarditis, or serum hepatitis. However, some drugs that are smoked have a high level of toxicity. Cocaine smokers, for example, can ingest lethal quantities through inhalation. Of particular public health concern is the damage done to fetuses by pregnant women who smoke crack.

The willingness of many people to smoke drugs played a major role in the crack epidemic of the eighties. The introduction of crack cocaine ready for smoking opened a large new marketplace for cocaine among people whose former drug choices were alcohol, marijuana, and nicotine.

Consumer Patterns of Illicit Drug Use

For drugs that volatilize at low temperatures, smoking can be an easy, efficient method of consumption, and large amounts of a drug can be rapidly delivered to the brain. Most psychoactive drugs exert the maximum subjective effects when blood levels of the drug are rapidly increasing. Since smokeable drugs enter the bloodstream rapidly through the lungs, inhalation can produce a sharp increase in the drugs's arterial concentration. The drug is then carried by arterial blood directly to the brain. A high concentration of any particular drug in the arterial blood can produce an intense psychoactive effect, which is qualitatively different from the drug's steady state effect. This intense psychoactive effect, often called a "rush," is desired by the abuser. Drug abusers who prefer to smoke rather than ingest a drug are in pursuit of this intense psychoactive effect. The "rush" has made smoking the most common method of introducing drugs into the bloodstream. Table 1 below shows the sources of some common smokeable drugs.

TABLE 1. Smokeable Drugs and their Sources

DRUG	SOURCE
Freebase cocaine (freebase crystals and crack)	Coca Plant
Opium	Poppy Plant
Freebase heroin	Opium
Phencyclidine (PCP)	Illicit Synthesis
Methamphetamine	Illicit Synthesis
Delta-9-Tetrahydrocannabinol (THC)	Cannabis Indica,
Marijuana (.1-9.5%) -9-THC*	Cannabis Sativa
Hashish (10-30%) -9-THC*	

*The Range of THC values are from Mikururija and Aldrich, 1988.

COCAINE

In the United States, cocaine is sold in two forms: the hydrochloride salt form and the form of freebase cocaine. Cocaine hydrochloride, which is water soluble, is used by snorting or by intravenous injection. Some cocaine abusers smoke cocaine hydrochloride; however, cocaine hydrochloride volatilizes at a high temperature and most of it is destroyed by burning. Therefore, most cocaine abusers who smoke cocaine use freebase cocaine. Cocaine freebase volatilizes at a lower temperature, and a greater percentage of it is spared during the smoking process. The form of freebase called crack has become the most popular form of cocaine that is smoked in the United States.

FREEBASE COCAINE

Freebase cocaine can be prepared from the hydrochloride salt form as either freebase crystals or as crack.

The preparation of freebase crystals involves dissolving the cocaine hydrochloride in water, converting the hydrochloride to its alkaloid form by addition of a strong base (such as sodium or ammonium hydroxide), extraction of the alkaloid with an organic solvent (such as petroleum ether), and crystallization into freebase. Before the current crack epidemic in the United States, most cocaine freebase users made their freebase from cocaine hydrochloride. The preparation of freebase crystals was part of the ritual of use. The freebase conversion also removed sugars and other water-soluble diluents used to "cut" the cocaine. Until the passage of drug paraphernalia laws, most users prepared their freebase with conversion kits purchased at drug paraphernalia shops or by mail order. The kits contained all the ingredients necessary for conversion of the cocaine—except, of course, the cocaine hydrochloride itself.

Crack cocaine is also made from cocaine hydrochloride. The cocaine hydrochloride is dissolved in water, mixed with baking soda or sodium bicarbonate, and heated. While the mixture is being heated, the "cooker" gently swirls or rotates the container. The freebase cocaine precipitates and coalesces into a soft mass that becomes hard when it is dried. Sugars and other water- soluble diluents remain in the water, which is then poured off, leaving the solid mass. Most crack users can now buy crack in the form of pellets or "rocks" that are already in the freebase form. Some users prefer to make their own crack from cocaine hydrochloride because they feel more confident of its purity.

Both crack and cocaine freebase crystals can be smoked in glass pipes. The glass pipe has a bowl fitted on the bottom with one or more fine-mesh copper screens, which support the cocaine. The user heats the side of the bowl with a small butane torch or lighter. The freebase then vaporizes and is drawn through the pipe. A pipe used in this manner gets very hot and users often burn their fingers or lips. Some freebase smokers have burns on their groins from hiding hot freebase pipes in their pockets.

It might be noted here that several years before the current crack epidemic, smoking cocaine paste became a major public health problem in Peru. Cocaine paste is a direct extract of coca leaves containing 40 to 85 percent cocaine sulfate; it is often smoked in marijuana or tobacco cigarettes. Subsequent to widespread use in Peru, cocaine paste smoking became popular in Bolivia, Columbia, and Ecuador as well (Jeri 1984).

COCAINE AND MARIJUANA IN COMBINATION

Cocaine is frequently used in combination with other drugs. One such combination rolls rock cocaine into a marijuana cigarette; this combination is called a "primo". A marijuana cigarette laced with crack is commonly known as a "grimmie." Crack is crushed between two coins, mixed with marijuana, and rolled into a "joint". Although smokers of grimmies are smoking crack, they seem to view it as a less intense and less severe form of use than smoking crack in a pipe. Many grimmie smokers do not realize that they are freebasing, as they associate freebasing with using a pipe. This association has led some freebasers to smoke grimmies as a means of controlling their cocaine use. When cocaine is smoked with marijuana, users report that there is less compulsion for continued use and less difficulty sleeping afterwards.

COCAINE AND TOBACCO

The combination of crack cocaine and a tobacco cigarette is known as "caviar" or "cavies". Cocaine hydrochloride is also used in this manner. The user makes the combination by reducing crack to a powder and using the cigarette as a straw, sucking the powdered crack into the tobacco. The advantage of this dosage form is that it can be smoked in public without revealing that the person is using cocaine.

Consumer Patterns of Illicit Drug Use

COCAINE AND PHENCYCLIDINE (PCP)

Cocaine and PCP are sometimes taken together by regular cocaine users. The combination is commonly known as "whack" or "spacebase." Some users intentionally create this combination for an intensified high; however, PCP is more often included because it is a less expensive substitute for cocaine. Thus, some cocaine users who believe they are using only cocaine are actually using cocaine that has been "cut" with PCP.

COCAINE SUBSTITUTES

The most widely used cocaine substitute, procaine, is commonly used as either a drug of deception or intentionally as a "poor man's cocaine." Sold under names such as "Snowcaine" or "Rock," procaine can be purchased in drug paraphernalia shops or by mail order. Sellers escape drug regulations by selling the substitute as incense. The label disclaimer gives directions for using the incense: "Do not inhale vapors, as it may cause stimulation."

PCP

Most users of PCP smoke the drug, often mixing it with parsley, tobacco, or marijuana. Sometimes users coat tobacco cigarettes with PCP by dipping the cigarette into a solution containing the drug. A dark-brown colored cigarette is frequently used for this purpose to hide the discoloration produced by the PCP. Rolled with dark brown paper, Sherman cigarettes appear to be the standard cigarette for this form of PCP smoking; hence, the street name of this combination, "shermans" or "shermies."

METHAMPHETAMINE (ICE)

Methamphetamine can be smoked in either the hydrochloride salt or freebase form. In the last decade, smoking the d-isomer of methamphetamine, called "ice," has become popular in Hawaii. Drug Enforcement Agency (DEA) seizures of ice began there in 1985. The ice sold in Hawaii probably originates in Korea; however, ice maufacturing seems to have begun in the U.S. as well. In 1990, the DEA reported a seizure of ice crystals manufactured in California.

Methamphetamine is often smoked in the following ways:

1. The methamphetamine is placed on aluminum foil, the foil is heated from below, and the methamphetamine vapors are inhaled. (As with heroin, this method of use is sometimes called "chasing the dragon.")

2. The methamphetamine is kindled and inhaled though a small, straight glass pipe. (Unlike freebase cocaine, which is not water soluble, methamphetamine cannot be smoked in water pipes since the water soluble methamphetamine would become trapped in the water.)

3. The methamphetamine is smoked in combination with tobacco or marijuana.

HEROIN AND OPIUM SMOKING

Smoking heroin is a dominant form of opiate use in Asia. The Asian form of freebase heroin prepared for smoking is designated by the U.S. Drug Enforcement Agency as heroin #3. Smoking freebase heroin also occurs in the United States and England.

In the early seventies, another freebase form of the drug, known as Persian heroin, was favored by cocaine freebase users on the West Coast, who used it to attenuate cocaine-induced anxiety, agitation, or paranoia. With continued, frequent use, some cocaine users who also used Persian heroin as a secondary drug became physically dependent on the heroin, much to their surprise, as they thought that physical dependency could only occur with intravenous injection.

Smoking opium itself continues to be a primary yet stable mode of drug use among some heroin users in England (Gossop et al. 1988). Opium smoking also occurs in the United States, particularly among immigrants from Southeast Asia.

STIMULANT AND OPIATE COMBINATIONS

Drug abusers have long used combinations of stimulants and opiates intravenously. As mentioned above, the combination is commonly called a "speedball." Methamphetamine or cocaine freebase can also be smoked with freebase heroin. The street term for smoking a mixture of cocaine and heroin is "chasing and basing." One of the new drugs of choice is a mixture of crack and smokeable heroin. It is called by a variety of names including "crank" and "speedball" though it bears little resemblance to street drugs that have similar names. The new mixture of crack cocaine and heroin is smoked in a pipe, rather than injected intravenously.

CIGARETTE SMOKING

The role of cigarette smoking in drug abuse relapse is worth some consideration. Often, patterns of drug abuse involve the combination of various drugs with cigarettes (as is shown above). In addition, many drug treatment patients report that they smoke more cigarettes when using other drugs such as cocaine. The role of continued cigarette smoking in inducing cravings for other drugs of abuse deserves careful clinical study. If researchers find that smoking cigarettes contributes to relapse, treatment programs should incorporate smoking cessation as part of drug abuse treatment.

INTERNATIONAL DRUG TRAFFIC

OPIUM AND ITS DERIVATIVES

In the past few years, Burma and Laos have overtaken Southwest Asia as prime sources of the U.S. heroin supply. Today, heroin from Southeast Asia accounts for approximately 40 to 50 percent of the flow into the United States. The Southeast Asian heroin entering the U.S. is also a more pure and potent form of the drug.

European officials say that the amount of Southeast Asian heroin being smuggled into Europe is also increasing. They estimate that up to 40 percent of the heroin reaching France and the Netherlands is from Southeast Asia. The comparable figure for Britain is 15 percent. Well-organized and powerful drug smuggling cartels, controlled mainly by the Chinese, are seeking to increase profits by developing new markets for heroin as well as enlarging established markets in the U.S., the European Community, Australia and New Zealand. Likely targets include Scandinavia, Eastern Europe, Canada,

Japan, South Korea and other industrialized countries of Asia where income levels are rising.

Likewise, opium production in Mexico is expanding. Even Lebanon, previously known only as a producer of cannabis, has become a site of increasing heroin production. Yet, the rise of heroin-related activities in these countries will not prevent Columbia, with its prime opium-growing climate, from continuing to be a major source country for heroin.

COCAINE

Despite determined law enforcement efforts, greater allocation of government funds in support of law enforcement, improved legal structures, and an increased awareness of the need for national and international cooperation, cocaine cartels have still managed to expand their operations and establish new consumer markets around the world.

Japanese drug-enforcement officials say they fear that Japan has been targeted by South American cocaine syndicates that view Japan's increasingly wealthy consumers as a potentially lucrative new market.

Amphetamines currently constitute a major drug-abuse problem in Japan. Use of this stimulant by the Japanese may be related to Japan's recent discovery of cocaine from Columbia and Bolivia. Due in part to the increase in wealth and leisure time, demand for cocaine among the Japanese appears to be growing. Overseas travel has also been an important factor in their exposure to this drug. For these reasons, cocaine prices in Japan are much higher than elsewhere in the world, bringing significant profits to drug dealers.

The principal growing areas of coca have remained unchanged. Among coca-producing countries, Peru continues to cultivate the highest total number of hectares. Average production has been estimated at two kilograms of cocaine hydrocholoride per hectare. Yet, Bolivia and Colombia are also expanding their capacity to cultivate, refine, and process the coca leaf into cocaine.

The principal method of cocaine trafficking is air transport, followed by land transport, sea transport, and the postal service. For air and land transport, false-bottomed suitcases are a commonly-used hiding place. Air tight containers are usually used for sea transport.

Traffickers have also hidden cocaine in their clothes and body orifices. Couriers frequently swallow condoms or the fingers of surgical gloves filled with cocaine. Between 100 and 500 grams of the drug can be transported in this manner.

In addition to refined methods of concealment and established trafficking routes, courier profiles are constantly changing. For example, not only are South American, North American, and European cocaine couriers active, but Africans, Indians and East Asians are also being discovered for possession of cocaine. In Africa alone, 32 different ethnic groups have been encountered by law enforcement authorities in a recent three-and-a-half year period of investigations.

Furthermore, law enforcement officers have often been out-flanked, out-gunned, and out-financed when combatting these powerful and professional drug-smuggling organizations. Due to increased smuggling activity and the violence associated with it, governments have had to establish stronger laws and better-coordinated intelligence and enforcement programs at national and international levels.

Fortunately, these efforts have had a certain impact on international cocaine-smuggling activities. Well-planned intelligence-gathering programs and sound law enforcement initiatives have resulted in the arrest of several major violators, the immobilization of some well-organized trafficking syndicates, and numerous seizures of cocaine. In addition to increasing quantities of confiscated cocaine, the number of South American traffickers arrested in Europe is on the rise.

CANNABIS (MARIJUANA)

Regardless of consumer preference for other illicit drugs, huge quantities of marijuana continue to be available throughout the world. Available data suggests that marijuana users are increasingly expanding their abuse of other drugs in conjunction with marijuana, contributing to a more complex poly-drug profile.

Thailand remains the principal Southeast Asian cannabis-producing area. Marijuana grown in Thailand is sometimes referred to as "Thai stick" or "ganji." For ease of distribution and guaranteed markets, the ganji produced in Thailand is financed, grown, and trafficked by Thai organizations working in cooperation with Western counterparts. Nonetheless, other primary cultivation areas have expanded rapidly during the past 10 years.

With respect to amounts seized and levels of abuse, the cannabis market in Europe has continued with little change in recent years.

Hashish production also continues at a stable pace in Afghanistan and Pakistan. The drug is primarily marketed to users located in these growing regions and in neighboring countries; however, hashish is also transported to Europe and North America by ship.

PSYCHOTROPIC SUBSTANCES

Interpol has recently reported an increase in the international use of psychotropic substances. The most frequently reported seizures of legally-produced psychotropic substances include benzodiazepine, fenethylline, methaqualone and secobarbital. As it has in the past, fenethylline continues to pose significant problems for law enforcement authorities in the Near and Middle East. With many countries reporting discoveries of heroin containing methaqualone, seizures of this psychotropic substance have also been expanding. Most of the methaqualone seized in recent years appears to be of illicit origin, rather than diverted from legitimate sources.

Among illegally-produced pyschotropic substances, amphetamine and methamphetamine continue to be seized the most frequently and in the largest quantities. However, the controlled substance analog, methylene dioxymethamphetamine (MDMA or "Ecstasy") has seen increasing seizures throughout Europe and the United States.

In the category of hallucinogenic psychotropic substances, LSD is still the most frequently seized.

Reports indicate that over 850 clandestine laboratories producing various psychotropic substances were seized during 1989. This statistic emphasizes the extent of illegal activity in psychotropic substances as well as the availability of precursors and essential chemicals which have kept the international drug trade active in recent years.

REFERENCES:

Ball, Saffer, Nurco. "Day-to-Day Criminality of Heroin Addicts in Baltimore," 1983.

Buzzeo, Ronald. "Chemical Diversion and Trafficking Up-Date." Office of Diversion Control, Washington, D.C. *The Narc Officer*, INEOA, April 1991.

California Narcotic Officers Association. *The California Narcotic Officer.* Vol. 8, No. 4, Oct. 1991; Spring 1989, Santa Clarita, CA 91350.

General Accounting Office. "The Crack Cocaine Epidemic: Health Consequences and Treatment," 1990.

________. Report GAO/HRD-91-55FS. GAO, P.O. Box 6015, Gaithersburg, MD 20877.

Gossop, M., P. Griffiths, and J. Strang. "Chasing the Dragon: Characteristics of Heroin Chasers." *Br J Addict.* 83:1159-1162, 1988.

International Narcotic Enforcement Officers Association. *International Drug Report.* Vol. 3, No. 7, July 1990.

________. *International Drug Report.* "Trends in Traffic: Heroin."

Jeri, F.R. "Coca-paste smoking in some Latin American countries: A severe and unabated form of addiction." *Bull Narc.* 36(2):15-31, 1984.

Mikuriya, T.H., and M.R. Aldrich. "Cannabis 1988: Old drug, new dangers: The potency question." *J. Psychoactive Drugs.* 20(1):47-55, 1988.

National Clearinghouse for Alcohol and Drug Information. "Drugs in the Workplace, Research and Evaluation Data." National Institute on Drug Abuse Monograph 91, 1989.

________. "High School Senior Drug Use, 1975-1989." National Institute on Drug Abuse Capsule (CAP) No. 23, 1990.

________. "Highlights on Attitudes and Knowledge Survey About Illegal Drug Use." National Institute on Drug Abuse Capsule (CAP) No. 19, 1986.

________. "Overview of the National Household Survey on Drug Abuse, 1988." National Institute on Drug Abuse Capsule (CAP) No. 23, 1990.

________. "PCP (Phencyclidine)." National Institute on Drug Abuse Capsule (CAP) No. 13, 1986.

________. "Research on Drugs and the Workplace." Report CAP No. 24, 1990.

National Criminal Justice Reference Service. "Drugs in the Workplace," TB010620, No. 47.

Seigel, R.K. "Cocaine smoking." *J. Psychoactive Drugs.* 14(4):271-358, 1982.

U.S. Dept. of Justice, Office of Justice Programs, Bureau of Justice Statistics. "Drugs and Crime Data, Fact Sheet: Drug Data Summary." November 1991.

________. *Manual for Police Chiefs and Sheriffs, Reducing Crime by Reducing Drug Abuse.* June 1988.

U.S. Dept. of Justice, Office of the Attorney General. "Drug Trafficking: A Report to the President of the United States." August 3, 1989.

This page intentionally left blank.

CHAPTER II

DRUGS, CRIME, BEHAVIOR AND ADDICTION

INTRODUCTION

Shootings, stabbings, barroom fights, rapes, robberies, domestic violence, sexual assaults, abused children, highway accidents, overdoses—all are part of the routine workday for law enforcement officers. To a very alarming degree, these crimes also involve some form of alcohol or drug abuse.

Currently, it is estimated that two-thirds of the U.S. population uses alcohol. A third of these people are moderate or heavy users. Moreover, 25 percent of American young adults admit to recent marijuana use, and still another 10 percent admit to using some type of mind-altering chemical. Perhaps the worst estimate is that up to 80 percent of all Americans will try at least one illicit drug by their mid-20s.[1]

LINKS BETWEEN DRUGS AND CRIME

The links between drugs and crime are not yet fully understood. Yet, the belief that they are related is fundamental to the United States' efforts to control crime through drug prevention.

Several studies have researched the extent of the relationship between drugs and crime.[2] The studies indicate that different levels of drug abuse are directly related to criminal behavior at the level of the individual offender. Individuals who abuse drugs in differing degrees of severity will tend to have corresponding patterns of severity in criminal behavior. Even among high-risk individuals with established patterns of both drug abuse and criminality, an increase or reduction in the level of drug abuse will correspond to an increase or reduction in criminality.

For example, street-level heroin abusers tend to engage in a variety of criminal acts and other behaviors to support their drug habits. Daily heroin users, in particular, commit an extraordinary number of crimes. Among heroin abusers, recent studies reveal a lifestyle that is thoroughly enveloped in the physiological need to obtain heroin or similar opiates. A large majority of abusers have reported that, during their actively addicted periods, they were only sporadically employed, if employed at all; they were generally helped or financially supported by a relative or friend; and they had very little legally-generated income of their own.

---

[1] "National Household Survey on Drug Abuse." National Institute of Justice Reports, U.S. Dept. of Justice.

"National Youth Survey." National Institute of Mental Health and National Institute on Drug Abuse. U.S. Dept. of Health and Human Services.

"National Adolescent Student Health Survey." Public Health Service, Office of Disease Prevention and Health Promotion, and Center for Disease Control, 1987.

[2] For information on drugs and crime, contact Drugs and Crime Data Center and Clearinghouse, 1600 Research Blvd., Rockville, MD 20850, (800) 732-3277.

Although these narcotics users, as a group, engage in a great deal of crime, the number and types of crimes vary considerably among individuals. Nonetheless, the links between drug use and criminality indicate that treatment and education programs are most likely to have the greatest impact on drug-related crime by directing their efforts toward frequent and intensive users rather than casual use in the general population.

THE DRUG USE FORECASTING PROGRAM (DUF)

One population of drug users which exemplifies the links between drugs and crime is that of arrestees. This population has often been excluded from national surveys; however, through its Drug Use Forecasting program (DUF), the National Institute of Justice has provided the United States with its first objective measure of drug use among arrestees. Begun in 1987, the DUF research not only provides a more accurate census of illicit drug use in the United States by including this population, but also makes it possible to investigate the following areas of drug usage: the age of onset and intensified use, cyclical trends, the relationship between drug use and certain types of crimes, the validity of reports made by arrestees themselves, and AIDS-risk behaviors in arrestees.

Local officials also use DUF information to plan the allocation of law enforcement, treatment, and prevention resources, as well as to measure the impact of local drug-use reduction efforts. At the national level, the DUF test results can help in tracking the course different drugs take throughout the country.

Overall, the most striking statistic from DUF data is that drug use among arrestees is over 10 times higher than among persons in households or senior high schools.

1991 DUF RESULTS

In 1991, the DUF program collected data from male arrestees in 23 cities and from female arrestees in 21 of these cities. Response rates were consistently high, with more than 90 percent of the arrestees agreeing to be interviewed. Approximately 80 percent also provided a voluntary, anonymous urine specimen. The data and information gathered through these urine tests and interviews are the highlight of the report.

According to the 1991 DUF sample of male and female arrestees, more than half tested positively for at least one drug in 1991. As in 1988 through 1990, cocaine continued to be the most pervasive drug among those tested.

Overall drug use. The percentage of men testing positive for at least one drug at the time of arrest ranged from 42 percent in Omaha to 79 percent in San Diego. Among women, the tests resulted in a similar range of 57 percent in Indianapolis to 74 percent in Philadelphia. Overall, in 18 of these DUF testing sites, 50 percent or more of both males and females tested positive for at least one drug. The relationship of age and ethnicity to drug use differed little from city to city.

Cocaine. In the 1991 sample of arrestees, cocaine was the most commonly used drug. Among male arrestees, percentages of use ranged from 61 percent in Philadelphia and 64 percent in Manhattan to 9 percent in Omaha. Cocaine use among female arrestees was only slightly higher, ranging from 63 percent in Atlanta to 26 percent in Indianapolis.

Drugs, Crime, Behavior and Addiction

Multiple drug use. Approximately 20 percent of the male and female arrestees in DUF's 1991 sample tested positively for two or more drugs. The highest rate of multiple drug use was found in San Diego—39 percent for men and 37 percent for women. The lowest multiple drug use among arrestees of both genders was found in Omaha. Multiple drug use was not limited to any specific categories of age or ethnicity.

Marijuana. In several cities where both male and female arrestees were tested, men were more likely to test positive for marijuana. However, in 1991, the percentage of all arrestees testing positive for marijuana was lower than any other data collection period, except increases in marijuana use were detected among juveniles in many DUF cities.

Opiates (heroin). In 17 of the DUF cities, less than 10 percent of the male and female arrestees tested positive for opiates. For male arrestees, opiate use was most prevalent in San Antonio, where 18 percent tested positive. Female arrestees, on the other hand, tested highest for opiates in Washington, D.C. (24 percent).

PCP. The use of phencyclidine was found to be highest in male arrestees from Chicago (14 percent). Among female arrestees, three percent tested positive for PCP in San Jose. In the remaining cities, less than three percent of the arrestees tested positive for PCP.

Amphetamines. Amphetamine use was still concentrated in the western cities of San Diego, San Jose, Portland, and Phoenix. San Diego arrestees showed the highest use, with 25 percent of the males and 27 percent of the females testing positive for amphetamines. In other cities, less than 8 percent of the male and female arrestees tested positive for this drug.

During the last several years, statistics from the DUF program proved especially useful in assessing the prevalence of "ice" (smokeable methamphetamine) as a new drug of abuse. The findings generally showed that amphetamine levels among arrestees remained stable or fell slightly, indicating no severe problem with regard to the new drug. Those interviewed who had heard of "ice" reported that they learned about it from television and newspapers.

Other drugs detected in DUF's 1991 sample include Valium, methadone, methaqualone, Darvon and barbiturates.

USE OF THE 1991 DUF DATA

In 1991 and previous years, statistics from the Drug Use Forecasting program have been extremely useful to local government officials.

Below are two examples of how DUF statistics have been utilized:

1. DUF statistics strengthen and support law enforcement efforts, advocacy, and other endeavors to increase public awareness and encourage public action against drugs.

The findings from DUF have indicated that drug use is pervasive and persistent in the offender population. DUF statistics serve as objective measures of the extent of drug use. This information can be used to allocate resources for law enforcement, drug education, and judicial proceedings. In

San Diego, for example, information from the DUF program was a key factor in obtaining support for a special court to deal with drug-related cases.

2. The DUF data have also found geographical differences in drug use among arrestees.

Urinalysis findings indicate that arrestee drug use differs by geographical areas. PCP is found primarily in San Jose and until recently in Washington, D.C. Amphetamines, on the other hand, have been limited to West Coast cities, such as San Diego, Portland, and Phoenix.

In Los Angeles, the Public Health Foundation used DUF data to examine the types of drugs used and the relationship of age and drug use.

Since DUF calculates the type of drugs used by offenders, the information can expedite the development of treatment strategies and guide drug education and prevention efforts.

CRIMINAL CHARGES AND THEIR LINKS TO DRUG USE

For the majority of male and female arrestees sampled during the DUF data collection period, larceny or theft was the most frequent criminal charge. Following larceny, the most frequent charges for men in the sample were drug sale or possession, and burglary. Among women, approximately 20 percent of the charges were for drug sale or possession.

DRUG ADDICTION: CRIME OR DISEASE?

In the past, efforts to eliminate drug addiction have been aimed mainly at isolated aspects of the problem. The common focus upon the individual user as "the problem" has helped create the image of the user as an outcast and has frequently resulted in the stereotype of the drug-addicted criminal. Recently, addiction has been redefined as a disease.

In order to obtain some clarity about whether or not the addict is a criminal, or is suffering from a disease (or both) it is necessary to explore each of these concepts.

DRUG ADDICTION AS A CRIME

Since the pain-killer phase of the mid-1800s, the use of narcotic substances in the United States has evolved through the recognition of opiate addiction by 1910 to its definition as a criminal activity in 1914 by the passage of the Harrison Act, which is still this country's basic narcotics law. As part of the Internal Revenue Act, the Harrison Act is a tax law and is administered by the Drug Enforcement Administration. The law was designed to make narcotics distribution a matter of record. The Act does not make drug use illegal, nor does it allow or forbid a doctor to give drugs regularly to a user. Nevertheless, its vague terminology which states that drugs must be dispensed in "professional practice only" has never been legislatively defined, and the Act has become the basis for over fifty years of legal problems for the user, the doctor, and the community. The prosecution of many doctors who followed the Harrison Act had the effect of depriving the user of medically supervised treatment with opiates; it became legally impossible for a doctor to prescribe narcotics except for withdrawal. The user was then forced to turn to illegal channels to obtain drugs, and thus his or her dependence on the criminal world became established. Before the prosecution of physicians for medical treatment of users and the prosecution of users themselves for possession of narcotics, users were generally not involved in criminal behavior.

Some attempt was made between 1919 and 1923 to deal with drug abuse as a medical problem. Forty-four public outpatient narcotics clinics were opened throughout the country. By 1923, the last clinic was closed. The clinics were started as an emergency measure and were generally unsuccessful. On the basis of an alleged rise in narcotics arrests, it was claimed that the clinics spread drug use by making drugs easily available. In fact, the arrest rate climbed substantially after the clinics were closed due to increased criminal activity to obtain drugs.

Often when one thinks of drug addiction, the image of the heroin addict comes to mind. The addict is frequently thought of as someone who is motivated to crime by the physical and psychological effects of the heroin, someone who will do anything to get his "fix". Heroin addicts are defined as criminals not only because possession is a criminal offense, but also because heroin dependency motivates the addict to commit crimes.

DRUG ADDICTION AS A DISEASE

Another perspective on drug addiction sees it not as a crime, but as a disease. In 1960, E.M. Jellinek first proposed this concept with specific reference to alcohol.[3] Since then, the concept has been broadened to include all psychoactive drugs. This new approach to addiction has resulted in dramatic changes in the treatment of chemical dependency during the past decade. Several physicians now approach addictive disease as a biochemical/genetic disorder which is activated by the patient's environment.

In support of this perspective, the genetic predisposition to alcoholism has been well established. While genetic predispositions for other psychoactive drugs have been less well studied, there does appear to be a higher incidence of psychoactive drug addiction in the families of addicts than in the population at large.

ADOLESCENT DRUG USE

In addition to the question of whether or not drug addiction is a crime or a disease, the issue of widespread drug use among adolescents has also been a matter of some controversy since the 1960s. Public concern about drugs intensified during the campus turmoil of the 1960s, and since then there have been several Congressional hearings on drug use. At the grass-roots level, local organizations of parents who were worried about adolescent drug use sprang up in a few places in the mid-1970s, and soon mushroomed into a national movement (U.S. House of Representatives, 1982; U.S. Senate, 1982). That concern is based on the growing numbers of adolescents who take drugs while living at home.

Adolescent drug use is especially troubling because of the developmental risks involved in taking psychoactive substances. The principal risks are toxic effects, impairment of motor functions, the potential for physical or

---

[3] Jellinek, New Haven College and University Press, 1960.

psychic dependence, and the long-term psychological and emotional effects of addictive disease.

There are several grounds for concern about drug use by children and adolescents. First, all psychoactive drugs have acute effects on mood, concentration, and cognitive functioning. Since pyschoactive drugs have such a strong effect on memory, a major concern is that drug use may interfere with intellectual and emotional development and impair school performance.

Second, if it is inevitable that a young person will eventually use drugs, it is at least advisable to resist starting for as long as possible. Many toxic substances require prolonged exposure to produce an effect; some require a long incubation period for the effect to become manifest. Thus, postponing the onset of use by adolescents reduces the likelihood of adverse effects, and may reduce the adolescent's chance of becoming a chronic adult user.

Third, a conservative course of action is especially appropriate when dealing with adolescents and unsafe chemical substances. In medicine, it is generally accepted that a drug should not be administered when it is known to be unsafe. When safety is in doubt—for example, during pregnancy—special restrictions are often imposed to avoid harm. In the case of illicit drugs, none has been sufficiently studied to warrant a claim of safety. Therefore, both parents and children should be as cautious of illicit drugs as they would be of any other toxic substance.

DEFINING DRUGS

The dictionary offers two definitions of "drug." The first one is "a substance useful in the art and practice of medicine." The second is "a narcotic, usually habit forming." If one looks up "narcotic," it will generally be defined as "a drug which produces sleep and relieves pain." [4]

These definitions are based on society's concept of the use of drugs and their beliefs about drugs.

A scientific definition, on the other hand, must be both descriptive and objective. It must make no assumptions about proper or improper use, social factors, or value judgments. The following is a basic pharmacological definition: *A drug is a substance which by its chemical nature affects the structure and function of the living organism.*[5] This definition includes prescription drugs, over-the-counter drugs, illicit drugs, recreational drugs (drugs which in our wisdom or folly we prefer to call beverages, like alcohol and caffeine), food additives, industrial chemicals, agricultural chemicals, pollutants, and food.

This definition is a workable one since it will always remind us that a drug is a drug, no matter what we call it. They all operate according to the same basic pharmacological principles. It doesn't make any difference

---

[4] *Webster's New World Dictionary of the American Language, 2nd Ed.* World Publishing Company, New York, 1971.

[5] "Controlled Substances: Use, Abuse and Effect." U.S. Dept. of Justice, Drug Enforcement Administration.

whether it's a wonder drug, whether it's heroin, or whether it's food. There are basic principles according to which all of these substances act.

The largest single group of prescribed drugs is for modifying mood and feeling; these are minor tranquilizers and related drugs. Nonetheless, we are all drug users, not only of alcohol, caffeine and cigarettes—or nicotine, which is a drug—but also of over-the-counter drugs, or drugs that will relieve anything that ails us. Even these drugs may be used wisely or foolishly; these drugs may be abused.

WHY USE DRUGS?

The most popular drugs used today are caffeine, nicotine, and alcohol. In this context, popularity is measured by the following parameters: number of people who have ever used, number of regular users, number of daily users, number of work-hours spent under the influence of the drug, and money spent for the drug. It is worth mentioning here that the amount of harm done to the human body by nicotine and alcohol vastly exceeds the physical harm done by all of the other psychoactive drugs put together.

Moreover, the amount of damage done to the human mind by alcohol alone, as measured by psychiatric hospital admissions, vastly exceeds the psychological harm done by all of the other psychoactive drugs put together.

These facts are commonly masked by the exclusion of caffeine, nicotine, and alcohol from the category of "drugs." Many people think that drug abuse is new. However, drug abuse has been around since the beginning of recorded history. In ancient and medieval literature, there are numerous descriptions of the use of mushrooms, marijuana, opium, and alcohol.

Even in the past, drug abuse has led to attempts at legal regulation. For instance, in the Code of Hammurabi (2240 B.C.), problem drinking is addressed and is described as a problem of men with too much leisure time and lazy dispositions. The historical records of nearly every culture include some laws controlling the use of a wide range of drugs, including tobacco.

Since human beings have always experimented with natural drugs, the question to be answered is: Why does this experimentation occur? In response to this question, many users claim to be bored, frustrated, in pain, unable to enjoy life, or alienated. They turn to drugs in the hope of finding oblivion, peace, togetherness, or euphoria. The fact that few drugs actually cause the effects for which they are taken—or if they do, they do so for only a brief time—seems to be no deterrent to experimentation. People continue to take drugs outside of medical prescription because:

1. Drugs make them feel good.
2. Drugs may relieve stress or tension, or provide a temporary escape.
3. Peer pressure is strong, especially for young people. Drug use has become a "rite of passage" in some parts of our society. Frequently, it is part of the thrill of taking risks.
4. From an early age we are "programmed" to want to feel good; the media tell us that drugs are part of the technology that can help make life a little bit better. They urge us to seek "better living through chemistry." One national commission studying the drug-

abuse problem estimated that by the age of 18, the average American has seen 180,000 television commercials, many of which give the impression that pleasure and relief are to be found in sources outside oneself, sources including drugs.[6]

5. In some cases, drugs may enhance religious or mystical experiences. A few cultures teach their children how to use specific drugs for this purpose.

Considering these different reasons for the use of drugs throughout history and throughout various cultures, a distinction should be made between use and abuse. Almost everyone uses or has used a psychoactive substance, even if it is a socially acceptable substance such as alcohol, caffeine, tobacco, or over-the-counter drugs. Yet, not everyone misuses or abuses drugs.

Misusing a drug means using it in a way that can have detrimental effects. Getting drunk may be a misuse of alcohol, but it does not necessarily mean the drunk person is an alcoholic or that he or she has sustained bodily damage from the episode. Abuse, on the other hand, has many definitions. The National Institute on Drug Abuse (NIDA) defines drug abuse as *drug use that results in the physical, mental, emotional, or social impairment of the user.* Some other definitions have a stronger link to social relationships; for example, use becomes abuse if the drug has a negative effect not only on the user, but also on others with whom the person is in contact. The reasons for abusing a drug vary widely, but most drug abusers have at least one thing in common: *they use drugs to feel good.* Feeling good involves individual perception and interpretation. For some, feeling good means feeling good about yourself; for others, feeling good involves association with a peer group, or relieving boredom or pain.

Drugs might also be used as a substitute for the achievement of a goal, such as the satisfaction of a need for affection, the need for a sense of belonging, or the need for a feeling of self-confidence. If, to some extent, the drug satisfies the need, the user may not learn how to satisfy the other needs; in other words, he or she may displace the primary need onto the need for drugs and, therefore, not learn to give and receive affection, develop a sense of belonging, or develop self-confidence. Such a person would be stunted in his or her personality development by ignoring the primary needs and replacing those with the need for drugs.

Any attempt to understand why people take drugs should consider the following principles of drug use:

Principle I. — People take drugs because they want to.

Principle II. — People use drugs to "feel better" or to "get high". Individuals experiment with drugs out of curiosity or out of the hope that using drugs can make them feel better.

[6] "National Commission on Drug Free Schools and Toward a Drug Free Generation: A Nation's Responsibility, Final Report." September 1990. U.S. Government Printing Office.

Principle III. — People have been taught by cultural example and the media that drugs are an effective way to make them feel better.

Principle IV. — "Feeling better" encompasses a huge range of shifts in mood or consciousness, including such aspects as oblivion or sleep, emotional shifts, energy modification, and visions of the Divine, etc.

Principle V. — With many mind- or mood-altering drugs, taken principally for that purpose, individuals may temporarily feel better. However, drugs have substantial short- and long-term disadvantages related to the motive for their use. These include possible physiological, psychological, or cognitive deterioration. The psychoactive effects of drugs also tend to be temporary, relatively devoid of adequate translation to the ordinary non-drug state of consciousness, and siphon off energy necessary for long-term constructive growth.

Principle VI. — Individuals do not stop using drugs until they discover "something better."

Principle VII. — The keys to meeting the problems of drug abuse are to focus on the "something better" and to maximize opportunities for experiencing satisfying nonchemical experimentation or, more likely, to keep experimentation from progressing to dependency.

FACTS ABOUT DRUG DEPENDENCE

Given that drugs make people feel good, each time a person takes that drug, the experience is rewarding and the behavior is positively reinforced. In the case of depressants, continued use may cause physical dependence and, as a result, secondary psychological dependence. Secondary psychological dependence is a negative experience, an avoidance, as it is sometimes called. It is also called "aversive reinforcement" because the feeling of withdrawal from the depressant is unpleasant, and the depressant drug is taken to prevent the occurrence of withdrawal symptoms. For example, once an alcoholic starts to experience the symptoms of withdrawal, the alcoholic is motivated to drink in order to avert the symptoms. The use of depressants is especially difficult to stop because of tolerance. As tolerance increases the dosage needed must be increased, and the reward of taking the drug becomes less important. Consequently, the need to prevent the occurrence of withdrawal, or secondary psychological dependence, becomes the most important factor that will encourage further use of the drug.

Drugs have multiple effects that vary with the amount of the drug used and the personality of the user, as well as the user's expectations of the drug's effects. As noted above, people take drugs to obtain a good feeling. However, whether or not a person decides to use drugs also depends on his or her background, present environment, and the availability of the drugs. The availability of drugs is a complicated problem. On the one hand, if drugs were not available, obviously no one would be using them; on the other hand, if the availability of drugs alone were the problem, we could solve it by simply shutting off the supply. The biggest problem, however, is not drugs, but people. People look for rapid solutions to problems, and drugs are one of the options our society makes available.

ADDICTIVE DISEASE

The latest and most productive approach to drug abuse is based on the concept that addiction is a psychological disease rather than a crime.

With this concept, addictive disease is defined as follows: the abuse of drugs which interferes with health, economic or social functioning, characterized by compulsion, loss of control, or continued use in spite of adverse consequences. In the past, most definitions of addiction were concerned with the chemical actions of drugs in the addict's body. Therefore, addiction was viewed as the result of physical withdrawal that compelled "hooked" users to continue using the drug. Drugs that caused physical dependence were addictive—others were not. This created a false picture of addiction. For example, cocaine was thought to be a "benign" drug compared to heroin. However, cocaine is a highly potent, central nervous system stimulant that can lead to compulsion; it is therefore extremely addictive. The most important principle of approaching addiction as a disease is shifting the focus from the physical effects of the chemical *drug* to the *person* using the drug. The question is not whether the drug is addictive but whether the user has an addictive disease.

Generally, a drug user has an addictive disease when there is present a compulsion, a loss of control, and continued use in spite of adverse consequences. You can tell if a person is addicted to a drug by his or her behavior. You look for a compulsive individual—a person who has a drive to get the drug and to use it continually. You look for a person who has lost control over the drug, a person who cannot say no. Drug addiction is manifest in the thought processes of the addict. In the beginning, they think of ways to control their drug use; for example, don't drink before noon, only drink beer, etc. Eventually, the loss of control is evident because the addict begins to recognize how powerless he or she is over the drug. In a sense, the addict surrenders to the power. The last behavior you look for in the addicted person is continued use of the drug in spite of adverse consequences such as deteriorating health, loss of job, family problems, or incarceration.[7]

Addiction cannot be cured. But, it can be brought under remission. Remission is known as recovery. It is brought about by learning to live a comfortable, rewarding, and satisfying life that does not include drugs. Methods used to bring about recovery are: long-term counseling, A.A. and other support groups, long-term residential care, and individual as well as family treatment programs. Recovery is not the same as *cured.* Cured implies that the disease is gone and will never come back. However, since people with addictive disease will inevitably escalate drug use to toxic levels, addiction cannot be cured, only controlled or recovered from.

Many individuals with addictive disease are in a state of denial about the severity of their addiction. Family, friends and employers should intervene to break through this denial system to get the person into treatment. In treatment, the addiction can be dealt with as a disease to be recovered from rather than to be cured. Due to the frequent loss of control by drug users, the primary treatment is simply no drugs—a chemical-free philosophy.

---

[7] Inaba and Cohen. *Uppers, Downers, All Arounders.* The Haight-Ashbury Detox Clinic, 529 Clayton St., San Francisco, CA 94117, 1989, p. 218.

Drugs, Crime, Behavior and Addiction

Researchers agree that addiction—whether to cocaine, heroin, amphetamines, or some other chemical substance—is a single disease. According to much of the latest evidence, addicts will switch drugs when their choice is not available.[8] Addiction is a psychological rather than a physical disease.

An addict will compulsively attempt to repeat and even to intensify the feeling produced by drugs—no matter what the consequences. The key to the diagnosis of addictive disease is in the observation that the addict persists in using drugs in spite of the adverse consequences. Simply taking away drugs, even if it could be done, would not solve the problem of drug addiction. At treatment centers across the country, it has been learned that if the addict's cocaine is taken away, the addict will become addicted to alcohol; if the alcohol is taken away, he or she will become addicted to Valium; if the Valium is taken away, you will find him or her somewhere down the line taking heroin; and if the heroin is taken away, he or she will find morphine, Demerol, codeine, Talwin, Percodan, Dialaudid . . . the list is endless.

With this approach to addiction, addicts are taught that the particular drugs they have been using are not the essential problem; once they have developed addictive disease, they are equally vulnerable to all mood-altering drugs. The recovering cocaine addict cannot go out and become a social drinker. The recovering heroin addict cannot smoke an occasional joint. Even going to the hospital for surgery can be risky, because a shot of morphine that would not affect most people could adversely trigger the cycle of addictive behavior.

The only treatment for addictive disease is to give up all mood-altering chemicals. It used to be thought that taking drugs or drinking to excess was a symptom of some other disorder, but it is not. It is an illness in its own right—the cause, not the effect.

ADDICTIONOLOGY

In the medical field, addictionology is a subspecialty focusing on the study and treatment of addictive disease. Until a few years ago, the concept of addictive disease did not exist. No one had suggested that all addictions were the same. Yet, most descriptions of the feeling of addiction are similar. In "Cocaine: A Special Report" (Playboy, September 1984), Contributing Editor Lawrence Gonzales wrote:

> Cocaine somehow gets access to the areas of the brain (the amygdalae and lateral hypothalamus) in which those chemical changes occur and allows you to make those changes at will. In addition, cocaine takes control of the use and manufacture within the body of essential chemical message transmitters, such as dopamine, which transmits sexual and feeding signals, and norepinephrine, which transmits signals to flee in the face of danger. When you take cocaine, it feels as if it is the most important function in life, because cocaine causes your body and brain to send those essential life protecting and life-producing signals: the need for sex, food, water, flight. So, of course, you take more.

---

[8] *Ibid.*

Artificially stimulating those areas of the brain has serious psychological consequences which are symptomatic of addictive disease. For one thing, after being over-stimulated, the pleasure circuits do not work anymore. Pleasure cannot be had. Pain is all that is left—pain and craving. The result is often the classic clinical picture of addictive behavior: continued compulsive use of the drug despite the adverse consequences.

When the pleasure circuits in the brain no longer produce pleasure, the result is depression, anxiety, and panic. The brain says, "You are dying of thirst. Get cocaine or you will die."

Later, when the chemicals are gone from the brain, the addict cannot believe he or she took the drug. The addict cannot remember why the drug was taken in the first place, because the memory states do not match. Remorse and anxiety set in. And not even getting high will make everything all right again. That is why addicts talk about needing to take drugs just to feel normal.

One of the most difficult jobs in treating addicts is to convince them that they cannot recover unless they avoid all mood-altering chemicals, forever. Cocaine addicts will want to be treated only for cocaine addiction. They may say: "Hey, I've never had a problem with drinking a few beers." Therapists hear it all the time: "How did this happen to me?" "I cannot understand it. I never drank before." Or, even worse for the addict, "Hey, what is the problem if I smoke a joint after work? Grass isn't even addictive." But it's not the drug, it's the person; and any mood-altering drug can initiate the cycle of addiction again. Indeed, animal tests bear out that fact. No laboratory monkey, when offered a particular drug, says, "No thanks, I use only Peruvian flake." An animal addicted to cocaine will substitute alcohol if it is deprived of its coke. If you substitute heroin; the animal will become a junkie. Give it the choice of any drug and it will choose cocaine. Cocaine appears to be the most dangerous because it is most efficient in triggering the reward circuitry of the brain.

Mood-altering drugs even interfere with the addict's ability to remember why not to use drugs. That sets the addict up for relapse. In fact, even while abstaining, most addicts have to be reminded daily why they cannot use drugs: because their worst experiences happened while they were high. Since memory is dependent upon a state of mind, those mood-altered memories are not readily accessible to the sober brain.

Once you are an addict, you are always at risk for relapse. What that means to a scientist is that relapse is a biological imperative. This is more or less a new principle of drug addiction: There is an active drive to relapse.

We can now understand a few of the mysteries of addictive disease. For example, why is the first drug experience free? It is free because it is free of anxiety. To inebriate is to exhilarate and then to stupefy. That is why the first high is free, because the first one is the exhilarating one. Then comes the stupefaction. The first experience gives direct access to the controls in the brain that operate the most fundamental circuitry of pleasure and happiness. The first time out, the addict is God, with his or her hand on the throttle of ecstasy.

Why, then, doesn't everyone repeat this ecstatic process over and over again? No one knows. As Dr. David E. Smith, founder of the Haight-Ashbury Clinic in San Francisco and one of the pioneers of addiction research, said: the potential addict "responds differently the very first time he uses" a drug. Most addicts interviewed said the same thing: "I was hooked the first time I got high. I was no longer lonely, no longer self-conscious; I could be with people; I was not afraid." [9] People without addictive disease do not react to chemicals that way when they first take them. That is why people without addictive disease can take drugs or leave them.

What, then, are the new scientific secrets of treatment? If, say, cocaine depletes dopamine, a chemical messenger to the brain, then is there some nonaddictive, benign drug that we can use to replace dopamine? The answer is yes: there is an approved treatment for low-dopamine diseases called bromocriptine. It is used in cocaine withdrawal and it works. It is given during the first ten days of abstinence. Similarly, the drug clonidine is used for heroin addiction.

TREATMENT

Given that a major characteristic of addictive disease is denial of its existence, it can be difficult to persuade an addict to seek treatment. Denial is one reason that drug-treatment centers use what is known as the Minnesota Model of therapy. The Minnesota Model is the method of treatment developed by Hazelden.[10]

An essential part of the Minnesota Model treatment is direct intervention in the addict's life. Since denial is a central characteristic in addiction, the Minnesota Model supports getting the practicing addict into treatment through constructive coercion if necessary, by using either involuntary commitment or "voluntary" admission resulting from an arranged crisis confrontation. The addict is a motivated person, motivated to feel better, and drug taking is used as a means of trying to feel better. Once the denial system is dismantled, the motivation to feel better can be used constructively in the rehabilitation process.

The most important fact about intervention is that it works. People who seek treatment voluntarily do no better than people coerced into it.

A typical intervention involves getting the addict's relatives, friends, employer—anyone who has influence over him or her—to have, as it were, a surprise party for him coordinated by a professional counselor. Each person has a prepared list of what the addict has done lately to make life miserable. (For example, a daughter might be enlisted to say, "Mom, I brought my new boyfriend over and you came out of the bathroom naked." Or "Dad, you missed my graduation because you couldn't get out of bed.") Each person also has an ultimatum. (A boss might be brought in to say, "Jim, if you do

---

[9] Smith, David E. and Arnold R. Wesson. "Treating the Cocaine Abuser." Hazelden Foundation, 1985.

[10] Hazelden Foundation, Center City, MN.

not get into this treatment program, you are going to be fired.") This is organized coercion. And that is really what it comes down to, short of catastrophic intervention, such as a serious accident, hitting the rock bottom of depression, or being arrested. Your family may have called the local police department to arrange an involuntary commitment. They will call the local police and say, "I will turn in my loved one if you promise me that you will give him the choice of treatment or prosecution." This happens all the time. Once the addict's relationship to the drug is stronger than any other relationships, then you need some organized intervention. Timing may be of the essence. There may be a particularly opportune moment when the person is truly receptive to getting help.

However, once the addict is in treatment, it appears that the person is never more than 51 percent in favor of getting better. "There really are these two forces within the addict: the drug speaking and trying to preserve itself—the parasite trying to remain in some equilibrium with the host—and the other side of the person that is getting all this support from work, from friends, from loved ones, to try to bolster itself, to make it assert itself so that treatment becomes possible." [11]

The essential aim of Hazelden's treatment plan—the Minnesota Model—is to get the addict fully involved in A.A. or one of its sister organizations, so that when the addict leaves treatment, he or she will continue going to meetings. The same is true of Gateway, Fair Oaks, the Betty Ford Center, Comprehensive Care Units, and every responsible treatment facility. In fact, one measure of a treatment program's effectiveness is how far it will go to get the addict to join after his or her insurance money is gone. At some hospitals, a staff member will hand the phone to the addict when the 28 days are up and say, "Call A.A. Here is the number. Good luck." Others have A.A. meetings in the hospital throughout the treatment program and insist upon follow-up meetings on hospital grounds. Some private programs will not accept anyone who cannot commit him- or herself to at least a year of treatment. Another key to good treatment is when the family is included. The addict cannot do it alone. Addiction is a disease that affects the entire family. Being married to an addict, or being the child or parent of an addict makes one ill as well. Family members must also be treated, or the patient will relapse.[12] And even with A.A., there is a 50 percent chance of relapse within 24 months.

RELAPSE

The small percentage of people in any society who suffer from addictive disease suffer greatly. Part of the reason is relapse. The American Medical Association includes in its definition of alcoholism the fact that it is a disease "characterized by a tendency to relapse." The same is true of addiction to any other drug. Of those who are treated, half to two-thirds relapse within

---

[11] "Drug Abuse Treatment." National Institute on Drug Abuse, Report CAP 27, 1988.

[12] Nelson, Charles. "Styles of Enabling in Codependents of Cocaine Abusers." United States International University, San Diego, CA, 1984.

Byrne, M.M. and J.H. Holes. "The Co-Alcoholic Syndrome." *Labor-Management Alcoholism Journal 9,* No. 2, 1979.

two years, whatever their method of treatment. Yet few treatment facilities address that issue, either before or during treatment; and few programs provide the long-term therapy necessary to give the patient the best chance against relapse. The reason for that is simple: treatment costs money; and most insurance policies cover only 28 easy treatments in the hospital and extremely limited follow-up and outpatient treatment.

When relapse occurs, it seems to come out of the blue, blanking out all reason, all experience, all logic. But there are warning signs. It may begin as anger or depression. It may begin as a sense of well-being, confidence, a warm glow of pride at how well everything is going. As one A.A. member said, "In my 30 years, no one ever called me to ask to be prevented from taking a drink. I myself never called for help at the threshold of relapse, probably because I did not want to be stopped." Here is another A.A. description of relapse after a promising period of sobriety:

> I felt hungry, so I stopped at a roadside place where they have a bar. I had no intention of drinking. I just thought I would get a sandwich . . . I had eaten there many times during the months I was sober. I sat down at a table and ordered a sandwich and a glass of milk, still with no thought of drinking. I ordered another sandwich and decided to have another glass of milk. Suddenly the thought crossed my mind that if I were to put an ounce of whiskey in my milk, it could not hurt me on a full stomach. I ordered a whiskey and poured it into the milk. I vaguely sensed I was not being any too smart but felt reassured as I was taking the whiskey on a full stomach. The experiment went so well that I ordered another whiskey and poured it into more milk. That did not seem to bother me, so I tried another.

The scientists would call what happened to him selective memory or euphoric recall, in which the addict suddenly remembers the good times he had while high. It is a cunning, baffling, and cruel trick of neurochemistry. The tendency to relapse should receive as much attention as does initial recovery. In other words, any program that slights the importance of a deep and lifelong involvement in A.A. (or Cocaine Anonymous or Narcotics Anonymous) is not for the addict who is serious about protecting his or her recovery.

One other important aspect of treatment that helps to prevent relapse is storytelling. The A.A. tradition of telling stories is not for the benefit of the persons to whom they are told. It is for the benefit of the person telling them. The sober alcoholic above told his own story out of the conviction that such honesty was required by and necessary only to his own sobriety. This example is evidence of the understanding among A.A. members that honesty is necessary to maintain sobriety. The happy byproduct of self-therapy for the one who has already attained sobriety is that the would-be A.A. member identifies with the stories he hears. He says, "Hey, this guy was almost as pan-fried as I was. And look at him now. How did he get sober?" Once that moment of identification—of constructive envy—is achieved, the addict is on his or her way to recovery.

Becoming addicted is like being in a near-fatal car accident and having both legs cut off. In relative terms, it does not happen to many people, and it should not discourage everyone else from driving. But for those unfortunate enough to be victims, there is no quick fix, only a lifetime of coping; and any advertisement that suggests otherwise is misleading people.

There is only one proven way to maintain abstinence: one day at a time for a lifetime. Drug treatment has become big business, but no one stays in business providing lifelong treatment. No one could afford it, and no insurance company would cover it. Not even the nonprofit places offer unlimited treatment. And that is why, no matter where an addict goes for initial treatment or detoxification, he or she will find the same thing: All roads lead to A.A. (or C.A. or N.A.). The reason is simple. It is free and it works.

THE EXTENT OF ADDICTION

Addiction is found in all races, religions, and social strata. The only difference is that some social classes have greater percentages of addiction to particular types of drugs.

Alcohol addiction is the drug dependency that affects the greatest number of professionals (and laypersons). A study by the American Medical Association estimated that 400 doctors are lost from the medical profession each year because of alcoholism. That does not sound like a significant number until you realize that it is the equivalent of the graduating classes from four large medical schools each year. This figure does not include those doctors lost because of use of narcotics or other drugs. Of the professionals addicted to drugs other than alcohol, physicians have one of the highest addiction rates. This is partly due to their access to narcotics and other potent drugs and partly due to the stress of the medical profession.

The nursing profession has also had similar problems with certain kinds of addiction, particularly tranquilizers, narcotics (to a lesser extent than physicians), and stimulants. Nurses have the opportunity to divert drugs prescribed for patients, and this diversion appears to provide the major drug supply. Furthermore, nurses often receive little professional respect and may be pressured by physicians, which, combined with irregular working schedules, leads to considerable job-related stress. It becomes extremely easy to pop a prescription tranquilizer when one cannot scream back at a surgeon having a bad day, or to ingest a stimulant to keep going through a double shift.

The Catholic Church has for years had special rehabilitation centers for priests with alcohol problems. The usual causes of alcoholism are reported to be the use of alcohol for socialization and for the psychological stresses and pressures of handling the problems of the congregation. The legal profession has also developed programs to help lawyers who are having difficulty performing well because of heavy use of alcohol and other drugs. Furthermore, the armed forces have admitted, in the last decade, that there are many service personnel with serious drug problems. Part of the drive to develop treatment programs in the armed forces began with the realization that many of the service personnel in Vietnam were using narcotics. Subsequently, a great deal of money was funnelled into the Veterans' Administration (VA) hospitals to help treat addicts.

Substance abuse in the workplace has recently become an issue of widespread public interest and pandemic media attention. It is commonly believed that drug abuse in the workplace is increasing in prevalence, but this is difficult to substantiate. Although drug abuse in industry—particularly the abuse of alcohol—has been recognized as a cause of industry-worker dysfunction since the beginning of the industrial revolution, why is drug abuse surfacing *now* as a major issue?

One important factor to consider is *who* is using drugs in the workplace. It may be noted that those who grew up in the late 1960s and have accepting attitudes towards drugs are now assuming positions of technical, professional, and executive responsibility. As the complexity of industrial and managerial tasks continues to increase, so do the economic and safety risks to both employers and employees. The serious consequences resulting from errors of judgment are making drug-induced impairment unacceptable at all levels of employment.

For many industries and corporations (as well as the U.S. military) technological improvements in urinalysis have led to large-scale drug testing. However, the promise of urinalysis to provide an objective appraisal of an individual's drug use has proved illusive. Drug testing has also raised some civil rights, legal and technological challenges. One challenge was recently brought about by the U.S. Army, which has questioned the efficacy of urinalysis due to "improper processing, handling, or recordkeeping" of samples.

Unsurprisingly, industry has been the most visible nexus of the increasingly litigious climate of the last 15 years. Drug abuse by employees significantly increases an industry's vulnerability to suits from employees disciplined for drug use, liability suits from employees injured by other employees under the influence of drugs, and worker's compensation disputes.

Fortunately, employee assistance programs (EAPs), which provide an alternative to disciplining employees with alcohol or other drug problems, have resulted in numerous individuals seeking treatment. In some industries, EAPs have increased the visibility of drug-impaired employees.

The net result of all these factors has been significant. Most notably, there has been an increasing sensitivity on the part of management, EAPs, medical and legal departments, industrial security officers, and unions toward employees who come to work impaired by the use of drugs. For instance, the alcohol or drug addiction problem among women was ignored for many years. According to various estimates, anywhere from 24 to 50 percent of problem drinkers are women. When you consider that the National Institute on Alcohol Abuse and Alcoholism (NIAAA) estimates that 15 percent of the total population has a drinking problem, then you are talking about a large number of people in the United States. The use of prescription sedatives combined with alcohol is also likely to be more common among women than men. Sixty percent of psychoactive drugs and 71 percent of antidepressant drugs are prescribed for women in response to symptoms of anxiety. Apparently, physicians are more likely to prescribe psychoactive drugs (Valium is number one) for women than for men. Due to the widespread availability of these drugs (and the availability of alcohol) many women develop poly-drug addictions which affect the home and the workplace.

Another population affected by addiction is that of the elderly. As many as 90 percent of those over age 65 (about 25 million people) have suffered side effects from drugs. About 20 percent have been hospitalized for these effects. Frequently, exposure to or use of drugs results in addiction. At one time, people believed that there were no elderly narcotics addicts. We now know that there are drug abusers and addicts throughout all levels of the population—young, old, blue-collar workers, professionals, male, and female.

DRUGS AND BEHAVIOR

We have already discussed why people take drugs. We have seen that drug use is as old as recorded history and has occurred in all civilizations. The most important point of this discussion is that drug use is an established part of human behavior, and as such it follows the same rules and principles of any other behavioral pattern. One basic behavioral principle is that behavior persists when it either increases the individual's pleasure or reduces his or her discomfort (psychic or physical). People do not take just any drug—they take only those substances that affect them pleasurably or that make a situation less intolerable. Furthermore, of those drugs that do increase pleasure or decrease discomfort, the ones chosen must be acceptable within the user's cultural setting.

Thus, there is no single cause of drug abuse. Studies with laboratory animals show that susceptibility to narcotics addiction is at least partially determined by genetics. Strains of laboratory animals have been bred that are either susceptible or resistant to induced addiction. Similarly, strains of laboratory animals have been developed that prefer alcoholic solutions over drinking water, whereas most animals will select tap water if given the choice. This finding suggests that alcoholism in humans may be partially based on hereditary predisposition.

Drug use, whether influenced by genetic factors or not, is also the result of a complex interaction of past experiences and present environments. This principle is true of any behavior. It is possible to group some persons together by a common history and environment, thus to predict whether or not they will have a predisposition to drug use, and to predict whether or not they will have a predisposition to a particular type of drug. This fact does not mean that potential users can be readily identified; rather, it means that some groups of individuals can be identified according to the *probability* of their becoming drug users. Various types of drug users may also be classified according to differences in personality and background. For example, narcotics addicts usually start drinking alcoholic beverages in their early teens, before their age and social-class peers do. After experimenting with alcohol, narcotics addicts often try marijuana or inhalants, such as those found in model airplane glue. The average age of first narcotics use is the late teens. As one drug becomes more acceptable in society—for example, marijuana—the next drug selected is usually less socially acceptable than the previous one.

PARENTS AND PEERS

Many parents have recently become concerned with the use of drugs among children and youth. Parents often believe that their authority is being undermined by various socializing elements such as the media, the government, and the peer group. Although many parents may see the media and the government as the main sources of socialization which erode their parental control, it is with the more proximate and accessible peer group that most parents are primarily concerned. They feel that more can be accomplished through intervention on a local, manageable level while continuing to exert pressure on the more nationally-oriented media and government.

This conflict between parents and peers is, of course, nothing new. It is one of the most predictable and, in Western society, probably the least avoidable of developmental conflicts. What is new, however, is the sharp focus upon the influence of parents and peers on drug use by adolescents. This focus is not surprising since drug use has increased substantially over the past several years and attitudes toward drug use provide what is one of the most distinctive and emotional conflicts between the generations.

Many researchers have studied adolescent drug use and abuse. In particular, there is extensive and growing literature on the role of the family. For example, parental drinking patterns are the single most important element in predicting adolescent drinking patterns. Thus, parental drinking behavior strongly influences the initiation of adolescents into alcohol use. However, parental influence on adolescent marijuana use is quite small. Whatever influence was found appeared to be based on parental attitudes and the strength of the parents' relationships with their children. In other words, parents who strongly discouraged marijuana use and still held the relationship together were more successful in minimizing initiation than those parents whose attitudes and behavior were more permissive.

In the case of illicit drugs other than marijuana, adolescent initiation into use appears to be strongly related to parental influences. The quality of the parent-child relationship is particularly important. Generally, the adolescent's feelings of closeness and loyalty to the family result in a low likelihood of initiation into other illicit drugs, while strict controls and parental disagreement about discipline result in a higher likelihood of initiation. Parental drug use is, again, an important factor which increases the possibility of the child's initiation into similar drug use.

Another finding with respect to the relative authority of parents is that the influence of the family differs in each stage of adolescent drug use. Parents appear to have a high degree of influence over adolescents' initiation into hard liquor use and, in particular, their initiation into use of illicit drugs other than marijuana. Parental influence appears to be somewhat diminished, however, with regard to initiation into the use of marijuana.

Peer influences on adolescent drug use have received less research attention. The role of peers has not been ignored; rather, it has been considered one among many factors influencing adolescent drug use. Nevertheless, some researchers have examined the role of peer influence. In the case of hard liquor, the more important peer factors influencing initiation into use are adolescents' and their peer groups' *perceptions* of how many of their friends are using hard liquor, *actual* use of hard liquor by friends, best friends' attitudes about the harmfulness of hard liquor, and the degree of adolescent involvement in peer activities such as going to parties or driving around. The single most important factor influencing initiation has proven to be the modeling effect, which is based on the *actual* use of hard liquor by an adolescent's friends.

With regard to marijuana, friends' actual and perceived use, friends' actual and perceived espousal of values and attitudes conducive to use, and the availability of the drug are peer factors that strongly predict adolescent initiation. As opposed to alcohol, which is associated with adulthood, marijuana is a substance associated with youth and rebellion; thus, the range and importance of peer factors in predicting use are considerably greater for marijuana than for alcohol. Exposure to peers who use marijuana and/or have favorable attitudes toward the drug has become a primary source of adolescent socialization.

The strength of direct and indirect peer influence on marijuana use plays a significant role in studies of adolescent drug use.[13] As attachment to parents diminishes, peer orientation grows and, therefore, the possibility of socialization into marijuana use increases.

In comparison to alcohol and marijuana, when considering the use of other illicit drugs, the influence of the peer group as a whole is considerably smaller. Rather, it is the actual use of any particular drug by the adolescent's *best friend*, and low levels of intimacy with that best friend, that is the strongest influence on adolescent use of other illicit drugs.

IN SUMMARY

Parental alcohol use has proven to be the strongest interpersonal predictor of adolescent alcohol use; likewise, peer marijuana use is the strongest interpersonal predictor of marijuana use; and the use of other illicit drugs by family and best friends is also the best predictor of adolescent use of these substances. Therefore, the problem of adolescent drug use is, to a great extent, the result of the adolescent's environment and interpersonal influences.

CHARACTERISTICS OF DRUG ABUSERS

According to Richard Blum,[14] the majority of drug abusers have the following characteristics in common:

> Their drug use usually follows clear-cut developmental steps and sequences. Use of one of the legal drugs, such as alcohol, almost always precedes use of illegal drugs.
>
> The dysfunctional attributes of drug use usually appear to precede rather than to derive from drug use. In other words, the "amotivational syndrome" often attributed to a person's heavy marijuana use was probably part of that person's personality before he or she started the drug.
>
> Immaturity and maladjustment usually precede the use of marijuana and of other illicit drugs.
>
> Those who will try illicit drugs usually have a history of poor school performance.
>
> Delinquent and deviant activities usually precede involvement with illicit drugs.

---

[13] "Preventing Adolescent Drug Abuse." National Institute on Drug Abuse. Research Monograph Series, No. 47, 1985.

[14] Richard Blum served as the Director of the Joint Program in Drugs, Crime and Community Studies at the Institute of Public Policy Analysis. He is a consulting Professor of Psychology at Stanford University.

> A constellation of attitudes and values that facilitate the development of deviant behavior exists before the person tries illicit drugs.
>
> There is a process of anticipatory socialization during which youngsters who will later try drugs first develop attitudes favorable to the use of legal and illegal drugs. A social setting favorable to drug use usually reinforces and increases individual predisposition to use.
>
> Drug behavior and drug-related attitudes of peers are usually among the most potent predictors of subsequent drug involvement.
>
> Parents' behaviors, attitudes, and closeness to their children usually have varying influence at different stages of their children's involvement in drugs.
>
> Highly deviant children start using drugs at a younger age than less deviant children.
>
> When drug use begins at a later age, the user is less likely to become intensely involved and more likely to eventually cease drug use. The period of greatest risk of initiation into illicit drug use is usually over by the mid-20s.[15]

In addition to these characteristics of drug abuse, it might be noted that a certain amount of rebelliousness is not unusual in teenagers as they try to assert themselves and gain self-identity. Some adolescents experiment with drugs for the sole purpose of annoying and upsetting their parents.

Others use illegal drugs because they offer the individual some benefits. The benefit is usually a short-term gain, such as increased positive feelings or a decrease in discomfort. However, the disadvantages are multiple. For example, there is a decrease in the chance of reaching permanent solutions to underlying problems. In the United States, there is also a probable decrease in the rewards an individual can obtain if he or she persists in drug use.

Notwithstanding these advantages and disadvantages, approximately 70 percent of the U.S. adult population are able to use alcohol—a potent psychoactive agent—in moderation, even to the point of strong psychological dependence, with minimal personal injury and social consequence. Likewise, many persons use other powerful psychoactive drugs under the supervision of a physician without becoming drug dependent. Morphine, for example, produces no significant pain relief in as much as 25 percent of the persons given it. Some people can take small amounts of heroin for years without becoming dependent on it, whereas some become physically addicted after a few intravenous doses. As the approach to addictive disease verifies, all controlled substances do not necessarily lead to drug dependency; addiction depends largely upon the individual and his or her environment.

---

[15] Blum, Richard H. *Society and Drugs.* San Francisco, CA: Jassey-Bass Press, 1969.

REFERENCES:

Ball, J.C., J.W. Shaffer, and D. Nurco. "Day to Day Criminality of Heroin Addicts in Baltimore — A Study in the Continuity of Offense Rates." *Drug and Alcohol Dependence*, 1983.

Blum, Richard H. *Society and Drugs*. San Francisco, CA: Jassey-Bass Press, 1969.

Byrne, M.M. and J.H. Holes. "The Co-Alcoholic Syndrome." *Labor-Management Alcoholism Journal* 9, No. 2, 1979.

Gandossy, R.P., J.R. Williams, and J. Cohen. *Drugs and Crime: A Survey and Analysis of the Literature*. National Institute of Justice Report, 1980.

Gonzales, Laurence. "Cocaine: A Special Report." *Playboy,* September 1984.

Goodwin, D.W. "Alcoholism and Heredity, A Hypothesis." *Arch Gen Psychiatry*. 36:57-61, 1979.

Inaba and Cohen. *Uppers, Downers, All Arounders*. The Haight-Ashbury Detox Clinic, San Francisco, CA, 1989.

Inciardi, J.A. "Heroin Use and Street Crime." *Crime and Delinquency*, Vol. 25, 1979.

Jellinek, E.M. *The Disease Concept of Alcoholism*. New Haven, CT: College and University Press, 1960.

National Institute on Drug Abuse. "Drug Abuse Treatment." Report CAP 27, 1988.

________. "Preventing Adolescent Drug Abuse." Research Monograph Series, No. 47, 1985.

Nelson, Charles. "Styles of Enabling in Codependents of Cocaine Abusers." United States International University, San Diego, CA, 1984.

Public Health Services, Office of Disease Prevention and Health Promotion, and Center for Disease Control. "National Adolescent Student Health Survey." 1987.

Smith, David. *A Multicultural View of Drug Abuse*. Cambridge, MA: Schemkman Publishing, Inc., 1978.

Smith, David E. and Arnold R. Wesson. "Treating the Cocaine Abuser." Hazelden Foundation, 1985.

U.S. Dept of Health and Human Services. National Institute of Mental Health and National Institute on Drug Abuse. "National Youth Survey."

U.S. Dept of Justice. Bureau of Justice Statistics, Special Report, July 1988. "Drug Use and Crime, State Prison Inmate Survey, 1986."

________. Bureau of Justice Statistics. Report on "Drugs and Crime Facts." 1991 NCJ 134371 and 1990 NCJ 128662.

________. Drug Enforcement Administration. "Controlled Substances: Use, Abuse and Effect."

________. National Institute of Justice. "Drug Use Forecasting." Research in Action, First Quarter 1991.

________. National Institute of Justice. "Probing the Links between Drugs and Crime." Research in Brief, February 1985.

________. National Institute of Justice Reports. "National Household Survey on Drug Abuse."

Vaillant, G.E. *The National History of Alcoholism*. Cambridge, MA: Harvard University Press, 1983.

CHAPTER III

DRUG LAWS AND PREVENTION PROGRAMS

INTRODUCTION

In the United States, the importation, distribution, and consumption of illegal drugs is often assumed to be concentrated only in major cities. However, the General Accounting Office (GAO) has recently released a report on drug abuse in rural communities which indicates that arrest rates for substance abuse were as high in rural areas as in nonrural areas.[1] As previous chapters have discussed, drug use undermines the health, economic well-being, and social responsibility of drug users; it threatens the civility of community and city life; it undermines parenting. In addition to controlling the violence and crime which accompany illegal drug trafficking, controlling drug use has long been the focus of law enforcement activity, due to the fact that it reduces robberies and burglaries.

Faced with growing drug-related violence, crime, and mounting public concern, police departments across the country are devising new approaches for combating drug dealing. The strategies include enlisting the support of community groups, seizing assets of both sellers and users, and cracking down on street sales.

Police and other experts have determined that rising crime is linked to crack sales. Violence by drug dealers is a growing concern. Homicides associated with the control of drug markets are up in many cities, with residents of high-crime/drug-sales areas living in constant fear. In some places, community residents are afraid to call the police because of threatened retaliation by drug dealers. Some drug dealers are reported to have forced public housing residents out of their homes so they could use the vacated apartments for temporary drug distribution or consumption.

The importation and distribution of illegal drugs follow a well-organized, four-step process. Producers of illegal drugs, or "kingpins," funnel narcotics to mid-level distributors. These, in turn, pass the drugs to lower level distributors who control street sellers.

Although this four-step process applies to most importation and distribution rings, the entire importation and distribution process can become far more complex; many individuals may be involved as drugs move from stage to stage in a series of complicated relationships that vary according to geographical location and type of drug distributed. For example, in many cities, gangs control street sales. These gangs include the "Crips" and the "Bloods" of the West Coast, Jamaican "posses," and several ethnic minority gangs in other areas.

---

[1] *Rural Drug Abuse: Prevalence, Relation To Crime, and Programs*. U.S. General Accounting Office, P.O. Box 6015, Gaithersburg, MD 20877, Dept. PEMD-90-24.

Even particular drugs have established systems of distribution. Street sales of powdered cocaine and crack follow several patterns. One of the most common means of distribution is through "crack houses." Typically, these are abandoned houses, some highly fortified against police intrusion and easily identified by both police and local citizens. In "open" crack houses, users can purchase and consume crack or other drugs on the premises. Hotels, motels, and apartments in rental buildings or public housing projects form yet another distribution avenue. On-the-corner street sales are also commonplace.

Due to the high volume and high visibility of illegal drug sales, police in many jurisdictions have been besieged with complaints from residents of neighborhoods where drug dealers and "dope houses" operate. Metropolitan police departments and Federal law enforcement agencies have also been pressured by the government and the media to "do something" about drug sales in U.S. cities.

LAW ENFORCEMENT INITIATIVES

At all levels, law enforcement agencies are stepping up their activities. They are joining hands with schools to help children resist drugs in prevention efforts such as Project DARE. Local law enforcement agencies are cooperating with each other in the fight. The International Association of Chiefs of Police recently reported that approximately 72 percent of the departments they surveyed participated in multijurisdictional drug enforcement task forces.[2]

A number of police departments, particularly in large metropolitan areas, are using new approaches in conjunction with more traditional ones. They are targeting alternative strategies against street sales and users and retaining traditional strategies for enforcement efforts against the kingpins and producers.

Control of drug supplies is generally a Federal responsibility, but Federal law enforcement agencies regularly receive help from state and local personnel through regional, statewide, or citywide task forces. Supply control efforts at the Federal level include source crop eradication, shipment interdiction, asset seizure and forfeiture, and investigations into organized crime and money laundering. These strategies are often interrelated.

In dealing with mid-level distribution, local law enforcement agencies use some of these same traditional approaches. They form task forces and employ interdiction strategies. They also use the traditional undercover and surveillance techniques that lead to search and arrest warrants against mid-level distributors. Where mid-level distribution is controlled by gangs, police emphasize gang enforcement investigations.

Street sales enforcement is almost exclusively a local responsibility. Traditional tactics include undercover surveillance and "buy busts," in which undercover officers buy drugs on the street and then arrest the sellers. Arresting drug dealers for possession and for possession with intent to distribute are other strategies traditionally employed at this stage.

---

[2] International Association of Chiefs of Police. *Reducing Crime by Reducing Drug Abuse: A Manual for Police Chiefs and Sheriffs*. Gaithersburg, MD 20878, IACP, June 1988, p. 65.

Finally, at the end of the distribution chain, police arrest individual users for possession.

NEW STRATEGIES OF ENFORCEMENT

A number of new approaches are being tried against street sales and users, primarily by larger metropolitan police departments under funding from the Bureau of Justice Assistance and the National Institute of Justice. The newer approaches are not necessarily discrete; some departments combine several to mount a comprehensive attack on drug sales.

Nor are all of the "new" techniques entirely new. For example, crackdowns and civil abatement procedures are refinements of techniques police have long been using to deal with such crimes as prostitution. The innovation is their application to combating drug sales. The new approaches, like the old ones, are designed to disrupt drug distribution through incapacitation and deterrence, with the ultimate goal of reducing drug consumption, street and property crime, and violence.

At the street-sales level, the new efforts can be roughly categorized as street enforcement, crack enforcement, problem-oriented policing, and citizen-oriented enforcement. Asset seizure and forfeiture also play a role, most often as integral parts of these other strategies. Figure 1 presents a summary of both traditional and innovative strategies for local enforcement of drug laws.

Figure 1.
Local law enforcement strategies against drugs

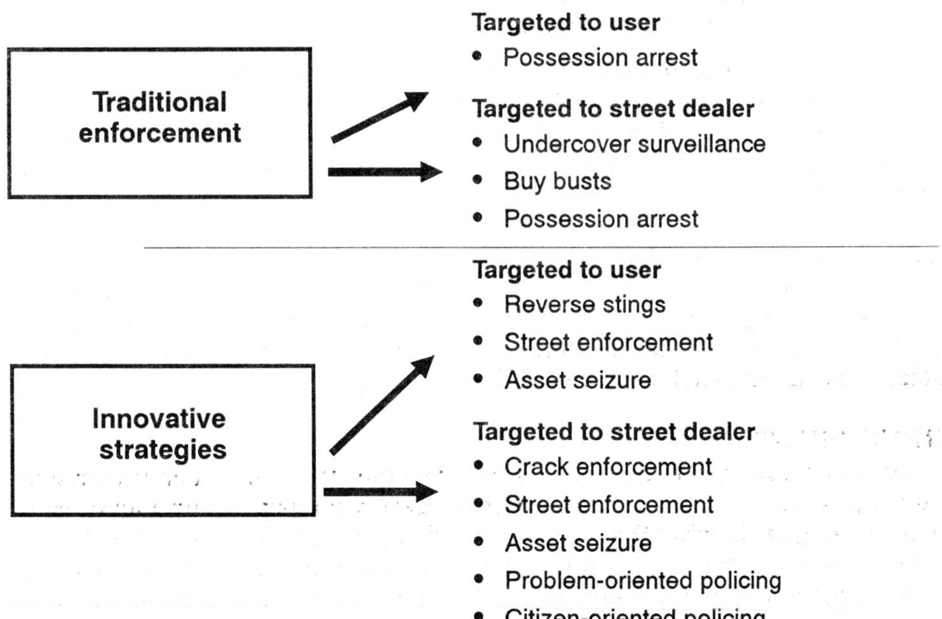

More and more, local law enforcement agencies are diversifying their strategies for combating drugs, variably targeting users and street sellers, and combining traditional techniques with newer approaches.

STREET AND CRACK ENFORCEMENT

Both street enforcement and crack enforcement are street-sales oriented; street programs deal with all types of drug sales, and crack programs focus on sales of this increasingly popular drug. These programs target drug sales locations and the street distributors themselves. Police use surveillance, informants, and information from drug hotlines to locate street sales and identify sellers.

Undertaking street enforcement and crack enforcement programs means increasing police personnel hours for narcotics control. Narcotics staff or tactical squads may work overtime, or patrol officers may be assigned to street-sales enforcement duty.

Specific law enforcement strategies depend on the nature of the drug problem. In cities where distribution takes place primarily through fortified crack houses, tactical or narcotics squads use search and arrest warrants, sometimes gaining entry by using heavy construction equipment. Where street sales are commonplace, the police may conduct saturation patrols or periodic large-scale arrests of suspected dealers in drug hot spots. These are frequently referred to as "sweeps" or "roundups."

CIVIL ENFORCEMENT

Civil enforcement procedures are gaining acceptance as well, and police are relying more and more on asset seizure at this distribution level. For example, if a house is being used as a crack house, the police typically notify the owner—through the public works department or the city attorney's office—that the property is being used for illegal drug sales. If the owner fails to take action, civil seizure of the property takes place and the house may be forfeited or even destroyed.

Street and crack enforcement strategies make use of building and fire code enforcement, along with tenant eviction if the property is rented. In jurisdictions where public housing projects are the center of drug sales, the police and public housing authorities cooperate in securing tenant evictions and enforcing lease conditions.

SELECTIVE ENFORCEMENT

Many innovative street enforcement programs focus on the purchaser and user of illegal narcotics. Police keep drug sales hotspots under surveillance and arrest both purchasers and sellers. Where it is permitted, police seize user assets, such as automobiles.

REVERSE STING

Another innovative approach is the "reverse sting," in which undercover police pose as drug dealers and arrest users who ask to buy narcotics or actually engage in what they assume is a drug transaction. User arrests may take place at the time of the sale or later in large-scale roundups of suspects, depending on the users' transience. This strategy is not as common as some of the others because of legal and operational concerns about police posing as dealers and engaging in what looks like actual drug sales.

PROBLEM-ORIENTED NARCOTICS ENFORCEMENT

Law enforcement agencies across the country are increasingly turning to policing that relies on a closer link to the community and a more systematic analysis of the conditions underlying deterioration in urban neighborhoods. Research has shown the benefits of the new approach in tackling a wide range of concerns about crime and disorder. One ingredient of the community-oriented approach is the use of systematic problem-solving techniques by police to bring a coordinated community response to counteract the devastating impact of drugs on neighborhood life.

Problem-oriented approaches apply the model successfully developed in Newport News, Virginia.[3] Under this approach, the first step in developing prevention or enforcement strategies is to collect and analyze data on individuals, incidents, and police responses to crimes.

Instead of relying on subjective or anecdotal assessment of their local drug problems, law enforcement agencies employing problem-oriented policing techniques collect and analyze objective data like crime statistics and citizen surveys. By looking at drug-arrest data, police in some cities have found that young adults are the group most actively involved in the drug trade; in other cities, they have found juveniles to be the more heavily involved group.

Problem analysis often shows that many conditions that are not the responsibility of the police—such as the presence of abandoned buildings and the lack of recreational facilities—contribute to a city's drug problem.

CITIZEN-ORIENTED POLICING

The premise of the citizen-oriented model of policing is that the police cannot solve the drug problem alone but must join with the community in controlling crime and ensuring public safety.

Local citizens establish community groups to eliminate the conditions that contribute to neighborhood drug sales. In Seattle, for example, citizens have set up their own drug hotline, pressured the legislature for new abatement laws and jail space, and conducted neighborhood cleanup projects. The distinctive feature of this approach is that a major responsibility for breaking the drug distribution chain rests not just with the police but also with neighborhood groups who work hand in hand with the police.

CASE STUDIES

The following case studies exemplify the approaches that are now working in cities and countries across the United States. They illustrate how to mobilize a variety of agencies—not just criminal justice, but health, education, business and citizen organizations—to join forces against drug abuse.

---

[3] Spelman, William and John E. Eck, 1987. *Newport News Tests Problem-Oriented Policing*, NIJ Reports, No. 201, p. 2, January/February 1987. Washington, D.C.
Eck, J.E., and W. Spelman, 1987. "Problem-oriented Policing In Newport News." *Police Executive Research Forum*. Washington D.C.
Goldstein, H., 1990, *Problem-oriented Policing*. New York: McGraw Hill.

And they explain how to focus programs on the most serious problems, devise appropriate tactics, and marshal needed resources.

Drugs affect communities in different ways. While programs from one community can't always be transplanted to another, the concepts, strategies, and lessons learned can be widely shared for the benefit of all.

Three types of enforcement strategies will be identified. Case-oriented drug law enforcement, network-oriented drug law enforcement, and comprehensive problem-reduction strategies.

Case-oriented drug law enforcement is essentially reactive and seeks sufficient evidence to arrest, prosecute, and convict known drug distributors. Methods for building cases include use of informants, undercover and surveillance methods, and "buy and bust" operations. Virtually all police departments with narcotics or dangerous drug units carry out this type of enforcement.

Network-oriented drug law enforcement is a proactive effort in which distribution is traced from street-level drug sellers through mid-level and high-level distributors, and at times to top-level kingpin distributors. This type of enforcement also requires the use of undercover and surveillance methods, but often also involves complex financial investigations to build prosecutable interlocking cases.

Comprehensive problem-reduction strategies are proactive initiatives taken to reduce harm to the community resulting from both the supply and demand for drugs. They typically involve not only law enforcement agencies but also community members and relevant community agencies such as those providing education, health, and mental health services for high-risk populations involved in the problem. Law enforcement agencies that participate in comprehensive problem-reduction strategies ordinarily also participate simultaneously in case-oriented and network-oriented drug law enforcement strategies.

The following case studies will incorporate the above approaches with enough detail to show what portions of them might be applicable to your jurisdiction.

COOPERATIVE LAW ENFORCEMENT STRATEGIES FOR DEMAND REDUCTION: A CASE STUDY IN MARICOPA COUNTY, ARIZONA

The Maricopa County Demand Reduction Program is an example of a comprehensive problem-reduction strategy that utilizes both horizontal and vertical coordination,[4] combines law enforcement, prosecution, education, and treatment components, and entails cooperation among Federal, county, and local public and private agencies. The county, whose major city is Phoenix, started its demand-reduction program in March 1989. It now has the following components:

[4] Horizontal coordination means that agencies work together in a cooperative effort in the sharing and investigation of cases and information, while vertical coordination means that information and coordination come from the chief of police.

Drug Laws and Programs

Periodically (usually two or more times each month), a location in the county where drugs are known to be used openly is targeted for a "user accountability" strike. During the selected time period, ranging from several hours to a few days, a task force of law enforcement officers from nearby communities arrests persons at the targeted location for drug possession and begins proceedings for seizing their vehicles and other property related to their drug possession.

Each of the county's law enforcement agencies has instituted a policy of encouraging arrests to be made under any circumstances when a person is found to possess illegal drugs (e.g., during the course of routine traffic stops). These offenses are all felonies in Arizona.

Persons arrested on drug charges are formally booked (not given a summons or otherwise diverted from the arrest procedure), so that they necessarily spend some time locked up in the county jail's intake facility.

The county prosecutor's office screens arrest reports for drug offenses to determine whether the arrestee meets criteria specified for participation in drug treatment as an alternative to prosecution. Typical arrestees who meet the criteria are first-time felony drug offenders over the age of 18 without a prior history of other felonies or recent misdemeanors involving drugs. Prosecution is temporarily suspended for qualifying arrestees, who are later sent a letter from the county attorney explaining the conditions which they must meet in order to avoid subsequent filing of criminal charges.

The alternative offered to the arrestee typically entails filing a written "statement of facts" admitting to the offense charge, participating in a period of drug-abuse treatment and mandatory drug testing, paying a treatment program fee, paying additional fees and assessments, and paying the sheriff for the costs of having been housed in the county jail's intake facility.

Eligible arrestees who opt for the treatment alternative undergo up to two years of group therapy, seminars, and routinely repeated urinalysis. At the end of the assigned period, arrestees who complete the treatment program and remain drug-free have their charges dropped.

Arrestees who are ineligible for the treatment alternative or who fail to complete it successfully are handled by the county attorney's normal procedures for prosecuting drug arrests. Arrestees who do not respond to the letter offering them the treatment alternative have an arrest warrant or summons issued against them.

An imaginative media campaign continually reminds the county's populace about the program through television, billboards, and print media. The message is: If you're caught with drugs, you're going to jail. "You then face felony charges, a prison sentence, and stiff financial penalties. Or pay to enter a year-long rehab program." The media are well informed about task force operations in progress, and their coverage helps demonstrate that the "Do Drugs, Do Time" campaign is more than rhetoric.

The demand-reduction program is based on the assumption that a large proportion of drugs purchased in the county are consumed by casual or infrequent drug users. By reducing the number of casual drug users, law enforcement agencies hope to disrupt the drug markets in their communities. Once the county's criminal justice agencies had decided to target a population that was assumed to have had little prior contact with the criminal justice system, they concluded that even modest interventions could alter patterns of drug abuse. Spending a few hours in jail, or even just seeing television commercials of casual users behind bars, could possible produce major behavioral changes. Surveys have shown very high public awareness of the demand-reduction program and its slogan.

One potentially conflicting goal of the county attorney's office was to avoid processing large numbers of persons arrested for drug possession or use. In fact, the diversion program incorporated as part of the demand-reduction strategy was intended to reduce work for county attorneys and the courts, for example, by eliminating the filing of a criminal case and having it later dismissed. The key to this aspect of the program was pre-filing diversion—eligible arrestees' cases are simply not filed in court if arrestees accept the conditions of the diversion program. Whether this sort of reduction in the prosecutor's workload can continue over a long period of time is not yet clear. Those arrested on minor drug possession charges who fail to respond to the letter offering the diversion option must be rearrested and prosecuted; they represent a potential future burden on the criminal justice system.

The county prosecutor's participation, and willingness to impose suitably structured sanctions on arrested users, was considered vital for initiating and maintaining the county's user accountability program. Otherwise, probable cause for arrest would have been undermined and law enforcement officers would have lost motivation to make arrests that were merely going to be dismissed by the prosecutor. Many thorny legal issues were researched by the county attorney's staff before procedures for arrests and pre-filing diversions were established, and these were continually fine-tuned over the following year.

The treatment component of the program is operated under a county contract by TASC, a private, non-profit, outpatient facility that has been incorporated for more than ten years. (TASC stands for "Treatment Assessment Screening Center," but the organization is otherwise similar to the Treatment Alternatives to Street Crime units found in many other jurisdictions.) TASC operates various educational programs, client assessments, counseling, urinalysis and breathalyzer testing, and statewide treatment services for agencies such as Arizona's supreme court and corrections department. TASC's ongoing operation in both the jail intake facility and in the community facilitated rapid establishment of an efficient diversion program. The main problem faced by TASC management in providing drug treatment is covering the expenses of indigent clients.

Educational components of the demand-reduction program are coordinated by a Drug Enforcement Administration (DEA) agent in Phoenix, who supplies schools and other community agencies with materials available through DEA and other national distributors. However, the current demand-reduction program in Maricopa County does not have other activities oriented specifically toward drug possession among juveniles. Juvenile arrests are uncommon under the demand-reduction program because the strike force targets are places frequented by adults. Still, juvenile arrestees in Maricopa County are unlikely to be undetected drug users; the county has one of the few programs in the country for universal urinalysis of juvenile arrestees who enter detention.

The drug test results of arrested juveniles are made available to assigned probation officers, who may make the information available to others, such as parents, teachers, or attorneys, at their discretion. Probation staff are enthusiastic about the juvenile arrestee urinalysis program. They find that their previous impressions of juvenile detainees in their custody did not give them a good perspective for distinguishing drug abusers from nonusers.

COOPERATIVE LAW ENFORCEMENT STRATEGIES FOR STREET-LEVEL TO MID-LEVEL DISTRIBUTION: A CASE STUDY IN COOK COUNTY, ILLINOIS

Originally founded in 1971, the Northeastern Metropolitan Narcotics and Dangerous Drugs Enforcement Group (NEMEG) is a horizontally-coordinated, case-oriented cooperative effort of municipal police departments that also includes the Illinois State Police and the Cook County Sheriff's Department. NEMEG, covering an area that encircles Chicago to the north, west, and south, does not include participation by all Cook County communities. Also, Chicago is not considered part of the NEMEG region. Currently, most nonparticipating agencies are either in large cities that believe themselves to be self-sufficient regarding drug law enforcement, or in small villages with no identifiable drug law enforcement. Participating agencies share in the following NEMEG resources:

— Training of officers to investigate and arrest persons involved in drug-related crimes.

— Ongoing access to and use of NEMEG officers experienced in special forms of investigation and activities, such as financial investigations and asset seizures.

— Realistic educational materials for residents about drug abuse, including information about "new" forms of drugs such as crack cocaine.

— Relatively rapid response to requests for NEMEG officers and other resources needed for crackdowns on local problems with drug dealers.

The command staff of NEMEG consists primarily of officers on a long-term assignment from the Illinois State Police or the Cook County Sheriff's Department. However, most NEMEG officers are provided by member police departments in communities in Cook County. Some communities join NEMEG directly, some join as part of a coalition administered by the South Suburban Mayors and Managers Association (SSMMA), and a couple of communities do both. Some members participate by sending a sworn officer to be a member of the NEMEG staff, while other members contribute only financially.

In the last few years, NEMEG has almost doubled the number of participating agencies through the combined efforts of SSMMA, the NEMEG director, and local chiefs of police. The SSMMA plays two major functions in promoting interagency cooperation for drug law enforcement: it relieves local agencies of the task of fiscal administration and provides participating agencies' chiefs with information about NEMEG activities, while ensuring that NEMEG commanders are aware of the chiefs' needs for services.

The main advantages to participating communities are:

- Fast response to local problems
- Centralized fiscal administration
- Training of officers
- Availability of drug enforcement officers unknown to local dealers
- Access to special investigation units
- Greater safety for law enforcement officers
- Shared resources
- Solid information for public education

COOPERATIVE LAW ENFORCEMENT STRATEGIES FOR REDUCING MID-LEVEL DISTRIBUTION: A CASE STUDY IN SAN DIEGO COUNTY

Founded in 1973 by the San Diego County Sheriff and the City of San Diego Chief of Police, and joined early on by the DEA, the San Diego County Narcotics Task Force (NTF) is a vertically and horizontally coordinated cooperative arrangement focusing on network-oriented drug enforcement. Task force operations are targeted primarily on mid-level drug dealers and are carried out jointly by members of all municipal police departments in the county, the sheriff's department, and the DEA. On-going cooperation for task force operations is provided by the staffs of the district attorney and U.S. Attorney.

This task force is known among law enforcement officials nationwide as an excellent example of interagency cooperation. On-site observations confirmed that interagency contacts are frequent, intense, productive, and highly cooperative. Factors that foster this kind of cooperation in San Diego County include the following:

- Rapid interagency communication, enhanced by insistence on a "team effort," direct access to agency supervisors, and an emphasis on innovation rather than routinization
- Coordination of actions taken by individual agencies on the same case, including coordination of issuing warrants, arrests, and civil and criminal prosecution
- Cross-designation of law enforcement staff from different agencies and of prosecuting attorneys from different agencies
- Continuous rotation of officers between local law enforcement agencies and the task force
- Formal procedures for selecting task force officers, coupled with informal procedures for ensuring compatibility between officers from different agencies

- Clear-cut criteria for assigning responsibility for cases, including specific amounts of drugs and money involved
- Pooling resources, including information, expertise, money, and equipment
- Sharing rewards, including seized and forfeited assets

UPPER-LEVEL DISTRIBUTION: FEDERALLY ORGANIZED EFFORTS

Drug task forces are the principal vehicles of Federally organized cooperation. The organizational arrangements of task forces vary, but there are two principal types of Federal task forces that involve state and local agencies:

- DEA state and local task forces. These are created by DEA and include DEA personnel as well as state and/or local agency personnel operating under DEA supervision and organizational direction.
- Organized Crime Drug Enforcement Task Forces (OCDETFs). These highly formalized, ongoing Federal arrangements are housed in selected U.S. Attorney's offices in major cities throughout the country. They may involve state or local agencies routinely or on a case-by-case basis.

The precursors of DEA state and local task forces were actually launched in 1970, prior to the DEA's creation. In that year, a pilot Federal task force was set up in New York City by the DEA's predecessor, the Bureau of Narcotics and Dangerous Drugs (BNDD). The task force was created in response to drug traffic that spilled beyond municipal, county, and state boundaries in metropolitan New York.

The early state and local task forces were based on the concept of "creative federalism." In order to foster mutual respect among levels of government, with each treated as an equal, creative federalism relied heavily on the notion of "coordination," which was never formally defined. The Federal agencies that first tried to hammer out working definitions of coordination found the experience frustrating.

Nowadays, formal cooperation in DEA state and local task forces has matured into a routine bureaucratic arrangement documented by compacts, memoranda of understanding, and sometimes contracts binding Federal and non-Federal jurisdictions. Federal agency staff now believe that a clear delineation of roles and responsibilities is vital to successful drug investigations, to the leadership and to personal communication among the participating investigators.

Organized Crime Drug Enforcement Task Forces (OCDETFs), first created in 1984 as a Presidential initiative, are charged with targeting major national and international trafficking organizations, the highest levels of importing and wholesale distribution. OCDETFs are administrative clusters of Federal investigative and prosecutive agencies. A U.S. Attorney's office that has an OCDETF designates coordinators who oversee OCDETF investigations. The coordinators work with both the participating Federal law enforcement agencies and the lead Assistant U.S. Attorney to see that cases are developed in a prosecutable manner.

The composition of investigators in a particular OCDETF investigation is determined by the initiating agency. In one case, the lead could be the FBI, and in another, Customs or DEA. OCDETF Assistant U.S. Attorneys become involved early in complex narcotics investigations. Working with the initiating law enforcement agencies, they help establish electronic surveillance, investigative grand jury proceedings, asset forfeiture, and the other investigative and prosecutive components typically needed in large-scale cases.

In contrast with DEA state and local task forces, OCDETFs infrequently involve non-Federal investigators. In general, OCDETFs focus on dealers one or two trafficking levels above those targeted by state or local investigators. When state or local investigators work on an OCDETF case, they are deputized only for the duration of the specified investigation. This provision contrasts with DEA policy, where the state or local investigators are deputized for the full length of their participation in a task force. State or local investigators who are invited to participate in an OCDETF case work with a special Federal agency, such as the FBI, and only for the period of time necessary to make the case. Although the case development period may be lengthy, at the close of the case the investigators return to their departments.

According to the FBI coordinator of OCDETFs and interviewed DEA agents, good working relationships have now been established among Federal, state, and local law enforcement agencies in many task force arrangements around the country.

THE DETROIT POLICE DEPARTMENT

The Detroit Police Department has a number of drug enforcement strategies such as:

BUY AND BUST

The investigation of an alleged narcotics distribution location where an undercover narcotics purchase is made and followed by an immediate arrest of the seller and recovery of the evidence.

CONSPIRACY CASE

A prolonged investigation to determine those responsible for the source and distribution of illegal drugs within an organization in order to prosecute those persons on charges of operating a continuing criminal enterprise. This strategy is aimed at mid- and higher-level drug traffickers.

CRACK DOWN

A massive enforcement effort conducted by local, state, and Federal law enforcement agencies whereby a series of arrest and search warrants are executed on a specified day in an effort to dismantle the illegal drug distribution network of a particular individual or organization. This effort usually marks the conclusion of a conspiracy investigation.

PADLOCK

The seizure of a drug distribution establishment after three consecutive enforcement efforts. The establishment is seized under the "nuisance abatement" act, and control and ownership of property can later be forfeited over to that agency's use. Padlocking is the actual securing of the establishment to prevent entry by unauthorized persons.

PRESSURE POINT
An enforcement operation where several planned raids are executed simultaneously within a targeted geographical area in an effort to maximize police effectiveness. This tactic is performed in response to complaints and information received from various community-based sources, i.e., police-community relations meetings, telephone complaints, and other sources.

RIP RIDE OPERATION
An enforcement strategy conducted in areas of high illegal drug activity where, while under police surveillance, customers that make drug transaction while using a vehicle are detained. Upon recovery of the purchased drug, the customer is arrested and the vehicle is confiscated and forfeited for police department use.

STREET ENFORCEMENT
The application of the various provisions of the Controlled Substances Act against the "open air" street corner merchant who distributes illegal drugs from street locations.

WRAP AROUND OPERATION
A follow-up action taken by the regular police patrol force in the aftermath of a recent enforcement action at a drug distribution establishment to insure that there is no resumption of illegal drug activity.

IMPLEMENTING COOPERATIVE DRUG LAW ENFORCEMENT STRATEGIES IN YOUR AREA

Potential obstacles to implementation of multijurisdictional drug enforcement strategies include:

— Corruption

— Violations of civil rights

— Differing agency accountability practices

— Maintaining operational secrecy

With sufficient advance planning and legal research, problems can be anticipated and avoided. The successes and difficulties experienced with the program suggest the following strategy for considering the establishment of multijurisdictional drug law enforcement programs.

Get the facts. A community-wide effort should be made to gain specific knowledge of the extent of the drug use problem.

Identify the problem. Multijurisdictional cooperation for drug law enforcement requires identifying a problem that all participating agencies agree is serious.

Evaluate the various cooperation strategies. The choice of which strategy to use (case-oriented drug law enforcement, network-oriented drug law enforcement, or a comprehensive problem-reduction strategy) depends on the problem to be addressed. Each strategy requires different types and levels of resources and different levels of interagency cooperation. A comprehensive problem-reduction strategy, for instance, requires active involvement by agencies and groups outside the criminal justice system, while case-oriented and network-oriented strategies operate primarily within the criminal justice system.

Involve top leadership in initial stages. Regardless of the type of cooperation undertaken, the top leadership of criminal justice agencies should be involved in designing a strategy to combat the problem.

Finalize important details. The detail of cooperation need not be nailed down before beginning a multijurisdictional effort. However, the following considerations must eventually be addressed.

- Written interagency agreements
- Personnel issues such as overtime, workers' compensation, pay rates, liability, and insurance
- Selection criteria for staff, and tenure and rotation policy
- Training
- Policies on use of weapons
- Sharing seized assets
- Handling informants
- Access to systems with confidential information

Do your own networking. Everyone contemplating establishment of a new multijurisdictional cooperative effort for drug enforcement could benefit from contact with practitioners who have already been through the experience.

Another program to combat drug abuse is the involvement of police officers within the schools to educate students about drugs.

Another program involves training police to become drug recognition experts.

THE DRUG RECOGNITION EXPERT PROGRAM (DRE)

The Drug Recognition Expert Program was started as a Federal grant for the Los Angeles Police Department to remove DUI (Driving Under the Influence) drivers from the road.[5] The program is divided into Preliminary Training, DRE Phase I and Certification Stage Phase II.

Preliminary Training (Pre-school)

The Preliminary Training section consists of 16 hours of classroom lectures and practical exercises. Topics covered include: standardized procedures in administration of the Field Sobriety Test, measurement and significance of the vital signs, and drug sign and symptom overview. DRE students are given a few weeks off to practice the skills before Phase I commences.

DRE School (Phase I)

Phase I involves some 56 hours of classroom lectures, practical exercises, role playing, and viewing video-taped drug suspects. The most difficult phase is made up of 30 formal classroom modules.

---

[5] Smith, Charles. Director, Bureau of Justice Statistics. "Drug Recognition Program." U.S. Dept. of Justice, Office of Justice Programs, 1990.

Certification Stage (Phase II)

The Certification Stage is based in jail facilities and involves a minimum of 40 hours. Arrestees in the jail are evaluated for drug use. A minimum of 15 evaluations, which include at least four of the seven drug categories, must be completed under the direct supervision of an experienced DRE. The student DREs' opinions must be compatible with the toxicological results.

Certification is granted following a comprehensive final examination and the recommendation of two DRE instructors.

DREs In The Field

During an involved 30-minute process, the DRE officer evaluates the individual suspected of being under the influence of drugs. After determining that no medical problems are present, vital signs are monitored and a physical exam is conducted. A chemical test is administered and the DRE forms a professional opinion based on the total picture provided by the results.

Evaluation

Two major studies have confirmed the accuracy of DREs on the street. The DRE program has been validated by researchers at the prestigious John Hopkins University. A 1984 study confirmed that the DRE can accurately distinguish between drug-impaired and non-drug-impaired individuals.

In 1985, the National Highway Traffic Safety Administration (NHTSA) then conducted a Field Validations Study consisting of 173 cases.[6] Evaluations regarding the accuracy of DREs in actual arrest situations were made by comparing DRE opinions with an independent laboratory's analysis of blood samples. The NHTSA found that the DREs were very successful in identifying both the drug-impaired individual and the types of drugs causing the impairment.

An expanding roster of states including the District of Columbia now utilize DREs for drug law enforcement.

NATIONAL DRUG ENFORCEMENT EFFORTS

The Drug Enforcement Administration (DEA) focuses its efforts to reduce the demand for drugs on its Sports Drug Awareness Program. This program was launched on June 27, 1984 and seeks to prevent drug abuse among school age youth, with special emphasis on the role of the coach and student athlete.

The Sports Drug Awareness Program includes brochures to inform coaches about the drug problem and to provide guidelines and an action plan to start a drug abuse prevention program for student athletes. In addition, DEA and Federal Bureau of Investigation (FBI) Special Agents and Public Affairs staff, players, and officials from professional sports, and high school coaches who have implemented successful prevention programs present

---

[6] Compton. "Field Evaluation of the Los Angeles Police Department Drug Detection Program." National Highway Traffic Safety Administration, Report No. DOT HS807012, U.S. Dept. of Transportation, 1986.

clinics for coaches to help them understand the drug abuse problem and develop a program in their high schools.

In conjunction with the U.S. Customs Service, the DEA also participates in the Law Enforcement Exploring Program of the Boy Scouts of America. The Customs Service sponsors approximately 30 Explorer posts throughout the country, teaching the participants about all areas of Customs activity. The program includes drug awareness and encourages Boy Scouts to spread the "no drug use" message to their peers. DEA worked with the Boy Scouts of America and Texans' War on Drugs to sponsor a drug abuse prevention training seminar for Explorer posts in six Texas communities.

United States Attorneys are another powerful force in efforts to reduce the demand for drugs. A mechanism within the U.S. Attorneys' Office to direct their prevention efforts is the Law Enforcement Coordinating Committee (LECC) program, which coordinates Federal, state, and local law enforcement activity. For example, under the leadership of the U.S. Attorney from the District of Hawaii, the LECC established the Hawaii Coalition on Substance Abuse, a statewide coalition of community and business leaders, working with drug abuse professionals and law enforcement officers.

THE BUSINESS OF DRUGS AND NARCOTICS ENFORCEMENT

Drug trafficking is big business. It is organized to earn huge profits. Today, the income from illegal activity is estimated at $100 billion.

All businesses need money and property to create products, to deliver them to their customers, to promote sales and to grow. Criminal businesses are no different. Drug dealers need money to buy silence from witnesses, to pay bribes, to expand into other illegal activities, to move into new towns and cities, and to pay for all their other illegal expenses.

Money and property are at the heart of all businesses. As long as assets and profits go untouched, lost workers and lost products can always be quickly replaced. Even with leaders in jail, confederates continue the business of drug trafficking by using the wealth and property left behind. Moreover, those imprisoned quickly return to drug dealing after being released, since criminals making huge profits see jail as an acceptable risk as long as they get to keep their earnings. They can invest their illegal fortunes while in jail, and the money will be waiting for them, with interest, when they get out.

Today's narcotics agents can no longer confine their activities to the "who, what, where, when and why" of drug enforcement. During every phase of their investigation they must ask an additional question, "What about the dollars?" "What about the assets?"

One of the attempts to seize the profits of crimes was the passage of the Bank Secrecy Act of 1970. The Bank Secrecy Act was passed in 1970 to ensure the maintenance of records by financial institutions and to require reports of certain financial activities where those records and reports "have a high degree of usefulness in criminal, tax or regulatory investigations or proceedings."

The need for the Act was well documented during the Congressional hearings which preceded its passage. Representatives of major Federal law enforcement agencies testified about the problems of investigating the financial activities of criminals, especially when foreign transactions are involved. Witnesses from Defense, Justice, State, Treasury and the Securities and Exchange Commission described how foreign accounts are used in black marketing, bribery, smuggling, securities violations, and tax evasion. One of the more sensational cases cited involved heroin disguised as canned food and smuggled into the United States from Europe. The money from this deal was moved in ways that remain common. The proceeds, amounting to $950,000 were sent to a European bank account of a Latin American shell company known as the "Me Too Corporation." Couriers delivered $800,000 in currency to two foreign exchange firms in New York. From there, the funds were transferred to the European bank account. The other $150,000 in currency was deposited with a large New York bank for the account of a South American brokerage firm. Those funds were later transferred by check to the same European bank.

On the strength of such testimony, the Bank Secrecy Act was passed and regulations were issued by the Treasury Department in 1972. Those regulations contain the following provisions:

> Banks and other financial institutions are required to maintain basic records such as signature cards, statements and cancelled checks for five years.
>
> Financial institutions are required to report currency transactions in excess of $10,000 to the IRS (Form 4789).
>
> Persons transporting or causing the transportation of currency and other monetary instruments in excess of $5,000 into or out of the U.S. are required to report it to the Customs Service (Form 4790).
>
> Everyone who has a financial interest in or signature authority over a foreign bank account must report it annually to the Treasury (Form 90-22.1).

It is clear that these provisions provide real tools in the fight against the traffic in drugs. They assist in following cash movements and provide obstacles to the "laundering" of funds. Crime is a cash business and illegal drugs appear to be one of the most widespread and lucrative underworld activities.

If money is carried out of the U.S. to pay for drugs, it must be reported. Unless money comes back through the banking system, it must also be reported when it is returned to the United States. Failure to do so is a crime, a crime which sometimes can be prosecuted more easily than narcotics charges. If drug receipts are deposited in large amounts in domestic banks, the banks must report the deposits.

There is a requirement that domestic financial institutions report currency transactions in excess of $10,000. The Federal bank supervisory agencies are responsible for ensuring that banks comply with these provisions. The IRS, however, has been delegated the responsibility of investigating potential criminal violations. The most publicized case so far has been the Chemical Bank case in New York. In 1977, the bank pled guilty to 445 misdemeanor counts of failing to file reports and was fined $222,500. The case arose from a narcotics investigation. Apparently, a number of branch bank managers went into business for themselves. For a small commission, they gave traffickers large denomination bills, $50's and $100's, for smaller ones.

In addition to the Bank Secrecy Act, the Federal government passed a civil law in 1978 (21 U.S.C. 881 (a) (6)) declaring that all monies used in, and all assets acquired from the illicit drug trade belong to the United States government and are subject to civil seizure under power of forfeiture. In effect, Congress authorized Federal attorneys to file civil lawsuits asserting the government's right to such property. Although the same evidence gathered in a criminal investigation can be used in these civil suits, they are independent of any criminal trials. Dismissal of criminal charges against an owner due to some technicality does not prevent the government from civilly suing for return of the property. Civil forfeiture suits are not burdened by the complex procedures of criminal cases; the level of proof needed in civil forfeiture suits is significantly less than the "proof beyond a reasonable doubt" required in criminal trials. Therefore, the government can introduce more types of evidence in these civil cases.

MONEY LAUNDERING

Today, money laundering is a runaway global industry that serves customers ranging from cocaine cartels to tax-dodging corporations. The coke smugglers can accomplish this feat because they have plenty of help.

The money laundering system depends on the collaboration, or often just the negligence, of bankers and other moneymen who can use electronic-funds networks and the secrecy laws of tax havens to shuffle assets with alacrity. The very institutions that could do the most to stop money laundering have the least incentive to do so. According to police and launderers, the basic fee for recycling money of dubious origin is 4 percent, while the rate for drug cash and other "hot" money is 7 to 10 percent.

Much is at stake as the powerful flow of narcodollars is recycled through the world's financial system. Drug lords and other lawbreakers are believed to be buying valuable chunks of the American economy, but clever money-laundering schemes make it almost impossible for U.S. authorities to track foreign investors. A case in point: blind corporations based in the Netherlands Antilles control more than one-third of all foreign-owned U.S. farmland, many of the newest office towers in downtown Los Angeles, and a substantial number of independent movie companies producing films like Sylvester Stallone's "Rambo" pictures.

While businesses and individuals may conceal their assets for purposes that are completely legal, or dubious at worst, the systems set up for their convenience can be perversely efficient at helping drug barons launder as much as $100 billion a year in U.S. proceeds.

What makes law enforcement so difficult is a financial rat's nest of loopholes that has long frustrated tax collectors as they search for dirty money afloat in the world's oceans of legitimate payments. The multibillion-dollar flow of black money (the profits from criminal enterprises) moves through the world's financial institutions as part of a vastly larger quantity of "gray money," as bankers call it. This dubious, laundered cash amounts to an estimated $1 trillion or more each year. Often legitimately earned, this money has an endless variety of sources: an Argentine businessman who dodges currency-control laws to get his savings out of the country; a multinational corporation that seeks to "minimize" its tax burden by dumping its profits in taxfree havens; a South African investor who wants to avoid economic sanctions.

The world's prosperity depends on a fluid and unfettered financial system, yet the lack of supervision is producing a large gray area in the economy. The IRS estimates that tax cheats skim as much as $50 billion a year from legitimate cash-generating businesses and launder the money to avoid detection. Banking experts calculate that the private citizens of debt-ridden Latin American countries have smuggled more than $200 billion of their savings abroad in the past decade.

Especially in the drug trade, the money-laundering process begins with greenbacks. Much of the cash simply leaves the U.S. in luggage, since departing travelers are rarely searched. Larger shipments are flown out on private planes or packed in ocean-going freight containers, which are almost never inspected. That explains, in part, why U.S. officials are unable to fully locate 80 percent of all the bills printed by the Treasury. Once overseas, the cash is easy to funnel into black markets, especially in unstable economies where the dollar is the favored underground currency.

However, narcotraffickers see America as a safe and profitable haven for their assets; they often launder and invest their cash in the U.S. The first and trickiest step is depositing the hot cash in a U.S. financial institution. The reason for this first step is that the IRS requires all banks to file Currency Transactions Reports for deposits of $10,000 or more. During the early 1980s, launderers got around this scrutiny by employing couriers called Smurfs, named for the restless cartoon characters, who would fan out and make multiple deposits of slightly less than $10,000.

The government now requires banks to keep an eye out for Smurfs, but launderers have developed new techniques. Since retail businesses that collect large amounts of cash are often exempt from the $10,000 rule, launderers have created front companies or collaborated with employees of small businesses or chain stores. To drug dealers, an exempt rating is like gold. A restaurant that accepts no checks or credit cards can be an ideal laundering machine. Even a front business with no exemptions is valuable because launderers can file the CTRs (Currency Transaction Reports) with the knowledge that they are unlikely to attract scrutiny, since the government is swamped with 7 million such reports a year, up from fewer than 100,000 a decade ago. Other places where drug dealers can often dump their cash include the currency-exchange houses along the Southwest border and urban check-cashing and money-transmittal stores.

Once the money is in a financial institution, it can be moved with blinding speed. Communicating with the bank via fax machine or personal computer, a launderer can have wire transfers sent around the world without ever speaking to a banking officer. The goal of many launderers is to get their money into the maelstrom of global money movements, where the volume is so great that no regulators can really monitor it all. Such traffic has exploded because of the globalization of the world economy, which has multiplied the volume of international trade and currency trading. On an average working day, the Manhattan-based Clearing House for Interbank

Payments System handles 145,500 transactions worth more than $700 billion, a 40 percent increase in just two years.

Much of the electronic money zips into a secret banking industry that got its start in Switzerland in the 1930s as worried Europeans began shifting their savings beyond the reach of Hitler's Third Reich. Later, the country's infamous numbered accounts became a hugely profitable business.

In 1986, money laundering became a specifically identifiable crime. Later, it became illegal to evade the $10,000 currency-reporting requirements by making groups of smaller deposits. Banks have begun to exercise more internal supervision as well, prodded by a series of investigations in the mid-1980s in which such institutions as the Bank of America and the Bank of Boston were forced to pay hefty fines for their involvement in laundering schemes. Yet, many major banks are still participants, wittingly or not, in increasingly subtle and sophisticated laundering operations.

There are many types of money-laundering schemes. For example, a customer could go to the Caribbean island of Netherlands Antilles; there, a French-owned bank would set up a corporation in Rotterdam where cash would be deposited in a local bank. The customer would control the recently created Dutch corporation through an Antilles trust company. The identity of the customer as the owner is protected by the island's secrecy laws. The Caribbean bank branch would then "lend" the customer his own money held in Rotterdam. If the customer was questioned by the IRS about his source of wealth, he could point to his respected loan-front international bank.

To help prevent this sort of laundering, the 1988 anti-drug abuse act included the Kerry Amendment. This amendment required the Treasury Secretary to negotiate bilateral agreements on money-laundering detection and prevention with all U.S. trading partners. Countries that refuse to participate or that negotiate in bad faith could conceivably be excluded from the U.S. banking network and clearing houses.

However, the administration is reluctant to enforce the law zealously for fear of hampering the U.S. banking industry. Nevertheless, there is more at risk than the dislocation of business as usual. Many experts believe the financial stability and national security of whole countries will be in jeopardy until the problem is solved. Some lawmakers have begun worrying about the impact of billions of drug dollars invested in U.S. institutions and wonder what influences the drug barons might eventually exert.

ASSET SEIZURE AND FORFEITURE

Forfeiture, the ancient legal practice of government seizure of property used in criminal activity, may prove to be a particularly useful weapon against illicit narcotics trafficking. Virtually all states authorize forfeiture in connection with drug trafficking and manufacture; four states also include cultivation of drugs in their forfeiture procedures. For purposes of forfeiture, other states group drug crimes with other offenses such as gambling and hazardous waste violations.

TYPES OF PROPERTY SEIZED

Once a state defines the type of criminal activity for which forfeiture may be invoked, it must define what property can be seized. All states authorize the forfeiture of drugs. Statutes also define properties that may not be illegal per se but may be seized because they were used to commit the crime.

Common provisions permit seizure of these types of property:

— Conveyances (aircraft, vessels, vehicles) used to transport, conceal, or facilitate the crime.

— Raw materials, products, and equipment used in manufacturing, trafficking, or cultivation, and the containers used to store or transport drugs.

— Drug paraphernalia used to consume or administer the controlled substance.

— Criminal research and records, including formulas, microfilm, tapes, and data that can be used to violate drug laws.

In practice, vehicles and cash are the most frequent forfeiture targets; a few states also authorize pursuit of real and personal property. A growing number of states are adding "traceable assets" (purchased with drug profits), such as jewelry and houses. A financial investigation is often required to link such assets to drug profits. The investigative expense may be cost effective, however, because the property is valuable and the potential for disrupting the criminal organization is high.

DISPOSITION OF FORFEITED PROPERTY

An important and controversial aspect of a forfeiture law involves the disposition of forfeited property. Most state statutes provide that outstanding liens be paid first. Next come the administrative costs of forfeiture, such as storing, maintaining, and selling the property. Some states require that, after administrative costs are reimbursed, the costs of law enforcement and prosecution must be paid.

More than half the states provide that confiscated property goes to the state or local treasury, or part to each. In some states, however, law enforcement agencies may keep the property for official use. If the property is sold or if it is cash, then the money goes to the state or local treasury. In some states, law enforcement agencies can keep all property, cash, and sales proceeds.

The legislative rationale for allowing law enforcement agencies to benefit from forfeiture seems clear. It is the belief that police departments will be more likely to allocate resources to pursue forfeiture of criminal property if the department can gain an automobile for undercover work or cash to supplement the drug "buy fund." Indeed, a few statutes not only allow the police department to keep all forfeited property but explicitly state that forfeited moneys and property cannot be used to reduce appropriations for the police budget.

In addition to allocating forfeiture proceeds to government treasuries and to law enforcement agencies, legislatures have provided for other interests to benefit. A few states earmark a percentage of forfeitures for drug rehabilitation and prevention programs. New York's law provides funds for restitution to victims, while Washington state allocates 50 percent of proceeds to its Criminal Justice Training Fund.

LIMITATIONS TO FORFEITURE PROVISIONS

Because it involves surrender of property rights, forfeiture is a severe penalty. For this reason, legislatures often include exceptions to forfeiture laws, most of them designed explicitly to prevent innocent people from losing their property.

The most common of such provisions concern forfeiture of conveyances; they protect innocent owners, lienholders, and common carriers. Exceptions are invoked for a person with interest in the property who neither knew of nor consented to its illegal use.

INFORMATION ON ASSET SEIZURE

The National Criminal Justice Association has issued a 100-page book called *Assets Seizure & Forfeiture: Developing and Maintaining a State Capability*. Despite the reference to states in the title, the book is also useful for local police executives. It was funded by the Florence V. Burden Foundation and the National Institute of Justice.

The book is available from the National Criminal Justice Assn., 44 N. Capital St. N.W., Suite 608, Washington, D.C. 20001. The publication is free with a charge for postage and handling.

The book is designed primarily for prosecutors and law enforcement executives who want to know the "hows" and "whys" of asset seizure. It covers in detail the necessary steps from the initial investigation or arrest through the actual taking of assets. The book points out, as many law enforcement executives have discovered, that "forfeiture is a complex, time-consuming, and resource-intensive process." In fact, the process may be beyond the abilities of small police agencies and prosecutors' offices, and so a regional or statewide pooling of resources may be needed for an effective asset seizure program.

Usually, a forfeiture action begins when a police officer makes a drug arrest or discovers potentially forfeitable property in the course of surveillance. It is important for the officer to be familiar with state and Federal laws governing forfeiture. That familiarity, say the authors, "includes understanding what evidence to look for, what information to see, and what questions to ask to develop the necessary information for a successful prosecution." Thus, it is advisable to train line officers in the concept and law of forfeiture.

This training is especially useful when police supervisors have to make judgments about whether or not to seize a dealer's assets. If, for example, a small-time drug dealer used a car worth $1,000 in his business, but the cost of prosecuting him would be $2,000, it would not make economic sense to seize the car. It would make even less sense if it turned out that an innocent third party held a lien on the car, because he would have first call on proceeds from its sale.

There have been a few well-publicized cases of forfeiture of very valuable properties from big drug traffickers—stores, horse-breeding farms, seaside mansions, and yachts. But most forfeiture cases have involved only cash and cars found at the scene of the arrest or serving of a search warrant. According to *Assets Seizure & Forfeiture*, that fact is a shame. The book notes that potentially forfeitable proceeds of drug transactions go far beyond the conveyances and cash found at the scene of searches or arrests.

The trouble is that establishing a case for seizing hidden assets from drug dealers may require a financial investigation that small agencies are unable to handle. The paper trail may lead through bank statements, credit card records, stockbrokers' records, lease agreements, business ledgers and a host of other trail markers.

Somewhat simpler than a full-blown financial investigation is a "net worth analysis." The purpose of this analysis is to establish that the person being investigated received and spent more money than he could have gotten from legitimate sources. This can often be done by checking public records such as property deeds, taxes paid, and business licenses issued; it can also be done by interviewing vendors, trash collectors, and suppliers of business services. If the forfeiture proceeding is in civil court, the suspect himself may have to give information about his assets.

Assets Seizure & Forfeiture also points out that white-collar crime investigators are well-equipped to handle such investigations. "For agency investigators with no experience in these types of investigations . . . training is a necessary first step in developing a capability to develop financial evidence," the authors say. Even when the investigators are trained, a police agency might hire an investigative accountant to help with a major case.

The book includes chapters on managing seized assets while court proceedings are under way, interagency cooperation in forfeitures, and a model curriculum to train investigators and police managers. It tells prosecutors where to look in their state's statutes for provisions governing forfeitures and gives the U.S. Attorney General's guidelines on seized and forfeited property.

Assets Seizure & Forfeiture is not exactly light reading, but it is a valuable resource for law enforcement executives who want to improve their chances of hitting drug dealers in the pocketbook and swelling the public treasury, if not that of their own agency. And, as the book's introduction puts it: "Law enforcement strategies aimed at attacking the profitability of crime may be the most effective means of disrupting criminal operations, and the seizure and forfeiture of criminals' assets may be the most effective of those strategies."

SOME PROBLEMS WITH ASSET SEIZURE

Since the advent in recent years of Federal and state statutes allowing local sharing of assets seized from narcotics violators, narcotics enforcement has been affected in both a beneficial and non-beneficial manner. The original intent of these laws was simple: they were written to be used as another tool for law enforcement in stemming the ever-growing tide of narcotics trafficking. They were designed to financially impact, in a negative manner, narcotics dealers at all levels. Lastly, they were enacted to financially support law enforcement in obtaining the necessary personnel, training and equipment.

Local law enforcement administrators have found that when asset-sharing funds are received by their agency, they are called upon by local city councils or boards of supervision to deduct a like amount from their annual budget requests. This was not the intent of the asset forfeiture laws. They were not designed to supplant existing personnel, training or equipment.

Some public governmental agencies and non-governmental, non-profit organizations peripherally associated with narcotics enforcement have also been successful in obtaining asset-sharing funds. If asset funds are diverted from law enforcement, they should be directed to viable anti-drug education programs within our schools. Prevention, by means of educating our young people in the inherent dangers of drug experimentation or abuse, is imperative.

Law enforcement itself is not without fault when it comes to asset sharing. Agencies which previously openly shared information on cases of mutual interest or that were multijurisdictional, have ceased communicating with one another. They are attempting to keep the asset sharing with any other agency to a minimum. In some instances, agencies that have had minimal participation in a major asset seizure have submitted exorbitant sharing claims for their assistance. If this type of philosophy is allowed to continue and grow from agency to agency, there is only one group of individuals who will really benefit, and that's the illicit narcotics dealers.

Furthermore, since the cash seizures come primarily from cocaine investigation, the emphasis has shifted away from other drugs. Heroin use and sales have become a lower priority because of the relatively low cash flow compared to cocaine. Finally, because the investigation of large dealers is complicated and very time-consuming, there is frequently insufficient staff available to investigate small dealers and other local problems.

To overcome these problems it is recommended that:

1. Agencies should join together to form interagency task forces, or larger agencies should designate specialized units to investigate major drug traffickers and seize their assets.

These dedicated units must be large enough to conduct the complex investigations and thus generate revenue. The task force approach should reduce the likelihood of interagency conflicts and free the local narcotics units to investigate local crimes.

2. The mission of the local narcotics unit should be established to include a well-rounded enforcement of drug problems within the community.

The nature of police work and police officers is that they will gravitate to the biggest and best cases. Therefore, the mission of the local narcotics unit must be clearly stated. The focus must be aimed toward investigating local problems and controlling the drug problems within its jurisdiction, avoiding the temptation to become involved in the glamorous major investigations that could monopolize the unit and destroy flexibility. The schools, and battling drug-related crime should be realized as the two most important missions. The purpose of the asset seizure unit should be that of providing support and revenue for the efforts of the local unit.

3. A portion of the assets seized from drug dealers should be used to support drug prevention and intervention programs within the community.

This policy recommendation addresses the importance of attacking the demand side of the drug equation. Rather than continuing to invest the seized funds in more equipment and manpower, part of the resources should be directed towards the implementation and support of drug prevention and intervention programs. By using the drug dealer's assets to support drug intervention programs such as Drug Awareness Resistance Education (DARE), law enforcement can take an important step toward reducing the future drug appetite of the community.

4. A portion of the assets seized from drug dealers should be used to finance drug enforcement training and equipment for patrol officers.

The recommended policy further addresses the demand side by allocating assets to the training of patrol officers in narcotics enforcement with the goal of turning each patrol officer into a street drug enforcement expert. Well-trained patrol officers would increase the risk to the possessor and/or user of illegal drugs by increasing the likelihood of arrest and successful prosecution.

In summary, it should be mentioned that asset seizure is an important emerging issue that offers great promise as well as some potential challenges. Continuing the present trend of increased asset seizure emphasis, without considering the potential problems, may lead to severe complications requiring reactive problem solving* at some future date. Managing the future through proactive strategic policy* assessment and implementation places narcotics enforcement in a position to enhance its opportunities, while avoiding future problems. Any law enforcement agency implementing asset seizure initiatives should consider these advantages and disadvantages with careful planning and caution.

DRUG FREE ZONES

While asset seizure is becoming an effective method of curtailing narcotic trafficking, other approaches such as Drug Free Zones continue to decrease the local distribution of such illicit drugs. Drug Free Zones are established by law, and were established to provide penalty enhancements (1 to 3 years) to adults who committed drug violations within Drug Free Zones.

One example of this approach may be cited from the city of Cypress, California which adopted a resolution establishing a Drug Free Zone within the city.

The California Health & Safety Code section 11353 describes Drug Free Zones in some detail. The policy focuses most on the prevention of drug use

* Reactive problem solving is dealing with a problem after someone brings it to your attention; for example, responding to a dispatcher call of a 211 (robbery) in progress. Proactive problem solving is not waiting for the crime to happen, but preventing the crime or going out and finding the criminal; for example, undercover narcotics enforcement, sting operations, etc.

by minors. Since minors are especially susceptible to coercion by older persons in their community, Drug Free Zones have been established to deter adults from distributing drugs in areas where minors are often located. The regulations involved in violations within a Drug Free Zone most often include a person 18 or older soliciting, inducing, encouraging, or intimidating a minor to commit any violation involving heroin, cocaine, cocaine base, PCP or methamphetamine.

The section has a broad definition of Drug Free Zones which includes: upon the grounds of or within a church or synagogue, playground, public or private youth center, a public swimming pool, during hours in which the facility is open for business, classes, or school-related programs or at any time when minors are using the facility, and within 1,000 feet of the grounds of any public or private elementary, vocational, junior high, or high school, during hours that the school is open for classes or school-related programs or at any time when minors are using the facility.[7]

The section also describes a "Youth Center" as including video arcades (any premises with 10 or more video games).

DRUG FREE ZONE SIGNS

The Health and Safety Code expressly states that Drug Free Zones need not be posted. However, it is hoped that posting signs (as many cities have already done) will discourage violations and enhance the likelihood that prosecutors will pursue the penalty enhancements. With the resolution, the Cypress City Council approved the purchase of 100, 12″ x 18″ "Drug Free Zone" signs. These signs were placed in the areas described above; they were also posted at the city limits. However, as previously stated, no sign need be posted to pursue the penalty enhancement.

PROSECUTION

As the District Attorney may not be aware that a particular defendant is eligible for penalty enhancements because of violation of the Drug Free Zone statute, it is incumbent upon the reporting officer to bring this to the attention of the prosecuting attorney. This can most easily be done in the initial crime report. An appropriate paragraph might read as follows:

CASE CLOSED BY ARREST.

Note: Pursuant to California Health and Safety Code Section 11353, this violation occurred in a (posted) Drug Free Zone.

If you do not have such a law, you might consider one.

Drug Free Zones statutes have been tested in the courts.

Rejecting a challenge to Virginia's Drug-Free Zone Act, the Virginia Supreme Court has held that the Act applies to sales even when school is closed and children are not present. *Virginia v. Burns*, No. 90-0495 (July 30, 1990).

---

[7] Gould Publications. *Penal Code Handbook of California*, 1992.

Drug Laws and Programs

The Drug-Free Zone Act, Virginia Code 18.2-255.2, makes it unlawful to distribute any controlled substance on the property "of any public, private or parochial elementary, secondary, or post secondary school, . . . [or] upon public property or any property open to public use within 1,000 feet of such school property . . ."[8] Violation of the section is a separate and distinct felony carrying a separate sentence of one to five years and a fine or not more than $100,000. In 1990, the Virginia General Assembly made the section's provisions applicable to drug transactions occurring "at any time."

NEEDLE EXCHANGE PROGRAM

One controversial drug-related initiative is the needle exchange program. The goal of this program is to reduce the spread of AIDS and other diseases. In its policy declaration, the International Association of Chiefs of Police stated that the exchange program sends conflicting messages to society. On the one hand, drug abuse is not tolerated; yet, on the other hand, we give out drug paraphernalia to use drugs. The Association suggests that law enforcement should adopt the following response:

> "Providing such paraphernalia will discredit anti-drug programs and is unlikely to have any effect on decreasing the spread of disease among addicts. Hygiene is not a priority for addicts who rarely sterilize drug paraphernalia. In fact, most addicts are willing to share needles with other addicts even if free needles are available."[9]

Even though there is some truth to the statement, needle exchange programs are worthy of implementation. For example, after 3 years in operation, the program in Vancouver, Canada has succeeded in reducing the spread of AIDS. The program began in 1989 because many IV drug users were infected with AIDS. It was recognized that AIDS was a major risk factor for IV drug users and their sexual partners. Among the IV drug users tested for AIDS, 1½ percent are positive in Vancouver. This compares to a rate of 14 percent in Montreal, Canada. The Director of the exchange program credits the giving out of clean needles and having a 95 to 100 percent return rate for the low number of AIDS cases in Vancouver.[10]

As for such programs in the continental United States, the first one authorized by state legislative action began in Connecticut. The New Haven Department of Health initiated its landmark needle exchange program on November 13, 1990. The program was then established in July, when Connecticut Governor William O'Neil signed into law a measure which allowed state officials to supply non-prescription needles and syringes through a pilot program. The New Haven needle exchange program represents a joint state-municipal effort, for which the state legislature authorized $25,000.

---

[8] Gould Publications of Florida, Inc. *Virginia Criminal Law and Motor Vehicle Handbook*, 1992.

[9] International Association of Chiefs of Police. *Reducing Crime by Reducing Drug Abuse: A Manual for Police Chiefs and Sheriffs.* Gaithersburg, MD 20878, IACP, June 1988, p. 51.

[10] "Vancouver's Needle Exchange Program." Canadian Centre on Substance Abuse. Reported in the *International Drug Report*, International Narcotics Enforcement Officers Association, January 1992.

According to Elaine O'Keefe, director of the department's AIDS division, these funds are used to purchase supplies for the program. New Haven is also providing staff for the program, which represents an expansion of the city's existing AIDS outreach program.

AIDS COUNSELING AVAILABLE

The mobile needle exchange program operates out of a van that travels to areas of the city known for high drug use. Clean needles and AIDS information are exchanged for used needles on an anonymous basis, with a limit of five units per exchange. Non-current IV-drug users are excluded from the program.

Also on duty in the van is an AIDS counselor who is available to talk with clients or refer them to other counseling and treatment programs. The state legislature mandated that counseling and education be provided as part of the program.

While clients are not required to provide their names, they are asked for information on their history of drug use and safe sex practices to provide baseline information on their habits. Users are later re-surveyed to detect changes in self-reported behavior.

When the legislation was adopted, legislators said that one of the prime objectives of the controversial program would be the gathering of data on the incidence of drug use and the impact of the exchange program.

Elaine O'Keefe calls the creation of the program a remarkable achievement and says she believes it will be successful not only in reducing the risk of AIDS, but in helping some drug users obtain treatment. She also hopes that, if the program works, a panel will be able to argue for statewide expansion of it. At that point, O'Keefe says she would push to decriminalize the statewide sale and possession of needles and syringes.

OPERATION "WEED and SEED" [11]
"Reclaiming America's Neighborhoods"

". . . the fight against crime is everyone's business. Families and neighborhoods, schools and churches, drug shelters and businesses and the media—everyone must joint in this fight."

President George Bush
August 14, 1991

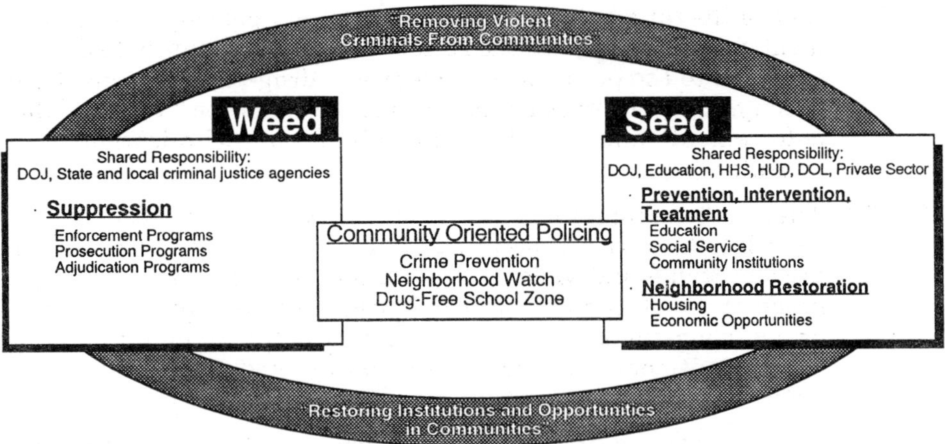

INTRODUCTION

Operation Weed and Seed is a comprehensive, multi-agency approach to combating violent crime, drug use, and gang activity in high-crime neighborhoods. The goal is to "weed out" crime from targeted neighborhoods and then to "seed" the targeted sites with a wide range of crime and drug prevention programs and human service agency resources to prevent crime from reoccurring.

The strategy further emphasizes the importance of community involvement in combating the problems of drugs and violent crime. Community

---

[11]U.S. Dept. of Justice. Office of the Attorney General. Reported in *The Narc Officer*. International Narcotic Enforcement Officers Association, Albany, NY. June 1992, pp. 11-16.

residents need to be empowered to assist in solving crime-related problems in their neighborhoods. In addition, the private sector must get involved in reducing crime. All of these entities, Federal, state and local government, the community and the private sector must work together in partnership to create a safe, drug-free environment.

The Weed and Seed strategy involves four basic elements:

1. Law enforcement must "weed out" the most violent offenders by coordinating and integrating the efforts of Federal, state and local law enforcement agencies in targeted high-crime neighborhoods. No social program or community activity can flourish in an atmosphere poisoned by violent crime and drug abuse. One effective law enforcement strategy, for example, is Project Triggerlock, a Department of Justice initiative that targets the violent offender for prosecution in Federal court to take advantage of tough Federal firearms laws. Between April and August of 1991, Triggerlock resulted in more than 2,600 arrests and had a 91 percent conviction rate.

2. Local police departments should implement community policing in each of the targeted sites. Under community policing, law enforcement works closely with the residents of the community to develop solutions to the problems of violent and drug-related crime. Community policing serves as the "bridge" between the "weeding" (law enforcement) and "seeding" (neighborhood revitalization) components.

3. After the "weeding" takes place, law enforcement and social service agencies, the private sector and the community must work to prevent crime and violence from reoccurring by concentrating a broad array of human services—drug and crime prevention programs, educational opportunities, drug treatment, family services, and recreational activities—into the targeted sites to create an environment where crime cannot thrive.

4. Federal, state, local and private sector resources must be focused on revitalizing distressed neighborhoods through economic development and by providing economic opportunities for residents.

GOALS:

- To eliminate violent crime, drug trafficking and drug-related crime from targeted high crime neighborhoods.
- To provide a safe environment, free of crime, for law-abiding citizens to live, work and raise a family.

OBJECTIVES:

- To develop a comprehensive, multi-agency strategy to control and prevent violent crime, drug trafficking and drug-related crime in targeted high crime neighborhoods.
- To coordinate and integrate existing as well as new Federal, state, local and private sector resources and concentrate those resources

in the project sites to maximize their impact on reducing and preventing violent crime, drug trafficking and drug-related crime.

- To mobilize community residents in the targeted sites to assist law enforcement in identifying and removing violent offenders and drug traffickers from their neighborhoods.

PROGRAM DESCRIPTION:

WEED—LAW ENFORCEMENT/REMOVAL OF VIOLENT CRIMINAL PROGRAM

Often, narcotics traffickers and violent criminals, once arrested, are almost immediately returned to the streets to continue their business of distributing drugs and terrorizing local residents. This environment of violence makes potential witnesses fear for their lives. Far too often, there is a lengthy delay between arrest and disposition of narcotic cases prosecuted at the local level. Moreover, even when such cases are resolved through a guilty plea or conviction, the criminal may serve little, if any, time in county or state correctional facilities. This cycle of arrest, delay, and mild or no punishment breeds frustration and despair in the community. The **Weed and Seed** initiative is designed to address this disturbing cycle.

Under this program, the local United States Attorney will play a central role in coordinating Federal, state and local law enforcement agencies to prosecute certain drug and/or violent offenders in Federal court, where they will be subject to pretrial detention, a speedy trial and mandatory minimum sentences. The advantages to this approach are:

- the offender is immediately removed from the streets, and the public immediately sees that these law enforcement efforts are effective;
- the offender is met with swift justice; and
- those convicted serve longer sentences mandated by Federal law and are prevented from committing further criminal acts for years to come.

BRIDGE Between "WEED" and "SEED"—COMMUNITY-ORIENTED POLICING

Community-oriented policing activities will focus on increasing police visibility and developing cooperative relationships between the police and the citizenry in the target areas. This strategy will support the suppression activities and provide a "bridge" to prevention, intervention and treatment, as well as the neighborhood reclamation and revitalization components. Techniques such as officer foot patrols, citizen neighborhood watches, targeted mobile units and community relations activities will increase positive interaction between the police and the community. The objective is to raise the level of citizen and community involvement in crime prevention activities and other partnership efforts, and to help solve drug-related problems in neighborhoods. This community-oriented approach will ensure that reduced levels of drug use, trafficking and related crime, which result from the "Weed" activities, are maintained. This effort will also enhance public safety and lead to reduced fear in the community so that socio-economic development and related services can be implemented successfully.

SEED—NEIGHBORHOOD REVITALIZATION PROGRAM

Neighborhoods, especially in urban areas, deteriorate when heavy narcotics trafficking thrives. The removal of violent criminals and the eradication of drug trafficking in such areas cannot be accomplished by law enforcement alone. Without addressing other existing social and economic problems, such communities remain fertile ground for still more drug trafficking groups. Accordingly, **Operation Weed and Seed** is designed to address the social and economic problems in communities where narcotics trafficking is prevalent, and to provide a comprehensive and focused framework under which public agencies, community organizations and citizens can form partnerships to enhance public safety and the overall quality of life.

Prevention, Intervention, and Treatment

In order to prevent crime and drug abuse at the local level, it is important to foster a sense of individual responsibility among community members, especially school-aged youth. Alternative activities for high-risk youth are needed to prevent them from being lured into narcotics trafficking. Consequently, programs involving recreational activities, job and life skills development, mentoring, service projects and education are needed. In addition, on-going support services for victims and survivors of violent crime should be stressed. Such programs may be coordinated through:

- Key state and local agencies
- Key Federal agencies such as:
  - Department of Housing and Urban Development
  - Department of Commerce
  - Department of Health and Human Services
  - Department of Education
  - Small Business Administration
  - Department of Labor
- Private sector
- Community-based organizations

Neighborhood Restoration

In addition, it is essential that Federal agencies, such as those listed above, provide resources that will enable neighborhood reclamation and restoration activities and improved community services to follow. This will include programs to enhance home ownership through housing rehabilitation and promote new business opportunities.

While the Federal government may provide initial assistance to implement **Weed and Seed** initiatives, state and local governments and the communities themselves must ultimately be responsible for long-term and sustained economic and social improvements.

STRATEGIES

The **Weed and Seed** program includes four major strategies:

1. Suppression Strategy

This strategy will consist primarily of enforcement, adjudication, prosecution, and supervision activities designed to target, apprehend and incapacitate violent street criminals who terrorize neighborhoods and account for a disproportionate percentage of criminal activity. Such criminals will be prosecuted under the Department of Justice initiative, Operation Triggerlock. Some of these activities will focus on special enforcement operations such as "street sweeps," repeat or violent offenders, intensified narcotics investigations, targeted prosecutions, victim/witness protection and services, and elimination of narcotics trafficking organizations operating in these areas.

2. Community-Oriented Policing Strategy

This strategy operates in support of intensive law enforcement suppression and containment activities and provides a "bridge" to the prevention, intervention, treatment components as well as the neighborhood reclamation and revitalization components. Community-oriented policing activities will focus on increasing police visibility and developing cooperative relationships between the police and the citizenry in the target areas. Techniques such as foot patrols, targeted mobile units, victim referrals to support services and community relations activities will increase positive interactions between the police and the community. The objective is to raise the level of citizen and community involvement in crime prevention activities to solve drug-related problems in neighborhoods and to enhance the level of community security.

3. Prevention, Intervention, and Treatment Strategy

This strategy will focus on activities such as youth services, school programs, community and social programs, and support groups designed to develop positive community attitudes toward combating narcotics use and trafficking. It will also provide opportunities for neighborhood residents.

4. Neighborhood Restoration Strategy

This strategy will focus on economic development activities designed to strengthen legitimate community institutions. Programs will be developed in partnership with law enforcement to organize and train citizens and resident groups to resist and repel the drug culture. These programs will improve living conditions, enhance home security procedures, allow for low-cost physical improvements, develop long-term efforts to renovate and maintain housing as well as provide educational, economic, social, recreational and other vital opportunities. A key feature of this strategy will be the fostering of self-worth and individual responsibility among community members.

SIX STEP IMPLEMENTATION PLAN

The program strategy consists of six basic steps for implementation:

1. Organize the Law Enforcement Task Force and Neighborhood Revitalization Coordinating Committee

The United States Attorney will chair both the Law Enforcement Task Force and the Neighborhood Revitalization Committee. The suggested participants listed below should have the authority, and control the necessary resources, to develop and implement a Weed and Seed strategy through the dedication of new resources and redeployment of existing services into the targeted neighborhood:

Law Enforcement

U.S. Attorney
State Attorney General
Mayor
State Drug Czar
Chief of Police
Sheriff
District Attorney
Presiding State District Judge
Chief Probation Officer
Chief Corrections Officer
Federal Law Enforcement Agencies
Victim/Witness Coordinator
State Criminal Justice
  Administrator – BJA
State Formula Funds

Neighborhood Revitalization

U.S. Attorney
Mayor
School Superintendent
Directors of Departments of:
  Social Services
  Housing
  Health/Mental Health
  Recreation
  Employment
Director of United Way
Directors of Private Community-
  based organizations
Private Industry Council
Representative – Federal Job
  Training Partnership Act
Regional Administrator HUD
Regional Administrator SBA
Regional Directors of Community
  Relations Service (CRS)

2. Selection of Target Neighborhood

The following suggested criteria should provide sufficient information to identify and expedite the selection of a high crime neighborhood.

- Incidents of gang-related violence
- Homicides/aggravated assaults/rapes and other incidents of violent crime
- Drug arrests
- High school dropout rates
- High unemployment rate
- High percentage of population on public assistance and
- Percentage of population on probation and parole

3. Conduct a Needs Assessment of Targeted Neighborhood

The type of information developed in step two will be used to assess the problems and needs of the targeted neighborhood in relationship to the

 md

program goals and objectives. The assessment will identify the problems in the targeted neighborhood and inventory the available resources to address those problems.

4. Select Resources

Specify the existing and new resources that will be needed to meet the objectives selected in step 3.

5. Identify Implementation Activities

Identify the program activities and human services that will be implemented to achieve each of the objectives, specifying **who** will be responsible for administering the activity, **what will it involve, where** will the activity be conducted, **when** will it be done, **how** will it be implemented and **how much** will it cost.

6. Develop Implementation Schedule

Develop a time-task plan that includes a schedule for the completion of major activities.

DEPARTMENT OF JUSTICE PILOT DEMONSTRATION PROGRAMS

The following describes the Phases I and II for implementation of **Operation Weed and Seed** in the Department of Justice:

Phase I—Fiscal Year 1991

In fiscal year 1991, the Bureau of Justice Assistance, a component of the Department's Office of Justice Programs, funded three pilot sites under this initiative.

1. **Trenton, New Jersey**, was awarded $284,000 from the Bureau of Justice Assistance, Office of Justice Programs, in September 1991. This **Weed and Seed** project is targeted at four neighborhoods and is proceeding with very good results. The City of Trenton has developed a four-pronged approach to fighting the war on drugs and crime in these neighborhoods:

(1) The Violent Offender Removal Program (VORP) is designed to target, apprehend, and incapacitate violent street gang members and disrupt drug trafficking networks in and around the designated Safe Haven Zones. VORP has resulted in the arrest of 69 persons since the beginning on this program.

(2) The Trenton **Weed and Seed** Program was recently awarded an additional $743,142 to fund community policing activities. The Community Policing Program is designed to emphasize the need for police officers and residents within the community to work together in creative ways to address the problems of crime at the neighborhood level. Community policing has been implemented in each of the four targeted neighborhoods.

(3) The Safe Haven Program is designed to bring together education, community, law enforcement, health, recreation and other groups to provide alternative activities for high-risk youth and other residents of the community. Three public middle schools in three of the targeted neighborhoods are being held open after regular hours from 3 p.m. to 9 p.m. to house these programs. In addition to programs for high-risk youth, the Safe Haven Project also includes a number of programs that are adult-oriented. The

number of community participants at one of the Safe Haven sites has averaged between 85 and 125 per evening, with as many as 200, on several occasions.

(4) The Community Revitalization and Empowerment Program is in the planning stages and should be underway soon.

A number of human services agencies have been identified to participate in the "Seed" effort, including: the Delaware Valley United Way, Urban League of Greater Trenton, Boys and Girls Clubs, DARE (Drug Abuse Resistance Education) program, and the Trenton School District, among others. In addition, the mayor of Trenton has held a number of town meetings in the targeted areas to assess community needs and the types of social services to be made available in the "Safe Havens." Project participants also have signed a memorandum of agreement specifying their commitment to the program.

The OJP Office of Juvenile Justice and Delinquency Prevention has agreed to establish Boys and Girls Clubs in public housing projects in the Trenton **Weed and Seed** sites. OJP's National Institute of Justice will be evaluating the **Weed and Seed** pilot projects.

2. **Kansas City, Missouri**, was awarded $200,000 in August 1991 from the Bureau of Justice Assistance, Office of Justice Programs, for a program organized by the U.S. Attorney and the Kansas City Police Department. The Kansas City **Weed and Seed** program has been expanded and BJA has received a preliminary draft of an extensive "Weeding" program that should be finalized and operational by February 1992. The working group, comprised of law enforcement, human service agencies and community organizations, is making much progress in developing its implementation plan for both the "Weeding" and "Seeding" components. A target neighborhood has been selected. The "Seeding" plan will feature forfeiture of houses used for drug trafficking and abandoned property, and conversion of these properties into affordable housing. Key participants under the "Seeding" component, at this time, are: the Regional Office of the U.S. Department of Housing and Urban Development; the Small Business Administration; the Kansas City Neighborhood Alliance; and the Ad Hoc Group Against Crime, a neighborhood-based organization.

The OJP Office of Juvenile Justice and Delinquency Prevention has agreed to establish Boys and Girls Clubs in public housing projects with the Kansas City **Weed and Seed** site. Further, OJP's National Institute of Justice will be evaluating the Kansas City **Weed and Seed** site.

3. **Omaha, Nebraska**, was awarded $25,000 in September 1991 from the Bureau of Justice Assistance, Office of Justice Programs. These funds were provided to the Community Partnership of a **Weed and Seed** pilot project. The Committee represents a broad cross-section of the community and has created an elaborate structure to develop this initiative. BJA expects to receive a full application from Omaha by the end of February 1992. OJP's National Institute of Justice will be evaluating the Omaha **Weed and Seed** site.

Drug Laws and Programs

In fiscal year 1992, the Department is expanding the pilot phase of **Weed and Seed** to additional sites. This initiative shows great promise, but much work remains to be done relative to refining the design of the program. While resources are limited in fiscal year 1992, approximately eight to ten additional sites will be funded under a limited competition involving 16 cities. Some of the factors that were considered in selecting the 16 cities that have been invited to participate under this limited competition are: the existence of a severe crime problem within the city; the presence of successful Department of Justice and/or other anti-drug programs; geographical diversity of sites in Phase II; and balance of large and mid-size cities. The cities under consideration are:

Atlanta, Ga.	Los Angeles, Calif.	San Antonio, Tex.
Boston, Mass.	Madison, Wis.	San Diego, Calif.
Charleston, S.C.	Philadelphia, Pa.	Seattle, Wash.
Chicago, Ill.	Pittsburgh, Pa.	Washington, D.C.
Denver, Colo.	Richmond, Va.	Wilmington, Del.
Fort Worth, Tex.		

Those cities that are not selected as the final eight grantees will receive training and technical assistance to assist them in developing and implementing comprehensive strategies, such as in the area of community policing, and will be eligible to compete for funding in fiscal year 1993.

On January 7-8, 1992, United States Attorneys from the 16 cities participated in a Planning Conference hosted by the Department. At the planning conference, the U.S. Attorneys were fully briefed on the **Weed and Seed** Program.

PRESIDENT'S FISCAL YEAR 1993 INITIATIVE

The President's budget proposes a substantially expanded **Weed and Seed** effort in fiscal year 1993. In the Administrations's fiscal year 1993 budget, $500 million has been proposed for **Operation Weed and Seed**. Under the Attorney General's leadership, the Office of National Drug Control Policy and the Departments of Education, Health and Human Services, Housing and Urban Development, Labor and Transportation will coordinate social services and community assistance programs, including those to expand drug treatment, provide job training, keep schools open in the afternoon and evening, offer alternative activities for high-risk youth, modernize public housing and improve the local community infrastructure.

Of the total $500 million in Federal resources, up to $400 million will go to neighborhoods that are designated as Urban Enterprise Zones by the Secretary of Housing and Urban Development. Fifty Enterprise Zones are proposed over the next four years, with two-thirds of them in urban areas. Up to $100 million will go to **Weed and Seed** neighborhoods that are not designated as Enterprise Zones. **Weed and Seed** Zones will be designated pursuant to guidelines issued by the Attorney General.

The Weed and Seed Initiative in 1993

1. **Law Enforcement: Eliminating Crime and Violence**. Under **Weed and Seed**, a total of $30 billion in specifically-targeted Department of Justice 1993 funds will help finance state and local law enforcement activities in over 30 neighborhoods. The features of this approach are:

- Immediate removal of offenders from the streets, providing visual proof to the community that law enforcement is effective.
- Stiff mandatory sentences for offenders prosecuted in Federal court, preventing further criminal acts and allowing communities to rebuild the social and economic infrastructure of their neighborhoods.
- Use of sophisticated case-building techniques such as audio-visual evidence gathering and witness protection, substantially increasing the efficiency and effectiveness of case development.

2. **Social Services: Providing Hope and Assistance**. A broad range of social service programs and resources will be available for use in the targeted neighborhoods, including:

- Educational and Prevention Programs, such as school drug use prevention, after-hours tutoring and dropout prevention programs.
- Job Training for high-risk youth and adults, including counseling, skills assessment and training, day care assistance, referral to Job Corps and job placement.
- Drug Treatment, including central intake and referral, specialized treatment for adolescents and pregnant women, after care, and referrals to education, literacy training, job training, and other social services.
- Access to Health Care, including primary and prenatal care, nutrition assistance, HIV counseling and testing and transportation services.
- Head Start for one year for eligible children.

3. **Creating Job and Economic Opportunities**. **Weed and Seed** areas will benefit from tax incentives in the Administration's Enterprise Zone proposal. Enterprise Zones will lay the foundation for successful supportive service programs.

4. **Housing and Community Development**. Public housing developments in **Weed and Seed** areas will be eligible for drug elimination grants to help rid the housing complexes of drug users. The targeted sites will also be eligible to receive specially-designated modernization funds to make necessary repairs. A special set-aside of housing vouchers will be available for very low-income families in need of assistance in those areas. Community development block grant funds will be available for such purposes as street and sidewalk repair, street lighting, park and recreational area improvements, as well as economic development activities.

How Weed and Seed Will Work

Pursuant to program guidelines promulgated by the Attorney General, local entities will submit joint applications to the Department of Justice that:

- Target previously designated Enterprise Zones with documented drug, gang and violent crime problems;
- Identify existing Federal, state and local resources for the targeted community that will be dedicated to the **Weed and Seed** effort;
- Identify private sector resources, including corporate contributions and individual commitments, to be included in the **Weed and Seed** effort; and
- Demonstrate a balanced, comprehensive plan, which addresses getting violent offenders off the streets, supports drug and crime prevention, and includes other efforts at neighborhood revitalization through strategies to create jobs and opportunities.

Drug use and crime are often deeply rooted in poor or economically deprived neighborhoods and act as barriers to the success of social service programs. **Weed and Seed** is a concerted effort to assist these areas by stripping away crime and drugs and replacing them with the tools to create opportunity. By evaluating carefully what happens through this effort, the foundation can be laid for the future.

PROGRAM POSSIBILITIES

The following is a list of potential projects and activities that a local jurisdiction might integrate into a local **Weed and Seed** initiative.

WEEDING

Law Enforcement
Project Triggerlock
Project Achilles
Street Sales (sweeps, reverse buys, buy-bust, etc.)
Multi-jurisdictional Task Forces
Crack Task Forces
Organized Crime/Narcotics
Serious Habitual Offenders Comprehensive Action Plan (SHOCAP)
Gang Identification/Intervention
Directed Patrols
Sector Integrity
Victim/Witness Coordination

Prosecution/Adjudication/Supervision
Project Triggerlock
Career Criminal
Repeat Offender
Drug Night Courts
Differentiated Case Management
Supervision/Reintegration

Pretrial Drug Testing
Comprehensive Drug Testing
Treatment Alternatives to Street Crime
Intensive Supervision
Boot Camps
Judges Training in Victims Issues
Prosecution-based Victim/Witness Programs

User Accountability
Civil Penalties
Denial of Federal Benefits User Accountability Program
Structured Fines
Community Service Programs

BRIDGE BETWEEN "WEED" and "SEED"

Law Enforcement
Crime Prevention Through Environmental Design
Hot Spot Cards (utilizing citizens to anonymously tip-off police to drug traffickers)
Nuisance Abatement
Landlord-Tenant Training
Police Mini-Stations/Kobans
Comprehensive approach to closing drug houses
Drug Paraphernalia Laws
Drop-In Centers
Offender Supervision and Victim Restitution Projects
Foot Patrols
Community-oriented Policing
Problem-oriented Policing
Innovative Neighborhood-oriented Policing
Law Enforcement Training in Victims Assistance and Protection
Law Enforcement Training to Improve the Treatment of Sexual Assault Victims

Community-oriented
Community Relations Service
Community Clergy Coalitions
Neighborhood Task Forces
Drug Free School Zones
Adopt-A-School
Adopt-A-Park
School Watch
Neighborhood Watch
Business Watch
Drug Free Recreational Centers (youth and adult)
Senior Citizens Programs
Volunteer Programs (graffiti clean-up, etc.)
Marches/Rallies
Drug Free Neighborhood/Community
Training and Technical Assistance:
    For Victims of Drug-Related Crime
    For Victim Service Providers

Drug Laws and Programs

For Clergy Response to Crime Victims
To Serve Parents of Murdered Children
To Serve Children of Murdered Parents
In Mental Health Treatment for Victims

Community Partnership Program (HHS)

SEEDING

Prevention/Intervention

Community Partnership Program (HHS)
Head Start Programs
Police Athletic Leagues (PAL)
Explorer Scouts
Boys and Girls Clubs
Law-related Education
After School Recreational Programs
Career Youth Development Programs
Conflict Resolution/Mediation Programs (grades 9-12)
Parent Awareness Programs
PTA/Parent Support Groups
Job Corps (DOL)
Victims of Drug Related Crime
Training and Technical Assistance to Address Child Sexual Exploitation
Peer Counseling

Educational Programs

Individual Responsibility Programs
Respect for Oneself and for the Rights of Others Programs
Drug Abuse Resistance Education (K-8)
McGruff Elementary School Drug Prevention Program - Curriculum (K-6)
Here's Looking At You 2000 (K-12)
Project Smart (6-10)
Refusal Skills (6-8)
Teens, Crime and the Community (9-12)
Literacy Programs

Housing/Community Redevelopment/Economic Development

Affordable Housing/Low Income Housing Programs (HUD)
Landlord-Tenant Training
Nuisance Abatement
Beat Health
Tenant Associations
Housing Ministries (building and remodeling affordable homes for low-income families)
Community Economic Development Programs (HHS)
8-a Program (SBA)
Small Business Investment Corporation (SBA)
Economic Development Administration (Commerce)
Chamber of Commerce
Operation Clean Sweep (HUD)

IN CONCLUSION

This chapter has discussed several of the programs that have been developed to effectively combat the drug use and abuse problem in the United States. In addition to various law enforcement initiatives, these include needle exchange programs, Drug Free Zoning, and Operation Weed and Seed. No one program by itself will be effective. Only through the combined resources of all levels of government, all components of the justice system and its administration, and the involvement of education, prevention and treatment efforts, will we truly experience a reduction in the problem of drug abuse.

REFERENCES:

Beasley, James O. Special Agent FBI, *The Analysis of Illicit Drugs and Money Laundering Records.* Laboratory Division, Racketeering Records Analysis Unit, RM 1B089, 10th Street and Pennsylvania Ave N.W., Washington, D.C. 20535.

Canadian Centre on Substance Abuse. "Vancouver's Needle Exchange Program." Reported in the *International Drug Report.* International Narcotic Enforcement Officers Association, Albany NY, January 1992.

Compton. "Field Evaluations of the Los Angeles Police Department Drug Detection Program." National Highway Traffic Safety Administration. Report No. DOT HS807012, U.S. Dept. of Transportation, 1986.

Eck, J.E., and W. Spelman. "Problem-oriented Policing in Newport News." *Police Executive Research Forum.* Washington, D.C., 1987.

Goldstein, H. *Problem-oriented Policing.* New York: McGraw Hill, 1990.

Gould Publications. *Penal Code Handbook of California,* 1992.

________. *Virginia Criminal Law and Motor Vehicle Handbook,* 1992.

House Committee on the Judiciary. Subcommittee on Crime. Money Laundering Legislation. July 24, 1985.

International Association of Chiefs of Police. *Reducing Crime by Reducing Drug Abuse: A Manual for Police Chiefs and Sheriffs.* Gaithersburg, MD 20878, June 1988.

International Narcotic Enforcement Officers Association. *The Narc Officer.* June 1992, pp. 11-16.

National Criminal Justice Association. *Assets Seizure & Forfeiture: Developing and Maintaining a State Capability.* Washington, D.C.

Senate Committee on Banking, Housing and Urban Affairs. Drug Money Laundering, S571. January 28, 1985, New York, NY.

Smith, Charles. Director, Bureau of Justice Statistics. "Drug Recognition Program." U.S. Dept. of Justice, Office of Justice Programs, 1990.

Spelman, W., and J.E. Eck. "Newport News Tests Problem-oriented Policing." *NIJ Reports.* No. 201, Washington, D.C., January/February 1987.

U.S. Dept. of Justice. National Institute of Justice, "AIDS and Intravenous Drug Use." *AIDS Bulletin.* February 1988.

________. National Institute of Justice. "Controlling Street-Level Drug Trafficking." Research in Brief, 1992.

Drug Laws and Programs

_______. National Institute of Justice. Police Foundation. "Modern Policing and the Control of Illegal Drugs: Testing New Strategies, Research Report." May 1992.

_______. National Institute of Justice. "The Police and Drugs, Perspectives on Policing." No. 11, September 1989.

U.S. General Accounting Office. *Rural Drug Abuse: Prevalence, Relation to Crime, and Programs.* Gaithersburg, MD.

A series of articles reported in *The Narc Officer*, official publication of the International Narcotic Enforcement Officers Association (INEOA), June 1991.

Chartier and Karchmer. "Multijurisdictional Drug Law Enforcement Strategies: Reducing Supply and Demand," pp. 29-34.

"Cooperative Law Enforcement Strategies in Demand Reduction: A Case Study in Maricopa County, Arizona," pp. 35-50.

"Cooperative Law Enforcement Strategies in Reducing Street to Mid-Level Distribution: A Case Study in Cook County, Illinois," pp. 51-59.

This page intentionally left blank.

CHAPTER IV

DRUG PHARMACOLOGY, CLASSIFICATION, AND TESTING

PHARMACOLOGY

The branch of science that deals with the interaction of chemical agents and living organisms is known as pharmacology. Traditionally, the major concern of pharmacology has been the study of drugs intended for medicinal use, i.e., drugs used to diagnose, prevent, treat, or cure disease. Even when such chemicals were misused and abused, sometimes for recreational purposes rather than for treating disease, the standard description of a drug was considered adequate. However, with the introduction of oral contraceptives in the mid-1950s, pharmacologists had to revise their definition of a drug. The "pill" was not used in the diagnosis, prevention, treatment, or cure of disease—unless pregnancy was to be considered a disease.

Consequently, pharmacologists have revised their definition of drugs to include ". . . all chemicals that affect living processes." This newer definition seems more appropriate, especially with the increased use of "street drugs," many of which never had any intended medical use.

The science of pharmacology has given rise to three major subdivisions now recognized as special areas of study and practice:

1. Psychopharmacology—The study of where and how drugs act in the body, how drugs are changed by the body, and how drug action affects behavior.
2. Therapeutics—the use of drugs in treating disease. When drugs are used specifically to destroy or weaken invading organisms, the treatment is referred to as chemotherapy.
3. Toxicology—the study of poisons and the treatment of drug poisoning, including intoxication, resulting from the presence of harmful chemicals in the body.

THE NERVOUS SYSTEM

In order to understand the impact of various drugs on the human body, one must first understand the uniqueness and processes of the nervous system. People take drugs recreationally to feel good and to alter their consciousness. Consciousness takes place through the nervous system.

All drugs are capable of producing more than a single response. Psychoactive drugs or substances have their primary effect on the human nervous system.

The nervous system is separated into three major divisions. It is important to realize however, that these divisions are not independent of each other. They interact; they are subsystems of the total system of our body.

The three major divisions include the central nervous system, the autonomic nervous system, and the peripheral nervous system.

THE CENTRAL NERVOUS SYSTEM (CNS)

The central nervous system (CNS) is composed of the brain and spinal cord. The central nervous system is encased in bone; the brain is covered by the skull, and the spinal cord resides within the vertebral column. The spinal cord serves as the conduit of information bringing signals to the brain from organs (including sensory organs) and muscles. In turn, the brain sends messages to motor fiber, which effect change in the activity of glands and muscles.

THE AUTONOMIC NERVOUS SYSTEM (ANS)

The autonomic nervous system (ANS) is a regulatory system for smooth muscles, which form much of the viscera and internal organs. Smooth muscles are specialized for slow, sustained functions, such as digestive movement. The autonomic nervous system is regulated by hypothalamic activity and is divided into the parasympathetic and sympathetic systems. These two systems act in opposite ways. The parasympathetic nervous system is primarily concerned with maintaining organ function; the sympathetic nervous system takes over under conditions of excitation, stress, or threat.

Although several drugs affect the central nervous system, their effects are most often observed in the autonomic nervous system. Drugs that have effects similar to adrenalin activate the sympathetic system of the ANS. Since these drugs mimic the effects of adrenalin and therefore stimulate the sympathetic nervous system, they are called sympathomimetic agents. Activation of the sympathetic system in the ANS produces the fight or flight response, which includes the following signs: increased respiration, increased cardiovascular output, dilation of the pupils, constriction of blood flow in the digestive system, and other stimulating effects.

THE PERIPHERAL NERVOUS SYSTEM (PNS)

To be precise, the ANS is actually a specialized portion of the peripheral nervous system. The nerves of the body that connect the brain and spinal cord to the sense organs and muscles make up the peripheral (motor-somatic) nervous system. When a receptor nerve is stimulated, it carries this excitation from the receptor to the central nervous system. When the brain has deciphered the message and acted on the information, it in turn activates motor nerves that carry excitation from the CNS to the glands and muscles. These nerves are known as effectors: they "effect" or stimulate the action required by the central nervous system in the peripheral nervous system.

Interestingly, many drugs (such as certain muscle relaxants) have what are called "peripheral effects," since their action is on the peripheral nervous system. A drug may have only peripheral effects, only central effects, or peripheral and central effects in combination.

SUMMARY

The complex functions of the nervous system are capable of producing several pleasurable states in human consciousness. Drugs are often used for the sole purpose of altering consciousness and producing such states. To better understand how these states are produced, it is necessary to explore the inner workings of the nervous system's three subsystems—the central, autonomic, and peripheral systems.

Within these subsystems the actual activity is begun by communication between nerve cells called neurons. This communication is carried out by electrical impulses within the cells and by neurotransmitters between the cells. Since drugs can affect both cells and neurotransmitters, sometimes causing profound behavioral and/or physical effects, the higher-order brain functions are the most susceptible to destruction by drug abuse.

NEUROTRANSMITTERS: MEDIATORS OF THE NERVOUS SYSTEM

A neurotransmitter is a naturally occurring chemical in the nervous system which carries electrical impulses between neurons (brain cells).

The brain and peripheral nervous system is comprised of neurons separated by small gaps called "synapses". Neurotransmitters act within the synapses to determine the quantity and quality of electrical impulses that will be transmitted.

Although there are over one hundred chemicals in the brain, no more than about two dozen are probably true neurotransmitters. Research to date indicates that some of these are very important in the development and continuation of drug dependence.

Some transmitters implicated in drug dependence are: Dopamine, Acetylcholine, Serotonin, Norepinephrine, and Gamma Amino Butyric Acid (GABA).

NEUROHORMONES: THE REGULATORS OF THE BODY

A neurohormone is a chemical that is made in a gland, leaves it, and acts on nervous tissue and/or other glands to maintain equilibrium in the body. Many neurohormones are made in the pituitary gland which is located at the base of the brain. The pituitary gland makes hormones which regulate most of the body's other glands. These include: thymus, thyroid, pancreas, ovary, testicle, adrenal, and breast glands. The pituitary gland also makes the neurohormones that are greatly responsible for pain relief, stress relief, and mental stability.

DIAGRAM OF HOW A NEUROTRANSMITTER WORKS

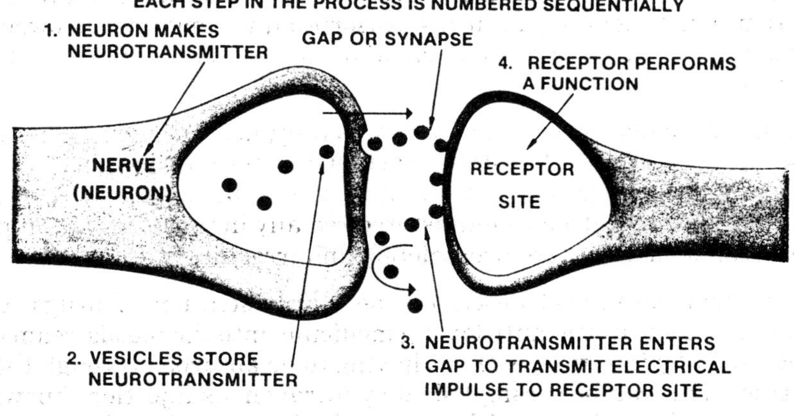

RECEPTOR SITES:

In 1974, the opioid receptor site was discovered. Opioids are opium derivatives which include heroin, morphine, codeine, Talwin, Darvon, Dilaudid, Demerol, Methadone, Percodan, and Fentanyl. When one of these drugs is taken, it goes to the brain and attaches to the opioid receptor site.

The opioid receptor site is known to help the brain perform the following functions:

Relieve Pain
Promote Mental Stability
Regulate Food Intake
Produce Euphoria
Control Stress
Prevent Depression
Control Breathing Rate

Receptor sites have also been discovered for benzodiazepines.

During natural brain activity, neurotransmitters and neurohormones attach to specific brain receptor sites to carry out different functions. Drugs of abuse mimic the brain's natural neurotransmitters and neurohormones in that they have similar chemical effects on the nervous system.

HOW DRUGS ENTER THE BODY

In order for a drug to have any more than a superficial effect, such as antacids in the stomach or antidandruff shampoos on the scalp, the chemical agent must enter the blood-vascular system. It must be absorbed or transported from the site of administration into the bloodstream, and then distributed by the blood throughout the body to various tissues and fluids. The manner in which the drug is introduced (the route of administration) is an important factor in determining how fast the drug acts, how long its effects will be sustained, the intensity of the drug's action, and the degree of localization of the drug's action.

Although drugs can be administered in several ways, they are usually given orally, rectally, parenterally, and by inhalation. Most often, drugs are taken into the body by way of the mouth. From the mouth, the liquid or solid drug passes into the stomach, and eventually into the intestine where most of the chemicals are absorbed (transferred) into the bloodstream. Oral administration is convenient, permits self-medication, and avoids the physical and psychological discomforts of injection. However, this route of administration is not ideal for all drugs. Absorption is sometimes slowed by the presence of food in the stomach and the excessive movement of the gastrointestinal tract.

Less commonly, drugs can be given rectally, i.e., through the rectum, the terminal end of the digestive tract. This method is particularly advantageous if the person is unconscious, has difficulty in swallowing, or is vomiting. However, drugs administered rectally in the form of a suppository or even an enema may be incompletely and irregularly absorbed.

The term parenteral describes the administration of drugs, such as antibiotics, insulin, and anticlotting medicine, into the bloodstream directly or indirectly by injection, without having to be absorbed through the digestive tract. This can be accomplished by intravenous injection (known as an IV or "mainlining," by which a drug in inserted directly into a vein);

intramuscular injection or IM (directly into muscle tissue); or by subcutaneous injection or "skin-popping" (just beneath the skin's surface). While each of these routes of administration has its distinct advantages and disadvantages, some features are commonly shared, as noted below.

Administration of drugs by injection:

1. Produces a more rapid response than can be obtained by oral or rectal administration.
2. Achieves more accurate dosage, since drug destruction in the digestive tract is avoided.
3. Bypasses the unpredictable absorption processes occurring in the stomach and intestine.
4. Provides insufficient time, in comparison with orally administered drugs, to counteract unexpected drug reactions or accidental overdose. Once given, an injection cannot be recalled.
5. Requires sterile conditions in order to avoid infectious disease caused by bacteria and viruses that can damage the liver, heart, and other body organs.
6. Presents a potentially painful situation for the drug taker.

Certain drugs can be administered by *inhalation* in which chemicals are absorbed into the blood stream by passing through the lungs. Volatile anesthetic gases, paint thinner and gasoline vapors, and non-volatile aerosols, as well as tobacco, marijuana smoke and crack cocaine can pass through the thin membranes of the lung's air sacs and readily enter the bloodstream. In certain instances, inhalation of drugs produces an effect nearly as fast as, or faster than, intravenous injection. Consequently, control of dose is a major advantage of inhaling or breathing in drug vapors and drug smoke.

A variation of inhalation is known as snorting, the intranasal administration of drugs. In this route of entry, a water-soluble drug such as cocaine is snorted or sniffed, being absorbed through the moist mucous membranes that line the nasal passages. The drug enters the blood vessels near the surface lining.

While most psychoactive drugs are administered by mouth, rectum, injection, or inhaling, the future of drug use could be changed dramatically by a relatively new form of administration. The U.S. Food and Drug Administration has recently authorized use of the first rate-controlled, transdermal drug system—a drug that is absorbed through the skin. Worn on the skin's surface as a disk or patch, the drug is absorbed directly into the bloodstream at programmed rates.

DRUG DISTRIBUTION AND ELIMINATION IN THE BODY

After a drug has been absorbed into the bloodstream, it is widely distributed throughout the body. Such dispersal, however, reflects the physical and chemical nature of the drug and its ability to pass through various membranes—cell walls, capillaries, the brain, and the placenta.

Four basic patterns of drug distribution have been identified:

1. Some drugs, including blood-plasma substitutes, remain largely within the bloodstream.
2. Other compounds, such as ethyl alcohol and certain sulfa drugs, become almost uniformly distributed throughout each and every body cell.
3. Most drugs are unevenly distributed in the body in accordance with their ability to penetrate different membranes of the body.
4. Very few drugs actually concentrate in one or more body tissues or organs that may not even be the sites of drug action.

It should be noted that although psychoactive drugs affect mood and behavior—functions controlled by the nervous system—most of these chemicals will be found outside the brain at any given time, even during states of drug intoxication and poisoning.

As drugs are circulated throughout the body, they undergo processes of metabolism and excretion, both of which are responsible for the elimination of the drugs and the termination of drug action.

The complex chemical changes that alter drugs and convert them to substances that can be eliminated from the body are known collectively as metabolism. A special system of enzymes in the liver cells carries out these metabolic reactions. Thus, the liver is an important body organ that functions in detoxification, the natural process of making substances non-poisonous.

When the recently detoxified substances are carried by the blood to the kidneys, the metabolized drug by-products are excreted, i.e., eliminated from the body in the urine. Consequently, the kidneys with their filtering action are the major route of eliminating toxic substances from the human body. This action of the kidneys helps maintain the body's chemical homeostasis, that internal state of constancy or equilibrium necessary for normal functioning.

Although most drugs are excreted by the kidneys, small amounts will also be eliminated via several minor pathways of excretion. These routes include sweat, saliva, gastric secretions, bile, feces, breast milk, and the lungs. Though several psychoactive substances are absorbed through the lungs, including nicotine and marijuana, only the highly volatile drugs, such as anesthetic gases and alcohol, are excreted through the lungs.

DRUG ACTIONS AND EFFECTS

Although there are technical differences between drug actions and drug effects, these terms will be used interchangeably throughout this section.

Drug actions are the result of a chemical interaction with some part of the human organism. In general, drugs change cell function by one or more of the following actions:

1. Stimulation — an increase in the rate of functional activity. Cocaine and amphetamines speed up central nervous system function.

2. Depression — a reduction in the rate of functional activity. Ethyl alcohol and barbiturates slow down or depress the function of the central nervous system.
3. Blocking — an obstruction that effectively prevents a particular action or response. This action is probably the consequence of depression. Antihistamine drugs block typical allergic reactions.
4. Replacement — the provision of a substitute or equivalent substance to restore an optimal condition. The administration of insulin to diabetics is an example of replacement therapy.
5. Killing or inactivating organisms — the destructions or prevention of the growth of disease-causing organisms. Antibiotics kill bacteria by interfering with the manufacture of bacterial cell walls.
6. Irritation — the abnormal excitation of some body part or function. This action may be an exaggerated form of stimulation. Laxatives irritate the large intestine to initiate defecation.

FACTORS INFLUENCING DRUG ACTIONS

In addition to the route of administration, drug distribution throughout the body, and processes of drug metabolism and elimination, the following factors should also be noted as influencing drug responses.

Dose

The quantity or amount of drug that is taken at any particular time is called the dose or dosage. The greater the dose, the greater will be the drug effect. Threshold dose or minimal dose refers to the smallest amount of a given drug capable of producing a detectable response. By contrast, the median effective dose describes the dose required to produce a specific response in one-half or 50 percent of test subjects. If the response to a dosage is death, it is described as the lethal dose. Drugs are also said to have a maximum effect, the greatest response produced by a specific drug, regardless of the dose administered.

Age

In comparison with so-called average 18- to 65-year-old adults, both infants and the elderly generally display more sensitivity to the effects of drugs. Infants tend to have underdeveloped abilities to metabolize and excrete drugs. As a consequence, drug actions within their bodies tend to be prolonged. The elderly, too, are likely to have impaired ability to metabolize and eliminate drugs from their bodies, part of the phenomenon of aging. Poor absorption in some older people is also a factor in reducing the effects of certain drugs. In another instance, one drug has a special reputation for reacting differently in children than in adults. Ritalin, a powerful stimulant for adults, acts as a depressant in children.

Body Weight

Placing the same amount of a drug in a 90-pound person and a 200-pound person is likely to produce significantly different results because of the greater concentration of the drug in the blood of the lighter-weighted individual. Lightweighted people usually experience a greater drug effect than heavier people, when all other factors, including dosage, are similar.

By contrast, the heavier individual with more blood and body fluids to dilute an absorbed drug has a reduced concentration of the dissolved drug—the amount of the drug contained per unit volume of body fluid.

Sex

Contrary to popular belief, the sex of a drug taker has very little influence on the effect of a drug. Males and females tend to respond equivalently to drugs. However, women should be extremely cautious about taking any drugs during pregnancy, because many drugs, including beverage alcohol, cross the placenta and can damage the embryo and fetus.

Time

The length of time between the taking of a drug and the observation of the anticipated effect is referred to as the "onset of action." Some drugs act shortly after entering the body; others may require several hours or even days before their effects become apparent. After the onset of action, drugs will vary in terms of the time required to achieve their maximum effects, as well as the duration of time during which drugs continue to have an effect.

Disease

The presence or absence of a disease condition will often alter a person's response to a drug. For instance, aspirin reduces fever, but has no effect in lowering normal temperature. People with impaired liver and kidney function often have difficulty in metabolizing and excreting drugs, and thus experience prolonged drug effects. Such people are unable to eliminate drugs from their bodies in a normal period of time. On the other hand, when a condition of diarrhea exists, some drugs are transported through the gastrointestinal tract so rapidly that drug absorption is significantly reduced.

Mind-set

One's emotional state or climate, often referred to as the mind-set, is now recognized as having a potentially significant impact on drug responses. Temperament marked by anger, fear, sadness, joy, or any other emotion can bring about changes in various body processes, namely, secretion of gastric juices and hormones, and alteration of blood pressure, heart rate, pulse, and respiration. These bodily processes, in turn, influence drug absorption, distribution, metabolism, and excretion—all of which can modify the response to a drug.

Taking a drug, especially a psychoactive one, in anticipation of "getting high," feeling more powerful or secure, or experiencing a new, altered state of consciousness, can also result in an exaggerated behavioral effect. Similarly, the use of a fake or inert substance that produces a drug response (the placebo effect) is also based upon a mind-set of trust, belief in a physician's judgment, and expectation of relief.

Environmental Setting

Closely related to mind-set in changing a drug response are the various factors of the environmental setting. The environment includes not only the physical place in which a drug is taken, but also the psychosocial circumstances surrounding the drug use.

The impact of the environment on drug action can be very significant with mood- and behavior-modifying chemicals. For example, using a psychedelic drug in a controlled laboratory situation or among caring, protective friends will likely result in fewer "bad trips" than would be experienced in "street use" of the same drug.

DRUG DEPENDENCE

Described as a state of psychological or physical need, or both, drug dependence can occur in an individual who uses a drug periodically or on a continual basis. Even though drug dependence is not exclusively associated with psychoactive drugs, the term is often used in reference to chemical modifiers which affect mood and behavior.

For many years, the word *addiction* was used to define compulsive use of drug substances, especially narcotics and alcohol. During the recent past, considerable difficulty arose in distinguishing among the various interpretations of addiction and habituation, especially as differences in the newer drugs and recreational ones became apparent. Eventually, the World Health Organization proposed substituting the more neutral term *drug dependence* for addiction. More recent variations in drug-abuse terminology include *chemical dependence*, *substance abuse*, and *addictive behavior*.

Although not everyone who uses psychoactive agents develops a drug dependency, such a condition is a distinct possibility. The most extreme form of drug dependence is characterized by: (1) psychological dependence, (2) the development of tolerance, and (3) physical dependence. Fortunately, not all of these phenomena occur in each instance of drug dependency. Some drugs carry the potential for psychological dependence only, whereas others involve the aspect of physical dependence as well.

PSYCHOLOGICAL DEPENDENCE

This sort of dependence occurs when a person takes a drug primarily for its effects. An individual who develops psychological dependence on a particular drug has a strong desire to repeat the use of that drug either occasionally or continuously. Although the body may not require the drug in a physical sense, the person has an intense craving for it to maintain drug-induced pleasure, a feeling of well-being, to achieve a maximum level of functioning, to reduce tensions, or to alter reality. When drug seeking becomes a compulsive and regular behavioral pattern, psychological dependence has reached its peak intensity. Deprived of the drug, the user will usually experience a period of readjustment, accompanied by some degree of anxiety, irritability, and restlessness.

TOLERANCE

With the repeated use of certain drugs, a condition known as tolerance develops. Tolerance is defined as taking more and more of the drug to obtain the same effect. Put another way, it is the development of body or tissue resistance to the effects of a drug so that larger doses are required to reproduce the original effect.

The onset of tolerance may be rapid or gradual, depending upon the drug used. However, this condition is not an all-or-none phenomenon, since a person may develop a tolerance to one aspect of a particular drug's action, but not to another. It should also be noted that tolerance can accompany psychological dependence upon a drug without the occurrence of physical dependence.

Theories that explain the mechanisms of physiological or tissue tolerance may appear both contradictory or complementary. One major theory holds that tolerance is the result of alterations in how a drug is processed in the body after repeated doses are taken. Changes occur in the normal processes of drug absorption, distribution, metabolism, or elimination. For instance, the liver begins to destroy the drug substance more quickly. As a result less of the drug reaches the site of its action. Another contrasting theory is based on the reduced sensitivity of nerve-cell receptor sites that takes place over a long period of drug taking. This represents a form of cellular or tissue adaptation in which reaction to the drug is diminished.

One additional concern with tolerance is the development of cross-tolerance, a condition in which the reduced pharmacological response to one drug results in a lessened response to another drug. Cross-tolerance, however, typically occurs among drugs belonging to the same class of chemical agents. For example, persons tolerant to morphine are also tolerant to heroin, methadone, and other narcotic agents, but not to alcohol or barbiturates, which belong to another class of drugs, the sedatives. One the other hand, persons tolerant to alcohol have a degree of tolerance to barbiturates and vice versa, but have no tolerance to narcotics.

With some drugs, tolerance develops very rapidly after the first dose; with others, it may occur more slowly.

Rate of Tolerance Development

Fast Tolerance Development	Intermediate	Slow
Opioids (Heroin, etc.)	PCP Amphetamines	Benzodiazepines (Valium, etc.)
Cocaine	Marijuana	Nicotine Caffeine

PHYSICAL DEPENDENCE

Simply stated, physical dependence is the presence of a withdrawal syndrome. One can also define physical dependence as the dependence of the body tissues on the continued presence of a drug revealed by withdrawal symptoms that develop when the drug is discontinued.

Thus, physical dependence is a state of functional adaptation to a drug in which the presence of a foreign chemical becomes "normal" and necessary. For the physically dependent, absence of the drug would constitute an abnormality, while presence of the drug would be required for normal functioning.

The condition of physical dependence is revealed only when drug use is discontinued. If the drug is removed abruptly, "normal" cell function is disturbed, resulting in hyperexcitability or overactivity of the nervous system. These drastic alterations in physical functions and behavior, observed or experienced after drug use is terminated, are known collectively as withdrawal or the abstinence syndrome.

DRUG DEPENDENCIES WHICH HAVE RECOGNIZED WITHDRAWAL TREATMENTS

Standard Medical Withdrawal Treatments	Recognized Withdrawal Treatments
Alcohol	Benzodiazepines
Heroin	Methadone (Clonidine)
Nicotine	Nicotine Gum

Drug dependencies which have no standard medical withdrawal treatments are caffeine, cocaine, marijuana, Phencyclindine (PCP) and amphetamines.

Antagonists for Drug Dependence

Antagonists are drugs which can neutralize a drug and prevent relapse. In contrast to medical agents which help a drug dependent person stop using the drug, antagonists actually prevent the re-use of a drug once someone has completely stopped use.

There are two antagonists now available for use in preventing relapse to drug dependence.

Drug Dependence	Antagonist
Alcohol	Disulfiram (Antabuse)
Heroin	Naltrexone (Trexan)

There are also experimental antagonists for nicotine and benzodiazepines.

WHY LEARN ABOUT DRUG DEPENDENCIES?

Understanding drug characteristics will help you to understand what will happen to users of particular drugs. For example, users of drugs with strong pleasurable effects, tolerance, and physical dependence will no doubt continue to use the drug for the pleasurable effects, will increase the dosage to obtain the pleasurable effects, and will at some point in time experience withdrawal when the drug is discontinued.

WHAT IS PLASMA LIFE?

Plasma life is the length of time that a drug will remain in the plasma, which is the clear part of the blood.

Knowing the plasma life of a drug is critical for the following reasons:

This is the approximate length of time that a drug produces maximal activity or influence; for example, pupil constriction with heroin, or pupil dilation with cocaine.

This is the approximate length of time that a drug will saturate the target areas or receptor sites in the brain.

Near the end of the plasma life, an addicted person will take a drug again. For example, the average heroin addict will want a fix every 4 to 6 hours, and the average nicotine addict about every 20 to 40 minutes.

PLASMA LIFE OF SOME COMMON DRUGS OF ABUSE

Drugs	Approximate Maximal Plasma Life
Heroin (morphine)	4 to 6 hours
Cocaine	3 to 5 hours
Amphetamines	4 to 6 hours
Phencyclidine	15 to 24 hours

WHAT ARE METABOLITES OR SECONDARY DRUGS?

A metabolite is a new drug that is formed when the drug originally taken comes into contact with enzymes and/or other reactors in the blood.

Drugs and/or their fat-soluble metabolites stay in the plasma for long periods of time.

SOME IMPORTANT METABOLIC CONVERSIONS WITH DRUGS OF ABUSE

Primary Drug	Metabolite(s)	Importance of Conversion
Heroin	Morphine	Changes to morphine in blood after 2 or 3 minutes and found in urine as morphine.
Cocaine	Benzoyle-cognine	Changes to benzoyle-cognine in blood and found in urine in this form.
Marijuana (Tetrahydro-cannabinol-THC)	A. 11-Hydroxy THC B. Carboxy THC	THC is active for only about two hours and produces euphoria. The metabolites are fat-soluble, non-euphoric, and stay in plasma 5 to 8 days. They are found in urine for 30 or more days.
Nicotine	Cotinine	Nicotine is active for 20 to 40 minutes. Cotinine lasts about 18 hours, which explains why a nicotine addict can sleep all night and not need a cigarette.

THE DIAGNOSIS OF ADDICTION

In dealing with drug abusers, the first consideration must be determining whether or not the individual is addicted.

You can usually make a diagnosis of addiction simply by knowing how often a person uses the drug. If addicted, the individual will reuse the drug within an interval which will approximate the plasma life of the drug the addict is dependent upon.

Once a diagnosis of addiction is made, stopping drug use is best accomplished by gradually reducing the daily intake of the drug over a 4 to 8 week period. If stopping is to be done in a shorter time-period, medical assistance to suppress withdrawal symptoms will almost always be necessary or the individual will relapse.

Unfortunately, a medical agent to assist withdrawal by suppressing symptoms is not available for all drugs which produce addiction.

POST-DRUG IMPAIRMENT SYNDROME (PDIS)

One of the most exciting findings regarding addiction was found by Dr. Forest Tennant[1]; he refers to it as the Post-Drug Impairment Syndrome. It is a combination of signs and symptoms found in persons who have taken certain drugs and developed a permanent chemical imbalance of the brain. It is thought that drug abuse may damage specific receptor sites, neurotransmitters, and metabolism in the brain. If a receptor site is damaged, one of the brain's natural neurotransmitters cannot attach to it and perform its natural function. When the metabolism of a neurotransmitter is altered, the brain will either have too much or too little brain chemical or neurotransmitter. Thus, PDIS is basically a permanent imbalance of the chemical equilibrium of the brain.

The drugs that commonly produce PDIS are phencyclidine (PCP), marijuana, amphetamines, cocaine, hallucinogens (MDMA, mescaline, LSD, psilocybin).

When one knows the signs and symptoms of PDIS, it is relatively easy to recognize. Today, many parents, relatives, employers, and friends realize that there is something wrong with an individual who has previously used drugs, but they do not quite know how to characterize it or understand what has happened.

A primary symptom of PDIS is the inability of the individual to maintain patterns of consistency; e.g., hold a job, engage in marital relationships, save money, complete school, or take care of personal belongings (such as a car) for very long. This inability is partially related to the fact that the PDIS-impaired individual cannot withstand much stress. This inability is often manifested in sudden outbursts of temper, depression, or bizarre behavior that may include delusions. Further, this inability is sometimes manifested by these individuals moving from town to town, or house to house, never living in one place very long. Oftentimes, they will stay with their parents for a few weeks, suddenly disappear for a few weeks, and then show up without warning—completely oblivious to the fact that they left, and they

---

[1] Dr. Forest Tennant, Jr. is the Executive Director of Community Health Projects, Inc. located at 338 South Glendora Avenue, West Covina, CA, 91790. He is an Associate Professor at UCLA School of Public Health. He has been a drug abuse consultant in the NFL and Training Consultant to the California Department of Justice. He has been on the Drug Abuse Advisory Committee for the U.S. Food and Drug Administration. In California he is considered one of the leading experts on drug addicition, recognition and treatment.

cannot understand their parents' concern. These individuals frequently join communes, residential groups, or religious cults because there they experience less stress and less responsibility.

Another typical symptom is the inability to concentrate or maintain attention. This results in the PDIS person constantly changing his or her mind or not completing tasks.

Although these individuals state that they have "lots of friends," close observation reveals the contrary; they have only one or two persons of either sex that they stay in close contact with for very long. In other words, they are very much "loners," but do not perceive themselves as such. In general, the PDIS individual does not perceive the world as most people do.

There are many situations in which PDIS individuals exhibit faulty perception. They generally feel that there is absolutely nothing wrong with them or any behavior they exhibit. These individuals do not respond well to any type of authority or advice and may not understand what is told to them by an employer, teacher, or parent. The reason for these symptoms is obvious. The ability of the PDIS individual to comprehend is impaired due to a chemical imbalance of the nervous system. It is important to emphasize that PDIS may vary in intensity from person to person.

DRUG PHENOMENON

Drugs of abuse produce dependence and promote relapse. They also produce a phenomenon of taking a chemical substance (that mimics a naturally produced substance) into the body which causes the body to stop producing the natural substance.

WELL KNOWN EXAMPLES ARE:

Thyroid	Stops Thyroid Production
Estrogen	Stops Ovary Production
Testosterone	Stops Testicle Production
Cortisone	Stops Adrenal Production

A dramatic example is cortisone. This natural drug, and particularly its potent analogs like Predisone, may suppress and atrophy the adrenal gland so much that the adrenal gland may stop producing cortisone after just 10 to 20 days of continuous treatment. This may result in some individuals taking cortisone for the rest of their lives.

GENETIC THEORY

Just as alcoholism is known to run in some families, there is also preliminary scientific evidence that this phenomenon may occur in families who are dependent upon other drugs.

The working genetic theory (not a proven fact) recommended by most authorities on drug dependence suggests that some persons may be born with excesses or deficiencies of either neurotransmitters, neurohormones, or receptor sites.

It is hypothesized that some genetic defects may be at least partially responsible for the following:

— Low resistance to peer pressure.

— Willingness to try drugs at a young age.

— Susceptibility to drug phenomenon.

— Childhood hyperactivity, deviancy, poor response to adult authority, inability to develop interpersonal relationships.

— Other poor health habits almost always observed in drug abusers: for example, failure to brush teeth, maintain diet, drive safely, etc.

PHARMACOLOGICAL DRUG CLASSIFICATION

There are many different drug classifications, including a legal classification. In the California Controlled Substances Act, a legal classification can be found. For example, narcotic drugs (Section 11019 of the Health and Safety Code) include such substances as opium, opiates, coca leaves and cocaine. Drugs are also classified in the Controlled Substances Act under certain schedules as to their medical usage, potential for abuse and dependencies.

For our purposes, a pharmacological drug classification is more useful because it groups drugs together for their effects. Pharmacology is the study of a drug, the action the drug has on the body, how the cells of the body are changed because of the drug, and how the modifications affect the body overall. By grouping drugs as to their effects (a pharmacological classification), it is easier to remember that, for the most part, drugs listed under a certain classification will have similar effects on the body (the differences might only be in intensity and duration of action).

Therefore, there are many reasons to classify drugs pharmacologically. First, if one drug of a class is physically addicting, it is very likely that other drugs of that class will also share this property. Second, if one drug of a group is likely to be associated with severe psychotic symptoms (e.g. cocaine), similar symptoms are likely to be observed with abuse of other drugs of the same group (e.g. amphetamines). Third, if an individual develops tolerance to one drug of a group, when the first drug is stopped and a second substance of that same category is taken within a relatively short period of time, cross-tolerance for the second drug is likely to be observed (e.g. tolerance developed to alcohol can result in cross-tolerance to diazepam or Valium). Finally, if two drugs of the same class are taken at the same time, they are likely to boost or potentiate the effects of each other with a potentially lethal overdose as a consequence (e.g. the concomitant mixing of ethanol, alcohol and diazepam).

Narcotics (Opiates)

These drugs have as their most prominent actions at the usual doses a dampening of pain with comparatively weak, general CNS depression (sedation). Substances that fall into this category include opium and all of its derivatives (e.g. morphine, heroin, codeine, etc.) and almost all non-anti-inflammatory prescription analgesics (e.g. meperidine or Demerol, propoxyphene or Darvon, etc.). Each of these drugs can be dangerous in overdose; all are physically addicting. These substances share cross-tolerance and can potentiate the other's actions, but the opiates are unlikely to precipitate psychoses, major depressions, or major anxiety syndromes. A narcotic is defined as a substance that relieves pain and produces sleep.

Hallucinogens (Psychedelics)

These substances share the ability to induce intense emotional feeling states characterized by a magnification of sensory perceptions and possible visual hallucinations at relatively low doses. They include drugs such as LSD, psilocybin, mescaline or peyote, MDA, MDMA or ecstasy, and STP. Hallucinogens do not produce prominent tolerance, have no clinically relevant physical withdrawal syndromes and are not likely to (but can) induce death in overdose. The symptoms of overdose are likely to resemble a CNS stimulant overdose. Hallucinogens do produce emotional instability and flashbacks (an unwanted recurrence of drug effects), a hyperstimulated state that includes panic and can produce states of confusion at doses close to those that induce a toxic reaction. Psychedelic is defined as mind-expanding or mind-altering.

Phencyclidine

This drug cannot logically be placed in any of the other groups. An analog of this agent was first developed as a dissociative anesthetic, but the human form, Ketamine, is now rarely used because a substantial proportion of people develop a state of extreme agitation and confusion when emerging from surgery. A similar drug, Sernyl, is still used as a veterinary anesthetic. Based on its clinical use, one would have predicted PCP would be a CNS depressant, but it is abused on the streets primarily as a hallucinogen or stimulant, or as a substitute for other drugs that are more expensive or more difficult to manufacture (e.g. THC). The clinical effects observed at a relatively low dose include changes in sensory perceptions and visual hallucinations similar to those described for the hallucinogens. At slightly higher doses, patients exhibit a syndrome, however, of mixed cholinergic and adrenergic disturbances marked by intense agitation and confusion. Thus, the most prominent clinical syndrome associated with this drug is a severe organic brain syndrome (OBS) that (as is true with all confused states) can be associated with hallucinations and/or delusions. Contrary to the general rules appropriate to other substances where acute drug-induced psychiatric syndromes are likely to disappear within several days to several weeks, the PCP-induced OBS can last several months or more.

Cannabis

All drugs deriving from cannabis have one active ingredient: delta-9 tetrahydrocannabinol (THC). All cannabis derivatives originate in the marijuana plant. At usual doses, the most prominent effects of these drugs are a change in the sense of time, an increase in appetite, and a floating sensation, similar to sedation or mild euphoria. At clinical doses, cannabis derviatives do not produce hallucination, although this psychedelic effect may occur at very high levels of intake.

Central Nervous System (CNS) Stimulants

The CNS stimulants are a group of drugs for which the most prominent effects at the usual doses center on enhancement or stimulation of nervous tissue activity. These agents include all forms of cocaine (including cocaine hydrochloride, "freebase" cocaine, and rock), all forms of amphetamines (e.g. methedrine and benzedrine), prescription weight-reducing products, amphetamine-like drugs such as methylphenidate (Ritalin), and even some over-the-counter weight-reducing drugs (e.g. Dexatrim), if taken in very high doses. The more potent agents have been listed first (i.e. the ones most likely to induce states of severe psychopathology and medical problems) while the less potent (e.g. weight-reducing products) require very high doses in the average individual to cause the same pattern of problems. These difficulties include possible lethal overdoses, physical addiction, dramatic psychoses, severe depressions, and all anxiety syndromes including panic attacks and obsessions. Although caffeine and nicotine are included here because they can induce and exacerbate anxiety, they are not capable of producing intense psychiatric syndromes, such as psychoses and major depressions.

Central Nervous System (CNS) Depressants

These drugs are named for the most prominent property at the usual doses of dampening CNS activity, while carrying relatively weak analgesic effects. Included among the CNS depressants are ethanol (beverage alcohol), barbiturates, barbiturate-like hypnotics (e.g. methaqualone or Quaalude), meprobamate (Miltown or Equanil), and all benzodiazepines (e.g. alprazolam or Xanax; diazepam or Valium, etc.). In other words, the CNS depressants include all prescription hypnotics and all prescription antianxiety drugs except for buspirone (Buspar). All drugs in this class share the properties of lethality in overdose, physical addiction, cross-tolerance, potentiation, the ability to induce severe depressions, prominent anxiety during withdrawal, and so on.

Solvents

All drugs in this category are capable of dissolving stains and oils and some are used as fuels or industrial solvents. The most prominent psychological actions of these drugs at the usual doses are feelings of excitement and confusion. Substances in this class include gasoline, toluene, paints and paint thinners, some glues, and the solvent used in typing correction fluid, and so on. The problems associated with these agents include the potential for severe cardiac arrhythmias, liver damage and kidney failure, while psychiatrically the most frequent clinical picture is confusion.

Miscellaneous Substances

It is unlikely that any simple categorization will fit all substances likely to be abused. Other drugs with relatively distinct side effect profiles include nitrous oxide (with effects and problems somewhat similar to mild CNS depressants), amyl nitrite (inducing mood swings and confusion), and anticholinergic type prescription antiparkinsonian drugs (e.g. procyclidine or Kemadrin, trihexphenidyl or Artane, benztropine or Cogentin), producing states of mild euphoria and confusion. Also not discussed in the abbreviated overview are over-the-counter (OTC) drugs on which people can at least demonstrate psychological dependence, including laxatives and antihistamines, the latter being the major component of OTC sleeping pills, and sedatives.

PSYCHIATRIC PROBLEMS AND SUBSTANCE ABUSERS

All substances of abuse affect the brain and produce changes in a person's normal level of functioning. Therefore, it is not surprising that such drugs are likely to show alterations in mood, ability to reason, and content of cognition.

We have already discussed how drugs placed into pharmacological classes have similar effects on the body. For example, if one member of a class is likely to induce states of psychosis, others are likely to produce this problem as well. Out of the listing of relevant drug classifications, the two categories of substances most intimately tied to states of psychiatric symptoms are the brain depressants (e.g., alcohol, the benzodiazepines, and the barbiturates) and the brain stimulants (e.g., cocaine, all forms of amphetamine, methylphenidate or Ritalin, and all prescription, as well as most over-the-counter, weight-reducing products).

It should also be mentioned that people who take large amounts of opiates or depressants risk the possibility of overdose.

Often, a person may show signs of psychic instability that indicate intoxification by a particular drug. For instance, when a person shows confusion about who and where he or she is, or what is going on around him or her, this is most likely caused by PCP, some psychedelics, toluene, paint thinner, or alcohol.

When a person shows no obvious signs of confusion, has stable vital signs, but has hallucinations (e.g. hearing things that are not there and believing they are real) or delusions (e.g., believing people are plotting against him or her and trying to harm him or her), such auditory hallucinations and/or paranoid delusions without confusion are likely to be seen with abuse of brain stimulants or brain depressants. The stimulants (especially the more potent ones such as cocaine and amphetamines) are likely to produce a severe psychosis in anyone after hours to days of escalating doses. Although this level of severe psychiatric impairment can mimic schizophrenia, the psychosis developed in the context of drug abuse is likely to disappear within several days to several weeks of abstinence, even if antipsychotic medications (e.g., haloperidol or Haldol) are not used. Identical symptoms may develop in the context of abuse of brain depressants such as alcohol, although this is much less common among alcoholics than among stimulant abusers.

Severe depression involving suicidal tendencies most often occurs among abusers of brain depressants during active intoxication and withdrawal. This level of depression is also likely to be a symptom of stimulant withdrawal.

On the other hand, a state of anxiety (panic attacks, paranoia, obsessive thinking, etc.) is most often caused during intoxication with such brain stimulants (cocaine and amphetamines, for example). Also, signs of general anxiety, panic, and phobia are likely to occur during the acute withdrawal from brain depressants such as alcohol.

ILLUSTRATION I
Pharmacological Drug Classification

NARCOTICS (OPIATES)

NATURAL
- OPIUM
- MORPHINE
- HEROIN (DIACETYLMORPINE)
- CODEINE (METHYLMORPHINE)

SYNTHETIC
- DEMEROL
- PERCODAN (OXYCODONE)
- METHADONE (DOLOPHINE)
- DILAUDID (HYDROMORPHONE)

HALLUCINOGENS (PSYCHEDELICS)

- PEYOTE (MESCALINE)
- PSILOCYBIN
- LSD (D-LYSERGIC ACID DIETHYLAMIDE)

PHENCYCLIDINE

- PCP
- KETAMINE
- SERNYL

SOLVENTS

- GASOLINE
- TOLUENE
- PAINTS
- GLUE
- PAINT THINNERS

CENTRAL NERVOUS SYSTEM (CNS) STIMULANTS

- AMPHETAMINES (BENZEDRINE)
- DEXTROAMPHETAMINE (DEXEDRINE)
- METHAMPHETAMINE (DESOXYN)
- RITALIN
- PRELUDIN
- PARNATE
- COCAINE (HYDROCHLORIDE)
- CRACK COCAINE
- CAFFEINE
- NICOTINE

CANNABIS

- MARIJUANA
- HASHISH
- HASHOIL
- THC
- SINSEMILLA (BUDS)

CENTRAL NERVOUS SYSTEM (CNS) DEPRESSANTS

BARBITURATES
1. SECOBARBITAL (SECONAL)
2. AMOBARBITAL (AMYLAL)
3. PHENOBARBITAL

NON-BARBITURATE SEDATIVES
1. DORIDAN

BENZODIAZEPINES
1. LIBRIUM (CLORDIAZEPOXIDE)
2. VALIUM (DIAZEPAM)
3. MILTOWN OR EQUANTIL (MEPROBAMATE)

METHAQUALONE (QUAALUDE)

CHLORAL HYDRATE

ALCOHOL

MISCELLANEOUS SUBSTANCES

AMYL NITRITE

GENERAL ANESTHETIC
1. ETHER
2. NITROUS OXIDE

MORNING GLORY SEEDS (LYSERGIC ACID AMIDE)

OTC (OVER-THE-COUNTER) DRUGS

IDENTIFYING THE DRUG ABUSER

Despite the prevalence of drug abuse and associated health problems in criminals, not much attention has been given to the use of urine testing for the purpose of identifying drug abusers who have been arrested. There are several reasons for identifying the drug abuse criminal.

To target active criminals. Researchers have found that drug-abusing offenders are among the most active criminals. Addicts commit more crimes during periods when they are frequently using drugs than during periods of lesser drug use. The association between high rates of criminality and drug abuse has been found predominantly in persons who use expensive dependence-producing drugs like cocaine and heroin. Less is known about the criminal activities of people who abuse PCP or other illicit drugs. In youths, however, heavy marijuana use is also associated with problem behavior and is often accompanied by the use of other illicit drugs.

To protect the public from crimes by persons released to the community. Judges are often faulted when persons they have released pending trial or on probation are found to have committed another crime, especially a violent crime. If persons who are released to the community before trial or through parole were tested for illicit drug use, it might be possible to initiate treatment or urine monitoring for those who test positively. Due to the links between drug use and criminality, effective programs for controlling or monitoring drug use may be a means of reducing the crimes of released arrestees and offenders.

To reduce jail or prison crowding. Jail and prison populations in large cities contain substantial numbers of drug-dependent persons. By identifying drug-dependent persons and placing them in residential treatment programs or urine monitoring programs, we may be able to reduce jail and prison populations and to lessen future drug abuse and crime. One jurisdiction in Indiana is adopting a program in which arrestees charged with minor offenses can be released without bail if they agree to participate in a urine monitoring program. The cost of testing is charged to the defendant but is less than the amount for bail and should result in the early release of more defendants. Judges in Washington, D.C. report that because of their pretrial testing program, they are more likely to release suspected drug users because they know that their drug problems are being addressed.

To reduce drug abuse and crime. There is growing evidence that criminal justice referral of offenders to drug abuse treatment programs, often accompanied by urine monitoring, can lead to a longer treatment period and to reductions in both drug abuse and crime. Because younger offenders are less likely than older offenders to inject hard drugs and to use heroin, identification of youthful offenders who are abusing drugs such as marijuana, PCP, or cocaine may hold promise for preventing more extensive drug use.

To address public health problems. Abusers of hard drugs, especially persons who inject drugs, are at high risk for health problems. Intravenous drug users are most at risk for contracting AIDS by sharing dirty needles that contain blood from other infected addicts. Prostitutes are also likely to have serious drug abuse and associated health problems. In a three year study, the Bureau of Justice Statistics (BJS) revealed in 1986 that 53 percent of probationers had a drug abuse problem.[2] In 1992, BJS reported that more than twice as many women as men in jail reported using a major drug daily.[3] The criminal justice system may have an unusual opportunity to identify persons with health problems.

To monitor community drug use trends. As illicit drugs become available in a community, persons known to be drug abusers may be expected to be among those who first use them. Thus, an ongoing urine testing program may provide warning of drug epidemics and information on changing patterns of drug availability. The results from a current urine testing program by the U.S. Department of Justice, Drug Use Forecasting (DUF) Program, has been useful for tracking the use of drugs in the United States.[4]

DRUG TESTING

In the current atmosphere of heightened concern about drug abuse in America, there is growing interest in the use of chemical tests, especially urine tests for identifying drug users. Public debate, often heated, has focused on the advisability and legality of using urine tests to identify drug use in athletes, celebrities, and employees performing sensitive jobs.

Increasingly, employers are warning employees that they will not tolerate drug use in or out of the workplace. Professional sports officials are also cracking down. Needless to say, the military already requires mandatory urinalysis.

In a recent survey of 390 companies, ranging from large to small, 17 percent reported that they test job applicants; 12 percent screen current employees, usually those in high-risk jobs or where the public's safety is of concern; and 26 percent plan to expand testing programs.

In 1989, two U.S. Supreme Court decisions upheld drug testing programs that were set up by the railroads and by the U.S. Customs Service. These programs allow employers to test employees for drugs without any belief that the employees in question have used drugs. Contrary to a long line of legal precedents, these programs were found to be constitutionally valid. The Supreme Court supported this constitutionality on two grounds: first, that present drug use is a major menace to our society which much be addressed, and second, that the mandatory testing programs were only minimal intrusions on an employee's privacy. The two cases were *Skinner v. Railroad Labor Executive Association*, March 21, 1989, No. 87-1555, 130 LRRM 2857, and *National Treasury Employees Union v. Von Raab,* 109 *S.Ct.* 1384 (1989).

---

[2] "Federal Criminal Case Processing, 1980-1989 with Preliminary Data for 1990." Bureau of Justice Statistics. NCJ-130526, October 1991, 29 pp.

[3] "Women in Jail, BJS Special Report." Bureau of Justice Statistics. NCJ-13432, March 1992, 12 pp.

[4] *Identifying the Drug Abuser: Drug Testing.* National Institute of Justice. Crime File Study Guide. U.S. Dept. of Justice.

For many employers, drug testing is a question of profit. Drug users cost industry an estimated $60 million annually in lost productivity, workers' compensation, and medical claims. The military argues that drug testing does work. According to a survey of 20,000 military personnel, drug use has fallen from 27 to 9 percent since testing began 1981.

It is quite clear from recent decisions about mandatory random drug testing of public safety employees that police officers, firefighters, and other guardians of the public welfare are held to a higher standard than other people. Even more specifically, the courts are consistently finding that law enforcement officers must conduct themselves (both on and off duty) in a manner consistent with the laws and practices they are sworn to uphold.

In a recent decision, *Penny v. Kennedy* (6th Cir., October 4, 1990), the Federal court expanded the employer's ability to conduct mandatory random drug tests of police officers and firefighters. Although recognizing that mandatory urinalysis testing infringes on an employee's privacy rights and is a Fourth Amendment search, the Court found that a city's interest in ensuring drug-free performance by firefighters and police officers overrides those employees' expectations of privacy.

Furthermore, the Court found that requiring particularized suspicion before drug testing would seriously impede the employer's ability to advance their compelling interest in ensuring that their employees are drug free.

It is important to note that these random and mandatory drug testing programs cannot be implemented without providing clear regulations that limit the discretion of the supervisor requesting the test. The city must specifically define its drug testing programs so that employees will know what procedures the city will follow in administering the testing program. In adopting drug testing programs, however, public employers must comply with their own administrative rules regarding new programs or policies.

Ominously, the Court's concurring opinion warns that law enforcement agents "should be exceedingly circumspect in their own behavior and comport their personal lives in accordance with the laws and practices they are sworn to uphold." Peace officers should, and must, keep this warning in mind and conduct themselves accordingly.

Drug use by police officers is now an important issue for every police chief in the nation. The problem is receiving media attention because of its potential threat to the integrity of law enforcement and the safety of the community.

To learn how law enforcement agencies are addressing this problem, the National Institute of Justice sponsored a telephone survey of 33 major police departments in 1986. The survey was conducted by Research Management Associates, Inc., of Alexandria, Virginia. Of the 33 departments surveyed, 24 had drug testing programs. These departments explained their testing procedures, selection process, and what procedures were used after a positive test. They also discussed whether treatment programs were available, and whether random testing had ever been considered. Departments provided information on the types of tests conducted, the administration of the tests, the procedures used to establish chain of custody, and the costs of the tests.

Key findings from the survey indicated the following:

73 percent of the departments surveyed were conducting applicant drug screening tests.

Virtually all departments had written policies and procedures for conducting tests when there was reason to suspect that officers were using illegal drugs.

21 percent said they were considering mandatory testing for all officers.

24 percent indicated that treatment rather than dismissal would be appropriate for officers under some circumstances, generally depending on the type of drug and severity of the problem.

These results show that many police managers are taking steps to make their departments as drug-free as possible.

Further impetus for action has come from the International Association of Chiefs of Police (IACP),[5] which recently developed a model drug testing policy for local police departments to consider in identifying and dealing with the use of illegal drugs by police officers. The policy calls for:

Testing applicants and recruits for drug or narcotics use as part of their pre-employment medical exams;

Testing a current employee when documentation indicates that the employee is impaired or incapable of performing assigned duties, or experiences reduced productivity, excessive vehicle accidents, high absenteeism, or other behavior inconsistent with previous performance;

Testing a current employee when an allegation involves the use, possession, or sale of drugs or narcotics, or the use of force, or when there is serious on-duty injury to the employee or another person;

Requiring current sworn employees assigned to drug, narcotics, or vice enforcement units to submit to periodic drug tests.

The U.S. Supreme Court voted on December 16th, 1991 to leave intact the Mandatory Drug Test Rules governing Federal employees. Without comment and with no dissents, the Court chose to bypass a Federal Appeals Court ruling which indicates that all levels of government may demand a drug test from every job applicant.

The Court refused to hear a constitutional challenge to the Justice Department's drug testing policy, under which lawyers tentatively accepted for employment with the department must submit to a urine test.

The challenge was brought by a lawyer who had been tentatively offered a job in the department's Anti-Trust Division. After the department refused to waive the requirement, the lawyer, Carl Willner, filed suit on the grounds that the drug test, in the absence of any suspicion of drug use, was an unreasonable search in violation of the Fourth Amendment. Judge Gerhard Gesell of the Federal District Court in Washington, D.C. agreed declaring

[5] International Association of Chiefs of Police, 13 Firstfield Rd., Gaithersburg, MD 20878.

the test unconstitutional, but the U.S. Court of Appeals for the District of Columbia Circuit overturned that ruling in a 2 to 1 decision.

Under the lower court ruling, a government agency is free to order mandatory tests for those seeking public jobs even if the individuals are seeking a position that has nothing to do with public safety, police work, or government secrets. The lower court indicated that as long as the agency believes that drug use is incompatible with an "efficient work force," it may require new job applicants to take a test.

CRITICISMS OF DRUG TESTING

Fourth Amendment rights against illegal search and seizure. Does the government have the right to impose mandatory testing on a person in the absence of individualized suspicion? It is argued that the invasion of privacy, the costs, and the intrusiveness of urine testing are too great to justify the testing of persons at random, when there is no clear suspicion that the person is using drugs. In some instances, mandatory urine testing has been sustained by the courts when unique institutional requirements existed. For example, such tests have been upheld for jockeys, in the context of regulation and reduction of criminal influence in the racetrack industry. Drug tests have also been approved for prison inmates, and in the military, to promote security.

Critics of mandatory urine testing argue that the need to watch the person providing the specimen is an unacceptable infringement of privacy. When an employee or offender who has received advance notice is tested, special precautions must be made to ensure that the person does not substitute someone else's urine.

Fourteenth Amendment due process rights. Considerable litigation has occurred over the accuracy of urine tests and whether punitive actions taken against a person on the basis of a single unconfirmed urine test violate the 14th Amendment's guarantees of due process. Because of the extensive use of the EMIT urine test,[6] most of this discussion has concerned the accuracy of that particular test.

When persons are repeatedly tested, other issues become relevant. For example, in Washington, D.C., a person on pretrial release tested positive for PCP on 16 tests over a 60-day period. A contempt of court ruling for this person was denied when expert witnesses could not specify the length of time that PCP could be detected in urine. Unlike cocaine and opiates, which are eliminated from the body within days after ingestion, PCP and marijuana may be stored and released weeks after use.

Another important issue is the confidentiality of test result information. For example, is information about drug use at arrests to be made available at the time of sentencing or parole? Furthermore, after a positive test result

---

[6] EMIT is Enzyme Multiplied Immunoassay Technique. EMIT is a popular test because it is relatively inexpensive and it has a reputation for accuracy. However, gas chromatography and gas chromatography/mass spectrometry are even more accurate and are considered necessary to ensure that the initial EMIT results are correct.

is obtained a person labeled a drug user is likely to suffer prolonged adverse consequences from that label.

Perhaps the greatest danger posed by urine testing programs is the belief that use of the tests will somehow solve the drug abuse problem. It is true that testing will uncover the magnitude of the drug problem in any particular jurisdiction and identify some of the affected persons. However, in the absence of pre-developed plans on how to assess a person's level of drug involvement and how to plan effective responses, the testing program may fail to achieve its goals of reducing drug abuse.

DRUG TESTING THROUGH URINALYSIS OR HAIR ANALYSIS

Drug testing is now big business in the United States and the stakes are high. As public concern over drug use has increased and employers and travelers recognize the impact that substance abuse can have on public safety, there is an increasing interest in the mandatory drug testing of employees, pilots, and others employed in sensitive positions. In addition, treatment programs have turned to drug monitoring in an attempt to measure the outcome on their patients and clients, thus gathering evidence of the efficacy of their particular program.

Urine samples for drug screens have many inherent assets. They are relatively easy to collect, not exorbitantly expensive, and are relatively accurate. At the same time, however, they are not perfect.

Drug testing or monitoring through urinalysis is a way of determining whether drugs have been used, but it is of little benefit if one wants to measure the amount of drug that was present in the body—that is, it is a qualitative rather than a quantitative test. In addition, there are difficulties that can lead to falsely negative results, including the possibility that a subject might give a sample that is not his own urine, and the possibility that, for drugs which stay in the body for very short periods of time, a urine sample might be falsely negative even when the drug has been ingested the same day. Additional problems relate to the inability to determine whether a positive sample indicates only one instance of drug use, or whether the subject has engaged in repeated drug intake over a matter of many days or weeks. This approach also has inherent dangers of false positive results due to contaminants such as poppy seeds. Finally, the careful supervision of gathering urine samples is embarrassing and may lead to a reluctance on the part of many programs to actually supervise the urine collection procedure.

While these difficulties are not insurmountable, they do underscore the reason why clinicians and other people interested in public health issues continue to search for additional approaches to drug monitoring. In this regard, the use of hair to determine drug intake patterns has many potential advantages. The samples are easy to gather under close supervision, thus decreasing the possibility of false negative results. Since hair grows steadily at approximately 1.3 cm. per month, the procedure offers the opportunity to observe sequential drug-taking patterns week by week. Because drugs finding their way into the hair follicles are there permanently until the hair is cut, this approach also minimizes the chance that the drug use will be missed because the substance is present in the blood or urine for a relatively short time.

Research on hair analysis for detecting drugs began in 1954, according to pharmacologists Martha R. Harkey and Gary L. Henderson of the University of California at Davis.

However, according to the consensus report of a conference on hair analysis held May 31, 1990 in Washington, D.C. by the Society of Forensic Toxicologists, Inc. and the National Institute on Drug Abuse, "there are no generally accepted procedures for hair analysis for drugs of abuse and there is no information on the accuracy, precision, sensitivity, specificity, or appropriate cutoffs that define potentially false positive or false negative results for either screening or confirmation procedures." The report notes that studies conducted so far are essentially anecdotal.[7]

One organization that does not consider hair analysis controversial is the Federal Bureau of Investigation, according to Special Agent Roger Martz, who heads the FBI's chemical toxicology unit and is its chief hair tester. He uses both gas chromatography/mass spectrometry (GC/MC) and a more advanced technology that analyzes hair with a tandem mass spectrometer.

In summary, there are many potential benefits to using samples of hair to determine drug-taking patterns. These would be of little use, however, unless there were data to demonstrate the relevance of this approach to real life situations.

The approach is based on the hypothesis and subsequent documentation that drugs circulating in the blood are incorporated into hair roots and follicles. Work with animals as well as some studies with humans indicates that the period of time when the drug was taken can be isolated in a specific area of the hair strand which grows out from the scalp at approximately 1.3 cm. per month. Work with animals exposed to drugs indicates that the amount of drug ingested is likely to impact the amount of the substance found in the hair strand, although there are even less impressive data regarding this quantitative association in humans.

The hair to be selected for analysis is ideally from the rear portion of the top of the head. It is usually suggested that a spot approximately 1 to 2 inches back from an imaginary line that could be drawn across the top of the head from ear to ear would be the ideal place for sampling between 10 and 20 hairs comprising a weight of approximately 10 milligrams. This point, also called the posterior vertex, is said to have hair growth that is least influenced by sex and age, as well as a more constant proportion of hair (perhaps 85 percent) that is in a growth phase.

The samples are subsequently taken and carefully washed. There are data to indicate that if this procedure is followed, it is not likely that hair dyes, shampoos, or any form of damage to the hair follicle will interfere markedly with the determination of the presence or absence of a drug. It is possible, however, that some of these factors might make a difference to the amount of drug present within the hair. After the hair is washed, the strands

[7] "Special Report, FDA, Psychemedics Reach Uneasy Truce Over RIA (Radioimmunoassay) Testing of Hair Samples." Reported in *International Drug Report,* International Narcotic Enforcement Officers Association, NY. Vol. 32, No. 11, November 1990.

can then be cut into segments that relate to a specific time period. This is made possible by cutting strands as close to the scalp as possible.

Next, the hair is dissolved through a series of steps. This procedure allows for the release of proteins related to the drugs used, proteins that can be identified by specific antibodies. The samples can then be scanned for the presence (and perhaps amount) of heroin, methadone, phencyclidine (PCP), cocaine, marijuana, nicotine, and benzodiazapines (like diazepam or Valium).

THE ACCURACY OF HAIR ANALYSIS

While few laboratories have developed data, there are indications that an impressive level of accuracy may exist. One group of investigators asserts that their analytic techniques will identify as little as 100 milligrams of cocaine per week (one "line" of "snorted" cocaine contains somewhere between 25 and 50 milligrams). Analysis of hair samples can also identify the use of as few as 3.5 "bags" of heroin per month and less than 2 "joints" of marijuana in a 30-day period. The authors state that even lower levels of drug use can be identified if larger samples of hair are obtained.[8]

There are also indications that the approach may be relatively reliable. One study gathered hair from 20 PCP users and 18 control persons, reporting that hair evaluations correctly identified all 38 people.[9] Another study compared the efficacy of urinalysis and hair evaluations on 60 patients with histories of prior drug use. Through hair analysis, positive results were obtained from all subjects; but with urine samples only 30 percent of the individuals tested positive. The latter result probably reflects the limited number of hours after drug intake when the substance still appears in the urine. Other data utilizing individual case reports have related remarkable correlations between the history of monthly drug use and specific hair segment evaluations which reflect that period of use.

Of course, as was true of urinalysis, hair evaluations are far from perfect. First, not many laboratories have this evaluation available, and it is likely to be quite expensive. Second, while the evaluations can tell us about drug intake on a weekly or monthly basis, it would be of little use regarding day-by-day or current use patterns.

More is known about urine and how the kidneys work than about hair. Hair has complicated structures which can be damaged by sun and chemicals, yielding varying results. There are also racial differences in the amount of a drug that is incorporated into hair, with one study finding that black hair is more absorbent of drugs than brown hair, and that certain drugs wash out of brown hair more easily than black hair. Some of the research is anecdotal, and much research has not yet been published.

---

[8] Baumgartner, W.A., et al. "Hair analysis for drugs of abuse." *Journal of Forensic Sciences*. 34:1433-1453, 1989.

[9] Sramek, J.J., et al. "Hair analysis for detection of PCP in newly admitted psychiatric patients." *American Journal of Psychiatry*. 142:950-953, 1985.

According to an FDA Announcement June 5, 1990 (55 Federal Register No. 23985) "There is no FDA regulated RIA product on the market that has been demonstrated to be effective in testing hair for the presence of drugs of abuse."

The following questions that need to be investigated before the results of hair analysis can be reliably interpreted:

— How are drugs incorporated into hair?

— What is the relationship between the amount of the drug used and the concentration of the drug or its metabolites in hair?

— What is the minimum dose required to produce a positive result?

— How is drug incorporation and retention in hair biased by race, age, sex, or other individual differences?

— To what extent is an externally applied drug (whether by sweat, glandular secretion, or environmental exposure) retained in the hair?

— What is the effect of various washing or hair treatment procedures in removing externally applied drugs and internally incorporated/bound drugs?

REFERENCES:

Addictive Behavior, Drug and Alcohol Abuse. Morton Publishing Company, 925 West Kenyon Ave., Unit 4, Englewood, Colorado, 80110, 1985.

Barnett, S. "Commercial hair analysis: Science or Scam?" *Journal of the American Medical Association.* 254:1041-1045, 1985.

Baumgartner, W.A., et al. "Hair analysis for drugs of abuse." *Journal of Forensic Sciences.* 34:1433-1453, 1989.

Inaba, Darryl and William Cohen. *Uppers, Downers, All Arounders.* The Haight-Ashbury Detox Clinic, 529 Clayton St., San Francisco, CA, 94117, 1990.

International Narcotic Enforcement Officers Association. "Special Report, FDA, Psychemedics Reach Uneasy Truce Over RIA (Radioimmunoassay) Testing of Hair Samples." *International Drug Report.* Vol. 32, No. 11, November 1990.

Manili, Barbara A. "Police Drug Testing." National Institute of Justice, Washington D.C., October 1987.

Maugh, T.H. "Hair: A diagnostic tool to complement blood serum and urine." *Science.* 202:1271-1273, 1978.

Schlaadt, Richard and Peter Shannon. *Drugs.* 3rd Ed. Prentice Hall, Englewood Cliffs, NJ 07032, 1990.

Sramek, J.J., et al. "Hair analysis for detection of PCP in newly admitted psychiatric patients." *American Journal of Psychiatry.* 142:950-953, 1985.

U.S. Dept. of Health and Human Services. National Institute on Drug Abuse. "Strategic Planning for Workplace Drug Abuse Programs," 1987.

U.S. Dept. of Justice. Bureau of Justice Statistics. "Federal Criminal Case Proceedings, 1980-1989, with Preliminary Data for 1990." NCJ-130526, October 1991, 29 pp.

________. "Women in Jail, A BJS Special Report." NCJ-134732, March 1992, 12 pp.

________. National Institute of Justice. *Identifying the Drug Abuser: Drug Testing.* Crime File Study Guide.

________. National Institute of Justice. Research in Brief. *Employee Drug Testing Policies in Police Departments.* October 1986.

Vista Hill Foundations. "Drug Testing: What it Can and Cannot Do." *Drug Abuse and Alcoholism Newsletter,* 3420 Comino Del Rio North, Suite 100, San Diego, CA 92108. Vol. 19, No. 2, March 1990.

White, Jason. *Drug Dependence.* Prentice Hall, Englewood Cliffs, NJ 07632, 1991.

Additional articles on Hair Analysis reported in *The Narc Officer,* a publication of the International Narcotic Enforcement Officers Association, Sept. 1990.

"Advantages of Hair Anaylsis Over Urinalysis."

"Legal Issues: NY Court Permits Hair Testing in Cocaine."

"Scientific Basis for RIAH (Radioimmunoassay of Hair)."

This page intentionally left blank.

CHAPTER V

SEDATIVES, HYPNOTICS, AND CENTRAL NERVOUS SYSTEM DEPRESSANTS

INTRODUCTION

Drugs that slow down mental and physical functions of the body are known generally as central nervous system (CNS) depressants. Since these chemical agents tend to produce a calming effect, relax muscles, and relieve feelings of tension, anxiety, and irritability, they are also described as having a sedative or sedating effect. Such drugs are referred to as sedatives.

At higher dose levels, sedatives also produce a drowsiness and eventually a state resembling natural sleep. Drugs that have such a sleep-inducing effect are called hypnotics. This hypnotic effect has nothing to do whatsoever with the artificially induced state of suggestibility often associated with the word "hypnosis." Nevertheless, the combination term of sedative/hypnotic appropriately identifies the major pharmacological effects of these drugs.

History of Depressants

Like other mood-altering substances, depressant drugs have long been used by humanity for a variety of reasons. Herbs and alcohol have often been used to produce stupor and sleep. During the early 1900s, ether, chloroform, and nitrous oxide were used to produce a "high."

Another drug used for specific medicinal purposes is Rauwolfia Serpintina, a snakeroot shrub common to India and Southeast Asia. This shrub has been used for centuries to treat several diseases, including high blood pressure and mental disorders. It was not until the 1950s that Rauwolfia's active ingredient, reserpine, was used clinically as an antipsychotic agent. Reserpine ushered in the age of the so-called "major tranquilizers" that revolutionized treatment of the mentally ill. Because of reserpine's adverse side effects, the derivative of the Indian snakeroot was soon replaced by the chlorpromazine family of antipsychotic agents.

The very first drug introduced as a sedative/hypnotic was bromide. In the 1860s, potassium bromide entered the practice of medicine as a treatment for epileptic convulsions. Due to its irritating effects on the gastrointestinal tract and its tendency to accumulate in the body, leading to chronic bromide intoxication (bromism), bromide was replaced by barbiturates upon their introduction in the early 1900s.

Supposedly synthesized by Adolph von Baeyer on December 4, 1862 (St. Barbara's Day), the name barbiturates was derived from the popular local saint's name. In 1903, barbiturates officially entered the field of medical practice under the name of barbital. Unlike barbituric acid from which it was derived, barbital not only sedated, but also induced sleep. Since the introduction of barbital, more than 2,500 barbiturates have been synthesized. Only about 50 of these drugs have ever been distributed as prescribed medications.

Although chloral hydrate and paraldehyde were synthesized and marketed before 1900, the barbiturates proved so successful as sedatives/hypnotics that they remained the number one depressant-type medication until 1960. Still prescribed today, barbiturates have been replaced in large measure by newer minor tranquilizers such as meprobamate (Miltown, Equanil) and its successors, the benzodiazepines (Librium, Valium, Dalmane).[1] These new antianxiety drugs, the anxiolytics, are generally less sedating, much safer, slower to induce tolerance, and demonstrate greater antianxiety effects with less sedation than the barbiturates. However, they are dependence-producing drugs.

Benzodiazepines

After the introduction of benzodiazepine compounds in the early 1960s, their use as sedatives and anxiolytics in the United States steadily increased through 1975 to a peak level of approximately 100 million prescriptions annually. Subsequently, benzodiazepine prescriptions decreased, to approximately 65 million prescriptions in 1981, and then leveled off. With the increased use of nonbenzodiazepine sedatives and anxiolytics (e.g., barbiturates and meprobamate) benzodiazepine prescriptions decreased markedly. Since most anxiolytics are benzodiazepines, trends in anxiolytic prescriptions have been similar to those of benzodiazepines. The recent trend of decreasing anxiolytic prescriptions is probably attributable to a decreased rate in refilling prescriptions, with little change in prescription size or proportion of the population receiving prescriptions each year. This tendency toward more conservative anxiolytic use is probably attributable to the substantial recent increase in negative attitudes of patients toward use.[2]

Five-year emergency room data, for the period ending with the second quarter of 1985, show a decreasing number of emergency room episodes for most major anxiolytics (total episodes for diazepam, chlordiazepoxide, chlorazepate, and meprobamate) and sedatives (barbiturate and nonbarbiturate); however, total episodes for lorazepam increased during that time period (unpublished Drug Abuse Warning Network (DAWN) data). These DAWN statistics are generally consistent with those of national surveys suggesting abuse of anxiolytic and sedative drugs in the United States has been decreasing in recent years.[3]

Tranquilizers

Tranquilizers are commonly abused depressant drugs. They have a variety of medical and trade names, but you need only recognize them and their effects as being those of the sedative/hypnotic group.

---

[1] Cohen, Sidney. "The Barbiturates—Has Their Time Gone." *Drug Abuse and Alcoholism Newsletter.* Vista Hill Foundation, San Diego, CA, Vol. VI, No. 5, June 1977.

[2] Bolter, M.D., J. Levine and D.I. Monheimer. "Cross-National Study of the Extent of Antianxiety/Sedative Drug Use." *New England Journal of Medicine.* 290:709-774, 1974.

Marko, J. *The Benzodiazepines: Use, Misuse, Abuse.* Lancaster, England: MTP Press Ltd., 1978.

[3] National Institute on Drug Abuse. "Benzodiazepines: A Review of Research Results, 1980." Research Monograph Series 33. Rockville, MD, 1985.

Central Nervous System Depressants

SHORT-ACTING DEPRESSANTS

Onset of effect: 10-20 minutes
Duration of effect: 4-5 hours
Length of physical withdrawal symptoms: 1-4 days

GENERIC	POPULAR BRAND NAME	STREET NAME
Pentobarbital	Nembutal	Yellows, Yellow Jackets
Secobarbital	Seconal	Reds, Red Devils
Ethchlorvynol	Placidyl	Dillies
Ethinamate	Valmid	
Paraldehyde	Paral	
Chloral hydrate	Noctec, Kessodrate	Mickey Finn, knock-out drops

INTERMEDIATE-ACTING DEPRESSANTS

Onset of effect: 20-40 minutes
Duration of effect: 6-8 hours
Length of physical withdrawal symptoms: 7-8 days

GENERIC NAME	POPULAR BRAND NAME	STREET NAME
Amobarbital	Amytal	Blues, Blue Heavens
Amo-secobarbital*	Tuinal	Rainbows, Tuies, Christmas trees
Butabarbital	Buticaps, Butisol	
Meprobamate	Miltown, Equanil	
Methaqualone	Quaalude, Supor, Parest, Mequin	Quaalude, Sopor's
Methyprylon	Noludar	
Glutethimide	Doriden	

*Short onset of action, 10-20 minutes - Intermediate duration of effect.

LONG-ACTING DEPRESSANTS

Onset of effect: 1 hour
Duration of effect: 8-14 hours
Length of physical withdrawal symptoms: 10-14 days

GENERIC NAME	POPULAR BRAND NAME	STREET NAME
Phenobarbital	Luminal	Pink Ladies

Effects of Tranquilizer Abuse

When abused, tranquilizers cause all of the objective symptoms displayed by a drunk person, except that there is generally no odor of alcohol. The degree of intoxication can produce symptoms which may vary from a euphoric "high," to sloppy drunkenness, to unconsciousness. The abuser may be drowsy, confused, and unable to think clearly. His or her coordination may be impaired when standing or walking. The abuser will be dangerous to him- or herself and to others when driving a car. The individual's speech will be thick and slurred. He or she will tremble. The abuser's eyes will "bounce" involuntarily upon movement to either side (called "nystagmus") and he or she will not be able to hold a fixed position for very long. The individual may be irritable and hostile. With large doses, the individual may fall into a deep sleep and/or a delirious state of consciousness. When taken with *alcohol*, tranquilizers *are* particularly deadly, because they increase the effects of both; this effect is called *synergism*. A person who is under the influence of alcohol may take a few pills and not survive. Tranquilizers can also be fatal when taken in combination with anesthetics and narcotics.

Objective Symptoms of Tranquilizer/Barbiturate Drug Influence

A person under the influence of a sedative/hypnotic drug may display all or some of the following objective symptoms:

— Drowsiness

— Staggered gait

— Impaired coordination

— Flushed face

— Thick and slurred speech

— Nystagmus (involuntary bouncing of the eyes)

— Confusion

When these symptoms are observed and investigation rules out alcohol as the lone intoxicant, the person is under the influence of a depressant drug.

Effects of Sedative/Hypnotic Withdrawal

Sedatives/hypnotics are highly addictive drugs. The abuser develops a tolerance to the drug so that he or she requires increasingly higher doses to achieve the same effects. The body develops a physical dependence on the drug, as well as a psychological dependence which is part of every drug abuse pattern. Continued use of the drug is required to prevent the characteristic symptoms which follow abrupt withdrawal.

Withdrawal from sedatives/hypnotics are more dangerous than withdrawal from narcotics. Under withdrawal of sedatives/hypnotics, the abuser will be nervous, anxious and delirious. He or she will tremble, feel nausea, and may have a headache. The abuser is quite likely to have convulsions. He or she may become unconscious, and may die. *If you are handling a person who seems to be experiencing severe withdrawal symptoms, transport him or her to a hospital immediately!*

Central Nervous System Depressants

Objective Symptoms of Sedative/Hypnotic Withdrawal

A person who is experiencing *withdrawal* from sedatives/hypnotics may display some or all of the following objective symptoms:

— Confusion - Abdominal cramps

— Anxiety - Delirium

— Hallucinations - Convulsions

— Tremors - Unconsciousness

— Insomnia - Possible Death

— Nausea and Vomiting

Methaqualone

Chemically, methaqualone is 2-methy-3-0-tolyl-4 (3H)-quinazolinone. In pharmacological terms, it is a non-barbiturate tranquilizer used medically as a sedative/hypnotic.

In 1978, the Lemmon Company bought the license to make Quaalude from the original maker, Rorer, Inc. Quaalude is marketed as Mequin. Only the brand name and the imprint on the white tablets are different from the original Rorer Quaalude tablet.

In 1984, methaqualone became a Schedule I drug on the Federal level.[4] However, according to the Federal government, methaqualone is no longer a prescription drug. Under Federal regulations, pharmacists must get rid of their remaining stock of methaqualone.

The psychological effects of methaqualone might explain the widespread popularity of the drug; it produces a sensual and somewhat euphoric state. After ingestion of 150 to 500 mg., the user first experiences a tingling sensation and the body becomes extremely relaxed. Inhibitions disappear, more candid flowing communication creates a feeling of intimacy; and the created mood is conducive to sharing. Users have often remarked that the drug has the effect of an aphrodisiac. Extreme muscle relaxation makes it difficult to walk without stumbling; the individual may have trouble coordinating movement of the arms and legs. He or she also experiences difficulty in talking, and speech is slow and slurred.

Undesirable effects include headache, hangover, dizziness, restlessness, dry mouth, nausea, vomiting, diarrhea, sweating, foul smelling perspiration, skin eruption, rashes and abnormal sensations such as burning. The exact route of chemical action is now known.

Methaqualone is metabolized in the liver and excreted in the urine and feces.

---

[4] A Schedule I drug, according to Title 21, §812, U.S. Code, is: (A) A drug or other substance that has a high potential for abuse; (B) a drug or other substance that has no currently accepted medical use in treatment in the United States; and (C) a drug or other substance where there is a lack of accepted safety for use under medical supervision.

Like short-acting barbiturates, methaqualone is dangerous when consumed with alcohol because the two substances act synergistically.

Most methaqualone-related deaths are the result of overdoses mixed with alcohol. Coma and convulsions can also result from an acute overdose (averaging 24 grams), and death has been known to occur following ingestion of 8 grams. However, with alcohol these averages are greatly reduced.

A person under the influence of methaqualone may exhibit objective symptoms similar to the barbiturate or alcohol user: slurred speech, unsteady gait, lack of coordination, irritability, etc.

As for the psychological effects of methaqualone, acute psychological dependence only develops with prolonged abuse, although tolerance usually develops with regular use. Methaqualone abuse is more likely to lead to authentic physical addiction with withdrawals characterized by epileptic-type seizures.

One of the more serious drugs, methaqualone causes physical dependency, tolerance, and psychological dependency. Withdrawal from the drug can result in death if detoxification is not properly supervised. Initial withdrawal signs are headaches and severe cramps, followed by convulsions and stomach hemorrhaging 3 to 5 days after discontinuing use of the drug.

For treatment of acute overdose, maintain an adequate oxygen supply. If possible, induce vomiting. Call for an ambulance or transport the individual to the hospital.

Counterfeit Quaaludes

One drug problem is counterfeit methaqualone. It is being counterfeited in Columbia and in clandestine manufacturing plants in Florida. "Ludes," as they are referred to in street traffic, are in high demand.

The counterfeit tablets marked "Lemmon 714," which is the Lemmon Company's legal trademark, are showing up in illicit drug traffic on the streets. These counterfeits contain only about 1.5 mg. each of methaqualone and diazepam, a central nervous system depressant, and 149 mg. of 4,4′-diamind dephenylmethane (methylenediplene, or MDA), a chemical used in industry as an epoxy resin hardener or in the preparation of dyes. Genuine Quaaludes contain 150-300 mg. of methaqualone. The toxic dose of MDA is 84.4 mg. per kilogram in body weight. Based on this, hepatitis could result if a 120 lb. person took a dose of 402 mg. of MDA or 4 tablets of counterfeit Quaaludes.

Alcohol Combined With Depressants

When more than one drug enters the body, a chemical interaction of some type may occur. One compound may offset the effects of another, which is known as *antagonism*. When two drugs enter the body that act in a similar fashion, this would increase the total effect and is known as an *additive effect*. If two drugs act together to give an effect that is greater than addition, it is known as *synergism* (sometimes referred to as potentiation). Coroners have found in a number of cases that the drug and alcohol levels in the blood were insufficient to cause death; however, the combined effect caused death. This effect is greatest when the short-acting depressants are combined with alcohol. Since the short-acting depressants are very similar in effect to alcohol, and because of the multiplying effect when the two drugs are combined, the result is a very potent depressant to the central nervous system.

The easiest way to distinguish an additive effect from a synergistic effect is the following: additive effect — 1 ounce of alcohol + 1 dosage of depressant is equivalent to 2 units of physical effect; synergism — 1 ounce of alcohol + 1 dosage of depressant is equivalent to 4 or more units of physical effect.

Depressant Abuse Orally or by Injection

The most common and easiest method of administering depressants is orally. The fast-acting depressants, which are the most commonly abused, begin taking effect within a very short period of time (10 to 20 minutes) when ingested orally. Because of this fact, intravenous injection is less common. Intravenous use of sedatives is usually used only by those deeply involved in the abuse of other drugs as well. Intravenous injection of sedatives is limited because the desired effect can be achieved almost as rapidly through oral administration; however, there is no orgasmic type "flash" or "rush" when taken orally.

Depressant Detection and Identification in the Body

For law enforcement purposes, drug detection is usually accomplished by urinalysis. Another efficient and accurate method for the detection of sedatives is through blood analysis.

When obtaining blood or urine samples, the following procedures should be followed:

1. Blood samples should only be drawn by qualified medical personnel.
2. The blood should be collected in vacutainers that contain a blood preservative.
3. Two full vacutainers of blood should be submitted to the laboratory for a complete analysis.
4. If amphetamines or opiates are suspected, a urine sample of at least three ounces of urine should be submitted.
5. If the identity of the drug is unknown, submit both urine and blood samples for analysis.
6. Any tablets, capsules, medications, or prescription vials taken from a suspect, or his or her vehicle, should be submitted to the laboratory with the blood and/or urine sample.
7. Specifically instruct the laboratory to check the blood alcohol level as well as drug levels. This is particularly important with respect to depressant drugs since the physical symptoms of intoxication are similar to alcohol.

When a person is suspected of driving under the influence of a sedative, and the suspect refuses to give either a blood or urine sample, law enforcement personnel should consider performing a breath-alcohol examination. This may show the absence of alcohol or it may show that the suspect's behavior is inconsistent with their alcohol level. By completing this examination, the officer can assume and support drug intoxication with more evidence.

Nystagmus Test

Nystagmus, according to Webster's Dictionary, is an involuntary rapid movement of the eyeball usually from side to side on the lateral/horizontal plane.

The nystagmus test has been widely used to identify the presence of PCP. More recently, law enforcement officers have come to realize the value of nystagmus testing for DUI arrests. Alcohol, as well as many other sedatives/hypnotics, will produce nystagmus. It can serve as a gauge to the user's level of intoxication.

When testing for horizontal gaze nystagmus, the angle of onset (where the eye begins to bounce) is the most critical point for diagnosing the person's internal level of drugs or alcohol.

The following factors assist administration of the test:

1. A reasonably well-lighted and safe area
2. A standing surface which is level and free of obstacles
3. A standard testing procedure. If possible, always give your tests in the same order. Always ask your subject the location and time and note the answers in your report.

When asked what gaze nystagmus is, the answer is simply a preliminary investigative technique in which the officer looks for an involuntary jerking of the eyes. In court, the officer should not get too technical and should avoid the use of medical terms unless thoroughly understood. The officer must be prepared to testify to his or her training and experience and keep a log to record the actual number of gaze nystamus exams conducted.

When performing the test, have the subject, if wearing glasses, remove them. Contact lenses do not need to be removed. Make sure that the subject can see you. There must also be enough light for you to see the reaction.

Follow these steps when administering a nystagmus test:

1. Direct the subject to hold his or her head still.
2. Hold your finger or pen approximately 12 inches from the tip of the subject's nose; then direct the subject to follow the testing object (your finger or pen).
3. Move the testing object rapidly from the front of the nose toward the side of the head, keeping the testing object 12 inches from the subject's head at all times.
4. Observe the right eye when moving the testing object to the subject's right. Observe the left eye when moving the testing object to the subject's left.

In the test called "rough pursuit," you are looking for the failure of the eye to follow the testing object smoothly. If not performed well, this is one of the objective indicators of intoxication or impairment.

Central Nervous System Depressants

Now repeat the test again, but move the testing object much slower. Watch for the point at which the eyes start to bounce or vibrate sideways. Stop and see if the bounce continues. If not, continue to move your finger or pen to the side of the head until you have a confirmed bounce which continues after your finger or pen has stopped.

For alcohol intoxication, the degree or angle of the eyes at this point is critical to determine the person's actual level of intoxication. The degree is determined by measuring from directly in front of the suspect to the side of the head, and any movement to the left or right would be an increase in the number of degrees. There are two devices available to determine the degrees involved. These devices are used in the DARTS Chart and the FOG Tool (folding onset gauge), two nysgatmus tests from Santa Clara. The FOG Tool has also been called the Grillimeter for its inventor.

You can approximate the degree by considering that moving the iris of the eye (the iris is the colored part of the eye) from directly in front of the nose to where it starts to touch the outside corner of the eye is movement from zero to 45 degrees. Nystagmus onset will occur between zero and 45 degrees.

Assume you have a subject who produces a nystagmus onset at 35 degrees. Subtract 35 degrees from the number 50. The difference of 15 degrees is equivalent to .15 BAC (blood alcohol content) (50 - 35° = .15 BAC).

To determine end point nystagmus, move the eyes to the right or left as far as you can and you are at the end point. End point nystagmus occurs between 45° and 50° or where the iris touches the outermost corner of the eye. About 50 percent of the general population will have end point nystagmus without any alcohol in their body.

For alcohol intoxication, the nystagmus test can be used as one tool which, coupled with other signs of impairment, may prove that the suspect is under the influence. However, do not base your arrest on the nystagmus test alone.

Some people will show nystagmus and not be under the influence of anything. About 4 percent of the population will have early onset nystagmus which can be mistaken for intoxication.

Check for eye injuries. Ask whether the subject has an artificial eye.

If the angle of the onset of nystagmus is not the same for each eye, check to see if the pupil sizes are different. The nystagmus may be the result of a head injury. If so, obtain immediate medical treatment for the subject.

Some people who are intoxicated will not show any apparent sign of nystagmus.

When using the nystagmus test in DUI situations, do not rely on it as the sole basis for determining driving under the influence. You must have other signs of alcohol intoxication.

Nystagmus tests are also useful for determining the bodily presence of drugs. Sedatives/hypnotics such as barbiturates, methaqualone, alcohol, and chloral hydrate cause horizontal nystagmus. PCP causes horizontal and vertical nystagmus. Tranquilizers such as Valium in large doses may also cause nystagmus. On the other hand, narcotics (heroin, methadone, etc.) and central nervous system stimulants (amphetamine, cocaine) do not cause nystagmus.

Illicit Packaging Methods

There are many forms of illicit drug packaging. The "jar", which is a one-thousand unit quantity, is often packaged in a paper or plastic bag. Other street jargon that is used frequently in referring to quantities of pills are: a "half jar", which refers to 500 pills, a "dime bag" which refers to the number of pills that can be bought or sold for $10-$20. The "nickel bag", which refers to $5-$10 worth of pills; and a "rack" which refers to 2 to 5 pills, and appears as a tinfoil wrapped packet. A "rack" is made by placing capsules side by side on a piece of tinfoil, which is wrapped around the capsules forming a rectangular packet.

Sedative/Hypnotic Use in Combination

The majority of emergency room incidents involving Valium, Librium, Dalmane, and other psychoactive drugs result from using these drugs in combination with alcohol or other drugs. Even aspirin, which ranks number three behind Valium and alcohol in emergency room incidents, can be dangerous, even fatal, to certain allergic individuals or when abused or taken in combination with other drugs.

The National Institute on Drug Abuse estimates that in a twelve month period of usage 900 people died of adverse reactions to Valium. Another estimated 200 deaths were attributed to Librium, 200 to Equanil and Miltown, 200 to Dalmane, 500 Luminal (phenobarbital), 200 to Mellaril, and 100 to Thorazine. Again, many of these deaths—94 percent in the case of Valium—were caused not by one single drug but by a combination of drugs, usually one or more of the prescription drugs in combination with alcohol. Not all of the victims were addicts, alcoholics, or abusers of drugs; some simply made the fatal mistake of taking a drink with a prescription drug.

The best way to avoid potential hazards is to avoid mixing alcohol with any prescription drug.

Glutethimide and Codeine

Codeine is widely available as a minor narcotic analgesic and cough suppressant. Glutethimide is a tranquilizer and sleeping aid. These two drugs when used together produce a high or euphoria. Users refer to this combination of drugs as "loads" or "fours and dors" [5] and use two to three times the therapeutic dosage. The two drugs interact in a synergistic way to intensify the sedative/hypnotic effect. Glutethimide is especially dangerous since it is not readily metabolized and can be reabsorbed. The abusers who use "loads" six or seven times a day, which is common, run the risk of overdose and death.

The "fours and dors" phenomena originated in the punk rock communities of Los Angeles. It became generally recognized that codeine products and glutethimide could be easily obtained through various diversion techniques,

---

[5] Dors means Doriden. Doriden is the trade name for glutethimide.

including fraudulent medical clinics, outright sale by physicians and pharmacists, theft, and prescription forgery.

In the northeastern United States, drug abusers refer to "loads" as "the New Jersey Set". In California, users obtain codeine tablets, while on the East Coast drug users get liquid codeine from cough syrup preparations which can be purchased over-the-counter.

The "load" phenomena has also been documented through an increase in codeine robberies. Two of the robberies resulted from the hijacking of large trailer trucks containing wholesale quantities. In another instance, a firm manager was kidnapped at gunpoint.

The Drug Abuse Warning Network (DAWN) has also substantiated the increased trafficking in "fours and dors". Emergency room admissions for codeine combination products has steadily increased over the last three years.

There has been no shortage of law enforcement activity related to this problem. In one case, law enforcement identified a physician who prescribed over 100,000 dosage units of codeine and glutethimide monthly. Undercover drug purchases implicated a local pharmacy in conspiracy with the physician.

This is a particularly dangerous mixture for overdose because it combines a narcotic with a potent sedative/hypnotic that approximates in lethality a short-acting barbiturate. Glutethimide can be deadly at only five to ten times the therapeutic dose used to induce sleep. In some people, glutethimide produces an atypical intoxication seizure. At five times the therapeutic dosage, daily use for over 30 days can produce physical dependence. Chronic use may cause stumbling, staggering and neurological impairments in the hands and legs which can eventually lead to paralysis. Psychiatric problems may also be precipitated or aggravated. High doses of the aspirin and acetaminophen found in codeine compounds can cause gastric ulcers, tinnitus and hearing loss, liver damage, and blood coagulation disorders. Other additives in high quantity can cause kidney damage, central nervous system (CNS) problems, and even death.

Due to the nature of glutethimide as a short-acting sedative/hypnotic, there is no specific antagonist for either overdose or dependence. Both conditions require the expertise and facilities of an emergency room, drug treatment clinic, or poison control center. If you are assisting an abuser of this drug, be sure that treatment personnel know what drugs are involved so they can take all proper precautionary and life-sustaining measures.

An overdose may be partially reversed by the administration of naloxone (Narcan), which, as a narcotic antagonist, will nullify only the effects of the codeine. Since there is no sedative/hypnotic antagonist, the effects of the glutethimide must be managed conservatively until it is excreted from the body. A life-support system for both the respiratory and cardiovascular systems is often necessary. Also, vigorous medical intervention and hospitalization are usually required.

Withdrawal from codeine dependence by itself is clinically no worse than a bad case of the flu. It can be managed on an outpatient basis with symptomatic non-narcotic medication. Glutethimide withdrawal, however, is much more complex than detoxification from codeine. Withdrawal can induce seizures, withdrawal psychosis, or death. The withdrawal syndrome is similar to that seen after the abrupt cessation of a short-acting barbiturate.

Doriden (Glutethimide)

Doriden is an oral hypnotic. It is a piperidinedione derivative that occurs in a white crystalline powder and a white scored tablet. Doriden is soluble in alcohol but practically insoluble in water. Its chemical name is 2-ethyl-2-phenylglutarimide, and is found in 0.5 gram and 0.25 gram tablets. Doriden is synergistic with other CNS depressants such as alcohol. With continued use of this drug, both physical and psychological dependence as well as tolerance will occur. Withdrawal symptoms include nausea, abdominal discomfort, tremors, convulsions, and delirium. In humans, the single acute lethal dose of Doriden ranges from 10g to 20g. Nonetheless, people have died from single doses as low as 5g and have recovered from single doses as high as 35g. A single oral dose of 5g usually produces severe intoxication.

The principal symptoms of Doriden intoxication vary in proportion to the ingested dosage. These symptoms are generally indistinguishable from those caused by barbituate intoxication and include the following: impaired memory, impaired concentration ability, impaired gait, tremors, slurring of speech, and ataxia (inability to coordinate voluntary muscular movements). Abrupt discontinuance of Doriden after prolonged use will also result in withdrawal reactions ranging from nervousness and anxiety to grand mal seizures.

Ethchloruynol (Placidyl)

Ethchloruynol is a non-barbiturate sedative/hypnotic marketed under the trade name Placidyl. Users report that, among the CNS depressants, Placidyl seems to have the most euphoriant effects.

This drug is available in 100-, 200-, 500-, and 750-mg. capsules. Since it is quickly absorbed from the gastrointestinal tract, Placidyl has an extremely rapid onset of action. Yet, its duration of action is relatively short (about 3 to 5 hours). Peak plasma concentrations of Placidyl are observed within 1 to 1½ hours after ingestion. During ingestion, the drug is metabolized by the liver and inactive metabolites are excreted in urine.

Placidyl also has some anticonvulsant and muscle-relaxant properties; it affects REM sleep only slightly, and compared to other sedatives/hypnotics, discontinuation of use produces less REM rebound. Many users report that Placidyl produces a mintlike aftertaste and, frequently, a hangover. Continued use of the drug results in concentrations of active metabolites stored in the body's fatty tissue.

Due to its euphoriant properties, Placidyl often produces giddiness, excitement, delirium, and incoordination. Recreational users describe Placidyl's effects as pleasant, calm, and happy with initial mild stimulation. However, if someone who is psychologically depressed takes Placidyl, his or her depression may increase. When it is available, this drug is usually the preferred sedative/hypnotic for more experienced CNS depressant users.

Since Placidyl is a preferred CNS depressant among frequent users, it should be mentioned that tolerance to Placidyl develops quickly; it readily produces physical dependence. With daily administration of one gram or more for four weeks, physical dependence usually occurs. Since one gram is only twice the hypnotic dose, the safety margin of Placidyl is quite small. Once physical dependence develops, continued administration is necessary if withdrawal symptoms are to be avoided. Chronic abusers may take up to 4 grams daily. After ingesting such a dosage, chronic dependent abusers show intoxication symptoms similar to those of an alcoholic. These symptoms include incoordination, tremors, slurred speech, and confusion. Abrupt discontinuation, on the other hand, results in withdrawal symptoms remarkably similar to delirium tremens (DT's), or the major abstinence syndrome seen in alcohol withdrawal.

Xanax (Alprazolam)

Xanax is a benzodiazepine. It is medically used for anxiety disorders and short-term relief of anxiety symptoms. Abuse of this drug is rapidly increasing. It is available in tablets of 0.25, 0.5, and 1 mg.

Effectiveness for long-term use of Xanax has not been established. Nonetheless, abrupt discontinuance or a rapid decrease in dosage can cause serious withdrawal seizures. Since Xanax is benzodiazepine, it may produce withdrawal effects similar to other benzodiazepines ranging from mild dysphoria and insomnia to a more severe withdrawal syndrome characterized by abdominal and muscle cramps, vomiting, sweating, tremors, and convulsions.

With prolonged use of Xanax, psychic and/or physical dependence may also develop. Discontinued use can cause agitation, increased muscle spasticity, sleep disturbances, and hallucinations. Although it is used for anxiety disorders and short-term anxiety relief, Xanax is of no value in the treatment of people with more complex pyschoses.

Summary

Over the last two decades, benzodiazepines have replaced barbiturates as the most frequently used anxiolytics, sedatives, and hypnotics. Benzodiazepines are among the safest, most effective, and widely prescribed psychotropic compounds. Despite increased overall use, the nonmedical use (i.e., abuse) of barbiturates and benzodiazepines has tended to decrease in recent years. When they are abused, benzodiazepines tend to be taken in combination with other drugs and are used most often by chronic polydrug abusers. Diazepam-opioid combinations appear to be the most glaring problem within this abuse pattern.

With regard to dependence and withdrawal, studies of laboratory animals and humans have shown that abrupt termination of high chronic doses of barbiturates and benzodiazepines can produce a severe withdrawal syndrome sometimes including delirium and/or grand mal convulsions. Some limited animal and human test data suggest that high doses of barbiturates may produce a more severe withdrawal syndrome than high doses of benzodiazepines. It has also become clear through these tests that benzodiazepines can even produce a withdrawal syndrome after prolonged treatment with normal therapeutic doses. Although additional research will be required to adequately address the risk/benefit ratio of long-term benzodiazepine use, there is an increasing clinical consensus that chronic maintenance of patients on anxiolytics is not desirable and that such patients should be regularly evaluated for termination of medication.

Slang Terminology

The following is a partial list of CNS depressant jargon used in California:

Bag	quantity of drugs packaged in various containers such as paper, balloons, baggies, etc.
Barbs	barbiturates
Barrel	100,000 pills
Bottle	100 pills
Cap	capsule
Cap up	transfer drug in bulk form into capsules
Downer	drug with depressant effect, usually means secobarbital
Dropped	taking drugs orally
Eat	to swallow drugs
Factory	location where illicit drugs are manufactured
Jar	1,000 pills
Jug	1,000 pills
Keg	50,000 pills
Knockout drops	chloral hydrate
Ludes	methaqualone
Mequin	methaqualone
Pill freak	user of any type of pills
Pillow	25,000 tablets usually packaged in a black plastic bag
Pink Lady	phenobarbital capsule
Q's	methaqualone
Rack	2 to 5 capsules wrapped in tinfoil
Sopors	methaqualone
Tabs	tablets

REFERENCES:

Bolter, M.D., J. Levine and D.I. Monheimer. "Cross-National Study of the Extent of Antianxiety/Sedative Drug Use." *New England Journal of Medicine.* 290:709-774, 1974.

Cohen, Sidney. "The Barbiturates—Has Their Time Gone." *Drug Abuse and Alcoholism Newsletter.* Vista Hill Foundation, San Diego, CA, Vol. VI, No. 5, June 1977.

Hecht, Annabel. "Tranquilizers: Use, Abuse, and Dependency: FDA Requirements." *FDA Consumer* 12, No. 8, October 1978, pp. 20-33.

Marko, J. *The Benzodiazepines: Use, Misuse, Abuse.* Lancaster, England: MTP Press Ltd., 1978.

National Institute on Drug Abuse. "Benzodiazepines: A Review of Research Results, 1980." Research Monograph Series 33. Rockville, MD, 1985.

Physician's Desk Reference, 45th ed. Medical Economics Data, N.J., 1991.

Stash Staff. *Downers: The Central Nervous System Depressant Drugs.* No. 21. Madison, Wisconsin: Stash Press, 1974.

________. "Methaqualone: A Dr. Jekyll and Mr. Hyde?" *Pharm Chem Newsletter*, II, No. 1, 1973, Palo Alto, CA, p. 4.

CHAPTER VI

ALCOHOL

INTRODUCTION

Although American culture generally accepts the use of alcoholic beverages, the misuse of alcohol is a major public health problem in the United States. Alcohol abuse is a matter of public concern because excessive drinking does not only affect the individual drinker; when compounded, excessive drinking also affects the drinker's family, friends, fellow workers, and neighbors. Even strangers may be put directly at risk by another person's excessive drinking.

HISTORY

The use and misuse of alcoholic beverages has long been a controversial issue in America. The issue has been contested by various interest groups and legislative bodies ever since (and even before) the birth of the country.

Efforts to control drinking have ranged from pulpit sermons and advice from physicians to legislative judgments by the courts. In fact, a large portion of the nation's political climate has been shaped by attitudes about drinking—attitudes as disparate as those which brought about the Whiskey Rebellion of 1794 and the Volstead Act of 1919.

America has even attempted to legislate nationwide prohibition by Federal law and has subsequently rejected it. Today, it is generally accepted that those adults who wish to drink have a right to do so within the limitations of local customs that are defined by written or unwritten laws. Written or unwritten legal rights, however, are not the only factors involved. Social rights and social pressures are also a major factor influencing the use of alcohol in the United States. These social factors vary from community to community throughout different regions and their local customs.

Given these circumstances, it is impossible to generalize about one national attitude toward moderate or social drinking. Perhaps there will never be such a nationwide agreement. Nevertheless, there is developing a common attitude concerning the excessive drinker, the problem drinker, and the alcoholic. This attitude is based in part on the growing awareness that excessive drinking does not affect the individual drinker alone; a drinking problem affects all those with whom the drinker comes into contact. This growing awareness is also based on the recognition that moral issues involved with alcoholism and excessive drinking are overshadowed by the more glaring health and medical complications which affect the individual and the society responsible for keeping that individual from causing harm to others.

This new look at drinking is not a renewal of hostilities between "wets" and "drys." Instead, there seems to be an appreciation among many intellectuals—including scientists, physicians, educators, jurists and religious leaders—that the solution of drinking-related problems requires an understanding of drinking in all its complex facets. It is essential to consider the chemistry and the physiological effects of the alcoholic beverages consumed in life by people, as well as the psychological and sociological implications to a society in which abstinence, moderate drinking, excessive drinking and alcoholism all occur as normal or abnormal behavioral patterns. Likewise, it is essential to clarify both the nature and scope of the problems, to assess their true impact on American society, and to arrive through study and research at new knowledge that can help prevent and control excessive drinking while continuing to improve the treatment and rehabilitation of the alcoholic.

Even though widespread public awareness of drinking problems is relatively new, the existence of alcohol and its abuse is exceedingly old.

As with natural phenomena such as fire and water, the discovery of alcoholic beverages cannot be assigned a date or a patent number, nor credited to any one person or place. Only a few basic ingredients—sugar, water, yeast and a mild degree of warmth—are required for alcohol production. Where these occur together, it is virtually impossible for alcohol not to be produced. According to paleontologists, all four of these ingredients were present on earth at least 200 million years ago in the Paleozoic era.

It seems obvious, therefore, that alcohol preceded humanity and that humans began using the substance long before the beginnings of written history. Since the earliest civilizations, alcoholic beverages have been regarded as nutritious foods, valuable medicines, and sacred liquids for religious ceremonies.

WHY PEOPLE DRINK

Alcoholic beverages have a long record of medical use and were at one time among the most widely prescribed drugs. Alcohol is still accepted as a useful, although not a curative, medical agent. While some of the health values once attributed to beer, wine, and distilled spirits have been disproved, others have been confirmed by modern scientific study. For example, certain alcoholic beverages are used by physicians as aids in the treatment of arthritis, digestive diseases, high blood pressure and coronary disease, and as tranquilizers or sedatives for convalescent and geriatric patients.

In one form or another, alcohol was probably the first tranquilizer known to human beings; today, it remains the most widely used. Despite its accepted religious uses, in the majority of instances, drinking stems from the desire for an antidote to unpleasant reality, the need for an ego boost, or as an aid to sociability. Quite apart from any physiological effects, the custom of drinking is often felt to be rewarding because of the social interrelationships, the status, and the behaviors and attitudes that accompany it.

EXCESSIVE DRINKING

Throughout the history of alcoholic beverages, in all its uses, drunkenness has been consistently regarded as a problem.

Alcoholic beverages were probably known in the New World long before Columbus. They were certainly brought to America in 1607 with the settling of the Virginia Colony. Twelve years later their excessive use was legislated against by a law decreeing that any person found drunk for the first time

 md

was to be reproved privately by the minister; the second time, the person would be reproved publicly; the third time, the person was to "lye tin halter" for twelve hours and pay a fine. Yet, in the same year, the Virginia Assembly passed other legislation encouraging the production of wines and distilled spirits in the colony. It should be mentioned that the custom of drinking was not unacceptable in early Virginia; drinking to excess, a very different activity, was unacceptable.[1]

Another early American settlement, the Massachusetts Bay Colony, had similar attitudes toward drinking. In the Bay Colony, brewing came to rank next in importance to milling and baking. As in Virginia, occasional drunkenness in Massachusetts was punished by whipping, fines and confinement in the stocks. Nonetheless, social drinking was acceptable and popular. As Norbert Kelly writes, "The Puritans neither disdained nor prohibited the use of beverage alcohol. They were emphatic, however, in urging moderation in drinking." [2]

The temperance movement—which grew out of the alcoholic excesses of England's Industrial Revolution—was not long in coming to America. It began with the goal of temperance in a literal sense: *moderation.* In the 1830s, at the peak of this early campaign, temperance leaders maintained that the remedy for intemperance was simply abstinence from distilled spirits. Several of these leaders, however, drank beer and wine.

Following this initial temperance movement, the next decades brought a significant change. The meaning of temperance was gradually altered from moderation to total abstinence. Instead of limiting the regulations to distilled spirits, all alcoholic beverages were then attacked as unnecessary, unhealthy, and inherently poisonous. The demand arose for total prohibition.

This demand culminated in the United States in the passage of the 18th Amendment, which prohibited the manufacture and sale of all alcoholic beverages. Beginning in 1920, national Prohibition lasted until 1933. Even now Prohibition remains a controversial subject. Its defenders claim that the 18th Amendment brought a substantial reduction in drinking and drunkenness, and a marked increase in the country's economic productivity. Those who oppose the concept say that the experiment curbed only the moderate drinker and brought new and dangerous glamor to drinking and manufacturing alcohol. They claim that it destroyed public respect for law enforcement officers and bred the crime, violence and general corruption that characterizes the Prohibition era's bootlegging of illicit liquor. Whatever the validity of these opposing views, one fact seemed fairly well established by the end of the Prohibition era: many Americans enjoyed drinking and

---

[1] Goode, Erick. *Drugs in American Society,* 3rd ed. Alfred N. Knopf, Inc., New York, 1989, pp. 118-126.

Oakley, Ray. S. *Drugs, Society and Human Behavior*. C.V. Mosby Co., St. Louis, 1972, pp. 79-94.

[2] Kelly, Norbet L. "Social & Legal Programs of Control in the United States." *McCarthy: Alcohol Education for Classroom and Community.*

would insist with considerable vehemence on their right to drink. Today, there are no signs that their views have changed.

Yet, while it has become clear that many and perhaps most Americans would continue to insist on their right to drink, people have become aware of the problem of drinking to excess. People realize that problem drinkers endanger the lives and the welfare of themselves, their families, and all those around them. Alcoholism is now recognized as a serious public health concern that urgently demands intelligent, practical action based on better knowledge of its causes and resolution of its associated problems.

VARIETIES OF ALCOHOL

Among the many varieties of alcohol, *methyl alcohol* (commonly called "wood alcohol") is the variety used in commercial products such as antifreezes and fuels. A second type of alcohol—also poisonous—is *isopropyl alcohol*. While isopropyl alcohol is usually called "rubbing alcohol," it is also used as a disinfectant and a solvent.

The only kind of alcohol that can be consumed safely in alcoholic drinks is *ethyl alcohol*, or "grain alcohol." "Denatured" alcohol is ethyl alcohol to which poisonous chemicals have been added. Since the removal of these poisons requires complex laboratory procedures, there is no household way to make denatured alcohol safe for drinking.

Ethyl alcohol manufactured for drinking is initially obtained through the fermentation of sugars and starches. The most common ethyl alcohols are beer and wine. Production of ethyl alcohols with a higher alcoholic content—for example, rum, gin, or whiskey—requires a process of distillation.

During distillation, a liquid mixture is vaporized and the components of the vapor are collected by differential cooling during condensation. In distilling a previously fermented solution containing a low concentration of alcohol in order to produce a beverage with a greater alcoholic content, heat must be applied to the solution until the alcohol (which has a lower boiling point than water) is changed to a vapor. This vapor is then collected and condensed into a liquid form resulting in a new beverage with a higher alcoholic *proof*. One-half of the proof equals the percent of actual alcohol content; in other words, 86 proof means that the alcohol is 43 percent of the total liquid content.

It is generally accepted today that alcohol, by strict definitions, is a food, since it is a source of calories. The caloric value of pure alcohol is 7 calories per gram. Thus, alcohol is nearly as high in calories as pure fat or oil, which contains 9 calories per gram. Apart from their calories, alcoholic beverages have no nutritional value; they contain only insignificant amounts of vitamins, minerals, and proteins. Therefore, alcohol is classified as an incomplete food.[3]

---

[3] Doweiko, Harold. *Concepts of Chemical Dependency*. Cole Publishing Co., Pacific Grove, CA, 1990, p. 17.

Alcohol

THE EFFECTS OF ALCOHOL ON THE CENTRAL NERVOUS SYSTEM

Since it is a drug, alcohol's effects are mainly exerted upon the central nervous system. As with other depressant drugs, the effects of alcohol follow a pattern in which the highest intellectual functions of the CNS are interfered with first. Those vital functions controlled by the brain stem regulatory centers are only affected later. Alcoholic depression of the CNS is characterized by a particularly long excitement, or delirium, stage. This prolonged hyperactivity results from depression of the inhibitory areas of the brain which usually operate to suppress the more physically stimulating functions of the CNS. Later, as the released areas of the CNS are themselves depressed, the drinker falls into a stupor and may become comatose.

Thus, contrary to the belief that still persists among many people, alcohol is not a stimulant; it is a tranquilizer. It was, in fact, once employed in preparing patients for surgery. However, although it can help to put a person to sleep, raise his pain threshold and finally produce unconsciousness, alcohol is not used as a general anesthetic in modern clinical practice.

The effects of alcohol on CNS functioning are proportional to the level of alcohol in the blood and the brain. Of course, individuals differ to some degree in their reactions to similar concentrations of alcohol in the CNS. Nevertheless, lower blood-alcohol levels produce less nervous function impairment. Likewise, higher concentrations of alcohol in the blood and brain produce more profound and widespread CNS depression. As is true with other drugs, the concentration of ingested alcohol in the brain at any given moment depends upon rates of absorption, distribution, and elimination—that is to say, it depends upon the individual drinker's metabolism.

METABOLISM

The average metabolic rate for alcohol in the body is approximately one drink per hour. One drink equals ⅓ of an ounce of 100 percent alcohol, the approximate equivalent of 1 ounce of whiskey, or 12 ounces of beer.

The rate of metabolism is important for two reasons: (1) determining the probable time length of a "hangover", and (2) determining the amount of time required to safely operate an automobile or other machinery after drinking. A hangover lasts approximately the same number of hours as the number of drinks ingested. Bear in mind that this is only a rule of thumb.

Since it takes approximately 1 hour for the body to metabolize the equivalent of 1 shot of whiskey or a 12-ounce can of beer, it is obvious how a person can fall "under the influence" of alcohol: by drinking more alcohol per unit of time than the body can metabolize. The greater the consumption per unit of time, the greater the increase in blood-alcohol concentration. The greater the concentration, the more noticeable the effects. However, at any given blood-alcohol level, the effects may differ greatly from person to person. Several people (often heavy drinkers) have learned to "hold" their liquor or behaviorally compensate for the effects of alcohol so that others cannot tell from outward appearance that they have been drinking to excess. The same person may even behave differently at different times given the same blood-alcohol level. This variation is a function of mood, setting, and expectations.

Absorption. After consuming alcohol, the body's first metabolic reaction is absorption. Since it requires no digestion and diffuses readily through the body, alcohol is a rapidly absorbed substance. About 20 percent of all ingested alcohol is absorbed from within the stomach, but the bulk of any drink makes its way into the blood stream only after it enters the small intestine. If a concentrated alcoholic drink is taken on an empty stomach, the effects can be felt very quickly in the CNS. On an empty stomach, absorption begins immediately and reaches a peak in as little as twenty minutes.

The period required for absorption may, however, be considerably delayed when the stomach contains a moderate amount of food. The presence of food tends to dilute the alcohol and interfere with its absorption from the stomach into the blood. In addition, milk or other fat-containing foods tend to slow down the rate at which the stomach empties into the first foot of the small intestine, from which most of the alcohol is absorbed into the bloodstream. Through this delayed absorption effect caused by food and/or milk, alcohol can be detoxified, keeping the alcohol's concentration in the blood and brain relatively low, and reducing its effects on the CNS. Similarly, sipping a drink over a period of time results in relatively low blood-alcohol concentrations and fewer CNS effects compared to the same amount of alcohol downed in one gulp.

Distribution. Once the alcohol enters the capillaries, it diffuses from the blood into all the body's tissues where it mixes with their water content. The better a tissue's blood supply, the more rapidly its concentration of alcohol increases. Thus, the level of alcohol in the brain quickly balances itself with that of the blood. Later, tissues that receive proportionally less blood or contain less water, finally take up their full share of the alcohol. Redistribution to secondary storage sites tends to draw some of the alcohol away from the brain and thus aids in the sobering process, provided that no further drinking is done.

Metabolic Breakdown. By far, the most important factor in the reduction of alcohol levels in the brain is the body's ability to burn up or oxidize the alcohol in its tissues. Between 90 and 95 percent of all the alcohol that is absorbed is broken down to carbon dioxide and water in a series of three steps catalyzed by enzymes. Most of the remaining alcohol leaves the body unchanged by way of the breath and urine.

The first step in the metabolic breakdown of alcohol takes place mainly in the liver. Two enzymes catalyze the conversion of alcohol, *first to acetaldehyde and then to acetate*. Ordinarily, the second step of conversion to acetate immediately follows the first, so that there is little or no accumulation of acetaldehyde. However, sometimes acetaldehyde may build up to toxic levels, particularly if the drinker's body contains drugs which suppress the activity of the oxidative enzymes.

The final step in the metabolism of alcohol takes place in all the body's cells. Here, the acetate derived from alcohol is fed into the cellular system for obtaining energy from foodstuffs. This step is known as the Krebs tricarboxylic acid cycle, the main chemical pathway used by the body's cells to burn the acetate fragments from foods. This cycle then produces energy and gives off water and carbon dioxide as waste products.[4]

RELATIONSHIP OF BLOOD-ALCOHOL LEVELS TO BEHAVIOR

When a person drinks more alcohol than his or her body can burn, the excess alcohol accumulates in the blood and brain. The increasing levels of alcohol then induce behavioral changes that—within limits—are correlative to the concentration of alcohol in the blood. The most important application of this principle has been determining a person's fitness to drive a motor vehicle.

Chemists have devised many tests for estimating the amount of alcohol in a person's brain by analyzing the blood, urine, and breath. Analysis of a person's breath is the basis for the intoxilizer test that drivers are required to take when suspected of driving under the influence. Such tests have nothing to do with the odor of a person's breath, which is caused not by alcohol itself but by other substances contained in alcoholic beverages. Rather, the breath serves as an index of the amount of alcohol in the person's blood, since the alcohol in the arteries is in balance with that of the air in the alveoli of the lungs.

Individuals vary in their ability to tolerate or withstand similar levels of alcohol in the brain; however, for most people, blood-alcohol levels do correspond to noticeable impairments in the ability to drive a car. For such purposes, blood-alcohol levels expressed in milligrams of alcohol per 100 milliliters of blood—that is, in mg.%—are related to probable fitness to drive.

BLOOD-ALCOHOL LEVELS RELATED TO FITNESS TO DRIVE

Hours spent drinking	TWO DRINKS Body Weight			FOUR DRINKS Body Weight			SIX DRINKS Body Weight			EIGHT DRINKS Body Weight		
	120	150	180	120	150	180	120	150	180	120	150	180
1 Hour . . .	.05	.04	.03	.11	.09	.07	.16	.13	.11	.21	.17	.14
2 Hours. . .	.02	.01	—	.08	.05	.04	.14	.10	.08	.20	.15	.12
3 Hours. . .				.06	.04	.02	.12	.08	.06	.18	.13	.10
4 Hours. . .				.05	.02	.01	.11	.07	.04	.17	.12	.09

NOTE: The number of drinks is based on one ounce of 86 proof alcohol or one 12 ounce bottle of beer. This is the typical strength of a bar or restaurant drink; home drinks tend to be about twice as strong.

HOW TO USE THIS CHART:

You can estimate figures that are not on this chart. For example, suppose you have been drinking for two hours, have had five drinks, and weigh 150

[4] Girdano and Dusek. *Drug Education: Content and Methods,* 4th ed. Random House, New York, 1988, pp. 80-81.

pounds. You would read down the left hand column to 2 hours, then read across. Four drinks would give you a blood-alcohol content of .05, and six drinks would give you a blood-alcohol content of .10. You could figure that your blood-alcohol content would be between these two figures, approximately .075. This blood-alcohol level indicates a loss of driving skill and the possibility that you could be charged with driving under the influence of alcohol.[5]

BLOOD-ALCOHOL LEVEL AND BEHAVIORAL EFFECTS

Present Blood-Alcohol	Average Effects
.02	Reached after approximately one drink: light or moderate drinkers experience some pleasant feelings; e.g., sense of warmth and well-being.
.04	Most people feel relaxed, energetic and happy. Time seems to pass quickly. Skin may flush, and motor skills may be slightly impaired.
.05	More observable effects begin to occur. Individual may experience lightheadedness, giddiness, lowered inhibitions, and impaired judgment. Coordination may be slightly altered.
.06	Further impairment of judgment; individual's ability to make rational decisions concerning personal capabilities is affected, e.g., driving a car. Individual may be subject to mood swings.
.08	Muscle coordination definitely impaired and reaction time affected; driving ability is suspect. Heavy pulse and slow breathing. Sensory feelings of numbness in the cheeks, lips, and extremities may occur.
.10	Clear deterioration of coordination and reaction time. Individual may stagger and speech may become fuzzy. Judgment and memory further affected (legally drunk, in most states).
.15	All individuals experience impairment of balance and movement. Severe impairment of reaction time.
.20	Marked depression in motor and sensory capability; slurred speech, double vision, difficulty standing and walking may all be present. Decidedly intoxicated.
.30	Individual is confused or stuporous; unable to comprehend what is seen or heard. May lose consciousness or pass out.

[5] Department of Motor Vehicles, State of California, Sacramento, California.

.40 Usually unconscious. Alcohol has become deep anesthetic. Skin may be sweaty and clammy.

.45 Circulatory and respiratory functions are depressed and may stop altogether.

.50 Near death.[6]

PHARMACOLOGICAL EFFECTS

What are the effects of alcohol on other parts of the body? One of its effects is to dilate the blood vessels close to the surface of the skin. This effect causes what people report as a warm feeling. However, this effect also *increases* heat loss. Therefore, alcohol consumption would not be advisable for a person trying to keep warm in a cold climate. A person drinking alcohol in a severely cold climate would freeze to death much sooner than someone who did not have alcohol in the bloodstream. Alcohol can also suppress the body's temperature regulatory mechanism, resulting in a sharp drop in body temperature.

Another effect of alcohol is to dilate the coronary arteries, thereby increasing blood flow. This effect, along with certain changes in blood lipoproteins, may explain the recent finding that moderate drinkers have fewer myocardial infarctions (heart attacks) than do either abstainers or heavy drinkers.

Alcohol also appears to have some anticoagulant properties. This effect may be a problem for automobile accident victims, because it increases the blood loss rate, adding to the risk of shock and/or bleeding to death.

Alcohol also acts as a diuretic. Diuretics are agents that increase the volume of urine. This effect is one reason why someone who has drunk to excess may be quite thirsty the next morning. The diuretic action of alcohol may disturb the electrolyte balance necessary for normal body functions.

Alcohol, like many other CNS depressants, also raises the seizure threshold. This effect helps to explain why seizures occur in some heavy drinkers who suddenly stop drinking. Individuals with seizure disorders should, of course, be urged to use alcohol with extreme caution.

A further effect of alcohol is the suppression of REM (Rapid Eye Movement) sleep. Very often people who have difficulty falling asleep have a "few drinks" in order to sleep. The greater the number of drinks, the more REM suppression. Of course, the first night the individual does not have this nightly "dose," he or she will experience a sleep with perhaps very disturbing dreams from which he or she awakens feeling quite unrefreshed.

---

[6] "Intoxication." *Drug Abuse and Alcoholism Newsletter.* Vista Hill Foundation, Vol. XV, No. 7, Sept. 1986.

Alcohol and Alcoholism: A Police Handbook. The Correctional Association of New York, the International Association of Chiefs of Police, New York, 1978, pp. 8-10.

TOLERANCE, DEPENDENCE, WITHDRAWAL

Tolerance for many effects of alcohol is easily developed, and is acquired by three mechanisms. First, alcohol is metabolized by the liver; it increases the formation and activity of the liver enzymes responsible for its metabolism. Therefore, chronic use requires higher "doses" if the user wants to continue certain effects. At the cellular level, chronic use results in the cells attempting to accommodate to the effects of alcohol. Therefore, the cells become dependent, because cellular accommodation continues whether or not alcohol is present. In the absence of alcohol, these cells are still "accommodating" by cell excitation to a drug that is not present. This is probably the mechanism by which abstinence symptoms occur. The heavy drinker who wants to avoid the "shakes" produced by cellular accommodation to a drug that is not present, drinks more. It's a vicious cycle.

Behavioral tolerance to alcohol is also acquired. Many people are able to "hold their liquor." They may drink far more alcohol than one suspects, because they do not *appear* drunk. Controlling drunken behavior in such a manner is an example of behavioral tolerance.

Tolerance, of course, can lead to both psychological and physical dependence. The heavy chronic drinker often feels that life cannot be lived without drinking. An important point is that psychological and physical dependence are not mutually exclusive. The chronic heavy drinker is at least psychologically dependent, but may also be physically dependent on alcohol.

Physical dependence is demonstrated by the appearance of abstinence symptoms when the alcoholic stops drinking. The severity of withdrawal symptoms is a function of the drinker's level of physical dependence.

ACUTE WITHDRAWAL SYNDROME

Many of the difficulties that occur after drinking are now recognized to be the result of withdrawal. Symptoms may range in severity and depend mainly upon how much and how long the individual has been drinking.

People with a relatively mild withdrawal syndrome may suffer only from what they call "the shakes," a state of tremulousness and relatively slight agitation. This is commonly managed by the parenteral administration of chlordiazepoxide (Librium), which reduces the person's psychomotor hyperactivity and tremors. The continued use of this minor tranquilizer during long-term convalescence may, however, be undesirable in alcoholic patients, if the alcoholic is also prone to abuse other general depressant drugs. Thus, some alcoholics have become addicted to the barbiturates, paraldehyde, chloral hydrate, and other sedatives/hypnotics with which they have been treated. Today, addiction to meprobamate, glutethimide, and other modern tranquilizers and sedatives is common among former alcoholics.[7]

The delirium tremens, or the D.T.s, develop after several weeks of heavy drinking, and seem to be precipitated when the person can no longer keep his or her blood-alcohol up to the accustomed level. This reduction of

---

[7] Schuckit, Marc. "Is there a Protracted Abstinence Syndrome with Drugs." *Drug Abuse and Alcoholism Newsletter*. Vista Hill Foundation, Vol. XX, No. 4, Aug. 1991.

blood-alcohol may occur as a result of persistent vomiting or other conditions that keep the person from continuing to drink. Users who are hospitalized for acute alcoholic intoxication, or alcoholics who are hospitalized for treatment of pneumonia or other conditions, may develop delirium tremens after a day or two of alcohol-free treatment.

The Hangover. Some experts contend that a hangover is actually an abstinence syndrome. The symptoms support this explanation because they are consistent with the symptoms of more minor abstinence syndromes discussed above. The most commonly reported symptoms include nausea, vomiting, shaking, profound thirst, fatigue, dizziness, perhaps anxiety and/or depression, skin pallor, and sweating. The severity of the symptoms are a direct function of how much was consumed and how quickly. The more consumed per unit of time, the worse the hangover.

Two factors contributing to the hangover are acetaldehyde and cogeners. Acetaldehyde is a by-product of the metabolism of alcohol in the liver and is very toxic, even in small quantities. It is thought to play a role in the severity of the hangover headache. Cogeners are naturally occurring by-products of the fermentation process that exist in alcoholic beverages and appear to contribute to an upset stomach, nausea, and headaches. The more cogeners, the greater the severity of these effects. Beer has the fewest cogeners, while bourbon and whiskey have the most. Usually, lighter colored hard liquors have fewer cogeners. Of course, nausea and vomiting could also be a function of the gastric irritation caused by large amounts of alcohol itself.

Unfortunately, there is no cure for a hangover other than time. An analgesic such as buffered aspirin may ease the headache, and drinking water may help replace any lost fluids. However, most home remedies that you may have heard of do little if anything to moderate the symptoms of hangover.

ALCOHOL AND DRUG INTERACTION

Alcohol interacts with many, if not most, drugs. One interactional effect is potentiation. Alcohol potentiates the actions of many CNS depressants. This effect can present a life-threatening risk to the drinker and drug user. In the presence of barbiturates, for example, even low or moderate amounts of alcohol can be lethal.

SUMMARY

Generally, the major pharmacological effects of alcohol are similar to those of the other CNS depressants. Alcohol is almost identical to the barbiturates in dependence and tolerance potential, toxic effects, and overdose risks. The absorption of alcohol takes place throughout the entire gastrointestinal tract and is affected by stomach contents and alcohol concentration and/or carbonation in the beverage. Alcohol crosses the blood-brain barrier quickly and is distributed through all body fluids, tissues, and organs. Its effects are clearly related to levels of dosage: the greater the consumption of alcohol per unit of time, the greater the blood-alcohol concentration. The Table on pages 137 and 138 shows the behavioral effects of alcohol at various blood-alcohol levels. Individual differences such as weight and tolerance affect blood serum levels. For instance, a person with great body mass will have less alcohol in the blood; therefore, that person will suffer fewer psychoactive effects. However, environment and setting may also cause a person to react differently at different times given the same blood-alcohol level.

Large amounts of alcohol can lead to acute and chronic tolerance in which higher and higher "doses" are needed to produce the desired effect. Tolerance can lead to both psychological and physical dependence, as demonstrated by abstinence symptoms ranging in severity from mild to life threatening. Chronic use can result in cellular accommodation to alcohol, blackouts, irreversible brain syndrome, digestive problems, gastritis, and liver problems, including cirrhosis and hepatitis. Prolonged use also increases the risk of cancer. Some recent findings indicate that genetics may be a contributing factor in alcoholism. It has been hypothesized that a physiological predisposition toward alcohol abuse, particularly in males, may result from genetic heritage.

ALCOHOL USE WITH NONALCOHOLICS

There is a growing body of literature on the beneficial effects of moderate drinking. This literature helps to explain how the effects of alcohol consumption can be extremely dangerous for some, yet mildly beneficial for others.[8]

PEOPLE WHO SHOULD NEVER DRINK

There are some groups of people who should never drink under any circumstances. These people should never drink because even as few as one to two drinks are likely to cause substantial problems. Among these individuals are pregnant women and recovering alcoholics or substance abusers. In addition, alcohol should be avoided by people taking any medication, especially those consuming antidepressants such as amitriptyline (Elavil), and those taking any drugs that make them drowsy such as the benzodizaepines (e.g., Diazepam or Valium). Several medical conditions can also be exacerbated by the consumption of alcohol; these conditions include any form of liver damage, immune system complications, or high blood pressure.

Individuals at an exceptionally high risk for the future development of alcoholism (e.g., children of alcoholics) should consider abstaining from alcoholic beverages altogether. Consumption of alcohol is also ill-advised for persons operating motor vehicles, machinery, or aircraft.

Given that alcohol is a potent drug with some serious consequences for personal health, how can alcohol still be consumed even in moderate amounts by people who are familiar with its deleterious effects? One explanation may rest with the data relating moderate alcohol intake to a diminished risk for heart attacks.

LOW DOSES OF ALCOHOL AND HEART DISEASE

Most studies of men and women in the general population show that, compared to nondrinkers, healthy individuals who consume 1 to 2 drinks

---

[8] Leiber, C.S. "To drink (moderately) or not to drink." *New England Journal of Medicine*. 105:124-126, 1986.

per day may have a lower risk of heart disease. A recent 4-year follow-up of over 87,000 nurses aged between 34 and 59 years old reported that those who consumed 5 to 14 grams of absolute alcohol per day (about 1 drink per day or 3 to 9 drinks per week) had almost half the risk of heart attacks than nondrinkers. This information is supported by the results of several other studies showing that the risk of cardiac arrest for moderate drinkers is 30 to 70 percent lower than the risk of heart attacks for abstainers.[9]

The relationship between light drinking and decreased heart disease holds true even after considering the potential benefits of youth and abstinence from cigarette smoking. It may also be possible that light drinkers have a decreased risk for strokes that are not related to bleeding in the brain (ischemic strokes).

The mechanisms through which low doses of alcohol produce "protective" effects against cardiac disease are still unknown.

Despite these recent findings, it is important to remember that higher doses of alcoholic beverages (perhaps in excess of 2 drinks per day) have adverse effects on blood fats. Higher alcohol intake is likely to multiply blood fats, including triglycerides and low-density lipoproteins, that are known to increase the risk of heart disease.

It is also important to carefully define the meaning of light or moderate drinking. While some British studies have suggested that up to 4 drinks per day may be considered moderate (defining a drink as the amount of alcohol found in approximately 12 ounces of beer, 4 ounces of wine, or 1.5 ounces of an 80-proof "shot" such as whiskey), most studies would show that this level of consumption is far too high.[10] Anything above 2 drinks per day is likely to increase the risk of liver disease, including cirrhosis. Furthermore, some reports indicate that as few as 2 to 3 drinks per day may increase the risk for rectal and lung cancers, while 3 or more daily drinks contribute significantly to the risk of high blood pressure.[11] As mentioned above, this data must be adjusted for body size; therefore, it is possible that lower doses of alcohol may increase these health risks for men and women whose body weights are a great deal below the respective averages for the sexes.

A review of the literature on alcohol's beneficial effects indicates that alcoholic beverages are not necessarily harmful to all people under all circumstances. Studies have been relatively consistent in demonstrating a decreased risk for heart attacks in men and women consuming 1 to 2 drinks per day compared to total abstainers. Nevertheless, abstinence is still advisable for recovering alcoholics and substance abusers, pregnant women, those taking medications, and people with certain medical disorders such as heart disease. The evidence suggests that even 1 to 2 drinks per day may

---

[9] Stampfer, M., et al. "A prospective study of moderate alcohol consumption and the risk of coronary disease and stroke in women." *New England Journal of Medicine*. 319:267-273, 1988.

[10] Shaper, A.G., et al. "Alcohol and Mortality in British Men." *The Lancet*. II:1267-1273, 1988.

[11] MacMahon, S.W., et al. "Alcohol and hypertension." *Annals of Internal Medicine*. 105:124-126, 1986.

adversely affect heart functioning in people with pre-existing heart disease. Some relatively new information also indicates that low doses of alcohol may increase the risk of breast cancer for women.[12]

ALCOHOL USE AND THE CRIMINAL JUSTICE SYSTEM

In the United States, alcohol use has posed particular problems for local, state, and Federal criminal justice agencies. These agencies are primarily concerned with the following issues regarding alcohol consumption:

1. Regulation - Law
2. Law enforcement
3. Driving under the influence of alcohol.

REGULATION

As early as 1100 B.C. in China there were laws regulating the sale and consumption of alcoholic beverages. In Europe, attempts to limit alcohol use have spanned from the fourteenth to the early part of the twentieth century. For example, in the sixth, fourteenth, and nineteenth centuries, British religious edicts and civil laws were enacted in an effort to institute temperance. However, the laws resulting from these outcries of alcohol's evil influences were relatively mild. In 1839, for example, the primary legislation of the public drunkenness act merely initiated a policy of weekend closing times and established a legal drinking age—one had to be at least sixteen years of age to drink.

Once the British colonies gained their independence, they became free to enact new Federal and state laws to regulate alcoholic beverages on their own. Thus, in 1791, a Federal excise tax was placed on whiskey; in 1834, a Congressional law was passed prohibiting the sale of alcoholic beverages to Indians; and in 1851, Maine enacted the first prohibition law.

Since the enactment of Maine's law, prohibition on local, state, and Federal levels became an American tradition. Following that first prohibition law, a series of regulations were passed and repealed until December 5, 1933, when the Twenty-first Amendment was ratified by thirty-six states, thus ending the "Great Prohibition."

Due to these frequent changes in the law, there was never any firm legislative stand taken against the use of alcohol. The lack of long-standing legislation possibly stems from the fact that alcoholic beverages had widely accepted uses in religious ceremonies and unwritten medical prescriptions; alcohol was also integrated into the fabric of American culture through its social use in the saloons and clubs that grew up around its consumption.

Today, the enforcement of regulations by criminal justice agencies involves violations arising from the sale of alcoholic beverages to minors, diluting alcohol by bars and restaurants, alcoholic beverage smuggling, tax

---

[12] Willet, W.C., et al. "Moderate alcohol consumption and the risk of breast cancer." *New England Journal of Medicine*. 316:1174-1180, 1987.

evasion activities, and enforcement of "blue laws" and closing times of alcoholic beverage outlets (stores, bars, and so forth).

However, enforcement agencies are primarily concerned with the problem of handling intoxicated persons, particularly those cited for driving under the influence of alcohol. Intoxication by alcohol accounts for a staggering number of the annual arrests in the U.S.: American police agencies make approximately two million arrests for the offense of public drunkenness each year. Nearly one-half of all fatal accidents involves alcohol; over 90 percent of short-term prisoners are confined because of their contact with alcohol; and the suicide rate for alcoholics compared to nonalcoholics is 58 to 1. Moreover, the Federal Bureau of Investigation reports that one out of every three arrests involves alcohol abuse.

HANDLING THE INTOXICATED PERSON OR THE ALCOHOLIC

Even in those few areas of the country where there are no specific laws against drunkenness, inebriates are often locked up under other charges such as vagrancy, loitering, or disorderly conduct. Maximum penalties for drunkenness range from five days to six months; for habitual drunkenness, some states even have statutes under which a person can be imprisoned for up to two years.

Until the laws are changed the peace officer will continue to be responsible for handling inebriates. To better enable police, sheriffs, and correction officers to deal with drunken individuals, information must be made available to help them undertake this task. In response to this need, the Christopher D. Smithers Foundation, Inc. has published a handbook on the subject, *Alcohol and Alcoholism: A Police Handbook.*[13] The following is an excerpt from the section titled "Handling the Intoxicated Person or Alcoholic":

> In handling the "drunk" or alcoholic in your course of duty as a police officer, you will encounter many different problems. Knowing how to handle these could, in some cases, mean the difference between life and death. Your very first problem will be to determine the extent of drunkenness. You must decide whether the person is in such a state as to be capable of hurting himself or others. If he does seem potentially dangerous, then he must be taken into custody, or at least protected.
>
> With the sleepy, depressed type, you must be especially careful. He may appear quite capable of sleeping off his current state of intoxication. But he may have downed a pint or more of whiskey, or some such drink, just before you arrested him—in which case, he will get more and more intoxicated in the following hour or two. If left alone in a cell and not watched, he could die from absorption of extra alcohol during that time. So your second problem involves your ability to recognize some of the common danger signs and complications of severe intoxication.

POSSIBLE COMPLICATIONS OF INTOXICATION:

Coma: Initially the victim is drowsy, very sad, and sick. He or she may become aggressive if disturbed. Later, the drinker may develop some definite physical symptoms, such as a change in skin pallor. He or she may complain

---

[13] Prepared by The Correctional Association of New York and the International Association of Chiefs of Police. Eleventh printing, March 1978.

of ringing in the ears, numbness "all over," and double or blurred vision. Later, the drinker will go into an increasing stupor, from which it is difficult to awaken, and he or she may die of two things:

Shock: Signs of shock are paleness, sweating, clammy skin, fainting, and weak pulse. Total anesthesia of the brain could also occur within two or three hours of first seeing the victim.

Convulsions: These are a potentially frightening and dangerous development of the hangover stage. The immediate dangers of convulsions are that the victim may fall and injure him or herself; the victim's airway may also become blocked, what is often called "swallowing the tongue." The greatest danger is that convulsions may indicate a very serious medical condition. After administering first aid, a physician should be called; the person should then be watched until medical advice is obtained.

Alcoholic Hallucinations: Delusions may last from minutes to days. The victim sees and hear things that are not really there. He or she is convinced that they are there, and those hallucinations may be vivid, frightening, and terrifying. Sometimes the drinker may become paranoid (feeling that someone is out to get him or her). Apart from these abnormalities, however, the drinker is generally rational, has the ability to talk, and knows who you are and what time of day it is. The drinker doesn't usually have a fast pulse, fever, or tremor, and is not sweating, pale, or flushed. In fact, he or she looks all right, but "sees things."

Delirium Tremens: The DTs are a serious complication of the hangover stage. The person suffering from delirium tremens is out of contact with his or her surroundings and does not know what is going on, though there may be moments of clear thinking. For instance, you may wear a uniform, but the person will not necessarily recognize this fact or realize what it means. The person may not know where he or she is, what time of day or what month it is, or even what nationality he or she is. The drinker generally doesn't "know" anything. He or she often has some fever, is flushed, has a rapid pulse and intense tremors. In addition, the drinker has the typical disturbing hallucinations and suffers from insomnia and great exhaustion. Usually the condition lasts from two to seven days. Fortunately, it is rare, but it is very serious and requires urgent medical attention.

In any of the above circumstances, after first aid is administered, the person should be taken to the nearest medical facility.

Another possible complication resulting from alcohol abuse is that inebriated persons are inclined to injure themselves. As mentioned above, the suicide rate among alcoholics is extremely high. Thus, an officer should be aware of how to deal with a person who is threatening suicide. The following suggestions may be useful when coming into contact with such a person:

1. Take all threats to commit suicide seriously.
2. Do not threaten someone who is threatening suicide.
3. Try to stimulate the "will to live" in the individual.

4. Do not make any sudden moves toward the person until you are close enough to grab a secure hold of him or her.

5. Send someone to get professional assistance (clergyman, doctor) while you are speaking to the suicidal person.

DRIVING UNDER THE INFLUENCE

Drunk driving is one of the most serious public health and safety problems facing the American people and their policy makers. In any given 2-year period, 50,000 Americans die as a result of drunk driving—almost as many American lives as were lost in the entire 10 years of the Vietnam War. Conservative estimates place the annual economic loss from drunk driving accidents at $21 billion to $24 billion for property damage alone.

The first identification of alcohol as a highway safety problem came through anecdotal evidence of alcohol involvement in automobile accidents. This evidence combined with the general societal knowledge of the effects of alcohol on human behavior led many to suspect an alcohol-automobile accident problem.

The suspicion of widespread alcohol-related accidents led to experimental studies of the effects of alcohol on driving skills. These experimental studies confirmed that alcohol, as it is commonly used, could impair driving performance. Chemical tests were then developed to measure the amount of alcohol in the body. These tests allowed researchers to determine the correlation of specific amounts of alcohol in the body to their direct effects on driving behavior.

The experimental studies were complemented by epidemiological studies which determined the incidence of alcohol in accident-involved drivers and in the general driving population. These studies revealed that alcohol was more frequently used by drivers involved in accidents and was used in greater amounts than by drivers who were not involved in accidents. The data obtained in the epidemiologic studies allowed researchers to make a much more precise statement about the relative risk of alcohol as a highway safety problem (i.e., the difference between the probability of being involved in an accident when not drinking and the probability of being involved after having had a certain amount to drink).

As evidence emerged that alcohol was a highway safety problem, countermeasures were developed and implemented. Laws were passed prohibiting alcohol-impaired driving. Soon chemical tests to measure blood-alcohol levels became more widely available and, as information correlating blood-alcohol levels with impairment of driving skills was scientifically proven, test results were gradually accepted in criminal trials as evidence of impairment.

At first, blood-alcohol measurements were used to establish the presumption of impairment. More recently, some State statutes have made it illegal to operate a motor vehicle with a level of alcohol in the body above a certain amount. Education and information efforts were undertaken to inform the public about alcohol and highway safety. These measures were taken to deter people from driving unsafely and to create public support for actions against those who drove while impaired. Sanctions against those convicted of alcohol-impaired driving included the traditional sanctions of fine and imprisonment, driver license suspension and revocation, and referral to health and education programs (sometimes called the health/legal approach).

The National Highway Traffic Safety Administration estimates that approximately half of all fatal traffic accidents involve the use of alcohol and/or drugs; 50 percent of drivers killed have a blood-alcohol level of .10 percent or above; and 60 to 75 percent of drivers in single vehicle collisions have a blood-alcohol level of .10 percent or above. The California Supreme Court has also recognized the gravity of this problem. While California has only 10 percent of the nation's licensed drivers on its roads, California drivers account for 30 percent of the nation's total arrests for driving under the influence.

DRUGS AND DRIVING

Alcohol is a drug, but a unique one. Alcohol is a single substance with a simple chemical structure, while the chemical makeup of most other drugs is fairly complex. Its absorption, distribution and elimination in the body are comparatively simple and well understood. Alcohol's use is almost entirely nonmedical. Although a drug of abuse, it is a legal drug whose social use is generally approved by society.

In contrast, other drugs may include many substances. Most are very complicated products of modern chemistry. In general, their absorption, distribution, and elimination within the human body are much more complex than that of alcohol. Some drugs are transformed by the body into new substances which themselves have effects on behavior.

Some drugs remain in the body for long periods of time; in some cases the drug's effects may continue even after the drug can no longer be detected in the blood. In other cases, presence of the drug itself may be detected long after the drug's action has ceased.

From the perspective of a highway patrol officer, there are several important differences between drugs and alcohol. First, even legitimate drug use can create a highway safety problem: drugs taken as directed can still impair driving ability. Second, the complex nature of many drugs may not allow the development and implementation of drug measurement techniques similar to those used for alcohol (i.e., breath analysis). Furthermore, even when drugs are detected, the consequences of that discovery may be unclear due to a lack of knowledge of the drugs' effect on driving behavior, and the lack of epidemiological research relating the use of particular drugs to impaired driving skills.

The nationwide experience of alcohol-related accidents has at least served as a starting point for examination of the drug and driving problem. However, the differences between alcohol and other drugs should not be forgotten.

Secobarbital (Seconal)

Secobarbital is a widely prescribed "short-acting" barbiturate typically used as a sleeping pill at 100 mg. or pre-operatively at 200 or 300 mg. Laboratory studies of skills associated with driving or flying have reported evidence of impairment after barbiturate use. The degree of behavioral impairment was found to be roughly proportional to the treatment dose level. The data as a whole showed impairment for extended time periods, with obvious impairment up to 6 hours and intermittent impairment beyond that time.

Diazepam (Valium)

Diazepam is the most frequently prescribed psychotropic drug in the world. Epidemiological studies have found diazepam present in approximately 10 percent of samples taken from fatally injured drivers.

Laboratory studies of the effects of diazepam and of alcohol-diazepam combinations clearly demonstrate that diazepam impairs psychomotor skills and that alcohol compounds the impairment. Studies have also shown that diazepam decreases the velocity and accuracy of eye movements, increases simulator accidents, and impairs tracking in a divided-attention situation.

Marijuana

In several laboratory studies, it has been proven that marijuana impairs perceptual and motor functions essential to adequate driving skills.

Since marijuana is used extensively, both alone and in combination with alcohol, the effects of marijuana have been examined under both these conditions. Three epidemiological studies (484 fatally injured drivers in Toronto, Canada; 267 drivers responsible for fatal accidents in Boston; and 600 operators killed in single-vehicle accidents in North Carolina) suggest that marijuana-alcohol interactions are of greater importance for traffic safety than marijuana alone. In all three studies, 70 percent or more of the fatally injured drivers found with marijuana in their blood also had alcohol in their blood.[14]

According to another study published in the June 1981 issue of *Psychopharmacology,* the effects of one marijuana cigarette are powerful enough to impair driving ability for up to eight hours.[15] Research for the study was funded and contracted by the National Institute on Drug Abuse (NIDA). Gene Barnett, an NIDA program officer and co-author of the study, emphasized that this study was the first to establish a definitive link between THC levels in the blood and the impairment of driving skills. THC, the metabolite formed when marijuana is broken down by the body, is the chemical agent responsible for most of marijuana's psychoactive effects. According to Dr. Travis Thompson, a University of Minnesota professor of psychology, the results indicated a one-to-one correspondence between the level of tetrahydrocannabinol (THC) and the level of impairment. "What that boils down to forensically," said Thompson, "is that if you know somebody's level, then you know the amount of impairment." He added that marijuana continues to impair driving ability even after the feeling of being intoxicated

---

[14] Reported in National Institute on Drug Abuse's Drug Concentrations and Driving Impairment: Consensus Development Panel. *Journal of American Medical Association.* 254:2018-2021, 1985.

[15] Coccheto, D.M., S.M. Owens, M. Perez-Reyes, et al. "Relationship Between Plasma Delta-9-THC Concentration and Pharmacological Effects in Man." *Psychopharmacology.* 75:158-64, June 1981.

has worn off. Although people say they feel high up to two hours after smoking marijuana, Thompson revealed that even when marijuana smokers no longer feel under the influence of the drug, their driving ability may be impaired for up to eight hours after smoking.

CONCLUSIONS

In both the marijuana-alcohol and the diazepam-alcohol studies, the addition of alcohol greatly increased the level of impairment that was already present when the other drug was used alone. Secobarbital, diazepam, marijuana, and alcohol were all found to impair a person's performance of various driving tasks. Drug levels tested for secobarbital and diazepam were therapeutic doses; the marijuana doses were considered moderate to strong by the subject population used; the alcohol effects were reported for levels up to and slightly above the legal limit. Among the drugs tested, researchers found no definitive differences in the pattern of effects on driving ability. All of the drugs tested impaired perceptual-motor skills (e.g., tracking, speed, and headway control), response time, detection ability, and decision-making tasks.

DRINKING AND DRIVING

The National Safety Council has stated that, while alcoholics account for most alcohol-related deaths on the highway, many accidents are still caused by nonalcoholics who drive under the influence. Many drivers in this condition refuse to believe that as few as two drinks can cause impaired judgment, distorted vision, and slower reaction time. These drinkers somehow feel that they are immune to the effects of alcohol. However, when such drinkers are stopped by the police on the highway and asked to take the drunk-driving test, they may be subject to the same penalties given alcoholics who cause serious automobile accidents.

LEGAL DECISIONS ABOUT DRUNK DRIVERS

Under the current laws, determining whether a person is too inebriated to drive is based on a 1935 decision by the Arizona Supreme Court. This decision has been endorsed by the American Medical Association and the National Safety Council.

The expression "under the influence of intoxicating liquor" refers to any abnormal mental or physical condition which is the result of indulging to any degree in intoxicating liquors and which tends to deprive the individual of the clear judgment and motor coordination that he or she would otherwise possess. If the ability of an automobile driver has been lessened in the slightest degree by the use of intoxicating liquors, then the driver is deemed to be under the influence of intoxicating liquor. The mere fact that a driver has taken a drink does not place the driver under the ban of the statute unless such drink has some influence upon him or her, lessening in some degree the ability to handle an automobile.

For example, California has interpreted this decision in the following manner:[16]

The Presumptive Level of being under the influence of an alcoholic beverage under the California Vehicle Code is 0.08 (January 1, 1992).

Remember, this is a vehicle code standard, and is intended for vehicle code situations.

§23155 of the California Vehicle Code: Driving While Intoxicated (Presumption)

1. 0.00 to less than .05 = It is presumed that the motorist is NOT under the influence.

2. 0.05 to less than .08 = This level "shall not give rise to any presumption."

(a) The law doesn't say whether the suspect is under the influence or not.

(b) A person could be prosecuted for driving under the influence, and a number have been convicted.

(c) Prosecution would, really, depend on the lack of driving skill, poor performance during field sobriety tests (FSTs), and other signs of impairment for a District Attorney to decide.

3. 0.08 or more = "It shall be presumed that the person was under the influence of an alcoholic beverage. . ." It is a Legal Presumption.

Percent of weight of alcohol in the blood shall be based upon grams of alcohol per 100 milliliters of blood.

DETECTING THE DRUNK DRIVER

Detection of the driver who is possibly "driving under the influence" is usually initiated in one of four ways:

direct observation of the individual while driving;

a report from some other person of the individual's driving;

as a result of a call to the scene of an accident; or

as a result of stopping the individual for a traffic violation.

The police officer must mentally record, with accuracy, not only the normal actions which should be expected, but also the individual's abnormal or unusual actions.

While parked, officers can easily keep moving traffic under surveillance to spot hazardous or unusual operation of a vehicle. The signs the officers are looking for that would warrant stopping a motorist are fairly straightforward, for they are similar to the signs manifested by a driver under the influence of drugs, or by one who is an habitual reckless driver.

Once an officer has decided to stop a vehicle, he or she should signal the operator to pull over, and then watch for a number of possible reactions in addition to the normal one in which the driver pulls over correctly. These include failure to stop soon after being signaled; attempted escape; an abrupt

[16] Gould Publications. *Vehicle Code of California.* 1992.

stop in the middle of the road; and/or a swerving, dangerous stop. How the person reacts after being signaled to stop can provide the first clue that the person may be intoxicated. By the time the motorist has pulled off the road, the officer has already had time to gather information about the driver—based on the manner in which the driver was acting prior to being signaled to pull over and the way in which the driver responded once requested to stop.

The next set of clues can be observed just prior to the driver's exiting the vehicle. First, the driver may attempt to change seats with the person in the passenger seat. The driver may also try to quickly conceal alcoholic beverages in the glove compartment, under the seat, or by throwing them out of the window; sometimes the motorist exits from the car immediately in an attempt to prove that everything is under control, and occasionally the driver may attempt to escape.

Once the officer comes into contact with the motorist, there are a number of signs that he or she should look for—again, these are usually quite evident and fairly easy to detect.

Some of the common physical signs of intoxication are:

1. Flushed, pale, or bruised face
2. Bloodshot or crossed eyes
3. Alcohol on the breath
4. Belching, hiccuping, vomiting, or shallow and heavy breathing
5. Uncoordinated gait, stumbling, walking into objects
6. Profuse sweating
7. Unkempt appearance
8. Incontinence
9. Uncontrollable waving of the arms and hands

Some of the common psychological signs of intoxication are:

1. Inappropriate laughing, crying, or talking
2. Inappropriate hospitality or lightheartedness
3. Incoherent speech or mumbling
4. General disorientation; the suspect may not know the time of day or where he or she is
5. Inappropriate behavior in response to the officer's requests

DETECTING DRUNK DRIVERS AT NIGHT

To detect drunk drivers at night a study was conducted in which cues observed in 4,600 patrol stops were correlated with driver blood-alcohol concentration (BAC). The 20 cues below are the best ones for discriminating night-time drunk drivers from night-time sober drivers.[17] These cues account for more than 90 percent of all DUI detections. The cues are listed in descending order of probability that the person observed is driving while intoxicated. The number given after each cue is the probability that a driver exhibiting that cue has a BAC equal to or greater than .10 (the legal limit). For example, the number 65 corresponding to the first cue, turning with wide radius, means that chances are 65 out of 100 that the driver will have a BAC of .10.

		Probability %
1.	Turning with wide radius	65
2.	Straddling center of lane marker	65
3.	Appearing to be drunk	60
4.	Almost striking object or vehicle	60
5.	Weaving	60
6.	Driving on other than designated roadway	55
7.	Swerving	55
8.	Speed more than 10 mph below limit	50
9.	Stopping without cause in traffic lane	50
10.	Following too closely	50
11.	Drifting	50
12.	Tires on center or lane marker	45
13.	Braking erratically	45
14.	Driving into opposing or crossing traffic	45
15.	Signaling inconsistent with driving actions	40
16.	Slow response to traffic signals	40
17.	Stopping inappropriately (other than in lane)	35
18.	Turning abruptly or illegally	35
19.	Accelerating or decelerating rapidly	30
20.	Headlights off	30

If the physical signs of intoxication are present they will be observable when the motorist gets out of the vehicle and responds to a request to show a driver's license and registration. (Naturally, officers should visually survey the inside of the vehicle and its other occupants when approaching the vehicle and during the initial contact with the motorist.) If the driver does not appear to be intoxicated (but possibly just sleepy from travelling for a long time), and if motor vehicle documents are in order and the driver hasn't

---

[17] "Guide for Detecting Drunk Drivers at Night." U.S. Dept. of Transportation. National Highway Administration. DOT HS 805-711, 2nd ed., January 1982.

broken any traffic laws, the driver would naturally be permitted to proceed—with a warning if it is deemed necessary.

If, on the other hand, the driver appears to be intoxicated, then the officer should immediately advise the driver of legal rights and ask the driver to move to an area away from the vehicle and moving traffic so that dexterity and physical coordination tests can be administered immediately.

After these tests, if the officer feels he or she does not have sufficient evidence of intoxication, and if the driver appears sober enough to drive safely, but has broken a moving traffic law, a citation should be issued and the driver should be allowed to proceed. If there is sufficient evidence of intoxication, the driver should be appropriately placed under arrest, hand-cuffed, searched for alcohol, drugs, and weapons, placed in the patrol car, and advised of legal rights under the implied consent law. Following this procedure, any other occupants of the car should be interviewed, the suspect's car should be searched, and any evidence should be collected and receipted according to standard procedures.

Following the arrest, the violator's car should be secured until it can be moved to safety. Arrangements must also be made for transportation of the other occupants of the car. The suspect should then be taken either to a hospital—in the event that there is a severe alcohol-related problem requiring immediate medical attention, such as alcohol hallucinosis or convulsions—or to a detention facility for chemical tests, temporary incarceration, if necessary, and the booking procedure.

During an accident investigation, police officers must also suspect the possibility that one or more of the drivers involved might be under the influence of alcohol. In addition to the presence of open bottles in the vehicle, other signs which may indicate possible alcohol use on the part of a driver include failure to have lights on, reports by witnesses indicating that the driver was swerving or driving on the wrong side of the road, or an actual failure on the part of the motorist to comprehend how the accident occurred or that it even occurred at all (however, this sign may be a symptom of shock as well).

If officers are sensitive to the signs that a person is or has been drinking while driving, much can be done to prevent alcohol-related accidents. Of course, most states do have an efficient, well-organized training program for their officers in the area of detection, investigation, and arrest of intoxicated drivers. Although the procedure is complex, the work of removing the intoxicated driver from the road is vitally important to highway safety. Therefore, the methods and techniques presented in this chapter are at the very least meant to reinforce the importance of this police operation.

The other major decision affecting the detection of inebriation is the implied consent law. This law contains two important provisions:

1. Upon receiving a license to drive, the motorist agrees as well to submit to a chemical test, if so requested by an officer.
2. If the driver refuses to be tested for being under the influence of alcohol, his or her license may be revoked.

EXAMPLES OF DEXTERITY/PHYSICAL COORDINATION TESTS ADMINISTERED TO SUSPECTED INTOXICATED DRIVERS

Romberg Test:	The suspect is asked to stand with feet together, arms at the side, and eyes closed. He or she is then asked to tilt the head to one side for ten seconds.
Finger-to-Nose Test:	Standing, feet together, eyes closed, and arms outstretched at a right angle to the body, the suspect is asked to extend the index finger, making a fist with the rest of the fingers, and then to attempt to touch the tip of the nose with the finger by bending the arm at the elbow; this process is then repeated with the other arm.
Balancing on One Leg:	Standing, feet together, arms at the side, looking straight ahead, the suspect is asked to extend the left leg forward without bending it and to hold it approximately one foot off the ground for ten seconds; this process is then repeated with the other foot.
Walking a Straight Line:	The suspect is asked to walk heel to toe in a straight line for several steps, then to turn on command and walk heel to toe back to the original position.

DO TOUGH DRUNK-DRIVER LAWS WORK?

In the last few years, many states have reformed both their laws and their law enforcement as a result of the growing awareness that drunk driving is a serious nationwide problem. Several citizen action groups have contributed to these changes in drunk-driver law enforcement. Since 1981, more than 30 states have enacted legislation directed at drunk driving control, most often by prescribing more severe sanctions such as mandatory confinement.

To gauge the impact of tougher sanctions on the criminal justice system, National Institute of Justice researchers examined the effects of mandatory confinement for drunk driving in certain jurisdictions of Washington, Tennessee, Ohio, and Minnesota. The findings revealed the following:

> Drunk driver arrests increase, especially when drunk driving and the new sanctions are well-publicized through various media outlets.
>
> Court workloads increase, due to mandatory confinement for drunk drivers.
>
> More defendants contest. With the introduction of mandatory confinement for drunk driving, more defendants are likely to challenge, postpone, or avoid compliance with court procedures and decisions. Several of the study jurisdictions experienced increases in "not guilty" pleas and requests for jury trials.
>
> Conviction rates vary. The effects of mandatory confinement sanctions on conviction rates for arrested drunk drivers varied in the different study sites.
>
> Rates remained stable in Memphis. In Seattle, they declined, due to the greater use of deferred prosecutions and to the fact that more defendants failed to appear for trial.

Incarceration rates increase. In each of the four jurisdictions, the study found a dramatic increase in incarceration rates for convicted drunk drivers. This clear and consistent finding includes drunk drivers convicted of their first offense.

Strains on corrections facilities increase. The National Institute findings clearly show that mandatory confinement has its greatest criminal justice impact upon incarceration facilities.

Strains on probation services increase. Since Tennessee law stipulates that all convicted drunk drivers must be placed on probation, Memphis probation officers have experienced a dramatic increase in their caseload. The same is true in Seattle, where drunk drivers now represent about 70 percent of the probation department caseload.

Special programs and facilities are required. Due to their previous "noncriminal" history, drunk drivers are frequently confined in a building located away from buildings housing other offenders. Drunk drivers are often also placed in special "confinement" programs for alcohol treatment, traffic safety education, or community service.

Fatalities may decline. Generally, the jurisdictions in the study experienced a decrease in overall traffic fatalities following the adoption of mandatory confinement sanctions. However, a direct cause-and-effect relationship cannot be assumed.

Publicity of driving safety increased. In most jurisdictions, enactment of new sanctions was accompanied by publicity focusing on drunk driving safety. It is difficult to determine the extent to which the decline in traffic fatalities resulted either from improved driving practices arising from heightened public awareness or from the imposition of mandatory confinement sanctions and enforcement.

It should be noted that traffic fatalities began a general decline in 1981, both nationally and in the case-study jurisdictions, although the decline in fatalities was considerably sharper in the study sites than in the nation as a whole.

SOCIAL DRINKERS AND ALCOHOLICS

The transition from abstainer to alcoholic is extremely unusual. It is much more common for someone with a steady, moderate drinking pattern to shift the pattern to one of problem drinking or alcoholism.

Many students of the alcohol phenomenon separate alcoholism from problem drinking. *Alcoholism* is generally considered to be a physical addiction to alcohol: the build-up of tolerance over time and an alcohol withdrawal syndrome varying from shakiness to DTs upon the sudden reduction or discontinuance of alcohol consumption. A strong desire to continue to drink heavily is an associated effect of alcoholism. *Problem drinking,* on the other hand, consists of difficulties in living directly related to overdrinking. Marital, job, social, or health problems are some of the areas affected. Addiction may or may no co-exist. In this discussion, alcoholism refers to both problem drinking and alcohol addiction.

It is highly unlikely that an alcoholic person will make a deliberate decision to become an alcoholic. Rather, he or she slips imperceptibly, without conscious intent, into excessive drinking styles that culminate in alcoholism. This transformation period is important to identify by the individual and by the clinician.

Drinkers in a pre-alcoholic phase may be able to correct their drinking behavior more readily if they become aware of their progression toward a destructive mode of use. But exactly how can an early warning system be developed to alert the drinker of his or her approach to hazardous levels of consumption?

The transition to problem drinking is not a simple one; it consists of more than a quantitative change in consumption patterns. Some people can become impaired by consuming daily amounts of alcohol that would produce no impairments in others. Also, it is possible that a fatty liver or alcoholic hepatitis may develop in a person whose patterns of consumption are consistent with other relatively healthy drinkers. Many occupational and social groups consume alcohol rather heavily and consistently. Some of their members will get into difficulties early. Others may go indefinitely without encountering alcohol-related adverse effects.

Usually, an escalation of drinking practices occurs during a period of increased stress. A few extra drinks are taken to unwind, to forget, or to sleep. When the stressful period is past, the newly established drinking routine continues. Under conditions of further stress, alcohol consumption then increases again. Eventually, the drinker reaches a point at which attempts to cut down or stop fail because of early withdrawal symptoms like the shakes or insomnia; these symptoms require alcohol for relief.

Another factor contributing to the development of problem drinking patterns is the entrapping quality of casual drinking. The mild euphoria and social relaxation provided by a few drinks produce feelings of amiable fellowship and good cheer. This state of mind is very attractive; it causes some people to make the error of assuming that the additional ingestion of alcoholic beverages will increase the fun. The guarantee of immediate pleasure is apparently of greater importance than the knowledge of adverse effects.

With additional amounts, the mild and pleasant stimulation changes to an increasing depression and then to substantial loss of control over behavior. This up-and-down effect of ethanol on the central nervous system mirrors the effect of alcohol used as an antianxiety agent. Initially, alcohol reduces tension and anxiety. As heavy drinking becomes chronic, anxiety levels are elevated. It may be that this increase in anxiety perpetuates drinking in a vain search for relief. Using alcohol to evade an unpleasant reality, to forget one's worries, or to achieve mastery over life's stresses usually turns out to be a poor effort at self-treatment. This effort is compounded not only by the period of intoxication, but also by post-intoxication ineffectiveness or debilitation and the pre-intoxicated drive to escape from unpleasant circumstances.

Unfortunately, the socially drinking individual has few guidelines to indicate that he or she may be at risk when the drinking patterns gradually change. If the individual drinks less than two drinks a day and does not save up the drinks to go on a binge, impairment over the years is not likely to occur. However, many people in this culture drink more than two drinks a day and appear to manage without adverse consequences. Where is one's personal danger zone? The answer lies not only in the amount of ethanol ingested over time, but also in how and why one drinks and what effects are experienced by the drinker.

Even two drinks a day are too much for some people. Some are hypersensitive to very small amounts of ethanol, reacting with a flush, hypotension, tachycardia, and chest constriction. Others are pathologic drinkers who become violent under the influence of one or two glasses. In addition, a long list of drugs interact adversely when combined with alcohol. These range from antibiotics, antihypertensives, and anticonvulsant to anticoagulants, diuretics, and sleeping pills. Of course, people with peptic ulcer, pancreatitis, and liver ailments may increase the severity of their usual disorder by exposing themselves to alcohol. Diabetics and epileptics would be unwise to use alcohol, if only because of the risk of smelling like a drunk during a period of unconsciousness, let alone the deleterious effects of alcohol in such conditions.

As a rule, the shift to dysfunctional drinking is a gradual one. In large doses, alcohol is a protoplasmic poison, but the dangerous level varies for each individual. To tell a person who has been drinking four drinks a day, and who has crept up to eight a day, that he or she is at risk will accomplish little. In fact, the usual responses to this approach are anger at being unjustly accused or a complete denial that a problem exists. The advice is interpreted as nagging and may in itself lead to additional drinking. It is far more desirable for each person who drinks to regularly examine his or her own drinking practices and to be willing to change those practices if there is any suspicion of overdrinking.

Self-examination should be a part of the drinking person's routine and every effort should be made to be as candid with oneself as possible. Examples of questions that may indicate a pre-alcoholic or an early alcoholic situation include:

1. Do I get drunk when I intend to stay sober?

   This question speaks to early loss of control over one's drinking. The inability to stop once drinking has commenced is an ominous sign. Even an occasional loss of control may be a warning signal. Some confirmed alcoholics are unable to stop drinking after a single drink has been consumed.

2. When things get rough do I need a drink or two to quiet my nerves?

   Using alcohol as a tranquilizer can be precarious, because the dose is difficult to adjust and no other person is supervising the medication.

3. Do other people say I am drinking too much?

   If the negative effects of drinking are evident to more than one person or to a single person on a number of occasions, this means that one's behavior is exceeding the social limits. It is advisable to listen to such comments, remembering that most people are reluctant to talk about the drinking troubles of their friends and relatives.

4. Have I gotten into trouble with the law, my family, or my business associates as a result of drinking?

   Being arrested for drunk driving or drunk and disorderly conduct are not reliable early signs of excessive drinking. Only a minority of these acts are apprehended, so it is unlikely that this was the first such offense. Being confronted with difficulties at home or at work also tend to be the cumulative effect of a long series of objectionable behaviors.

5. Is it impossible for me to stop drinking for a week or more?

   Resolving to stop and not being able to carry it off would indicate a definite psychological or physical dependence and points to potential problems in the future. Being able to stop is encouraging, but does not eliminate the possibility of a binge or other types of destructive drinking. Many alcoholics remain dry for long intervals. Therefore, being able to stop is not indicative of a dangerous situation.

6. Do I sometimes not remember what happened during a drinking episode?

   Blackouts due to alcohol consist of variable periods of amnesia. They are to be differentiated from passing out into unconsciousness, which is the end state of intoxication. Blackouts, which are complete and cover periods of hours or more, are definite evidence of alcoholism. Passing out is moreso an unfavorable sign of excessive drinking.

7. Has a doctor ever said that my drinking was impairing my health?

   Although it is now possible to pick up early signs of harmful drinking, by the time a medical examination reveals abnormalities attributable to alcohol, it is clear that continuing current drinking patterns will further damage one's health. Abnormalities of amino acid ratios, plasma lipoproteins, or hepatitic enzymes are signs that the liver cannot adequately metabolize the amount of ethanol being ingested.

8. Do I take a few drinks before going to a social gathering just in case there won't be much to drink?

   Assuring oneself of a sufficient supply of alcohol, "just in case," is evidence of an unhealthy preoccupation with such beverages and speaks for a need to feel "loaded" on social occasions.

9. Am I impatient while waiting for my drink to be served?

   The urgency to obtain a drink reflects a craving. Gulping drinks is another sign of overinvolvement with alcohol.

10. Have I tried to cut down but failed?

    As with the inability to stop drinking for periods of time, the inability to cut down is a warning that dependence is present or impending. Cutting down successfully but eventually slipping back up is another sign of possible future trouble.

11. Do I have to have a drink in the morning because I feel queasy or have the shakes?

The relief obtained from a drink after arising is often a relief of early, mild withdrawal symptoms. Therefore, drinking when one wakes up is a clear sign of increasing physical dependence.

12. Can I hold my liquor better than other people?

    Being able to hold one's liquor is not necessarily evidence of freedom from the complications of drinking. Holding one's liquor may indicate the development of tolerance due to the persistent consumption of large quantities. Although social disabilities may be avoided by holding one's liquor, physical impairment due to the amount consumed is inevitable.

13. Have many members of my family been alcoholics?

    There is some medical evidence of a genetic component to some instances of alcoholism. People whose parents or siblings had serious problems with alcohol have reason to be extra careful of their drinking habits. Not only may there be an inherited vulnerability, but the early life experience of an alcoholic parent may predispose the child to seek out consciousness-changing drugs or alcohol in later life.

The 13 indicators mentioned above range from early to advanced signs of alcoholism. They should be assessed seriously by the individual concerned or by the health professional who is evaluating the individual. The first step is recognizing that a threat to one's future does exists. The second step is taking realistic action on the basis of that threat. The third step is sustaining the new behavior. The following reactions to those three steps are critical blocks to altering the course of destructive drinking: refusal to accept the information, refusal to do anything about it, and refusal to maintain a corrective course of action once it is initiated.

SHOULD ALCOHOL BE PROHIBITED?

Alcohol addiction is second only to nicotine addiction in incidence and prevalence in the United States today. A conservative estimate is that ten million Americans are alcoholics, but figures of as high as fifteen million alcoholics and "problem drinkers" are also cited. Alcoholics are unable to refrain from their drug even though they decide to, want to, and try to quit drinking alcohol; those who succeed for a time remain in imminent danger of relapse. To the millions of alcoholics must be added millions of "spree drinkers" who are not addicted but who get roaring drunk from time to time.

Alcohol addiction is destructive to the capabilities of the human mind. In many states, alcoholic disorders lead to other diseases requiring mental hospital admission.

Alcohol abuse is also destructive to the human body. High concentrations of alcohol are directly irritating to the mucosal lining of the stomach, causing acute and chronic gastritis. Acute and chronic liver disease is common in people who have been drinking large amounts of alcohol for a long time. There is also a progressive disturbance in neurological functioning which results from an episode of acute alcohol intoxication. Furthermore, withdrawal from alcohol may set off a variety of nervous system disturbances, including delirium and convulsions.

Alcohol

In some of these disorders, the bodily damage is mainly due to malnutrition rather than to the direct effects of alcohol for a long time. Such nutritional disorders include Wernicke's encephalopathy, Korsakoff's psychosis, and alcoholic polyneuropathy.

Wernicke's disease. This disease is characterized by the sudden onset of three clinical symptoms: muscle paralysis, ataxia, and mental confusion.

Korsakoff's Psychosis. Some patients continue to show mental symptoms even after they have recovered from the acute phase. These alcoholics are suffering from a peculiar kind of intellectual impairment called Koraskoff's psychosis. This impairment is characterized by a disturbance in memory, especially the memory of recent events, as well as an inability to learn new material.

Alcoholic Polyneuropathy. Many patients show signs of damage to the motor and sensory fibers of peripheral nerves. Most complain of muscle weakness of the legs and arms or numbness and tingling of the skin. A few suffer from burning pain in the feet or hands, or deep aching of the legs.

One issue of debate is whether alcohol is solely responsible for this damage to mind and body, or whether defective nutrition also plays a role. Alcohol does contain calories; indeed, a heavy drinker may consume half or more of his or her caloric needs in the form of alcohol. Consequently, the drinker will drastically reduce his or her consumption of proteins, vitamins, and other essential nutrients. The two effects march hand in hand; irreversible brain and liver damage, for example, is less severe in the alcoholic who maintains adequate nutrition—but it can occur all the same. Making alcohol unavailable would thus contribute enormously to physical as well as mental health.

By a wide margin, alcohol is the biggest law enforcement problem in the United States today. Forty percent of all arrests are for being drunk in public or for drunk driving. Many homicides are alcohol-related. Alcohol is also a significant factor in child abuse. Likewise, the relationship between alcohol and suicide is very close.

One of the most powerful and rarely advanced arguments in favor of alcohol prohibition is that it is useless to prohibit other drugs so long as alcohol remains freely available.

This discussion hardly exhausts the arguments for alcohol prohibition, but it is perhaps sufficient to demonstrate the logic of such a proposal. From the humanitarian as well as the societal points of view, for the benefit of drinkers, potential drinkers, teetotalers, ex-heroin addicts and users of other drugs, and especially for the benefit of young people, alcohol should be prohibited—except for one consideration.

In contrast to the many logical arguments in favor of alcohol prohibition, the one decisive argument *against* such a measure is purely pragmatic: prohibition doesn't work. It should work, but it doesn't.

The evidence for the argument against prohibition was accumulated during the thirteen-year period 1920-1933. Before 1920, the arguments in favor of prohibition were overwhelming. The Eighteenth (Prohibition) Amendment passed both houses of Congress by the required two-thirds majority in December 1917, and was ratified by the required three-fourths of the forty-eight state legislatures a bare thirteen months later. After experiencing alcohol prohibition for thirteen years, however, the nation rebelled. The twenty-first (Prohibition Repeal) Amendment passed both houses of Congress by the required two-thirds majority in February 1933—and this time it took less than ten months to secure ratification by three-fourths of the forty-eight state legislatures.

Alcohol prohibition *was* repealed because people decided that alcohol was a harmless drug. On the contrary, the United States learned during Prohibition, even more than in prior decades, the true horrors of the drug. In fact, the repeal was brought about by the slowly dawning awareness that alcohol prohibition wasn't working.

Despite the law, alcohol remained available during Prohibition. People still got drunk, still became alcoholics, still suffered delirium tremens. Drunken drivers remained a frequent menace on the highways. Drunks continued to commit suicide, to kill others, and to be killed by others. They continued to beat their own children, sometimes fatally. The courts, jails, hospitals, and mental hospitals were still filled with drunks. In some respects and some parts of the country, perhaps, the situation was a little better during Prohibition—but in other respects it was unquestionably worse.

Instead of consuming alcoholic beverages manufactured under the safeguards of state and Federal standards, for example, people now drank "rotgut," some of it adulterated, some of it contaminated. The use of methyl alcohol, a poison, because ethyl alcohol was unavailable or too costly, led sometimes to blindness and death; "ginger jake," an adulterant found in bootleg beverages produced paralysis and death. The disreputable saloon was replaced by the even less savory speakeasy. There was also a shift from relatively mild light wines and beers to hard liquors—less bulky and therefore less hazardous to manufacture, transport, and sell on the black market. Young people—especially respectable young women, who rarely got drunk in public before 1920—now staggered out of speakeasies and reeled down the streets. While there were legal closing hours for saloons, the speakeasies stayed open night and day. Organized crime syndicates took control of alcohol distribution, establishing power bases that (it is alleged) still survive. Furthermore, a drug little used in the United States prior to Prohibition, marijuana, was first popularized during this period; ether was also imbibed. The use of other drugs increased as well; coffee consumption, for example, soared from 9 pounds per capita in 1919 to 12.9 pounds in 1920. The list is long and could be be lengthened—but we need not belabor the obvious.

During the early years of alcohol Prohibition, it was argued that better law enforcement would overcome resistance to the law. Therefore, enforcement budgets were increased, more Prohibition agents were hired, arrests were facilitated by giving agents more power, and penalties were escalated. However, Prohibition still didn't work.

Thus, the United States learned its lesson. More remarkably, years after repeal, the mere memory of Prohibition is still so repellent that no proposal to revive it would be taken seriously.

Alcohol

The Twenty-first (Repeal) Amendment left power in the states to retain statewide alcohol prohibition; it also made it a Federal offense to ship alcoholic beverages into a dry state. State after state repealed its statewide alcohol prohibition laws; in 1966, Mississippi's was the last to go.

In summary, it might be argued that far more could be gained by making alcohol unavailable than by making any other drug unavailable. Blocking access to alcohol would not only decrease the many problems growing out of alcohol abuse, it would also assist in reducing the initiation into and abuse of other drugs. Yet the United States, after a thirteen-year trial period, resolutely turned its face against alcohol prohibition. Society recognized that prohibition does not in fact prohibit; unfortunately, it brings additional adverse effects in its wake.

DRUNK DRIVING LAWS

INTRODUCTION

The National Highway Traffic Administration estimates that approximately half of all fatal traffic accidents involve the use of alcohol and/or drugs; 50 percent of all drivers killed have a blood-alcohol level of .10 percent or above; and 60 to 75 percent of drivers in single-vehicle collisions have a blood-alcohol level of .10 percent or above.

The California Supreme Court has responded to the gravity of this problem by (1) upholding the blood-alcohol level provision of Vehicle Code section 23152 (*Burg,* 35 *Cal.*3d 257 (1983)), and (2) by approving the use of "sobriety checkpoints" if certain safeguards are followed (*Ingersoll,* 43 *Cal.*3d 1321 (1987)). Checkpoints have also been upheld by the United States Supreme Court (*Sitz,* 110 *S.Ct.* 2481 (1990)).

Detection

Detection of the driver who is possibly "driving under the influence" is usually initiated in one of four ways:

— direct observation of the individual while driving;

— a report from some other person of the individual's driving;

— as a result of a call to the scene of an accident; or

— as a result of stopping the individual for a traffic violation.

When observing a person suspected of drunk driving, you must mentally record, with accuracy, not only the person's normal actions, but also the individual's abnormal or unusual actions.

Apprehension

Immediately stop any driver who is operating a vehicle in any manner which raises a doubt as to the driver's sobriety. Noticing this or any other abnormal condition, question the driver and ascertain the cause of his or her erratic driving.

Once you have detained the driver, your "reasonable suspicion" may develop into probable cause to arrest as a result of questioning, closer observation of the suspect, and administration of filed sobriety tests and/or the lateral gaze nystagmus test.

Note: When you testify in court, be aware of *Loomis*, 156 *Cal.App*.3d Supp. 1 (1984). It held that even an experienced officer may not use the nystagmus test as the basis for estimating a *specific* alcohol content or range, like ".17 or .18." However, the nystagmus test remains a perfectly valid tool, just like the roadside tests, in forming your *general* opinion that the driver is under the influence.

OFFENSES INVOLVING ALCOHOL AND DRUGS

The United States Supreme Court has upheld the practice of videotaping (with audio) the routine booking of DUI suspects. The tape, reflecting the suspect's slurred speech, attempts to perform non-verbal sobriety tests, and any remarks he or she may blurt out, is not considered "testimonial" and therefore may be admitted into evidence, even though no *Miranda* warning has been given. However, any incriminating *verbal* responses which you have solicited (such as asking him "the date of his sixth birthday," or asking him to count, or to recite the alphabet) will not be admissible, due to the right against self-incrimination, unless *Miranda* warnings have first been given (*Muniz,* 110 *S.Ct.* 2638 (1990)).

The primary elements of the misdemeanor labeled "Driving Under the Influence" are as follows (Calif. Veh. Code, §23152):[18]

(a) It is unlawful for any person who is under the influence of an alcoholic beverage or any drug, or under the combined influence of an alcoholic beverage and any drug, to drive a vehicle.

(b) It is unlawful for any person who has a 0.08 percent or more, by weight, of alcohol in his or her blood to drive a vehicle.

Note: The constitutionality of this subdivision was upheld by the California Supreme Court in *Burg,* 35 Cal.3d 257 (1983).

(c) It is unlawful for any person who is addicted to the use of any drug to drive a vehicle, except for a person who is participating in an approved methadone maintenance treatment program.

DRIVING UNDER THE INFLUENCE DEFINED

Within the meaning of the Vehicle Code, for a person to be "under the influence" the liquor or combination of liquor and drugs must have so far affected that person's nervous system, brain, or muscles as to impair the person's ability to operate a vehicle in a manner like that of an ordinarily prudent and cautious person in full possession of his or her faculties using reasonable care under similar conditions. It is not necessary to prove any specific degree of intoxication. A person is impaired to an "appreciable degree" if intoxication causes him or her to operate a vehicle in a manner different from that in which it would be operated by an ordinarily cautious and prudent person. "Under the influence" does not require being affected to the extent commonly associated with terms like "intoxicated" or "drunk".

---

[18] Gould Publications. *Vehicle Code of California*. 1992.

Alcohol

A person's driving ability may be impaired even though others who see the driver may not readily know that he or she is intoxicated.

OFFENSES IN AN OFFICER'S PRESENCE

Ordinarily in California, to justify a misdemeanor arrest without a warrant, an officer must have reasonable cause to believe a driving under the influence offense has occurred in his presence. (Penal Code, §836.) Since all of section 23152 offenses are misdemeanors, these driving under the influence offenses must be committed in the presence of the arresting officer.

CIRCUMSTANTIAL EVIDENCE OF A DRIVER'S IDENTITY

Remember, however, that only the identity of the driver is established by circumstantial evidence. The actual act of driving itself must occur in the officer's presence, unless the situation comes under any of the exceptions discussed below. Normally, this will mean that the officer must actually see the car move—although, in theory, "driving" can be determined through some other senses.

IMPLIED CONSENT LAW

Purpose

The best scientific evidence of intoxication is a sample of the driver's blood, breath, or urine taken soon after the act of driving. This evidence will supplement fallible human observation (*Sudduth,* 65 *Cal.*2d 543 (1966); *Zidell,* 264 *Cal.App.*2d 867 (1968)). The sample must be taken soon after the arrest since the amount of alcohol or drugs in the blood begins to diminish soon after drinking or ingestion stops, as the body functions eliminate it from the system (*Schmerber,* 384 *U.S.* 757 (1966); *Skinner,* 58 *Cal.App.*3d 591 (1976)).

Chemical, Blood, Breath, and Urine Tests

The following California statute contains most of the language and provisions contained in the Vehicle Codes of other states:

> Any person who drives a motor vehicle shall be deemed to have given his or her consent to chemical testing of his or her blood, breath, or urine for the purpose of determining the alcoholic content of his or her blood, and to have given his or her consent to chemical testing of his or her blood or urine for the purpose of determining the drug content of his or her blood, if lawfully arrested for any drunk driving offense. The testing shall be incidental to a lawful arrest and administered at the direction of a peace officer having reasonable cause to believe the person was driving drunk. The person shall be told that his or her refusal to submit to or complete the required chemical testing will result in a fine and mandatory imprisonment if the person is convicted.

What the Driver Must be Told:

> refusal to submit to, or failure to complete, a chemical test will result in a fine and mandatory imprisonment if convicted, and suspension or revocation of driving privileges for a period of one to three years, depending on the driver's prior record;
>
> the driver has a choice of either a blood, breath, or urine test;

Note: If taken to a medical facility for treatment, the driver must submit to whatever tests are available.

refusal to take, or failure to complete, a test may be used as evidence against the driver in court, and will result in a fine and imprisonment if this arrest results in a conviction;

the driver has no right to counsel in connection with the test;

if unable to complete one test, the driver must submit to one of the remaining tests.

The best method for giving this admonition is to read it.

Chemical Test

Chemical tests are incidental to arrest and are administered at the direction of a peace officer who has reasonable cause to believe the person was driving a motor vehicle in violation of drunk driving statutes.

Blood Test

A blood sample must be drawn by medically qualified persons; this includes physicians, registered nurses, licensed vocational nurses, licensed clinical technologists or bioanalysts, or certified paramedics authorized by their employer.

Breath Test

Ordinarily, the operator should be certified by a forensic alcohol supervisor, analyst or trainee, employed by a licensed forsenic alcohol laboratory whose breath testing instrument is being used. (Cal.Admin.Code, title 17, §1221.4.)

Urine Test

A urine sample shall be collected giving the subject such privacy as will ensure accuracy of the specimen while maintaining the dignity of the person involved. To avoid dilution of the sample with water, an officer or other person may remain and observe from several feet away. Women should be observed by a female officer or employee while the sample is being taken, rather than having the complete privacy of a stall. The only "privacy" necessary is that which is common to toilets found in a public restroom, school, military establishment, or similar places. The sample should be collected at a place where there are both toilet and handwashing facilities.

A urine test sample is collected no sooner than 20 minutes after the driver has first voided his or her bladder. The bladder is initially emptied to remove the urine which has accumulated over a period of time and therefore cannot serve as a basis for accurately determining the blood-alcohol level. This initial quantity of urine need not be retained and may be discarded (*Miles,* 118 *Cal.App.*3d 555 (1981)). However, some agencies request retention; therefore, the local practice should be checked. Failure to produce a urine sample after the 20 minute period has passed is considered a refusal. (*Smith,* 25 *Cal.App.*3d 300 (1972.))

Once 20 minutes have passed, you need only wait a short but reasonable time before insisting on either a urine sample or requesting that the driver choose one of the other tests.

ELIMINATION OF ALCOHOL FROM THE BODY

Approximately 90 percent of the alcohol consumed is eliminated from the body by oxidation metabolism occurring primarily in the liver. The remaining alcohol is excreted through the breath, urine and perspiration.

Elimination through urine consists of water and metabolic wastes that are removed from the blood in the kidneys. The small amount of water that is removed will carry with it the same concentration of alcohol as the blood. This is because alcohol and water are infinitely soluble. It has been well-established that the concentration of alcohol found in the urine will reflect the concentration of alcohol in the blood by a ratio that has been determined to be 1.3 to 1.

Since urine is constantly being produced by the kidneys, it is necessary to have a subject void his or her bladder before giving a urine sample for analysis. The void eliminates urine that would reflect the average blood alcohol level from the time since the previous urination (which could have been several hours prior). The sample collected at least 20 minutes after the void reflects the blood-alcohol level over those 20 minutes.

Elimination of alcohol through the breath involves an exchange of gases in the lungs. Since circulating blood travels throughout the lung tissues, the blood is constantly exchanging gases with air in the lungs. At body temperature (37° C) a small amount of alcohol will become a gas. This amount has been determined to one part of alcohol as gas for every 2,100 parts of alcohol that stays in the blood as liquid. This equilibrium between blood and breath is established almost instantly in millions of tiny "pockets" which lead to the alveoli (throat, trachea, bronchial tubes, etc.) and contain various mixtures of room air and deeper lung air. Consequently, the "top lung" air does not reflect the true blood-breath equilibrium. This air reflects less alcohol concentration and more deep lung breath. For this reason the first part of an exhale has the lowest concentration of alcohol in the breath. The highest concentration is reached from the last part of an exhale and contains the breath that reflects the true blood-alcohol concentration.

The total rate of elimination of alcohol (metabolism, breath, and excretion) varies from person to person, but is reasonably constant for any one individual. This rate is about .02 percent of blood-alcohol concentration per hour, or about 1 ounce of 100 proof alcohol by a 150-pound male per hour.

TESTS FOR DRUGS

Breath test instruments are designed only to detect alcohol and will not detect or measure other drugs. If you have reasonable cause to believe that the driver is under the influence of drugs, or a combination of alcohol and drugs, and you have a clear indication that a blood or urine test would reveal that fact, then you may require a person who has already given a breath test to also submit to an additional blood or urine test.

Set out in your report the facts giving rise to your belief that the driver is under the influence of drugs, or the combined influence of drugs and alcohol, as well as those facts giving you a clear indication that a blood or urine test will so reveal. It is initially difficult to tell whether an intoxicated driver has ingested alcohol, drugs, or a combination (*Rice,* 118 *Cal.App.*3d 30 (1981)). "Track marks" coupled with an impaired condition are obvious enough signs of drug use (*Roach,* 108 *Cal.App.*3d 228 (1980)). When the subject is obviously intoxicated with an odor of alcohol, but a breath test results in a reading lower than would be expected of a person exhibiting those symptoms of intoxication, then a combination is likely and further testing is in order (*Roach,* 108 *Cal.App.*3d 891 (1980)).

THE BEST TEST RULE FOR DRUGS

Drugs for which blood is the preferred test sample are primarily the sedative/hypnotic substances such as barbiturates (Seconal, Amytal, Tri-unal, etc.), benzodiazepines (Valium and Librium), carbonates (Equinal, Valmid), non-barbiturates (Dilantin, Doriden, methaqualone), and Darvon. Remember to obtain 10 ml. or more (two vacutainer tubes) of blood with preservative and anticoagulant.

Drugs for which urine is the preferred test sample are more various. As a rule of thumb, if the preferred sample is not blood, then collect urine. Drugs in this category would include amphetamines, cocaine, PCP, methadone, heroin, morphine, and codeine.

There is no test sample for LSD (Lysergic Acid Diethylamide).

If you suspect marijuana intoxication, then obtain a blood sample. The lab will be able to detect the presence of THC in the blood. Some labs can also detect THC in the urine.

BRAIN SCANNER USED TO DETECT DRUG AND ALCOHOL IMPAIRMENT

Giving new meaning to the concept of a non-invasive test, brain waves are joining blood, breath, urine and saliva as indicators of drugs or alcohol in the body. New Jersey law enforcement and medical authorities are currently using a brain wave test system designed to pinpoint the particular type of substance ingested. Called the ADMIT System (Alcohol Drug Motor-sensory Impairment Test), the device was first marketed in January 1985 by the Pharmometrics Corporation, a subsidiary of the National Patent Development Corporation.

To administer the test, a disposable headband is placed on the subject and connected to a microprocessor, which displays his or her brain waves on a screen and produces a printout. As the brain waves are displayed, so is the analysis, which indicates whether or not the subject is impaired and with what substance.

The device is a modification of an electronystagmograph, a machine that measures eye movements and gives the results in waveforms. According to Paramometrics, it was noted several years ago that the presence of drugs affected the results of the electronystagmograph; it was furthermore noticed that the affected waveforms corresponded to particular types of drugs.

Dr. S. Thomas Westerman, credited by Pharmometrics with developing the ADMIT System, worked out eight classifications of substances which showed specific brain waves. These substances are alcohol, hallucinogens, tranquilizers, barbiturates, opiates, marijuana, cocaine and amphetamines. When the ADMIT System was first marketed, the software was equipped to detect only alcohol and marijuana. During January 1990, the engineers added programming to allow detection of hallucinogens, opiates, and cocaine as well. According to Selig Solomon, President of Pharmometrics, programs to detect the presence of barbiturates, amphetamines, and tranquilizers were to have been completed by the end of February 1991.

Whether or not brain wave tests can be used as evidence in drunk driving cases still remains to be seen. The Monmouth County prosecutor's office in New Jersey is coordinating efforts with six police departments in the county to qualify the ADMIT System for use as court evidence.

SIGNS OF DRUGS (SYMPTOMS)

When conducting field sobriety tests (FST's) on a suspected impaired driver, you will find, more often than not, that your drug user will be mixing drugs and alcohol. The eyes are one of the best indicators of being under the influence of drugs.

Use the following list of drugs and their corresponding effects on the eyes when testing a driver for drug-induced impairment:

1. Cocaine — pupils will be dilated and will stay dilated in a well-lit area.
2. Heroin and Opiates — pupils will constrict and remain constricted in a dark area.
3. Marijuana — blood vessels of the eye will be dilated, producing a reddening effect. Also observe an increase in heart rate and the noticeable smell of marijuana.
4. PCP — produces vertical nystagmus. The eye will appear to bounce up and down on a vertical plane. Vertical nystagmus will occur when the subject has ingested small or large amounts of PCP.

   Note: A high blood-alcohol level or a high concentration of barbiturates in the blood will also produce this vertical bounce or nystagmus. This effect has been determined from both field experience and laboratory testing

REFERENCES:

Bogan, Joseph. *A Drinker's Guide to Drinking and Driving.* Kendall/Hunt Publishing Company, Dubuque, Iowa, 1988.

Coccheto, D.M., S.M. Owens, M. Perez-Reyes, et al. "Relationship Between Plasma Delta-9-THC Concentration and Pharmacological Effects in Man." *Psychopharmacology.* 75:158-64, 1981.

Colquett, M., et al. "Drunk Drivers and Medical and Social Injury." *New England Journal of Medicine.* 317:1262-1266, 1987.

Doweiko, Harold. *Concepts of Chemical Dependency.* Cole Publishing Co., Pacific Grove, CA, 1990.

Girdano and Dusek. *Drug Education: Content and Methods,* 4th ed. Random House, New York, 1988.

Goode, Erick. *Drugs in American Society,* 3rd ed. Alfred N. Knopf, Inc., New York, 1989.

Gould Publications. *Vehicle Code of California.* 1992.

Hollister, I.E., H.K. Gillespie, A. Olson, et al. "Do Plasma Concentrations of Delta-9-THC Reflect the Degree of Intoxication." *Journal of Clinical Pharmacology.* 21:1715-1775, 1981.

Honsteer, R.W., R.D. Miller, and Tomero. "Impairment of Performance with Low Doses of Marijuana." *Journal of Clinical Pharmacology.* 14:936-940, 1973.

International Association of Chiefs of Police and the Correctional Association of New York. *Alcohol and Alcoholism: A Police Handbook.* Christopher D. Smithers Foundations, Inc. Eleventh printing. New York, 1978.

Kelly, Norbert L. "Social & Legal Programs of Control in the United States." *McCarthy: Alcohol Education for Classroom and Community.*

Leiber, C.S. "To drink (moderately) or not to drink?" *New England Journal of Medicine.* 310:846-848, 1984.

MacMahon, S.W., et al. "Alcohol and hypertension." *Annals of Internal Medicine.* 105:124-126, 1986.

Miller, B., et al. "Alcoholism Diagnosis for Convicted Drunk Drivers." *Alcoholism: Clinical and Experimental Research.* 10:651-656, 1986.

Moskowitz, H. *Alcohol, Drugs and Driving.* 5:173-228, 1989.

National Institute on Drug Abuse. Drug Concentrations and Driving Impairment: Consensus Development Panel. *Journal of American Medical Association.* 284:2018-2021, 1985.

National Public Services Research Institute. *One For The Road.* Aug. 1977, reproduced by DMV Sacramento, California.

Oakley, Ray S. *Drugs, Society and Human Behavior.* C.V. Mosby Co., St. Louis, 1972.

Shaper, A.G., et al. "Alcohol and mortality in British men." *The Lancet.* II:1267-1273, 1988.

Stampfer, M., et al. "A prospective study of moderate alcohol consumption and the risk of coronary disease and stroke in women." *New England Journal of Medicine.* 319:267-273, 1988.

U.S. Dept. of Justice. "Drinking and Crime." National Institute of Justice File Study Guide, NCJ 97221.

U.S. Department of Transportation. National Highway Administration. "Guide for Detecting Drunk Drivers at Night." DOT HS 805-711, 2nd ed., Jan. 1982.

Vista Hill Foundation. "Intoxication." *Drug Abuse and Alcoholism Newsletter.* Vol. XV, No. 7, Sept. 1986.

________. "Is there a Protracted Abstinence Syndrome with Drugs." *Drug Abuse and Alcoholism Newsletter.* Vol. XX, No. 4, Aug. 1991.

Willett, W.C., et al. "Moderate alcohol consumption and the risk of breast cancer." *New England Journal of Medicine.* 316:1174-1180, 1987.

Yesevage, J.A., V.O. Keirer, M. Denari, et al. "Carry-over Effects of Marijuana Intoxication on Aircraft Pilot Performance: A Preliminary Report." *American Journal of Psychiatry.* 142:1325-29, 1985.

________. "Drinking, Driving and Health Promotion." *Health Education Journal.* 16:224-440, 1989.

CHAPTER VII

THE NARCOTIC DRUGS OF ABUSE

INTRODUCTION

In current usage, the *narcotic drugs* (which originally referred to a variety of substances which relieve pain and produce sleep) include the following substances: 1) opium and its derivatives (heroin, morphine, and codeine), and 2) synthetic narcotics (such as methadone, Demerol, Talwin) which have properties similar to the opium derivatives.

Narcotic drugs are the most effective pain relievers known. They are among the most valuable drugs available to physicians, and are widely used to relieve short-term acute pain, reduce suffering during terminal illnesses, and promote rest so the body can restore itself. Because of the physical and/or psychological addiction which results from their abuse, the use of these substances is controlled. Heroin, however, is illegal for anyone to use.

This chapter will discuss the narcotics most commonly abused. Codeine, Darvon, methadone, opium, heroin and fentanyl have been selected for coverage. There are many narcotic substances of abuse. However, these drugs present particular problems for law enforcement agencies and deserve special consideration.

CODEINE (METHYLMORPHINE)

Codeine is the most commonly used narcotic analgesic. It is a naturally occurring narcotic originating in the opium poppy. It may be used in its natural state or it may be modified chemically to form a semi-synthetic opiate such as heroin (diacetylmopine).

Dr. Forest Tennant, Executive Director of Community Health Projects, states that codeine has replaced Valium as the most abused prescription drug in California. He outlines the problem in "Codeine Abuse in California: Aggravation by Well-Meaning Government Regulations." His contentions on abuse are supported by local and national health statistics showing recent upswings in overdose deaths and emergency room cases.

Codeine is generally used in combination with other substances such as aspirin and acetaminophen.

Abuse and Dependence: Codeine can produce drug dependence of the morphine type, and therefore, has the potential for being abused. Psychic dependence, physical dependence, and tolerance may develop upon repeated administration of this drug and it should be prescribed and administered with the same degree of caution appropriate to the use of other oral narcotic-containing medications. Like other narcotic-containing medications, the drug is subject to the Federal Controlled Substances Act and is a Schedule V product.

Overdose Signs and Symptoms: Codeine in sufficient overdosage produces narcosis sometimes preceded by a feeling of exhilaration and followed by convulsions. Nausea and vomiting are also common side effects. The pupils are constricted and the pulse rate is usually increased. In increasingly severe overdoses, cardiorespiratory depression and cyanosis occur, followed by a drop in body temperature, circulatory collapse, coma and even death.

DARVON (PROPOXYPHENE)

In the 1960s, Darvon was claimed to be a non-addicting, non-narcotic analgesic equal to codeine in pain-relieving potency for the relief of mild to moderate degrees of pain. In its chemical structure, Darvon is similar to methadone. Darvon is sold under trade names such as Darvon Compound, Davocet-N, and under its scientific name, propoxyphene. In the United States, Darvon is a frequently prescribed drug. Propoxyphene is generally not dangerous when taken as directed but it can be a dangerous drug when misused. It is second only to barbiturates as the prescription drug most often associated with suicides. Since Darvon use is not only widespread but is also known to lead to suicides, accidental deaths, and addictions, it has raised serious concerns among law enforcement agencies.

Several Darvon-related deaths have been reported to the Drug Enforcement Administration's Drug Abuse Warning Network (DAWN). The exact cause of these deaths is still uncertain. The best evidence thus far is that propoxyphene is no more effective than aspirin, codeine, and other pain relievers. It is occasionally used in county jails to give heroin addicts some relief from the pains of heroin withdrawal. Since it is no better than other narcotic pain relievers, overuse of Darvon may help to explain why users frequently become addicted or suicidal.

TALWIN (PENTAZOCINE)

Talwin was first synthesized in 1958. It is considered a safe and effective oral analgesic for the relief of moderate to severe pain. When it was first used, it was found to have several advantages over morphine-like drugs. For example, its use produces less vomiting, constipation, respiratory depression, and euphoria than do opiates. As a result, Talwin 50 found significant clinical application in post-operative care and trauma, obstetrics, treatment of gastro-intestinal pain, treatment of the elderly, and treatment of those in chronic pain.

After 1969, with broad acceptance and extensive use of Talwin, reports of dependence and abuse began to appear. Throughout most of the 1970s, Talwin 50 abuse was relatively small. However, by the end of 1977, Talwin 50 began to be combined with PBZ, a prescription antihistamine. On the street, PBZ is known as "Blue Velvet" and the combination of PBZ with Talwin 50 is known as "T's and Blues."

The T's and Blues phenomenon has been limited chiefly to hardcore addict populations. However, this misuse of PBZ with Talwin 50 has drawn media and law enforcement attention.

WINTHROP LABS REFORMULTION OF TALWIN ELIMINATES POTENTIAL FOR MISUSE

Fortunately, Winthrop Laboratories (makers of Talwin) has come up with an effective contribution toward the resolution of the T's and Blues problem. They have developed Talwin with naloxone tablets, named Talwin Nx.

Naloxone is a narcotic antagonist. In brief, the naloxone will precipitate withdrawal symptoms in addicts who are dependent on narcotics, such as heroin, morphine and methadone. It will also precipitate withdrawal symptoms in those who have become dependent upon T's and Blues, using Talwin 50 that has been formulated without naloxone.

The addition of naloxone does not affect or alter the safety of Talwin when it is taken orally. Naloxone is inactive when taken by mouth. However, when injected, naloxone will precipitate withdrawals.

Since 1983, Talwin Nx has replaced Talwin 50. Since then the the abuse of Talwin has dropped dramatically. Information from clinics and addicts confirms the fact that Talwin Nx is considered an unsuitable drug for misuse.

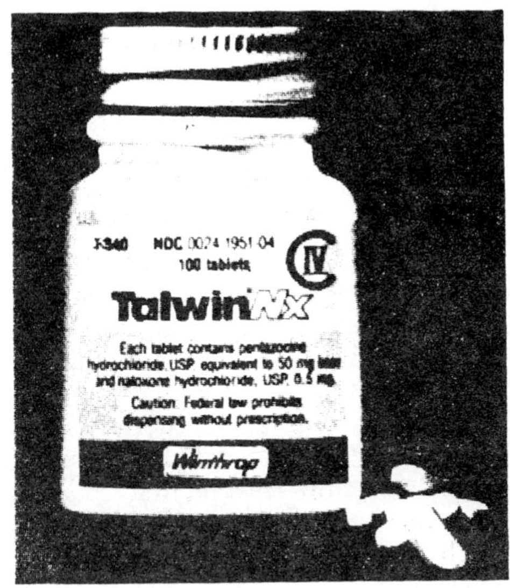

Talwin® 50IV (pentazocine HCl) tablets have been reformulated to include naloxone (0.5mg). The reformulation was undertaken to discourage misuse through injection. The new formulation is called Talwin® NxIV. The color and shape of Talwin Nx is new. Talwin Nx is a pale, oblong-shaped, scored tablet bearing the embossed identification "T-51." Talwin 50 will be discontinued as stocks are exhausted.

NALTREXONE

Naltrexone, a new drug which has been touted by the *New York Times* as an effective and nonaddictive replacement for methadone in the treatment of opiate addiction has now gone into full-time production as a prescription drug. Naltrexone has been termed "a chemical straitjacket" and "the ultimate brain-control drug" by both methadone counselors and clients. Since it exerts virtually no measurable effects of its own, psychologically at least, but only blocks the effects of opiate drugs such as heroin, methadone, Dilaudid, Percodan, Darvon and so on, naltrexone might not be expected to find much demand on the drugstore market. In fact, the Dupont company of Maryland, which will market it as "Trexan," claims to be providing it primarily as a public service, without expecting to garner any substantial profit from this "orphan drug". Even drug-treatment officials who have been opposed to methadone maintenance therapy for years, are fiercely promoting naltrexone as a replacement for it.

Essentially, naltrexone is a long-lasting adaption of the classic "narcotic antagonist" drug naloxone, which has been in use since the 1960s. Produced by Dupont under the brandname, Narcan, naloxone is used in hospital emergency wards everywhere to bring patients out of overdoses on heroin or other opiate drugs. Used in this manner, naloxone has saved thousands of lives. "The patient will appear to be dead when brought into the emergency room," says a veteran physician; "his lips bright blue, no motion, no respiration, no detectable pulse. One shot of Narcan, and instantly the guy comes back to life with a "bang", sitting straight up on the gurney, coughing and spitting quite often taking a swing at the ER intern who just brought him back from the dead. These naloxone-precipitated withdrawals are irreversible, although they only last for 20 minutes.

Naltrexone specialist, Dr. Ginzberg at NIDA tends to agree that the drug will not work well in circumstances of coercion; the patient has to volunteer for the therapy, and believe in it strongly, and the administering therapists have to be prepared to actively "cheerlead" their clients through the roughest parts of the first couple months of abstinence. Highly motivated clients are bound to benefit from the therapy, but Ginzberg notes that the converse is also true, since "poor motivation predicts failure." The simple fact is that the drug, unlike methadone, does not have the specific effect of abolishing an addict's craving for heroin, Demeral, Percodan, etc. In fact, the specific point of naltrexone therapy is to help the addict directly confront and (hopefully) vanquish his or her drug-craving, even if it takes months or years.

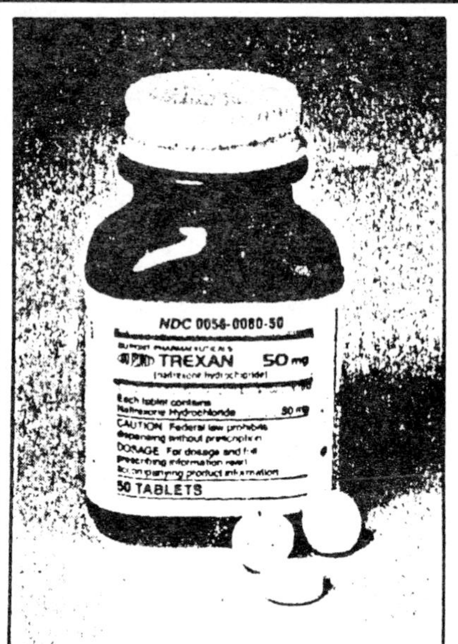

WARNING

"Drug abusers share medication," it is noted in NIDA's latest monograph on naltrexone. In fact, there have been several cases since 1973 of naltrexone clients slipping a dose of the drug to friends who were on methadone or street heroin. The results have been pretty spectacular: Instant withdrawals so drastic they required intensive hospital treatment.

Each white Trexan tablet will counteract a dose of 25 milligrams of heroin for 24 hours, the Dupont company warns; two Trexan tabs will last 48 hours, three tabs 72 hours, and so on. Opiate addicts who take Trexan will be in withdrawals for as long as the dose lasts.

"Symptoms of withdrawal have usually appeared within five minutes of ingestion of Trexan," cautions the Dupont product information in very small print, "and have lasted up to 48 hours. Mental status changes including confusion, somnolence and visual hallucinations have occurred." Such drastic mental changes are not typical at all of ordinary opiate withdrawals, and suggest that naltrexone's main active metabolic—6-Beta naltrexol—has special psychotrophic effects in people who are actively addicted.

Naltrexone-Induced withdrawals need to be managed carefully by physicians, titrating into the patient just enough hydromorphone Dilaudid to overcome the naltrexone blockade, but not enough to overdose the patient dead. The same delicate and complicated routine must be undertaken when naltrexone clients accidentally injure themselves so badly that they require opiates for pain relief.

Naltrexone is not entirely devoid of side-effects, at least in one-time, acute doses. In a 1982 NIDA article, Dr. Charles O'Brien stated that "Normal human males given an acute dose of 50 mg of naltrexone reported irritability, dysphoria, sexual ideation, and penile erections." At such doses, in first time subjects, naltrexone promotes a "rapid and significant" increase of the hormones ACTH, cortisol, and luteinizing hormones, which could account for these effects. Therefore, administrators typically start patients at 25 mg. doses and work gradually upward over a period of weeks, so that the client develops "tolerance" to these side-effects. If the drug is ever given to scores of thousands of people—say, the entire methadone-maintenance population—a percentage of them is sure to encounter significant medical problems with these unwanted side-effects. Therefore, every responsible party agrees that naltrexone will not replace methadone as the treatment of choice for most recovering opiate addicts.

On the other hand, the clinical history of naltrexone since 1973 has shown that it works well for addicted physicians. At the Haight-Ashbury Free Medical Clinic in San Francisco, Dr. Donald Wesson has proven an astonishing 60-percent success rate, working strictly with addicted doctors and nurses. Combined with appropriate personal therapy, naltrexone is virtually tailored for addicted physicians.

METHADONE

Methadone is a synthetic narcotic. In an effort to improve on the properties of the natural alkaloids of opium, a number of such synthetic compounds have been developed and tested. Methadone's longer duration of action (24 hours), makes it distinct from morphine. With prolonged use of methadone, the withdrawal state becomes more drawn out, but of lesser intensity than heroin. Methadone has a cross-dependence with morphine and heroin; therefore, it can forestall the morphine or heroin abstinence syndrome (withdrawals). During the 1960s, methadone came into widespread use for heroin detoxification. This process takes place through the transference from heroin to equivalent doses of methadone, followed by a gradual reduction of the daily methadone dose. The 1973 FDA regulations define methadone detoxification as the administration of methadone in decreasing doses to reach a drug-free state in a period not to exceed 21 days. Administering methadone for more than 21 days is deemed maintenance treatment.

Why Methadone Maintenance?

In an ideal world, there would be no need for drug treatment programs because no one would become addicted to heroin or other drugs in the first place. Even in the world as it is, there would be no need for maintenance treatment if there existed drug-free treatment programs capable of helping heroin addicts to become responsible, self-respecting, ex-addicts able to live without opiates.

Drug-free treatment programs do not work for everybody. In fact, the rehabilitated addicts emerging from treatment programs and living drug-free each year represent only a small portion of the addict population.

Something must be done for addicts who refuse to enter drug-free programs, for addicts who are denied admission to drug-free programs, and for those who fail in drug-free programs. This population should be targeted for methadone maintenance.

For several reasons, methadone is superior to both morphine and heroin as a maintenance drug. First, methadone is highly effective when taken by mouth rather than by injection. This method of administration avoids the hazards of infection, AIDS, and the many other drawbacks associated with daily intravenous injection of drugs. Second, methadone is a *long-acting* drug. An average oral dose of methadone keeps the user from experiencing withdrawal for up to 24 hours. Addicts on morphine or heroin, on the other hand, must "shoot up" or inject the drug 3 to 4 times a day.

As a *long-acting* drug, methadone has a slower and more gradual onset of effect, especially when taken orally. Therefore, patients receiving oral methadone do not experience the "rush" or "bang" often felt soon after heroin is injected directly into a vein. After the initial "rush" of a heroin injection, a period of somnolence or lethargy usually follows. Then, after a relatively brief period of feeling more or less "normal," the heroin addict begins to experience withdrawal anxiety, followed by withdrawal distress or the abstinence syndrome.

Therefore, a patient on heroin tends to "bounce" from one physiological state to another throughout the day. Some heroin addicts go through this cycle, or portions of it, two or three times in 24 hours. However, since methadone is taken orally and has a more gradual effect on the body, patients on this maintenance drug do not experience this cycle of "rush" or "bang" followed by severe withdrawal anxiety. [1]

By relieving the acute effects of heroin withdrawal, methadone also keeps the addict from feeling anxiety about where the next "fix" or shot of heroin is coming from. Patients on stable daily doses of methadone no longer have to engage in compulsive drug-seeking behavior; they no longer have to engage in crime to support their heroin habits.

Another reason for methadone's superiority is that some addicts have a tendency to escalate their doses of heroin. But once stabilized on an adequate daily dose of methadone, patients are content to remain on that dose year after year.

A fifth advantage is that methadone blocks the heroin effect. A patient stabilized on a daily dose of methadone who uses heroin at the same time discovers that the heroin has no effect. The larger the dose of methadone, the larger the dose of heroin that is blocked. There is nothing mysterious about this blocking effect; it is a case of cross-tolerance. The effect of any opiate or synthetic narcotic is blocked when one dose is substantially higher than the other.

The key characteristic which makes methadone a useful maintenance drug, however, is one shared by morphine and heroin. Patients on uniform daily doses of methadone begin to perceive fewer and fewer initial effects of the drug; they develop tolerance. As with morphine and heroin, the effects which remain are experienced to a lessened degree. However, the patient on

---

[1] It should be pointed out that the euphoria of a drug rush often depends upon how the drug is used. For example, even though oral methadone does not produce a "rush" or "euphoria," administering methadone by intravenous injection will produce a heroin-like euphoria.

methadone does not need larger and larger doses to satisfy his or her drug dependence.

After tolerance has developed—that is, after a patient has been stabilized on a uniform daily dose—patients on methadone cannot be distinguished from drug-free men and women. They look and act "normal," and they report that they feel "normal." However, methadone patients report that this drug can cause some side effects. Supporting these reports, Drs. William Bloom and Brian Butcher of Tulane University have documented the following side effects of methadone:

Drowsiness—tended to disappear in all patients as they achieved a stable dose level.

Decreased sexual interest—reported in both men and women. In some patients, however, sexual interest increased.

Nausea—eventually grew less in long-term maintenance patients.

Alcohol abuse—older addicts and those on high methadone doses tended to drink more.

Difficulty in urination—experienced most by younger patients and those taking higher doses.

In addition, addicts have reported constipation, swelling of feet and ankles, blurring of vision, numbness of hands and feet, and weight gain.

Despite the advantages of methadone discussed above, there have been many complaints about methadone addicts continuing to commit crimes while on the methadone maintenance program. It should be remembered that the majority of methadone patients are people who have, for the most part, lived a life of crime to support their heroin addiction. Thus, many of the addicts do not change their lifestyle and continue their criminal behavior while on methadone maintenance. Nonetheless, these criticisms should cause methadone maintenance treatment programs to re-evaluate their effectiveness and re-organize their methodology in order to meet their targeted goals.

In March of 1990 the U.S. General Accounting Office issued a report on methadone maintenance programs.[2] In summary, the report stated that methadone maintenance is the most commonly used treatment for heroin addiction. One hundred thousand addicts receive treatment in over 650 programs nationwide. The GAO reviewed the activity of 24 methadone programs in 8 states: California, Florida, Illinois, Maryland, New Jersey, New York, Texas and Washington. The report found the following:

Program policies, goals, and practices differed. Since the fine details of each program are decided on by the programs themselves, their individual characteristics vary greatly.

---

[2] "Methadone Maintenance Report." GAO/T-HRD-90-19, U.S. General Accounting Office, March 23, 1990.

Most programs are not effectively treating heroin addiction. A substantial percentage of patients continued to use heroin after 6 months of treatment.

None of the 24 programs evaluate their effectiveness. With one exception, the programs did not know the extent to which their treatment goals were met or the overall level of continued drug use in the programs.

Federal oversight of methadone maintenance treatment programs has been very limited since 1983. There are no Federal treatment effectiveness standards for these programs. Instead, Federal regulations have primarily established administrative requirements.

Interim maintenance, without other support services, is not effective. The GAO concluded that interim maintenance—the provision of methadone without any counseling or rehabilitative services—would not significantly reduce heroin use.

OPIUM

As an opiate, heroin originates in the flower of the opium poppy. The opium poppy is an annual plant (lives only one season and must be replanted every year) that is native to the Mediterranean region. In addition to its native region, the opium poppy can be grown in most parts of the world between the latitudes of 56 degrees north and 56 degrees south (approximately the Canadian border to the tip of South America). Although the opium poppy grows well in any warm dry climate, India, Turkey, Laos, Thailand, Burma, Iran, Yugoslavia, Bulgaria, Hungary, Greece, Afghanistan, Pakistan, China, Indochina, and Mexico are the principal growers. India and Turkey are probably the largest producers of opium for legal use.

Cultivation of the Opium Poppy (Papaver Somniferium L.)

The opium poppy is usually planted in the late summer or fall, although in some locations it can be planted twice a year. The opium farmer cultivates the land and then scatters handfuls of tiny poppy seeds across its surface. These fields are often weeded and cultivated to keep all foreign plants from the poppy. The poppy takes approximately three months to mature to its normal height of three to four feet. The plant has one main tubular stem from which a number of off-shoot stems grow. The mature green plant has seed pods located at the end of the stems with a flower appearing on the top of seed pods. The flower has petals that may be singular or double, plain or fringed and many vary in color from white to pink and red to purple or a combination of these. The color has no bearing on the opium content within the plant. The seeds of the poppy which are located in the seed pods contain no opium and are therefore not illegal.

According to Section 11019 of the Health and Safety Code of California, the opium poppy and poppy straw are defined as a narcotic drug. In Section 11021 of the Health and Safety Code, opium poppy means the plant of the species Papaver Somniferium L., except the seeds. In Section 11025 of the Health and Safety Code, poppy straw means all parts except the seeds of the opium poppy, after mowing.

The seeds are used as an edible commodity such as in bird seed and food stock. The seeds are also used in the production of oils that are used in lamps, cooking, and the manufacture of paint. Even though the seed contains no opium, it does produce the opium that can be found within the pod. The pod is actually the greatest source of opium within the poppy. The stems and leaves of the poppy do contain opium although not enough to make complete harvesting of the plant worthwhile.

After the flower appears on the seed pods, the petals of the flower begin dropping off leaving the green pod completely exposed. It is at this time that the pod has reached its maximum degree of growth and is ready to be harvested for its opium content. The harvesters go through the fields and manually cut shallow incisions into the pods using a sharp, shallow knife-like instrument. This instrument will vary with individual harvesters from a single blade to a triple blade instrument.

The incisions cut into the pods can be either vertical or circular and are usually made in the cool, late afternoon or early evening hours, which is apparently conducive to greater production of opium.

Once the incisions have been made, a white gummy sap appears on the outer surface of the pod. The sap (raw opium) is produced by the seeds contained within the pods. When the white gummy sap is exposed to air, it turns dark brown. The bleeding of the sap usually takes several hours depending on the climate, although any heavy dew or rain could be fatal to the crop. The next day the harvesters go back through the fields and collect the sap, either using a special metal scraping instrument or their fingers, taking the sap off the pod and putting it into containers usually fastened to the harvester's belt. Some harvesters scrape the sap into a cuplike container that fits under the pod. Since the pods ripen unevenly, the harvesters often rework the rows time and time again.

Opium poppy plants will grow well in various parts of the United States, particularly in the mountainous regions of Humboldt County in Northern California. The geography in this region is very similar to the mountainous regions of Mexico where opium poppy plants proliferate. There have been numerous seizures of opium poppy fields in these California mountains, but at the present time, these fields have not been considered an opium source for the manufacture of heroin due to a lack of laboratory facilities and a lack of cheap labor. Since the harvesting of opium requires hand labor and is a very tedious, low-yielding process, it is feasible only in areas where hand labor is available and extremely cheap. It takes approximately three acres of poppies to produce 10 kilograms (22 pounds) of opium. Many of the opium fields in Northern California are believed to be "volunteer" crops which nature causes to reproduce each year from original crops planted by Chinese immigrants in the late 1800s and early 1900s.

For some time, it has been suggested that Colombia will become a future heroin source country. A laboratory was purported to be in existence in the country, converting raw opium into morphine base and heroin. The venture was said to be financed and backed by a cocaine cartel to allow them to diversify into another highly profitable drug trafficking area.

The latest reports from Colombia and America support and verify the fact that Colombia is now a source country for heroin production. A recent operation by the Colombian police resulted in the discovery and destruction of 450,000 opium poppy plants. Furthermore, opium poppy cultivation has been identified in four states of Colombia: Cundinamaraca, Antioquia, Cauca, and Tomila.

In Cundinamaraca and Antioquia, active poppy fields have been located; while plantations and processing laboratories have been detected in Cauca. Recently 10 kilograms of morphine were seized in Cauca. In Tomila, 25 hectares of poppy plants and three hectares of seedlings were found, which resulted in the destruction of 1.5 million plants. Intelligence obtained from this particular operation shows that the raw opium produced in this case was being exported to Mexico to be processed into "dark heroin."

Smoking Opium

Smoking opium is a simple refinement of raw or crude opium. One pound of opium will yield approximately 3/4 lb. of smoking opium. The procedure consists of boiling out the impurities and adding glycerine to give it a more pliable consistency. Smoking opium is very popular in many parts of the world, but not as popular in the United States. It was first introduced in the United States in the late 1800s with the immigration of the Asian community into San Francisco.

Opium smoking dens were quite popular in the San Francisco area but enforcement efforts have essentially phased them out. There may be an occasional opium den or facsimile encountered today, but their popularity has not been a significant problem as it was in late 1800s and early 1900s. These opium dens were premises where opium users would meet and participate in the rituals of opium smoking. There was generally a leader or practitioner who would tend to the user by providing smoking paraphernalia and keeping the opium lighted. The word "opium" comes from the Greek term "opos" which means juice. Users would often lie upon the floor and form a circle by placing one's head on another's hip and so on. Another method was to lay their heads on a special pillow. These pillows are still encountered on occasion, which suggests the probability that some opium smoking still exists. While lying on the floor, the smoker would lie on his side and smoke through the opium pipe. The smoker's head would be elevated and on its side. The opium does not actually burn, but rather smolders and the user inhales the fumes through a pipe.

The alkaloid of opium is morphine. Opium usually contains 10 percent morphine, 0.5 percent codeine, 1.2 percent thebaine, and 1 percent papaverine. There are also approximately 20 other alkaloids in opium.

MORPHINE

The chemical formula of morphine is $C_{17}H_{19}NO_3$. Morphine was named after the Greek god of dreams, Morpheus, by the German researcher Serturner, who first isolated the drug from opium in 1805.

Illicit morphine is produced from opium through a fairly simple process. This process usually yields one pound of morphine per 10 pounds of opium. Likewise, one kilo of morphine will produce one kilo of heroin.

The opium chemist heats water in an oil drum over a wood fire until the proper temperature is reached. The chemist then dumps raw opium into the oil drum and stirs it with a heavy stick until it dissolves. At this time, ordinary lime fertilizer is added to the steaming solution, precipitating organic waste and leaving the morphine suspended in a chalky white liquid near the surface. The chemist then pours the solution into another oil drum through cheesecloth or a piece of flannel cloth, removing any waste matter. The solution is again heated and stirred as concentrated ammonia is added, causing the morphine to solidify and drop to the bottom. This solution is then filtered through cheesecloth or flannel, leaving chunky white kernels of morphine on the cloth. The morphine, called free morphine base, is dried and packaged for shipment to make into heroin.

Medical morphine, despite developments of various synthetic narcotics, is still the most widely used drug for relief of severe pain. It is desirable for the following reasons: 1) it raises the patient's pain perception threshold; 2) it relieves the anxiety and fear that are natural emotional reactions to painful stimuli and are largely responsible for the unpleasantness of the pain experience, and 3) it can produce sleep even in the presence of severe pain.

There are a number of preparations that contain morphine, such as morphine sulphate, morphine hydrochloride, morphine acetate, and morphine tartrate. Of the morphine preparations, morphine sulphate is the most common. It appears as a white, chrystalline powder. It is odorless, has a bitter taste, and darkens upon long exposure to light. It acts as a depressant on the central nervous system, and when injected for the relief of pain, acts almost immediately.

Morphine sulphate is manufactured in tablet and liquid form. An average dose is 1/6 to 1/4 grain, with a fatal dose known to be as low as one grain, if the individual has developed no tolerance. The average morphine addict uses from two to ten grains, 4 times a day. Morphine sulphate legally comes in 1/12, 1/8, 1/6, 1/4, and 1/2 grain quantities.

HEROIN (DIACETYLMORPHINE)

A milestone in the history of opiate use was the chemical modification of morphine to diacetylmorphine.

Heroin was first produced in 1874 by an English researcher, D.P. Wright. Wright experimented with heroin on dogs as an ideal non-addicting substitute for morphine, but later discontinued any further research. In 1898, the Bayer Chemical Company of Germany manufactured diacetylmorphine under the brand name of Heroin for its mass marketing campaign. One of the original advertising slogans was "Heroin - A Sedative for Coughs." Heroin soon became one of the most popular patent medicines on the market. In the United States, the St. Louis Pharmaceutical Company offered a sample box of heroin tablets free to physicians and in 1906 the American Medical Association approved heroin for general use and advised that it be used in place of morphine for various painful infections. Due to the unrestricted distribution by physicians and pharmacists in 1920, an enormous drug problem arose, that of heroin addiction. In 1924 the importation and manufacture of heroin was prohibited in the United States. However, the first comprehensive control of heroin in the United States was established with the Harrison Act of 1914.

Chapter VII

THE MANUFACTURING PROCESS FOR HEROIN

The manufacturing process for heroin is more complicated than that of opium or morphine. The centers for heroin laboratories are Iran, Hong Kong, Mexico, Southeast Asia, and the Philippines. The goal of the five-stage manufacturing process is to chemically bond morphine molecules with acetic acid and then process the compound into a fluffy white powder that can be injected by the use of a syringe and hypodermic needle. The process is as follows:

1. To produce ten kilos of pure heroin (the normal daily output of some labs) the chemist heats ten kilos of morphine and ten kilos of acetic anhydride in an enamel bin or glass flask. This mixture is heated for six hours at exactly 185 degrees. The morphine and acid become chemically bonded creating an impure form of diacetylmorphine, or heroin.
2. To remove the impurities of the compound, the solution is treated with water and chloroform until the impurities precipitate out leaving a higher grade of diacetylmorphine.
3. The solution is then drained into another container and sodium carbonate is added until the crude heroin particles begin to solidify and drop to the bottom.
4. After the heroin particles are filtered out of the sodium carbonate solution under pressure from a small suction pump, they are purified in a solution of alcohol and activated charcoal. The mixture is then heated until the alcohol begins to evaporate, leaving relatively pure granules of heroin at the bottom of the flask.
5. The final stage produces the fine white powder known as heroin and requires considerable skill on the part of the chemist. The heroin is placed in a large flask and dissolved with alcohol. As ether and hydrocholric acid are added to the solution, tiny white flakes begin to form. After the flakes are filtered out under pressure and dried through a special process, the end result is a white powder 80 to 100 percent pure, known as Heroin No. 4. Under the hands of a careless chemist, the volatile ether may ignite and produce a violent explosion.

The heroin produced from the labs in Hong Kong and France is usually white and pure. In the crude clandestine laboratories in Mexico, Mexican heroin is brown in color because the manufacturing process leaves impurities in the heroin. Raw opium is converted to heroin in a continuous three-way process. In contrast to the classical French procedures, morphine hydrocholride is produced instead of morphine base, simply by adding water, lime, salt, and hydrochloric acid. The morphine product is then filtered by squeezing it in a cloth. On the third day it is acetylated to produce heroin hydrochloride.

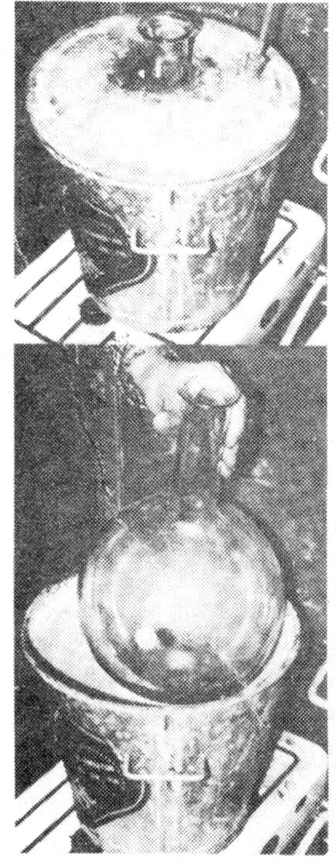

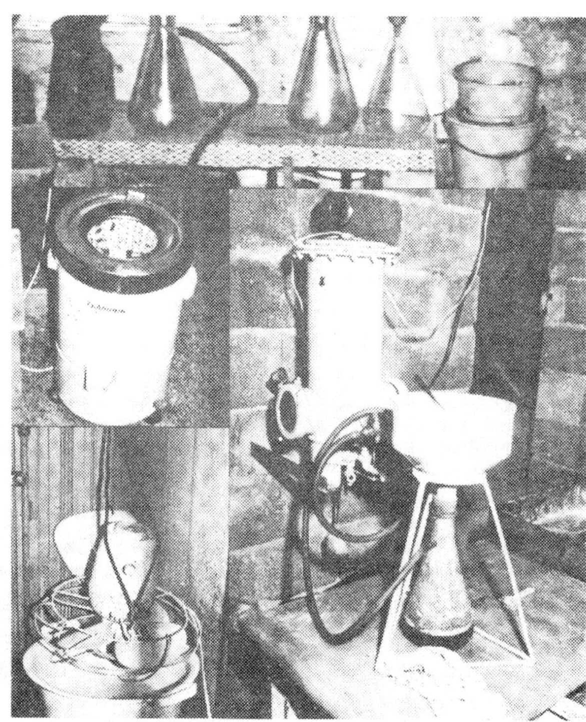

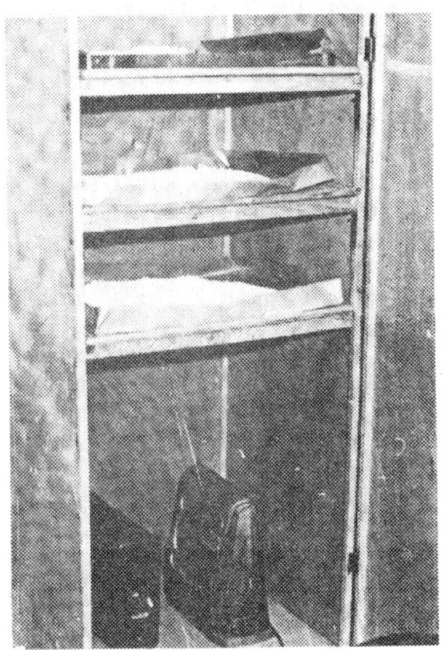

THE CONVERSION PROCESS REQUIRES A SERIES OF SUCCESSIVE STEPS. SHOWN ABOVE IS SOME OF THE EQUIPMENT USED.

TYPES OF HEROIN

Types of heroin are traditionally numbered according to the four steps in the heroin production process. Heroin No. 1, a tan-to-brown colored powder, is actually crude morphine base extracted from raw opium. It is the starting material for the various heroin products. Heroin No. 2, a white-to-gray powder, is a transitional product in the conversion of morphine base to heroin. Two marketable products are derived from Heroin No. 2: smokeable heroin and injectable heroin—both maufactured for illicit markets. Heroin No. 3, smoking heroin, is also known as "White Dragon Pearl." It is tan-to-gray in color, yet commonly seen in several shades of gray, blue, and light brown; it has a granular or lumpy composition. Heroin No. 4 is a mixture of heroin hydrochloride (50 to 60 percent), caffeine (30 to 50 percent), and often strychnine hydrochloride (0.5 to 10 percent). Heroin No. 4 also has other impurities such as 3 or 6 monocetylmorphine, codeine, and thebaine. No. 3 Heroin is more available than No. 4 Heroin. Heroin No. 3 is easier to make than Heroin No. 4 because Heroin No. 3 is manufactured without the final step in the production process. The final stage is not only dangerous but doubles the time required to make the heroin.

Heroin No. 4, injectable heroin hydrochloride, is usually marketed as a fluffy white powder (the famous "China White" of the United States), and may vary in color from a bright white to a creamy yellow. Since it is sold by volume rather than by weight, it is less dense than European-produced heroin.

Despite the availability of the highly processed Heroin No. 4, street heroin found in the United States is probably the lowest quality of any heroin available on the world's illicit drug market. On the average, U.S. street heroin contains 3 to 10 percent (out of a 0-85 percentage range) pure heroin. Canadian illicit heroin, prepared for street sale, contains approximately 35 percent (out of a 0.5-96 percentage range) of the drug. A study of the composition and potency of street heroin in Amsterdam reported that the average heroin content was 40 percent (out of a 10-60 percentage range).

It has recently been reported that in 1992 heroin is pouring into the United States from the Pacific Rim in record amounts, at extraordinarily high purity levels and at bargain prices, spurring the fears of drug enforcement agencies that heroin addiction is poised to become the drug epidemic of the 1990s.

The highly addictive drug, sold on city streets from Boston to Washington, D.C., is now so inexpensive that users have taken to smoking and snorting it, rather than using the traditional more effective method of injecting it into the vein. That change, according to Federal agents, has made the drug far more attractive to a potential new market of abusers who do not want the stigma and danger of using a needle in the age of AIDS.

"As the price of heroin drops, people can afford to use it in less efficient ways that don't involve needles," said Mark Kleinman, a drug analyst at Harvard's John F. Kennedy School of Government. He added that "Now people will believe they can't get hooked by snorting. And a lot of people who would never use a needle now may start."

Mexican Brown

Beyond the basic numbered types, there are varieties of heroin commonly sold in the United States. "Mexican Brown" heroin, a phenomenon of the western U.S., is usually pinkish brown in color, a fine powder with dark brown flecks and/or white particles. The color may vary from a rather light brown to almost chocolate. The product's name does not necessarily mean that it originates in Mexico; initially, heroin from Mexico was a characteristic brown due to a particular method of manufacture, hence the name "Mexican Brown". Apparently, the name and the color both make the product more marketable, as this type of street heroin is one of the most avidly sought by consumers. One ex-dealer and user reported that he used instant coffee to make "Mexican Brown from China White. . . I couldn't deal China White. It had to be brown." The active ingredients in this preparation are usually procaine, 55 percent and heroin, 30 percent; diluents may be talc, flour, cornstarch, lactose and/or mannitol.[3]

Although Mexican Brown heroin does not necessarily originate in Mexico, the major source of brown heroin is Mexico. Asian heroin is also entering the United States through various channels. Asian heroin may first be smuggled into Europe (Paris, Amsterdam and/or Brussels) and then brought into the U.S. by air or sea transportation; or it may enter via Canada, South America or Mexico.

Persian Heroin

Law enforcement agencies have recently encountered another type of heroin variously called "Persian Heroin," "Lemon Heroin," "Persian Morphine," and "Salt n' Pepper." As analyzed by the Drug Enforcement Administration laboratory in San Francisco, Persian Heroin displayed the following characteristics: it is a "base" substance, not a hydrocholoride. This means that it is not soluble in water. It is commonly light tan to near pink to reddish in color. Instead of adding water to the powder prior to "cooking," lemon juice (containing citric acid) or vinegar (containing acetic acid) is used to dissolve the heroin. The traditional solution and heating procedure is used for manufacture. Seizures of Persian Heroin have revealed consistently high percentages of pure heroin. Seizures of even small amounts have been as high as 98 percent pure.

It is possible that Persian Heroin is a crude morphine base. In Iran, there is a common practice of "chasing the dragon"—that is, smoking this morphine base. It has been stated by Persian Heroin dealers in San Francisco that they receive their supply from Iranians who brought the habit of smoking with them to California. They have connections in the homeland and receive the drug many different ways. The percentage of the morphine in the drug must be high in order to get the psychoactive effect from smoking. In the last several years, Persian Heroin has been cut to decrease potency and increase profits. Consequently, users have started injecting the drug to get more of an effect.

---

[3] For a complete discussion of heroin adulteration see the *PharmChem Newsletter*, Vol. 3, No. 2, 1974.

Black Tar Heroin

Black tar heroin has been found in steadily increasing amounts in the United States. It began to appear in wholesale quantities in the United States in about 1979, two years after the Drug Enforcement Administration stopped eradication efforts in Mexico.

The Drug Enforcement Administration has, over the past several years, encountered black tar heroin in 27 of the 50 states. It is believed that the material originates in the Mexican states of Durango, Sinaloa, Sonora, and Guerrero. The growing acceptance of this form of heroin over traditional forms is believed to be due to its high purity at the "street" level. The purity has been found to be as high as 93 percent. Although purities as low as 2 percent have been encountered, the purities most frequently seen range between 40 and 80 percent pure. The smaller marketable quantities of black tar heroin are normally packaged in plastic bags, balloons, and aluminum foil and the heroin conforms to the shape of the packaging.

Even "brown" or "Mexican Brown" heroin is now almost always tar that has been cut and blended.

Due to the different varieties of brown heroin, several street names for tar have emerged. These include: gum, goma, chiva, raw heroin, and Mexican mud.

High purity and low volume account for the demand for tar. Most uncut tar ranges from 50 to 70 percent purity and is commonly injected at full strength in areas of California, Oregon, and Washington. A match-head size piece usually sells for about $25 and will give an experienced user one to five doses, depending on purity. Since a gram is about the size of a pea, a dealer can easily hide five or six grams of tar in a sock and, from this amount, sell the tar to fifty or sixty customers. If the same dealer wanted to conceal a comparable supply of white heroin he would have to carry 25 to 30 grams. Street dealers have been known to carry a couple of grams of tar in a balloon in the mouth. If approached by law enforcement, they simply swallow the balloon and recover it later.

Along with the high purity of tar there has come a rash of overdoses and overdose-related deaths. It is not unusual for an area dense in black tar heroin to experience double or triple the amount of these incidents, but normally this happens only during the initial influx of tar. A consistently high incidence of overdoses usually occurs where tar is sold both cut and uncut and purity fluctuates significantly.

Manufacturing Tar Heroin

The processes used to manufacture tar heroin are easier than those used for the white crystalline variety and take about one-third of the time. Moreover, there are no controls on any of the chemicals needed. Impurities such as hydrochloride, opium alkaloids, acetylated opium, acetylated codeine and insoluble plant products are not removed. They substances are responsible for the final tar-like form and for some of the inflammation infection, and the scarring that occurs on the skin and veins of the intravenous user. The production process below results in a product that is about 60 to 70 percent heroin and 10 to 20 percent morphine:

1. Score poppies and gather opium.

 md

2. Dissolve the opium in water and one of the following base solutions:
   a) Butanol and Ammonia.
   b) Hydroxide
   c) Lye
   d) Lime and/or Ammonia.

   This will cause the active alkaloids (morphine, caffeine, etc) to separate from the organic debris.
3. Cook with one of the following chemicals to convert the morphine to heroin:
   a) Acetic Anhydride
   b) Acetylchloride
4. Add baking soda
5. To clean the heroin, heat with acetone or alcohol and activated charcoal.
6. Add hydrochloric acid and ether to change the heroin base to heroin hydrochloride, a water-soluble salt suitable for injection.

Characteristics of Tar Heroin

A street level "bag" or "paper" of tar heroin is most often described as looking "like a rat turd." It is usually very dark brown, nearly black in color, and could be mistaken for a piece of hash. When cut excessively, it may become lighter in color or even translucent, like a chip off a beer bottle. The tar-like, sticky form is very common and is often pressed flat. Opinions differ on the significance of the degree of hardness. It may be hard when old or dry or when high in purity. Hardened tar can resemble a piece of obsidian, hardened roofing tar, or charcoal. Tar heroin smells strongly of vinegar but this does not begin until two or three hours after the manufacturing process is completed. During that time, it is possible for a smuggler to walk a small amount across the border without alerting drug detecting dogs.

To cut tar heroin, the dealer may use any of the common cutting agents such as lactose, inositol, or brown sugar; however, chocolate milk powder, instant coffee, raisins, molasses, and powdered Vitamins A, B3, and C have also been reported. Blenders and coffee grinders are often used to combine the heroin with the cutter.

Freezing or drying the tar first to harden it will facilitate the cutting process. Sometimes the heroin is spread on tin foil, then a cutting agent is sprinkled on top and melted in. Using a cutting agent usually alters the originally viscous form, which may be undesirable in some areas. One ingenious dealer reported that he burned cornstarch in a cast-iron skillet until it was black, then rolled the ball of heroin in it until the desired amount of cutter was absorbed. The tar still looks the same, but if the user cooks his heroin instead of dissolving it in cold water, the cornstarch will gel. (Lemon or lime juice are also often used to dissolve tar heroin prior to injection.)

Cut tar heroin is most often packaged in balloons while uncut tar is wrapped in cellophane, tin foil, or both.

An Analysis of Black Tar Heroin

The Idaho State Crime Laboratory in Pocatello, Idaho, has analyzed black tar heroin in exhibits submitted over a period of approximately two years. The purity has ranged from 4 percent to 100 percent heroin. Most frequently the purity is between 70 percent and 90 percent. Sample weights have ranged from 50 milligrams to 2 ounces. To date, the smaller samples are usually soft and gummy, while the larger samples have been received as hard blocks. The weight of the individual samples was approximately 0.24 grams. There have been two documented cases of overdose deaths associated with this type of heroin in the 1980s. The Los Angeles County Sheriffs Criminalistics laboratory recently tested an exhibit of 12 balloons containing a brown pliable substance similar to tar heroin with a greyish coating on it. The analysis of this material showed it to contain a mixture of cocaine and heroin.

China White vs. Fentanyl

China White heroin, or Heroin No. 4, is the most refined form of heroin since it has gone through the fifth and most dangerous step in the manufacturing process. This step turns the opium solution into injectable heroin hydrochloride. Although it has been the heroin variety of choice in the past, China White is currently not as popular as the different varieties of tar heroin on the street. Nonetheless, China White is still available.

The continuing availability and popularity of China White may have caused the confusion in 1980 regarding a white powder sold on the street as heroin. The powder first appeared on the streets of California's major cities in June, 1980. In December, 1980 this powder was analyzed by a DEA lab in Washington as fentanyl; it was believed to have been manufactured in clandestine labs in southern California, probably in San Diego. Fentanyl is a synthetic, narcotic analgesic similar to morphine and meperidine (Demerol). Since this fentanyl was sold as heroin (most likely as China White heroin), the white powder caused a number of overdoses up and down the state.

Alpha methyl fentanyl is a very potent drug. In analgesic activity, one mg. (2.0 ml) is equal to 10 mg. of morphine or 75 mg. of Demerol. Even if fentanyl were cut or diluted to 1 percent, it would still be equivalent to buying 75 to 80 percent pure heroin in street doses. Like morphine, fentanyl's onset of action is almost immediate if injected. The duration of action is 30 to 60 minutes after a simple IV dose of 0.1 mg. The duration of the drug's respiratory depressant effect is longer than its analgesic effect. The peak respiratory depressant effect is 5-15 minutes following injection. When fentanyl is combined with CNS depressants such as barbiturates, tranquilizers, or other narcotics, it may even have an addictive or potentiating effect. The drug's medical use is limited to cases in which an analgesic action of short duration is needed. Fentanyl is sold under brand names such as Sublimaze and Innovar.

Red Rock

Red Rock is No. 3 Heroin manufactured in the Philippines and combined with barbital, strychnine and caffeine. This combined form of heroin looks like small red rocks and is consumed by smoking.

Once the heroin has been manufactured, it is packaged and smuggled to various parts of the world. The majority of shipments comes to the United States.

Heroin is usually smuggled into California in hermetically sealed plastic bags or rubber condoms; however, there are a variety of other methods employed in smuggling due to the establishment of well-defined trafficking routes throughout the world. Before shipment, the wholesaler will most likely dilute the heroin with some powdered agent to increase its profitability (and decrease its quality). Depending upon the wholesaler's dilution, the original heroin shipment could enter its destination country with a pure heroin percentage of only 50 or 25 percent. From the wholesaler, who deals in pounds and kilos, down to the ounce dealer, through the gram dealer, and finally to the heroin user, the drug is often "cut," diluted, or "stepped on" a number of times leaving the street quality of the drug at .5 to 5 percent. That means that only .5 to 5 percent of the total powder is actually heroin.

CUTTING HEROIN

The basic paraphernalia for adulteration of heroin include the following: the cut (lactose, etc.), scales, measuring spoons, flat nonporous surface, razor blade or playing card, sifter or nylon stocking, funnel, and packing containers (toy balloons, paper bindles, plastic bags, etc.).

A common diluting agent is lactose or dextrose, a white powdered milk sugar that is used as a baby food supplement and can be purchased in any drug store. Lactose is also used by druggists as a filler for capsules. Often heroin addicts have what they call a "milk sugar habit," causing them to crave sweets, soda pops, etc. It is not uncommon for a heroin addict to add three or four spoons of sugar to his/her coffee.

Besides lactose, any soluble powder that is not disruptive to the body can be used as a cutting agent. Dealers of Mexican Brown heroin will often use brown-colored diluting agents such as chocolate cake mix, cocoa and instant coffee, instead of white milk sugars. This maintains the brown color of their product and gives the visual impression of better quality. Other cutting agents include powdered quinine (which has a bitter taste similar to heroin, making it an ideal cutting agent), procaine, baking soda, powdered sugar, powdered milk, menita, mannitol, starch, and Darvon.

The individual dealer will be able to approximate the percentage of heroin that he has purchased by injecting either himself or a second party. Some dealers use chemical testing kits that are now available on the street or in many paraphernalia shops. In an elaborate operation, a chemist will ascertain the percentage of the heroin by chemical analysis.

Once a dealer has a general idea of the heroin's purity, he will mix a small quantity of the heroin and cutting agent in the desired proportions and retest the heroin as a final check. When the dealer is sure of the ratio he wishes to use, he proceeds to dilute the remaining heroin. When a dealer cuts the heroin he may use one of any number of dilution formulas. Two basic formulas are as follows:

Formula 1

1 ounce of lactose added to 1 ounce of 100 percent heroin = 2 ounces of 50 percent heroin.

2 ounces of lactose added to 2 ounces of 50 percent heroin = 4 ounces of 25 percent heroin.

4 ounces of lactose added to 4 ounces of 25 percent heroin = 8 ounces of 12-1/2 percent heroin.

8 ounces of lactose added to 8 ounces of 12-1/2 percent heroin = 16 ounces of 6-1/4 percent heroin.

16 ounces of lactose added to 16 ounces of 6-1/4 percent heroin = 32 ounces of 3-1/8 percent heroin.

32 ounces of lactose added to 32 ounces of 3-1/8 percent heroin = 65 ounces of approximately 1-1/2 percent heroin.

Formula 2

Cutting Agent added to 100 percent heroin = Heroin

Cutting Agent	100 percent heroin	Heroin
1 oz.	1 oz.	2 oz. of 50 percent heroin
2 oz.	1 oz.	3 oz. of 33-1/2 percent heroin
3 oz.	1 oz.	4 oz. of 25 percent heroin
4 oz.	1 oz.	5 oz. of 20 percent heroin
5 oz.	1 oz.	6 oz. of 17 percent heroin
6 oz.	1 oz.	7 oz. of 14 percent heroin
7 oz.	1 oz.	8 oz. of 12-1/2 percent heroin
8 oz.	1 oz.	9 oz. of 11 percent heroin
9 oz.	1 oz.	10 oz. of 10 percent heroin
10 oz.	1 oz.	11 oz. of 9 percent heroin
11 oz.	1 oz.	12 oz. of 8-1/3 percent heroin
12 oz.	1 oz.	13 oz. of 7-1/2 percent heroin
13 oz.	1 oz.	14 oz. of 7 percent heroin
14 oz.	1 oz.	15 oz. of 6-2/3 percent heroin
15 oz.	1 oz.	16 oz. of 6-1/4 percent heroin
16 oz.	1 oz.	17 oz. of 5-3/4 percent heroin
17 oz.	1 oz.	18 oz. of 5-1/2 percent heroin
18 oz.	1 oz.	19 oz. of 5-1/4 percent heroin
19 oz.	1 oz.	20 oz. of 5 percent heroin
20 oz.	1 oz.	21 oz. of 4-3/4 percent heroin

This dilution formula could be continued until 64 oz. were created, which would result in 1-1/2 percent heroin.

To cut the heroin, the dealer will measure out the desired amount of heroin, for instance five level teaspoons, and place it in a pile on a flat nonporous surface such as a record album, mirror, or glass plate. He will then measure out the desired amount of lactose and place it in a separate pile on the same surface. Using a playing card, razor blade, knife, or any sharp-edged instrument, the dealer chops the heroin to take out all the lumps and make it a fine powder. The heroin is then sifted through a sifter or nylon stocking producing a fluffy powder and removing foreign material from the substance. Once it has been fluffed, the heroin usually has a little more volume.

The same process of chopping, sifting, and refining is then repeated with the diluting agent. After sifting both the heroin and the diluting agent, the dealer will then mix the two piles. Once the piles are mixed, the diluted heroin is sifted to combine the mixture as equally as possible. At this point, the dealer may resift the diluted heroin several times to assure an equally distributed mixture and to produce a little more volume by increasing its fluffiness. The sifted heroin is then placed in a single pile. Now the dealer is ready to place the heroin into packages for sale.

PACKAGING HEROIN FOR SALE

In larger quantities, heroin is packed in plastic bags or rubber condoms which generally hold from ½ oz to 3 oz. of the drug. On the West Coast of the United States, smaller amounts are packaged in penny balloons and paper bindles. On the East Coast, heroin is packaged in 2 ½ x 2 ½ " glassine envelopes and number 5 gelatine capsules. The dealer will weigh the desired quantity of heroin on a scale or use a measuring spoon. When packaging in balloons, the balloons will be placed at the end of the funnel while the desired amount of heroin is funnelled into the balloon. In the dope business, the amount received is usually less than the amount represented. For example, a "spoon" of heroin represents a level teaspoon of approximately 2 grams. However, most "spoons" have been found to contain from .7 to 1.5 grams. If the dealer is packaging ounces (referred to as "pieces") he will first measure an ounce on a scale, then measure an ounce in teaspoons. One ounce is 14 teaspoons. The dealer will commonly measure out as little as 11 level teaspoons to the "piece," instead of the required 14 teaspoons that equal an ounce. The usual weight of a measured and packaged "piece" is 22-25 grams.

Paper bindles are also used for packaging small amounts of heroin. The paper bindle is simply a square piece of paper—often the glossy paper cut from a magazine. Paper bindles can even be commercially purchased with directions on how to fold them. They have names such as Snow Seals, which are usually purchased to package cocaine. When used for heroin, the size of the paper will depend upon how much heroin is to be sold in the bindle. Once the paper is cut to size, the heroin is placed in the middle of the bindle. The paper will then be folded to make a triangle. The base of the triangle is usually folded once or twice; then the outer wings of the paper are folded inside, and the top of the triangle is folded and tucked into the wings.

Another form of packaging is the penny balloon. The heroin is placed into the bottom of the balloon and the balloon is then knotted or twisted and rolled up to the end. At this point, the end is folded back over to form a ball. Sometimes rubber condoms are then folded over the ball for added protection from breakage. Once the heroin has been packaged in this container, it is ready for sale. The penny balloon is probably the most common form of packaging for street heroin since the heroin is well protected and the dealer or user can carry the balloon in his or her mouth. If the dealer or user is approached by a police officer, he or she can swallow the balloon and retrieve it later.

In many geographical areas of the United States, the larger dealers (distributors) will have several small-time user/dealers working for them. The distributor will often "front" (or furnish on a credit basis) several "bags" (balloons) to each of his or her user/dealers who will sell the bags of heroin to other users and return the money to the distributor to pay for the initially "fronted" drugs. This user/dealer's payment is usually some free heroin from the distributor. For example, a distributor will "front" the user/dealer 30 balloons of streetlevel quality, ready-to-use heroin. The user/dealer will then sell 20 of the balloons and keep 10 for his own personal use and payment. He will then take the proceeds from the 20 balloons back to the distributor and get 30 more balloons. This cycle continues until the distributor develops a trust in the user/dealer. After a trust is devloped, the distributor will "front" the user/dealer several packages of 30 each time.

Another example may be illustrated through the package size of 12 balloons. In this case, the user/dealer sells ten of the balloons and keeps two for himself. The same process of credit and future payment continues as the distributor develops a trust for the user/dealer, resulting in larger and larger loans of "fronted" heroin to be sold on the street. Regardless of their size, these packages are often referred to as "paquettes," a Spanish term translated as "packages." Throughout California, there are a variety of packaging trends which may be unique to certain geographical areas. For example, these packages or packets will vary in size from one community to the next, while the principal relationship between the distributor and the user/dealer remains the same.

REFERENCES:

National Institute on Drug Abuse. "1990 Annual Data from the Drug Abuse Warning Network." Rockville, MD.

Sternlicht, Deborah. "The Prescribing of Darvon." *Street Phamacologist.* Vol. 2, No. 3, June-July 1979, pp. 4-8.

Tenant, Forest, M.D. "Codeine Abuse in California: Aggravation by Well-Meaning Government Regulations." Reported in the *LA Times*, 1980.

U.S. Dept. of Justice. Drug Enforcement Administration. "Drugs of Abuse." *Drug Enforcement.* Vol. 6, No. 2, 1980.

U.S. General Accounting Office. "Methadone Maintenance Report." GAO/T-HRD-90-19, March 23, 1990.

________. "Stir over Darvon." *Time.* Vol. 112, No. 23, December 4, 1978, p. 96.

CHAPTER VIII

HEROIN INFLUENCE

THE LAW AGAINST HEROIN USE

Being under the influence of heroin is a crime in all states of the United States. In California, the law is found in Section 11550 of the Health and Safety Code. Under section (a) it reads:

> No person shall use, or be under the influence of any controlled substance which is (1) specified in subdivision (b) [opiates], (c) [opium derivatives], (e) [depressants], or paragraph (1) of subdivision (f) [cocaine base stimulants] of Section 11054, specified in paragraph (14) [Mescaline], (15) [Peyote], (21) [Phencyclidine], (22) [PHP-PCP Analog], or (23) [TPCP, TCP-PCP analog] of subdivision (d) [hallucinogenics] of Section 11054, specified in subdivision (b) [Raw opium, Morphine, Opium, Codeine, Cocaine] or (c) [Methadone, Fentanyl, etc.] of Section 11055, or specified in paragraph (1) [Amphetamine] or (2) [Methamphetamine] of subdivision (d) or in paragraph (3) [PCP] of subdivision (e) of Section 11055; or (2) a narcotic drug classified in Schedule III, IV, or V, except where administered by or under the direction of a person licensed by the state to dispense, prescribe, or administer controlled substances. It shall be the burden of the defense to show that it comes within the exception. Any person convicted of violating any provision of this subdivision is guilty of a misdemeanor and shall be sentenced to serve a term of not less than 90 days or more than one year in the county jail. The court may place a person convicted under this subdivision on probation for a period not to exceed five years and, except as provided in subdivision (c) [opium derivatives], shall in all cases in which probation is granted require, as a condition thereof, that such person be confined in the county jail for at least 90 days. Other than as provided by subdivision (c), in no event does the court have the power to absolve a person who violates this subdivision from the obligation of spending at least 90 days in confinement in the county jail.[1]

Although the above quoted material is the law against narcotic influence, this section is not to be used for arresting a narcotic addict for addiction. In a 1962 U.S. Supreme Court decision, *Robinson v. California*, 370 *U.S.* 660, the court held that it was unconstitutional and against the 8th Amendment of the U.S. Constitution, cruel and unusual punishment, to arrest a narcotic addict for addiction. Therefore, officers are said to be arresting narcotic users not for addiction but for being under the influence of a narcotic.

Legally, what is the difference between arresting a person for using heroin and arresting a person for being under the influence of heroin? According to jury instructions (Cal JIC 16.060), if a controlled substance is appreciably affecting the nervous system, brain, muscles and other parts of a person's body, or is creating in him or her any perceptible abnormal mental or physical condition, such a person is considered under the influence of a controlled substance. Generally, a person is considered under the influence of heroin when you can identify the physiological symptoms of heroin use:

---

[1]Gould Publications. *California Penal Code.* 1992.

constricted pupils, scratching, dry mouth, dull and indifferent, unsteady, needle marks, clammy skin, etc. You must also prove venue; in other words, the crime must have occurred within the county that brings the case to trial. When you observe the suspect under the influence, a crime is being committed in your presence. The prosecutor will establish jurisdiction by asking you where you observed the defendant under the influence. Almost all 11550 Health and Safety Code arrests are for influence.

It is confusing whether heroin withdrawals constitute heroin use or influence. Below is a diagram of the physiological effects of heroin.

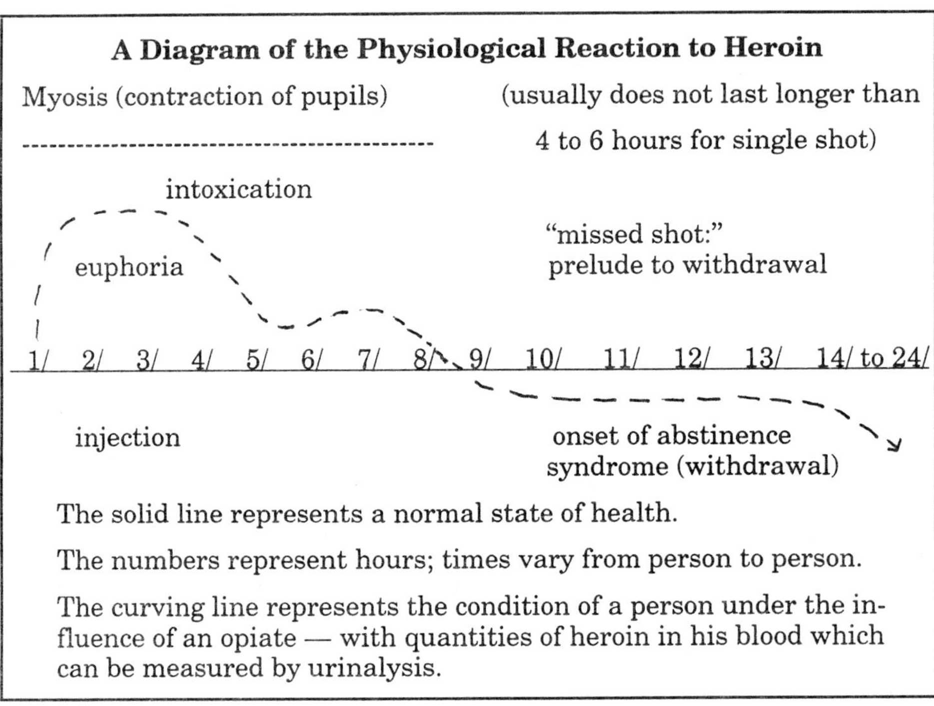
A Diagram of the Physiological Reaction to Heroin
Myosis (contraction of pupils)
(usually does not last longer than 4 to 6 hours for single shot)
intoxication
euphoria
"missed shot:" prelude to withdrawal
1/ 2/ 3/ 4/ 5/ 6/ 7/ 8/ 9/ 10/ 11/ 12/ 13/ 14/ to 24/
injection
onset of abstinence syndrome (withdrawal)
The solid line represents a normal state of health.
The numbers represent hours; times vary from person to person.
The curving line represents the condition of a person under the influence of an opiate — with quantities of heroin in his blood which can be measured by urinalysis.

When does the law recognize that a person uses a controlled substance such as heroin? When a person is observed with fresh needle marks, scar tissue, and admission of use, it is reasonable to conclude that the person committed the crime of heroin use. When a person is charged with use of heroin, venue must be established. There must be evidence of where the suspect used heroin. To establish this, ask the suspect, "where did you have your last fix?" If the suspect refuses to talk, then venue must be proven by a preponderance of the evidence. For example, the apartment manager can state that the suspect lived in the apartment for one year and has seen the suspect daily for two weeks.

We know that heroin influence begins at the point of injection and continues for up to 4 to 6 hours afterwards, or until the user begins to experience the onset of an abstinence syndrome. Is the state of heroin withdrawal considered to be heroin use or influence? It could be successfully prosecuted that withdrawal symptoms fall within the scope of heroin influence. Medically, however, the question could be phrased as follows: is a person under the influence of an opiate while experiencing withdrawal symptoms? Withdrawal is actually the addict feeling the absence of an opiate. Therefore, the absence of the opiate is affecting the addict's body. If the addict had not become addicted to heroin, the withdrawal symptoms would not be present. Therefore, the use of heroin is creating a perceptible mental and physical condition, i.e., runny nose, dilated pupils, vomiting, cramps, fever, etc.

However, in *People v. Gutierrez*, 72 *Cal*.3d 397, Gutierrez was arrested for heroin use while being observed in a state of withdrawal. The court stated that to arrest for use, the crime must be committed in the officer's presence. Since Gutierrez did not inject the opiate in the officer's presence, the arrest was illegal. Another problem in arresting an addict during the withdrawal stage for heroin use is the officer's initial observations of the withdrawal syndrome. Withdrawal from opiates starts out similar to the symptoms of a common cold and progresses (if the tolerance is high enough) to the symptoms of a severe case of influenza or the flu. The point is this, a police officer cannot arrest a citizen for having a cold or the flu.

It has been established that heroin use in Section 11550 of the Health and Safety Code means withdrawals. Most prosecutors will not prosecute a use case only.

However, when a person is arrested for heroin influence, it is suggested that both influence and use be charged. Heroin influence relates to symptoms of heroin use from the moment of injection up to 4 to 6 hours later, (constricted pupils, recent needle puncture wounds, etc.). If the prosecutor charges only influence, then it is possible that only the most recent needle marks can be admitted into evidence, which may be one fresh needle mark you could find. However if use is also charged, then all the marks are evidence that the addict had been using heroin on the other days prior to the time the defendant was observed to be under the influence.

It sounds confusing and juries also get confused with the terms "use of" and "under the influence". If the evidence shows that the defendant is a user of heroin (within several days prior to arrest) and the defendant was under the influence at the time of the arrest, then the defendant should be charged with two counts of Section 11550 of the Health and Safety Code.

Count I: Did willfully and unlawfully use heroin.

Count II: Was willfully and unlawfully under the influence of heroin.

ARRESTS FOR NARCOTIC INFLUENCE

To secure an arrest for narcotic influence, an officer should be able to articulate the facts that justify the contact or detention of an individual, and to investigate the readily observable symptoms which are possible narcotic indicators by doing the following:

establishing reasons for the person's condition which confirm or eliminate the possible use of heroin;

detaining the person for a pupilometer test; if person refuses, conduct the test at the police station.

The officer can form the conclusion that the person is under the influence of heroin (or a narcotic or controlled substance) when his investigation shows that no physical or mental illnesses or other intoxicants are involved. This conclusion is probable cause for an arrest. Once the officer reaches this conclusion, the subject should be admonished before questioning continues.

Viewing areas of the body (e.g., the arms) which are in plain sight does not constitute a search. The officer is permitted to obtain the subject's voluntary consent to view unexposed parts of the body. If the subject refuses consent, the officer may only demand such exposure as incident to an arrest, i.e. as a search for further evidence of the crime. *Provided* that the officer has *first* formed the intention to arrest, the officer may make this demand before informing the person that he or she is under arrest.

Probable Cause

An officer's reasons for contacting, stopping, or investigating a subject must always be stated clearly in the crime report. This contact may be the result of a vehicle stop, non-vehicle contact or residential investigations.

Vehicle Stop

Reasons for a vehicle stop include: moving violations, equipment violation, occupant resembles wanted suspect, near scene of recently reported crime, stolen vehicle.

Non-vehicle Stop

Reason for a non-vehicle stop: received prior information of suspicious person in area, person appears lost or ill, person appears under the influence of something, person resembles wanted suspect, pedestrian vehicle code violation.

Residential Investigations

If you receive information on suspicious circumstances at a residence, 415 P.C.,[2] etc., knock on the door and allow the occupant to open it. You cannot enter the residence without consent unless you see a crime being committed or enter to check on the safety of a victim (if your call was 242 P.C.[3] in progress, shot fired, etc.). If you have probable cause to arrest, make an entry into the residence after knocking, identifying yourself, and stating your purpose.

Contact with a private citizen need not necessarily be based on a suspicion of criminal activity. It may be initiated due to a need for service or aid, such as traffic advice, directions, etc. For example, an officer has encountered a situation which calls for an investigation when he observes a person whose conduct or demeanor gives a reasonable indication that the person is:

sick

in need of help

under the influence of an intoxicant (whether alcohol or a narcotic).

---

[2] 415 P.C. in California means disturbing the peace, domestic disturbance, party, etc.

[3] 242 P.C. in California means assault and battery.

Heroin Influence

It is proper for the officer to contact a person falling into one of these categories.

If, during the contact, the officer develops a reasonable suspicion that the person has committed, is committing, or is about to commit a crime, the officer has the authority to detain (stop) the person long enough to complete his or her investigation. An officer may exercise this authority anywhere the officer has a right to be. Possible violation of Section 11550 of the Health and Safety Code of California is a valid basis for a stop.

When the contact or stop begins under other circumstances (e.g., the issuance of a citation for a motor vehicle violation), if the officer observes narcotic indicators, he or she has probable cause for a self-initiated investigation of the subject's condition.

An officer will also have probable cause to begin an investigation on the basis of information supplied by personal knowledge of the area, knowledge of the suspect, police sources, or informers.

Note that to violate the statute a person must be "under the influence" of a controlled substance or "narcotic drug" on the date (at the time) he or she is charged with the violation.

PRELIMINARY INFLUENCE INDICATORS

There are several preliminary narcotic indicators. A section of the Oakland Police Department Narcotics Influence Report[4] lists some of these narcotic indicators according to major areas of eyes, balance, coordination, skin, mental state, and speed.

The indicators under these headings are not, in and by themselves, conclusive. A combination of several from different categories is necessary before one has a probable indication of the influence of narcotics. A combination is necessary because prolonged addiction produces a tolerance which can cause some indicators to become less visible, such as the disruption of coordination.

---

[4] "11550 H.S. Enforcement Manual, Training Bulletin." Oakland Police Department, California, June 1977.

NARCOTICS INFLUENCE REPORT
Oakland Police Department

DATE	TIME	LOCATION OF ARREST	R.D. NUMBER
DEFENDANT'S NAME		SEX—RACE—D.O.B.	DEFENDANT'S ADDRESS

PART I: PHYSICAL OBSERVATIONS (check as applicable)

EYES (PUPILS)
__ Constricted
__ Dilated
__ Watery
__ Sensitive to Light
__ Reaction Test
____ mm. to ____ mm
Comparision: _____
__ No Reaction Observed
__ Eyelids Droop
__ Squints
__ Glassy Appearance
__ Other: _________

LIGHTING CONDITIONS
__ Daylight
__ Nighttime
__ Artifical Light
__ Other: __________

BALANCE COORDINATION
__ Normal
__ Sways
__ Staggers
__ Unable to Stand
__ Other: _________

SKIN
__ Scabs
__ Cold-Clammy
__ Sweating
__ Other: _________

OTHER
__ Nose - runny, sniffling
__ Yawning
__ Scratching
__ Dry Mouth
__ Drowsy ("On the Nod")
__ Drooling
__ Nauseated
__ No Odor Alcoholic Beverage
__ Other: _________

MENTAL STATE
__ Cooperative
__ Depressed
__ Confused
__ Passive
__ Argumentative
__ Nervous
__ Other: _________

SPEECH
__ Normal
__ Slurred
__ Incoherent
__ Excited
__ Other: ___________

MECHANICAL AIDS USED
__ Flashlight
__ Pupilometer
__ Photos taken by _____
__ Other: ___________

EYES (PUPILS)

Pupil size is extremely important in determining the status of a narcotic user. In the case of a heroin addict, a constricted pupil indicates recent use (within about 4 to 6 hours), while a dilated pupil usually means the addict is entering or is already in active physical withdrawal.

The size of normal pupils changes according to lighting conditions. In a very bright light, the pupils constrict; they become smaller. When the light diminishes, the pupils dilate; they become larger. The size of a normal pupil varies with each person, but the normal range of variation is between 2 and 5 mm. in diameter.

Heroin Influence

Below is a graph showing pupil size of a normal human under very bright and very dark experimental conditions. It can be seen in this graph that the pupil does not go beyond a normal range of 2.9 mm. and 6.5 mm., despite a high range of illumination.

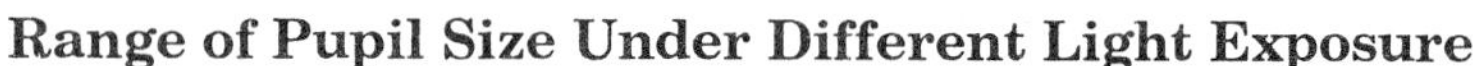

Range of Pupil Size Under Different Light Exposure

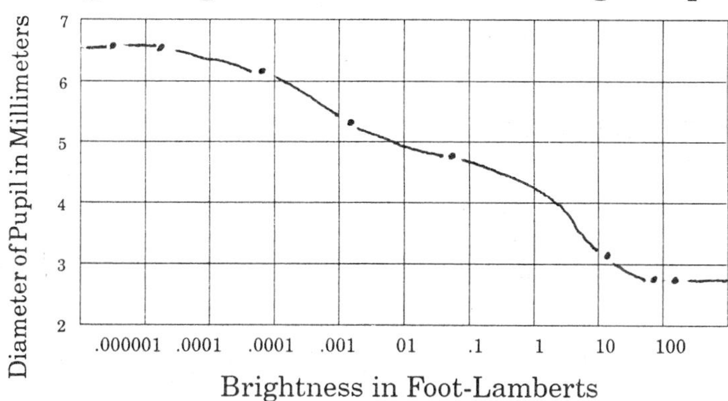

Most narcotic drugs constrict the pupil below the normal range (below 2.9 mm.) for a short period of time.

Although each narcotic has a predictable, consistent effect on pupil size as indicated in the Pupil Size with Use of Some Common Opioids chart on the next page, there are some drug interactions that may alter the expected result.

No matter how long an individual has used an opiate, its influence will always cause the pupils of his or her eyes to constrict. The only exception to this rule is Demerol, which causes the pupils to dilate. Sometimes the pupils of a person "under the influence" will have become so small that they are described as being "pinpointed." This particular term, however, is medically and legally imprecise.

In their constricted state, the user's pupils do not respond normally to changes in light. They do not visibly constrict when a light is focused on them suddenly. (Medical instruments could record changes in the pupils, but these changes are so slight that they are almost undetectable to an unaided observer.) When the pupils of someone not under the influence of an opiate are subjected to the same changes in light, the pupils will show plainly visible changes in size.

In conjunction with any combination of the narcotic indicators discussed previously, constricted pupils furnish reasonable grounds for an arrest of violation of Section 11550 of the Health and Safety Code of California. When the condition of the pupils has been verified by comparison with those of another officer, the subject may be placed under arrest and admonished (see Admonition of Rights below). The officer with whom the subject's eyes have been compared must be identified in the crime report.

PART IV: ADMONITION OF RIGHTS

1. YOU HAVE THE RIGHT TO REMAIN SILENT 2. ANYTHING YOU SAY CAN AND WILL BE USED AGAINST YOU IN A COURT OF LAW	3. YOU HAVE THE RIGHT TO TALK TO A LAWYER AND HAVE HIM PRESENT WITH YOU WHILE YOU ARE BEING QUESTIONED	4. IF YOU CANNOT AFFORD TO HIRE A LAWYER ONE WILL BE APPOINTED TO REPRESENT YOU BEFORE QUESTIONING, IF YOU WISH ONE
THE ABOVE STATEMENT WAS READ TO THE ARRESTEE BY Smith, A.	SERIAL NO. 1001 P	TIME 1930
DO YOUR UNDERSTAND EACH OF THESE RIGHTS I HAVE EXPLAINED TO YOU? Yea, I know them.	HAVING THESE RIGHTS IN MIND, DO YOU WISH TO TALK TO US NOW? (WAIVER STATEMENT) Sure. You got me now.	

PUPIL SIZE WITH USE OF SOME COMMON OPIOIDS[5]

Opioid	Approximate Minimal Dose Required to Produce Constriction Below 3 mm. Diameter	Approximate Length of Time Between Dose and Constriction	Approximate Length of Time Constriction Lasts
Heroin	4-6 mg.	15 minutes	4-6 hours
Morphine	10-20 mg.	15 minutes	4-6 hours
Codeine	200-300 mg.	30-60 minutes	3-4 hours
Propoxyphene	400-600 mg.	1-2 hours	4-6 hours
Methadone	10-20 mg.	1-2 hours	Variable
Meperidine (Demerol) Pentazocine Nalbuphine Butorphanol	May produce no change or even dilation	N/A	N/A

[5] Tennant, Forest S. *Identifying the Heroin User.* Veract, Inc., West Covina, CA, 1985.

CAUSES OF NON-NARCOTIC PUPILLARY CONSTRICTION[6]

CAUSE	WAY TO IDENTIFY CAUSE
Medication for glaucoma	Individual will have doctor's prescription and obtainable medical records.
Tertiary (neuro-) syphilis	Condition is usually permanent and affects only one eye, while narcotics always affect both. Iris around pupil gives "eroded" or "degenerated" appearance. Have subject wait 4 hours to see if dilation occurs. This dilation will occur when heroin influence wears off.
Injury to eye or nerves	Will have past history of injury or disease, usually on one side. Will not dilate even in the darkness. Have subject wait for 4 hours as with syphilis.
Congenital	Condition is permanent and subject will know this. Usually on one side. Will not dilate even in darkness. Have subject wait for 4 hours as with syphilis.
Phencyclidine (PCP)	Will produce constriction in some individuals. Determine PCP presence by urine test.
Age under 18 years or over 65 years	Young and older persons have naturally constricted pupils under 2.9 mm. in diameter.
Excessively high doses of barbiturates and benzodiazepines	These individuals are usually in a coma or so intoxicated they cannot walk.
Hippus	Hippus is an abnormally exaggerated rhythmic contraction and dilation of the pupil. It is occasionally seen when the pupil dilates in narcotic withdrawal. Since Hippus is not a consistent and predictable finding, it does not have many medico-legal implications.

[6] *Ibid.*

MEASUREMENT OF PUPIL SIZE

Although pupil size can be photographed, it can be measured quite accurately with a simple card called a pupilometer. With the card, simply measure the pupil size to determine whether or not it is outside the normal range (2.9 to 6.5 mm.). A pupil size smaller than 2.9 mm. in diameter most likely indicates recent narcotic use. Below are some test procedures for measuring pupil size for medico-legal purposes.

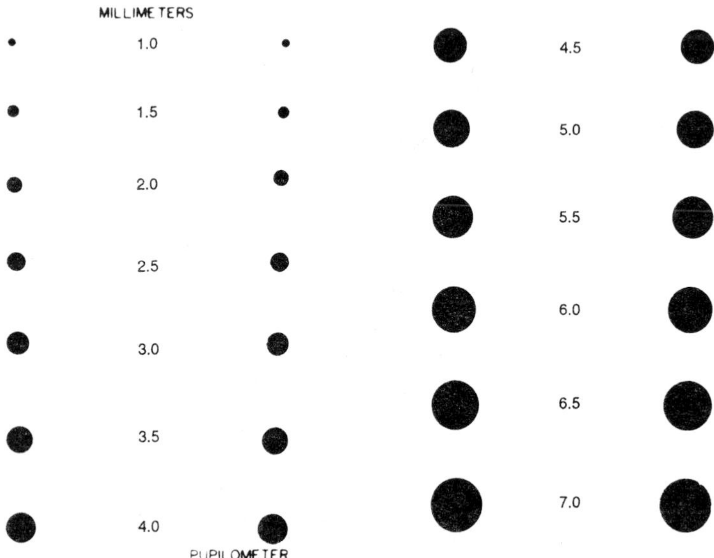

PUPIL TEST PROCEDURES

1. During the day, test the subject away from bright sun. At night test the subject in light. Plain room lighting is best.
2. Measure pupil size by holding a flashlight at a 45 degree angle from the subject's lateral side. Never shine the light directly into the eye from the front, or the pupil will constrict and destroy the measurement.
3. Compare subject's pupil size to a pupilometer. Note sizes in millimeters.
4. Keep flashlight about 1 foot away.
5. Note the reaction or absence of reaction in subject's pupils by "flicking" the light beam on and off the pupil.
6. Repeat above procedures on at least one non-drug-using person in the same light and note results for comparison.
7. Remember that those few persons with a very dark iris surrounding the pupil cannot be adequately measured.

Heroin Influence

After using the pupilometer, you will need to verify your procedures in court. The following is a sample courtroom testimony:

> Defendant and I (officer) then entered a small interview room. I dimmed the lights. After waiting a few minutes I performed a light reflex test on the defendant's eyes by directing a flashlight above the left eye and then above the right eye. I observed the response of his pupils. The pupils of the defendant's eyes remained at approximately 1.5 millimeters in size despite the change in the amount of light to which his eyes were exposed.

PHOTOGRAPHIC DOCUMENTATION OF PUPIL SIZE AND REACTION

There are some legal and clinical occasions when photographic evidence of pupil size and/or reaction may be advantageous. Consult the following key points when using this procedure:

1. A standard camera with a flash is sufficient, since it reacts faster than the pupil can.
2. Take photograph with pupilometer next to the eye for comparison.
3. Make sure room light is satisfactory. Avoid bright light or darkness.
4. To demonstrate non-reactivity by photograph, take a picture in room light. Then place the subject in a very dark room for 5 minutes and repeat the same photograph. A non-reactive pupil will not dilate in darkness. It is advisable to take photographs of a control subject at the same time and in the same light to demonstrate the difference.

SUMMARY

The normal pupil diameter of an adult (age 18-65 years) is considered to be 2.9 to 6.5 mm. Teenagers and persons over age 65 years may naturally have very small pupils under 2.9 mm. in diameter. These statistics proliferate in pertinent scientific literature dating back to 1941.

Pupil size under 2.9 mm. in diameter is one of the most reliable indicators of acute heroin influence.

If a pupil is constricted under 2.9 mm. in diameter, its reactions to light will usually be imperceptible to the common observer.

Even if a pupil is not constricted under 2.9 mm. in diameter with heroin, the pupil may still be non-reactive. In addition, non-reactivity of the pupil lasts slightly longer than constriction.

The pupil usually constricts within 10 to 15 minutes after intravenous heroin use, and it usually remains constricted for 4 to 6 hours. It may remain constricted 8 to 10 hours if a very high heroin dose is used.

For unknown reasons, little tolerance develops to the pupillary effects of heroin. Therefore, pupillary constriction and non-reactivity may be present in a user who shows no other influence signs, such as droopy eyelids, slow speech, or itching.

NEEDLE MARKS

In addition to constricted pupils, some corroborating physical evidence of narcotic use can be found on the arms in the form of needle marks. The needle marks, scar tissue, "tracks," or "tattooing" can usually be found over the veins.

When checking for needle marks, examine the veins of the arms carefully. Feel for scar tissue. Make a close inspection of the scabbed areas if any are present. Press raised areas gently and ask about pain or tenderness. During the investigation, ask the user if he fixes himself and how he feels. Is he going to get sick (withdrawals)? Ask simple questions to make the user feel comfortable during the interview.

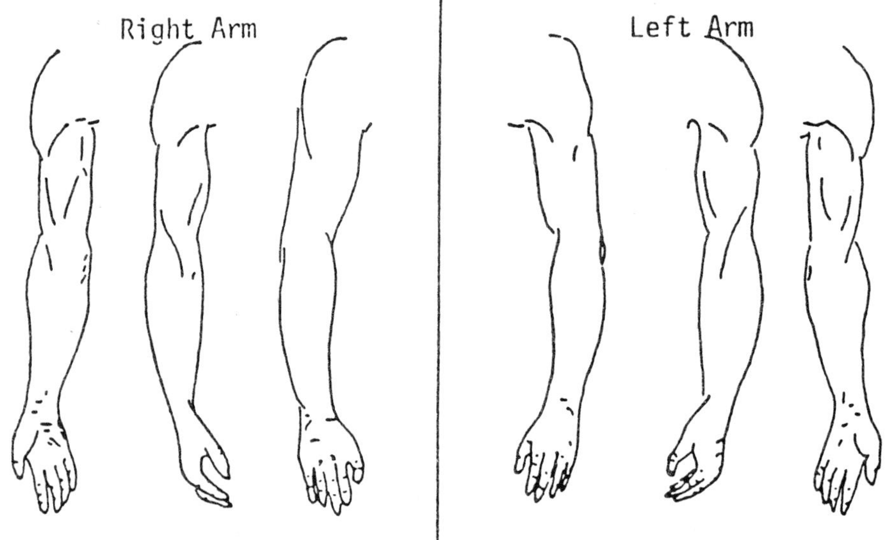

Scar tissue (the "tracks") will form over a vein after a period of repeated injections in the same spot. Some sources estimate that it takes approximately 50 injections to form one inch of permanent scar tissue. Repeated injections into the scar tissue will cause the skin to abscess. The same injections cause hardening (sclerosis) and collapse of the vein.

Old needle marks, scabs, tattooing, bruises and tracks may be signs of addiction, but they do not prove present use. Only indications of a recent injection confirm that the person is "under the influence."

Most addicts inject heroin into the inner folds of the arm and the back of the hand. Veins in places other than the arm are very thin and can seldom be used.

Addicts rarely, if ever, use proper medical procedures to administer drugs intravenously. Most heroin addicts have scabs (crusts of hardened blood and serum), inflammatory tissue, and scar tissue, over their veins from constant injections, many of which are unsterile.

Heroin Influence

Immediately after an addict "fixes" himself, a small pink swelling will occur at the point of injection. This forms a scab which is a distinctive light pinkish-orange in color. The swelling may appear as a tiny hole, and sometimes it will have clotted blood around it. The injection site may bleed, leaving a stain on the user's shirt sleeve. If the site is pressed after a recent injection, it may ooze. A scab can normally form within 24 hours after injection. The approximate age of a scab can be estimated by its color and by the condition of the tissue around it. After three or four days, it becomes predominantly orange. As it grows older, the color darkens. A scab may last as long as 21 days.

If the tissue around a scab swells, the swelling will be pronounced for the first two days after the injection. It will then subside. Since a bruise is essentially bleeding under the skin, a bruise has about the same life span as a scab, which results from bleeding above the skin. A bruise forms within about 24 hours and dissolves by 14 to 21 days.

Blue dots will occasionally be observed over the veins of Caucasian addicts. The dots are caused by attempts to sterilize the injection needle with a burning match. During the injection, carbon from the match flame is deposited under the skin. The resulting blue dots are commonly referred to as "tattooing."

Injection may also cause abscesses, infection of the vein (Thrombophlebitis), or infection of the skin, which is sometimes referred to as blood poisoning or cellulitis.

NEEDLE MARK CLASSIFICATION AND DESCRIPTION[7]

Classification	Approximate Time After Injection	Major Appearance Characteristic	Major Texture of Site
Fresh	0-24 hours	Red dot	Oozing
Early	24-96 hours	Light scab Light bruise Reddened border	Mild elevation
Late	5-14 days Dark bruise	Dark scab ("tracks")	Elevated ridges
Healing	14 days and older	Scar/fiber formation ("silver streaks")	Indentation

Withdrawals (not an indicator for heroin influence)

While questioning the addict, watch for obvious withdrawal symptoms: yawning, sniffling and/or excreting through the nasal passages, perspiration, gooseflesh, chills, restlessness, clearing of the throat and the desire to expectorate. These signs will give the officer an idea of what to expect in the way of marks and an estimate of the daily amount of narcotics being used. Quantity used will vary with the quality currently being sold. These obser-

---

[7] *Ibid.*

vations will assist in overcoming declarations of weekend use, commonly referred to as "only chippying." The term "chippying" has also been used recently to refer to the use of only one or two injections or "hits" a day. Therefore, the original definition of sporadic use with varying intervals between injections cannot always be confirmed.

Withdrawal symptoms (or the abstinence syndrome as it is called in the medical profession) varies in intensity depending on the amount of narcotic used.

At the United States Government Hospital in Lexington Kentucky, doctors Himmelsbach and Small conducted extensive research into opiate addiction and the abstinence syndrome from 1939 to 1943. The withdrawal studies were made under controlled conditions with specific doses at regular periods—circumstances a narcotic officer will not encounter. Himmelsbach and Small described withdrawal symptoms and their severity as follows:

MILD (+)	MODERATE (++)	MARKED (+++)	SEVERE (++++)
Symptoms include:	Additional symptoms:	Additional symptoms:	Additional symptoms
Yawning	Loss of appetite	Deep breathing	Vomiting
Watery eyes	Dilated pupils	Fever	Diarrhea
Runny nose	Tremors	Insomnia	Weight loss
Sneezing	Gooseflesh	Restlessness	
Perspiration		Rise in blood pressure	

Experience and observation will be the only methods the officer has to evaluate the admissions made to him by the user. For example, a user may say he uses a cap a day, but shows mild (+) through severe (++++) symptoms; also, his arms may be decidedly marked. It is then obvious that he is lying. Another user may say he is using a gram a day and exhibits mild (+) symptoms or none at all. The dealer he is buying from is probably adulterating the heroin to the point where the user has what is known as a "mild sugar habit." These are extreme examples, but they are nonetheless true. The officer may not always observe all the symptoms, but only some of those listed in the four categories above. From these symptoms, the officer can make an estimate of the user's habit.

Even though an arrest for heroin influence cannot be based on the presence of withdrawals (since withdrawals indicate use, not influence), it is still very important that, as an officer, you understand the degrees of withdrawal and observe withdrawal symptoms during the interview process for corroborating evidence.

Problems of Recognition

A person under the influence of opiates shows a distinctly different combination of symptoms than a person in some other condition. Some problems of recognizing opiate influence may involve the following:

- long-time addicts
- the symptoms of other drugs

 md

— non-drug abuse situations

Prolonged addiction — The primary difficulty in recognizing a chronic addict lies in the fact that, because the addict has developed an abnormal tolerance for the drug, he or she may not display many of the visible indicators of opiate abuse as clearly as someone who has less tolerance. This principle parallels alcohol tolerance, wherein an alcoholic may show fewer outward signs of intoxication when compared to an equally intoxicated non-alcoholic.

As a consequence, a chronic addict may or may not exhibit the following symptoms:

— reduced coordination

— impaired comprehension

— drowsiness

In such cases of tolerance, the officer must rely on other narcotic indicators, such as the subject's familiarity with the argot of drug abusers, the wearing of warmer clothing than necessary for the weather, prior arrests, etc. It should be emphasized, however, that problems of recognition are limited to the preliminary indicators. Every user of opiates, no matter how tolerant of the drugs, will have constricted pupils.

Summary of Heroin Influence

To validly state that a person is under the influence of heroin, an officer must have physical evidence of heroin activity (such as constricted pupils, non-reactive pupils, or muscle relaxation) and laboratory evidence of heroin activity (evidence of heroin or a heroin derivative such as morphine in the blood or urine).

More than one item of evidence must be found in order to make the diagnosis of heroin influence.

If an officer observes a constricted pupil below 2.9 mm., he or she has probable cause to arrest the suspect for violation of Section 11550 of the Health and Safety Code of California. If, after a blood or urine analysis, a heroin derivative (morphine) is detected, the individual is definitely under the influence of heroin.

In another situation the pupil may be under 4.0 mm. and be non-reactive. In this case, photograph the pupils in lighted and darkened conditions; also photograph a control subject under the same conditions with the same camera. Find fresh needle marks or heroin present in the nasal passage. Find heroin or a derivative in the urine. Meeting these conditions, the person is under the influence of heroin.

In a third situation, you may find a suspect who exhibits muscle relaxation including one or more of the following symptoms: droopy eyelids, slurred or slow speech, abnormal gait, nodding. You find fresh needle marks and the person is negative on alcohol breath, blood or urine; yet, a heroin derivative is found in the urine. In this case, the person is under the influence of heroin.

Summary of Narcotic Indicators

Narcotic indicators are signs and symptoms of opiate use that you can observe with your eyes. It should be reminded that no narcotic indicator alone is conclusive; a combination of indicators is required for probable cause to arrest. Below is a list of narcotic indicators that might be observed by an officer while performing law enforcement duties:

1. Poor coordination
   a. A user under the influence may exhibit poor physical coordination and poor balance (stumbling).
   b. Chronic users become tolerant to this effect unless they use enough of the drug to exceed their tolerance level.
2. Drowsiness or sleepiness ("on the nod")
   a. A tendency to sit looking off into space (known to addicts as "goofing") may indicate the use of heroin, barbiturates, or both. Head may bob back and forth.
   b. Slow, shallow breathing, a dry mouth, slow reflexes, and a general retardation of physical activity.
3. Appearance and clothing
   a. Excessively warm clothing on a warm day (to counteract hypothermia, the lowered temperature of the skin caused by opiates). On a hot day may be carrying a jacket. Unkempt appearance.
4. Malnutrition
   a. More interested in feeding the heroin habit than in feeding the body necessary nutrients.
   b. Thin, frail, or run-down bodily appearance.
5. Pupils of the eyes
   a. Sun glasses to conceal myosis (constricted pupils). (This phenomenon is encountered less frequently now than in the past.)
   b. Droopy eyelids from sedation.
6. Flushed complexion (caused by dilation of the facial blood vessels after an injection)
   a. A tendency to scratch facial areas, particularly the nose, may indicate a slight overdose or an allergic response to the drug.
   b. Scratching other areas of the body, particularly the sites of injection (scratching of the arms.)
   c. Sweating due to relaxation of the blood vessels.

Heroin Influence

7. Excessive desire for sugar

    a. The mild sugar diluent in heroin causes hyperglycemia (excess sugar in the blood stream), and an addict becomes habituated to this condition; hence, the "milk sugar habit."

8. Impaired comprehension

    a. The subject's mind may function rationally but very slowly; subject may become easily confused during a conversation carried on at a normal speed.

    b. Some addicts become very talkative when under the influence.

    c. Inhibited speech that is slow and deliberate but understandable.

9. Use of the characteristic vocabulary of heroin addicts

10. Needle marks and tracks on the arms, hands and other areas where veins can be reached by a person who injects himself

    a. Long sleeve shirts (to hide needle marks)

    b. Blood stains on clothing near or at the site of an injection.

11. The subject's own statement that he is an addict or is under the influence of a drug

12. Possession of prescription drugs without adequate medical explanation

13. Possession of paraphernalia associated with the sale or use of drugs

    a. An "outfit" including a spoon, a hypodermic syringe (pharmaceutical or homemade), a needle, a tourniquet, matches and other miscellaneous items.

    b. The spoon will have a characteristically bent handle, and may be blackened from being held over lighted matches.

    c. A belt used as a "tie rag" (tourniquet) will have teeth marks at one end. Other tie rags include rubber tubing, neckties, and ripped t-shirts.

14. Withdrawal symptoms (see text). No known deaths have been recorded due to withdrawal symptoms.

15. Overdose symptoms (see text).

WHAT IS HEROIN?

Heroin is chemically known as diacetylmorphine; it is made by the chemical conversion of morphine which has been synthesized from opium.

Heroin is classified as an "opioid." This term is now preferred over "narcotic" since it is more descriptive in that "narcosis" refers to sleep and sedation which is produced by many drugs rather then specifically relating to the unique characteristics of an opioid.

An opioid is any drug that:

1. Will relieve pain.

2. Will produce withdrawal symptoms when the drug is withheld after chronic administration.
3. Will suppress withdrawal symptoms which occur as a result of withholding chronic opioid administration.

Opioids come from three sources:

1. Opium poppy plant, e.g., heroin
2. Synthetic manufacturer, e.g., propoxyphene
3. Nervous tissue in human body, i.e., endorphin

HOW IS HEROIN USED?

Proper identification of heroin use can only be made by understanding its various use patterns.

Heroin is most frequently used intravenously, but it can be smoked, sniffed, taken orally, or by rectal suppository.

Most single doses of street heroin contain about 4 to 8 mg. For example, a 2 percent street sample that weighs 250 mg. or ¼ gm. contains 5 mg. of heroin, as does a 1 percent sample which weighs 500 mg. or ½ gm.

Most persons dependent upon heroin begin to use it in their late teenage years after they have experiences with nicotine, alcohol, caffeine, marijuana, and one or more other illicit drugs such as PCP, cocaine, and/or amphetamines.

A few heroin users may begin to use in late adolescence or in adulthood and may not have extensive experience with other abusable drugs.

Once addicted to intravenous heroin, approximately 70 to 80 percent of addicts continue intermittent use for many years, or for life.

Addiction periods or "runs" usually last 4-6 months, and the cessation of a "run" is often brought about by arrest or entry into treatment. Periods of abstinence usually last no more than a few weeks or months, and relapse is usually precipitated by physical or mental stress.

HOW DOES HEROIN WORK?

Heroin is converted to morphine within about 2 to 3 minutes after it is injected into the blood stream.

Before total conversion to morphine, heroin enters the brain and helps produce a brief yet intense euphoria called a "rush."

Heroin and morphine attach to small areas in the brain known as receptor sites. Upon drug use, these sites are triggered to help produce the following signs and symptoms, defined as "being under the influence":

— Constricted pupils (less than 2.9 mm. diameter)

— Non-reactive pupils

— Muscle relaxation (e.g., droopy eyelids, slurred speech, slow gait, sleepy appearance, etc.)

— Decrease in pulse, reflexes, blood pressure, and respiration rate.

Heroin Influence

In addition to the "under-the-influence" signs listed above, the user may experience pain relief, euphoria, and psychic stimulation.

HEROIN METABOLISM

Ever since the increased use of heroin, research has identified how the human body accepts, deactivates, and eliminates the drug. The process of acceptance, deactivation, and elimination is usually called "metabolism" or "pharmacokinetics."

SCHEMATIC DIAGRAM OF HEROIN METABOLISM

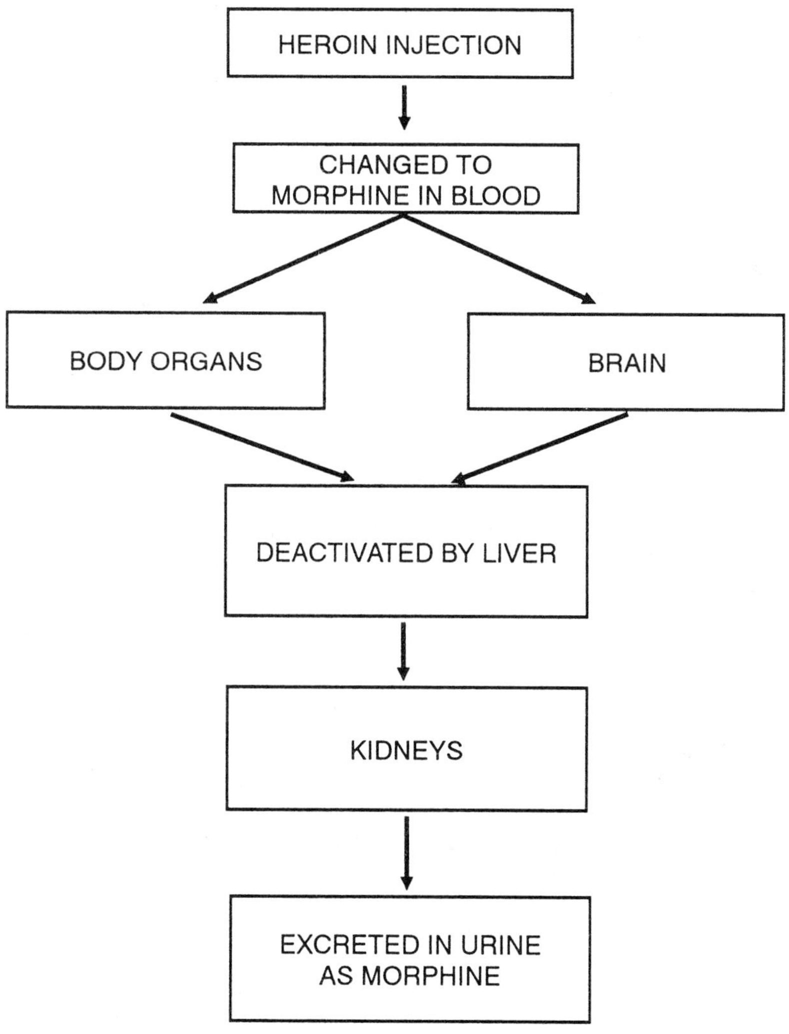

It takes approximately 1 to 2 hours for heroin-morphine to reach the urine after heroin is injected. Yet, after a single injection of heroin, morphine can be found in the urine for 48 to 72 hours.

After heroin reaches the blood stream through intravenous, oral, anal, nasal, or respiratory routes, most of the drug is transformed to morphine within 2 to 3 minutes. After 4 to 6 hours the liver deactivates most of the heroin-morphine; it is then eliminated primarily through the bile and urine.

Although a small amount of codeine will often be found in urine specimens from heroin addicts, it is due to codeine mixed into street heroin; it is not caused by metabolism.

TOLERANCE, PHYSICAL DEPENDENCE AND WITHDRAWAL

The chronic administration of a therapeutic dose of heroin over a period of a few weeks will reduce the respiratory depressant, analgesic, sedative and euphoric effects initially introduced by the drug. Larger doses will become necessary to produce the same effects elicited by earlier use of the drug. At this point, the user is said to have become tolerant. The rate at which tolerance develops is a result of the size of the heroin dose and the frequency of administration. Development of tolerance may considerably elevate the dosage which is lethal to the individual; yet, death by respiratory depression can occur even in the chronic user. Tolerance does not, however, alter all the effects of heroin; highly tolerant persons will continue to have constricted pupils and constipation. After complete withdrawal of the drug, tolerance will disappear. Thus, after weeks or months of total abstinence, a previously dependent user's "regular" dose may be fatal.

Physical dependence may be defined as a condition that requires the regular administration of heroin, at higher than therapeutic doses, to prevent the appearance of withdrawal syndrome. Even regular administrations of heroin at therapeutic doses for one or two weeks precipitate mild withdrawal symptoms when they are discontinued. If the usual dose of heroin is withheld from a physically dependent person, a predictable sequence of responses will usually occur, many of which are opposite to the effects produced by the drug. The severity of these withdrawal responses will depend upon the degree of tolerance, the duration of chronic administration, and the usual dose of the drug. About 8 to 12 hours after the last dose, lacrimation, rhinorrhea (runny nose), yawning, and perspiration will appear. About 12 to 14 hours afterward, the individual may fall into a tossing, restless sleep which may last for several hours. Upon awakening, she/he is more restless and miserable. As the syndrome progresses, the following additional signs appear: dilated pupils, anorexia (no appetite for food), gooseflesh, restlessness, irritability, and tremors. These responses usually reach their intensity as the individual shows increasing irritability, marked anorexia, incessant yawning, severe sneezing, lacrimation, and stuffy nose. Nausea, vomiting, intestinal spasms, and diarrhea are signs of prolonged withdrawal. At this point, the individual's heart rate and blood pressure are elevated, and he or she may feel chills, alternating with periods of flushing and excessive sweating. Other symptoms of prolonged withdrawal include abdominal cramps, pains in the bones and muscles of the back and extremities, muscle spasms, and kicking movements.

Heroin Influence

Without treatment or drug use, the symptoms usually subside in 72 hours. Restoring physiological equilibrium takes considerably longer. Over a protracted period of abstinence, more subtle behavioral manifestations will appear, including: failure to tolerate stress, nearly paranoid concern over discomfort, and poor self-image. Following withdrawal, these factors contribute significantly to the tendency of the compulsive user to relapse.

From a medico-legal viewpoint, it is generally incorrect to describe an individual as being "under-the-influence," since withdrawal does not occur until there is essentially no narcotic left in the blood stream. Remember that all narcotics develop physical dependency or withdrawals.

MINIMAL TIME AND DOSAGE REQUIREMENTS FOR DEPENDENCE UPON SOME OPIOIDS[8]

Drug	Usual Dose	Approximate Daily Dose Required to Produce Dependency	Minimal Length of Time Required to Produce Dependency
HEROIN	4-8 mg.	20-25 mg.	1-2 Weeks
MORPHINE	8-20 mg.	50-100 mg.	1-2 Weeks
CODEINE	30-60 mg.	1200-1800 mg.	1-3 Weeks
PROPOXYPHENE	65-130 mg.	800-1000 mg.	2-3 Weeks
MEPERIDINE	50-1000 mg.	Over 1000 mg.	2-3 Weeks
METHADONE	5-10 mg.	20-40 mg.	1-2 Weeks

Note: Lower dosages given over a longer period of time may also produce dependence. Furthermore, intravenous administration will produce tolerance and dependence faster than will oral administration.

WITHDRAWAL SYMPTOMS AND SIGNS FROM HEROIN ADDICTION[9]

Symptoms: Feelings experienced by the addict 4 to 6 hours after last use:

- Insomnia
- Aching muscles (mylagia)
- Nausea
- Chills
- Aching joints (arthragia)

Symptoms perceptible to an observer 8 to 12 hours after last use:

Sweating (diaphoresis)	Usually first sign to appear
Gooseflesh (piloerection)	Usually second sign to appear
Hyperactive reflexes	Usually third sign to appear
Yawning	Only occurs after prolonged withdrawal
Tearing (lacrimation)	Only occurs after prolonged withdrawal

[8] *Ibid.*
[9] *Ibid.*

Runny nose (rhinorrhea)	Only occurs after prolonged withdrawal
Vomitting	Only occurs after prolonged withdrawal
Diarrhea	Only occurs after prolonged withdrawal
Pupil dilates above 6.5 mm.	Only occurs after prolonged withdrawal

Other Physiological Symptoms

Often after the addict has injected the opiate, there is a tendency to itch the skin, particularly around the face. The addict's mouth will be dry, his face will be flushed and his skin temperature lowered. In addition to a flushing of the skin, opiates often cause sweating due to the relaxation of the blood vessels. Since the continual use of opiates cause a general dehydration of fluids, the skin of the addicted person will become dry, the fingernails pale or brittle, and the lips dry. The opiates have a direct effect on the gastrointestinal tract causing constipation. This is one reason why opiates are very common for the relief of diarrhea. Opiates also tend to diminish sexual desire.

Due to the fact that opiates generally depress the central nervous system, the addict's movements, pulse, breathing, and heartbeat will be slower than normal.

Distinguishing Between New Users and Chronic Users

Not all addicts are the same. There are differences in the observable and unobservable effects of the intravenous use of heroin.

OBSERVABLE EFFECTS OF INTRAVENOUS HEROIN ON NEW USERS AND CHRONIC USERS[10]

New User	Approx. Time After Last Injection	Chronic User	Approx. Time After Last Injection
Sedation "nodding"	.25-4 hours	Little or no sedation	.25-4 hours
Poor motor coordination (slurred speech)	.25-4 hours	Little or no motor loss (slurred speech)	.25-4 hours
Pupillary Constriction	.5-6 hours	Pupillary Constriction	.5-6 hours
Depressed Reflexes	.5-4 hours	Depressed Reflexes	.5-4 hours
Scratching	.25-6 hours	Scratching	.25-6 hours
Vomiting	.25-2 hours		
Relaxation	.25-12 hours	Relaxation	.25-6 hours
Decreased Respiratory Rate	.5-4 hours	Decreased Respiratory Rate	.5-4 hours

[10] *Ibid.*

Heroin Influence

No Withdrawal Signs		Withdrawal Signs: runny nose, gooseflesh, dilated pupil	8-72 hours
"Rush"	30 seconds - 5 minutes	"Rush"	30 seconds - 5 minutes (Depending on amount used over tolerance)
Euphoria & Psychic Stimulation	.25-6 hours	Little Euphoria & Psychic Stimulation	.25-6 hours
Pain Relief	.25-6 hours	Little Pain Relief	.25-6 hours
Constipation	—	Constipation	Constant
Suppressed Cough	.25-6 hours	Suppressed Cough	.25-6 hours
Morphine in Blood	.25-12 hours	Morphine in Blood	.25-12 hours
Morphine in Urine	2-4 hours	Morphine in Urine	2-24 hours

How Much Heroin Does An Addict Use?

An addict will use several balloons or bindles a day to support his habit. A balloon of heroin contains about a ½ gram, enough heroin for one or two injections, depending upon the extent of the user's habit. A ½ gram equals 500 mg. of total weight. If there is 1 percent heroin in the ½ gram, then there is actually 5 mg. of heroin in the ½ gram or ¼ spoon.

Heroin Paraphernalia

Heroin can be taken orally (although it is not very effective), snorted in the nose, or injected. The most common method of using heroin is injecting it into the veins. Paraphernalia for injecting heroin is variously called an "outfit," "kit," "rig," or the "works," and includes a spoon or bottle cap, syringe, needle, needle sheath, cotton, tourniquet and matches.

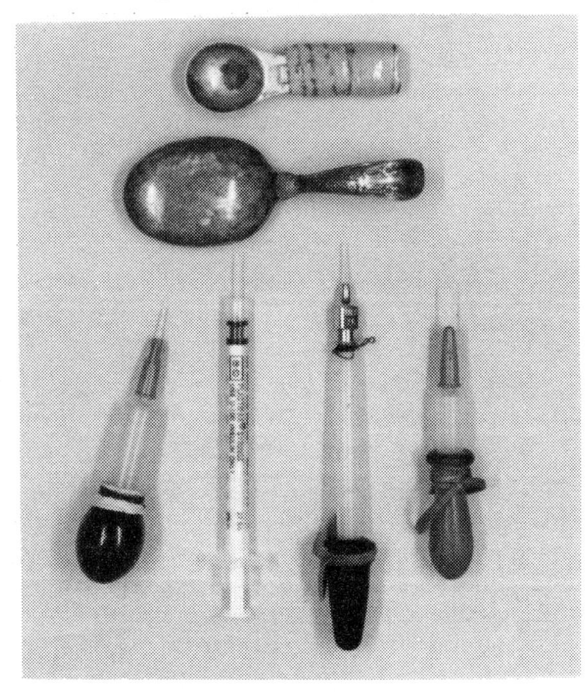

A Spoon - The heroin addict will take a teaspoon, tablespoon, measuring spoon or the metal top of a bottle and use any one of

 md

these items to hold the heroin solution. The spoon will typically be burnt on the bottom from heating the solution and crimped up in the center to make the spoon more stable, thereby decreasing the chances of spilling the heroin. Sometimes the spoon handle will be bent back in a U-shape, leaving the bowl off the surface so the solution can be heated without the addict holding it. Depending on the cleanliness of the addict, some heroin residue or a dirty piece of cotton may remain inside the spoon.

Hypodermic Syringe - The syringe may be a medical type syringe, such as one used to inject insulin, with a plunger or an eyedropper with the rubber suction bulb. However, the medical type syringes were at one time unpopular, especially if the addict injects himself, since depressing and releasing the plunger with one hand is cumbersome.

Therefore, addicts will often obtain a professional syringe, take out the plunger and cut the syringe smaller. For an air source, the addict will use a plastic grape or a baby pacifier and this "home made" outfit enables the addict to "work" or "play" with the bulb while injecting heroin.

In many states, the law requiring syringes to be obtained through a doctor's prescription has been changed, enabling a person to purchase the insulin-type disposable syringes over the counter. Under the new law, addicts no longer had to use the same precious but dirty, misused needle and syringe that they had shared with other addicts. They could now use a new, sharp and sterile needle and syringe each time they injected—if they chose to do so. Clean and sterile needles decrease the incidents of infection, diseases such as hepatitis, AIDS, and a host of other problems. With clean needles, the injection sites also heal more quickly, thereby reducing the chances of having the "marks" of telltale heroin use.

Addicts enjoy not only the effects from the heroin after it is injected, but also the foreplay which precedes the actual injection. They derive much pleasure from watching the needle penetrate the vein while holding the bulb of the syringe between the thumb and fingers. When the needle "registers" (the blood enters the syringe indicating that the needle has entered the vein) the addict can manipulate the bulb with one available hand. The addict will often manipulate or "play" with the bulb, squeezing and then backing off, to allow his blood and the heroin to intermix. Many addicts refer to this foreplay as "jacking off." This particular part of the ritual could not be accomplished with the medical type (plunger) syringe. In most cases, the addict will use the syringe over and over again until the needle bends or until the syringe becomes inoperative. Other addicts, however, have opted to purchase or obtain the insulin-type syringes and will use them.

Hypodermic Needle - The needle is usually a #25 or #26 pharmaceutical needle, the preferred size and opening for injecting heroin. The higher the number, the smaller the needle.

Needle Sheath or Cover - The needle sheath usually comes with a hypodermic needle and is a plastic covering used to protect the needle. If a needle sheath is not available, the addict will often use the back part of a matchbook cover by rolling it up, tying it with a rubber band, and placing the needle directly inside. Sometimes the plastic needle sheath is used to stir the heroin while it is being dissolved in water.

Heroin Influence

Cotton - Common cotton is formed into a ball and used as a filter between the needle and the heroin solution when the heroin solution is drawn into the syringe. The cotton balls are often saved so that when the addict is desperate, he can dissolve them in water and remove any residual heroin they contain.

Tourniquet - The tourniquet or "tie rag" may be a piece of rubber tubing, a necktie, a belt, a piece of cloth, a nylon stocking, or any strong, soft elongated material. The tourniquet stops the flow of blood and forces the vein to the surface, making it easier for the addict to locate the vein for injection.

A Book of Matches - the addict uses any kind of heating device, usually matches, to heat the heroin in water.

Injection paraphernalia sometimes include miscellaneous items such as a small container for water, tissue paper or cloth to wipe blood, and a special container for the outfit.

Injecting Heroin

Once the addict is in possession of the injection paraphernalia and the heroin (which is most commonly packaged in toy balloons), he is ready to "fix" himself (inject the heroin into his veins).

The proper amount of heroin will be taken out of the balloon and put in the empty spoon. The amount will depend on the addict's habit, the purity of the heroin, and how much heroin the addict could get. The addict will put water in the syringe and then put the water from the syringe into the spoon containing the heroin. The mixture is then heated with matches (four or five matches) until the first bubble rises to the surface of the solution and the powder dissolves. Below is an illustration of cooking up heroin.

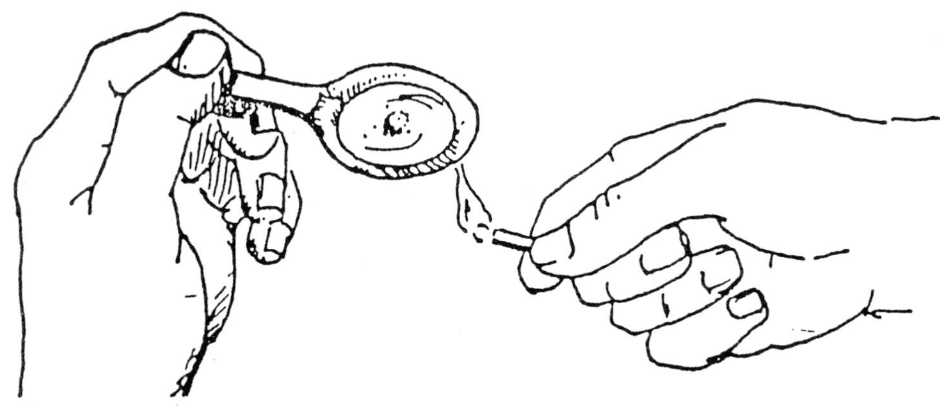

 md

Before drawing the solution into a syringe, a small amount of cotton is placed in the bowl of the spoon to prevent clogging of the needle. The syringe or eyedropper with its hypodermic needle attached is then stuck into the cotton, and the solution is drawn into the syringe or tube of the eyedropper through the cotton.

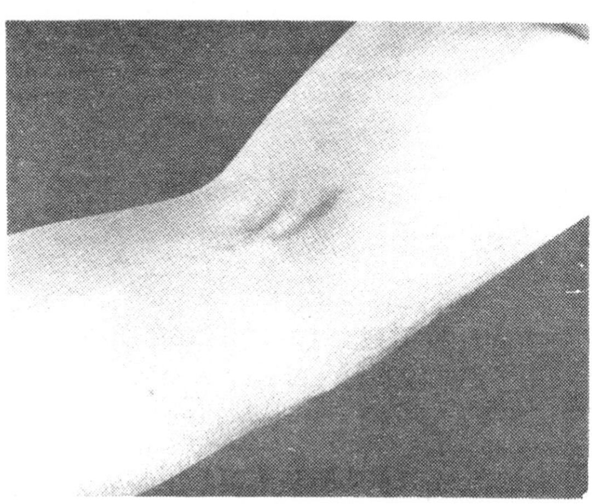

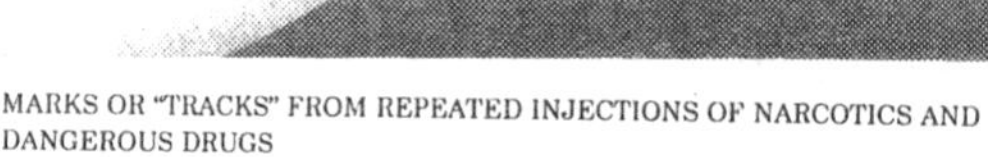

MARKS OR "TRACKS" FROM REPEATED INJECTIONS OF NARCOTICS AND DANGEROUS DRUGS

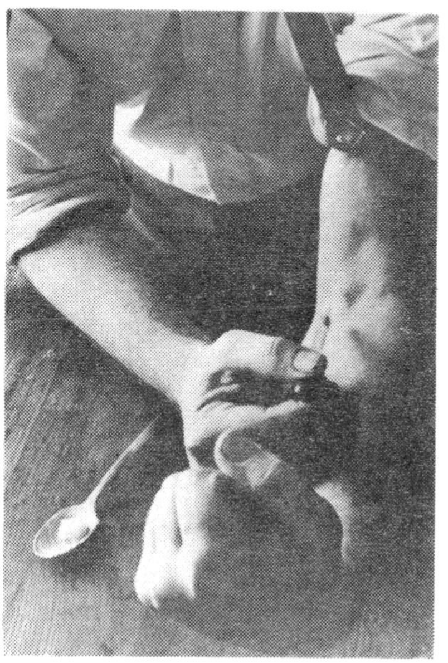

Most addicts inject the heroin into the inner elbow area. The injection is made easier by tying a rag, belt, or rope around the arm above the elbow, which causes the veins to swell and stand out. The needle is then placed on top of a vein and the puncture is made. When blood appears in the eyedropper or syringe, the addict knows that the needle is inside the vein.

Some addicts will "clean" their "works" by running water back and forth through the syringe a number of times. Other addicts will just put the outfit away dirty.

Psychological Effects Of Heroin

Immediately after injecting the heroin, the addict describes a feeling of intense pleasure or euphoric feeling sometimes described as a sexual climax lasting several minutes and centered in the abdomen. The intensity of this euphoria depends on a number of things including the addict's habit, the amount of tolerance developed, the normal amount and purity of the heroin injected, and the user's psychological state of mind. An addict who is heavily addicted and beginning withdrawal symptoms may only experience a slight euphoric effect after injection. In this case, the injection only negates the sickness, allowing the addict to feel normal. He will normally feel relief from pain and a mental sluggishness or drowsiness (a dream-like state) often called "on the nod." Psychologically, he may feel relief from problems and responsibilities. The feeling of ease and a floating sensation are common. Some heroin addicts become very talkative after fixing. Generally, both male and female addicts have a reduced sexual desire after using opiates.

Heroin Influence

The central nervous system and analgesic effects of heroin (diacetylmorphine) depend upon the conversion of heroin to morphine in the body. This conversion occurs rapidly in a two-step process: the first stage produces 6-monoacetylmorphine; the second produces morphine. A study of the metabolism of intravenously-administered heroin showed that significant quantities of morphine were excreted in the urine within two hours of administration.[11] Thus, when considering the pharmacological activities of injected heroin, it is actually morphine which is studied. Morphine is the point of reference for all narcotic analgesics, including heroin; extensive use and study of morphine over many years has made it a standard of comparison.

Intramuscular administration of the therapeutic dose (10-20 mg.) of morphine (equivalent to 5-10 mg. of heroin) in a "normal" adult (weight approximately 150 lbs.) will cause a range of effects from drowsiness and euphoria to anxiety and nausea. One of the most significant effects produced by heroin and morphine is depression of the respiratory center. The degree of depression is usually dose-dependent, particularly in the non-tolerant (non-dependent) individual; although in hypersensitive individuals, a drastic depression may result, regardless of dosage.

Another effect which appears after administration of morphine or heroin is constricted pupils. Despite tolerance to other effects, chronic users do not develop tolerance to the pupillary constricting action of the drug. Opiates also have a marked constipating effect. While morphine tends to increase the tone of intestinal smooth muscle, it decreases propulsive movement and thereby delays gastric emptying. Morphine also effects the smooth muscle of the urinary tract and tends to contract the ureter and the detrusor muscle of the bladder. Due to difficult urination, urinary retention results, which then depresses the response to the stimulus of a full bladder.

Heroin High

The small amount of heroin that goes to the brain is probably what produces the heroin high. The high or euphoria can last for 30 seconds to 5 minutes. It seems that addicts become tolerant to this euphoria and eventually inject heroin only to prevent withdrawals (getting sick) with very little high or euphoria from the drug.

---

[11] Yeh, S.Y., and R.L. McQuinn. "GLC Determinations of Heroin and its Metabolites in Human Urine." *Journal of Pharmacology Science.* 64:1237-1239, 1975.

VISIBLE EFFECTS OF ACUTE HEROIN INFLUENCE

Basic Physiologic Effect	Signs / Symptoms
Autonomic nervous system suppression	Decrease in pulse, respiration, reflexes, blood pressure, body temperature
Muscle relaxation in:	
Neck	"Nodding"
Eyelids	Droopy
Face / mouth	Licking of lips, Sleepy appearance Drooling
Larynx	Slurred or slow speech
Extremities	Slow gait
Release of histamine	Itching
Stimulation of eye center in brain	Constricted pupils, Non-reactive pupils

The acute physiologic effects of heroin usually begin within 15 minutes after heroin is injected, and they usually last about 4-6 hours with a normal dosage. If dosages of 8 mg. or more are used, effects may be slightly longer than 6 hours. Persons who are tolerant to heroin may show few, if any, physiologic effects, with the exception of the eye signs.

NON-VISIBLE EFFECTS OF ACUTE HEROIN INFLUENCE

Heroin has many effects that are not visible to an observer.

Acute or Immediate Effects

- Euphoria
- Psychic stimulation
- Nausea
- Pain relief
- Emotional stabilization
- Cough suppression
- Bowel and bladder suppression

If heroin is taken chronically and the user becomes tolerant, most of the above effects disappear, although emotional stabilization may persist. Constipation may also develop and be persistent.

CRITERIA FOR PHYSICAL EVIDENCE OF ACUTE HEROIN INFLUENCE[12]

PUPIL SIZE:	Under 2.9 mm. in. diameter *(normal adult is 2.9 to 6.5)*
PULSE:	Under 60 beats per minute *(normal is 72/min.)*
BLOOD PRESSURE:	Systolic under 100 mm. Hg. *(normal is 80 mm. Hg.)*
	Diastolic under 60 mm. Hg. *(normal is 80 mm. Hg.)*
RESPIRATORY RATE:	Under 12 respirations per minute *(normal is 20/min.)*
TEMPERATURE:	Under 97° F *(normal is 98.6° F)*

Body Fluids

A urine or blood test will detect the presence of narcotics. Heroin, codeine, methadone, Darvon, and Demerol can be readily tested in the urine of most toxicologic laboratories. It takes two hours from the time of the injection for the morphine to be found in the urine. Ninety percent of the morphine is gone from the urine within 24 hours and 98 percent is gone within 48 hours. Be sure to obtain at least 10cc. of urine. The white powder in the urine bottle is boric acid, which acts as a preservative. The lab will tell you if the urine is positive or negative for morphine (heroin) but will not identify the percentage of the drug.

A person charged with being under the influence of a narcotic may request a urine test (which will be given at the jail). The reporting officer should offer the subject an opportunity to request the test and record his decision on the report form in the space provided (see figure below).

PART VI: CHEMICAL TEST

Statement to Defendant: You may take a chemical test to determine the presence or absence of a narcotic in your body. If you wish to take a chemical test, it will be provided at the Jail upon your request.

I ☐ *request* / ☒ *refuse* *to take a chemical test.*

John Doe
SIGNATURE OF DEFENDANT

REPORTING OFFICER	SERIAL NO.	NO. SECOND OFFICER	WITNESS
A. Smith	1001 P	1002 P	9001 T

TF-680

[12] Tennant, Forest S. *Identifying the Heroin User.* Veract, Inc., West Covina, CA, 1985.

The officer should urge the person to sign the form, whether he requests or refuses the test because it is not unusual for the defendant to take the stand and deny having had the opportunity. Be sure to explain the purpose of the test in that it will prove or disprove the presence of opiates. Also, point out that a refusal can be used against him and may show consciousness of guilt. Occasionally, a lab report will indicate negative urinalysis. There are several reasons for this. It is possible that the individual was under the influence of something else. A negative urine might mean that the suspect had taken only a small amount of heroin 24 hours prior to giving the sample. Also, quality and accuracy of the lab may be questionable.

Frequently, you will find a person who appears to be under the influence of something but you cannot identify the substance. In this case, bear in mind that many drug users are "poly-drug users." It is not unusual for users to mix or combine different drugs.

If you have arrested a person who is in such a condition that he is unable to care for himself but you suspect possible heroin and/or other drug use, you should request both a urine and a blood test. The medical technician should draw at least two vials of blood. Have the suspect take an intoxilyzer test to eliminate alcohol as the cause of the condition. There are also tests available to detect marijuana in the body.

Body Fluids Required for Testing Narcotic and Drug Cases

Due to the confusion among police personnel over the type of body fluids (blood or urine) to be obtained from drug suspects, drug analysis laboratories have made the following recommendations:

BEST DRUG TEST

Drug	Blood Test	Urine Test
Amphetamines		Yes
Heroin		Yes
Cocaine		Yes
Codeine		Yes
Chlorpromazine (Thorazine)		Yes
Meperidine (Demerol)		Yes
Phencyclidine (PCP)		Yes
Barbiturates	Yes	
Chlordiazepoxide (Librium)		Yes
Diazepam (Valium)	Yes	
LSD	Yes	
Marijuana	Yes	

The Best Test List reflects the substances that most labs are able to detect in a sample of either urine or blood. However, some labs can find LSD in the blood and urine and marijuana in the urine. Also, some narcotics can be detected in the blood.

Heroin Influence

If you have a clear narcotic influence case, only a urine sample is necessary. However, if you are unsure, it is advisable to take both blood and urine samples from the suspect(s), since many drugs on the market are a combination of amphetamines, barbiturates, or tranquilizers, and users often take these substances in conjunction with one another.

Quantity of Blood or Urine Sample

Blood - Volume is handled by the technician (usually 2 vials)

Urine - As much as possible. The minimum: 1½ ounces

a. Drugs - Just take the first urine sample for evidence

b. Alcohol - Take a sample of the latest bladder void for evidence, but wait at least 20 minutes and take a second sample. Keep both samples for your lab sample.

If the suspect requires a blood sample, it will take place in a hospital setting. At this time, have the nurse or lab technician write on their medical records their observations and the suspect's condition, arms, needle tracks, etc. Medical personnel have seen many addicts and know how difficult it is to find a vein to draw blood. Get a copy of the suspect's medical records at the time of the test and include it in the police report. The nurse or lab technician can be subpoenaed as a witness for the prosecution.

URINE TEST CHARACTERISTICS OF SOME OPIOIDS[13]

Drug	Form Found in Urine	Approximate Time It Shows in Urine After Consumption	Approximate Length of Time It Can be Found in Urine
Heroin	Morphine Sulfate	1 - 2 Hours	24 Hours - About 90% gone
			48 Hours - About 98% gone
			72 Hours - Trace amount, sometimes detectable
Codeine	1-2 Hours (about 95%)	6 Hours	About 65% gone
	Morphine Sulfate (about 5%)		24 Hours - About 99% gone
			48 Hours - Trace amount, sometimes detectable

[13] *Ibid.*

Methadone	2-4 Hours	24 Hours	About 80% gone
			48 Hours - About 98% gone
Propoxyphene	2-4 Hours	Same as Methadone	

CAUSES OF NEGATIVE URINE TESTS

Urine specimen collected too soon. Most abusable drugs will not show in urine for about 1-2 hours after use.

Urine specimen collected too late. About 90% is eliminated by 48 hours after last use.

Too little drug in urine specimen to detect, i.e. below .20 μg./ml. This commonly occurs when low dosages of drugs are used.

Laboratory error.

How To Avoid Negative Urine Tests

Take more than one urine sample. Wait about an hour between collections.

Ask laboratory how they want samples processed and labeled.

Wait until the pupil is reactive and has returned to normal size to insure that enough time has passed to allow the drug to reach the urine.

Urine Test Standards

There are several techniques which will measure the qualitative presence of abusable drugs in urine. The techniques have different costs, sensitivities, methodologies, and can detect the presence of different drugs.

Urine testing can be done through one of the following techniques:

— Thin Layer Chromatography (TLC)

— Radioimmunoassay

— Enzyme Immunoassay

— Gas Layer Chromatography (GLC)

— Gas Chromatography/Mass Spectroscopy (GC/MS)

— High Performance Gas Liquid Chromatography (HPLC)

USE OF HEROIN AND COCAINE

It is fairly common for people to use heroin and cocaine or other central nervous system stimulants (such as amphetamines) in combination. To some law enforcement officers, this combination presents a confusing picture and makes the arrest situation difficult to handle. However, it is quite easy to make an arrest for being under the influence of narcotics when you understand a few facts. First of all, the pupils may not be constricted below 2.9 mm. because cocaine dilates the pupil. However, since the activity level of cocaine is shorter (2-3 hours) than heroin (4-6 hours) pupillary constriction may occur after the cocaine wears off. Cocaine and amphetamines usually will *not* effect the sedating and muscle relaxant properties of heroin.

Heroin Influence

In order to make an arrest for being under the influence of heroin and cocaine/amphetamines, you will need either the admission of use, fresh needle marks or the evidence of sedation or muscle relaxation, droopy eyelids, slurred or slowed speech, abnormal gait, or nodding. You will also need a positive blood and/or urine sample showing a heroin or cocaine derivative.

USE OF HEROIN AND METHADONE

Occasionally, you will be involved with a methadone addict who is also using heroin. In this case it should be remembered that doses of methadone given in methadone maintenance programs are not enough to sedate or cause droopy eyelids, slurred or slowed speech, or abnormal gait of a heroin addict. Like heroin, methadone causes pupil constriction; however, methadone pupil constriction may last up to 18 hours after a methadone dose. When checking for signs of heroin influence, also recall that methadone is not given by injection and that methadone appears as "methadone" in urine tests rather than as morphine or codeine.

If the person you have stopped claims to be on a methadone maintenance program but appears to be sedated by the appearance of muscle relaxation, droopy eyelids, slurred or slowed speech, or abnormal gait, then you have probable cause to arrest. Check for pupillary constriction below 2.9 mm. Also, take a blood or urine test. If a heroin derivative and methadone are found, then the person is under the influence of a combination of heroin and methadone. In this case, look for fresh needle marks.

The following conditions are necessary for making a diagnosis of heroin influence in a methadone patient:

1. Fresh needle mark.
2. Sedation or muscle relaxation as indicated by droopy eyelids, slurred or slowed speech, or abnormal gait.
3. Heroin derivative in urine or blood.

USE OF HEROIN AND CRACK

Among some drug users, a mixture of crack and smokeable heroin is emerging as a new drug of choice. Since it combines the physical addiction to both heroin and cocaine with the intense high of crack, this mixture threatens to addict a new generation of drug users to heroin.

The mixture of heroin and crack is called by a variety of names such as "crack" and "speedball," though it bears little resemblance to street drugs that have similar names but are used differently. "Speedball" usually refers to the intravenous injection of cocaine and heroin. However, the new mixture of crack and heroin is smoked in a pipe.

One reason for the mixture's popularity is the nature of the high from crack, which is a stimulant. The high is brief, from 8-10 minutes, and extremely intense. Some crack users refer to the high as all the pleasurable feelings they have ever had crammed into a few minutes. Yet, once the high abates, users say they become jittery and depressed.

To escape the depression or "crash," crack addicts are turning to a range of sedatives including marijuana, alcohol, and heroin. Smoking heroin has only recently become economically practical since heroin has become more abundant and pure. Therefore, the main attraction to this drug combination is that the smokeable heroin lengthens the crack high and reduces the intensity of the depression that follows it.

"It is not at all surprising that heroin is making a comeback," said Dr. Mitchell S. Rosenthal, president of Phoenix House, which operates 10 drug-treatment centers in New York and California. "We've been expecting something like this for the past three years. Crack users need some way to come down from that racing high," he said, "and it was inevitable for a large number to eventually turn to heroin. But we didn't expect to see so much so quickly." Users at the Phoenix house said that the combination of crack and heroin is sometimes sold premixed and generally costs about $10 a dose—roughly twice as much as a dose of regular crack. Lisa, a 28-year-old former crack addict enrolled in a Harlem drug-treatment center, said it was common to see people "chasing the dragon," an old term newly applied to smoking heroin with crack. "Crack hypes you up," she said. "The heroin gives you a calm, drowsy high. A lot of people," Lisa said, "are chasing the dragon now."

USE OF HEROIN WITH CODEINE PROPOXYPHENE (DARVON) OR PENTAZOCINE (TALWIN)

Law enforcement officers are often confused when a person states that their heroin influence signs are due to pain medications, such as codeine (Empirin), propoxyphene (Darvon), or pentazocine (Talwin). The diagnosis of "under-the-influence" of heroin, however, is relatively simple when a few pertinent facts are known.

PERTINENT FACTS

1. The doses of codeine, propoxyphene, and pentazocine prescribed by doctors and dentists for pain are not high enough (by multiples of 2 to 5 times) to cause the pupil to constrict under 2.9 mm. in diameter.
2. The prescribed dose of the oral analgesics mentioned above are not high enough to produce sedation and muscle relaxation, e.g., droopy eyelids and slowed speech.
3. Regardless of the presence of codeine, propoxyphene, or pentazocine in blood or urine, a heroin derivative will still be present as will fresh needle marks on the arm from the injection of heroin. If heroin and codeine have both been used, ask the laboratory to determine which drug predominates in the urine.
4. Physicians do not normally prescribe codeine, propoxyphene, or methadone by injection, and so a fresh needle mark is usually evidence of heroin use.

USE OF HEROIN WITH ALCOHOL, PHENCYCLIDINE (PCP), MARIJUANA, DIAZEPAM (VALIUM), OR OTHER SEDATIVES

It can also be confusing when a person states that their heroin influence signs are due to alcohol, PCP, marijuana, or diazepam (Valium or other sedative-type drugs.) Again, diagnosing whether or not someone is "under-the-influence" of heroin becomes relatively simple when a few pertinent facts are known.

PERTINENT FACTS

1. The drugs listed above (including alcohol, but with the exception of PCP) rarely constrict an adult's pupils below 2.9 mm. in diameter.
2. The dosage of diazepam (Valium) normally prescribed by physicians rarely produces visible evidence of sedation or muscle relaxation if the drug is taken as prescribed and not mixed with alcohol or other drugs.
3. Nevertheless, all the drugs listed above can produce the identical sedation and muscle-relaxing effects that heroin does.
4. All the drugs listed here, including alcohol, can produce nystagmus and cause non-reaction of the pupil.

Even if the above drugs or alcohol are taken, to make a diagnosis of heroin influence the subject must have constricted pupils and morphine in the urine. Sedation, muscle relaxation, and non-reactive pupils cannot be used as evidence by themselves since the above-listed drugs and alcohol may produce these symptoms.

Heroin/Morphine Overdose

It is difficult to state the exact amount of morphine that is toxic or lethal to man. In general, a normal, pain-free adult is not likely to die after oral doses of less than 120 mg. or to have serious toxicity with less than 30 mg. parenterally.

Dreisbach lists the minimum lethal dose of morphine for a non-tolerant adult as 200 mg.[14] However, the lethal dose may be up to 2,000 mg. in a narcotic-tolerant individual and as little as 2 mg. in an infant. Toxic and lethal dosage levels of morphine may be drastically reduced by the concomitant use of barbiturates, alcohol, phenothiazines, monoamine oxidase inhibitors[15] and imipramine-like drugs.

Constricted pupils, coma, and respiratory depression strongly suggest opiate poisoning (overdose). An individual who has taken an excessive (toxic) dose of morphine or heroin will be stuporous or comatose. He or she may be unresponsive to painful stimuli. The individual's respiratory rate is usually low and cyanosis may be present. As the respiratory exchange becomes poorer, blood pressure falls progressively. The pupils are symmetrical and pinpoint in size. Urine formation is depressed. Body temperature falls, the skin becomes cold and clammy, skeletal muscles are flaccid and the jaw is relaxed. The tongue may roll back, causing obstruction of air passages. If

---

[14] Dreisbach, R. H. *Handbook of Poisoning: Diagnosis & Treatment*. 8th ed. Los Altos, CA: Lange Medical Publications, 1974, pp. 285-289.

[15] Monoamine oxidase (MAO) is a complex enzyme system widely distributed throughout the body. There are drugs that inhibit MAO in the body such as Nardic, Eutonyl, Parnate, etc.

death occurs, it is usually due to respiratory failure; this is usually not the case in users of street heroin, where death is often due to unknown causes.

The most common reason addicts die is overdose. The second most common cause is accidents, i.e., suicide, auto accidents, homicide. Due to intravenous injection of heroin, the sharing of "outfits" (injection paraphernalia), and the failure to use hygienic techniques, there is a high incident of endocarditis, hepatitis, and other infections among heroin abusers.

Opiate overdose itself is caused by severe respiratory depression. Generally, respiration does not stop immediately; rather, it decreases over a prolonged period of lethargy, stupor, and coma. Sometimes, however, collapse and death are so rapid that the syringe is found in the vein and the tourniquet is still in place on the arm. In these cases, the lungs are suddenly and massively flooded with fluid. This flooding is called pulmonary edema. Cerebral edema, or accumulation of fluid in the brain, may also cause death. Although sudden collapse and death may be called an overdose, it may not be a genuine overdose caused solely by the opiate. Since addicts are poly-drug users, sudden overdoses are more often caused by mixing substances.

For example, a heroin addict long accustomed to injecting heroin got drunk one day, took his customary injection of heroin, then collapsed and died. Subsequent X-rays showed pulmonary edema. In another case reported by the Haight-Ashbury medical clinic, an addict shot some "reds" (barbiturate acid) and then "fixed" himself with heroin. The cause of death was declared an "overdose of heroin," although the drug combination exacerbated the effects of the heroin itself. Autopsies have even shown that some deaths were caused by injections of heroin that left little or no heroin (morphine) in the body. In these cases, death is most likely caused by the adulterants (such as quinine) in the heroin mixture or by an allergic reaction to the heroin. In any event, the end result of these drug combinations is the same—death.

Since police officers often receive blind calls revealing only that someone is sick or in need of assistance, and since officers frequently find individuals on the sidewalk or alleyway unconscious, they should be aware of how to diagnosis an overdose. Clinical signs of an overdose include the following:

pinpointed pupils (unresponsive to light); however, due to other factors, pupils may not be constricted.

nausea, vomiting

dry mouth

sweating

hypothermia; cold, clammy skin (lowered temperature)

muscle twitching

flaccid muscles

marked respiratory depression

slow, weak regular pulse

convulsions in some cases (from codeine and Demerol)

unconsciousness; coma

Heroin Influence

What to do first in cases of drug overdose depends chiefly on how well the person is breathing. If the person is conscious and there is no problem with breathing, either call an ambulance or take the person as quickly as possible to the emergency room of a hospital. There should be at least 10 reasonable deep breaths a minute. If necessary, administer artificial respiration. Use a mask with a one-way air value. If there is any blood, make sure to put on latex gloves to prevent any transmission of the AIDS virus. Any drugs, bottles, etc. found near the person should be taken with the person to the hospital. If there are witnesses, ask what happened and what drug was involved. Does the person have a medical history of problems? If no such evidence is found, look in the person's jacket, on the bedside table, or in the medicine cabinet for a bottle or container carrying the name of the persons's physician or pharmacy. Fast and accurate information about a person's medications and medical condition can be life-saving. Remember to protect the person, cover him or her lightly, turn the person onto his or her stomach if vomiting (face down on floor with the head turned to one side). Keep the person's mouth and airway open and clean; keep the person breathing; call an ambulance or take the person to a hospital emergency room.

The problem of drug overdose is frequently complicated by the use of drugs in combination. The classical signs and symptoms of overdose with one drug may be altered or masked by the effect of the other drug or drugs present. An otherwise safe dose may be lethal in combination with other drugs. Disease, exposure, and serious cerebral or visceral injury may further obscure the picture. However, the preservation of life and vital functions is always more important than immediate specific drug identification.

In a five-year study done in San Francisco, the incidence of acute, fatal narcotism was determined to be 3.2 percent of all deaths (10,882) subject to a medical examiner's inquiry. Heroin was responsible for the greatest number of these deaths, usually accompanied by alcohol or other drugs of abuse. In these fatal cases, the median blood-concentration of the heroin metabolite known as morphine was 20 µg./dL. Death from propoxyphene, the second most frequently encountered narcotic, was generally determined to be suicidal, while death from heroin was judged to be accidental. The highest fatality rate occurred in black males between the ages of 21 and 30 years of age. The three most consistent findings were positive identification of the narcotic in the body (100 percent of the cases), pulmonary edema (90.4 percent of the cases), and microscopic liver changes (71.1 percent of the cases).

OBTAINING AN ARREST WARRANT FOR PERSONS WHO HAVE OVERDOSED ON HEROIN

When officers respond to the scene of a suspected heroin overdose, they should note all the objective symptoms of opiate influence. For example, note the condition of the suspect's eyes; look for fresh hypodermic needle puncture wounds and their location on the body; check the pulse and/or breathing rate of the suspect; and observe the suspect's general appearance (i.e., lethargic, unconscious, or stuporous).

If the paramedics are in attendance at the scene of the overdose, officers should obtain the name and identification number of each paramedic that treats the suspect, and their fire station assignment. If the paramedics administer Narcan to the suspect, the officer should note the reaction the suspect had to the drug, and how much Narcan was administered to the suspect. It is also recommended that the officers obtain an opinion from the paramedics as to whether or not the suspect is, in fact, under the influence of an opiate.

When Narcan is administered and the suspect responds to the treatment, he will probably require additional evaluation at a medical facility. Following a doctor's evaluation, the suspect may be released to the officer who can transport him to the County Jail facility for formal booking. Should the suspect need to stay at the hospital for further treatment, the officer will be required to submit the information obtained in his investigation on a formal crime report and request the issuance of a warrant.

Once the suspect is transported to a hospital, it is very important for the officer to obtain a sample of the suspect's blood. The officer should have medical personnel (if available) remove the blood sample. If a technician from the crime lab removes the sample, he will retain it and deliver it to the crime lab for analysis. If hospital personnel removes the sample, the officer will retain custody of the sample and deliver it to the crime lab at the earliest opportunity for analysis. The officer should also obtain a urine specimen if possible. Both samples will enable the crime lab to perform a full drug screen and prevent a defense that the suspect was under the influence of other drugs. For corroborating evidence, obtain the name of the attending physician and his medical opinion as to whether the suspect is or is not under the influence of an opiate. *Miranda* warnings will apply to initiate questioning of the suspect.

Field Test

There are a number of presumptive color tests which can assist in the identification of opiates such as formaldehyde, nitric acid, ferric chloride, and marquis. The marquis reagent is the most common test and consists of formaldehyde in concentrated sulfuric acid. This reagent is available to law enforcement in commercially produced drug testing kits and is also sold in packets of small glass vials. The officer should carefully read all instructions before conducting the test. The procedure consists of placing the suspected opiate into the reagent or a few drops of the reagent into the suspected opiate. If the reagent turns a red to violet color, the results are positive for opiates. Amphetamines will turn the marquis reagent to an orangey brown. The officer should handle the reagent with care since it is an acid; he or she should also bear in mind that this test is only a preliminary indication of opiates. For positive identification, the substance must be analyzed by a qualified chemist.

REPORT WRITING

To arrest a suspect for narcotic influence, an officer must do the following:

1. be able to articulate the probable cause to contact and detain the suspect
2. investigate the observable physical symptoms of drug influence and establish reasons for the suspect's condition
3. conduct a pupilometer test and a nystagmus test

 md

Heroin Influence

If the conclusion is that the person is under the influence of heroin (or another narcotic or controlled substance) then an arrest should be made. After the arrest, the suspect should be *Mirandized* before further questioning. Photos of injection sites and eyes should be taken; photos of the eyes of a control subject should also be taken for comparison. Injection sites, if present, should be diagrammed on the California Health and Safety Section 11550 report form.

Obtain a Blood or Urine Sample From Suspect

An officer's reasons for contacting, stopping, or investigating a subject must always be clearly stated in the Crime Report.

Contact with a citizen need not be based on a suspicion of criminal activity. It may be initiated due to a need for service or aid, such as traffic advice, directions, etc. For example, if an officer observes a person whose conduct or demeanor gives a reasonable indication that the person is sick, in need of help, or under the influence of an intoxicant, the situation calls for an investigation. It is then proper for the officer to contact that person.

If, during the contact, the officer develops a reasonable suspicion that the person has committed, is committing, or is about to commit a crime, the officer has the authority to detain the person long enough to complete his investigation. An officer may exercise this authority anywhere he has a right to be. A suspicion of narcotic influence is a valid basis for a stop.

When the contact or stop begins under other circumstances (e.g., a moving violation), if the officer observes symptoms of narcotic influence, he has probable cause for a self-initiated investigation of the subject's condition. An officer will also have probable cause to begin an investigation on the basis of information supplied by his personal knowledge of the area, knowledge of the suspect, police sources, or informants.

Once an officer develops cause for the stop of the individual and an investigation into the subject's condition, the officer next should investigate the observable physical symptoms of drug influence. The first step in the examination is to observe the subject's balance, coordination, mental state, speech, and skin. If the subject shows signs of intoxication, the officer has sufficient cause to investigate the condition of the subject's eyes.

The subject's eyes should be examined in two ways, determining the size of the pupils using a pupilometer, and determining reaction to light by observation. The pupilometer is used to determine the size of the subject's pupils. The size of normal pupils changes according to lighting condition. In a very bright light the pupils constrict (become smaller); as the light diminishes, the pupils dilate (become larger). The size of normal pupils varies with each person, but the normal range of variation is between 2.9 and 6.5 mm. in diameter.

In the report, the officer should include all the symptoms of narcotic influence that he or she found during the investigation. To make a narcotic influence arrest, the officer must have evidence of influence such as constrictive pupils, droopy eyelids, or a positive blood or urine sample showing the presence of heroin or a heroin derivative such as morphine.

Heroin Slang

Bag . . . . quantity of drugs packaged in various containers such as paper, balloons, baggies, etc.
Balloon . . . . quantity of drugs, usually heroin, packaged in toy balloons
Behind stuff . . . . using heroin
Bindle . . . . quantity of drugs packaged in various containers, same as bag
Brown stuff . . . . heroin from Mexico with brown coloration
Cap . . . . capsule
Chiva . . . . heroin
Cold turkey . . . . stop using heroin suddenly with no assistance from other medicine
Cook, Cook up . . . . . . prepare heroin for injection by heating it in water to dissolve
Cotton . . . . small pieces of cotton with drug residue from using the cotton as a filter when preparing the drug for injection
Cut . . . . adulterate drugs to obtain a larger quantity
Do up . . . . inject
Down . . . . "get down"—inject a drug
Dried out . . . . detoxified, withdrawn from a drug
Fit . . . . injection paraphernalia
Fix . . . . to inject a drug
Gee . . . . gasket between needle and syringe
Geeze . . . . to inject a drug
H . . . . heroin
Habit . . . . need for a drug; addiction
Hard stuff . . . . heroin, cocaine, morphine
Hit up . . . . to inject a drug; to borrow or attempt to borrow
Hooked . . . . addicted
Joy Pop . . . . irregular use of narcotics
Junk . . . . heroin
Junkie . . . . heroin addict
Kick . . . . stop; to stop taking a particular drug especially heroin
Kit . . . . injection paraphernalia
Mainline . . . . to inject the drug directly into the vein
Marks . . . . supravenous scars caused by injection of drugs
Mexican Brown . . . . . Mexican heroin
Needle freak . . . . one who injects drugs into the vein or skin
Nod . . . . dozing as a result of drugs, usually heroin
O.D. . . . . overdose of a drug, many times fatal
Outfit . . . . injection paraphernalia
Piece . . . . one ounce of a narcotic, usually heroin
Quarter . . . . twenty-five dollars
Quarter piece . . . . . . 1/4 ounce of a certain drug
Rig . . . . injection paraphernalia
Shit . . . . heroin
Shoot (up) . . . . inject a drug
Shooting gallery . . . . place used by users to inject drugs
Skin pop . . . . inject drugs into the skin rather than into the vein

Heroin Influence

Smack . . . . heroin
Spike . . . . needle
Spoon . . . . quantity of a drug, approximately a gram to two grams
Step on . . . . adulterate drugs to obtain a larger quantity
Strung out . . . . addicted
Stuff . . . . heroin
Sugar (milk) . . . . addict's desire for sweets due to heavy habit; amount of sugar mixed with everyday heroin.
Tar . . . . tar heroin
Tie off . . . . prepare for injection by placing a tourniquet on the arm to be used
Tie rag . . . . homemade or makeshift tourniquet used during the injection of drugs
Tools . . . . injection paraphernalia
Tracks . . . . supravenous scars from injection of drugs
White stuff . . . . heroin, usually Chinese
Withdraw . . . . stop using narcotics
Works . . . . injection paraphernalia

Terms Related to Black Tar Heroin

Aceite . . . . Spanish word for "oil"
Ball
Black gum
Black heroin
Black tar
Brown gummy balls
Brown heroin
Bugger
Candy
Carga . . . . Spanish word for "load"
Chapapote . . . . Spanish word for "tar"
Chiclosa . . . . Spanish word for "Chicklet" (gum)
Chocolate
Chiva . . . . Spanish word for "goat" (due to its smell)
Cocoa
Dog food
Goma . . . . Spanish word for "gum"
Gomero . . . . Spanish word for "rubbery"
Gum
Gumball
Gummy
Mexican mud
Mexican tar
Mud
Peanut butter
Pedazo . . . . Spanish word for "piece"
Poison
Raw heroin
Redrock
Tar
Tootsie roll

Sample Jury Instructions on Urine Tests as Evidence

PEOPLE'S PROPOSED JURY INSTRUCTION NO. ____________

REFUSAL TO PROVIDE URINE SAMPLE AND CONSCIOUSNESS OF GUILT

You are instructed that in a case where a defendant is accused of violating section 11550 of the Health & Safety Code, it is permissible to prove that the defendant was offered a urine test after he or she had been made aware of the nature of the test and its effects. The fact that the test is refused under such circumstances is not sufficient standing alone and by itself to establish the guilt of a defendant; however, refusal to submit to the test is a fact which, if proven, may be considered by you in the light of all other proven facts in deciding the question of guilt or innocence. Whether or not such conduct shows a consciousness of guilt and the significance to be attached to such a circumstance are matters for your determination.

People v. Sudduth, 65 CAL. 2D 543 (1966)
Whalen v. Municipal Court, 274CAL.2D 809 (1969)

GIVEN ______

GIVEN AS MODIFIED ______

REFUSED ______

____
JUDGE

 md

Heroin Influence

Sample Examiner's Admonition of Urine Test

EXAMINER'S ADMONITION OF URINE TEST
PER PEOPLE V. SUDDUTH, 65 CAL. 2D 543

DATE ____________________ TIME ______________

NAME ____

You have been placed under arrest for a violation of Section 11550 of the Health and Safety Code, under the influence of a controlled substance. Incident to that arrest you are requested to submit to a urine test to determine the presence of heroin in your body. UNDER CALIFORNIA LAW AND THE UNITED STATES CONSTITUTION YOU DO NOT HAVE THE RIGHT TO REFUSE TO SUBMIT TO SUCH A TEST. When you submit to such a test the results will be made available to you and if the test indicates that there is no heroin in your body you can and will be able to use such evidence to demonstrate your innocence; but if the test indicates a presence of an opiate in your body such evidence can and will be used against you in court. If you refuse to submit to a urine test it constitutes a wrongful refusal to cooperate with law enforcement officers in their investigation and your refusal can and will be used against you in court as an indication of your consciousness of guilt in attempting to suppress evidence. You do not have the right to talk to an attorney or to have an attorney present before stating whether you will submit to a test or during the administration of the test.

I acknowledge that I have been advised by _________________ of my obligation to submit to a urine test. Having this obligation in mind I choose:

______________ to submit to a urine test.

______________ to refuse to submit to a urine test.

____
Examiner

____
Signature of Arrestee

____
Witness

 md

EXAMPLES OF ARREST AND NARCOTIC INFLUENCE REPORTS

CONSOLIDATED ARREST REPORT 212-536-252 (4/75) CA00109 Oakland Police Department

1. DEFENDANT'S TRUE NAME (Leave Blank)	2. PFN	3. RD NUMBER	4. BKG AGENCY

5. DEFENDANT'S NAME	6. ARREST NUMBER	7. CODING
Doe, John M.		

8. AKA or NICKNAME	9. OCCUPATION
Prune	None

10. DOB	POB	HEIGHT	WEIGHT	HAIR	EYES	RACE	SEX	AGE	11. JAIL USE
06 Aug 46	Tx	6'	165	Blk	Bro	N	M	30	

12. SALIENT CHARACTERISTICS	13. CLOTHING	14. HOLD FOR
Pockmarked face	Blu/Whi long sleeve shirt, Blu levis, Bro cap	

15. DEFENDANT'S RESIDENCE ADDRESS	16. RES. PHONE
1210 Union Street	N/P

17. DEFENDANT'S BUSINESS ADDRESS	SCHOOL	18. BUS. PHONE
- -		

19. DRIVER'S LICENSE NO.	20. SOCIAL SECURITY NO.	21. DATE ARRESTED	22. TIME ARRESTED
- -	- -	01 Jan 77	1930

RIGHT INDEX FINGER

23. CODE SEC.	M/F	COURT	CC	WARRANT NO.	BAIL	CEN	PIN NUMBER
11550 H&S	M		1				

CII NUMBER

FBI NUMBER

CASH AT BOOKING

ID CONFIRMED BY

CHECK ☐ PIN ☐ NCIC

CITATION NUMBER

COURT

COURT DATE/TIME

SIGNATURE OF PERSON PRINTED X

SIGNATURE OF PERSON TAKING PRINTS

24. LOCATION OF ARREST	TOTAL	25. SUPERVISOR
IFO 1850 San Pablo Ave.		3/1

26. ARRESTING OFFICER	SERIAL NO.	ARRESTING OFFICER	SERIAL NO.
A. Smith	1001 P	1002 P	

27. TRANSPORTING OFFICER	SERIAL NO.	TRANSPORTING OFFICER	SERIAL NO.
1003 P		1004 P	

28. VEH. LIC. NO.	STATE	YEAR	29. YEAR	MAKE	MODEL	COLOR	30. TOWED TO	HOLD FOR	TOW TAG

I HEREBY ARREST THE ABOVE DEFENDANT ON THE CHARGE INDICATED AND REQUEST A PEACE OFFICER TAKE HIM INTO CUSTODY. I WILL APPEAR TO SIGN A COMPLAINT AGAINST THE PERSON I HAVE ARRESTED (SEE REVERSE SIDE FOR INSTRUCTIONS)

31. SIGNATURE OF ARRESTING CITIZEN	32. ARRESTING CITIZEN'S RES. ADDRESS	33. RES. PHONE

34. ARRESTING CITIZEN'S NAME	SEX–RACE–AGE	35. ARRESTING CITIZEN'S BUS. ADDRESS	36. BUS. PHONE

37. COMPLAINANT'S NAME	SEX–RACE–AGE	38. COMPLAINANT'S ADDRESS	CITY	39. ABC PREM. INVOLVED
A/O				

40. CO-DEFENDANT	SEX–RACE–AGE	CO-DEFENDANT	SEX–RACE–AGE	CO-DEFENDANT	SEX–RACE–AGE

41. ☐ ARMED WITH DEADLY WEAPON ☐ USED A WEAPON ☐ CAUSED GREAT BODILY HARM ☐ ACTED IN CONCERT

42. BURGLARY CLASSIFICATION

43. VALUE OF LOSS (Petty Theft Only)

44. INSTRUCTIONS: List charges by name and code section. Document your admonishment of the arrested person. Enter the names and charges of other arrested persons who are not co-defendants. Enter the reason for physical arrest (misdemeanors only). If you are completing an offense or continuation report, DO NOT start the narrative on this sheet.

11550 H&S Under the Influence of Narcotic

Quoted TF 361 -- Verbal statement taken.

Refused to submit to chemical test. Signed form.

REPORT ATTACHED: ☐ OFFENSE ☐ CONTINUATION ☐ NONE

EXTRA COPIES TO:

 md

NARCOTICS INFLUENCE REPORT
Oakland Police Department

DATE	TIME	LOCATION OF ARREST	R.D. NUMBER
01 Jan 77	1930	IFO 1850 San Pablo Ave	

DEFENDANT'S NAME	SEX-RACE-D.O.B.	DEFENDANT'S ADDRESS
Doe, John M.	M N 06 Aug 46	1210 Union Street

PART I: PHYSICAL OBSERVATIONS (check as applicable)

EYES (PUPILS)
- x Constricted
- ___ Dilated
- ___ Watery
- ___ Sensitive to Light
- ___ Reaction Test
  - 1.0 mm to 1.5 mm
  - Comparison: 9001 T
  - 4.0 mm to 4.5 mm
  - No Reaction Observed
- x Eyelids Droop
- ___ Squints
- x Glassy Appearance
- ___ Other:

LIGHTING CONDITIONS
- ___ Daylight
- x Nighttime
- x Artificial Light
- ___ Other:

BALANCE COORDINATION
- ___ Normal
- x Sways
- x Staggers
- ___ Unable to Stand
- ___ Other:

SKIN
- ___ Normal
- x Scabs
- x Cold-Clammy
- ___ Sweating
- ___ Other:

OTHER
- ___ Nose - runny, sniffing
- ___ Yawning
- ___ Scratching
- x Dry Mouth
- x Drowsy ("On the Nod")
- ___ Drooling
- ___ Nauseated
- x No Odor Alcoholic beverage
- ___ Other:

MENTAL STATE
- ___ Cooperative
- ___ Depressed
- x Confused
- x Passive
- ___ Argumentative
- ___ Nervous
- ___ Other:

SPEECH
- ___ Normal
- x Slurred
- x Incoherent
- ___ Excited
- ___ Other:

MECHANICAL AIDS USED
- x Flashlight
- x Pupilometer
- x Photos taken by 2001T
- ___ Other:

PART II: LOCATION OF MARKS

 md

PART III: ADDITIONAL INFORMATION

(Note defendant's remarks; clothing condition; describe additional symptoms.)

1. Susp's shirt, BLU/Whi Long Sleeve, depicting Blood Stains at Left Arm, inner area. Suspected as being worn when Susp Fixed.

2. Susp voluntarily stated he couldn't be "loaded" because he only fixed half a T and normally he has to shoot more heroin to get loaded.

3. (Search of Susp's person revealed injection paraphernalia -- if applicable)

(see reverse side)

PART IV: ADMONITION OF RIGHTS

1 YOU HAVE THE RIGHT TO REMAIN SILENT
2 ANYTHING YOU SAY CAN AND WILL BE USED AGAINST YOU IN A COURT OF LAW
3 YOU HAVE THE RIGHT TO TALK TO A LAWYER AND HAVE HIM PRESENT WITH YOU WHILE YOU ARE BEING QUESTIONED
4. IF YOU CANNOT AFFORD TO HIRE A LAWYER, ONE WILL BE APPOINTED TO REPRESENT YOU BEFORE QUESTIONING, IF YOU WISH ONE.

THE ABOVE STATEMENT WAS READ TO THE ARRESTEE BY Smith, A. SERIAL NO 1001 P TIME 1930

DO YOU UNDERSTAND EACH OF THESE RIGHTS I HAVE EXPLAINED TO YOU?	HAVING THESE RIGHTS IN MIND, DO YOU WISH TO TALK TO US NOW? (WAIVER STATEMENT)
Yea, I know them.	Sure. You got me now.

PART V: INTERVIEW

Are you under a doctor's care? By Whom and Why? No.

Are you taking medication? What? When? Yes. Valium, Methadone

When did you first use narcotics? What Kind? When I was 18, in the Marines.

What kind of narcotics, if any, are you using now? Stuff, H., Little coke when I can get it.

Have you ever used heroin? When did you start?

When did you last "fix" and with what? About 2 hours ago.

What part of your body do you inject? In my left arm.

How much do you use? How often? About 1/2 a T

PART VI: CHEMICAL TEST

Statement to Defendant: You may take a chemical test to determine the presence or absence of a narcotic in your body. If you wish to take a chemical test, it will be provided at the Jail upon your request.

I ☐ *request* ☒ *refuse* *to take a chemical test.*

John Doe

SIGNATURE OF DEFENDANT

REPORTING OFFICER	SERIAL NO.	NO. SECOND OFFICER	WITNESS
A. Smith	1001 P	1002 P	9001 T

TF-680 (12/76)

 md

REFERENCES:

Carter, R.L., and A. Wiler. "Chronic Meperidine Intoxication and Intact and Chronic Spinal Dogs." *Fed Proc.* 14:955, 1955.

Day, D.C., C.W. Gorodetzky, and W.R. Martin. "Comparative Effects of Codeine and Morphine in Man." *J. Pharmacol Exp Ther.* 156:101-106, 1967.

Dole, V.P., and M.E. Nyawander. "Narcotic Blockage—A Medical Technique for Stopping Heroin Use by Addicts." *Transactions of Association of American Physicians.* 79:132, 1966.

________. "Rehabilitation of Heroin Addicts after Blockage with Methadone." *New York State Journal of Medicine.* August 1, 1966, p. 2015.

Dreisbach, R.H. *Handbook of Poisoning: Diagnosis & Treatment.* 8th ed., Los Altos, CA: Lange Medical Publications, 1974, pp. 285-289.

Fraser H.F., and H. Isbell. "Pharmacology and Addiction Liability of DL-and D-propoxyphene." *Bull Narcot.* 12:9-14, 1960.

Goth, A. *Medical Pharmacology.* 4th ed., St. Louis: The C.V. Mosby Company, 1968, pp. 306-323.

Himmelsbach, C.K. "Further Studies of the Addiction Liability of Demerol (1-Methyl 4-Phenyl Piperidine 4-Carboxylic Acid Ethyl Ester Hydrochloride)." *J. Pharmacol Exp Ther.* 79:5, 1943.

________. "Studies of Certain Addiction Characteristics of (a) Dihydromorphine (Paramorphan), (b) Dihydrodesoxymorphine-D (Desomorphine) (c) Dehydrodesoxycodeine-C (Desocodeine), and (d) Methyldihydromorphine (Metopon)." *J. Pharmacol Exp Ther.* 67:239-249, 1939.

________. "Studies of the Addiction Liability of Demerol (D-140)." *J. Pharmacol Exp Ther.* 75:64, 1942.

Himmelsbach, C.K., and H.L. Andrews. "Studies on Codeine Addiction. II. Studies of Physical Dependence on Codeine." *Public Health Rep Suppl.* 158:11, 1941.

Hine, C.H., J.A. Wright, D.J. Allison, B.G. Stephens, and A. Pasi. "Analysis of Fatalities from Acute Narcotism in a Major Urban Area." *Journal of Forensic Sciences.* JFSCA, Vol. 27, No. 2, April, 1982, pp. 372-384.

Isbell, H. "Withdrawal Symptoms in Primary Meperidine Addicts." *Fed Proc.* 14:354, 1955.

Jaffe, J.H. "Drug Addiction and Drug Abuse." *The Pharmacological Basis of Therapeutics.* L.S. Goodman and A. Gilman, Ed., 4th ed., New York: The MacMillan Company, 1970, pp. 276-313.

________. "Narcotic Analgesics." *The Pharmacological Basis of: Therapeutics,* L.S. Goodman and A. Gilman, Ed., 4th ed., New York: The MacMillan Company, 1970, pp. 237-275.

Jasinski, D.R., J.D. Griffith, C.B. Carr, et al. "Progress Report From the Clinical Pharmacology Section of the Addiction Research Center." *Committee on Problem of Drug Dependence.* National Academy of Sciences, Washington, D.C., 88-115, 1974.

Kay, C.D., C.W. Gorodetzky, and W.R. Martin. "Comparative Effects of Codeine and Morphine in Man." *J. Pharmacol Exp Ther.* 156:101, 1967.

Kurland, A.S., L. Wurmser, F. Derman, et al. "Urine Detection Tests Management of the Narcotic Addict." *Am J Psychiat.* 122:737-742, 1966.

Lasagna, L., and H.K. Beecher. "The Analgesic Effectiveness of Codeine and Meperidine (Demerol)." *J. Pharmacol Exp Ther.* 112:306, 1954.

Martin, W.R., and H.F. Fraser. "A Comparative Study of Physiological and Subjective Effects of Heroin and Morphine Administered Intravenously in Post-Addicts." *J. Pharmac Exp Ther.* 133:388-399, 1961.

Martin, W.R., F.R. Jasinski, C.A. Haertzen, et al. "Methadone: A Reevaluation." *Arch Gen Psychiatry.* 28:286-298, 1973.

Mule, S.J. "Identification of Narcotics, Barbiturates, Amphetamines, Tranquilizers, and Psychotomimetics in Human Urine." *J Chromatogr.* 39:302-311.

Olsen, G.D., H.A. Wendel, J.D. Livermore, et al. "Clinical Effects and Pharmacokinetics of Racemic Methadone and its Optical Isomers." *Clin Pharm and Ther.* 21:147-157, 1977.

Seevers, M.H., and C.C. Pfeiffer. "A Study of the Analgesia, Subjective Depression, and Euphoria Produced by Morphine, Heroin, Dilaudid, and Codeine in the Normal Human Subject." *J. Pharmacol Exp Ther.* 56:166, 1936.

Shuster, M.M., and M.C. Lewin. "Needle Tracks in Narcotic Addicts." *New York St. J Med.* 68:3134, 1968.

Tennant, Forest S. *Identifying the Heroin User.* Veract, Inc., West Covina, CA, 1985.

Yeh, S.Y., and R.L. McQuinn. "GLC Determinations of Heroin and its Metabolites in Human Urine." *Journal of Pharamcology Science.* 64:1237-1239, 1975.

Yeh, S.Y., C.W. Gorodetzky, and R.L. McQuinn. "Urinary Excretion of Heroin and its Metabolites in Man." *J. Pharmacol Exp. Ther.* 196(2):249-256, 1976.

Young, A.W., and F.R. Rosenberg. "Cutaneous Stigmas of Heroin Addiction." *Arch Derm.* 104:80-86, 1971.

CHAPTER IX

DESIGNER DRUGS/ANABOLIC STEROIDS

INTRODUCTION

The term "designer drugs" was coined in the laboratory of Dr. Gary Henderson at the University of California, Davis. Originally, the term referred to the increasing sophistication of illicit drug chemists who were developing the ability to produce drugs designed to fit the tastes of individual clients.

Since then, a more clinical synonym has come into use; the term "controlled substance analogs" refers to substances of abuse that are allegedly "designed" by clandestine chemists. The aim of these chemists is to manufacture chemical compounds that produce the "high" of controlled substances (such as narcotics, depressants, stimulants or hallucinogens). However, these compounds are chemically different from controlled substances; therefore, they are not subject to the provisions of the Controlled Substances Act (CSA). By selling these chemical variants (analogs), the clandestine manufacturer can profit from the distribution of dangerous abusable compounds while avoiding the penalties that would be levied against those illegally trafficking the controlled substance.

This concept of designing pharmacologically active, chemically related substances, is neither new nor restricted to illicit clandestine laboratories. In fact, most controlled substance analogs were first developed by legitimate pharmaceutical chemists and publicized through articles in scientific journals. In the quest for better medicinal agents, pharmaceutical companies will synthesize and test numerous analogs of a parent compound. These analogs mimic the qualitative actions of the original compound, but may vary in potency (the dose required to produce maximal effects) and in duration of action. For example, within the benzodiazepine family there are numerous variations on the "parent" drug, chlordiazepoxide (Librium). These Librium analogs (e.g. Valium, Dalmane, Serax, Ativan, Centrax, etc.) are now on the market and have similar psychoactive and therapeutic effects.

The use of chemical analogs for the purpose of avoiding the laws regulating controlled substances was first noticed in the 1960s with the synthesis and sale of amphetamine analogs of mescaline (MDA, MMDA, DOM, TMA, PMA, DOB and DMA). Within this group of hallucinogenic amphetamines, MDA, MMDA, DOM, and TMA were controlled under the Drug Abuse Control Amendments (a predecessor to the CSA). Since then, PMA, DOB, and DMA have been controlled administratively under the Controlled Substance Act. In the 1970s, three PCP analogs (thiophene analog, PCE and PHP) and the methaqualone analog (mecloqualone) were all controlled administratively via the CSA. An amphetamine analog, N-ethylamphetamine was later controlled in 1982.

NARCOTIC ANALOGS

The current wave of controlled substance analogs is focusing on the production of narcotic analogs. These substances consist of variations of the parent compounds fentanyl and meperidine (pethidine). Fentanyl (marketed as Sublimaze and Innovar) is a short-acting highly potent narcotic which, in humans, is about 100 times as strong as morphine. It is used medically as an anesthetic during surgery.

Fentanyl is favored by some anesthesiologists because its effects wear off fairly quickly after surgery. Since it produces a high like that of heroin, fentanyl is one of the drugs most frequently abused by anesthesiology staff, who sometimes illegally tap hospital supplies for their own recreational use. The manufacturer of fentanyl is Janssen Pharmaceutica in Piscataway, New Jersey.

Several fentanyl analogs are so potent that one gram is sufficient to make about 50,000 doses (approximately 250 times stronger than heroin). Since 1979, fentanyl analogs have been trafficked on the street as "heroin," "synthetic heroin," or "China White" (referring to a strong form of Southeast Asian heroin). In California, these analogs have been associated with more than 100 overdose deaths.

Other fentanyl overdoses have been reported in Boston, Philadelphia, Newark, and Baltimore; most of these have occurred since January 1, 1992. The State Medical Examiners' Office in Baltimore has confirmed 23 fentanyl overdose deaths in Maryland, 19 of those occurring in Baltimore. Recent fentanyl exhibits obtained by the Baltimore Police Department were packaged in either bright yellow or colorless glassine bags, without any log. Analysis by the police department's laboratory showed that most of these exhibits contained about one percent fentanyl hydrochloride, forty percent quinine, and sugars.

Although only anecdotal information is currently available, it is hypothesized that much of the fentanyl being distributed on the East Coast originated from a single source of supply and is being introduced into the heroin distribution chain at the wholesale level.

In the New York City metropolitan area, a recent rash of deaths and hospitalizations has been attributed to a subsance being sold as heroin under the brand name "Tango and Cash." Analysis by a DEA Special Testing and Research Laboratory determined that the powder consisted of fentanyl hydrochloride (12 percent), N-1-phenylethyl-4 piperidyl aniline (the immediate precursor to fentanyl), mannitol, and a trace of caffeine.

This particular form of fentanyl is contained in glassine bags rubber stamped with the logo "Tango and Cash" in Old English style lettering. Above the lettering in the logo is an image of one hand holding a hat and a second hand holding a sheet of paper with four dollar-signs ($). Below is an image of the logo.

It is possible that other deaths have been caused by fentanyl analog overdoses, but since the tissue levels of these substances are extremely low, regular toxicological methods have failed to identify them.

Of the clandestine fentanyl analogs identified to date, only alpha-methylfentanyl (CSA 1981) has been controlled using the regular scheduling process. A total of ten other fentanyl analogs have been controlled in Schedule I, using the emergency scheduling provision of the Comprehensive Crime Control Act of 1984. The first substance of any type to be controlled using emergency scheduling was the powerful fentanyl analog, 3-methylfentanyl (CSA 1985). Since then, nine more fentanyl analogs have been placed in Schedule I on an emergency basis. These fentanyl analogs include acetyl-alpha-methylfentanyl, alpha-methyl-thiofentanyl, benzylfentanyl, beta-hydroxy-fentanyl, beta-hydroxy-3-methyl-fentanyl, 3-methyl-thiofentanyl, para-fluorofentanyl, thiofentanyl, and thenylfentanyl.

Another synthetic narcotic drug which has been mimicked by clandestine laboratory operators is known as both meperidine and Demerol. The first meperidine analog, termed MPPP, was identified by a DEA laboratory in 1982. The MPPP compound is about 5 to 10 times more potent than meperidine; thus, its dosage should be similar to morphine. Samples of the MPPP analog have also been found to contain a neurotoxic by-product, MPTP. This by-product is formed during the synthesis of MPPP. At least seven persons who used an MPPP/MPTP mixture developed a severe physiological disease similar to Parkinson's disease. The neurological damage caused by exposure to MPTP appears to be irreversible and has been proven to worsen with time.

DEA laboratories have recently analyzed a second meperidine analog in confiscated samples, termed PEPAP. These samples also contained a by-product that is chemically related to the neurotoxin, MPTP. Since MPTP has caused such severe neurological damage, in August of 1985 the DEA used emergency scheduling to control these substances by placing both MPPP and PEPAP into Schedule I.

In the class of hallucinogenic amphetamines, the parent drug MDA has two principal analogs; these are MDMA (also known as Ecstasy) and MDE (also known as Eve). While MDMA has been clandestinely produced, trafficked, and abused in several areas of the country, MDE manufacture and usage appears to be much more limited. Animal experiments have shown that MDA, MDMA, and MDE have similar pharmacological effects. Recent experiments with MDA and MDMA indicate that a single high dose of either drug produces brain damage in rats. For these reasons, on July 1, 1985, MDMA was placed in Schedule I of the Controlled Substances Act on an emergency basis.

SYNTHETIC NARCOTIC PHARMACOLOGY AND TOXICOLOGY

Synthetic narcotic substances such as meperidine and fentanyl derivatives are pharmacologically similar to opium-based narcotics such as morphine. Like morphine, the synthetic narcotics primarily act on the central nervous system (CNS) and the gastrointestinal (GI) tract. In addition to producing analgesia, drowsiness, and euphoria, these substances also produce varying degrees of respiratory depression, constipation, nausea, vomiting (except fentanyl), muscular rigidity, and changes in the tone of the autonomic nervous system.

The actions of both natural and synthetic narcotic substances are mediated by way of biological molecules called opioid receptors. These opioid receptors are found on the surfaces of neurons and other types of cells. The narcotic substances bind to these opioid receptors and stimulate a cellular response. In general, the more tightly a narcotic substance binds to these receptors, the more potent it is (i.e., the lower the dose required to produce a response). The opioid receptors consist of a number of different subtypes (delta, kappa, mu, sigma) and each subtype mediates different parts of the diverse actions of narcotics. At the present time, the mu subtype of opioid receptor is considered to be especially involved in the analgesic and addicting properties of narcotics.

Opioid receptors are found in high numbers in some areas of the brain; they are also present in the gastrointestinal tract. Narcotic analgesia is most likely exerted through the opioid receptors located in CNS areas such as the spinal cord and the thalamus (areas involved in pain transmission and perception). The euphoric effects, on the other hand, are more likely to involve stimulation of opioid receptors found in the limbic regions of the brain (areas that mediate mood and emotion). Morphine-like narcotics also have toxic actions; these actions create respiratory depression and release histamine (except fentanyl) into the circulation.

Respiratory depression is caused by the effect of narcotics on brain stem centers which sense carbon dioxide levels in the blood. Although this respiratory arrest is the most common cause of overdose fatalities, the interaction of depressed respiration and released histamine may be responsible for some of those deaths. The hypoxia (lack of oxygen) which follows severe respiratory depression may lead to a drop in blood pressure, and any release of histamine will produce further hypotension. Blood pressure may eventually become so low that cardiovascular collapse occurs and death results.

Some additional toxic effects may result from prolonged use of meperidine. These effects include tremors, muscle twitches, hallucinations, seizures, and tissue fibrosis at injection sites.

Fentanyl and its derivatives also depress respiration; however, the respiratory effects of fentanyl are much shorter in duration. Moreover, fentanyl differs from morphine in that it does not provoke a release of histamine; it thereby allows for greater cardiovascular stability.

MEDICAL USES OF FENTANYL DERIVATIVES

Below is a brief description of the fentanyl derivatives used in human and veterinary medicine:

Fentanyl - This drug was introduced into the United States in 1968 as an intravenous analgesic-anesthetic under the trade names Sublimaze and Innovar. Fentanyl now occupies a major place in therapeutics as a pre-anesthetic, an anesthetic, and a post-surgical analgesic. Fentanyl is a very potent and short-acting drug; it is approximately 100 times as potent as morphine and its duration of action is roughly 30 minutes. Fentanyl is used in approximately 70 percent of all surgeries in the United States.

Alfentanyl - At 20 to 30 times the strength of morphine, this very short-acting substance (15 minutes) is less potent than fentanyl. Alfentanyl is currently tested in clinical trials as an ultra-short-acting analgesic to be used in diagnostic, dental, and minor surgical procedures.

Sufentanyl - This fentanyl derivative is very potent (2,000 to 4,000 times the strength of morphine). With such a potency, Sufentanyl is used as an anesthetic-analgesic agent for cardiac surgery.

Carfentanyl - This substance is an extrememly potent fentanyl derivative (3,200 times the strength of morphine) which is used only in "capture guns" for immobilizing wild animals.

Lofentanyl - This substance is the most potent fentanyl derivative (6,000 times the strength of morphine) and is very long-acting. Lofentanyl is currently being evaluated for use when prolonged analgesia and respiratory depression are required in such applications as tetanus and multiple trauma.

ILLICIT FENTANYL DERIVATIVES

Very little is known about the biological effects of the illicit derivatives. At best only preliminary data is available from studies conducted in laboratory animals. Virtually nothing is known about their effects in humans.

Alpha-methyl Fentanyl - was the first illicit fentanyl derivative to appear on the streets. It is a very simple modification of the fentanyl structure and is about 200 times as potent as morphine. As a new drug entity, it was not at first on any international, federal, or state restricted drug list and was in essence "street legal." However, it is now classified as a Schedule I drug by the DEA. Alpha-methyl Fentanyl is a Schedule I drug because it has no approved medical uses and a high addiction liability.

Para-fluoro Fentanyl - was the second illicit derivative to appear on the streets. It is a simple derivative of fentanyl and has about the same potency. Para-fluoro Fentanyl is presently classified as a Schedule I drug by the DEA. Little is known about the compound; it appeared only briefly and does not seem to be in use at this time.

Alpha-methyl Acetylfentanyl - first appeared on the streets in 1983. This very simple derivative of fentanyl is a new chemical entity; therefore, it escapes classification as a restricted drug. At this time, it is not a restricted drug and nothing is known about its pharmacological properties.

Alpha-methyl Fentanyl Acrylate - has been identified in samples containing acetyl alpha-methyl fentanyl. It may be a new derivative but is more likely a contaminant or a by-product of synthetics. Nothing is known about its pharmacological properties.

Benzyl Fentanyl - has recently appeared mixed with other fentanyl derivatives in street samples. It is possibly an unwanted synthetic by-product or an intermediate used in the synthesis of other fentanyl derivatives. It has no narcotic effects.

Fentanyl - itself has appeared in street samples and has long been associated with overdose deaths in California. The fentanyl sold on the streets is most likely synthesized in illicit laboratories and not diverted from pharmaceutical supplies. All fentanyl sold on the streets is in powder form and all fentanyl sold as a pharmaceutical is in dilute, liquid form. Although abuse of Sublimaze by medical personnel in hospitals and clinics has been documented, the extent of the problem has not been adequately researched.

3-Methyl Fentanyl - is the latest derivative to be introduced onto the streets; it is certainly one of the most potent fentanyl derivatives (3,000 times as potent as morphine). This analog appeared in California sometime between the fall of 1983 and the spring of 1984 and is thought to be responsible for over a dozen overdose deaths in the San Francisco Bay area, the highest incidence of fentanyl-related deaths to date.

PHYSICAL DESCRIPTION OF "CHINA WHITE"

Since the fentanyls are cut (diluted) with large amounts of lactose or sucrose (powdered sugar) before they are sold on the street, the amount of active drug present is exceedingly small, less than 1 percent. These amounts are so small they contribute nothing to the color, odor or taste of the sample.

Color - The color of the samples obtained to date has ranged from pure white (sold as "Persian White") to light tan (sold as "China White," "Synthetic Heroin," or "Fentanyl") to light brown (sold as "Mexican Brown"). The brown color results from the lactose which becomes slightly carmelized though heating.

Texture - The texture of the samples observed in the laboratory has ranged from light and finely powdered to somewhat coarse, cake-like and crumbly, resembling powdered milk.

Odor - Occasional samples will have a medicinal or chemical odor, but this is not characteristic.

In summary, the fentanyls appear in all the various forms that heroin does, and there is nothing characteristic about the appearance of any sample that will identify it as fentanyl instead of heroin. Therefore, it is often sold as heroin. This substitution is partly responsible for the numerous overdose deaths associated with the fentanyls.

ROUTES OF ADMINISTRATION

Intravenous injection is the most common route of administration for the fentanyls; however, they may be smoked or snorted as well. In fact, because of their high lipid solubility, the fentanyls should be excellent drugs for snorting and may become increasingly popular drugs among cocaine users. At least one overdose fatality was identified in which snorting was the only route of administration. Fentanyl has also been detected in the urine of individuals who used the drug only by smoking it.

PHARMACOLOGICAL EFFECTS OF FENTANYL

It should be remembered that although the fentanyls are chemically quite distinct from other narcotics (morphine, heroin, methadone, etc), they are pharmacologically equivalent; that is, they have all the effects and toxicity of a classical narcotic. Since the fentanyls are pharmacologically equivalent to other narcotics, all of their effects can be reversed by naloxone (Narcan), although higher doses of the antagonist may be required.

Euphoria

The euphoria or "rush" from the fentanyls should be qualitatively similar to that of heroin; the intensity of the effect would depend upon the dose and the particular derivative used.

Analgesia

Profound analgesia (absence of pain) is a characteristic effect of all the fentanyls. As little as 50 micrograms of fentanyl will produce analgesia while only 3 micrograms of the 3-methyl derivative would be required.

Side effects and toxicity

Respiratory Depression - This is the most significant acute toxic effect of the fentanyls. The depth and duration of respiratory depression will depend on the dose and the derivative used. However, compared with other narcotics this effect is relatively short-lived. For example, following 200 micrograms of fentanyl given intravenously, maximum depression occurs within 5 to 10 minutes; normal respiration returns within 15 to 30 minutes.

Antidote - Naloxone (Narcan) is the antidote of choice for respiratory depression (or any other effect) produced by the fentanyls.

Bradycardia - Fentanyl produces a dose-dependent decrease in heart rate of up to 25 percent with a parallel drop in blood pressure of up to 20 percent. This effect is thought to be due to vagal stimulation (stimulation of vagus nerves) and can be blocked by atrophine. The role of this response in overdose deaths is not known.

Muscle Rigidity - Sometimes called "wooden chest," muscle rigidity is the response common to high doses of all narcotics. Individuals using the fentanyls may describe this effect as a muscle tightness or tingling.

Addiction Liability - The fentanyls produce both *tolerance* and *physiological dependence* following repeated administration. Controlled studies have shown that addicts perceive fentanyl derivatives as having heroin-like effects. In California, many individuals enrolling in methadone treatment programs have only fentanyl in their urine upon admission, yet are convinced they use only very high grade heroin. Therefore, when pharmacologically equivalent doses are used, most users probably cannot tell the difference between heroin and the fentanyls.

Abuse Potential - As a pharmaceutical, fentanyl (Sublimaze) was always thought to have a low abuse potential because of its short duration of action and its restricted availability. Also, Sublimaze is available only in injectable, aqueous formulations containing either 100 micrograms or 500 micrograms per vial (50 micrograms/milliliter). These relatively small amounts and low concentrations make it difficult for a tolerant addict to administer a euphoric dose conveniently.

Until now, the only documented illicit use of fentanyl was in "doping" race horses. Narcotics are frequently used to dope horses because they produce excitation in the horse (and other animals such as the cat and mouse). Fentanyl's short duration of action and its very low, nearly undetectable concentrations in blood and urine make it an ideal doping agent. Fentanyl has been used in this manner for nearly a decade.

Now, the fentanyls are available throughout most of California. Since they are potent, not easily detected by routine analytical methods, and, in the case of the newer analogs, quite legal, they may become the drug of choice for many heroin users. Fentanyl use is likely to increase in California; its use may then spread to other states, and new derivatives may appear periodically.

OVERDOSE DEATHS

To date there have been more than 200 overdose deaths caused by the fentanyls. In all the cases, known heroin users were involved, injection sites and accompanying paraphernalia were found, and autopsies showed typical signs of narcotic overdose such as pulmonary edema and congestion. Routine toxicological analysis of the body fluids revealed no narcotics, sedative or stimulant drugs present; however, analysis of these fluids in the laboratory (using methods specifically developed for the fentanyls) revealed very low levels of these synthetic narcotics. Traces of the fentanyls were also found in the accompanying paraphernalia.

OTHER HAZARDS OF FENTANYL

The fentanyls are very difficult to detect either in body fluids or paraphernalia because the amounts present are very small and because they do not react with the reagents routinely used for the analysis of narcotics.

Why do the fentanyls represent such a hazard and public health problem? There are several clear-cut reasons. First, these drugs are much less expensive to make than traditional narcotics. Secondly, they do not require importation and all the expenses incurred thereby. Thirdly, those making and selling synthetic narcotics are rarely prosecuted because the substance may not be illegal. Fortunately, the DEA has recently been able to take swift action to control some of these substances. It is estimated that, using the more potent fentanyl derivatives, a single chemist working an eight-hour day could supply the entire nation's heroin market on an on-going basis. A single 6-month supply for the United States could be stored in a closet. Hence, from the perspective of those on the production side of the illicit drug market, one can see the immense attractiveness of this approach in terms of cost and liability.

What are the hazards? There are basically three. First, these chemists are obviously not required to carry safety trials with these new compounds as a legitimate drug company would be. Hence, the first subjects to receive them are not laboratory animals, but human beings using these compounds on the street. Secondly, there are no quality controls in the laboratories as there would be in a legitimate drug company. Hence, contaminants or unwanted compounds are not removed, and probably often not even detected. Thirdly, there is the issue of potency. Due to their potency, the fentanyl variants must be cut in microgram amounts.

A dose of fentanyl as small as 40 to 80 micrograms will induce a heroin-like euphoria; a 200 microgram dosage is used in surgery; and about 300 micrograms can kill. By comparison, a standard aspirin tablet weighs slightly over 300,000 micrograms. A postage stamp weighs about 60,000 micrograms. Hence, overdoses of this synthetic narcotic are common.

Even the analysis of fentanyl can be dangerous. Since it is an airborne substance in small amounts, fentanyl can be absorbed through the skin or mucous membranes causing illness or possibly death. Full self-contained skin and respiratory protection should be worn by all investigative and laboratory personnel whenever handling fentanyl or substances believed to contain fentanyl. These protective precautions should be taken especially when investigating clandestine manufacturing or distribution sites.

Most fentanyl that enters the illicit drug market is believed to be clandestinely manufactured. However, since fentanyl is often sold by distributors as heroin or mixed with heroin, analysis of samples can be complicated. The standard field test for analyzing heroin will differentiate between samples of heroin and samples of fentanyl when they are not mixed. The heroin test produces a purple color, while fentanyl produces a dull orange color. However, if fentanyl is mixed with heroin, the purple color of heroin will mask the dull orange given by the fentanyl. This masking allows small but potent amounts of the synthetic narcotic to go virtually undetected in samples of heroin.

Due to the fact that fentanyl is often sold as heroin, its dangers have increased even more. Fentanyl is 25 times as strong as heroin and 100 times as strong as morphine. Regular heroin users who substitute fentanyl or one of its derivatives may not be aware of its potency and overdose unknowingly.

During early February 1991, a series of drug-related deaths and injuries caused by apparent heroin overdoses occurred in the New York metropolitan area. Approximately six deaths and 69 overdoses occurred in New York, two deaths and 30 overdoses in Connecticut, and ten deaths and 114 overdoses in New Jersey. Further inquiry disclosed that fentanyl, sold in the south Bronx as heroin under the brand names "Tango and Cash" and "Goodfellas," was the cause of these deaths and overdoses. One "Tango and Cash" sample analyzed by the DEA's Special Testing and Research Laboratory was found to be 20 to 25 times stronger than the Sublimaze dosage used for surgery.

When it became apparent that fentanyl was being sold as heroin at known heroin sale locations, the New York City Police department (NYPD) mobilized with a response designed to 1) immediately warn potential heroin users of the danger and 2) to locate and immobilize the supplier(s) via traditional investigative methods. Several squads of NYPD officers utilized bullhorns and sound tracks to go through the potential sale areas alerting people of the dangers of the heroin being sold under the brand names of "Tango and Cash" and "Goodfellas."

DEA laboratories have been involved with the analysis of two fentanyl samples related to this New York investigation. The first exhibit consisted of the initial sample of "Tango and Cash" seized by the New York Police Department. An examination of this sample at the DEA Northeastern Regional Laboratory confirmed the presence of fentanyl hydrochloride, mannitol (a common heroin cut), a trace of caffeine, and traces of an intermediate chemical. A second exhibit, obtained in New Jersey, was submitted to the DEA Special Testing and Research Laboratory in Virginia. Their analysis confirmed the presence of the same substances. The glassine envelope contained a total 35 milligrams of powder consisting of 12.5 percent fentanyl hydrochloride, approximately 86 percent mannitol, a trace of caffeine, and a trace of an intermediate chemical identified as N-1-phenylethyl-4-piperidyl aniline. The amount of fentanyl present in this sample is approximately the equivalent of 100 milligrams of pure heroin.

Two circumstances lead a DEA Senior Forensic Chemist involved in the investigation to speculate that the samples were clandestinely manufactured:

1. The fentanyl present was fentanyl hydrochloride, a form not commercially available. The type of fentanyl used in the manufacture of Sublimaze is fentanyl citrate.
2. The presence of the intermediate would be highly unlikely in commercially produced fentanyl.

OUTLOOK

Despite the 1991 series of fentanyl-related deaths and injuries in the New York metropolitan area, fentanyl and its analogs are not known to be distributed on an organized, continuous basis on the East Coast of the United States. Hopefully, the investigations precipitated by these overdoses and deaths will soon be identified and dismantled. In the mean time, however, the profit potential of the fentanyls is still astronomical and law enforcement officers should be aware of the drugs' increasing use nationwide. Fentanyl itself, probably one of the least potent of the analogs, is less expensive to produce than heroin. Production of a kilogram requires only a small expense for lab equipment, approximately $1,000 for intermediate chemicals, and the ability to perform two chemical reactions. One kilogram of fentanyl is the approximate equivalent of 25 kilograms of heroin. This equivalency translates to a street value of $5,000,000 to $112,500,000.

In addition to its profitability, domestically produced fentanyl is also easier to distribute than heroin. Fentanyl distribution does not require an international smuggling infrastructure to send shipments over long distances and circumvent customs inspections as does heroin. Fentanyl's ease of production, distribution, and its profitability make it an attractive drug to manufacture. However, fentanyl's concentrated strength occasionally creates a significant problem for manufacturers. It is difficult for traffickers to properly "cut" fentanyl (with substances such as mannitol) to keep the mix from being so strong that it causes overdoses, while providing the microgram-sized quantity necessary for a heroin-like high. This difficulty has resulted in several cases, such as those involving "Tango and Cash" and "Goodfellas," in which the fentanyl was not cut enough. Nonetheless, should one or several traffickers perfect the cutting process and develop a trafficking infrastructure, fentanyl's availability on the street could increase dramatically and provide an already expanding heroin market with an additional supply.

MPTP

It was only a matter of time before a true poison "hit the streets". This is precisely what happened in northern California in 1982, when a highly toxic compound known as MPTP was circulated. The MPTP compound is neurotoxic to a group of cells in the brain known as the substantia nigra. By pure coincidence, this happens to be the same area that is damaged by Parkinson's disease. Two years ago, a group of young adults came to the

Santa Clara Valley Medical Center who, in every way, resembled elderly patients with end-stage Parkinson's disease. These young drug users had literally frozen up. Parkinsonian therapy was probably life-saving for three of them; however, these patients continue to be severely disabled and require medication every one to three hours, simply to enable them to move, eat, and drink. Two of the patients have recently undergone prolonged hospitalization; the outlook for their futures is not very promising.

While there are currently only twenty young adults who have been permanently crippled by this first "designer drug disaster," law enforcement has identified an additional 500 people who have been exposed to MPTP, believing it to be a new "synthetic heroin." With increased research, evidence has shown that damage to the substantia nigra area of brain, even if it does not cause immediate symptoms, may act like a time bomb with changes in the brain slowly ticking away. In other words, these young adults exposed to MPTP could eventually develop a neurological condition that is nearly identical to Parkinson's disease.

Until recently, this concern was just theoretical. However, in the last several months, officers investigating this new drug problem have witnessed a group of young people at Santa Clara Valley Medical Center who used MPTP two years ago and are now developing a myriad of symptoms, all suggestive of early Parkinson's disease. If the number of drug users diagnosed with these symptoms continues to increase, northern California may be facing an epidemic as a result of this catastrophe.

MPPP

Methyl-phenylpropionoxpiperidine (MPPP) is an illicit analog of meperidine, a legal, federally controlled painkiller which goes by the trade name Demerol. Heroin addicts who have used the drug experienced the same effects as would victims of Parkinson's disease who were without medication. The neurological damage caused by MPPP is actually done by the neurotoxin MPTP, a contaminant unintentionally created in the MPPP manufacturing process. Unless clandestine chemists assay their batches, they cannot know if it is contaminated with MPTP.

MPPP and MPTP help to explain the growing numbers of hospitalized patients with symptoms strikingly similar to Parkinson's disease. In an advanced case, Parkinson's can turn a person into a statue. Sometimes the rigidity has an "on-off" effect. With respect to the symptoms of this disease, it has been verified by California medical examiners that over 70 people who injected themselves with the synthetic heroin MPPP were turned into living statues. Their chances of recovery are slim.

The urgency of this drug problem came to the attention of California law enforcement after a 42-year-old heroin user was brought to Valley Medical Center in Santa Clara, California in a frozen state after injecting himself with MPPP. According to Dr. William Langston, chairman of the neurology department at Valley Medical Center, the symptoms exhibited by the user when he was brought into the hospital were quite dramatic. "He had completely frozen almost overnight," Langston said. The doctor then learned that the user's girlfriend was in the same condition. For the previous two weeks, her family had been washing and feeding her three times a day. "It was like having a store mannequin around the house," he said.

At first, doctors in Santa Clara assumed that the patients brought in with rigid, distorted faces were merely unconscious, until a man who was assumed to be unconscious moved his fingers enough to write: "I have no idea what is going on. I just can't move." Several stories were subsequently reported. One member of the medical team researching MPPP heard a story of two brothers who were shooting up heroin and froze. They would have starved to death if their mother had not come to visit them. In another case, a police technician called in to report a medical student who had become paralyzed after injecting himself with a drug he had synthesized in his own lab. After obtaining a drug sample from one of the frozen users brought into the hospital, the doctors in Santa Clara confirmed it was MPPP. The student had mistakenly synthesized MPPP instead of the pain-killer Demerol.

Approximately 300 people have been identified by Langston as MPPP users. Most are between 20 and 40 years old; some, he said, are only now beginning to show the symptoms of this drug's effects, although they may have taken the drug several years ago. Some of these symptoms include tremors of the hands, loss of motor control, and paralysis.

Although MPPP appears to be sold primarily in California, the manufacturers and distributors are still unknown. According to Frank Sapienza, a chemist with the drug control division of the DEA, it has not yet been determined whether one or several mystery chemists are responsible for the drug's production. Despite the remaining questions, the DEA has confirmed that in 1985 they arrested operators of a clandestine drug lab in Brownsville, Texas, where materials and instructions for manufacturing MPPP were found.

Since so many problems have been caused by MPPP/MPTP in Northern California, some clinics are distributing flyers identifying the health problem. The following is an example of such a flyer:

HEALTH WARNING

If you have injected anything called "synthetic heroin" or noticed a burning sensation when injecting any drug over the past two or three years, there is a good chance you may have taken MPTP. This is "bad heroin." *Possibly,* it has been on the streets on and off since 1981. *Definitely* it was on the streets during January through July of 1982. This "bad heroin" has caused Parkinson's disease in some users, ranging from mild to severely disabling symptoms. The color of the heroin containing MPTP has most often been light beige or China White, although other colors have been reported. Some symptoms of this drug's effects include: 1) a burning sensation upon fixing, sent 7 or 8 inches up and down the arm, 2) jerking of limbs during and after fixing, 3) stiffening, from immediately after fixing up to months later, 4) visual blurring, during and/or after fixing, 5) strange or unusual high, 6) drooling after the high, 7) oiliness of skin much later, and 8) freezing.

It is *very* important that you find out if you took this drug because it may cause you to develop this disease in the future. If you think you may have taken MPTP, EVEN ONCE, or if you know anyone who may have taken the drug, please call the Department of Neurology, Santa Clara Valley Medical Center, San Jose, California, telephone number (408) 299-5246, and we will discuss it with you.

This is not a controlled substance, so no legal action could or would be taken against those who used it or sold it. We are strictly concerned with MPTP as a medical emergency. Anything you tell us will be kept strictly confidential under protection of the Public Health Service Act. Law enforcement or other government agencies will not be allowed access to anything you say, and the information *cannot* be used against you or anyone you try to help, in any criminal or civil proceedings.

You may already have symptoms of this disease and *not know it. ONLY* a doctor's examination can eliminate this possibility (these are general physical examinations and involve little or no discomfort or payment). If we find you have this disease, we can help you. You need not suffer from many of the problems listed above. Furthermore, by examining you, we come that much closer to understanding this disease and devising a cure for it. If you know anyone who may have taken MPTP, please pass this information on to them.

WE REPEAT: IF YOU TOOK THIS "BAD HEROIN," EVEN ONCE, YOU MAY BE AT RISK FOR PARKINSON'S DISEASE AND SHOULD SEEK MEDICAL ATTENTION IMMEDIATELY.

CONTROLLED SUBSTANCES ANALOGS

ABBREVIATIONS

BDMPEA = 4-bromo-2,5-dimethoxyphenethylamine

DOB = 4-bromo-2,5-dimethoxyphenylisopropylamine

DOM = 4-methyl-2,5-dimethoxyphenylisopropylamine; STP

MDA = 3,4-methylenedioxyamphetamine

MDE = 3,4-methylenedioxy-N-ethylamphetamine

MDMA = 3,4-methylenedioxymethamphetamine; Ecstasy; XTC

MPPP = 1-methyl-4-phenyl-4-propionoxy-piperidine

MPTP = 1-methyl-4-phenyl-1,2,5,6-tetrahydropyridine

PEPAP = 1-phenethyl-4-phenyl-4-acetoxy-piperidine

ANABOLIC STEROIDS, BETA AGONISTS AND GAMMA HYDROXYBUTYRATE

INTRODUCTION

An estimated 2 to 3 million abusers of anabolic steroids support a $100 million dollar annual sales market that is nearly evenly divided between unscrupulous medical professionals, smugglers, and counterfeit clandestine laboratory operators. This unique form of drug abuse incorporates the diversion of pharmaceutical drugs from proper health care uses to illicit "street" uses with international black market smuggling and manufacturing operations.

Anabolic steroids are not generally thought of as drugs of abuse. Therein lies the problem. Adolescents rushing to physically become adults and athletes willing to win at any cost have discovered a short cut to achieve their goals, while the coaches, cops, and clinicians have slept. Tragically, this chemical time-saver destroys both body and mind to varying degrees and relegates premier performers to a "hall of shame."

Recent research has determined that the nationwide abuse of anabolic steroids, particularly by adolescents, is a significant problem. The abuse of steroids among male high school seniors is displayed in the chart below. The survey's finding that 6.6 percent of the seniors had used anabolic steroids, coupled with the report that two-thirds of the abusers began using steroids at or before the age of 16, indicates a serious drug abuse concern.

NATIONWIDE SURVEY OF ANABOLIC STEROID USE AMONG MALE HIGH SCHOOL SENIORS [1]

SAMPLE: 3403 twelfth graders from 46 private and public high schools

Age at First Use of Anabolic Steroids

15 or less	38.3%
16	3.0%
17	24.0%
18 or over	4.7%

Reasons for Using Anabolic Steroids

Improve Athletic Performance	47.1%
Appearance	26.7%
Prevent/Treat Injury	10.7%
Social and Other	15.5%

Primary Source of Anabolic Steroids

Black Market	60.5%
Physicians, Pharmacists, and Veterinarian	21.0%
Mail Order	9.0%

It is generally believed that anabolic steroid abuse is significantly underreported and misunderstood by the users, the public, medical practitioners, and the police. The ease with which researchers can obtain study sample information supports the contention of widespread use. With increased research and action by enforcement authorities, the problem of anabolic steroid abuse will be overcome.

The purpose of law enforcement involvement is to assure that anabolic steroids are not ignored, particularly by adolescents. Some authorities profess that anabolic steroids are more dangerous to America's youth than other recreational drugs.

WHAT ARE ANABOLIC STEROIDS?

Steroids are hormones naturally secreted by the endocrine glands, a complex system that influences and controls important bodily functions. Although the chemical nature of hormones is varied, a large proportion of

---

[1] Buckley, William E., et al. "Estimated Prevalence of Anabolic Steroid Use Among Male High School Seniors." *Journal of the American Medical Association* 260, No. 23, December 16, 1988, 3442-2444.

the body's hormones are steroids. Steroidal hormones are characterized by their basic cyclopentanoperhydrophenanthrene ring structure.

Steroidal hormones in humans are generally grouped into three main classes: (1) androgens, the primary male sex hormones, (2) estrogens, the primary female sex hormones, and (3) adrenocortical steroids by the adrenal cortex of both sexes. Similar steroids, generally referred to as sterols, are found in plants.

HISTORY OF STEROID DEVELOPMENT

The history of steroid development is fascinating. In the 1930s, steroid hormones were tediously extracted in small quantities from urine, or from animal tissues such as the adrenals and ovaries. This tedious extraction was extremely costly. As the study of the biological activity of steroids evolved rapidly, there was great incentive to find inexpensive starting materials, preferably from reliable plant sources. The first such material identified was diosgenin, obtained from the Mexican yam of the Dioscorea species.

Through the 1950s diosgenin continued to be the starting material for steroid production through partial synthesis. Another inexpensive material, cholesterol, from wool or animal fat, was also found to be a suitable starting material. Both materials undergo transformations, some of which are facilitated by microbial/fermentation methods.

As the price of the yam (then available only from Mexico) rose and led to eventual "nationalization," there ensued feverish activity to find alternative natural sources and more practical, totally synthetic routes. This activity was fueled by the discovery of the anti-inflammatory activity of cortisone in 1948 and the introduction of oral contraceptives in the early 1960s.

Nearly all steroids are currently derived commercially from either of two sources: (a) stigmasterol, the principal sterol from the unsaponifiable portion of soybean oil or (b) diosgenin from the Mexican yam. The Mexican yam can be grown in China but to date has not been successfully grown elsewhere. The diosgenin in the Mexican yam is the basis of the Diosynth, Roussel Uclag, Syntex, and Schering AG (Germany) methods of steroid production, while stigmasterol is the basis of Upjohn's production.

HISTORY OF STEROID USE

Steroids were first introduced to athletes in the United States by a physician and weightlifter, Dr. John Ziegler. Dr. Ziegler was appointed as the team physician for U.S. weightlifters at the world championships of 1954 in Vienna, Austria. While on that trip, he discovered the use of testosterone among Soviet weightlifters. He and some close associates tried testosterone and found that it increased their muscle development. With the help of a pharmaceutical company, Dr. Ziegler developed Dianobol (methandrostenolone) in the late 1950s. Soon after he adminstered Dianabol to some of the athletes training at the York Barbell Club, the rage began. Seeing the dangerous side effects of this new drug, Dr. Ziegler tried to stop its use, but it was too late.

A few of the more well-known anabolic agents are Dianabol, Winstrol, Durabolin 50, Decadurabolin, and Nilavar. Human growth hormone (HGH) or Somatotropin could be added to the list today. Since the development of these anabolic agents, the use of steroids to increase muscle growth has become a massive, worldwide phenomenon.

ANDROGENIC/ANABOLIC STEROIDS

Testosterone is the principal androgen of the testes. Kochakian and Murlin (1935) first demonstrated that androgens also promote nitrogen retention and protein synthesis. Papanicolaou and Falk (1938) then showed that male muscle development was mediated by androgens. This growth-promoting property or "anabolic" activity led to the term anabolic steroids. The discovery of this dual androgenic/anabolic activity led some researchers to attempt a dissociation of the two types of activity; this research then led to various theories of structure-activity relationships. However, these efforts have met with only partial success (Vida 1969). Thus far, it has not been possible to totally eliminate either type of activity; it has only been possible to enhance one type over another. Thus, the term androgenic/anabolic steroid became an accepted descripter for this class of steroids.

LEGAL STATUS OF ANABOLIC STEROIDS

By act of Congress in October 1990, anabolic steroids were placed in Schedule III of the Controlled Substances Act. The Act was signed into law in November of 1990 and became effective on February 27, 1991. Anabolic steroids are legally defined in 21 U.S.C. 802 (41)(A) and in 21 CFR §1308.02 as any drug or hormonal substance "chemically and pharmacologically related to testosterone" that promotes muscle growth.[2] The definition mentions twenty-seven specific anabolic steroids and includes their salts, esters, and optical isomers. These can be classified on a structural basis into two general groups: (1) androstand and its derivatives, and (2) 19-norandrostance (or estrance) and its derivatives.

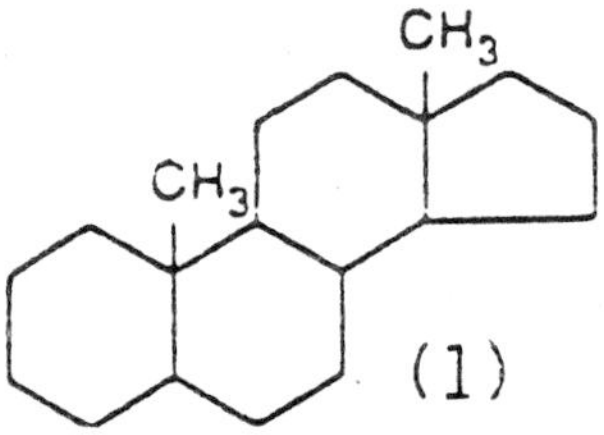

CH_3 CH_3 (1)

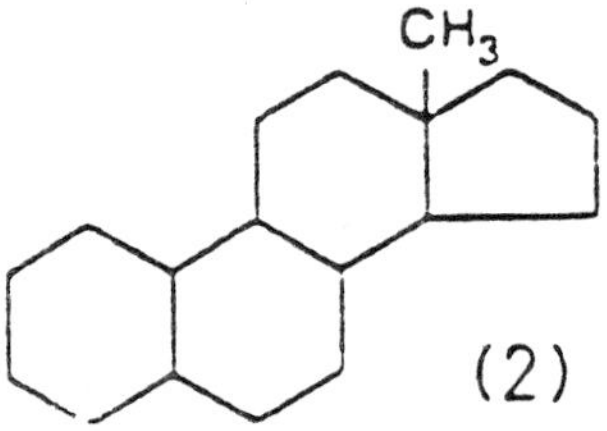

CH_3 (2)

Controlled anabolic steroids are classified as compounds structurally related to the following:

(I) testosterone

(II) methyltestosterone

(III) northesosterone or nandrolone

(IV) compounds having structurally unique features in addition to their commonality with testosterone.

A review of the controlled substance steroid list determined that, in three instances, individual steroids were listed under duplicate names. The fol-

---

[2] Gould Publications. *United States Code Unannotated.* Vol. 4. 1992.

lowing steroid types are actually one and the same steroid: 1) chlorotestosterone and clostebol, 2) dihydrotestosterone and stanolone, and 3) methandienone and methandrostenolone. Additionally, methandranone is incorrectly listed, since there is no such steroid. Thus, after calculating the misinformation, there are a total of twenty-three anabolic steroids—including their salts, esters, or isomers—listed in Schedule III. Several other anabolic steroids are being considered for addition to this list.

The following titles and sections of the U.S. Code are applicable in determining the legal liability of manufacturing, distributing, marketing, administering, and using those steroids listed in Schedule III of the Controlled Substances Act:

USC Title and Section	Related Offense
18 USC 2	Aiding and Abetting
18 USC 371	Conspiracy to Commit an Offense or Defraud the United States
19 USC 1497	Failure to Declare Merchandise
19 USC 2595(a)	Forfeiture Statue
21 USC 321	FDA Trademark Violation
21 USC 331(a)(b)	Adulterated/Misbranded Products
21 USC 331(i)(3)	Counterfeit Products
21 USC 333(b)	Counterfeit Products
21 USC 333(e)	Distributing Anabolic Steroids
21 USC 353(b)(1)	No Prescription
21 CFR 1306.04(a)	Prescribing Without Medical Purpose

USC - United States Code
CFR - Code of Federal Regulations

NOTE: Steroids intended for adminstration through implants to cattle or other non-human species are excluded.

STEROID SOURCES AND PRODUCTS

Most of the steroids currently on the market are smuggled in Mexican products. In addition, steroids diverted from medical uses have come from physicians, veterinarians, and pharmacists. Counterfeit steroids are also sold by gynasium and tanning salon entrepreneurs who purchase bottles, stoppers, and labels from unsuspecting medical supply houses and private printers. These unscrupulous entrepreneurs then fill the bottles with only corn or cottonseed oil.

Anabolic steroids that have been recently purchased and recovered by law enforcement investigation include:

— Primobolon

— Nandrolone Decanoate*

— Methandrostenolone*

— Stanozolol

— Oxymetholone*

— Testosterone-Cypionate*

— Depo-Testosterone*

— Testosterone Enanthate

— Sten

— Primotestin Depot

— Winstrol-V

— Sostenone-250

— Methyltestosterone

— Halotestin-Fluoxymesterone*

— Testosterone Suspension

*Known Counterfeits

Prices for individual steroid products range from $10.00 to $150.00, depending upon mg./ml. strength, manufacturer, and quantity. The most popular variety of steroids sold on the market are oil-based injectables, followed by tablets and water-based injectables. Syringes used for injection tend to be 22-gauge. Analysis of these syringes has shown that some steroid users combine the drug with other substances. In these poly-drug combinations the following substances have been found:

— Cocaine

— Marijuana

— Tenormin Atenolol (A prescription beta blocker for hypertension)

— Cyanocabalamin (A prescription B-12 vitamin)

— Forosemide (A prescription diuretic)

DISTRIBUTOR AND ABUSER TRENDS

Local work-out gyms are the primary location of anabolic steroid distribution activity. Dealers are contacted at the gyms and transactions occur at the gym, in the parking lot, or at the dealer's residence. The undercover buyer needs a good working knowledge of steroid products, prices, and abuse techniques, i.e., stacking, cycling, etc.

Counterfeit production of anabolic steroids has also been discovered in motel rooms and home garages of sellers. The counterfeit products are then distributed at or near local gym sites. Another popular distribution route is by mail order. Both nationally and internationally, steroid distributors utilize overnight express carriers and post office boxes to distribute the drug to both local dealers and individual users.

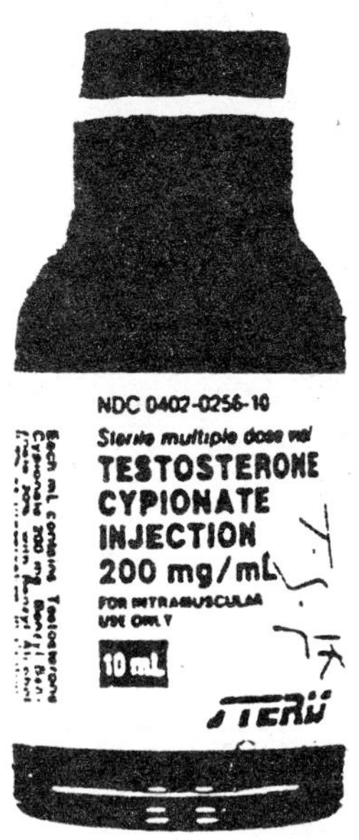

NDC 0402-0256-10
TESTOSTERONE
CYPIONATE
INJECTION
200 mg/mL
10 mL

Shown here is one of six crimp-top sealed vials analyzed by the Scientific Investigation Bureau of the Nassau County Police Department of New York. The vials were purchased for $1,200 as part of an undercover buy/bust operation by the Nassau County Police. After analysis, instead of the contents labelled "STERIS, 200 mg./ml. Testosterone Cypionate in cottonseed oil," the vials were found to contain only sesame seed oil. The vials were thoroughly counterfeit. These bottles had a red liner under the crimp-top where the authentic ones have a gray liner. The overall shape of the vials is also different, and the bottoms of the vials have a raised "number and dot" configuration which authentic vials do not have.

In addition to the scam of counterfeit steroids and the physical dangers of steroid abuse, one final concern is the involvement of public safety personnel in the distribution and use of this drug. Firemen, corrections officers, security guards, policemen, and deputy sheriffs have all been investigative targets for possession and sales of anabolic steroids. During covert operations and internal affairs follow-up, cases involving public safety professionals pose special concerns. Public safety personnel who abuse anabolic steroids also present unique liability concerns for department managers. In any case, however, the abuse of this drug is unlawful.

ANABOLIC STEROID PERIODS OF ACTION[3]

Steroid Type	Half Life	Preparation	Abuse Rate
Orals	few hours	Anavar	3-4 times daily (20-100 mg./day)
		Winstrol Dianabol Maxibolin Halotestin Adroyd	
Injectable Oils	1-3 days	Testosterone Propionate Testosterone Cypionate Durabolin Decadurabolin Primabolin	2-3 times weekly (200 mg./week)
Injectable Waters	few hours	Testosterone Methandriol	4 time weekly (400 mg./week)

SIDE EFFECTS OF ANABOLIC STEROIDS

A great deal has been written about the potential problems associated with anabolic steroid use. The two main side effects are changes in liver functioning and an increased risk of cardiovascular disease. Other dangerous side effects include: increase in irritability (aggressiveness), impaired pituitary and thyroid function, increase in blood pressure or nervous tension, disorder of the prostrate gland, changes in reproductive systems (testicular atrophy or clitoral enlargement), sex drive fluctuations, increased body and facial hair (thinning of hair on scalp), acne, skin rash, Gynecosmastia (development of breastlike tissue in males), sore nipples, headaches, dizziness, nose bleeds, drowsiness, muscle cramps, and spasms.

Women who use anabolics face most of the side effects listed above. Other side effects for women include: menstural irregularities, deepening of the voice (nonreversible), increased collagen (the fibrous component of connective tissue), and increased body and facial hair (nonreversible).[4]

Hormonal, Liver, and Cardiovascular Damage

The first area of concern for anabolic-androgenic steroid users is their hormonal effect. Steroids are synthetic derivatives of testosterone, the male hormone responsible for the development of masculine sex characteristics.

[3] Goldman, Bob, D.O. *Death in the Locker Room.* Tucson: The Body Press, 1984.
Taylor, William N., M.D. *Anabolic Steroids and the Athlete.* Jefferson: McFarland & Company, 1982.

[4] Miller, Roger W. "Athletes and Steroids: Playing a Deadly Game." *FDA Consumer.* November, 1987, 19 pp.
Voy, Robert, M.D. "Illicit Drugs and the Athlete." *American Pharmacy.* NS 26, No. 11, November, 1986, 41-44.
Windsor, Robert E., M.D. and D. Dumitru, M.D. "Anabolic steroid use by athletes. How serious are the health hazards?" *Postgraduate Medicine* 84, No. 4:37-49, September 15, 1988.

Designer Drugs/Anabolic Steroids

One of the most sought after functions of testosterone is the promotion of increased nitrogen retention and skeletal muscle growth.[5] It has been known for sometime that when a person takes steroids, the body's natural testosterone level will decrease. This effect is due in part to the the delicate balance in the negative feedback system mediated by the pituitary gland and the hypothalamus. (This balance is also known as the central effect.) In other words, the increased level of circulating synthetic testosterone tells the brain (more specifically, the hypothalamus and pituitary gland) that there is too much testosterone on board and production should stop. As a result, these areas of the brain shut down the synthesis of certain hormones (gonadotropins) whose job it is to regulate the testosterone production by the testes. The effect, then, is decreased stimulation for the testes to produce testosterone, since the anabolics have already satisfied this role.

The second main side effect of androgenic/anabolic steroid use is liver damage. Due to their method of absorption in the body, oral anabolics produce more liver problems than do the injectibles. Many body builders are already familiar with the elevated LFTs (liver function tests) seen in conjunction with anabolic steroids, especially those C-17 alpha alkyl oral derivatives of testosterone (Dianabol, Anavar, Anadrol, etc.). A review of the sources cited below indicates that 50 percent of all individuals using oral steroids in their training regimens demonstrate LFT figures above the acceptable range.

Steroids have several effects on the liver that are not reversible. The two life-threatening conditions of peliosis hepatis (not to be confused with hepatitis) and liver tumors are both well-documented in medical literature on steroid use. Peliosis hepatis, characterized by the formulation of multiple, small blood-filled cystic lesions within the liver, was found in 23 steroid abuse cases extending into 1984. In addition, 36 cases of liver tumors were investigated. Of all these cases of severe hepatic complications, only one involved a body builder using steroids. The others were associated with steroids administered for medical therapy.[6]

This one case is very significant, however, because it is the first report of severe liver dysfunction due to anabolic steroids used for athletic purposes. The subject, a competitive body-builder with apparently no previous history of liver disease, had self-administered various steroids, including Dianabol, Anavar, and Winstrol, during the four years before his hospitalization for unexplained weight loss. In a shocking turn of events, he was overcome by widespread liver cancer only three months after admission. This case further supports the premise that severe liver dysfunction is primarily associated with the prolonged use of the orally active C-17 alpha alkyl anabolic steroids.

---

[5] Papnicolaou, G.N., and E.A. Falk. "General Muscular Hypertrophy Induced by Androgenic Hormones." *Science* 87, 238 (1938).

[6] Kuipers, H. "Influence of anabolic steroids on body composition, blood pressure, liquid profile, and liver functions in body builders." *International Journal of Sports Medicine.* 12:413-418, 1991.

The third problem resulting from steroid use is an increased risk of cardiovascular complications.[7] Multiple independent studies were conducted in 1984 in hopes of settling this issue. The results, to say the least, are alarming. In essence, steroids were found to cause a dramatic reduction of high density lipoproteins (HDL-C) and an increase in low density lipoproteins (LDL-C) in the body. The problem is that low HDL-cholesterol values are an independent risk factor for the development of coronary artery disease. This adverse effect takes place through a mediating enzyme, hepatic triglyceride lipase, found in the liver. Apparently, anabolic steroids increase this enzyme; the enzyme then removes HDL particles from the body's circulatory processes. After only eight weeks of steroid use, the level of HDL cholesterol can drop by 50 percent. There is also evidence that LDL cholesterol levels can rise by as much as 20 to 25 percent during this time. The problem with an LDL increase is that high levels of LDL cholesterol contribute to the development of heart disease. Thus, the double effect of steroids on the body's cholesterol levels results in serious cardiovascular complications.

There is no doubt about the damaging effects of anabolic steroids on testosterone levels, the liver, and the cardiovascular system. Yet, there are several other effects such as skin problems, fluid retention, baldness, severe depression, and extreme aggressiveness.

SIGNS AND SYMPTOMS OF STEROID USE

When investigating steroid use, one should look for the following warning signs: sudden weight gain, male breast enlargement or shrinkage of the testicles, unusual muscular injuries of the chest or arms; jaundice, severe acne, thinning hair on the forehead or temples, sudden adult male characteristics such as change in voice or facial hair, mood swings (such as euphoria, giddiness, aggressiveness or depression), and curiosity about steroid use. Since adolescents are particularly vulnerable to steroid dealers and stand to suffer the most long-range bodily damage from steroid abuse, they should be watched carefully for these warning signs.

SLANG TERMINOLOGY

Some slang terms for steroids include: Blast, Ball, Depo, G, Growth, Roids, Maxi, Primo, and Test.

BETA AGONISTS

In addition to steroids, there is a new group of body-altering drugs on the market—the beta agonists. The most common beta antagonist is clenbuterol. Although these drugs are primarily for use in animals, there is one exception: certain beta agonists have specialized medical uses as specific bronchiodilators used by asthmatics to relax the muscles of the bronchi.

---

[7] Kautor, Mark A. "Androgens Reduce HDL2-Cholesterol and Increase Hepatic Triglyceride Lipase Activity." *Medicine and Science in Sports and Exercise.* Vol. 17, August, 1985.

Alen, M. "Androgenic Steroid Effects on Liver and Red Cells." *British J. of Sports Med.* Vol. 5 (6), March 1985.

Designer Drugs/Anabolic Steroids

Some of the research on animals indicates that administration of large dosages of beta agonists may enhance lean body mass and reduce the animal's bodyfat. This is an effect that many people are interested in obtaining. However, there is a down side to beta agonists.

MINOR SIDE EFFECTS

Here is a list of documented beta agonist side effects that can be dangerous but are most likely not life-threatening:

Heart palpitations

Heart rate increase

Severe headaches

Nosebleeds

Dizziness

Nausea and vomiting

Alternating fever and chills

Muscle aches and pains

Extreme irritability

Nervousness

Dramatic increase in sensitivity to stress

MAJOR SIDE EFFECTS

Some of the documented life-threatening side effects (and only those that we know of so far) of beta agonist use are listed below:[8]

Fatalities from myocardial infarctions (heart attacks)

Strokes

Violent muscle tremors

Severe hemorrhaging

Tachycardia (could double resting heart rate)

Cancerous tumors

Interestingly, these major side effects were not seen in the animals themselves, but in their offspring. In second generation animal studies, an

---

[8] Stock, M.J., and N.J. Rothwell. "Effects of beta-adrenergic agonists on metabolism and body composition." *Control and Metabolism of Animal Growth.* London: Butterworth Pub. Co., 249-257, 1986.

elevated incidence of tumors was well-documented. Due to these findings, most companies working with clenbuterol and cimaterol have dropped them.

Although the researchers have only clinically studied beta agonists in animals, it has been determined that the same side effects will occur in humans.[9] These findings were the result of an isolated health epidemic in Europe.

In the spring of 1990, medical authorities in Spain and France were dismayed by an alarming number of violently ill people in certain areas of their countries. Exhibiting strikingly similar symptoms (tremors, heart palpitations, fever, tachycardis, vomitting, etc.), these individuals appeared to have been poisoned by a beta agonist. As it turned out, they were. The patients did not self-administer the beta antagonist; rather, they ingested the substance by eating the liver of cattle that had been treated with clenbuterol. One hundred thirty-five people in Spain and 22 in France received medical attention for clenbuterol poisoning, attracting the attention of the U.S. Department of Agriculture, which now condemns meat found to contain any residues of clenbuterol.[10]

Given that these victims of clenbuterol poisoning did not administer the drug themselves, the potential for permanent damage through self-administration is alarming. If clenbuterol or other beta agonists are ever marketed toward athletes, both law enforcement and physicians may have a serious health problem with which to contend.

GAMMA HYDROXY BUTYRATE

Several U.S. states have recently reported outbreaks of poisoning associated with the illicit use of Gamma Hydroxy Butyrate (GHB). These reports were made to the National Center for Disease Control. The Center's records reveal that from June through November 28, 1990, at least 57 cases of illness attributed to GHB exposure were reported. California reported 25 cases, 17 of which were from the San Francisco area; Georgia reported 15 cases, all of which were from the greater Atlanta area; Florida reported seven, six of which were from the greater Tampa area; South Carolina reported three; Minnesota reported two; Arizona, two; and Ohio, Texas and Virginia, one each.

Although no deaths were reported, most patients required emergency room care; at least 11 of the victims were hospitalized, and nine required ventilator support or other intensive care. The adverse effects of GHB

---

[9] Forsberg, N.E., M.A. Ilian, et al. "Effects of cimaterol on growth and myofibrillar protein degradation and on calcium-dependent proteinase and calpastatin activities in skeletal muscle." *J. Anim. Sci.* 68:652-658, 1989.

Harper, J.M.M., I. Mackinson, et al. "The effects of beta agonists on muscle cells in culture." *Dom. Anim. Edno.* 7:477-484, 1990.

Timmerman, H. "Beta-adrenergics: Physiology, pharmacology, applications, structure, and structure activity relationships." *Beta Agonists and Their Effects on Animal Growth and Carcass Quality*. New York: Elsevier Appl. Sci. Pub., pp. 13-28, 1987.

[10] Bechet, D.M., A. Listrat, et al. "Cimaterol reduce cathepsin activities but has no anbolic effect in cultured myotubes." *Am. J. Phys.* 259:E827, 1990.

Reeds, P.J., S.M. Hay, et al. "Stimulation of muscle growth by clenbuterol: Lack of effect on muscle protein biosynthesis." *Jr. J. Nutr.* 56:249-258, 1986.

poisoning include vomitting, drowsiness, a hypotonic state, loss of consciousness, irregular and depressed respiration, tremors, seizure-like activity, hypotension, and respiratory arrest.

GHB is a normal metabolite produced by the body and is not a nutritional requirement. Since at least May, 1990, GHB has been marketed illicitly to body builders. It has also been promoted illicitly for weight control and insomnia. Despite its lack of nutritional value, GHB has even been illicitly touted as a "replacement" for L-tryptophan, which had been marketed as a food supplement. It is alleged that GHB produces a "high" (a trance-like state). The promotion of this effect has led to the further use of GHB as an illicit drug. Investigations conducted by the State Food and Drug Branch in San Jose, California revealed that some of the same distributors involved in illegally marketing GHB are also involved in illegally marketing steroids.

GHB is sold through mail order outlets, health food stores, body building gyms, and fitness centers. GHB has been illegally marketed under a variety of names, including Gamma Hydroxybutric Acid, Sodium Oxybate, Sodium Oxybutyrate, Gamma Hydroxybutrate Sodium, Gamma-OH, 4-Hydroxy Butyrate, Gamma Hydrate, and Somatomax PM. It is distributed as a sodium salt in powder or tablet form and is commonly dissolved in water. GHB may also be offered in other forms or in combination with other ingredients.

In the United States, the only legal use of GHB has been under specific FDA exemptions for investigational research protocols (e.g., treatment of narcolepsy). In Europe, GHB has also been used as an anesthetic adjunct and experimentally as a treatment for prosthypoxic cerebral edema and ethanol withdrawal.

Due to its adverse poisoning effects, GHB was banned by California on November 8, 1990. In California, GHB is an unapproved drug product and is therefore illegal to sell, advertise for sale, or possess. Anyone advertising, selling or possessing GHB is in violation of the Sherman Food, Drug and Cosmetic Law, Division 21 of the Health and Safety Code, Sections 26000 through 26851.

DEFINITION OF TERMS RELATED TO STEROIDS:

Anabolic .... To build and cause synthesis of body tissue.

Anabolic Steroids ... Synthetic derivatives of the natural male sex hormone, testosterone.

Androgenic .... To cause virilization or male sexual characteristics. All anabolic steroids have some androgenic qualities.

Cortical Steroids .... Natural hormones formed in the cortex (outer layer) of the adrenal gland located on top of each kidney. These steroids are used to suppress inflammation, treat asthma, and for replacement therapy for people with adrenal insufficiency.

Cycling .... A periodic repetition of anabolic steroid abuse. Cycles may last from 6 to 12 weeks of drug use followed by 8 to 10 weeks of drug free periods.

Ergogenic Aids ..... Any substance, whether naturally formed or synthesized, that can be used to increase strength, flexibility, or endurance.

Estrogen .... Female sex hormones produced chiefly by the ovaries.

Human Growth Hormone (HGH) ... A polypeptide hormone secreted by the pituitary gland or synthetically available through commercial genetic engineering. One of the most powerful hormones in controlling human growth and development.

Hormone .... A chemical produced by a gland, secreted in the blood stream, and affecting the function of distant cells or organs. The three types of hormones classified on a structural basis are polypeptide, protein, and steroid hormones.

Stacking .... The simultaneous use of different anabolic steroid preparations (both oral and injectable), with the expectation of saturating and stimulating multiple receptor sites while limiting the aggregate dose or side effects.

Steroids .... A classification of fat-soluble organic compounds based upon molecular structure and including some of the natural and synthetic hormones.

Testosterone .... Male sex hormones with anabolic and androgenic effects produced by the testes.

Steroids: A Selected Bibliography

Introduction

This bibliography is not comprehensive but is intended to provide some important sources of information on steroids and beta agonists.

Alen, M. "Androgenic Steroid Effects on Liver and Red Cells." *British J. of Sports Med.* Vol. 5 (6), March 1985.

Alen, M., and P. Rahkila. "Reduced HDL Cholesterol in Power Athletes." *Int. J. Sports Med.* Vol. 5 (6), Dec., 1984.

Alen, Marrku., et al. "Response of Serum Hormones to Androgen Administration." *Medicine and Science in Sports and Exercise.* Vol. 17, June, 1985.

American Medical Association. Council on Scientific Affairs. "Drug abuse in athletes: anabolic steroids and human growth hormone." *Journal of the American Medical Association* 259, No. 11:1703-1705, March 18, 1988.

_____. Council on Scientific Affairs. "Medical and nonmedical uses of anabolic-androgenic steroids." *Journal of the American Medical Association* 264, No. 22-2923-2927, December 12, 1990.

"Anabolic Steroids Control Act of 1990." (104 Stat. 4851. The Anabolic Steroids Control Act of 1990 is Title XIX of the Crime Control Act of 1990, P.L. 101-647, November 29, 1990.)

Bahrke, Michael S. "Anabolic-androgenic steroid use by soldiers: the U.S. Army steroid testing policy." *Military Medicine.* 155:573-574, November 1990.

Bechet, D.M., A. Listrat, et al. "Cimaterol reduce cathepsin activities but has no anbolic effect in cultured myotubes." *Am. J. Phys.* 259:E827, 1990.

Bero, Dennis L. "Of MDs and muscles—lessons from two 'retired steroid doctors.'" *Journal of the American Medical Association* 263, No. 12:1697-1705, March 23/30, 1990.

Brower, Kirk J. "Addictive potential of anabolic steroids." *Psychiatric Annals* 22, No. 1:30-34, January 1992.

________. "Clinical assessment and urine testing for anabolic-androgenic steroid abuse and dependence." *American Journal of Drug and Alcohol Abuse* 17, No. 2:161-171, 1991.

Buckley, William E. "Estimated prevalence of anabolic steroid use among male high school seniors." *Journal of the American Medical Association* 260, No. 23:3441-3445, December 16, 1988.

Catlin, Don H. "Analytical chemistry at the Games of the XXIIIrd Olympiad in Los Angeles, 1984." *Clinical Chemistry* 33, No. 2:319-327, 1987.

Chelminski, Rudolph. "'The shocking stain on international athletics." *Reader's Digest.* 133:131-135, August, 1988.

Choi, P.Y.L. "High-dose anabolic steroids in strength athletes: effects upon hostility and aggression." *Human Psychopharmacology.* 5:349-356, 1990.

Committee on Sports Medicine. "Anabolic steroids and the adolescent athlete." *Pediatrics* 83, No. 1:127-128, January, 1989.

Cowart, Virginia S. "Athletes and steroids: the bad bargain." *Saturday Evening Post.* 259:56-59, April, 1987.

_____. "Bunting 'steroid epidemic' requires alternatives, innovative education." *Journal of the American Medical Association* 264, No. 13:1641, October 3, 1990.

_____. "Ethical, as well as physiological, questions continue to arise over athletes' steroid abuse." *Journal of the American Medical Association* 261, No. 23:3362-3367, June 16, 1989.

_____. "Would controlled substance status affect steroid trafficking?" *Physician and Sportsmedicine* 15, No. 5:151-154, May, 1987.

Dart, Roland C. "Anabolic steroid abuse among law enforcement officers." *Police Chief* 58, No. 7:18, July 1991.

Donohoe, Tom and Neil Johnson. *Foul play: drug abuse in sports.* New York: Basil Blackwell, 1986. 189 pp.

Duda, Marty. "Do anabolic steroids pose an ethical dilemma for U.S. physicians?" *Physician and Sports Medicine* 14, No. 11:173-175, November 1986.

Dyment, Paul G. "Steroids: breakfast of champions." *Pediatrics in Review* 12, No. 4:103-105, October 1990.

Elashoff, Janet D. "Effects of anabolic-androgenic steroids on muscular strength." *Annals of Internal Medicine* 115, No. 5:387-393, September 1, 1991.

Forsberg, N.E., M.A. Ilian, et al. "Effects of cimaterol on growth and myofibrillar protein degradation and on calcium-dependent proteinase and calpastatin activities in skeletal muscle." *J. Anim. Sci.* 68:652-658, 1989.

Fuller, John R. "Performance-enhancing drugs in sport: a different form of drug abuse." *Adolescence* 22, No. 88:969-976, Winter 1987.

Fultz, Oliver. "Roid rage: anabolic steroid use is exploding with shattering consequences." *American Health.* 10:60-65, May 1991.

GAO Report B-235236. "Anabolic steroids and Human Growth Hormone." 1989.

Goldman, Bob, D.O. *Death in the locker room: steroids, cocaine & sports.* Tucson, AZ: The Body Press, 1987. 370 p.; 1984, pp. 113-135.

Goodwin, Frederick K. "Anabolic steroids and dependence." *Journals of the American Medical Association* 266, No. 12:1619, September 25, 1991.

Graham, Stewart. "Recent developments in the toxicology of anabolic steroids." *Drug Safety* 5, No. 6:459-476, 1990.

Groves, David. "The Rambo drug: steroids. . . " *American Health* 43-48, September, 1987.

Harper, J.M.M., I. Mackinson, et al. "The effects of beta agonists on muscle cells in culture." *Dom. Anim. Edno.* 7:477-484, 1990.

Haupt, Herbert A. "Anabolic steroids: a review of the literature." *American Journal of Sports Medicine* 12, No. 6:469-484, 1984.

Haupt, H.A., and G.D. Rovere. "Anabolic Steroids." *American Journal of Sports Medicine.* Vol. 12 (6), Nov-Dec., 1984.

Hickson, Robert C. "Adverse effects of anabolic steroids." *Medical Toxicology and Adverse Drug Experience* 4, No. 4:254-271, 1989.

Johnson, Mimi D. "Anabolic steroid use in adolescent athletes." *Pediatric Clinics of North America* 37, No. 5:1111-1123, October, 1990.

Kautor, Mark A. "Androgens Reduce HDL2-Cholesterol and Increase Hepatic Triglyceride Lipase Activity." *Medicine and Science in Sports and Exercise.* Vol. 17, August, 1985.

Kochakian, C.D., and J.R. Murlin. "The effects of male hormone on the protein and energy metabolism of castrate dogs." *J. Nutr.* 10, 437 (1935).

Designer Drugs/Anabolic Steroids

Kuipers, H. "Influence of anabolic steroids on body composition, blood pressure, liquid profile, and liver functions in body builders." *International Journal of Sports Medicine.* 12:413-418, 1991.

Lamb, David R. "Anabolic steroids in athletics: how well do they work and how dangerous are they?" *American Journal of Sports Medicine* 12, No. 1:31-38, 1984.

Landry, Gregory L. "Anabolic steroid abuse." *Advances in Pediatrics.* 37:185-205, 1990.

Lin, Geraldine C. (ed.). *Anabolic steroid abuse.* Rockville, MD: National Institute on Drug Abuse, 1990. 249 pp. NIDA Research Monograph 102, DDS Publication No. ADM 91-1720.

Lopez, Mike. "Steroids in athletics: one university's experience." *Journal of College Student Development.* 31:523-530, November, 1990.

Lubbell, Adele. "Does steroid abuse cause—or excuse—violence?" *Physician & Sportsmedicine* 17, No. 2:176-185, 1989.

May, Jon R. (ed.). *State laws/regulations pertaining to the control of anabolic steroids.* Rockville, MD: U.S. Food and Drug Administration, Division of Federal-State Relations, Office of Regional Operations, 1991.

Miller, Roger W. "Athletes and Steroids: Playing a Deadly Game." *FDA Consumer.* November, 1987, 19 pp.

Moore, Wayne V. "Anabolic steroid use in adolescence." *Journal of the American Medical Association* 260, No. 23:3484-3486, December 16, 1988.

Narducci, Warren A. "Anabolic steroids—a review of the clinical toxicology and diagnostic screening." *Journal of Toxicology/Clinical Toxicology* 28, No. 3:287-310, 1990.

Nemechek, Patrick M. "Anabolic steroid users—another potential risk group for HIV infection." *New England Journal of Medicine* 325, No. 5:357, August 1, 1991.

O'Connor, John S. "Blood chemistry of current and previous anabolic steroid users." *Military Medicine.* 155:72-75, February, 1990.

Papnicolaou, G.N., and E.A. Falk. "General Muscular Hypertrophy Induced by Androgenic Hormones." *Science* 87, 238 (1938).

Perry, Paul J. "Illicit anabolic steroid use in athletes: a case series analysis." *American Journal of Sports Medicine* 18, No. 4:422-428, July-August, 1990.

Reeds, P.J., S.M. Hay, et al. "Stimulation of muscle growth by clenbuterol: Lack of effect on muscle protein biosynthesis." *Jr. J. Nutr.* 56:249-258, 1986.

Stehlin, Dori. "For athletes and dealers: black market steroids are risky business." *FDA Consumer* 21, No. 7:24-25, September, 1987.

"Steroids in sports. Part I: System accused of failing test posed by drugs." *New York Times.* Thursday, November 17, 1988.

"Steroids in sports. Part II: On the black market, drugs are in easy reach of public." *New York Times* Friday, November 18, 1988.

"Steroids in sports. Part III: A 'guru' who spreads the gospel of steroids." *New York Times.* Saturday, November 19, 1988.

"Steroids in sports. Part IV: New 'breakfast of champions': a recipe for victory or disaster?" *New York Times.* Sunday, November 20, 1988.

"Steroids in sports. Part V: Victory at any cost: drug pressure growing." *New York Times.* Monday, November 21, 1988.

Stock, M.J., and N.J. Rothwell. "Effects of beta-adrenergic agonists on metabolism and body composition." *Control and Metabolism of Animal Growth.* London: Butterworth Pub. Co., 249-257, 1986.

Strauss, Richard H. (ed.). *Drugs & performance in sports.* Philadelphia: Saunders, 1987. 221 pp.

Strickland, A.L. "Steroids: do they enhance athletic performance?" *Journal of the South Carolina Medical Association* 84, No. 2:59-62, February 1988.

Swanson, Charles. "Abuse of anabolic steroids." FBI Law Enforcement Buletin 60. No. 8:19-23, August 1991.

Taylor, William N. *Anabolic steroids and the athlete.* Jefferson, NC: McFarland, 1982. 116 pp.

_____. "Drug issues in sports medicine. Part I: Steroid abuse and NSAID selection in athletic/active patients." *Journal of Neurological & Orthopaedic Medicine & Surgery* 9, No. 2:159-164, July, 1988.

_____. "Drug issues in sports medicine. Part II: Growth hormone abuse and anti-hypertensive drug selection in athletic/active patients." *Journal of Neurological & Orthopaedic Medicine & Surgery* 9, No. 2:159-164, July, 1988.

_____. "Synthetic anabolic-androgenic steroids: a plea for controlled substance status." *Physicians and Sportsmedicine* 15, No. 5:140-150, May 1987.

Timmerman, H. "Beta-adrenergics: Physiology, pharmacology, applications, structure, and structure activity relationships." *Beta Agonists and Their Effects on Animal Growth and Carcass Quality.* New York: Elsevier Appl. Sci. Pub., pp. 13-28, 1987.

Tricker, Ray. "The incidence of anabolic steroid use among competitive body builders." *Journal of Drug Education* 19, No. 4:313-325, 1989.

Turner, A.B. "Steroids: reactions and partial syntheses." *Natural Products Reports* 6, No. 6:539-575, December, 1989.

U.S. Comptroller General. *Drug Misuse: anabolic steroids and the human growth hormone.* Washington: General Accounting Office, 1989. 43 pp. (GAO/HRD-89-109) (B-235236).

U.S. Congress. House Committee on Energy and Commerce. *Medical devices and drug issues.* Hearings before the Subcommittee on Health and the Environment. 100th Congress, 1st session, 1987. Washington, US GPO, 1987. 400 pp.

_____. House Committee on the Judiciary. *Abuse of steroids in amateur and professional athletics.* Hearings before the Subcommittee on Crime. 101st Congress, 2nd session, 1990. Washington: US GPO, 1990. 163 pp. (Serial No. 92).

_____. House Committee on the Judiciary. *Anabolic steroid restriction act of 1989.* Hearing before the Subcommittee on Crime. 101st Congress, 1st session, 1989. Washington: US GPO, 1989. 90 pp.

_____. House Committee on the Judiciary. *Anabolic steroids control act of 1990.* Hearing before the Subcommittee on Crime. 101st Congress, 2nd session, 1990. Washington: US GPO, 1990. 48 pp. (Serial No. 90).

_____. House Committee on the Judiciary. *Legislation to amend the Controlled Substances Act (anabolic steroids).* Hearing before the Subcommittee on Crime. 100th Congress, 2nd session, 1988. Washington: US GPO, 1989. 105 pp.

U.S. Dept. of Justice. Drug Enforcement Administration. "Schedules of controlled substances; anabolic steroids." Federal Register 56, No. 30:5753-5754, February 13, 1991.

Designer Drugs/Anabolic Steroids

Vida, J.A. "Androgens and Anabolic Agents." New York: Academic Press, 1969.

Voy, Robert, M.D. "Illicit Drugs and the Athlete." *American Pharmacy.* NS 26, No. 11, November, 1986, 41-44.

Voy, Robert O. *Drugs, sport, and politics.* Champaign, IL: Leisure Press, 1991. 227 pp.

Walters, Milda. "Analysis of illegally distributed anabolic steroid products by liquid chromatography with identity confirmation by mass spectrometry or infrared spectrophotometry." *Journal of the Association of Official Analytical Chemists* 73, No. 6:904-926, November/December, 1990.

White, George L. "Preventing steroid abuse in youth: the health educator's role." *Health Education* 18, No. 4:32-35, August/September, 1987.

Windsor, Robert E., M.D. and D. Dumitru, M.D. "Anabolic steroid use by athletes. How serious are the health hazards?" *Postgraduate Medicine* 84, No. 4:37-49, September 15, 1988.

Woolley, Bruce. "The use and misuse of drugs by athletes." *Houston Medical Journal.* 2:29-35, March, 1986.

Wright, James E. "Anabolic steroids and athletics." *Exercise & Sports Sciences Reviews.* 8:149-202, 1980.

Yesalis, Charles R. "Epidemiology and patterns of anabolic-androgenic steroid use." *Psychiatric Annals* 22, No. 1:7-18, January 1992.

Zurer, Pamela S. "Drugs in sports." *Chemical & Engineering News* 62, No. 18:69-78, April 30, 1984.

________. "Pumped up." *U.S. News & World Report 112.* No. 21:54-56, 59, 61-63, June 1, 1992.

This page intentionally left blank.

CHAPTER X

CENTRAL NERVOUS SYSTEM STIMULANTS

The stimulant drugs are so named because they excite the body's normal functions and work directly on the central nervous system. Their ability to produce increased activity, alertness, and excitation has prompted people to call them "pep pills," or more commonly, "uppers." Their medical uses include treatment of depression, weight control, and warding off fatigue during dangerous and prolonged tasks by astronauts, pilots, etc. Some criminals have reported that they use stimulant drugs to bolster their courage before committing a crime.

The stimulant drugs most frequently abused are cocaine and the amphetamines (which include drugs chemically related to amphetamines). Two additional drugs gaining popularity (but not covered here) are phenmetrazine (known as Preludin) and methylphenidate (known as Ritalin).

COCAINE (ERYTHROXYLON COCA)

INTRODUCTION

Cocaine (Benzoylmethyl ecognine - $C_{17}H_{21}NO_4$) is a white crystalline alkaloid found in the leaves of the coca bush (Erythroxylon coca). This substance acts as a stimulant on the central nervous system.

Cocaine is the principal active ingredient of the South American coca plant. The coca plant is an evergreen native to South America, particularly the countries of Peru, Bolivia, Brazil, Chile, and Columbia. It has also been successfully cultivated in Java, West Indies, India, and Australia.

THE ILLICIT PROCESSING OF COCA

There are some very important differences between the legitimate and illegitimate processing of coca. The illicit processor rarely has access to the wide range of quality chemicals available to legitimate processors in the United States and Europe. The illicit process is carried out by "cooks" who know little about chemistry and routinely use substitute solvents and chemicals, depending on what is available.

As a South American "cook" once said, "All you need to make cocaine is three buckets and two sheets." Many cooks actually use this method. The work is done in makeshift laboratories more reminiscent of kitchens, and the sheets (complete with multiple kilos) are often hung on a clothesline to dry in the sun. Time is of the essence, and one never knows when a cocaine kitchen may have to be moved at a moment's notice. Lengthy procedures are abbreviated to meet this criterion and quality is often sacrificed in the process.

There are three kinds of laboratories that deal with the different stages of coca processing. Usually located at or near the growing area is the pasta lab, which is used to extract all the alkaloids from the coca leaf in the form of a water soluble paste. This crude cocaine sulfate, called pasta, is far less bulky than the leaves themselves, and the extraction procedure and laboratory requirements are simple enough to be performed by the coca growers themselves. The pasta maker simply soaks the dried leaves in water, adds a strong alkali (such as lime) to release the alkaloids, and stirs in a solvent like kerosene or gasoline, which will dissolve the alkaloids while remaining separate from the water. The water is then drained out the bottom of the container and the solvent (gasoline or kerosene) is poured off the top. Once the gasoline has been separated, sulfuric acid is added to precipitate the alkaloids. The precipitate—the pasta—is separated from the gasoline by filtration and put out in the sun to dry. On the average, it takes 100 to 150 kilos of dry leaves to produce one kilo of dry pasta.

The dry pasta is usually tannish brown, resulting from plant material, dirt, or other substances on the coca leaves. Usually all the pasta's compounds will precipitate with lime and dissolve in gasoline. If a stronger alkali is used, more compounds will be present.

The next step of the process is to convert the pasta to cocaine base. This step usually takes place in a base lab located in Columbia. The conversion process is critical since it determines the amount and proportions of different alkaloids that will be present in the finished product. Due to the time involved, weight losses, and the potential risk to the cocaine, some parts of this conversion process are routinely left out. When properly performed, however, the conversion of pasta to cocaine base will eliminate cinnamylcocaine, hygrine, and most organic impurities.

The conversion is properly performed by dissolving the pasta in water and adding sulfuric acid to further acidify the solution. Potassium permanganate is then added to the solution, causing it to turn a violet color. During this oxidation process, the cocaine is not appreciably affected, but the oils and impurities are attacked almost immediately. The critical part of the process is deciding when to stop the action of the permanganate by adding an alkali. If the decision is made too early, the resultant base will contain more impurities and other alkaloids; if the decision is made too late, some cocaine will be destroyed by the permanganate.

There is hardly an experienced cook who has not over-oxidized the pasta at one time or another. Therefore, this part of the conversion process is often eliminated. The owners of the pasta do not want to take the chance of losing any cocaine. It will sell anyway, so why risk the loss of profits by oxidizing the pasta?

However, pasta converted to base without being oxidized rarely results in cocaine hydrochloride (the final product) which is over 60 percent cocaine base. Cocaine hydrochloride made from properly oxidized base, on the other hand, may contain as much as 82 percent cocaine base. By eliminating the oxidation process, the cooks are actually decreasing the content of cocaine base in the finished product. Nonetheless, the un-oxidized finished product will sell equally well.

The last step of the process is to convert the base to "crystal," the South American term for cocaine hydrochloride. This step is usually done in a crystal lab located in or near a major city in Columbia. The base is dissolved in ether; hydrochloric acid is then added to precipitate the formation of cocaine hydrochloride crystals. These crystals are collected by filtration and then dried. This process will rarely be performed with less than 3 kilos, since as many as 50 kilos may be done at one time. The crystallization is performed as quickly as possible by illicit processors, taking as little as 15 minutes, whereas a more professional procedure might take hours.

Since most illicit cocaine is made the quick way, with the emphasis on quantity, it often contains an alkaloid proportion similar to that which existed in the leaves themselves. This alkaloid proportion is not necessarily bad, because most consumers of cocaine seem to prefer the mellower high of mixed-alkaloid cocaine to the speedy but clear high of the pharmaceutical product. It should be noted that, in medicine, cocaine is used as a local anesthetic; the presence of other alkaloids makes it less effective as such. However, when the cocaine is used as a recreational drug, the same reasoning may not hold true.

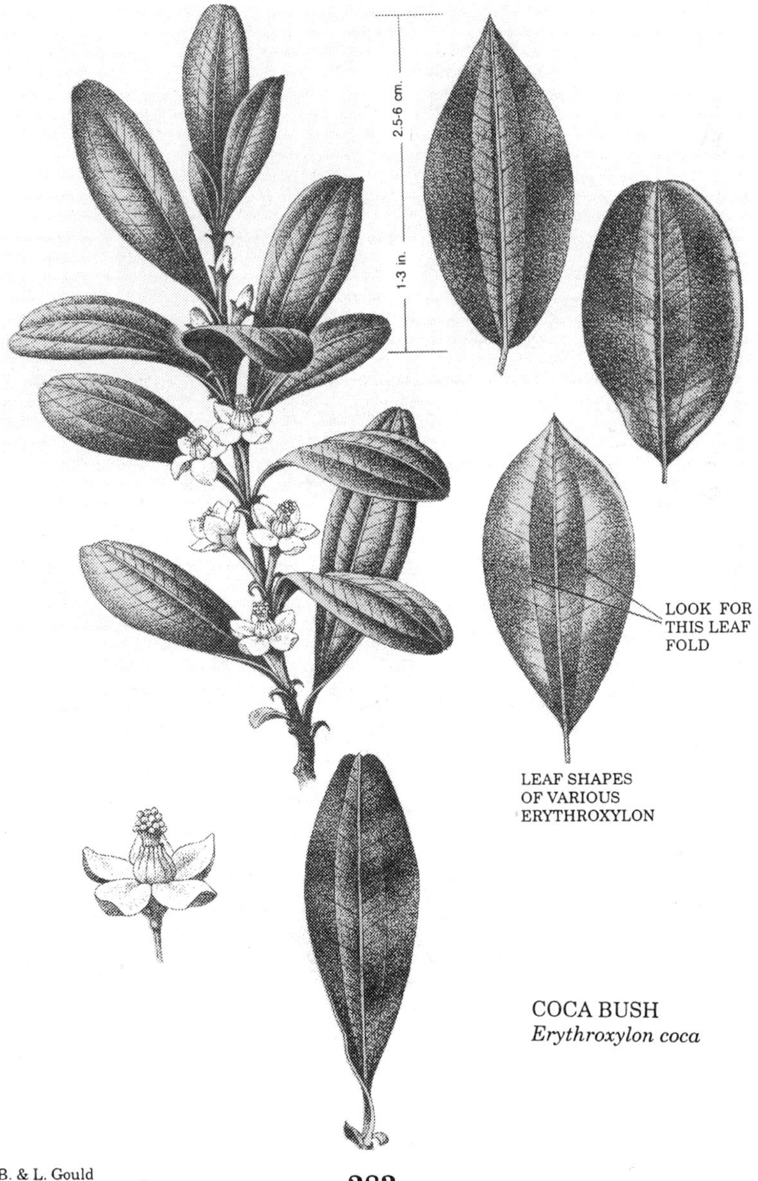

COCA BUSH
Erythroxylon coca

HISTORY OF COCA USE

The natives of South America have a long history of chewing on the leaf of the coca plant; it has been estimated that over 90 percent of all South American natives chew the coca leaf. They chew, on an average, about two ounces of coca leaf daily and are often characterized by blackish red deposits on their teeth. These deposits are caused by the alkaline ash sprinkled on the cocaine to increase its oral absorption. South Americans claim that, despite the bitter taste of the leaves, the cocaine depresses their hunger and increases their strength.

South American natives have explained how chewing the leaves of the coca plant gives them energy to withstand the long grueling hours needed to cultivate their rocky, unproductive terrain; it reduces hunger and keeps them warm. Cocaine raises the body's temperature and, by constricting surface blood vessels, holds on to the increased body heat. This effect of cocaine offsets the cold temperature of peaks such as those in the Andes mountains, allowing South Americans to cultivate their terrain for longer periods of time. Natives of South America also claim that cocaine is a gift from the gods, that it is necessary for their survival, since it increases oxygen intake. But, as often happens with a drug, it can have ill effects when transported from the culture which has safely assimilated it.

The majority of coca leaves grown in South America are either consumed by South Americans or exported to other countries for consumption. As explained above, another use of the leaf entails the extraction of cocaine for either illicit or medical purposes.

Cocaine took a long time to come down from the mountains. By 1840 most of the important medicinal alkaloids had already been isolated and were being used for medical purposes. These alkaloids included morphine and codeine from opium, nicotine from tobacco, and atropine from Belladonna. In 1860, cocaine was then extracted, identified, and named. But aside from the discovery that it numbed the tongue and the suggestion that it could have potential as a local anesthetic, it was not assigned a practical use until 1878.

In 1878, a medical report advocated the use of cocaine for the treatment of morphine addiction. In 1883, another report by a German physician was brought to the attention of the medical profession. This report upheld the beneficial effects of cocaine by demonstrating how cocaine relieved fatigue when issued to Bavarian soldiers during war maneuvers.[1]

By 1880, through the influence of these and other reports, cocaine was in many patent medicines and other products. It was touted as a cure for fatigue, asthma, stomach ailments, "women's illnesses," and nose inflammations. Park-Davis sold cocaine in cigarettes and tablets, while patent-medicine quacks peddled it from brightly painted wagons. One of the most popular forms of cocaine was the concoction created by John Pemberton, a Georgian pharmacist, containing kola nuts and cocaine: Coca-Cola. By 1906,

---

[1] Inaba, D. and W. Cohen. *Uppers, Downers, All Arounders.* San Francisco, CA: Haight-Ashbury Detox Clinic, 1989. 56-63.

the Coca-Cola Company had switched to decocanized coca leaves; however, even as late as 1920, the drink could be ordered by asking for a "shot in the arm." Buyers still sought the stimulation of cocaine which had been present in the original form of Coca-Cola.

Coca flower

Coca bean

By 1914, the addictive and psychoactive effects of cocaine became apparent. Cocaine was recognized nationwide as a dangerous substance. In New York State, for example, the illegal sale of opium or heroin was considered a misdemeanor, while the sale of cocaine was a felony. Likewise, on the Federal level, the Harrison Narcotic Act of 1914 restricted cocaine to doctor's prescriptions and imposed fines and imprisonment for those who illegally sold or distributed it.

Since then, the old Federal narcotic laws have been replaced by the Comprehensive Drug Abuse Prevention and Control Act. In 1970, this act placed cocaine in Schedule II, retaining it as a valid medical drug but with severe restrictions due to its high potential for abuse. A misnomer in both the new law and the old Harrison Act is that cocaine is a narcotic. Cocaine and coca are stimulants similar in effect to the amphetamines and are unrelated to the depressive narcotic drugs.

After the 1920s, cocaine use declined as a result of increased law enforcement, drug education, and the marketing—in 1932—of a cheaper synthetic stimulant named amphetamine. Regardless of these developments, cocaine use began to suddenly increase again in the 1970s.

CURRENT PATTERNS OF COCAINE USE

Many have said that cocaine has replaced marijuana as the drug of growing acceptance and is "the drug of the 1990s." The most conservative researchers estimate that 10 million Americans now use coke with some regularity, and another 5 million have probably experimented with it.[2] (Other estimates double that figure.)[3] According to surveys by the National

---

[2] "Drug Enforcement Report." Vol. 8, No. 7, Jan., 1992.

[3] U.S. Department of Justice. "Drug Use in the General Population." *Drugs and Crime Facts, 1991.* Rockville, MD: Drugs and Crime Data Center and Clearinghouse, 1991, pp.18-19.

Institute on Drug Abuse, about 40 percent of young adults (18 to 25 years old) have used cocaine. Of all drugs in the U.S., cocaine is now the biggest producer of illicit income due to its popularity among drug users.

The effects of cocaine on performance are still not clearly known. Jeffrey Rosecan, M.D., Director of the Cocaine Abuse Treatment Program at Columbia Presbyterian Medical Center, is a drug abuse consultant to the National Football League (NFL) and has also treated professional basketball players. In cocaine abuse, Dr. Rosecan could only find one study, done by Sigmund Freud in 1885, documenting the effects of cocaine on performance.[4] Freud administered the test on himself and found that cocaine increased muscular strength and decreased reactions over a four-hour span. Amazingly, the test has never been replicated on humans, according to Dr. Rosecan.

Arnold Washton, Ph.D. and executive director of the Washton Institute, consulted with the NBA on the formation of its drug policy. He treated basketball player Michael Ray Richardson for one and a half years, the only time he was drug-free, according to Dr. Washton.[5] Richardson subsequently relapsed and was banned from professional basketball for life.

When asked why players continue to risk lucrative careers by using drugs, Washton replied: "Most professional athletes have been pampered by coaches and others around them since a young age. Coming from small towns to the big city, in their early twenties with new-found riches and time on their hands, they maintain an adolescent fantasy of omnipotence."

Dr. Rosecan agrees: "They feel they are above the law," he says. "Cocaine is a stimulant. It increases performance in the short run, but not with chronic use. Once an athlete gets in the mind-set that the drug helps his game, he becomes addicted. It's just like a stockbroker or a lawyer working long hours under pressure. If cocaine helps them get more work done in less time, they tend to keep coming back for more."

Likewise, according to Washton, the fact that drug use in the NBA continues is "testimony to the power of addictive disease." "Let's not forget that cocaine takes control of brain functioning. It impairs judgment and even the survival instinct," Washton added.

NEW FORMS OF COCAINE

There are new forms of cocaine being used today; the most popular of these is crack. To explain the differences between crack and cocaine hydrochloride, it will be best to review the cocaine extraction and production processes.

As explained above, the first product to be made from the leaves of the coca plant is coca paste, which is then converted to cocaine base. Dried cocaine base is usually dissolved in either ethyl, acetone, or a mixture of both and then filtered to remove solid impurities. A mixture of concentrated

---

[4] Freud, Sigmund. "On the General Effects of Cocaine." Rpt. in *Drug Dependence*. Issue No. 5, Oct. 1970.

[5] Washton, A. and M. Gold. "Chronic Cocaine Abuse: Evidence for Adverse Effects on Health and Functioning." *Psychiatric Annals*. 14(10):733-743, 1984.

hydrochloric acid and either acetone or ethanol is then added to precipitate cocaine hydrochloride. The precipitate is filtered and dried carefully, using bright light to produce a white, crystalline powder; this powder is the finished product, cocaine hydrochloride, otherwise known as cocaine.

Cocaine hydrochloride, available on the street at 30 to 40 percent purity, remains the most common coca product in the United States. The predominant methods of cocaine abuse continue to be primarily through inhaling and, to some extent, injecting cocaine hydrochloride. In the past decade, however, the use of "crack" has become increasingly prevalent in the United States.

Crack is a purified form of cocaine which avoids the dangers of traditionally purified freebase cocaine. Since cocaine hydrochloride will largely decompose if smoked directly, the hydrochloride must be converted back to a relatively pure base state—or freebase—before it is suitable for smoking. Freebase is not quite the same substance as crack however.

Freebase is either made the traditional way by using volatile chemicals or by a heating and cooling method using baking soda. In traditional freebase production, cocaine hydrochloride is mixed with baking soda or ammonia, and then with water and ether. The ether then evaporates to produce a powdery cocaine base, which is smoked in a water pipe or sprinkled on a tobacco or marijuana cigarette and smoked.

The danger of freebase is that if it is heated before it is completely dry, the remaining ether—combined with the heat—may result in an explosion. On the other hand, since ether is not used to make crack, crack is safe from this sort of explosion. Crack is made by using only baking soda or ammonia.

The Appearance of Crack

Crack is an off-white color resembling coagulated soap powder or pieces of soap. Crack made either with baking soda or ammonia is smoked in a water pipe or sprinkled over a tobacco or marijuana cigarette and smoked. The word "crack" most likely comes from the crackling sound made when it is smoked before it dries; it may also come from its occasional resemblance to cracked paint chips or plaster.

Appearance of Cocaine Hydrochloride

Traditional cocaine sold on the street is in the form of a white powdery substance. It resembles snowflakes, crystals, or lactose and is more fine than the hard rock form of crack. This physical quality of cocaine accounts for two of its nicknames: "crystal" and "snow." Like heroin, cocaine is usually "cut" (diluted with some other substance) for street sale.

A gram of street cocaine contains approximately 10 "doses." This gram of cocaine does not contain the pure drug smuggled from Columbia or Peru; rather, it has been "stepped on" with sugar or other substances. Cocaine is cut with various substances including mannitol, lactose, insitol, B-2 vitamin, amphetamines, caffeine, pseudo-cocaine (Toot, super cocaine), and synthetic cocaine or local anesthetics such as Procaine, Benzocaine, Lidocaine.

The major visual indicator of traditional cocaine is the consistency of the crystal formation. Cocaine crystals are often called snowflakes for their appearance. This uniform appearance is sometimes the result of reconstitution in a lab. Reconstitution is a process whereby a pure cocaine product is broken down; adulterants are then added to make it impossible to distinguish crystal variations. Good cocaine, on the other hand, will come apart in layers. When cut with a razor blade it should be rather brittle and crumble easily. Moistness may indicate that the product has been recently stepped on. If you drop one of the crystals (clusters) on a mirror, you should hear a tile-like click and not a dull thud. When the cocaine is pushed along a mirror with the razor blade to make lines, the lines should be uniform and not clumpy with a filmy trace on the mirror (which could indicate the presence of mannite, a diluting agent). Generally, good street cocaine will have a uniform off-white color with a bit of pearl luster as opposed to a harsh, bleached out brightness.

METHODS OF COCAINE USE

Oral Use

As detailed above, the oral ingestion of cocaine by chewing coca leaves with lime has been used by the natives of Andean South America for thousands of years. Chewing coca is probably the best way to absorb cocaine. The effects are pleasingly different, more moderate, and less harmful to the body than sniffing coke. But coca leaves are hard to find outside the Andes.

Sigmund Freud's favorite method of taking cocaine was also oral; he dissolved 0.05 grams of the hydrochloride in water (1 percent solution) and drank it.

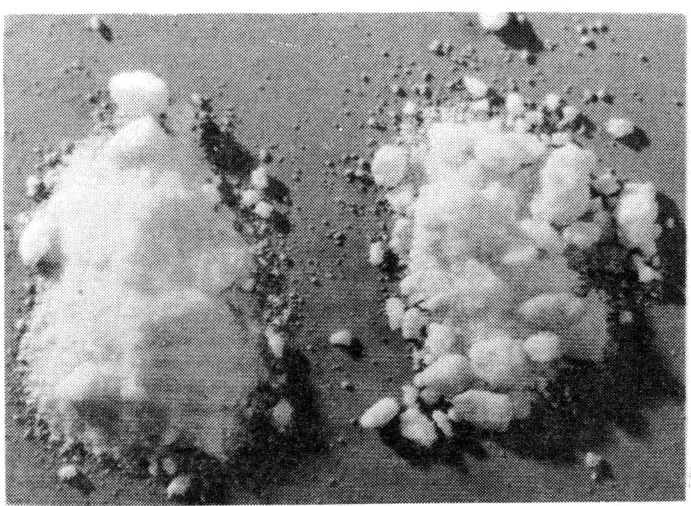

In about 3,000 B.C., the natives of Valdivia, Ecuador, discovered that alkalinizing the mouth greatly facilitated the release of cocaine from coca and improved its absorption through the oral membranes. They did this by chewing coca with lime made from burnt shells or plant ashes. Lime, however, is very caustic and can burn the lips and mouth severely. There is a much easier way to alkalinize the mouth for cocaine use.

Dissolve one-fourth teaspoon of fresh baking soda in a cup of warm water and gargle several times with this solution, washing it around and spitting it out. Or simply put the same amount of baking soda under the tongue and let it dissolve slowly. Alkalinizing the mouth in this way will facilitate the absorption of cocaine in the oral membranes.

For many years, researchers thought that oral cocaine was inactive because it was changed chemically in the gastrointestinal tract. Studies by Richard B. Resnick, M.D., and his co-workers have shown that oral coke gives a greater, though rather different, subjective high with fewer cardiovascular effects than does snorting the substance.[6]

The disadvantage of oral ingestion, however, is that it is difficult to control the dosage, increasing the possibility of cocaine poisoning. It has been well-documented in recent years that rubbing coke directly on the gums or membranes increases the likelihood of developing gum disease.

Another method of oral cocaine use is a hot-water infusion of coca sweetened with a little raw sugar, called "Agua De Coca" in the Andes. This method is usually used as a remedy for indigestion. In addition, coca leaves also make an excellent tea. Angelo Mariani's Coca Tea sustained President Ulysses S. Grant in his later days and gave him the strength to finish his memoirs, one of the best accounts we have of the Civil War. Mariani also concocted the most famous alternative of all in the 1860s—a comforting red wine made with coca-leaf extract added to a Bordeaux. In the 1880s, U.S. Surgeon General William Hammond, M.D., discovered that infinitesimally small doses of pure cocaine in wine—two grains of the hydrochloride to a pint of wine—was an excellent tonic for therapeutic purposes. Freud noticed this method of use and commented that Hammond himself "was for a long time in the habit of taking a wine glass full after the days work and found himself refreshed each time, without any subsequent depression." [7]

Another method related to traditional oral uses is when cocaine is used as a sex aid. It is applied to the genital organs. A sprinkle of coke on the clitoris or just below the head of the penis will anesthetize the tissues and retard sexual climax.

However, when cocaine was widely used as a surgical anesthetic around the turn of the century, doctors discovered that the urethra (the tube inside the penis or vulva through which urine is eliminated from the bladder) is very sensitive to cocaine: several patients died from constriction or collapse of the urethral canal. Also, cocaine severely dries some of the delicate membranes of the genitals.

Injecting Cocaine

Some users inject cocaine directly into the veins as one would inject heroin. They claim that when injecting cocaine, it is not advisable to heat the water solution since the heat and boiling tends to evaporate the cocaine. Also, cocaine is extremely soluble in water. Users report that, with injection

---

[6] Resnick, R.B. et al. "Acute Systemic Effects of Cocaine in Man." *Science.* 195:696-698, 1977.

[7] Byck, Robert, M.D. (ed.). *Cocaine Papers by Sigmund Freud.* New York: Stonehill, 1975.

of cocaine, the rush or immediate euphoria occurs within seconds and is very intense. Users claim that the high from injecting cocaine will last anywhere from 45 to 90 minutes.

One drawback to this method is that intravenous injection leads to paranoid states of consciousness more often than when equivalent amounts are inhaled. Intravenous cocaine injections are also likely to cause initial stages of dependence since the user would seek to repeat the immediate rush of the drug. The nasal route of intake does not cause such an immediate rush. Furthermore, the repetitious exposure of the cerebral neurons to high concentrations of cocaine from the veins produces alterations of brain metabolism that provoke distortions of thinking and perception in addition to the well-known emotional changes.

Snorting Cocaine

One of the most popular methods of using cocaine today is by snorting, i.e., inhaling the cocaine into the nostrils. In snorting cocaine, the immediate euphoric effect takes place within about 30 seconds and the user feels under the influence from 30 to 90 minutes. Users report that the rush from snorting cocaine is not quite as intensified as from injection or freebasing.

In snorting cocaine, the user will bring the powdered cocaine up to one nostril holding the other nostril closed and sniff the cocaine into the nose. The user may vary from one nostril to another, but usually holds the other nostril closed for better suction. The immediate effect of snorting cocaine is a burning or freezing of the nostril area depending on the purity of the cocaine and the substance the cocaine has been cut with. If it has been cut with Procaine there will be more of a freezing. The user will normally snort anywhere from 1⁄10 of a gram to ½ gram at one time. Some users who want to maintain a constant high can snort cocaine all day long. When the cocaine is snorted, a portion of the cocaine moves through the nasal passages and bits are taken down through the throat. Other portions are taken in by the small capillaries in the mucous membrane and carried and spread throughout the body to the brain. At times, however, some of the drug becomes lodged in the hairs of the nose and if it remains for any length of time, tends to irritate the membrane causing sores or bleeding. Cocaine constricts the blood vessels and anesthetizes the cilia which keep the mucous blanket moving over mucous membranes. Thus, the membranes dry out and stop functioning, leading very quickly to dryness, crusting, and ulceration in the nose. Small amounts of the drug can also become lodged in the sinus cavities resulting in congestion and related discomfort. In order to prevent such problems and maintain clear and unirritated nasal passages, many users will attempt to keep the cocaine very finely grained. This is achieved by chopping the cocaine with a razor blade or other sharp edged instrument, or grinding the powder with a mortar and pestle. It is alleged that the finer the grain, the smaller the possibility of some of the cocaine being lodged in the nose or sinus. Some users will snort or drop water into the nose to help dislodge and dissolve any piece that may be held by the hairs.

Smoking Cocaine Paste

Cocaine can be smoked, either by freebasing it or by mixing the paste into a cigarette. In South America, a cocanized tobacco cigarette is called a pistola, or if mixed with marijuana, a "banana with cheese." Chemists in

South American cocaine refineries often smoke paste, a crude and very impure form of cocaine sulfate, in this manner. But smoking paste, freebase, or hydrochloride can be very harmful to the lungs.

The first report of coca paste smoking came from Peru in 1974. Since then, the practice has spread to Columbia, Bolivia, Ecuador, Panama and other countries. Sporadic instances of use have been reported in Los Angeles, San Francisco and other cities. Coca paste is the first extraction product made during the manufacture of cocaine from the leaves of the coca bush. The paste, or "pasta," may contain up to 80 percent cocaine sulfate, benzoic acid, kerosene, sulfuric acid, and other alkaloids or impurities found in coca leaves. This paste is usually sprinkled on tobacco or marijuana and smoked.

Freebasing Cocaine

There is one popular form of cocaine use in the U.S. which resembles coca paste smoking. That form is freebasing, or smoking alkaloidal cocaine. The popularity of freebasing has been sufficient enough to generate an entire subindustry which markets freebasing kits designed to convert the cocaine hydrochloride from street cocaine to freebase. These freebase kits are advertised and sold in paraphernalia shops. Due to the widespread demand and the ease of home production, freebase cocaine is ordinarily made by the consumer.

Apparently originating in Marin County, California, where the needed ingredient—wealth—is found in abundance, freebase cocaine has spread throughout the country.

Freebase cocaine is never sold as freebase. Rather, street coke—containing cocaine hydrochloride (a salt), various sugars (mannitol, glucose), and other cutting agents (xylocaine)—is treated, reducing the mixture to pure cocaine alkaloid; a white, slightly shiny powder. This purifying process increases the potency of the drug.

Freebase is not soluble in water, not bitter to the taste, and is ineffective if snorted or eaten. What it does is vaporize more easily than cocaine hydrochloride, melting at body temperature making it readily suitable for smoking. Since freebase doesn't burn, it must be either sprinkled on a cigarette or consumed in a pipe designed for this purpose. These freebase pipes usually consist of a glass bowl with an extended drawing pipe, and a complex organization of multi-layer screens to hold the freebase over the bowl as it is heated. When applied to the bowl, the flame volitizes the drug as it melts and drips from screen to screen.

As it is inhaled, freebase enters the bloodstream through the lungs and the high may be felt even before the smoke is exhaled. The euphoria lasts for only a few minutes and the primary kick from the coke is the instantaneous and intense rush. So strong is the brief high that repetitive and excessive usage is common. Compulsive consumption of this form of cocaine is far greater among "baseballers" (freebasers) than among those who snort cocaine. Due to the increased purity, the more efficient route of administration, and the compulsive desire to re-experience the intense but short rush, overdosing is a significant risk for freebasers.

CRACK

Crack was first detected in Southern California in 1981 and documented in New York City during the summer of 1985. According to a recent survey conducted by the 800-COCAINE Helpline, 25 percent of crack users smoke the drug on the job. Most crack smokers in the survey (81 percent) have occasionally snorted cocaine before switching to crack. Eighty-two percent reported that they felt compelled to use crack again after the first time.

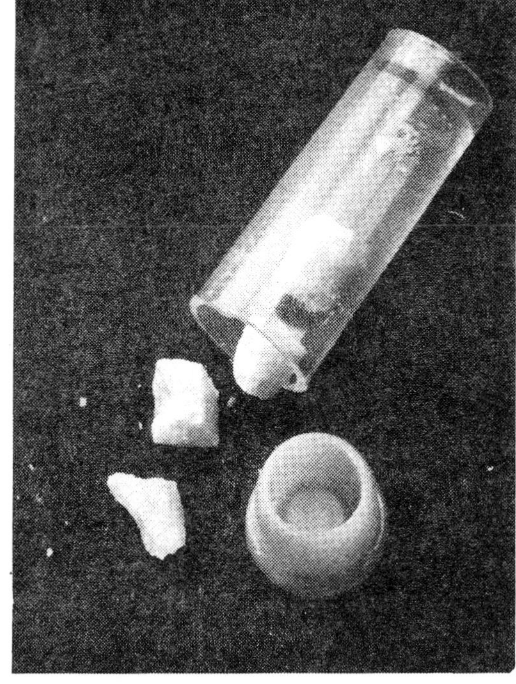

Although crack and freebase share the danger of addiction, there are several differences between smoking crack and traditional cocaine freebasing.

Freebasing is a process of converting cocaine hydrochloride (HCL) back to cocaine base for smoking. Traditional freebasing involves heating ether or other flammable solvents as the critical part of the extraction process. This procedure creates an extremely hazardous situation in which the risks of explosion and fire are quite high. Crack, on the other hand, eliminates the use of flammable solvents and the risks of explosion and fire.

Crack is made by adding baking soda (or ammonia) and water to cocaine HCL. The mixture is heated and cooled, then filtered to collect the crystals. The result of the process is a solidified form of cocaine base, or crack, which somewhat resembles parmesan cheese.

FREEBASE PROCESS	CRACK PROCESS
– Removes diluents	– Removes diluents
– Solvents used	– Does not require solvents
– Danger of explosion/fire	– No danger of explosion/fire
– Powdery material produced	– Hard flaky material produced
– End product is cocaine freebase	– End product is cocaine freebase

USE OF CRACK AND FREEBASE

Traditional cocaine freebase is smoked through a water pipe in which the substance was originally produced or is sprinkled on a marijuana or tobacco cigarette and smoked. Likewise, crack may be sprinkled on a marijuana or tobacco cigarette or mixed with either of these substances and smoked in a pipe.

Upon inhalation both freebase and crack are rapidly absorbed by the lungs and carried to the brain within a matter of seconds. The user experiences a sudden and very intense "rush" followed by a euphoria which suddenly subsides into a feeling of restlessness, irritability, and in cases of sustained use, post-euphoric depression. This post-euphoric period may be so uncomfortable that freebase and crack smokers continue smoking, often in marathon binges, until they become exhausted or run out of cocaine.

At purity levels between 60 and 90 percent, crack is usually sold on the streets in small vials, glassine envelopes, or sealed plastic bags. Although amounts vary, a small vial contains an average of 100 milligrams of crack. The average price for 250 milligrams of crack is $25, while 500 milligrams cost $40 to $50. A ten-dollar vial of 100 milligrams can provide one, two, or three inhalations when smoked in a pipe, depending on how deeply the user breathes.

This low price per dose attracts buyers, while giving the dealer a substantial profit. Since crack users often crave more of the drug immediately after smoking, they tend to purchase more cocaine in its crack form than they may have if they purchased the traditional powdered form of cocaine hydrochloride.

Crack is usually sold on the street or in crack houses and goes by several names including rock, base, or freebase. Crack houses, sometimes called smoke houses, are generally the average apartment or house. However, the definition of what constitutes a crack house varies from city to city. In some cities, a user can both purchase and smoke the drug on the premises. In others, a user can only purchase the drug and is not allowed entry. Still in others, a user must bring his own crack, because the drug is not sold on the premises; the house simply provides a room and a pipe for smoking crack.

It is generally believed that smoking crack has become such a popular method of cocaine use because it satisfies the desire for a more intense "high" without the complications and dangers involved in freebasing with ether or injecting cocaine with hypodermic needles.

POPULARITY OF CRACK

In the city of Los Angeles, crack accounts for 90 percent of all street-level cocaine seizures.

The advent of crack can be held responsible for the recent broadening of the cocaine market into lower-income populations, as it appears to be the almost exclusively preferred form of use by low-income cocaine users.

Some confusion has arisen, both in law enforcement and among laypersons, as to what purpose rock cocaine serves the user. Freebasing was uncommon during the original cocaine vogue of the 1970s and early 1980s. Cocaine hydrochloride is also a perfectly usable form of the drug. So why does today's user go to the trouble of making rock cocaine?

The main attractiveness of crack is that it renders cocaine smokeable. Cocaine in the bloodstream, regardless of its form before ingestion, is rapidly metabolized to its relatively inert components. The cocaine high is therefore dependent on how rapidly the drug can be absorbed. The serious cocaine user's goal is to get as much cocaine into his bloodstream as quickly as possible. Smoking is much more efficient in this respect than snorting, as the lungs give much more surface area for absorption than the nasal passages and deliver absorbed substances to the bloodstream much more directly. This reasoning also accounts for the swiftness of the freebase high. Smoking cocaine delivers the drug directly to the body all at once—where it is quickly eliminated. Snorting, by contrast, dribbles cocaine into the system a little at a time, giving a less intense but longer-lasting effect.

Cocaine must be freebased to be smokeable since normal cocaine hydrochloride vaporizes at a very high temperature. Freebase cocaine vaporizes at 187° C, a temperature within the reach of an ordinary butane lighter (and tolerable to the human lungs). Hydrochloride can be smoked, and occasionally is, but it will burn rather than vaporize, causing most of the drug to be wasted in the process. Conversely, freebase has to be smoked in order to be used efficiently, since it is not very soluble in water. Freebase cocaine works best when delivered through the lungs as a gas.

Another advantage of smoking crack over snorting cocaine is that by smoking the user protects himself from the famous "rat's nose" syndrome. By trying to absorb large quantities of cocaine through the small surface area of the nasal membranes, coke snorters often suffer severe corrosive damage to these tissues. Smoking freebase spreads the burden over the much larger surface area of the lungs. Of course, chronic smoking may turn out to be just as bad for the lungs as chronic snorting is for the nose.

NEW YORK CITY CRACK

In New York City, crack distribution began in the Harlem-Bronx areas, then spread throughout the rest of the city.

Most New York crack encountered for retail sale is packaged in small clear plastic vials with stoppers. These vials are similar to the glass vials used for perfume samples and are used legitimately for the packaging of extremely small items, such as semiconductors or watch parts. The vials are popular for crack distribution for several reasons. They are easy to transport and conceal on the person, including in body cavities, because the vials are waterproof. The vials also allow the buyer to visually inspect the product before purchase. Wholesale quantities of crack vials, usually 100, are packaged in large plastic bags, similar to freezer bags.[8]

In some areas of New York, crack is being sold in small glassine bags. Some crack vials are placed in glassine bags then sealed and stamped with a brand name, similar to the way heroin is marketed. This affords an illusion of quality control and gives the buyer a specific name to ask for when making a subsequent drug purchase. Some of the brand names encountered in the Lower East side of Manhattan are "White Cloud," "Cloud Nine," and "Super White." In the Washington Heights area of Manhattan, the brand names "Serpico," "Conan," "Lido," "Baseball," and "Handball" have been identified.

---

[8] Drug Enforcement Agency. New York Field Office, Unified Intelligence Division. "Trends in Traffic: Cocaine." *The Narc Officer*. Nov. 1988.

Crack vials have also been placed in small one-inch plastic bags and hermetically sealed. Sometimes crack has been marketed in assorted colored capsules as well. In Suffolk County, New York, crack is being sold in small pyrex tubes that can also be used to smoke the crack.

It has been discovered recently that even non-drug materials are being sold as crack. Small chunks of plaster of paris or brown soap, when placed in a vial, resemble crack. According to a report from Queens, one individual was placing the coconut section of a Mounds candy bar in small vials that were then sold to abusers as crack.

THE PURITY OF STREET CRACK

To date, the purity of seized crack ranges from 60 to 90 percent. Although this purity is higher than that found in street-level cocaine, the belief that crack is a purified form of cocaine is not accurate. Over 75 percent of the materials used to "cut" cocaine survive the crack conversion process and are present in crack. Adulterants, or "cuts," such as Procaine, Lidocaine and Benzocaine also enter the bloodstream directly when crack is smoked, thus posing additional health hazards to crack abusers over and above the hazards of crack itself.

The DEA Western Laboratory in San Francisco, California recently received an exhibit of crack cocaine containing 2418.5 grams of 69 percent cocaine base, while nearly all of the remaining balance consisted of Procaine base. The sample consisted of large solid chunks of a uniform yellowish-white waxy material. The material was collected in Oakland, California, and is referred to on the streets of Oakland as "Mr. Coffee." Some larger chunks of the material appeared to conform to the inside shape of the glass coffee pot used with the "Mr. Coffee" coffee machine.

The Western Laboratory has also received two additional samples of a similar material from the Seattle-Tacoma, Washington area. One of these samples consisted of 110 grams of 24 percent cocaine base with most of the remaining balance containing Procaine base. The other sample contained 28.5 grams of 45 percent cocaine base also mixed with Procaine base.[9]

The consistent presence of such adulterants in crack poses significant health hazards to the crack user. The increasing popularity of crack, coupled with the counterfeit sale of substances resembling crack, puts users at an additional risk.

CRACK HOUSES AND ADDICTION

Since smoking crack requires paraphernalia such as small glass pipes and a small acetylene or butane torch or other source of heat, base houses have come into existence. They provide a place for users to rent the paraphernalia and use their crack; these places are comparable to opium dens or heroin shooting galleries. These crack houses are usually located in a clubroom, apartment, or similar private place. There is usually a small

---

[9] U.S. Department of Justice. Office of Forensic Sciences. *Microgram*. Vol. 24, No. 6, June 1991.

admission charge to enter the base house and a separate charge for the use of rental paraphernalia.

In accordance with the rise of crack houses, attesting to the popularity of crack, there has also been a rise in the number of hospitalizations due to crack abuse. Most chronic crack abusers report symptoms and suffering similar to the adverse effects of intensified cocaine addiction. The addiction to crack takes place much faster and the adverse effects, such as depression and paranoia, are much stronger in a crack addict than in a traditional cocaine user. Most crack addicts report intense cravings for the drug and claim they will do nearly anything to get it. Many report committing street crimes to obtain money for crack. Several addicts report engaging in sexual activity, sometimes extensively, to obtain money for crack. In addition, the paranoia that is symptomatic of cocaine addicts may account for the violent crime that has often resulted from widespread crack use and distribution.

PHYSICAL EFFECTS OF FREEBASING COCAINE

Smoking freebase has a tremendously stimulating physical effect. The "rush" lasts only a short time, but users report extreme exhilaration. Some users have said that you get a sensation of floating off on a wonderful cloud of euphoria, a feeling that rivals a hang-glider ride or a cruise in a sailplane.

From a clinical viewpoint of the physical effects, the chronic cocaine user progresses through three phases: euphoria, dysphoria, and paranoid psychosis.

Smoking freebase with its two-minute superhigh evokes an enormous desire to keep on "basing." Again, the rapid shift from ecstasy to misery impels many users to keep smoking until they or their freebase are exhausted. This compulsion may be understood since relief from desolation is at hand from a single puff.

The results of smoking freebase, either in a special pipe or sprinkled on a cigarette, are identical to smoking coca paste or injecting cocaine hydrochloride intravenously. Mydriasis (dilation of the pupils), tachycardia, and increased blood pressure and respiration rates are the autonomic effects. The "rush" is sudden and intense. Feelings of energy, power and competence are described. The euphoric high subsides after a few minutes into a restless irritability. The residual "wired up" state is so intolerable that a heroin habit may be started to relieve the tense and overwrought feeling. Sleep is impossible during a freebase binge, but exhaustion eventually supervenes. Enormous weight loss takes place in heavy users due to the anorectic action of cocaine. Manic, paranoid, or depressive psychoses have also been seen. Due to cardiorespiratory arrest, severe overdoses can even cause death.

Chronic users of freebase sometimes report bizarre skin phenomena like amber crystals and/or (more commonly) black specks that appear to come right out of the skin. This experience is not commonplace and the casual or part-time user of freebase may never encounter them. Nonetheless, these experiences deserve mention because they are so rarely discussed yet they do occur and are therefore a possibility for anyone who freebases.

Ronald Siegel estimates that it takes about three months to lose control of cocaine use; at this point, the experience of the bizarre skin phenomena described above may begin to occur.[10] Siegel writes: "Unlike LSD, where you observe the hallucinations, with freebase the hallucinations become a direct part of your reality." Siegel, who does extensive counseling with drug abuse patients, goes on to recite the already famous case of his patient who became convinced that worms were crawling out of his body and brought Siegel bits of skin he had tweezed from his arms. "The guy was totally convinced the worms were real," Siegel writes. "All he wanted to know from me, in fact, was how they could have contaminated his cocaine supply to begin with."

MEDICAL USES OF COCAINE

For medicinal purposes, cocaine is a local anesthetic used to control topical pain; it is used in surgery on the nose, mouth, throat, and the eyes. Although it has largely been replaced in today's medical arsenal by synthetic anesthetics—Lidocaine, Procaine, etc.—cocaine still has some attractive capabilities. Cocaine lasts longer than synthetic anesthetics and its vasoconstricting properties prevent bleeding. However, even considering these advantages, the abuse potential has severely curtailed cocaine's medical application.

Nevertheless, there has been a recent renaissance in the medical use of cocaine, the result of a preparation whose value in terminal care is unsurpassed. Formulated in England and called "Bromptons Mixture," its British recipe contained heroin and cocaine with gin or brandy. Transported to America, it is generally prepared as morphine and cocaine with gin or another alcoholic vehicle. Most therapists working with the terminally ill report marked improvement in patients as a result of the cocaine mixture. The stimulating effect of the cocaine apparently counteracts the dull, lethargic effect of the pain killer morphine. With morphine and the other narcotics the price paid for freedom from pain is often a listless patient who can barely distinguish between the dreams induced by the narcotics and the real world around him. The addition of cocaine in many cases gives bed-ridden and incoherent patients the ability to become ambulatory and lucid.

While relief for the painfully dying is welcomed, the increased use of medical cocaine means greater opportunity for diversion and the need for increased monitoring by law enforcement agencies.

COCAINE COSTS AND RETAILING

Medicinal cocaine has little resemblance to street cocaine. The pure cocaine that Merek Co. sells to pharmacists for $1.35 a gram (1 oz. costs $39.00) is very different from the adulterated coke on the street. Pure cocaine is a light, extremely shiny, flaky white powder. Illicit cocaine is significantly dulled by the cut. The amount of remaining gleam is often in direct proportion to the percentage of pure cocaine in the powder.

The various measures of street cocaine are as confusing as the amount of pure cocaine in the "buy." Adulterated coke is generally sold by the gram, yet it is also retailed by "lines." Four lines, sometimes referred to as "two by

---

[10] Siegel, R. "Cocaine Freebase." *Journ. of Psychedelic Drugs.* 13:297-317, 1982.

two" may be sold as a unit. Cocaine is also sold in the unit referred to as a "spoon," which is approximately 1/4 of a teaspoonful.

THE CHEMISTRY OF COCAINE

The alkaloid content of the coca leaf ranges from about 0.5 to 2.0 percent with cocaine representing approximately 50 to 75 percent of the total alkaloid. The crude alkaloid may be extracted with dilute acid, then made alkaline and re-extracted into organic solvents. It is also quite possible to hydrolyze the alkaloid mixture to re-esterify and purify the cocaine through ethanolic recrystalization. In its free form, cocaine has a molecular weight of 303 and a melting point of 98° C. In it hydrochloride salt form, cocaine has a molecular weight of 339 and a melting point of 197° C. The hydrochloride is soluble in water and ethanol, while freebase cocaine is soluble in organic solvents such as ether or chloroform.

Studies on the bodily distribution of cocaine in various animals clearly show penetration of the drug into all tissues examined, with the highest levels in liver, kidney, heart, and fat tissues.[11] Significant concentrations of cocaine were present in the brain and appeared to persist at low levels for several weeks after use. The drug was readily metabolized and primarily excreted in the urine and feces during the first 24 hours. In the animals studied, cocaine is metabolized to norecgonine, ecgonine, and a host of hyphoxylated derivatives. All these compounds are quite active pharmacologically, except for ecgonine, which does not appear to exhibit cocaine-like effects.

Studies in humans, although limited in scope, indicate that peak plasma levels of cocaine are reached at the first sampling (five minutes) after IV administration.[12] Eight hours after injection, the drug was no longer detectable. Benzoylecgonine, however, was detectable for a period of at least 24 hours after IV use. Interestingly, the biological half-life of cocaine following either IV or intranasal use was about 2.6 hours. Although both cocaine and benzoylecgonine were detected in urine for a full eight hours, the cocaine levels were generally one-tenth that of the metabolite benzoylecgonine. Cocaine is generally excreted from humans in a form containing the following substances: the free drug itself, the metabolites benzoylecgonine, norcocaine, and ecgonine, as well as several hydroxylated derivatives of these metabolites.

---

[11] Dendow, G.A. et al. "Self-Administration of Psychoactive Substances by the Monkey: A Measure of Psychological Dependence." *Psychopharmacology*. 16:30-48, 1969.

Johanson, C.E. "Assesment of the Dependence Potential of Cocaine in Animals." J. Grabowski (ed.). *Cocaine Pharmacology, Effects, and Treatment of Abuse*. Washington DC: NIDA Research Monograph 50, 1984. 54-71.

[12] Fischman, M.W. et al. "Cardiovascular and Subjective Effects of Intravenous Cocaine in Humans." *Arch. Gen. Psychiatry*. 33:983-989, 1976.

PHYSIOLOGICAL EFFECTS

In the central nervous system, cocaine alters neurotransmitters and can concomitantly alter electrical activity in the brain. Although some conflicting data appears to exist regarding the effect of cocaine on neurotransmitters, it most likely stimulates the release of dopamine, norepinephrine and serotonin while blocking the return of these same substances into the nerve terminal.

Concerning the electrical alterations which occur following cocaine administration, some studies showed that persistent low voltage fast waves occurred in the electroencephalogram (EEG) with subsequent increases in alertness as well as heart and respiratory rates, which lasted for periods of one to two hours.[13] Chronic administration of cocaine caused permanent changes in the EEG and in behavioral depression, along with the apparent development of tolerance to the convulsant and cardiorespiratory effects of the drug.[14]

The effect of cocaine on the cardiovascular system is direct. The heart rate increases and the blood pressure is raised through vasoconstriction. Respiration, however, is stimulated primarily through a direct effect on the medullary respiratory center. Through peripheral vasoconstriction as well as increased muscular activity, cocaine also causes an increase in body temperature.[15]

Generally 1 to 2 grams of cocaine are considered to be a lethal dose in humans; however, the route of administration plays an important role in overall toxicity. Death through cocaine overdose normally consists of convulsions coupled with cardiorespiratory failure. However, the data available on cocaine deaths frequently indicate the involvement of other drugs (opiates, amphetamines, barbiturates).[16] Therefore, the actual percentage of deaths due to cocaine alone is smaller than the total number of deaths involving cocaine.

PSYCHOLOGICAL, NEUROCHEMICAL, BEHAVIORAL EFFECTS

As indicated previously, cocaine may be taken in a variety of ways: intravenous injection, oral ingestion, smoking, snorting (intranasal) or simply applied to a variety of mucous membranes—genital, oral or rectal. Certainly the immediacy, the intensity, and the duration of the cocaine effect is related to the mode of administration. These methods produce euphoria, hyperstimulation, increased heart rate, increased respiration, hyperflexion, alertness, and feelings of grandiosity and power. These effects are accom-

---

[13] Dackis, C.A. and M.F. Gold. "New Concepts in Cocaine Addiction: The Dopamine Depletion Hypothesis." *Neuroscience and Biobehavioral Review*. 9:469-477, 1985.

[14] Fischman, M.W. et al. "Acute Tolerance Development to the Cardiovascular and Subjective Effects of Cocaine." *The Journal of Pharmacology and Experimental Therapeutics*. 235:677-682, 1985.

[15] American Society for Pharmacology and Experimental Therapeutics. Committee on Problems of Drug Dependence. "Scientific Perspectives on Cocaine Abuse." *The Pharmacologist*. 29:20-27, 1987.

[16] "The Implications of Crack." *Drug Abuse and Alcoholism Newsletter*. Vol. 15, No. 6, July 1986.

panied by an increase in the level of 5-hydroxytryptophan and, to some extent, the levels of dopamine, norepinephrine and epinephrine in the brain.[17]

The tremendous desire to repeat the experience and counter any depressive effects often leads to compulsive chronic use of cocaine. Such activity usually causes a decrease or depletion in the neurotransmitters (DA=dopamine; E=norepinephrine; 5HT=5-hydroxtrytophan) and over time causes overt depression, dysphoria, paranoia, hallucinatory experiences and sometimes destructive anti-social behavior.

In addition to the primary neurotransmitters mentioned, cocaine has effects on acetylcholine, which may alter motor functioning and interfere with mental activity, often leading to confusion and poor coordination. In effect, cocaine can cause serious central neurochemical imbalances which must be restored in order to achieve normal functioning after sustained chronic use of the drug. Unfortunately, the myriad changes occurring in the CNS are not yet fully understood. Full knowledge of the central and peripheral neurochemical changes may well lead to more effective clinical treatments.

TOLERANCE

Most drug abusers show development of tolerance to the pharmacological effects of any given drug after continued chronic use. However, in the case of cocaine, it has been believed that chronic use by humans leads not to a decrease but to an increase in sensitivity. Animals, on the other hand, develop a definite tolerance to the convulsive dose and to the cardiovascular and respiratory action of cocaine when it is given repetitively. Despite the supposed lack of tolerance, physical dependence to cocaine still occurs in humans after chronic use. Certainly depression, insomnia, agitation, and lethargy (behavioral depression) can be observed following cessation of chronic cocaine use; these symptoms are indicative (along with the neurochemical changes) of some degree of physical dependence. Furthermore, the high level of drug-seeking behavior exhibited by regular cocaine users clearly demonstrates the existence of psychological dependence. The cause of this obsessive-compulsive behavior is most likely the psychic drive to repeat the cocaine experience; this psychic drive is the core problem associated with illicit cocaine use. It is this pernicious drug-seeking, drug-reinforcing effect of cocaine that engenders continued abuse by the user with subsequent detrimental effects to both the individual and to society.

COCAINE ADDICTION

Many scientists are now revising their notions about cocaine addiction. It has become more apparent that some form of tolerance does develop, which is part of the classical definition of addiction. It has been found more recently that chronic cocaine users need larger quantities of the drug to get high and may never again experience the ecstasy of their first episodes. Some researchers believe that a person's brain chemistry can make him an addict;

[17] Hammer, S. and L. Hazleton. "Cocaine and the Chemical Brain." *Addictive Behavior: Drug and Alcohol Abuse*. Colorado: Mortion Publishing Co., 1985, pp. 84-88.

they say, "The brain and cocaine may be like a lock and a key." Some users say of cocaine, "That's what's been missing from my life to make me feel wonderful," while others remain unaffected. Given these various effects on users, cocaine addiction, like alcoholism, cannot be considered a sign of psychological weakness. Cocaine addiction is a result of the drug's interaction with a person's brain chemistry.

Scientists concede that there are those who can use small amounts of cocaine infrequently without showing any obvious physical damage or becoming obsessed with the drug.[18] The latest hypothesis, however, is that cocaine may damage the brain by slow steps. Charles Schuster, a professor of pharmacology at the University of Chicago, has found that amphetamines lower the overall amounts of some neurotransmitters in the brains of rats, monkeys, and guinea pigs.[19] In Schuster's studies, the reduction persisted for as long as three years after the last time the animals were given the drugs, leading Schuster to believe that the neurons involved may be permanently incapacitated.[20] Although more experiments are under way, the prognosis doesn't look good. Schuster concludes, "I suspect that cocaine will also damage the brains of these animals. When something happens across several species, you think more seriously about the pertinence to humans."

Until more research has been completed, the exact addictive effects of cocaine in humans will not be known. Currently, doctors do not know how to predict who will develop a physiological need for cocaine and who will not.

COCAINE TOXICITY

Cocaine toxicity occurs regardless of the route of administration. Frequently, the cocaine toxicity is what actually brings a person in for medical treatment, rather than any great desire to stop using the drug. Due to its toxicity, cocaine can have an adverse effect on the mucous lining of any part of the body. In addition, it can adversely affect the sinuses, the trachea and the lungs. It is not uncommon for freebasers to report severe respiratory problems. Freebasers may destroy the ability of their lung cells to process gases, leaving them with a constant cough and shortness of breath. Some physicians believe that the side effects of freebasing are as much due to the propane torch used to heat the cocaine as from the drug itself. For those persons who snort cocaine, the toxic effects (beginning with simple irritation) usually occur in the iris and the conjunctivae. There have even been instances of cocaine crystals ending up in the retina, apparently as a result of retrograde circulation from the nasal cavity. Individuals who are referred to as "skin poppers" often develop skin abscesses and cellulitis as a result of cocaine's toxicity. After the veins of these individuals are destroyed, they will begin injecting the drug directly into the skin and subcutaneous tissue.

---

[18] Erickson, P. et al. *The Steel Drug: Cocaine in Perspective.* Toronto: Lexington Books, 1987, pp. 89-110.

[19] Wagner G.C., C.R. Shuster, and L.S. Seiden. "Methamphetamine-induced changes in brain catecholomines in rats and guinea pigs." *Drug and Alcohol Dependency.* 4:435-438, 1979.

[20] Preston, K.L. et al. "Long-term effects of repeated methamphetamine administration on monoamine neurons in the rhesus monkey brain." *Brain Res.* 338:243- 248, 1985.

For individuals who have a history of continuous cocaine snorting which is 6 months or longer, X-rays of the sinuses are taken. Sinus X-rays of a 23-year old referred to a hospital for cocaine abuse demonstrated a large abscess of the right maxillary sinus.[21] This sort of abscess is not at all uncommon. Three days after admission, this young man sneezed and saved the material in a tissue, as it was unlike anything he had ever sneezed out before. This material was discovered to be the remaining third of his nasal septum. Generally, ENT (ear, nose, and throat) surgeons do not surgically repair the nasal septums of cocaine abusers. Rather, they replace the nasal septum with a prosthetic device: the nasal septum button. This button is placed in the nasal cavity and rides on either side of the remaining bone. The person will wear this synthetic nasal septum for the rest of his or her life.

As mentioned above, another possible effect of cocaine's toxicity is death. Sudden death from cocaine use is usually a result of seizures of cardiac arrythmia.[22] This phenomenon of subcortical stimulation by a particular drug that results in seizures and sometimes death is referred to as "kindling." This is not a new phenomenon and has been identified in the past with amphetamine abuse.[23] However, there is a misconception that persons who snort cocaine cannot die from kindling. The misconception is founded on the apparent lowering of the seizure threshold in many people who have a long history of cocaine abuse. In the case of amphetamine, the minimum lethal dose, taken orally, has been demonstrated at 1.4 grams. Certainly, this is not a large amount of cocaine to be consumed on a one-time basis. Many cocaine abusers use several grams on a given day.

Acute fatalities generally occur in people who have been abusing cocaine over an extended period of time. Sometimes cocaine crystals are found around the nose, or the syringe with which the cocaine was administered may be still lodged in the vein. When death is caused by cocaine-induced seizure, the person very often has such a violent tetanic reaction that the fingernails will be buried in the palms of the hand and the teeth will have bitten through the lower lip and the distal third of the tongue; in some cases, the victims bite all the way through the tongue itself.

The route of cocaine administration will sometimes dictate compulsive use. It appears that as many as nine out of every ten individuals who abuse cocaine via the nasal route are able to continue to do so on a recreational basis. It also appears, however, that when users change from the nasal route to the system of freebasing, the brain is so enamored of the freebasing method that the person quickly develops a compulsive use habit. With this sort of change in the route of cocaine administration, a $300 per week habit may be quickly replaced by a $300 per day habit.

---

[21] "Cocaine: The Great Addicter and Deceiver." *Drug Awareness Information Newsletter*. Jan. 1990. Rpt. in *The Narc Officer*. June 1990.

[22] Wetli, C. and R. Wright. "Death Caused by Recreational Use of Cocaine." *JAMA*. 241(3):2519-2522, 1979.

[23] Inaba, D. and W. Cohen. *Uppers, Downers, All Arounders*. San Francisco: Haight-Ashbury Detox Clinic, 1989, p. 62.

SOME COCAINE TREATMENT PERSPECTIVES

Recently, treatment centers have noticed patterns of effects resulting from cocaine abuse. For example, in alcoholic patients, blackouts have long been recognized as a common amnesic episode. Likewise, the same phenomenon of blackouts in people who are cocaine abusers has recently been observed by drug treatment center personnel.

Craving is another common phenomenon during the abuse of cocaine and is especially intense during the first 6 months after cessation. The craving may be triggered by something so remote as a favorite song heard while abusing cocaine. Several factors can immediately trigger off intense craving, leading sometimes to the physical effects of palpitations and sweating.

Paranoia is also quite common during cocaine abuse and during the initial period of abstinence. The person will suddenly develop an intense paranoid state without provocation. This state will lessen with the passage of time and the person frequently will not respond to antidepressants.

Another pattern reported by treatment personnel consists of visual and auditory hallucinations experienced by the patient. Several patients have insisted that they see peripheral blue lights out of the lateral field of vision. Chronic cocaine users also report tactile hallucinations of "bug bites." The sensation that the skin is crawling with bugs is also seen in patients who abuse Talwin and Pyribenzamine. Treatment personnel believe that this phenomenon is related to the adulterants added to the cocaine, rather than to the cocaine itself.

Treatment centers have reported some other patterns among cocaine abusers; these include weight loss and a deterioration of personal hygiene.

Treatment professionals believe it is extremely important that patients who have completed their program of inpatient treatment and who are participating in NA and/or AA on a regular basis, receive reassurance that the overwhelming cocaine craving they experience is not abnormal and that this will lessen with time, though probably never completely disappear. Similar to the alcoholic who has "dry drunks," during their recovery, cocaine abusers frequently develop "dry-highs." The person may experience a sudden tachycardia, diaphoresis (perspiration), or an appearance of being "high"; some even believe they can taste the cocaine in their mouths and feel the numbness in their noses. This phenomenon is very common during the recovery process and requires reassurance from the assisting professionals that it will come and go frequently during the first 6 months of recovery, and will lessen with time.

Some treatment professionals hypothesize that these phenomena are caused by the depression of dopamine and norepinephrine during the abstinent phase. However, the distressing symptoms of the recovery period may also result from the unsteady and erratic production of these neurotransmitters which occurs after cessation of cocaine use. Some studies in progress indicate these neurotransmitters will be permanently suppressed in persons who continue to abuse cocaine.[24] With continued research on abstinence phenomena and developments in the necessary support systems such as NA, AA, and family education, it is hoped that recovering cocaine abusers will learn to deal with and eventually overcome the abstinence syndrome.

UNDER THE INFLUENCE

Although a person may exhibit warning signs of cocaine abuse, they may not necessarily be under the influence of cocaine. Under the influence of cocaine means that there is physical evidence of cocaine present in the body such as dilated pupils, hyperactive nervous system, muscle relaxation and, especially, cocaine found in blood or urine. Since cocaine's activity level in the body is 3 to 6 hours following use, the term "under the influence" is restricted to users who show physical evidence of cocaine during its activity period of 3 to 6 hours.

Although the activity period is 3 to 6 hours, cocaine can still be found in the blood for as long as 6 to 8 hours after a single dose. Since cocaine in the blood correlates with the activity of cocaine and "influence," the presence of cocaine in the blood should be considered absolute evidence of "influence."

In outward appearance, however, cocaine affects people differently. Therefore, law enforcement officers may encounter various situations in which it is appropriate to arrest a user for being under the influence of cocaine. In addition to evidence of cocaine in the urine or the blood, it is necessary for officers to have other types of corroborating evidence.

If a subject's pupils are dilated above 6.5 mm. and cocaine derivative is found in the urine, it is appropriate to arrest the subject for cocaine influence.

In another situation, however, a subject's pupils may be dilated between 5.0 and 6.5 mm. In this situation, the officer should have photographic documentation of the subject in question and 1 or 2 control subjects who have smaller pupils in the same light. The officer should also document the presence of fresh needle marks or cocaine residue in the nasal passage as well as cocaine derivative found in the urine.

To make an arrest for high dosage use of cocaine, it is necessary to observe evidence of muscle relaxation including droopy eyelids, slurred or slow speech, abnormal gait, and nodding. In this situation, it is also necessary to document the presence of cocaine residue in the nasal passage or fresh needle marks and a negative alcohol breath, blood, or urine test. This corroborating evidence is only additional to cocaine derivative found in the urine or blood.

In another situation, to make an arrest for cocaine influence, an officer must observe evidence of central nervous system hyperactivity including increased speech rate, excessive sweating, pulse over 110 per minute, respiration over 25 per minute (requires two observers) and the presence of

[24] Grabowski, J. and S.E. Devorkin. "Cocaine: An Overview of Current Issues." *Int. Journ. of Addictions.* 20:1065-1088, 1985.

cocaine in the nasal passage or fresh needle marks. Again, you must find cocaine derivative in the urine to arrest the subject for being under the influence.

One last situation in which an officer may arrest for cocaine influence is when there is corroborating evidence of paranoia, hallucinations, or delusions and the presence of cocaine in the nasal passage or fresh needle marks. This evidence is additional to the positive identification of cocaine derivative found in the urine or blood.

EXAMINATION OF A COCAINE SUSPECT

Law enforcement officers examining a cocaine suspect for evidence of cocaine use should look for the following symptoms:

Rapidity of speech (low dose)

Slowing or slurred speech (high dose)

Agitated or hyperstimulated appearance (low dose)

Sedated or sleepy appearance (high dose)

High pulse and respiration rate

Pupil size (compare the control subject in the same light)

Needle marks

Presence of cocaine in nasal passages

Hallucinations or delusions

Cocaine in blood or urine

Remember that cocaine's acute physical effects may last only 1 or 2 hours after use. Some acute effects of cocaine include rapid speech, local anesthesia, pupil dilation, increase in heart rate and blood pressure, mood elevation, increase in respiration and reflexes, relaxation, and impaired motor functions. However, when the physical effects are observed (such as an increase in speech rate, pulse, or pupil dilation) there is almost always direct physical evidence of cocaine in the nasal passage or a fresh needle mark. Officers should also bear in mind that cocaine has a short duration of activity which correlates with its influence on the human body. A single dose may last about 3 to 4 hours and cocaine cannot be found in the blood past about 6 hours.

For cocaine documentation, nasal examination is indispensable. After snorting cocaine, residue remains in the septum and is excellent evidence. The residue is brown, black, white, or gray. Often the residue looks like plain dirt. To examine for residue, have the subject lean head backward and look at the septum of nose with a flashlight.

PHYSICAL EFFECTS OF COCAINE

Hyperactivity. Since cocaine is a very powerful central nervous system stimulant, someone under the influence of cocaine will be "wired." They will be breathing rapidly, talking fast, acting excited, over-reacting to situations, or extremely agitated. Frequently, persons who use cocaine will be highly paranoid, or may even hallucinate.

Increased heart rate and blood pressure. The average pulse is around 65 to 75 beats per minute. Someone who is under the influence of cocaine might have a pulse as high as 130 beats per minute. A pulse exceeding 110 beats per minute is a good indication that the subject is under the influence of a stimulant, possibly cocaine. In an overdose situation, a doctor or paramedic is authorized to furnish both pulse and blood pressure information.

Pupil dilation. A normal pupil will dilate to a maximum of approximately 6.9 mm. Someone under the influence of cocaine may have pupils larger than 7.5 or 8.0 mm.

Increased respiration. The average person takes about 15 breaths per minute. Someone under the influence of cocaine will have a much higher respiration rate. A respiration rate of 25 breaths per minute is a good indication that the subject is under the influence of a stimulant, possibly cocaine; this information can easily be validated by medical personnel.

Signs of ingestion. If someone snorts cocaine, you might see irritation around the nose or actual cocaine residue inside the nose. If cocaine has been injected, you will find puncture wounds and scar tissues over the blood vessels, usually on the inner arm.

Other symptoms. Insomnia, depression, loss of appetite, and radical mood elevations are often found in cocaine users. In large doses, cocaine may cause someone to look drunk. The person will appear sedated, have slurred speech and impaired motor functions, but will still have dilated pupils, rapid pulse and rapid respiration. Tremors, convulsions, delusions and hallucinations are also consistent with high doses of cocaine. When someone comes down off cocaine, they will usually experience paranoia, depression, anxiety, and general discomfort.

THE EXAMINATION

When investigating for evidence of cocaine influence, make as many field observations as you can and follow this basic format:

1. Note how the subject is acting. Pay special attention to mood and speech. Look for signs of hyperactivity, paranoia, or over-excitement. Ask the subject how he or she is feeling.
2. Examine the pupils for dilation beyond the normal levels. Use your pupilometer to measure the subject's pupils and the pupils of your partner under the same conditions; note the difference in pupil sizes. Check the reaction of the pupils to the absence and presence of light. In this respect, both your field examination and in-custody workup are the same as if you were checking the subject for heroin.
3. Take the subject's pulse. The pulse can usually be felt on the wrist or neck; count how many times the heart beats per minute. Remember that people under the influence of cocaine may be extremely paranoid. Explain to them what you are going to do before you do it. Often reaching for their hand or their neck may cause a violent reaction.
4. Check for signs of ingestion. Have the suspect tilt his or her head back and shine your flashlight up his or her nose. Often you can see

cocaine on the nasal passage. Cocaine also tends to cause reddening or even ulcers in or around the nose, or on the septum. Check for puncture wounds over the veins or blood vessels. Describe them or chart them just as you would during a heroin examination. Do not try to identify the kind of substance that the suspect is injecting; however, it should be noted that cocaine usually causes more tissue damage than heroin. If someone is injecting cocaine, the skin around the wound will most likely be bruised or swollen.

5. Ask the suspect about his or her medical condition. This question should be asked to avoid a later defense in court. Ask the following questions:

   a. Are you injured or sick?

   b. Are you being treated by a doctor or dentist?

   c. Have you had any recent head injuries?

   d. Do you have anything wrong with your eyes?

   e. Are you taking any medication or applying any medication to your eyes?

   f. Do you have glaucoma or syphilis?

   g. Do you have any problems with your heart or blood pressure?

   h. Do you have any respiratory problems?

   i. Have you been drinking?

If the suspect answers "yes" to any of these questions, ask more questions to ascertain the exact condition.

CHEMICAL TEST

Cocaine can be detected in the blood for about 6 to 8 hours and in the urine for about 24 hours. Like heroin, however, it may take 2 hours after use to detect cocaine in the urine. Therefore it is best to take a blood sample.

THE REPORT

Once again, it is critical that you explain, in detail, the reason for your initial detention, your observations, and your evidence that the suspect is under the influence. Make sure you include a statement of what all your tests and observations mean (i.e., "based on my experience and training in the area of narcotics, I recognize the objective symptoms displayed by the suspect to be consistent with that of a person who is under the influence of cocaine.") Remember that once the handcuffs go on, anything you ask the suspect should be under *Miranda*. So *Mirandize* the subject and try to get a copout. Find out when, where, and how he or she got loaded, how much of the drug was used, and how it made him or her feel. Since cocaine users are frequently talkative, once you get them going, they'll usually lay everything out. In your questioning, be systematic, clear and concise.

COCAINE OVERDOSE

The average quantity of cocaine necessary to produce death by overdose is 1.2 grams ingested within 30 minutes. This amount may very considerably depending upon such factors as body weight, metabolic rate, or condition of health. One common symptom of overdose is a loss of control. Frequently the user will not be aware of his or her condition. The user may tremble yet say, "Oh, it's nothing"; they may tell you everything is fine, but they can't stop moving. Observe the following overdose symptoms as well:

Extremely nervous, irritable, and belligerent

Excessively cold

Dilated pupils

Unnaturally pale

Nauseated: feels queasy, throws up or tries to throw up

Seek medical aid immediately if the person:

Passes out (loses consciousness)

Has a seizure or convulsion

Is disoriented: Do they know who you are? Do they know who they are? Do they know where they are?

Is hallucinating, jumping up and down uncontrollably, hysterical, or babbling incoherently.

Has tachycardia (extremely rapid heartbeat).

If help is unavailable, get the person to lie down and remain calm in a quiet atmosphere. Elevate the legs and slightly lower the head. A person showing signs of overdose will continue to come on to the drug for at least another half an hour, so it is also important to remove the drug at the first sign of overdose.

In the event that the officer fears involvement for whatever reason, but does not want to simply abandon the overdosed person, the following option may be chosen: Take the overdosed person to a hospital emergency room. Put a note in the person's pocket briefly stating the problem (cocaine overdose) and leave immediately if you do not wish to answer questions.

Summary of signs indicating cocaine use:

1. Cocaine paraphernalia
2. Dilated pupils
3. Redness and sores around the nose
4. Rapid breathing and pulse rate
5. Hyperactive, bizarre and/or paranoid behavior
6. Itching of the skin
7. Perspiration on the forehead and neck
8. Extreme desire for liquid
9. Redness in the eyes due to lack of sleep
10. Dark brown deposits on the tongue and teeth
11. Needle marks and tracks
12. Sunglasses to shield the eyes

SYMPTOMS AND EFFECTS OF CHRONIC COCAINE USE

Only a blood or urine test will definitely diagnose cocaine use. However, you should suspect chronic cocaine use if you observe a combination of any of the following signs:

Dilated pupils

Talks and walks too fast

Nose may constantly run, appear red, or the person may sniff frequently

Sudden disappearances from work or school

Work or school performance deteriorates

Time distortion, including tardiness, unusual meal times, and missed appointments

Chronic forgetfulness or broken promises

Frequent auto accidents and/or traffic violations

Falls asleep during the day

Loss of interest and motivation at work or school

Needle marks with intravenous use

With freebasing, tips of fingers and nails may erode

Weight loss

Mental confusion or paranoia

Chronic cocaine use may cause the following health complications:

Rhinitis, sinusitis, bronchitis, and respiratory ailments

Nasal ulcers and/or perforation of nasal septum

Paranoia

Severe depression and lack of energy

Addiction or dependence

Chronic insomnia

Weight loss and malnutrition

Skin eruptions due to excessive itching

Some social problems associated with chronic cocaine use include the following:

Loss of desire to work or attend school

Disregard for time deadlines

Marital discord

Resorting to illegal activities to support habit

Switching to heroin or alcohol abuse

Accidents

Violence and fights

Although research is still underway, it has been observed by medical professionals that chronic cocaine use may deplete the brain of the chemicals norepinephrine and dopamine.[25] Loss of these brain chemicals provides a rational explanation for many of the behaviors and symptoms of the chronic cocaine user listed above. This loss may also explain some of the withdrawal symptoms experienced by habitual cocaine users.

COCAINE WITHDRAWAL SYMPTOMS

Below is a table of the most common cocaine withdrawal symptoms. These symptoms and their frequency among cocaine users were determined in a study of 49 cocaine-dependent persons conducted by Dr. Forest Tennant.*

Symptoms	Number Who Experienced Symptoms*
Craving for cocaine	41 (83.7%)
Depression	39 (79.6%)
Irritable	35 (71.4%)
Increased appetite	35 (71.4%)
Sleep increase	33 (67.3%)
Lethargy	32 (65.3%)
Weakness	23 (46.9%)
Confused thoughts	19 (38.8%)
Loss memory	19 (38.8%)
Abnormal taste and smell	19 (38.8%)
Anxious	13 (26.5%)

*It should be noted that subjects experienced and reported more than one symptom during withdrawal.

COCAINE METABOLISM AND DETECTION IN BODY FLUIDS

If taken intranasally, cocaine reaches its peak plasma level after about 30 to 60 minutes. If taken intravenously or by freebasing, it reaches peak plasma levels within 5 to 10 minutes.

Cocaine is converted in the blood to benzoylecgonine, and this metabolite is usually detected in the urine. Cocaine metabolite appears in the urine about one hour after it is used, and it can be detected in the urine for about 48 hours.

Cocaine can be found in the plasma for up to 4 to 6 hours after ingestion, although it is present in very low plasma concentrations after 1 to 1.5 hours. A plasma concentration of 10 ng/ml. or greater should be considered to be evidence of cocaine "influence."

* See p. 107.

[25] Smith, D.E. and D.R. Wesson. *Treating the Cocaine Abuser*. Center City, MN: Hazelden Education Materials, 1985.

Short, P.H. and L. Shuster. "Changes in brain norepinephrine associated with sensitization to d-amphetamine." *Psychopharmacology*. 48:59-67, 1976.

Central Nervous System Stimulants

It should be re-emphasized that urine or blood testing is essential for diagnosing cocaine use. There are several techniques that will accurately detect the qualitative presence of cocaine metabolite in urine. The amount of cocaine in the urine is not very important—only the fact that it is present or absent. Sometimes, however, this important piece of evidence may be difficult for officers to obtain.

Causes of negative urine tests:

Urine specimen collected too soon. Most abusable drugs will not show in urine for about 1 to 2 hours after use.

Urine specimen collected too late. About 90 percent is eliminated by 48 hours after last use.

Too little of the drug in urine specimen to detect, i.e., below 2.0 ng/ml. to detect. This commonly occurs when low dosages of drugs are used.

Laboratory error.

How to avoid negative urine tests:

Take more than one urine specimen. Wait about an hour between collections. Check with laboratory to see how they want samples processed and labeled.

Wait until the pupil is reactive and returned to normal size to ensure enough time has passed to allow the drug to reach the urine.

Hindrances to accurate blood testing:

Cost

Lack of equipment

No qualified blood drawers or technicians to operate equipment

Test performed too seldom for technician to be competent

Lack of adequate veins to draw blood from the user

If cocaine is present in plasma at a level above 10 ng/ml., cocaine activity can be assumed to be present.

STREET TESTS FOR COCAINE

Often cocaine traffickers check the purity of the drug by using chemicals. Cobalt thiocyanate, hydrochloric acid, and chloroform are the ingredients for the classical test for cocaine. Clorox tablets (sodium hypochlorite) is sometimes used as a test. When cocaine powder is dropped into a clorox solution, a white halo appears as the powder falls to the bottom of the glass. Any red coloring indicates a synthetic anesthetic. Another test involves heating the substance suspected to be cocaine. When heated on aluminum foil, pure cocaine produces a grey, or red-brown stain. A black residue indicates the presence of sugar. Sounds upon heating may also be significant; a popping sound means amphetamine and a sizzling sound indicates Procaine.

PRELIMINARY FIELD TESTS FOR LAW ENFORCEMENT

Until recently, investigative field testing for cocaine was a messy, complex procedure. However, many simple test kits are now available to drug-enforcement agents. B-D Co., Arlington Texas, makes a series of tests for controlled substances called "Nik." The cocaine test consists of a thick clear plastic envelope and three sealed glass tubes containing liquid. A small portion of the suspect powder is placed in the envelope, closed and the glass tubes broken in sequence; it is a simple, convenient procedure. While a positive indication by the test presumptively identifies cocaine and in most cases would warrant arrest, further assay is generally required for subsequent court proceedings. The preliminary field test is called a cobalt test.

COCAINE AND VIOLENCE

The association of cocaine with overt violence takes many forms. It begins in the growing fields and extends to assaults on concealed laboratories where coca paste and cocaine are made. It spreads to the transportation system protecting the material from hijackings by rival mobs. Its most visible and violent forms are seen in the capital cities. In Bogota, for example, the assassination of police, judges, and newspaper editors who would try to oppose or deter the "narcotrafficantes" is commonplace. The violence can also be random with bystanders in the field of fire murdered without compunction.

When cocaine arrives at the port of entry of the consuming nation, violence begins again, and it continues even after the ultimate consumer has delivered the drug to his brain. As one dealer said: "If you aren't paranoid in this business, you don't survive." Everyone carries a weapon and uses it without particular restraint. Some gangs specialize in "ripping off" cocaine dealers and transporters because "that's where the money is."

It might be recalled that the expression "dope fiend," coined during the first decades of this century, referred not to heroin addicts, but to cocaine addicts. It was supposed to denote the crazed, demonic assaultiveness of cocaine users.

The plight of the compulsive cocaine consumer is a difficult one. Cocaine hunger probably exceeds heroin hunger in intensity. If it is measured by what people will do for a fix, the drive to obtain cocaine is at least as great as that of a heroin-dependent person in withdrawal. When the craving is great, but money, liquid assets or cocaine are not at hand, cocaine users may become desperate. Their dysphoria is great, and cocaine represents the only possible relief. They are compelled to obtain cocaine just as the starving rat might deliver a dose of cocaine rather than go to the food pellets in the cage.

Cocaine psychosis is common. It varies in degree from mild suspiciousness to overwhelming delusions of death threats with subsequent attempts to defend one's self by aggression against the threatener or threateners. With mild delusional disorders, some ability to evaluate reality may be retained. When paranoid thinking overwhelms the ability to sort out reality from delusion, however, insight into the false ideas is absent. Appropriate hallucinatory incidents accompany the deluded thought process.

Cases are known of individuals in the post-cocaine state who have killed relatives or friends who refused to lend them money. Several cities have seen a new wave of armed robberies based on the simple need to obtain relief from cocaine withdrawal.

COCAINE AND ALCOHOL

The findings of two related studies of cocaine death, conducted by researchers at the University of Miami and the National Center for Disease Control in Atlanta, indicate that the combination of alcohol and cocaine appear to result not only in a more intense high but also in an increased risk of sudden death. According to researchers, the combination of cocaine and alcohol produces a third chemical believed to be cocaethylene.

Dr. Deborah Mash, Neuroscientist at the University of Miami is coordinating one of these leading studies on cocaine and alcohol. According to Dr. Mash, early research indicates that in a group of individuals who suffer from heart disease, the risk of death in using cocaine and alcohol is 21 times greater than those using cocaine alone. Dr. Mash's research also shows that people can die after consuming as little as one drink in combination with powder or crack cocaine (a common combination among weekend drug users).

In the past, cocaine has been considered a recreational drug with little risk for causing death. However, when reports of cocaine-related deaths involving casual users came to the surface (such as the case of the University of Maryland basketball player Len Bias), statistics of cocaine-related deaths began to soar throughout the nation. According to the National Institute on Drug Abuse, cocaine-related deaths rose from about 700 in 1985 to more than 3,000 in 1989.[26]

The chance discovery of the chemical cocaethylene was made by Dr. Lee Hearn, Chief Toxicologist at the Dade County Medical Examiner's Department. While looking for clues into the pattern of cocaine-related deaths, Dr. Hearn in a chance discovery identified the chemical cocaethylene in persons who died after consuming cocaine and alcohol. After studying 287 recent cocaine-related deaths in Dade County, it has been found that 62 percent tested positive for cocaethylene. This chemical substance, created in the liver when alcohol and cocaine meet, works much like cocaine. It turns on the flow of pleasure-producing chemicals in the brain and it creates an addiction which is very difficult to assuage.

Dr. Mash of the University of Miami noted that cocaethylene produces a "higher high" than cocaine alone. Corroborating this finding, Dr. Hearns indicated that cocaethylene packs a deadlier punch as its toxicity is strong enough to kill laboratory mice at lower doses than cocaine.

In humans, cocaethylene's threat may sneak up. While the body flushes cocaine from its system in a matter of hours, Drs. Mash and Hearn fear that cocaethylene may linger for longer periods, accumulating in bodily tissues. This accumulation could be deadly for those already at risk of heart failure. Cocaine is widely known to overload the heart by boosting blood pressure and constricting blood vessels, increasing the risk of death. With increased research, some more of our questions concerning the effects of cocaine may be answered.

---

[26] National Institute on Drug Abuse (NIDA). *Methamphetamine Abuse in the United States.* Washington: DHHS Pub. No. (ADM) 89-1608, 1989.

Chapter X

AMPHETAMINES

The first amphetamine-like compound was discovered in 1919 by a Japanese scientist named Ogato. Little use was found for the substance until 1927 when George Allas suggested its substitution for ephedrine. He was trying to find a way to more efficiently counteract depression in mental hospitals. Allas found that when patients started taking this drug, many lost their appetites. The loss of appetite proved to have a large market value; thus, amphetamine and its chemical analogs were once common ingredients in "diet pills."

In the early 1930s, when Smith, Kline & French Laboratories marketed the Benzedrine inhaler, dextroamphetamines became commercially feasible. Other amphetamines and amphetamine-like compounds were subsequently perfected and uses for them were "discovered." By the 1960s, the efficacy of amphetamines was being claimed by drug manufacturers for at least 11 uses:

1. To control symptoms of narcolepsy
2. To control certain hyperkinetic behaviorial disorders in children
3. To relieve or prevent fatigue in individuals with deteriorated psychomotor performance
4. To treat mild depression
5. To antagonize the pharmacological actions of depressant drugs (e.g. barbiturates, alcohol)
6. To control appetite
7. To induce insomnia and counteract fatigue in persons occasionally required to perform mental or physical tasks of long duration
8. To prevent and treat surgical shock
9. To maintenance blood pressure during surgery
10. To treat Parkinson's disease
11. To enhance the action of analgesic drugs

However, the American Medical Association's handbook on drug dependence published in 1969 did not accept these uses so readily. One section of the handbook read:

> With the exception of the first two items, the indications for the proper medical use of stimulants are subject to varying degrees of professional controversy. The debate, waged on both scientific and ethical grounds, is focused on the efficacy of these drugs as well as on the hazards involved. . . The usefulness of stimulants for reducing appetite, however, has been strongly challenged in many medical research circles. Paradoxically, the amphetamines also are used to reduce the overactivity and distractibility of hyperactive children.[27]

---

[27]American Medical Association. *Drug Dependence, A Guide for Physicians,* Chicago, 1969, p. 114.

In addition to these uses claimed by early manufacturers and physicians, amphetamines have also been used to improve athletic performance, to keep awake when driving a vehicle long distances, to cram for a test, or just for the euphoric effect.

The most extreme abuse is the use of the drug solely for its "rush" and euphoric effect. This effect can be achieved by "popping" (swallowing handfuls of pills), "snorting" (inhaling crushed pills or crystals through the nose), or "shooting" (injection under the skin or into a vein). Though oral use of amphetamines may cause difficulties, including dependence and paranoid psychosis, it is more likely that these effects will be maximized through intravenous injections. It is usually this route of administration and the compulsive taking or shooting of amphetamines that creates the phenomenon called the "speed freak." With each injection, the user experiences a "rush" or a "flash." The immediate result of those injections is euphoria, audio and visual hallucinations, and hyperactivity. This phase can be prolonged by repeated injections for several days. The only limitation on the length of the user's trip is when, because of exhaustion, he or she is forced to "come down."

The scene of abuse in the 1960s ran all the way from the Haight-Ashbury District of San Francisco through the cities and towns of America to the U.S. military establishment. Amphetamines were a popular substance of abuse at this time. The makeup of the Haight-Ashbury speed scene was vividly described by Roger C. Smith, Ph.D., a criminologist. Dr. Smith's monograph "The Marketplace of Speed: Violence and Compulsive Methamphetamine Abuse" is one of the best pieces of literature on the abuse of amphetamine-type central nervous system stimulants.[28] In an overview of amphetamine's rise to popularity, Dr. Smith stated:

> The amphetamine research project came into being during the early spring months of 1968. At that time, the relatively benign patterns of social and ritual use of marijuana and the psychedelics had given way to the compulsive use of methamphetamine or "speed." The level of violence in neighborhoods was beginning to spiral upward and the medical and psychiatric problems of young people were increasing geometrically. While my primary obligation was to gather data on patterns of amphetamine use, I also felt that I had some obligation as a human being to seek out help for the hundreds of "speed-freaks" that I talked with.

In another passage on the effects of amphetamine and the counter-effects of other substances of abuse, Dr. Smith wrote:

> Drug switching is especially prevalent in the speed scene because of specific drug effects. One cannot use amphetamine over an extended period of time without experiencing a variety of adverse effects, including the appearance of hallucinated "crank bugs" or tiny microanimals which appear to be crawling around under the skin, paranoia, malnutrition, serum hepatitis, and abscesses. Thus, one must either learn to control the length of a "run," or he must use other drugs in an instrumental fashion to counteract the central nervous system stimulation induced by the amphetamine. For most middle-class youngsters, the first such drugs used are barbiturates, a drug which immediately terminates the stimulation and allows the

---

[28] Smith, R.C. "The Marketplace of Speed: Violence and Compulsive Methamphetamine Abuse." *Journ. of Psychedelic Drugs*. 2:20-24, 1969.

> individual to sleep. However, barbiturates also induce bizarre and often assaultive behavior and if injected cause abscesses and cellulitis. Thus, the speed user continues to experiment until he discovers that heroin terminates the stimulative effects and has none of the adverse effects of barbiturates.

These passages from Dr. Smith's early writing on amphetamine still hold true today. Most likely, they were also true when amphetamines were used prior to the 1960s. In 1938, the use of amphetamines by the military to enhance and extend performance was first employed by the Germans. Subsequently, many countries on both sides during World War II used "pep pills" to increase the fighting effectiveness of their soldiers. Great Britain, for example, dispensed approximately 72 million "energy tablets" to military personnel during that period.

THE JAPANESE EXPERIENCE WITH AMPHETAMINES

In 1940, amphetamines were used in Japan to treat some psychiatric patients and to combat Parkinson's disease.[29] During World War II, amphetamine-like drugs were also used wholesale to increase the efficiency of Japanese soldiers and production workers.[30] By the end of the war, central nervous stimulants were used almost compulsively by the Air Force, airport construction workers, and munitions factory workers in order to maintain motivation and increase efficiency.[31]

By the end of World War II, some Japanese drug companies wanted to dispose of their surplus stock of amphetamine-like drugs. Using the slogan "elimination of drowsiness and repletion of the spirit," the advertising appealed to young people who had learned to use drugs during the war. This effort by the drug companies to rid themselves of surplus stock snowballed into an epidemic of amphetamine abuse.

In the early postwar period in Japan, amphetamine abuse was greatest among young people, although government authorities also detected abuse among members of distinct occupational groups, particularly artists, writers, students, entertainers, waitresses, bartenders, and night laborers. Examining physicians began to see chronic amphetamine abusers in the fall of 1946.

The Japanese government first attempted to control amphetamine abuse by enacting the drug control law of 1948 which designated central nervous system stimulants as dangerous drugs. The control of amphetamine manufacturing soon followed.

These control measures proved inadequate to stem what a Health and Welfare Ministry official called "the tide of this fast-spreading evil." Responding to an acknowledged emergency, in 1951 the Japanese enacted the central stimulant control law which paralleled the provisions of the

---

[29] Brill, H. and T. Hirose. "The Rise and Fall of a Methamphetamine Epidemic: Japan, 1945-55." *Seminars in Psychiatry*. 1:179-194, 1969.

[30] Hemmi, T. "How We Handled the Problem of Drug Abuse in Japan." *Use and Abuse of Amphetamines and its Substitutes*. Rockville, MD: NIDA Research, Issue 25, 1980.

[31] Suwaki, H. *Methamphetamine Abuse in Japan*. Rockville, MD: NIDA Research Monograph 115, 1991, pp. 84-98.

narcotics control law. The government had become convinced that amphetamines, despite their alleged medical usefulness, had the same dependence-inducing effect as narcotic drugs.

After the imposition of these controls, illicit manufacture of amphetamine burgeoned, black markets for their distribution and sale proliferated in number and complexity of organization, and the incidence of amphetamine abuse further increased. In response to this worsening situation, the Japanese government revised the central stimulant control law in 1954 to increase criminal penalties for violations of its provisions. In 1955, the central stimulant control law was further revised and amended to control chemical precursors and intermediates for the illicit manufacture of amphetamine-like central nervous system stimulants. Penalties for violations of the act were again increased. Likewise, detection efforts were intensified and many illicit manufacturers and traffickers were arrested, prosecuted, convicted, and jailed. The government of Japan also determined that amphetamine abusers would be treated in mental hospitals in accordance with the provisions of the Mental Hygiene Act. Finally, these stern measures against the illegal manufacture and sale of amphetamine-like drugs greatly reduced the epidemic.

Coincident with the 1955 amendments to the central stimulant law, a social campaign against amphetamines was organized and driven throughout Japan. Emphasizing the problem of youth, the principal objectives of the campaign were:

1. To put an end to abuse of amphetamines;
2. To strengthen the control system established by law;
3. To provide treatment for persons dependent upon amphetamines;
4. To inform the public about the dangers of amphetamine abuse and dependence; and
5. To collect and disseminate information on the treatment and other assistance available to amphetamine abusers.

The Japanese amphetamine epidemic lasted about 10 years and was not put to an end until the drug, as well as its chemical precursors, were strictly controlled, until violators were vigorously prosecuted, treatment for addicts was provided, and the public was educated to the dangers of these central nervous system stimulants.

Despite the passing of the epidemic, amphetamine abuse has never totally disappeared from Japan. Furthermore, it has been predicted that cocaine will soon become a popular drug among users there.

APPEARANCE OF AMPHETAMINES

Amphetamines are found as tablets, capsules, crystals, and liquids. The tablets are found in many colors, sizes, and shapes (round, heart, square, triangle, oval, etc.). These tablets may have a line indented into one of the flat surfaces. They may be scored once or twice in this manner so the tablet can be easily broken into two or four sections to decrease the dosage. The shape and color give rise to many of the slang terms for the amphetamines: "hearts," "cartwheels," "greenies," "oranges," "peaches," "roses," "whites," and many others. The amphetamine capsules also come in a variety of sizes and colors, but they generally resemble time-release cold capsules.

The crystalline form and liquid solution is almost always methamphetamine, known as "meth". The crystals are white, while the liquid is clear and contained in glass ampules. "Meth" is also found in tablet form.

"Crank" is the illicit manufacture of methamphetamine. It takes many forms including a yellow to white powder, a brown to reddish tarry-like substance, crystals resembling rock candy or shards of glass, or a yellowish-brown oily substance.

METHODS OF AMPHETAMINE USE

Amphetamine tablets and capsules are swallowed. Methedrine crystals are soluble in water, and like the liquid solution, are administered by injection. However, because the crystals are water soluble, the solution does not have to be "cooked" first, like heroin does. The methamphetamine crystals may also be sniffed into the nostrils (like cocaine).

The crystals can also be placed in a glass pipe and smoked or placed on tin foil, heated, and the vapors of the "meth" inhaled.

EFFECTS OF AMPHETAMINE USE

The medical community has not always accepted the belief that amphetamine can be physically addictive. The older medical literature suggested that amphetamines do not produce physical addiction. However, direct observation of amphetamine abusers in the 1960s, the so-called "speed freaks," made it clear that amphetamine addiction is more widespread, more incapacitating, more dangerous, and more socially disrupting than narcotics addiction.

In the 1960s, John Kramer, Chief of Medical Research at the California Rehabilitation Center in Corona, California pointed out that the intravenous use of amphetamines is medically indistinguishable from cocaine addiction.[32] Referring to patterns of amphetamine use in the 1960s, Kramer wrote:

> The use of hundreds of times the average dose of amphetamines is physically addicting, meaning that tolerance builds up, and definite withdrawal symptoms occur when the drug is discontinued.

Physical addiction is a distinct possibility since amphetamines affect the central nervous system like some other addictive drugs. Amphetamines stimulate the CNS, leading to increased wakefulness, alertness, arousal, activity, talkativeness, restlessness, pleasurable sensation, and reduced appetite. Larger doses may produce irritability, aggressiveness, anxiety, suspiciousness, excitement, auditory hallucinations, and paranoid fears (delusions, psychotic reactions).

Stimulants also dilate the pupils, increase sweating, quicken breathing, raise blood pressure, and produce tremors (shaking) of the hands. In addi-

---

[32] Kramer, J.C. "Introduction to Amphetamine Abuse." *Journ. of Psychedelic Drugs*. 2:8-13, 1969.

tion to the possibility of physical addiction, these drugs have a high potential for psychological dependence. Tolerance to normal dosages does develop (sometimes to an astonishing degree) and, after extremely high doses, some withdrawal effects can be observed.

AMPHETAMINE WITHDRAWAL SYMPTOMS

Since tolerance develops, requiring larger and larger doses, chronic users of amphetamines can experience withdrawal symptoms—generally a deep depression and debilitating fatigue. Due to these bodily reactions to the absence of the drug, extremely high doses taken over a long period of time can be considered physically addicting.

The stimulants produce high levels of pleasurable feelings and, occasionally, feelings of greatly increased power; they also produce sexually orgasmic experiences when taken intravenously. One is easily seduced into the repeated use of these substances. Overdosage can occur rapidly, with marked impairment of judgment, greatly increased suspiciousness (paranoia), aggressive behavior, and serious interruption of normal eating and sleeping patterns (which produces physical deterioration). Constant heavy use often leads to somewhat psychotic behavior which, in some cases, can be indistinguishable from paranoid schizophrenia. Thus, the cessation of use can cause the regular user to engage in very irregular behavior. Suicides have occasionally been triggered by the prolonged depressions of mood which follow the intense stimulation of continued heavy use. The deep depression which accompanies the withdrawal period can lead to any number of destructive behaviors. However, intravenous amphetamine users often learn that heroin produces similar orgasmic feelings when injected while producing none of the deteriorative effects of "speed" on health and performance. Thus, there is some tendency to switch from amphetamines to heroin use, which actually worsens the user's experience of withdrawal.

AMPHETAMINES AND VIOLENCE

Police reports and medical research indicate that amphetamines do tend to set up conditions in which violent behavior is likely to occur. Suspiciousness and hyperactivity may combine to induce unwarranted assaultative behavior. Under the influence of amphetamines, change of mood is common; for the most trivial reasons, the user abruptly shifts from warmly congenial to furiously hostile moods.

Most high-dose amphetamine users describe involvement, either as aggressor or victim, in episodes in which murder or mayhem was avoided by the slimmest of margins. There are, of course, instances in which violence actually occurred. It is clear from a number of reports by users that these instances would not have taken place had it not been for the use of amphetamines.[33]

---

[33] Asnis, S. F. and R.C. Smith. "Amphetamine Abuse and Violence." *Journ. of Psychedelic Drugs.* 10:371-377, 1978.

Ellinwood, E. H. "Assault and Homicide Associated With Amphetamine Abuse." *American Journ. of Psychiatry.* 127:1170-1175, 1971.

One testimony before the Select Committee on Crime in 1969 verified the relationship between amphetamine abuse and violence or crime. Joel Fort, M.D. and Professor at the School of Social Welfare, University of California at Berkley, told the Select Committee:

> On a typical run (prolonged heavy use) of speed, there develops severe paranoia (paranoia characterized by delusions and hallucinations, violence, etc.), a marked tendency to violence sometimes tragically leading to murder, and serious physical deterioration. . . Amphetamine should be very high on the list in the sense I have mentioned. . . in terms of crimes of property and sometimes violence associated with obtaining enough money to support . . . addiction.[34]

Other medical professionals have also explained their observance of this relationship between amphetamine use and violence or crime. Professor Gosta Rylander, a Swedish psychiatrist, has written at length on this relationship after observing and questioning her patients. I quote at length here to illustrate the alarming degree to which amphetamine abuse may lead to violence:

> The crime-causing influence of central stimulants . . . can be studied in the light of three different types of mental states.
>
> First, the increased self-assurance which can give a feeling of omnipotence, the stimulation of energy and heightened activity, the ignoring of difficulties and consequences, involve disposition to crime. This was expressed in the same words by two girls who did not know each other: "I always turn 'criminal' after Preludin (phenmetrazine) shots," they said. An addict with long experience of the drug declared that a crime was a natural outlet for the drug-induced overactivity, without any thought being given to the nature of the act committed. When caught red-handed, the addict may be astonished at the action of the (arresting) policemen. Of course, the addicts need money to buy tablets illegally, but even if that need is not acute, they may still commit crimes. "I would never have committed such a clumsy and stupid crime, if I hadn't been high," the addicts often say.
>
> Two of my patients with no crimes of violence in their records committed robberies when high on Preludin. One of them, a man, knocked down a jeweler in his shop; the other, a girl, inspired two foreigners, whom she met by chance, to a robbery and a holdup. She helped them in both cases. The crimes mentioned were quite ruthless and, from the criminal's point of view, very stupid. They committed the crimes without bothering about the obvious risks of being caught; in fact they were caught.
>
> Two of my addicts who had not been sentenced for crimes of violence before, committed murder under the influence of Preludin and a small amount of alcohol. This seems to be a very dangerous combination. . .
>
> In states of acute paranoid psychosis, a panic-filled addict can commit dangerous acts of different types. One of my addicts killed another addict because he felt sure this man was sent out by a gang to kill him. In a similar state, another of my patients drove through the central part of Stockholm at high speed against red lights and

---

[34] For a more complete discussion, see "Crime in America — Illicit and Dangerous Drugs." October 23, 24, 25 and 27, 1969, San Francisco, Calif. hearings before the Select Committee on Crime, U.S. House of Representatives; pp. 39-89.

> through a one-way street in the wrong direction until he ran into another car at a street corner, badly injuring both the passengers of this car and himself. Another one tried to force his way into the police headquarters in Stockholm with a knife in his hand, crying for help from the Swedish Secret Service against his persecutors.
>
> Finally, addicts who intravenously inject large doses of central nervous system stimulants decline socially more quickly than alcoholics. They become parasites, living on relatives, friends, or sometimes on sickness benefits, peddling alcohol or narcotics. They are inclined to all sorts of petty crimes and anti-social acts by which they can get some money with which to buy drugs. . .[35]

SUMMARY OF AMPHETAMINE ABUSE SYMPTOMS

1. Dilated pupils
2. Sweating (heavy perspiration)
3. Shaking - tremors of the hands
4. Talkativeness
5. Possibly thin (due to reduced appetite)
6. Paranoia (increased suspiciousness)
7. Quickened breathing
8. Aggressiveness
9. Irritability
10. Potentially violent

HANDLING PEOPLE UNDER THE INFLUENCE OF STIMULANTS

From the point of view of how dangerous a drug user may be, professionals in the medical, psychiatric, and law enforcement fields discuss four major categories of dangerous drugs: PCP, alcohol, cocaine, and amphetamines. Particularly in the case of amphetamine or cocaine users, you are dealing with people who are extremely dangerous. This kind of individual will be very jumpy, very reactive to minute distractions, and unable to keep still. He or she may be wringing his hands, talking very fast, talking about a disconnected set of ideas all at once, talking about people who have followed him or her, or chain-smoking. Long-term users of amphetamines or cocaine may be very withdrawn and emaciated. The user may be extremely suspicious of everything that is going on around him or her. The user may also lick his or her lips frequently, since one of the side effects of amphetamine/cocaine use is extreme dryness of the mouth and lips.

Users of stimulants can be very dangerous. This type of drug user is somebody you should never let out of your sight, and never turn your back on. The primary intervention is to immobilize the individual as soon as possible. If you don't, it is quite likely that someone will get hurt. Immobi-

---

[35] Rylander, Gosta. "Clinical and Medico-Criminological Aspects of Addiction to Central Stimulating Drugs," Symposium on Abuse of Central Stimulants, Stockholm: Alquist and Wiksell, 1969.

lizing the user should be undertaken with the recognition that (especially among males):

1. He's going to be very quick.
2. He's going to be very strong.
3. He's going to defend himself in every way that he conceivably can.

Immobilizing the user is probably going to take more officers than one would suspect it should. There is relatively little need for the kinds of reassurance and gentleness that you might want to exercise with the person on a bad trip. Remember to control the person as soon as possible. The chances of the user trying to escape and the potential for violence are both very high.

METHAMPHETAMINE HYDROCHLORIDE

As a form of amphetamine, methamphetamine is also a central nervous system stimulant. Stimulants are either natural, such as epinephrine and norepinephrine, or synthetic such as amphetamine and phenmetrazine. The first natural stimulant to be discovered was epinephrine (adrenalin) and the effects were first described in 1899. The first synthetic stimulant of any significance was prepared in 1919 by a Japanese chemist and was later identified as methamphetamine.

Methamphetamine is commonly available under the trade name "Desoxyn." It is a schedule II drug. Methamphetamine has often been called the poorman's cocaine and has traditionally been the drug of choice of outlaw motorcycle gangs. On the street it is usually called "Meth" or "Crystal." In Honolulu, "Crystal" or "Ice" is referred to as the rock methamphetamine while "Crank" is the term used for the powder form.

Illicit methamphetamine has been around for decades. In the 1960s, it was usually made in illicit makeshift labs by motorcycle gangs. It got a bad name in the late 1960s and early 1970s when many users learned the truth behind the phrase "speed kills."

In recent years, its use and supply have grown to rival cocaine in many areas of the country. This is due to a discovery in the early 1980s that using ephedrine made the manufacturing of methamphetamine much easier. Ephedrine has several advantages over the old process. It is easier, involving one-half the number of steps in its processing. Also, it does not smell bad, reducing the possibility of detection and allowing it to be cooked in cities.

For a while, ephedrine was unregulated and easy to buy, though California state legislators changed that in April 1987, when they required all ephedrine sales to be registered with the State Department of Justice. Still, its illegal use has transformed speed into a potential national drug crisis for the 1990s.[36]

---

[36] National Institute on Drug Abuse, Statistical Series. Data from the Drug Abuse Warning Network (DAWN), Semiannual Report Series G, N24, DHHS Pub. No. (ADM)90-1664, Washington, D.C., 1990.

SPEED LABS

Through the 1960s and 1970s, the illegal production and sale of speed was the exclusive domain of gangs like the Hell's Angels. The Hell's Angels continue to stay deeply involved in speed production, preferring their proven and pungent cooking method in the privacy of the country.

From about 1984 on, however, increasing numbers of non-gang members were found cooking crank. Narcotics agents began finding speed labs everywhere: in motels, mobile homes, houseboats, and rented homes. Most of those labs used the ephedrine method. In 1986, for example, 82 percent of the methamphetamine labs seized by narcotics agents in California used the ephedrine method, according to a report from the state's Bureau of Narcotics Enforcement. In 1988, that figure was 79 percent.[37]

The problem of methamphetamine production became so widespread that speed recipes were even turning up in state prisons. One inmate was found running a small speed lab in his cell.

Illegal methamphetamine production is a hazardous and environmentally destructive crime that is expensive to clean up. Producers, often with little understanding of chemistry, combine a variety of explosive and hazardous chemicals to make the stimulant in makeshift laboratories.

When they have finished, illicit processors secretly dump the leftover toxic soup down drains, in rivers, or by the roadside. Cleanup costs for each lab or dump site may run into the thousands, with taxpayers picking up most of the tab. According to the American Environmental Management Corp., the company contracted to dispose of lab waste in most of California, disposing of an operating lab can cost taxpayers from $4,000 to $20,000, although sites where labs and excess chemicals are dumped usually cost less.

Cleaning up these illicit labs is so costly because the methods used to produce speed include dangerous chemicals that are heavily regulated when used by legitimate businesses. These chemicals include:

Freon - A pressurized toxic liquid used in refrigeration, it adds to the destruction of the Earth's ozone layer when released.

Ether - An extremely flammable and explosive liquid, used legally in industry solvents and anesthetics.

Methlamine - A highly corrosive, flammable and explosive chemical that is a suspected carcinogen. It is used industrially in rocket propellants, insecticides, and to tan leather.

Lye - A corrosive powder used to unclog drains.

Hydriodic gas - A deadly gas if breathed. It is used in disinfectants.

When dumped down drains or into cesspools by illicit processors, these chemicals kill bacteria that neutralize raw sewage, allowing sewage and

---

[37] California Narcotic Officers Association. *The California Narcotic Officer*. Spring, 1988.

chemicals to seep into groundwater, posing hazards even for the person who touches the chemical combination.

The danger of these chemicals is also attested to by the fact that many labs are found due to fire. About three years ago, the frequency of such disasters led state regulators to rigorously analyze the chemicals used to produce speed. Subsequently, that analysis led to drastic and expensive changes in the ways speed labs were handled.

While vats of seized chemicals used to be carted into court along with the accused, they are now destroyed and cases are tried using photographs and sample bottles. Most police officers do not even enter speed labs. They cord off the area and wait for a state-licensed chemist to arrive. The chemist, in a fire-retardant jumpsuit and gas mask, takes samples of the evidence. He turns the rest over to workers from a private waste disposal firm, who remove and destroy the chemicals.

In 1988, California narcotics agents found 377 speed labs and a number of chemical dump sites. The cleanup costs were paid by the county, which was later reimbursed through state and federal funds.

APPEARANCE AND PACKAGING OF METHAMPHETAMINE

Methamphetamine is sold in various forms. Purchase may include glass vials, paper bundles, or clear heat-sealed cellophane packets. Most recently it has been found in pieces of plastic straws which are heat sealed at both ends.

Methamphetamine normally appears in the form of a white powder. The formula used and the amount of washing determines the color and consistency of the final product. For instance, using Copper Hydrocenenators in the manufacturing process produces a green color methamphetamine.

Methamphetamine "Ice", on the other hand, is a clear, or translucent crystal in rock form. This "Ice" rock resembles shave-ice, rock candy, pieces of glass, and Hawaiian rock salt. Other aspects of "Crystal Meth" or "Ice" are discussed below.

METHAMPHETAMINE USE AND PARAPHERNALIA

Methamphetamine can be taken orally, by injection, or smoked in either a glass pipe referred to as a "meth bowl" or "bong," or in folded aluminum foil. The "meth" or "Ice" pipe or "bong" has one section where the "Ice" or "meth" crystals are placed through a hole on the top of the bowl or the stem. The "meth" pipe or "bong" may have a vent hole on the stem between the chamber and mouthpiece. To avoid paraphernalia laws, this pipe is often available for "burning incense" through some liquor stores and tobacco shops.

METHAMPHETAMINE ABUSE SYMPTOMS

Persons under the influence of methamphetamine will display the same objective symptoms as someone who is under the influence of cocaine. They will be hyperactive, talkative, paranoid, and agitated. They will have dilated pupils, increased respiration and pulse rates, and have noticeable mood swings.

Compared to cocaine, however, methamphetamine appears to be more damaging to the skin tissue; injection sites are often characterized by extreme swelling, bruising, and infection.

If someone snorts this drug, often reddening, ulcers, or sores can be detected in and around the nose.

Persons who use methamphetamine also suffer more severe and quicker trauma to their body than persons who use cocaine. "Speed freaks" are characterized by being skinny and malnourished with rotten teeth, and poor personal hygiene. "Speed freaks" are highly paranoid, constantly believing that they are being watched, followed, and conspired against. This extreme paranoia can make a "speed freak" extremely dangerous.

ARREST REPORT

For methamphetamine, the officer's field examination and narcotics work-up will be the same as that of someone who is under the influence of cocaine. In the report, pay particular attention to the reason for your initial detention of the person, your observations, the examinations the subject performed, the results, and what they meant to you. Include a statement similar to, "Based on my experience and training in the area of narcotics, the person displayed objective symptoms consistent with that of a person who is under the influence of a stimulant, possibly methamphetamine."

When you suspect the person is under the influence of methamphetamine or cocaine, it is recommended that you describe his condition as being under the influence of a stimulant consistent with cocaine or methamphetamine. It is often embarrassing to describe someone as being under the influence of cocaine in your report, then to have the blood test results show methamphetamine, or vice-versa.

"CRYSTAL METH" OR "ICE"

"Crystal Meth" or "Ice" first appeared in Hawaii during 1985 but was not recognized as a problem until 1987. During that time, local Filipino gang members were the principal distributors for this form of methamphetamine. Due to the hydriodic acid/red phosphorus reduction of ephedrine, it is currently believed that "Ice" is prepared in the Far East, notably Korea, the Philippines, and Taiwan.

MANUFACTURING AND DISTRIBUTION

"Ice" is simply d-methamphetamine hydrochloride in very large, crystal-clear "rocks." It is prepared by slow evaporation of a saturated solution of the salt in water or isopropanol. The appearance of the resulting product is in dramatic contrast to the traditional crystalline white powder, prepared by "gassing" an etheric solution of the freebase with anhydrous hydrochloric acid.

"Ice" is reportedly being smuggled into the United States from the Far East (specifically Thailand, Hong Kong, and Korea) by way of Canada. The drugs are then smuggled to Seattle (WA), then to Portland (OR) and finally to Honolulu (HI). While "Ice" is being sold in the majority of the Hawaiian Islands, it is predominantly being sold and used on the island of Oahu. It should also be noted that several clandestine methamphetamine laboratories in the Western United States, possibly attempting synthesis of this variant, have been recently seized.[38]

HOW "ICE" IS SOLD

"Ice" is most frequently sold in heat-sealed cellophane packets. Sometimes it may also be carried in opaque glass vials or paper bindles. This form of methamphetamine is typically sold on the underground market in small "rocks," hence the additional street designation "crack meth." In addition to "Ice", some street names for the drug, used primarily on the West Coast and in the Far East, include "Slabu," and "Hiropong." It should be noted that in some areas of the eastern United States "Ice" is also the current street name for 4-methylaminorex (also known as "U4Euh"). Quite surprisingly, the street value of "Ice" is significantly higher than an equal amount of the powder form. This fact may lead to a rapid switch-over to "Ice" by clandestine methamphetamine cooks.

HOW IS "ICE" RECOGNIZED?

In California, methamphetamine is normally found as a white powder. "Ice," on the other hand, is the name for crystal methamphetamine in solid form. The slang term "Ice" was designated for the drug due to its appearance. It is generally a clear, crystal-shaped, solid form (of medium to large size) that looks like glass. It has also been designated "crystal" and "glass" by some users. "Crystal Meth" has been described as both transparent with a light yellowish cast—a translucent milky white—and an almost pure white (similar in appearance to rock candy or Hawaiian salt.) Although "Ice" is reported to be odorless, some samples have the very strong and distinctive odor of P2P.

The "Ice" found in Hawaii is 98 to 100 percent pure. Information gathered in the Honolulu area indicates that several forms of this relatively pure "Crystal Meth" are being used. The most prevalent form is the translucent or clear rock crystal. This form of "Meth" is water-based and burns quickly leaving a milky white residue on the inside of the smoking bowl. Reports from Hawaii also indicate that a yellowish "Crystal Meth" is available. This oil-based, yellow "Meth" is said to burn slower and last longer leaving behind a brownish or black residue in the pipe.

HOW IS "ICE" USED?

While methamphetamine can be injected, inhaled, smoked, or taken orally, the "Ice" form of this drug is ingested by smoking. This makes "Ice" extremely addictive.

Due to its alleged lack of odor, "Ice" is often smoked in public without detection. Smoking is usually done using a glass pipe called a bong, which is usually a circular bowl with an attached pipe stem (usually 5″ in length).

---

[38] "Clandestine Laboratory Seizures in the United States: Calendar Year 1990." U.S. Department of Justice, Drug Enforcement Administration, Office of Intelligence, 1991.

Central Nervous System Stimulants

The basic difference between a pipe used for cocaine and a pipe used for "Meth" is in the construction (see illustration below).

METHAMPHETAMINE PIPE (GLASS)

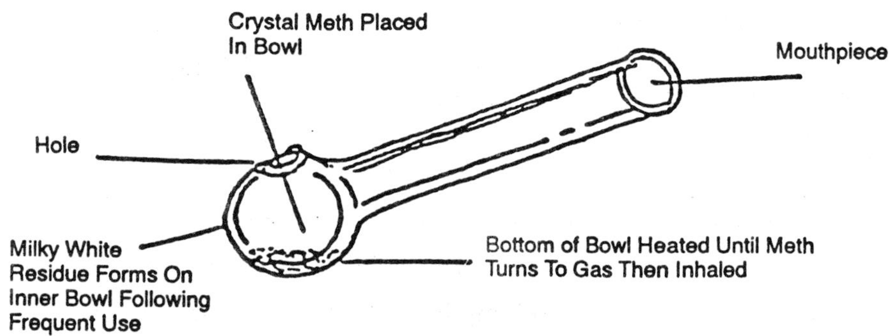

CRACK PIPE (GLASS)

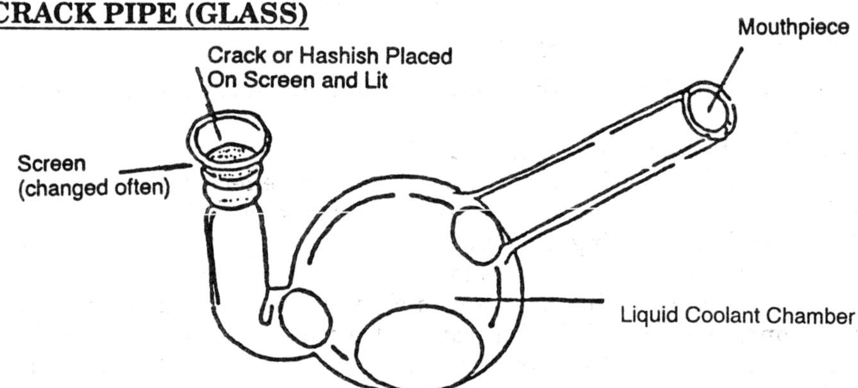

The cocaine pipe is made of two sections, one to hold the cocaine and the other section to hold a liquid coolant. The sections are separated by a screen or similar object. Cocaine smokers will ignite the cocaine in the top half of the glass pipe. The fumes are then inhaled, first through the coolant chamber and then into the mouth.

The "Meth" or "Ice" pipe, on the other hand, has only one section where the "Meth" is placed and heated. There are no screens and no coolants in the "Meth" pipe. The top of the bowl usually has a 1⁄8" hole leading to the main chamber and may have a vent on the stem that releases the "Meth" vapor when the bottom of the bowl is heated.

The "Ice" is first placed into the chamber and heated with a lighter or other heat source until it turns to a gas. The opening in the chamber and vent hole are sealed, usually with a finger, while the crystal is being heated. Once the crystal has turned to gas, it is inhaled by the user. With this method of ingestion, approximately 10 to 15 hits of "Meth" can be obtained from a one-gram dosage. It might be noted that a telltale sign of the "Meth" user is a burn mark on the finger(s) used to seal the hole in the main chamber.

 md

THE HIGH

The "high" gained from "Ice" lasts from 2 to 14 hours (some reports indicate 12 to 24 hours), depending on the amount ingested. When heated in a glass pipe, the crystals turn to liquid and produce a potent vapor that enters the bloodstream rapidly. As this happens, large doses may be excreted into the urine, unchanged, up to 72 hours after ingestion. When allowed to cool or cooled by a wet rag, the "Ice" reverts to its solid crystal state. It is then reusable and easy to transport.

The following factors are believed to have contributed to the growing popularity of "Ice":

* In quality, "Ice" is similar to or better than "Meth" used for injection.
* Smoking "Ice" eliminates the use of a needle.
* Methamphetamine enters the body faster when it is smoked.
* The drug's effects are long lasting when compared to other drugs (particularly in comparison to a cocaine "high" of about 20 minutes).
* "Ice" is often odorless, colorless, and tasteless.
* "Ice" is easy to transport.
* "Ice" sells for more than cocaine but is much cheaper to produce.

PHYSICAL/PSYCHOLOGICAL EFFECTS

It is too early to tell what the long-term physical effects of "Crystal Meth" or "Ice" will be. However, due to the potency of smokeable "Ice", it most likely will be worse than injecting methamphetamine. Symptoms of abuse include absences from work or school, paranoia, schizophrenia, and behavior that is unpredictable, uncontrollable, delusional, irrational, illogical, and often violent. Continued use of "Ice" for days at a time causes: 1) insomnia, 2) depletion of the body's stored energy, and 3) vitamin and mineral deficiencies. When the drug wears off, the user will then crash for 24 to 36 hours. Often the effects of the drug do not go away. In other words, some users do not return to normal health. Overdoses can lead to convulsions, coma, and eventually death. People often use this drug to lose weight quickly, to stay up all night working or studying, and for a feeling of excess energy.

Prolonged use can produce a high degree of tolerance and users find they need much heavier dosages to produce the same effects. Heavy use can also result in psychological dependence, leading to a psychotic state, anxiety, depression, and fatigue.

PROBLEMS ASSOCIATED WITH USE

Withdrawal from methamphetamine does not involve physical discomfort but can involve acute depression and fatigue. Depression can reach critical proportions, since life seems boring and unpleasant after cessation of use. Progressive toxic effects of methamphetamine abuse may include restlessness, tremor, talkativeness, irritability, insomnia, anxiety, delirium, panic states, paranoid ideation, palpitation, cardiac arrhythmia, hypertension, circulatory collapse, dry mouth, nausea, vomiting, abdominal cramps, convulsions, coma, and death.

Other problems include rapid deterioration of physical and psychological health, since methamphetamine disrupts the apprehension of time passing and creates the same sort of stress to the body that any long period of exertion creates. However, the user does not let his or her body recuperate; therefore, permanent damage or death may be the result.

Like crack, "Crystal Meth" has also affected newborn infants. As of August, 1989 a survey of all newborn infants in Hawaii showed that 25 percent had traces of "Crystal Meth" in their systems. Queens Hospital in Hawaii is averaging approximately a half dozen "Meth" overdoses a day compared to 1 a day last year. Furthermore, between January 1 and September 11, 1989, 23 percent of all narcotics arrests in Honolulu have been related to "Crystal Meth". It appears from these statistics that "Ice" has surpassed cocaine as the drug of choice in Hawaii.[39]

METHAMPHETAMINE AND THE TRUCKING INDUSTRY

Methamphetamine use is also spreading throughout the contiguous United States. Based on a year-long investigation of drug use in the trucking industry in California, it was found that the main drug being sold on the road is methamphetamine, which is frequently referred to as "go fast" by truckers. In addition to methamphetamine (known also as "speed," "crank," and "lucille cocaine,") heroin and other drugs have also been purchased from dealers working out of trucks.

The most remarkable aspect of this operation is how brazenly open the drug traffic is. Offers to buy and sell drugs crackle over the CB airwaves from one end of California to the other. However, the center of the action is right around the truck stops.

For the most part, these deals do not take place inside the truck stops. Much of the drug trafficking is conducted by prostitutes and small-time dealers who are not truckers. Yet, the truck stops generally have pretty good security; they don't allow non-truckers inside. So the truckers looking for action, and the pushers and hookers looking to provide it, congregate in nearby parking lots or alongside roads. Law enforcement officers have observed and overheard numerous transactions of this sort.

Those officers who drive California's highways can only be terrified by the results of this operation. Big 18-wheel rigs weighing up to 40 tons are whizzing down that highways at 50 to 70 miles an hour. The thought that their drivers might be under the influence of narcotics can be chilling.

In California, the statewide investigation of drug trafficking and the trucking industry began because law enforcement had been alerted to the problem by truck drivers who believe that drug use is the leading cause of truck accidents. So far, investigations have done little to allay those fears.

---

[39] Kouri, James. "Ice: New Drug of Choice in Hawaii." *The Narc Officer*. December, 1989, pp. 43-45.

Miller, Marissa. "Trends and Patterns of Methamphetamine Smoking in Hawaii." NIDA Research Monograph 115, Rockville, MD, 1991, pp. 72-83.

The truck drivers who informed law enforcement of the problem were much more typical of the population of hardworking men and women on the road than the relative handful of drug users and pushers that have been arrested. Only a small fraction of truckers are involved in activity of selling drugs, such as methamphetamine, on the road. Investigations have shown that the overwhelming majority of drivers do not sell or use drugs of any kind. During the investigations, law enforcement officers frequently heard clean truckers harassing the drug dealers over the air by saying things such as, "If you want to 'go fast,' go buy a bigger truck," or "Truckers for a drug-free America."

STIMULANT SLANG TERMS

Beans .... pills, commonly referring to benzedrine tablets or capsules
Basing .... baseballing; freebasing cocaine
Bennies .... benzedrine tablets
Black Beauty .... bi-phetamine capsules (methedrine capsule)
Blow .... cocaine
Bottle .... 100 pills
Bug .... to annoy, itching sensation, sensation due to cocaine poisoning
C .... cocaine
C & H .... cocaine and heroin
Cap .... capsule
Cartwheel .... benzedrine tablets
Cocaine Blues ...... depression from discontinuing the use of cocaine
Coke .... cocaine
Coke Out .... excessive use of cocaine to point of incoherence
Coke Spoon .... specially made tiny spoons for inhaling cocaine
Crack .... smoking cocaine
Crack cooler .... rock cocaine with wine cooler
Co-pilot .... benzedrine
Crank .... methamphetamine
Crash .... to sleep or come down from being under the influence of a stimulant
Crate .... large quantity of pills, usually 50,000
Cross-tops .... benzedrine tablets
Crystal .... methamphetamine
Dexies .... amphetamine tablets (dexedrine)
Diamonds .... amphetamine tablets
Flake .... cocaine
Flash powder .... methamphetamine
Freak .... heavy user of a drug; scared
Freeze .... the numbness caused by using cocaine
Girl .... cocaine
Glass .... crystal methamphetamine
Happy Dust .... cocaine
Hearts .... amphetamines (dexedrine)
Horn .... to inhale drugs through the nose
Hot Rock .... rock cocaine and tar heroin
Ice .... crystal methamphetamine
Jug .... 1,000 pills

 md

Central Nervous System Stimulants

Keg	50,000 pills
King's Habit	use of cocaine
Lady	cocaine
Leaf	cocaine
Line	cocaine poured out in a thin line on a table, book, album, etc., for inhaling into the nose with a straw.
Lucille	methamphetamine
Meth	methamphetamine
Merck	pharmaceutical cocaine
Mini Beans	small benzedrine tablets
Nose Candy	cocaine
Pep Pill	amphetamine
Peruvian	cocaine
Pill Freak	user of any type of pills
Pillow	25,000 amphetamines tablets usually packaged in black plastic bags.
Pop	to take a drug by either injecting or through the mouth
P-2-P	Phenyl-2-propanone (chemical used to manufacture meth)
Roll	ten pills sold in a roll (usually tinfoil)
Script	drug prescription
Sheet Rocks	liquid LSD with rock cocaine
Slabu	crystal methamphetamines
Snort	to sniff the drug through the nose
Snow	cocaine
Spacebasing	crack dipped in PCP and smoked
Speed	methamphetamine
Speedball	mixture of heroin and a stimulant drug
Super crank	cocaine crank
Tabs	tablets
Toot	cocaine
Upper	amphetamines
Whites	benzedrine
White Girl	cocaine
Wired	to be under the influence of a drug

REFERENCES:

American Medical Association. *Drug Dependence, A Guide for Physicians.* Chicago, 1969, p. 114

American Society for Pharmacology and Experimental Therapeutics. Committee on Problems of Drug Dependence. "Scientific Perspectives on Cocaine Abuse." *The Pharmacologist.* 29:20-27, 1987.

Asnis, S. F. and R.C. Smith. "Amphetamine Abuse and Violence." *Journ. of Psychedelic Drugs.* 10:371-377, 1978.

Bailey, D. N. and R.F. Shaw. "Cocaine and Methamphetamine – Related Deaths in San Diego County, 1987." *Journ. of Forensic Science.* 34:407-422, 1989.

Brill, H. and T. Hirose. "The Rise and Fall of a Methamphetamine Epidemic: Japan, 1945-55." *Seminars in Psychiatry.* 1:179-194, 1969.

Byck, Robert, M.D. (ed.) *Cocaine Papers by Sigmund Freud.* New York: Stonehill, 1975.

California Narcotic Officers Association. *The California Narcotic Officer.* Spring, 1988.

Dackis, C.A. and M.F. Gold. "New Concepts in Cocaine Addiction: The Dopamine Depletion Hypothesis." *Neuroscience and Biobehavioral Review.* 9:469-477, 1985.

Dendow, G.A. et al. "Self-Administration of Psychoactive Substances by the Monkey: A Measure of Psychological Dependence." *Psychopharmacology.* 16:30-48, 1969.

Drug Enforcement Agency. New York Field Office, Unified Intelligence Division. "Trends in Traffic: Cocaine." *The Narc Officer.* Nov. 1988.

Ellinwood, E. H. "Assault and Homicide Associated With Amphetamine Abuse." *American Journal of Psychiatry.* 127:1170-1175, 1971.

Erickson, P. et al. *The Steel Drug: Cocaine in Perspective.* Toronto: Lexington Books, 1987. 89-110.

Fischman, M.W. et al. "Acute Tolerance Development to the Cardiovascular and Subjective Effects of Cocaine." *The Journal of Pharmacology and Experimental Therapeutics.* 235:677-682, 1985.

________. "Cardiovascular and Subjective Effects of Intravenous Cocaine in Humans." *Arch. Gen. Psychiatry.* 33:983-989, 1976.

Freud, Sigmund. "On the General Effects of Cocaine." Rpt. in *Drug Dependence.* Issue No. 5, Oct. 1970.

Gawin, F., and H. Kleber. "Abstinence symptomatology and psychiatric diagnosis in cocaine abusers." *Archives of General Psychiatry.* 43:113, 1986.

Grabowski, J. and S.E. Devorkin. "Cocaine: An Overview of Current Issues." *Int. Journ. of Addictions.* 20:1065-1088, 1985.

Hammer, S. and L. Hazleton. "Cocaine and the Chemical Brain." *Addictive Behavior: Drug and Alcohol Abuse.* Colorado: Mortion Publishing Co., 1985.

Hemmi, T. "How We Handled the Problem of Drug Abuse in Japan." *Use and Abuse of Amphetamines and its Substitutes.* Rockville, MD: NIDA Research, Issue 25. 1980.

House Select Committe on Crime. "Crime in America—Illicit and Dangerous Drugs." San Francisco, California Hearings, October 23-27, 1969, pp. 39-89.

Inaba, D. and W. Cohen. *Uppers, Downers, All Arounders.* San Francisco, CA: Haight-Ashbury Detox Clinic, 1989.

Johanson, C.E. "Assesment of the Dependence Potential of Cocaine in Animals." J. Grabowski (ed.). *Cocaine Pharmacology, Effects, and Treatment of Abuse.* Washington DC: NIDA Research Monograph 50, 1984.

Kouri, James. "Ice: New Drug of Choice in Hawaii." *The Narc Officer.* December, 1989, pp. 43-45..

Kramer, John C. "Introduction to Amphetamine Abuse." *Journ. of Psychedelic Drugs.* 2:8-13, 1969.

Kramer, John C. and Robert Pinco. "Amphetamine Use and Misuse with Recommendations for Stimulant Control Policy." *Journ. of Psychedelic Drugs.* Vol. 5, No. 2, Winter, 1972, pp. 142-143.

Miller, Marissa. "Trends and Patterns of Methamphetamine Smoking in Hawaii." NIDA Research Monograph 115, Rockville, MD, 1991, pp. 72-83

National Institute on Drug Abuse (NIDA). *Methamphetamine Abuse in the United States.* DHHS Pub. No. (ADM) 89-1608, Washington, D.C., 1989.

_______. Statistical Series. Data from the Drug Abuse Warning Network (DAWN), Semiannual Report Series G, N24, DHHS Pub. No. (ADM)90-1664, Washington, D.C., 1990.

Preston, K.L. et al. "Long-term effects of repeated methamphetamine administration on monoamine neurons in the rhesus monkey brain." *Brain Res.* 338:243-248, 1985.

Resnick, R.B. et al. "Acute Systemic Effects of Cocaine in Man." *Science.* 195:696-698, 1977.

Rylander, Gosta. "Clinical and Medico-Criminological Aspects of Addiction to Central Stimulanting Drugs." Symposium on Abuse of Central Stimulants, Stockholm: Alquist and Wiksell, 1969.

Schuckit, M. *Drug and Alcohol Abuse.* 3rd Ed., New York: Plenum Press, 1989.

Short, P.H. and L. Shuster. "Changes in brain norepinephrine associated with sensitization to d-amphetamine." *Psychopharmacology.* 48:59-67, 1976.

Siegel, R. "Cocaine Freebase." *Journ. of Psychedelic Drugs.* 13:297-317, 1982.

Smith, D.E. and D.R. Wesson. *Treating the Cocaine Abuser.* Center City, MN: Hazelden Education Materials, 1985.

Smith, R.C. "The Marketplace of Speed: Violence and Compulsive Methamphetamine Abuse." *Journ. of Psychedelic Drugs.* 2:20-24, 1969.

Stash Staff. *The Adverse Effects of Amphetamines.* No. 205. Madison, Wisconsin: Stash Press, 1974, p. 7.

Suwaki, H. *Methamphetamine Abuse in Japan.* Rockville, MD: NIDA Research Monograph 115, 1991, pp. 84-98.

U.S. Department of Justice. "Drug Use in the General Population." *Drugs and Crime Facts, 1991.* Rockville, MD: Drugs and Crime Data Center and Clearinghouse, 1991.

U.S Department of Justice, Drug Enforcement Administration, Office of Intelligence. "Clandestine Laboratory Seizures in the United States: Calendar Year 1990."

_______. Office of Forensic Sciences. *Microgram.* Vol. 24, No. 6, June 1991.

Wagner G.C. et al. "Methamphetamine-induced changes in brain catecholomines in rats and guinea pigs." *Drug and Alcohol Dependency.* 4:435-438, 1979.

Washton, A. and M. Gold. "Chronic Cocaine Abuse: Evidence for Adverse Effects on Health and Functioning." *Psychiatric Annals.* 14(10):733-743, 1984.

Wetli, C. and R. Wright. "Death Caused by Recreational Use of Cocaine." *JAMA.* 241(3):2519-2522, 1979.

_______. "Cocaine: The Great Addicter and Deceiver." *Drug Awareness Information Newsletter.* Jan. 1990. Rpt. in *The Narc Officer.* June 1990.

_______. "Drug Enforcement Report." Vol. 8, No. 7, Jan., 1992.

_______. "The Implications of Crack." *Drug Abuse and Alcoholism Newsletter.* Vol. 15, No. 6, July 1986.

This page intentionally left blank.

CHAPTER XI

HALLUCINOGENIC/PSYCHEDELIC DRUGS

The chemical substances in this group are referred to as hallucinogenic drugs because they produce hallucinations. These drugs have also been referred to as psychotomimetic drugs since they mimic a psychological state. Psychedelic is a word that came out of the 1960s drug culture and means mind expanding. Even though these drugs do not necessarily expand the mind, the word psychedelic points to an area of the body on which these drugs do have their greatest effect: the brain.

The hallucinogens are a diverse group of compounds, most of which originate in plants, though some are produced by chemical synthesis. For many years, people have debated how to classify these compounds and which drugs should or should not be called hallucinogens. One problem is that some drugs not considered hallucinogenic do produce hallucinations if a sufficient dose is taken. For example, central nervous system stimulants such as amphetamines or cocaine are capable of producing hallucinations with long term heavy use. However, there is a main group of hallucinogenic drugs that share similar properties. In particular, the hallucinations they produce have similar characteristics and they have similar pharmacological effects.

The drugs grouped in this category all have the ability to induce visual, auditory or other hallucinations; they also have the ability to separate the individual from reality. They produce a wide range of behavioral alterations; thus, their classification by chemical structure is difficult. However, there is sufficient documentation of how these drugs alter synaptic transmission processes in the human brain. Therefore, it is possible to classify these compounds by the transmitter upon which the drug is thought to act.

Several chemical substances are commonly thought to serve as synaptic transmitters within the brain. Such substances include acetylcholine, norepinephrine and serotonin.

Thus, we could classify psychedelic drugs as follows:

I. ACETYLCHOLINE PSYCHEDELICS
Atropine, scopolamine, muscarine—from plants such as belladonna or deadly nightshade, jimpson-weed, stick weed, thorn apple and henbane. This group also includes muscarine from a mushroom (amanita muscaria) found in Europe and Scandinavia.

II. NOREPINEPHRINE PSYCHEDELICS
Mescaline, DOM (STP), MDA, MMDA, TMA, myristicin—from plants such as peyote and mescaline derivatives (DOM, TMA and MMDA); myristicin is from nutmeg and mace.

III. SEROTONIN PSYCHEDELICS
Phencyclidine (PCP), Ketamine. The neurotransmitters upon which these compounds exert their activity are unknown. These are synthetically manufactured compounds.

HISTORY

The various hallucinogens have very diverse histories. One of the interesting aspects is that these drugs are found almost all over the world and have been used by a wide range of peoples, at least at some stage of their history. It has been suggested that humans may have begun using hallucinogens after observing their effects on animals. The evidence for this hypothesis comes mainly from the folklore of different countries. Whatever the origins, people have a long history of using hallucinogens as medicines, in religious ceremonies, and for simple recreational purposes.

GENERAL EFFECTS OF HALLUCINOGENIC/PSYCHEDELIC DRUGS

The physiological changes produced by the hallucinogens are most prominent in the first few hours after the drug is taken. They include dilated pupils, lack of muscular coordination, muscular weakness, and tremors. Heart rate and blood pressure may rise, but the effects are small and variable. In this early part of the drug experience, the user may also experience dizziness, nausea, and even vomiting.

There are a number of perceptual changes that characterize the hallucinogens. They produce some simple distortions. For example, colors may be brighter and more intense, and objects around the person may change shape. Some users may experience synesthesia. This term refers to the translation of experiences from one sensory modality into another: sounds may be seen and tastes may be heard. Finally, there are the obvious hallucinations. These are mainly visions of objects and patterns that are usually in a constant state of change. Other senses may be involved, but visual hallucinations predominate.

Associated with the perceptual changes are feelings of de-personalization or of being "external to the self," almost as if one is looking at oneself from the outside. This de-personalization may provoke anxiety in some users, particularly those who are inexperienced. Users also report feelings of insightfulness, as though discovering great truths about the world. This belief may continue beyond the drug experience. Great emotional changes may accompany the drug-induced experience. These can vary from ecstasy to despair, possibly even in the same "trip."

This pattern of effects may be altered in one of two ways, both of which result in "bad trips." First, the individual may panic and feel a loss of control. Experiences may seem all too real, rather than being drug-induced phenomena. Panic may also result simply from unpleasant experiences; for instance, a common hallucination is that spiders are crawling all over the body. Another type of "bad trip" may involve psychotic reactions. Symptoms such as paranoia and delusions are common, but other schizophrenic-like symptoms may also result. In such cases, bizarre behavior, even suicide, can occur. Sometimes the psychosis may persist long after other symptoms of drug use have disappeared.

Another after-effect of hallucinogens is the recurrence of the drug-induced experience days, weeks, or even months later. The person may have an emotional or perceptual experience similar to one that occurred under the influence of the drug, seemingly without any provocation or inducement. These "flashbacks" are usually brief. Their cause is unknown.[1]

The greatest hazard of the psychedelics is that their effects are unpredictable each time they are taken.

The history of experimental work with LSD in the 1950s and 1960s has indicated that beneficial results do not occur from the mere administration of the drug; in fact, the indication is quite clear that without therapeutic intent, preparation, and management, administration of the drug to humans is definitely dangerous. These studies and others have concluded that there are no apparent medical uses for the hallucinogens. Some psychiatrists have conducted exploratory work with LSD, but without clear or validated success.[2]

WITHDRAWAL SYNDROME

There is no documented withdrawal syndrome related to abuse of the hallucinogenic drugs. For this reason, the psychedelics have been shown to produce no physical dependence.

This discussion will be confined to the most popular psychedelic drugs used—LSD, PCP, Peyote (mescaline), Psilocybin mushroom and some miscellaneous substances.

LYSERGIC ACID DIETHYLAMIDE

INTRODUCTION

In 1938, Dr. Albert Hofmann co-developed a fungal plant rust called ergot into a compound called lysergsaure-diathylamid (LSD). Five years later, Dr. Hofmann decided to see if LSD could be developed into an analeptic compound to stimulate blood circulation and respiration in elderly people. While crystallizing the LSD compound in the form of a tartrate, he absorbed "an immeasurable trace" of it through his fingertips. Dr. Hofmann described his first unintentional use as "a not unpleasant intoxicated-like condition" occupying two hours of interesting imagery. From 1943 to 1970, Hofmann used LSD about 15 times and concluded that there was simply no way to guarantee either a good or bad "trip." "The experience is handled best,"

[1] Shick, F., and D. Smith. "Analysis of the LSD Flashback." *Journal of Psychedelic Drugs.* Educational Off-Print Series. Vol. 3 No. 1, Sept. 1971.

See also Abraham, H.D. "Visual Phenomenology of the LSD Flashback." *Archives of General Psychiatry.* 40:884-889, 1983; and Silling, S.M., "LSD Flashbacks: An Overview of the Literature from Counselors." *American Mental Health Counselors Association Journal.* January, 1980. pp. 39-49.

[2] Savage, C. "Lysergic Acid Diethylamide (LSD-25): A Clinical-Psychological Study." *American Journal of Psychiatry.* 1952. In 1952, Savage reported the first study attempting to use LSD as a chemotherapeutic drug in the treatment of depression. He concluded that no significant therapeutic value could be attributed to the drug.

Hofmann cautiously counseled, "by a stabilized person with a meaningful reason for taking LSD."

Even though LSD is made from a fungus that grows on certain grains such as rye, it can be produced easily and synthetically in a laboratory.

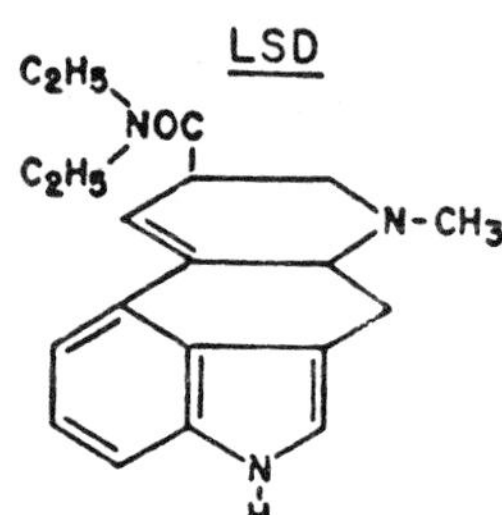

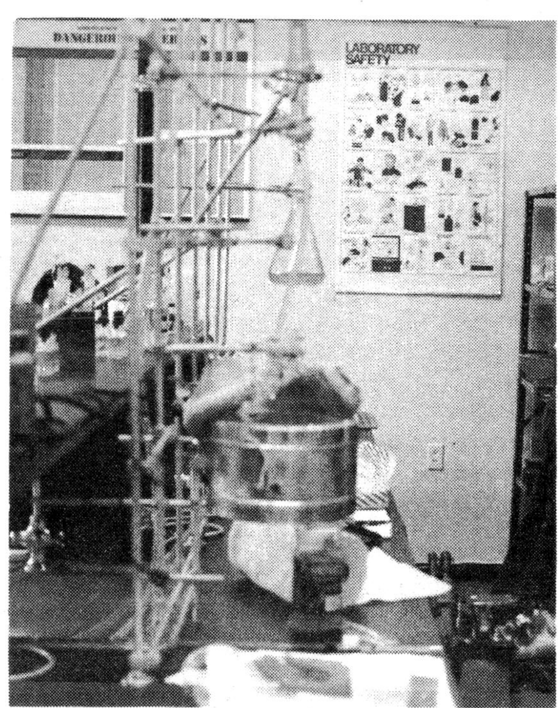

PHASES OF LSD USE

The first phase of LSD use mainly involved pharmacological and psychotomimetic studies. This phase consisted mainly of experiments on creativity, treatment of character disorders, and religious mysticism. The next phase (1965-1970) involved widespread indiscriminate use by mostly young people. This phase involved a combination of magical expectations created by the sensationalism of the mass media, the extremism of reactions by society, and by LSD's ready availability and ease of concealment. During this phase people talked about Augustus Stanley Ocusley III's purple haze, white lightning and blue cheer, and the orange sunshine barrels made by the Brotherhood of Eternal Love.

During the next phase (1970-78) LSD was not publicized in the media, law enforcement made few arrests and, though LSD use never disappeared, not much attention was given to the drug.

The next phase (1980s) involves more use of LSD than at any time since the early 1970s. Most of the "acid" used today is of the blotter variety. Wizards, political symbols, chemical equations, flying saucers, zodiac signs, flowers and a menagerie of animals and cartoon characters are found on blotter paper.

THE 1990s: THE "NEW AGE OF AQUARIUS"

Currently, LSD is relatively cheap. A hit that lasts 12 hours costs only about $5, compared with $70 for a quarter ounce of marijuana and $50 for a half gram of cocaine. Today's LSD is also marketed in smaller doses per unit—usually 20 to 80 micrograms—compared to the 150 to 250 microgram units sold in the 1960s.

For these reasons (as well as some others), LSD has regained popularity in the 1990s. A 1991 national NIDA survey of 26,000 high school seniors found that 9.3 percent of white males and 5 percent of white females had used a hallucinogen—almost always LSD—in the previous 12 months. Furthermore, the Washington, D.C. branch of the Drug Enforcement Administration confiscated 14 doses of LSD in 1990, while in 1991 it confiscated 5,600 doses.

The popularity of LSD decreased in the early 1970s because of problems with the purity of the LSD on the market. There were rumors that LSD was cut with strychnine or amphetamines. PCP and crude speeds were often represented as LSD. However, since 1973, according to the Pharm Chem Lab in Menlo Park, California, LSD has been consistently 87 to 95 percent pure, while the remaining ingredients are simple inert substances.[3]

Standardization of doses has gone a long way to increase the popularity of LSD. The big seller of LSD in 1979 was blotter acid featuring a tiny green or red dragon. However, some counterfeit dragon acid appeared in 1980 causing some users to be more cautious or stop purchasing the drug altogether. There was also the popular "wizard" or Mickey Mouse acid. It featured a four-color still image of Mickey Mouse, wand in hand, from the classic cartoon, "The Sorcerer's Apprentice." The printing is not easy to duplicate cheaply or quickly. A "package" of this acid is sold wholesale for $2,000+ in 40 sheets of absorbent blotter paper, each sheet divided by perforations into 100 individual hits. Each package of 40 blotter sheets is sealed in tin foil and put in a cardboard box which is sealed with wax. The package contains 4,000 hits equal to one gram. Most middle-level LSD dealers buy acid in bulk and produce their own brand of blotter LSD using a stamp or silkscreen to put their logo on the sheets. It was reported in *High Times* (August 1981) that one West Coast LSD dealer includes a marketing kit when a buyer purchases 100,000 hits of LSD in liquid form. The kit illustrates the finepoints of commercial LSD preparation, how to dilute LSD; if it is to be "windowpane" LSD, the kit illustrates how to mold the gelatin, at what temperature, and the logistics of impregnating and stamping blotter LSD.

In many areas of the United States in the 1990s, LSD is making a noticeable resurgence. This "new" LSD on blotter paper is a high purity LSD, unlike some of the LSD from the 1970s which was frequently cut with other substances. With high purity, "bad trips" are infrequent. The LSD is so expertly refined that impurities which may have caused bad trips are simply not present.

---

[3] *PharmChem Newsletter*. PharmChem Laboratories. July 1989.

By some accounts, today's LSD is much milder than it was a generation ago. Each dose of 1990s acid (often in the form of drug-permeated blotter paper, decorated with cartoon characters) contains about 20 to 80 micrograms of LSD, compared with about 150 to 250 micrograms in the 1960s. The threshold needed to trigger a classic LSD experience is 200 micrograms. Most teenagers take the smaller doses and use acid as "a social intoxicant" at parties. But users can quickly build up a tolerance for the drug, requiring greater quantity to achieve the same high.

Despite the high purity of the new LSD, this drug can cause several health complications. Physicians and counselors report seeing a new crop of young acid users suffering from persistent panic attacks, nightmares and even psychosis. "Four kids on my caseload came in and said they'd tried LSD over the holidays," says Joyce Schaller-Vitullo, a substance-abuse counselor at Oak Park-River Forest High School near Chicago. Two of them landed in the hospital after taking multiple hits. Dr. Henry Abraham, director of psychiatric research at St. Elizabeth's Hospital in Boston, has studied disastrous LSD reactions for 21 years. In the last year, he has seen 25 new patients, many of them young, with continuous visual hallucinations. Dr. Abraham believes that certain people are more susceptible than others to the harmful effects of LSD. He also says that a user may have a severe biological reaction on the first trip or the 101st.[4]

Unlike those involved with LSD in 1960s, current LSD traffickers and users are very well-informed about the drug. Packaging of LSD sheets or individual hits is in baggies or aluminum foil. Those handling it apparently know that touching and absorbing it may cause a trip. LSD has once again become popular because it is inexpensive, can be used sometimes without obvious signs, and it is perceived as non-addictive. Interestingly, the new generation of LSD abusers thinks of LSD as the new drug on the street. They are almost completely unaware of LSD's history in the 1960s.

It seems inevitable that LSD will again become a widespread social phenomenon. The U.S. Drug Enforcement Administration is taking the nation's latest drug trip seriously. Administrator Robert C. Bonner wants to intensify educational efforts. Since the drug fell out of fashion, he says, anti-drug publicity campaigns for the past 10 years rarely even mentioned it. Until such educational programs can take effect, however, LSD use is likely to proliferate. One person exemplifying this chronic use pattern is Timothy Leary, who urged us to "turn on, tune in and drop out" more than 20 years ago. Leary is now 71; he still takes the drug, he has said, for "noble, spiritual purposes."

FORMS OF LSD

In its pure form, LSD is an odorless, tasteless and colorless crystal. It dissolves in water and cannot be detected except by chemical analysis. The drug is combined with other ingredients to obtain bulk for packaging. These ingredients then contribute to the odor, taste and color of the LSD sold on the street.

---

[4] "Science and Medicine." *San Jose Mercury News*. 16 June, 1992.

Hallucinogenic/Psychedelic Drugs

LSD is mixed with or put on almost anything which can be swallowed: sugar cubes, candy (such as "Necco" wafers), animal crackers, chewing gum, paper, or any ingestable liquid. It has been placed on stamps and envelope flaps which are licked; it has also been mixed with gelatin and formed into thin squares (called "window panes") which are chewed. LSD has been put into tablet form—such as a distinctive orange tablet called Sunshine. It may also be seen on the street in clear capsules (smaller than the common time-release cold capsules), which contain LSD in a white or light blue powder.

In short, any substance which can be introduced into the body can contain LSD. Also, it is difficult to find because almost all forms of the drug are so easy to conceal.

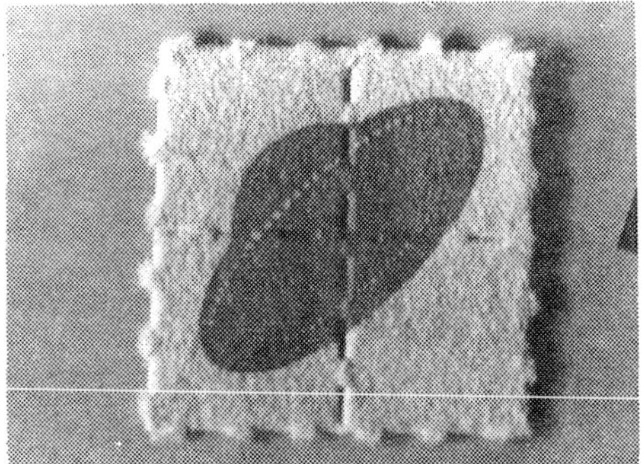

PHARMACOLOGY OF LSD

The effects of LSD vary according to the amount and its method of administration. With 1 to 2 μg./kg. ingested orally, the average period of onset for LSD's effects is 45 minutes (15 to 120 minutes). Almost all effects of LSD are gone after 8 to 12 hours; although, in some cases, it may take 24 hours. Very large doses may produce intense and substantial symptoms for 48 hours. When the drug is swallowed, there is a gradual build-up of physiological symptoms. These consist of numbness, a tingling of the extremities, chilliness, anorexia, nausea, and sometimes vomiting. Other symptoms include flushing of the face and dilation of the pupils. These symptoms usually subside by the time the psychic symptoms appear.

DISTRIBUTION OF LSD IN THE BODY

LSD readily crosses the blood-brain barrier but is not concentrated in the brain. Higher concentrations of the drug are found in the hypothalmus, the limbic system, and the visual and auditory reflect centers. LSD's half-life in humans (its period of activity in the body) is 175 minutes. Excretion of LSD proceeds by way of 2-oxidation of LSD in the liver, an inactive metabolite; it is then eliminated by the kidneys.

Since tolerance to LSD is lost as quickly as it develops, there is no tolerance when used twice weekly. However, cross-tolerance between mes-

Chapter XI

LSD-25 (Lysergic Acid Diethylamide)

caline, psilocybin, and DMT has been established by researchers.[5] Physical addiction characterized by withdrawal effects, on the other hand, does not occur with LSD.

It should be noted that stimulants tend to potentiate and increase the effects of LSD. Conversely, sedatives, tranquilizers, and narcotics counteract the LSD effect (despite a few exceptions).

The lethal dose of LSD for humans is unknown. If the human metabolism of LSD is similar to that of a rabbit, the calculated lethal dose would be 20 mg. (or 20,000 µg.). When death results in the course of an LSD experience (LSD behavioral toxicity), it is usually due to accident or suicide rather than the drug's intrinsic toxicity.

One example of an accidental LSD death occurred on January 1, 1988. Two white males, aged 24 and 25, died in an accidental apartment fire which apparently started when a dry Christmas tree overturned and the electrical lights burst into flames. Investigation by the Office of the Chief Medical Examiner (OCME) revealed that both victims were alive at the time of the fire.[6]

Upon examination of the 24 year old victim, a 3⁄8" x 3⁄8" piece of white blotter paper stamped with a globe emblem was discovered in the stomach. A blood alcohol concentration of 0.10 percent was also identified. No other common drugs of abuse, excluding lysergic acid diethylamide (LSD), were found in the urine. Additional toxicological studies revealed a 0.8 ng./ml. concentration of LSD in the victim's blood.

The second victim, a 25 year old white male, had a cosaturation level of 31 percent, an alcohol-blood concentration of 0.13 percent, while no drugs were detected in the blood and urine. Both deaths were ruled accidental and LSD intoxication was considered to have played a role in the incident.

This case exemplifies oral ingestion of LSD impregnated paper which resulted in intoxication and, subsequently, accidental death. LSD was not initially suspected as a contributing factor until examination of the stomach contents revealed the drug's characteristic blotter paper. In this case, the ink on the blotter paper remained intact, permitting identification.

Despite LSD's uniformity of distribution in the body, the effects of 100 µg. of LSD will vary widely. Ten percent of the population will not observe any substantial subjective changes; the great majority will report definite psychic effects. Women appear more sensitive to the drug than men. Schizophrenics and alcoholics are somewhat resistant to 100 µg. of LSD. Body weight is not a reliable index of LSD effects. There are, however, some variables that account for different effects of the drug. These variables include the personality and expectations of the user as well as the security of the environment in which the drug is taken.

---

[5] Rosenberg, D.E. et al. "Observations on Direct and Cross-Tolerance with LSD and D-Amphetamine in Man." *Psychopharmacology*. 5:1, 1963.

[6] Drug Enforcement Administration, Forensic Sciences Section. *Microgram*. Vol. XXV, No. 2, Feb. 1992.

Although the effects of LSD have been observed and documented, the question of human brain damage remains unresolved. The precise manner by which LSD exerts its psychic effects is still unknown.

THE LSD STATE

Perhaps the first psychological indication that LSD has started to act within the body is a loosening of emotional inhibitions. The user may feel spontaneous laughter, tears and smiling without cause, or relaxation of tensions. In general, the user's mood will be euphoric and expressive.

The user may also experience changes in visual perceptions and extreme changes of mood. He or she may lose the sense of time and depth perceptions. Size, movement, color, spatial arrangement, sound, touch and his or her own "body image" will be distorted. For example, the user might lose the ability to tell the difference between his or her body and the rest of the environment. The users might even believe he or she can fly or float in the air. Two very strong but opposite sensations might be felt at once; for example, the user might feel both heavy and light at the same time. Because this new world is so fascinating, abusers of LSD will usually lose their desire to eat or sleep until the trip is over. Nausea is also a frequent side-effect.

All of these psychological effects prevent the LSD user from making rational judgments about even the most common dangers; for example, he or she might walk in front of a moving car, or step out of a window several stories up. It is easy to see how accidental deaths can occur while a person is experiencing the effects of a "trip."

The same individual may experience different effects at different times. It should be remembered that responses to this drug cannot be predicted; abusers talk about "good trips" and "bad trips" or "bummers." Abusers can usually remember what happened to them while they were under the influence, but they are often not able to describe it. This is because some of the experiences are not in the verbal dimension; there are no words available to adequately describe their sensations.

SIDE EFFECTS FROM LSD

One of the most frequent side effects of LSD, for the user, is that the original drug-induced experience can recur days, weeks, months, and even years after the drug is taken. This is called a "flashback." Intensive use of the drug seems to cause this situation more often than infrequent use. This recurrence of symptoms may be startling or frightening and may cause the abuser to think he is losing his mind.

Another common side effect of LSD use is the fear or the panic that is experienced when the user is unable to cope with the usual effects brought on by the drug. This panic is often experienced by novice LSD users as opposed to individuals who have taken LSD frequently and are more familiar with the drug's effects. Medical and law enforcement personnel often encounter an individual who is experiencing this sort of LSD panic or "bummer"—the "bad trip."

The panic reaction that some individuals undergo during the LSD experience may include feelings of deep de-personalization and distorted perceptions. The content of the drug-induced illusions or hallucinations may be very alarming, leading to anxiety, to panic or uncontrolled excitement at the peak of the drug's effect. These reactions are most likely to occur in inexperienced users when in disturbing or threatening environments, in subjects who have ambivalent attitudes toward the drug experience, or in persons who are emotionally and mentally unstable.

LSD use can also cause an extended period of psychosis, which may occur after a single exposure, and usually involves a person who had a history of psychosis prior to ingestion of the drug.

One other effect is that LSD produces a suggestible state, making the user susceptible to several influences in his or her environment. This suggestibility can induce a bad reaction. The bad reaction may then become an overwhleming reality to the individual under the influence of the drug, who is then off on a "bummer."

In regard to prolonged psychotic episodes, there are many reports of this type of activity after LSD use. However, many drug-using communities attract disturbed people and it may be difficult sometimes to separate direct effects of the drug from episodes caused by a person who is already psychologically ill.

It has not yet been demonstrated conclusively that any permanent organic defects result from prolonged LSD use; however, there are studies that show chromosomal damage. A number of chemicals are known to have a chromosomal effect that is similar to LSD. Such drugs as alcohol, caffeine and even commonly-used pharmaceutical drugs will increase the incidence of chromosome damage at about the same rate as LSD.

Early laboratory studies have suggested that LSD would cause malformation of a fetus if the mother took LSD. There is no hard and fast proof to substantiate this hypothesis, as other drugs could cause the same effect during the first trimester of pregnancy. Nevertheless, LSD is an ergot derivative capable of contracting the pregnant uterus. Evidence suggests that this effect has caused fetal death and abortion; thus, pregnant women should not use LSD.

A BREAKDOWN OF THE LSD "TRIP"

The actual LSD experience or "trip" can be divided into four stages. The first stage begins when the drug is ingested and lasts until the full psychological effects are manifest. If LSD is taken orally, these psychological symptoms usually appear in thirty to forty-five minutes. The first phase, initial development of symptoms, usually lasts about an hour if a normal amount is taken, but the time can vary from twenty minutes to two hours.

In the second phase, the full effects of the drug are manifest; this period usually lasts about four to six hours. The length and intensity of the psychological experience depends upon several factors, which include:

1. Amount taken
2. Frequency of use (which may have led to tolerance)
3. Prior experience with the drug
4. Concurrent use of other drugs

5. Physical and psychological makeup of the user
6. "Setting" (environment in which the drug is taken)
7. "Set" (mental condition of the user—happy, depressed, etc.). Setting and set are important in reducing the incidence of "bummers" and "flashbacks."

The third phase, or the recovery, starts when symptoms of the drug experience begin to diminish. During this phase, the person experiences altering waves of LSD symptoms and waves of normal feelings. This period usually occurs seven to nine hours after drug ingestion.

The fourth and final phase of the LSD "trip" is the aftermath. This final phase is usually demonstrated by feelings of tension, restlessness, chilliness, and nausea. These feelings characterizing the recovery stage generally linger for several hours but are usually gone by the following day.

The impact of LSD on the senses is normally very striking. The function of perceiving, organizing, and interpreting sensory impressions that reach the brain can be severely altered by the drug. The user may become aware of the onset of LSD by noticing that objects have begun to waver and appear distorted. For example, a wall might begin to waver or grow larger, objects in a painting may begin to move, or ordinary objects may suddenly appear luminous as though surrounded by a halo.

The term "hallucinogenic" implies that the drug causes hallucinations. A true hallucination—auditory or visual—has no basis in fact but is very real to the individual experiencing the hallucination. While this occasionally happens with LSD, pseudo-hallucinations are more common. Pseudo-hallucination means that the user knows that what he sees or hears does not have a basis in external reality. For example, the user may see geometric forms, figures or brilliant colors, but he or she realizes that those visions do not really exist because they are drug-induced.

In short, LSD can seriously affect the grasp that a person has on the world; in some cases, this drug can altogether shatter what was once a firm relationship with that world. This is especially true when the user forgets that what he is seeing, hearing or feeling is drug induced and will, in time, disappear.

An LSD user's emotions are characterized by rapid swings from one mood to another. For example, it is not uncommon for users to laugh hysterically and then suddenly become very sad, depressed, and even cry for no apparent reason. Some users report feeling happy and sad at the same time. Such changes in emotions are not necessarily directly caused by LSD but may arise from the individual's own personality having been enhanced or altered by the drug.

The effect of LSD on other thought processes is just as pronounced as in the area of emotions. On many occasions, perception of time may be sharply altered. Time may appear to stand still, causing the user to feel cut off from the future. This feeling is often accompanied by a strong sense of living exclusively in the present. Foresight may become diminished or non-existent.

A second aspect of how LSD affects the thinking is in the way that a person perceives himself. Often the individual's body image becomes extremely distorted; the user may see himself as being totally dismembered, limb from limb. This effect can become terrifying and can lead to severe anxiety and panic.

LSD also causes a lack of ability to think in abstracts or in terms of ideas and concepts. One theory is that the user becomes so preoccupied with the LSD experience that he or she loses interest in other things.

It is common to hear the term "consciousness-expanding" or "mind-expanding" in discussions about LSD. Despite the claims of LSD advocates, a person under the influence of LSD has a restricted rather than an expanded range of consciousness. This belief of increased awareness or acuteness is caused by the blurring of certain psychological boundaries, perhaps between reality and fantasy. This blurring of boundaries ultimately results in the user falsely believing in an extension of his or her awareness, but actually rational judgment or critical reasoning is often greatly impaired.

TREATMENT FOR "BAD TRIPS"

Repetitive users of LSD often realize that they may experience a bad trip or "bummer." For this reason, users will often keep tranquilizers or barbiturates on hand. In the past, physicians administered these types of drugs to individuals experiencing "bad trips," but found these types of drugs were not antidotes. Illicit users may still keep a supply of these drugs in an attempt to counter adverse psychological reactions. A very real danger of using this type of drug when under the influence of LSD is the possibility of an overdose. An LSD user attempting to stop adverse effects by using hypnotics or tranquilizers may actually intensify his "bad trip," causing him to ingest still more "downers," leading to an overdose. Most physicians now agree that the best way of dealing with the "bad trip" is by using the "talk down" method of treatment. This method essentially involves a reassuring conversation with the individual regarding his well-being.

LAW ENFORCEMENT AND LSD

Law enforcement will frequently be called in to handle an individual who is having a bad trip on LSD or some other hallucinogenic/psychedelic substance. A bad trip usually occurs in someone who has taken a substance which produces some unpleasant effects; it may also occur in an unstable individual who now experiences psychological disturbance as a result of the drug.

The person on a bad trip is usually in a state of panic about what is going on within him or her. He may be talking about strange things, about seeing things in a peculiar way, or perceiving people or objects as changing shapes in front of his eyes. He may talk about strange sensations in relation to his environment, such as seeing the walls move or go in and out as if the room was breathing. He may talk about feeling the floor moving under him. All of these bizarre-sounding perceptions should indicate to an officer that the person is probably psychotic or having a drug-induced experience.

Intervening in this situation is similar to dealing with an authentic psychotic person. Approach the person calmly, in a way that is non-threatening; do not contribute to his or her feeling of panic. Keep in mind that you may be dealing with someone who fears police officers. It is especially important to approach the user very calmly and reassure him that he is going to be all right and that you are there for his protection and to help him. If there is a lot of noise around, a lot of movement or a lot of people, try to reduce the level of stimulation as much as possible.

The individual experiencing the effects of a psychedelic drug will be very sensitive to changes and to any kind of stimulation in the environment. The principal danger in this kind of situation is *not* that the individual is going to attack another person; rather, the danger is that the person's panic will cause him to inadvertently hurt himself or someone else. He or she may try to get away from something that appears terrifying. He may jump out a window because he doesn't know it is a window or because it seems that jumping through it is more desirable than being attacked by monsters. If there is some indication that the individual is a danger to himself or to others around him, you should restrain him. It is important to control the user so he won't hurt himself; at the same time try to reduce his panic through calming reassurance. Often, if you have the individual under control, a referral to a drug crisis center is appropriate. A less desirable alternative is the county hospital emergency room. Unless the hospital has considerable experience with such cases, however, this option may make the situation worse. The atmosphere may increase the individual's panic and treatment with drugs may produce serious reactions.

CURRENT REPORTS OF LSD EVIDENCE

As mentioned above, LSD soaked blotter paper has been recognized as the most popular vehicle for distribution and consumption of the drug. Although there are several different types of LSD blotter paper, law enforcement officers should be familiar with some of the most popular forms and designs.

The DEA Northeast Laboratory in New York City recently encountered twenty sheets of white, untextured paper approximately 2 1/2 x 2 1/2 inches.[7] The paper was printed on one side with a geometric design in red ink and the words "White Lightning" in blue ink, as shown right. Each sheet of paper showed perforation impressions that did not fully penetrate the paper and subdivided the paper into 1/4 x 1/4 inch square dosage units with a total of 100 dosage units per sheet. The perforation pattern consisted of eight two-millimeter long dashes per inch of perforation. Analysis showed each dosage unit to contain 19.8 micrograms of LSD.

[7] Drug Enforcement Administration, Forensic Sciences Section. *Microgram*. Vol. XXV, No.3, March 1992.

Hallucinogenic/Psychedelic Drugs

The Suffolk County Crime Laboratory's Chemistry Section in Long Island, New York reports receiving an exhibit of LSD blotter paper depicting the recently popular television character Bart Simpson. Analysis showed 38 micrograms of LSD per dosage unit.[8]

The DEA North Central Laboratory in Chicago, Illinois recently encountered an exhibit consisting of one rectangular piece of tan paper approximately 2 1/2 x 2 3/4 inches overall as shown below.[9] The design of a multi-armed figure on a surfboard is printed in purple ink on one side of the paper and two figures (male and female) with flowers and the words, "So You Say" are printed in black ink on the opposite side of the paper. All printing is done through the lithographic process. The sheet of paper shows perforation impressions that do not fully penetrate the paper and divide the paper into 1/4 x 1/4 inch square dosage units with a total of 106 extant dosage units. The perforation pattern is approximately 12 one-millimeter long dashes evenly spaced per inch of perforation. Analysis shows 42 micrograms of LSD per dosage unit.

---

[8] Ibid.

[9] Drug Enforcement Administration. *Microgram.* Vol. XXV, No. 5, May 1992.

The Sacramento County Crime Laboratory in Sacramento, California reports receiving submission of evidence confiscated at a "Grateful Dead" rock concert held from May 3-5, 1991 in Sacramento. Prior to the concert, intelligence officers reported that sellers were "waiting for deliveries."

The confiscated LSD blotter papers were perforated into 1⁄4 inch squares having the following designs: blue outlines of prancing unicorns on white paper (below left), gradual color transition (rust through gold to green) of "peace" symbols on off-white paper (below right), and dark blue-black ink beetle and bird on white paper (not pictured).

LSD was not detected on the following non-blotter, slick surfaced papers: red, no design, perforated into 1⁄2 inch squares, and brilliant blue, no design, perforated into 1⁄8 inch squares.

Numerous submissions of psilocybe mushrooms and "bunk" mushrooms were also associated with drug sales at the concert.

The Canton-Start County Crime Laboratory in Canton, Ohio reports a recent submission of LSD blotter paper with the two designs shown below. Both designs are on white paper with two colors of ink—purple and blue for the moon design, and blue and green for the pyramid design.[10]

[10] Ibid.

 md

Hallucinogenic/Psychedelic Drugs

The same laboratory has also encountered purple microtablets of LSD which had not been seen in the Canton, Ohio region since the early 1980s.

One other exhibit was received by the DEA Southeast Laboratory in Miami, Florida.[11] This exhibit contained 600 dosage units of LSD blotter paper with the design shown below. The exhibit originated in San Francisco, California and was sent to Jacksonville, Florida. The blotter paper is unlike any sample previously seen by the DEA. It is white, untextured paper, 2 1/2 by 2 1/2 inches, with the cartoon image of "bear-devil" and assorted party items rubber-stamped in orange, red, purple, blue, and green inks. The paper shows perforation impressions which do not fully penetrate the paper but subdivide it into 1/4 by 1/4 inch square dosage units, each containing 84 micrograms of LSD.

MUSHROOMS

Another substance that falls under the category of psychedelic drugs is the hallucinogenic mushroom. Fly agaric (amanita muscaria) is a hallucinogenic mushroom common to many parts of Europe and Asia. Its use dates back hundreds, perhaps thousands of years. Unfortunately, early evidence of its use has been more legend than established fact. One such legend is that it was used by certain Viking warriors prior to battle. The drug was supposed to increase their ferocity. Certainly, the Norse warriors were famous for their ferocity; whether it was due to fly agaric, alcohol, or some other means is not clear. It has also been argued that fly agaric was the drug known as "soma" in poetry from ancient India.[12] Soma was much celebrated, but the description has made it difficult to positively identify the drug, or even to be sure that it was a real drug.

---

[11] Drug Enforcement Administration. *Microgram*. Vol. XXV, No. 7, July 1992.

[12] Wasson, R.G. *Soma: Divine Mushroom of Immortality*. New York: Harcourt, 1968.

One interesting characteristic of fly agaric is that the active ingredient, probably muscimole, is excreted unchanged in the urine. Because of this, and the relative scarcity of the mushrooms, people often saved their drug-containing urine and reused it. Such practices have been reported amongst people in Siberia and elsewhere.

The sacred mushroom, teonanacatl (food of the Gods), has been used by Indian cultures of Mexico and Central America for centuries. The practice of incorporating divine mushrooms into semi-religious ceremonies dates back to 1500 B.C. This history is based on stone artifacts believed to represent mushrooms. The first verified recorded use of hallucinogenic mushrooms occurred during the coronation feast of Montezuma in 1502. However, with the introduction of Christianity to the New World, the use of mushrooms was driven underground. Mushroom use was thought to have died out by the 20th century, but its continued use by Oaxacan Indians was "re-discovered" in 1953 by R.G. Wasson.

PSILOCYBIN AND PSILOCIN

Psilocybin and psilocin are psychedelic agents obtained from the mushroom (Psilocybe Mexicana). Psilocybin is approximately 1 percent as potent as LSD; in other words, 10 mg. of psilocybin would produce the same degree of action as 0.1 mg. of LSD. Psilocybin is effectively absorbed when taken orally and the mushrooms are eaten raw. Apparently, after the mushroom has been ingested, the phosphoric acid is removed from psilocybin, producing psilocin, the active psychedelic agent.

PSILOCIN

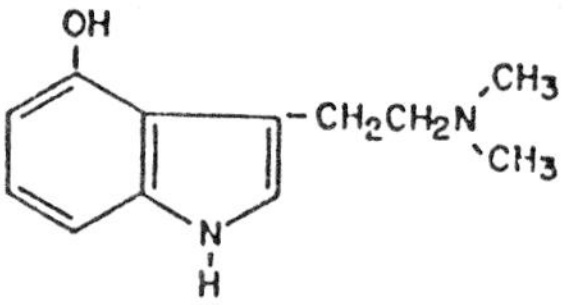

OH

$-CH_2CH_2N(CH_3)_2$

N
H

Until the 1960s, very little was known about the so-called "magic mushrooms" that grow in the southern portion of Mexico. Botanists have now identified at least 20 species of mushrooms from that area which contain psilocybin, the mind-altering drug in the mushroom.

The ingestion of 32 dried specimens of Psilocybe Mexicana, weighing 2.4 grams is considered a medium dose by Mexican Oaxaca Indian standards. To increase the dosage, it was possible to extract the active principals from the mushroom and to purify and crystallize them. The main active component was named psilocybin after the mushroom and the accompanying alkaloid was named psilocin. Using some of the ground-breaking research conducted by Dr. Albert Hofmann, other researchers have since identified other mushroom specimens which also contain psilocybin and psilocin.[13]

---

[13] Heim, R. et al. "Botanical and Chemical Characteristics of a Forensic Mushroom Specimen of the Genus Psilocybe." *Journ. of Forensic Science Society.* 6:192-210, 1966.

PSILOCYBE MUSHROOMS

THE AMERICAN HALLUCINOGENIC MUSHROOM

The most common and the strongest hallucinogenic mushroom in the United States is known as Psilocybe Cubensis. The top of this mushroom, known as the cap, varies in color from a light tannish gold to a light gold which appears almost white. The edge of the cap will be either a darker gold, if the center is white or a whiter color if the center is gold-tan. The gold color is similar to that of broom straw. The cap of the mushroom will be covered with a sticky, slimy substance. Most of the caps have a slight knob in the very center, although this is not always the case. A slight rise or discoloration can be observed in the center of this knob upon close examination. Since the size of the cap varies depending on the age of the mushroom, caps may range from 1/2 to 2 inches in diameter, with some as large as 5 inches.

As the Psilocybe Cubensis mushroom first begins to grow, it may show small, whitish spots that disappear as it matures. As it continues to grow, the stock becomes visible and the cap appears egg-shaped. The cap is curved inward and connects to the stem in order to protect the gills and spores that form on the underside of the cap. The gills are covered with millions of microscopic spores which later fall to the ground to produce more mushrooms. In a young mushroom, a white line appears where the cap joins the stem. After the cap opens up, this white line (called the annulus or skirt) forms around the upper portion of the stem.

Once the mushroom starts to mature, it does so quite rapidly. The maturation period is from 24 to 72 hours depending on the weather and the temperature conditions. The cap first becomes conical, then bell-shaped and finally flatter. As the mushroom gets older, the color becomes somewhat darker but it will retain the golden color until it dies, turns black and falls to the ground.

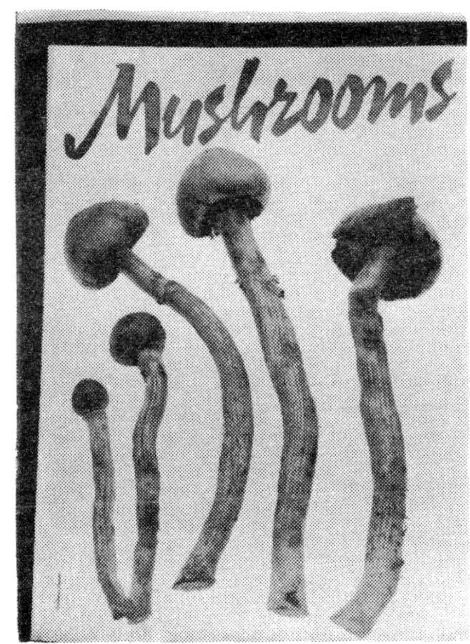

One of the more definite identification characteristics of this mushroom is that the cap will turn blue with age where it has been scratched. The bluing of the cap will appear strongest around the edges. When the cap expands with growth, the gills underneath the cap become visible. The gills will be grayish-white in young specimens and violet-grey to nearly black in mature specimens. The gills are attached to the stem and may be slightly notched. The mushrooms are quite firm to the touch. The size of the stem depends on the size of the mushroom.

The skirt around the upper portion of the stem will be purplish-black from the dropping spore. The stem will be a little larger at the base and will be covered with a mass of white moss-like matting. The stem is usually the first part of the mushroom to turn blue, especially toward the base where it is torn or broken.

METHOD OF INGESTION

Once the mushrooms have been collected, there are several methods of ingestion. The first method would be to eat the mushrooms fresh which includes the cap and the stem.

Another popular method is to dry the mushrooms on a piece of window-type screen, which is situated to allow air to circulate underneath the screen. Drying is accomplished in about three days. Once they are completely dry, the mushrooms can be stored in a container and will reportedly keep for a period of years without loss of potency. The weight of the mushroom is also greatly decreased during drying, as these mushrooms are 80 to 85 percent water. Some users freeze the mushrooms, but this is the least satisfactory method since the mushrooms spoil soon after they thaw.

Another method is to dry the mushrooms and grind them up in a blender or food grinder. The ground mushrooms are then placed in a shallow container, covered with methyl alcohol, and allowed to stand for 5 days. The alcohol is then strained off and the liquid placed in a dish until it evaporates. The remaining white crystalline substance is purportedly pure psilocybin.

PSYCHOLOGICAL EFFECTS

As one writer describes the effects of mushroom ingestion: "It permits you to travel backwards and forwards in time, to enter other places of existence, even to know God. . . Your body lies in darkness, heavy as lead, but your spirit seems to soar and leave the hut and with the speed of thought to travel where it listeth, in time and space accompanied by the shamans singing . . . at least you know what the ineffable is, and what ecstasy means. Ecstasy! For the Greeks, ecstasies meant the flight of the soul from the body. Can you find a better word to describe this state?"[14]

The hallucinations and distortions of time and space often produced by mushrooms are similar to LSD. Like LSD, side effects always precede development of the psychedelic action. Users feel symptoms associated with the fight/flight/fright response concomitantly with the psychological effect. With mushrooms, however, the duration of action is slightly shorter—2 to 4 hours.

The first clinical studies and analyses of the effects of psilocybin in humans were made at the University of Basle's Psychiatric Clinic in Basle, Switzerland. These studies were conducted on patients at the clinic by staff members of Sandoz Ltd. research laboratories.[15]

On the average, an oral dosage of 3 to 4 milligrams of psilocybin leads to changes in mental attitudes in 20 to 30 minutes. The psychological symptoms produced by doses of up to 5 milligrams cause mood alteration and frequently cause pleasant environmental contacts. This feeling of tactile sensation is usually accompanied by relaxing feelings in both the mind and the body; sometimes this feeling leads to a sense of detachment from the environmental contacts. Commonly, the user experiences tiredness and weariness or a concomitant feeling of lightness and floating.

When higher doses of 6 to 20 milligrams are orally ingested, the psychological changes are much more pronounced. These higher dosage levels frequently cause severe changes in perception of time and space. The awareness the individual has of his or her self or "body image" changes markedly. As with LSD, psilocybin also causes the individual to experience illusions, perceptual alterations and hallucinations. Psilocybin has been used in psychotherapy because during the drug-induced dream-like state, the user will often recall events as far back as early childhood.

---

[14] De Bald, R. and R.C. Leaf. *LSD, Man and Society*. Connecticut: Wesleyan University Press, 1968, pp. 69-70.

[15] Steiner, J.E. and F.G. Sulman. "Simultaneous Studies of Blood Sugar, Behavioral Changes and EEG on the Wake Rabbit after Administration of Psilocybin." *Arch. Int. Pharm.* 145:301-308, 1963.

THE PSILOCYBIN TRIP

The influence of expectation and mood seem to play an important part in any psychedelic experience including the use of psilocybin. Studies show that positive expectations before taking psilocybin usually lead to safe experiences during the drug "trip."[16] On the other hand, the reverse is also true. Anxiety or fear of the drug experience usually leads to an unpleasant "trip." Hence, the mood of an individual before the drug session is the best indicator of mood during the drug session. From this hypothesis, the following characteristics are said to be true of the psilocybin trip:

- Unpleasant, depressed, or anxious moods are intensified
- Pleasant moods provide a pleasant drug experience
- Religious expectations lead to a mystical or religious experience
- Ideas of gaining new insight reveal a drug experience that yields mind or consciousness expansion

From numerous studies conducted to date, it may be clearly seen that the type and depth of the drug experience depends to a decisive degree on the user's mental stability, expectations before the experience, and the environment in which the drug is used.

Another factor contributing to the success or failure of the drug experience is prior mental preparation. The drug will only release and activate that which is already present in the person taking it. An individual who does not realize a mental flaw in his or her character, yet has a positive expectation, may still experience the panic of a "bad trip."

THE QUESTION OF ADDICTION AND OTHER HAZARDS

Unlike narcotics, the hallucinogens do not give rise to true addiction marked by withdrawal symptoms. However, the hallucinogens are not less dangerous than other drugs of addiction. They are dangerous in a different way. The great danger associated with the use of hallucinogens without medical supervision is the possible occurrence of a "bad trip," characterized by the development of severe confusion, panic and anxiety. This may lead to suicide, or in a psychologically unstable or youthful person whose character is still not mature, a permanent psychological trauma may develop.

The power of the hallucinogens to completely transform perception and the dangers inherent in such a process readily explains why primitive people imposed a taboo on these organic substances. For these people, hallucinogenic substances were sacred and were reserved for the use of medicine men in religious, ceremonial situations. Since, in our society, these taboos no longer exist and the general trend is to throw aside the last inhibitions, government has no alternative but to impose strict controls on the use of hallucinogens.

---

[16] Fischer, R. "Sympathetic Excitation of Biological Chronometry." *Int. Journ. of Neuropsychiatry.* 2:116-121, 1966.

Fischer, R. et al. "Personality Traits: Dependent Performance Under Psilocybin." *Diseases of the Nervous System.* 31:91-101, 1970.

Metzner, R. et al. "The Relation of Expectation and Mood to Psilocybin Reactions." *Psychedelic Review.* 5:3-39, 1965.

PEYOTE AND MESCALINE

Peyote (Lophophora Williamsii), a plant common to the Southwestern United States and Mexico, is a spineless cactus with a small crown or "button" and a long root. For psychedelic use, the crown is cut from the cactus and dried to form a hard brown disc, referred to as a mescal button. The dried button is softened in the mouth and swallowed. Because of its bitter taste, it is often ingested with tea, coffee or milk.

The "button" is eaten by some Indians in their traditional religious ceremonies. For all other purposes, except legal research, peyote is illegal. Mescaline can be extracted from the peyote cactus, or produced synthetically in the laboratory. Its use is totally restricted.

PEYOTE CACTUS

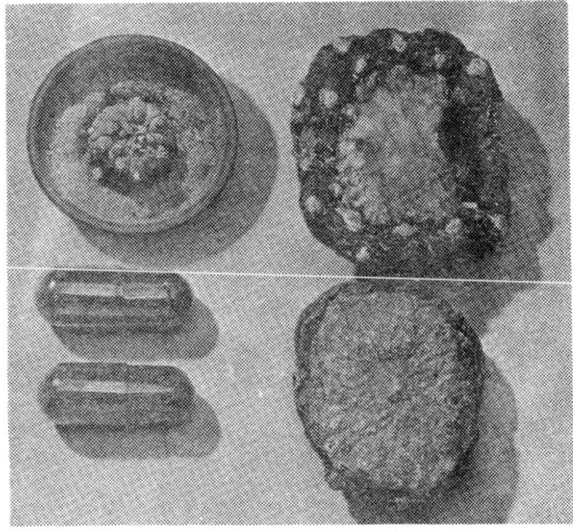

PEYOTE CACTUS, BUTTONS AND GROUND BUTTONS

SUPREME COURT DECISION ON PEYOTE

On April 17, 1990, a five-member majority of the U.S. Supreme Court decided that the First Amendment's guarantee of the free exercise of religion does not bar a state from applying its general criminal prohibition of peyote consumption to those individuals whose religion prescribes sacramental use of the substance. Below is a court case and decision involving this issue of peyote use.

OREGON DEPARTMENT OF HUMAN RESOURCES v. SMITH

U.S. Supreme Court, No. 88-1213, 4/17/90, 47 CrL 2001

The issue of peyote consumption came to the Supreme Court in the context of a dispute over unemployment benefits. Two employees were fired from their jobs because they ingested peyote at a religious ceremony of the Native American Church, to which they belonged. The state treated the grounds for their dismissal as "misconduct." On that basis, the state denied them unemployment benefits after the Oregon courts held that denial of benefits violates the Free Exercise Clause. The U.S. Supreme Court granted certiorari but declared that it could not resolve the case without knowing whether sacramental use of peyote violates the state's drug laws, 485 U.S. 660, 56 LW 4357 (1988). On remand, the Oregon Supreme Court held that state law makes no exception for sacramental use of peyote but that the First Amendment would forbid the state from using its criminal law to punish the good-faith religious use of peyote, 763 P2d 146 (1988).

Justice Scalia, speaking for the majority, disagreed with the state court's First Amendment analysis. The employees' religious motivation for using peyote does not place them beyond the reach of a criminal law that is not specifically directed at their religious practice, he said; as a general matter, the Free Exercise Clause does not prevent the state from promulgating and enforcing regulations of general application whose incidental effect may be to burden religiously motivated conduct. Otherwise, Scalia reasoned, professed doctrines of religious belief would be superior to the law of the land—an outcome that the Free Exercise Clause has never been interpreted to require.

Nor did Scalia accept the employees' argument that regulations touching upon the exercise of religious belief should be subjected to a balancing test that would require a showing of a compelling governmental interest. Such a test has been used in *Sherbert v. Verner*, 374 U.S. 398 (1963), and a few other cases to invalidate denials of unemployment compensation benefits. However, it has never been used to strike down any other form of government regulation, and it is particularly unsuited to application in a criminal context, Scalia said.

Justice O'Connor concurred in the result but did not use the majority's reasoning. Governmental regulations that burden the exercise of religious faith should be subjected to a "compelling state interest test," she insisted, and the majority's contrary conclusion requires both a "strained reading of the First Amendment" and a disregard of the court's "consistent application of free exercise doctrine to cases involving generally applicable regulations that burden religious conduct." She agreed with the state, however, that a religious exemption for peyote would impair the governmental interest in prohibiting possession of peyote.

Justice Blackmun, joined by Justices Brennan and Marshall, agreed with O'Connor's approach to the case but not her conclusion that the state had shown a compelling interest. Blackmun defined the state's interest narrowly, noting that there was no record evidence that peyote use is harmful to health or that peyote trafficking is widespread.

APPEARANCE OF PEYOTE

Peyote "buttons" are brown in color, approximately 1 to 2 inches in diameter, and resemble the underside of a dried mushroom. They are occasionally found on the blackmarket for street sale. The "buttons" are more often found ground up into a brown powder and sold in clear capsules.

 md

EFFECT OF MESCALINE

Mescaline is the active ingredient in peyote. Mescaline dilates the pupils and increases pulse rate and blood pressure. The highest psychedelic effect is 2 hours after oral use of 12 to 20 mescal buttons (500-1500 mg.). Twelve to 20 mescaline buttons is a common number for adults. Mescaline's half-life (activity of the drug in the body) is about 6 hours. Effects of a large dose may last up to 12 hours.

MESCALINE

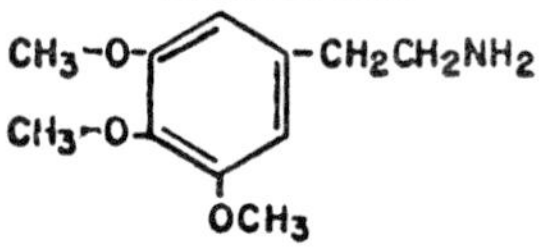

CH_3-O- $-CH_2CH_2NH_2$

CH_3-O-

OCH_3

In about 24 hours after administration approximately 87 percent of the mescaline is eliminated from the body by the kidneys. Repeated doses of mescaline have been shown to produce tolerance to the drug's psychological effects. For a high degree of tolerance to be established, a period of three to six days of use is required. Cross-tolerance between mescaline, LSD and psilocybin has been demonstrated, even though mescaline differs in molecular structure from the other two.

No known human deaths have been reported as a result of a mescaline overdose. However, when combined with certain other drugs such as insulin or barbiturates, there is a very pronounced additive effect which increases the mescaline's toxicity.

As for physiological symptoms of use, mescaline produces effects similar to those observed during the fight/flight/fright syndrome: dilation of pupils, increase in blood pressure, heart rate, body temperature, and EEG, as well as behavioral arousal and other excitatory symptoms similar to those produced by amphetamines. However, such actions are not the primary effects sought by users of mescaline. As one writer puts it:

> "Interest in mescaline centers on the fact that it causes unusual psychic effects and visual hallucinations. The usual oral dose, 5 mg., causes anxiety, sympathomimetic effects, hyper-reflexia of the limbs, static tremors and vivid hallucinations that are usually visual and consist of brightly colored lights, geometric designs, animals and occasionally people; color and space perception is often concomitantly impaired, but otherwise the sensorium is normal and insight is retained."[17]

In contrast to atropine and scopolamine, mescaline produces no delirium, amnesia or clouding of consciousness. Hallucinations are usually clear and vivid.

It has been known for a long time that "visions" are the most characteristic symptoms induced by mescaline. Like LSD, mescaline causes

---

[17] Block, W. "Pharmacological Aspects of Mescaline." M. Renkel and H.C. Denber (eds.). *Chemical Concepts of Psychosis*. New York: McDowell Obolensky, 1968, pp. 106-119.

marked alterations in perception. Individual objects may take on new colors, shapes and may even seem to come alive while they move, wave and ripple. Many users experience synesthesia. In these instances, the senses become mixed, and the user will see sounds and hear colors, etc. Also, objects normally seen in two dimensions may appear tri-dimensional. Likewise, tri-dimensional objects may appear more voluminous than usual. All objects, even the smallest and most unimportant ones, appear to stand out distinctly.

Unlike LSD users, who sometimes cannot distinguish between an authentic and a pseudo-hallucination, subjects under the influence of mescaline are usually aware that the perceptual alterations have no basis in reality and are due to the effects of the drug.

Subjective Effects

There are multitudes of subjective reactions that may be experienced following the ingestion of mescaline. Emotional instability, significant mood changes and unprovoked emotional changes are common. As with subjects taking other psychedelic drugs and reporting an increased perception of truth, introspective and religious experiences are also common with mescaline use.[18] Likewise, adverse or threatening reactions may also follow mescaline ingestion in both the naive and experienced user.[19] Bad trips on mescaline can usually be reversed or ended by a competent and supportive friend through the process of "talking down." This same technique is now employed in emergency hospitals for persons under the influence of LSD who experience a bad trip. Although chemical intervention has been widely practiced by emergency wards in the past, it has been found unnecessary except as a last resort.

THE STREET PACKAGING OF MESCALINE AND PEYOTE

Peyote buttons are normally sold on the street as brown, dried discs approximately two to three inches in diameter and between one-half and one inch thick. Normally, a person will hold a button in his mouth until it becomes soft enough to swallow without chewing, because of the bitter taste. Four peyote buttons are usually adequate for one trip. Substances sold in the street as mescaline are almost always found to be entirely different drugs with contaminant substances. Usually, mescaline will be packaged in a clear, gelatin capsule containing a brown-colored powder and sell for $2 to $5 per

---

[18] Kluver, H. *Mescal and Mechanisms of Hallucinations.* Chicago: University of Chicago Press, 1966.

[19] Pelner, L. "Peyote Cult, Mescaline Hallucinations, and Model Psychosis." *New York Journ. of Medicine.* 67:2833-2843, 1967.

capsule. Occasionally, peyote is seen in a ground-up form which is placed in large capsules to allow for ingestion without experiencing the bitter taste.

THE SYNTHESIS AND EXTRACTION OF MESCALINE

Mescaline can be extracted from peyote buttons or manufactured synthetically. The manufactured substance (mescaline sulfate) is chemically identical to the mescaline or 3,4,5-trimethoxyphenylethylamine extracted from peyote cactus and produces similar effects. The mescal button contains several alkaloids including mescaline, anhalomine, ankalamine and anhalidine. In his book *Mescal and Mechanisms of Hallucination,* Heinrich Kluver states that euphoria is one of the typical mescal symptoms. [20]

PCP—PHENCYCLIDINE

INTRODUCTION

PCP is a synthetic drug. The initials PCP come from its full chemical name, phenylcyclohexyl piperidine, monohydrochloride. This substance was first synthesized by researchers at Park, Davis and Company in 1956 from a new family of chemicals. The first clinical trial of the drug's effectiveness as an anesthetic agent for humans was conducted in 1957. Medically, PCP seemed to be more effective and safer than other anesthetics; but it did cause some other problems. When used as a surgical anesthetic, up to 30 percent of the patients manifested agitation, excitement and disorientation during the recovery period. People experienced body-image changes, de-personalization and feelings of loneliness, isolation and dependency. Their thinking was observed to become progressively disorganized. Due to these adverse reactions, PCP was taken off the market as an investigational drug in 1965 and clinical studies in humans were discontinued. Beginning in 1967, the drug became available for use in veterinary medicine as an anesthetic or immobilizing agent. All legitimate manufacturing of PCP in the U.S. was discontinued in April, 1978.

CLASSIFICATION OF PCP

Phencyclidine is sometimes referred to as an "upper" or "downer" with stimulant or depressant-like properties. Sometimes it is referred to as a "hallucinogen."

Despite these references, PCP is not related to any of the other chemically-manufactured or known street drugs. It has also been stated that PCP is

[20] Kluver, Heinrich. *Mescal and Mechanisms of Hallucinations.* Chicago: University of Chicago Press, 1966.) In spite of marked nausea, Kluver notes that many subjects have a good time. Being in a state of mental exhaustion, they become talkative and jocular, they commit social errors and enjoy committing them; harmless remarks, even a potato salad or a catsup bottle are considered unusually funny. Sometimes the euphoric state may have no foundation whatever in objective circumstances. One subject said: "Suddenly I noticed that I lost control over myself through my laughing and was forced to continue laughing without any stimulus object." Some subjects refer to "cosmic emotions and ecstatic states" in which exclamations of enjoyment become involuntary. Despite these euphoric effects, a few records indicate that mescal may cause fear and horrible depressions. The drug apparently does not influence the sexual sphere in any specific way. Nonetheless, Indian peyote-eaters maintain that it inhibits sexual desires.

in a unique pharmacological classification of its own called the phencyclidines. Over 30 analogs are included in this new classification of drugs. One of these analogs, ketamine, is currently used as a surgical anesthetic. The major difference between ketamine and phencyclidine is that ketamine has a shorter duration of action and produces convulsions much less frequently.

HISTORY OF PCP USE

The illicit use of phencyclidine was first discovered in Los Angeles in 1965.[21] In 1967, it appeared in the Haight-Ashbury area of San Francisco under the name "Peace Pill." PCP was not popular then because of some adverse physical reactions in users. Phencyclidine seemed to disappear from the drug scene in San Francisco, but in 1968, it re-surfaced on the East Coast under the name of Hog. In the early 1970s, PCP was still a relatively unknown drug. However, in a review by the Pharm Chem Research Foundation, it was determined that from 1972 to 1979 phencyclidine use increased markedly and spread throughout the United States.

The growing problem of PCP use was due to its simplicity of manufacture, its availability, large profits, and its effects on users. In California, PCP is still a popular street drug and appears under a variety of names including crystal, crystal joints, KJ, angel dust, rocket fuel, Shermans, PCP, ozone, dust, and elephant tranquilizers.

STREET PCP (WHERE DOES IT COME FROM?)

The PCP sold in the United States is made in illegal laboratories, in bathrooms, garages, and basements.[22] The person who makes it may or may not be a real chemist. It is not particularly difficult to make, but it does take many complicated steps, and some of those steps are dangerous. A man died in San Jose, California from the inhalation of cyanide fumes caused by his preparations in making PCP.

The cost of making PCP is not great. Each person who sells it, from the original chemist to the final dealer who sells a joint on the street, doubles the price. One typical joint purchased on the street for $15 to $25 actually costs the chemist about one cent to make.

Most of the PCP available on the street today is not pure PCP. Usually other things as lactose or baking soda have been added to stretch it out. In addition, it is often improperly made and processed. Needless to say, poor quality PCP results in more bad trips than does high quality PCP.

PHYSICAL CHARACTERISTICS OF PCP

PCP in its pure state is a clear liquid; as a powder, it is a white colored substance. However, due to impurities in the manufacturing process it often has a slight yellowish or brownish tint to it.

---

[21] "PCP (Phencyclidine): The New Delusionogen." *Educational Off-Print Series.* Madison Wisconsin: Stash Press, 1975.

[22] Rainey, J.M., and M.R. Crowder. "Prevalence of Phencyclidine: Street Drug Preparations." *New England Journ. of Med.* Vol. 290 (8):466-467, 1974.

Hallucinogenic/Psychedelic Drugs

Although most powdered PCP is white or yellowish, many dealers will alter this standard appearance. In an attempt to make his product unique and thereby establish a reliable clientele, some dealers will add food coloring or other adulterants to the PCP. Purchases of "blue crystal" or "strawberry crystal" have been made by narcotics officers. When investigating for possession of PCP, law enforcement officers should keep these possibilities in mind.

A substance suspected to be PCP can generally be detected by its distinctive chemical odor. The process of manufacturing PCP requires numerous chemicals, including ether, which is one of the strongest identifiable odors. The mere presence of this odor is a preliminary indication that the substance could be PCP. While the ether smell is telltale sign, the police officer will find various physical forms of PCP on the street.

Crystal PCP

The texture of the powder or "crystals" will range from a granular sugar to a loose powder to lumps. PCP crystals will be found packaged in zip-lock baggies, hermetically sealed in plastic, or wrapped in aluminum foil bindles. Crystals can be inhaled through the nose or, more rarely, sprinkled on a plant material and smoked. The terms crystals and powder are interchangeable.

Liquid PCP

Liquid phencyclidine is generally clear or yellow colored, but can be disguised by any color. It may be found in eye-drop and vanilla extract bottles, or similar containers. Phencyclidine may be sprayed, sprinkled or soaked into a leafy substance which, when dried, produces "angel dust." The leafy substance might be any of the following:

1. Mint leaves
2. Parsley, oregano, or other vegetable spices or materials
3. Marijuana

Liquid phencyclidine may also be injected; however, this method of administration is not common in most geographical areas.

Although PCP can be snorted and injected, the field officer will most often encounter PCP contained in the hand rolled cigarette or "joint." This PCP joint can be produced in two ways:

1. The typical "joint" encountered by officers is produced using powdered PCP crystals. Approximately 35 to 50 milligrams of the drug is sprinkled onto a vegetable matter such as parsley, mint leaves or oregano, and then hand rolled into a cigarette. It is very rare to see a marijuana cigarette sprinkled with PCP as users generally do not like the combined effects of the two drugs. The field officer should be able to see the small PCP crystals upon breaking open the suspected PCP cigarette.
2. A second method of manufacturing the PCP joint is by making use of liquid PCP. The PCP is reduced to liquid form, sprayed on vegetable matter, and the vegetable matter is allowed to dry. This dried vegetable matter is then hand rolled into cigarettes for smoking. Generally a joint made in this manner will contain about

half the quantity of PCP as that made with crystals and, as a result, will sell for about half as much on the street. Since it is difficult to detect the liquid PCP in a cigarette manufactured in this manner, the field officer should look for the obvious—a cigarette rolled with vegetable matter other than marijuana.

The police officer should also look for other containers holding vegetable matter which is not marijuana. Sprayed PCP has been found in plastic baggies, film canisters, tobacco pouches, and spice jars. While in and of itself there may not be probable cause for arrest, the officer should still seize the suspected material, write an offense report, and submit the material to the crime lab for analysis.

Users of liquid PCP have devised ways to get around the obvious hand-rolled cigarette. One of the most common is by using a needle and absorbent string. The string is dipped into liquid PCP, allowed to dry and then threaded through a commercial cigarette. This method makes it very difficult to detect the PCP and has been used to enable friends and relatives to smuggle PCP into jails.

PCP PACKAGING AND STORAGE

Phencyclidine is packaged in a number of ways. The most common packaging methods include tinfoil, plastic bags, and vials.

Tinfoil appears to be the most popular container for phencyclidine in both the powder/crystal form and when it is sprayed onto vegetable matter. When packaged in tinfoil, PCP is generally found in small quantities such as one gram or less. The larger quantities, such as full grams or more, are usually packaged in plastic zip-lock wrappers or baggies. Phencyclidine may also be found in either glass or plastic vials. These glass or plastic vials come in all sizes, but most commonly contain a gram or less. A popular glass vial is the eye drop bottle. It should be noted that paper bindles are rarely used to package PCP because they absorb moisture and the PCP soaks into the paper.

The most common quantity of PCP powder encountered on the street is the gram quantity. Generally packaged in the corners of plastic baggies which are then tied off and cut, PCP has also been seen compressed into small rocks and carried in any number of other containers. One gram of PCP is about the size of a dime and will enable the manufacture of approximately 20 to 25 cigarettes.

Although tinfoil is most common container for PCP, there are some differences of opinion concerning the storage of PCP in a damp or cool environment. Many persons arrested for possessing PCP have the misconception that the substance will lose its potency if subjected to heat for an extended period of time. In fact, PCP will remain moist and damp if refrigerated and this storage method will increase its profitability when sold in quantities by weight.

When searching locations for PCP, officers should pay particular attention to refrigerators, freezers, storage chests, and other areas where the temperature would remain cool and constant.

METHODS AND PATTERNS OF PCP USE

As discussed above, PCP is usually a dry powder or granular, light colored substance. In California, it is usually sprinkled on dried parsley leaves or marijuana; it may also be dissolved in liquid and sprayed on these leafy substances. The PCP is then rolled into a thin joint and smoked. Occasionally it is snorted (inhaled vigorously) or added to food or liquid and swallowed. Very rarely it is injected or smoked in a pipe. It might be noted that PCP can also be absorbed rectally.

In addition to these, there may be a variety of other methods of PCP use. The users are limited only by their imaginations. One such method which is gaining popularity in Los Angeles, California is placing liquid PCP in the eye with an eyedropper. In this manner, the many blood vessels and the delicate tissues of the eyes and inner eyelids are able to absorb the drug. This method allows the PCP to spread throughout a greater number of blood vessels in the user's skin.

Since PCP can be absorbed through the skin, police officers should be cautious when handling a substance believed to contain the drug. There is at least one case where a U.S. Navy pilot was accidentally subjected to the influence of PCP when his suitcase and clothing were contaminated by a liquid spill. Following the wearing of clothing from his suitcase, he exhibited bizarre behavior and had to be hospitalized for PCP toxicity.

With respect to PCP usage, there are three principal patterns. Each carries its own respective dangers. One kind of user smokes PCP occasionally at parties, dances, concerts and other social events. This person is least likely to know what he or she is getting, because a joint passed at a party contains an unknown dosage. Depending upon the amount used and the purity of the dose, the effect may be anything from a pleasant numbness to a violent physical reaction.

The second kind of user is considered a regular user. This person smokes PCP from twice a month up to three times a week. The regular user is likely to smoke on weekends and sometimes during the week. Most regular users are hesitant about accepting the idea that they are "addicted," "dependent," or have a problem with PCP. These individuals are "hidden users." Often, they maintain regular employment and appear to be functioning more or less normally. Their use of the drug can, however, result in tragedy. For example, in several cases single parents or housewives have ingested the drug in front of their children. This usage pattern has sometimes led to accidental ingestion of PCP by small children.

The third type of user is someone who uses PCP every day, or as often as it can be found. This person is much more likely to know what is being smoked because he or she is probably dealing PCP in order to support the expense of its use or is buying it in quantity and rolling his or her own joints. Therefore, with this type of user, problems do not arise out of not knowing what one is getting; rather, problems result from the fact that when someone uses PCP on a regular basis, their memory, reasoning, judgment, and common sense disappear. Thus, the user thinks he or she can drive while stoned; he or she may think nothing of selling joints on the corner in front of the local school. Continued use, then, results in increasingly bizarre behavior and ultimately in severe memory loss. Usually, it is the first type of user that is most likely to end up with a medical crisis. The second and third types are more likely to be arrested.

PHARMACOLOGY OF PCP

PCP is distributed in the body's tissues, metabolized by the liver and excreted unchanged in the urine. The drug is highly soluble in lipid (fat) tissues. The cardiovascular effects include increases in blood pressure, heart rate, and cardiac output. PCP effects include hypersalivation and increased bronchial secretion. PCP also increases body temperature. After PCP use, respiratory rate is usually normal or slightly increased.[23]

SIGNS AND SYMPTOMS OF PCP INTOXICATION

PCP shares the properties of many commonly used street drugs. It may act like a depressant, a stimulant, a psychedelic, and a tranquilizer. It produces a unique combination of these effects in addition to removing physical pain.

Physiological Effects

The physiological effects of PCP differ markedly with dose. At low doses, the most prominent effect is similar to that of alcohol intoxication—a generalized numbness. With increased doses, analgesia and then anesthesia can be observed. Large doses can produce convulsions, coma or even death. Most persons using PCP experience a confused state characterized by feelings of weightlessness, depression, anxiety, and hallucinations.[24] Users frequently report difficulty in reasoning and poor concentration.[25] At least one study published in *Clinical Toxicology* has documented these physiological effects of PCP intoxication.[26] The study observed the effects of acute PCP intoxication in 18 individuals. On the next page is a summary of the study's results.

---

[23] Johnson, K.M. "Neurochemical Pharmacology of Phencyclidine." R.C. Peterson and R. Stillman (eds.). *Phencyclidine Abuse: An Appraisal.* NIDA Report. Rockville, MD: 1978.

Leonard, B.E. and S.R. Tonge. "Some Effects of an Hallucinogenic Drug (PCP) on Neurohumoral Substances." *Life Sciences.* 9:1141-1152, 1970.

Lindgren, J.E. et al. "The Chemical Identity of 'Hog'—A New Hallucinogen." *American Journal of Pharmacy.* 141:86-90, 1969. ("Hog" is a slang term for PCP.)

[24] Rainey, J.M. and M.K. Crowder. "Ketamine or Phencyclidine." *JAMA.* 230:824, 1974.

[25] Reed, A. and A.W. Kene. "Phencyclidine (PCP): Another Illicit Drug." *Journ. of Psychedelic Drugs.* 5:8-12, 1972.

[26] *Clinical Toxicology.* Vol. 9, Issue 4, 1976.

Hallucinogenic/Psychedelic Drugs

	LOW to MEDIUM DOSE (Acute Confusional State)	HIGH DOSE (Stupor or Coma)
Clinical Features:		
A. *Responsiveness*	Initially uncommunicative, may respond to simple commands with nodding or eye movement; later incomplete verbal responses and then becomes talkative.	Appears awake; Unresponsive to verbal stimuli, responds to deep pain with movement.
B. *Orientation*	Disoriented for time and place, appears confused or fearful; amnesia for episode.	------------------
C. *Behavior*	Agitated, excited, combative; aggressive, self-destructive or bizarre behavior; insomnia, loss of appetite, incontinence, followed by depression, irritability.	------------------
D. *Speech*	Slurred, intermittently unable to articulate.	Moaning, groaning inability to articulate.
E. *Eyes*	Open "stare appearance" with drooping of eyelids, very little effect on pupil size.	--------------
F. *Nystagmus*	Bilateral, horizontal, and vertical	Same. More jerky nystagmus.
Motor System:		
A. *Gait*	Unable to tandem walk; some muscle rigidity.	--------------
B. *Muscle Tone*	Rigidity.	--------------
C. *Movements*	Restlessness, repetitive movements	Twitching movements, facial grimace.
Other:		
A. *Increased Secretions*	Drooling	Same.

Psychological Effects

The best subjective information on the psychological effects of PCP was published in a report by Doctors Baker and Amini in the *Journal of Psychedelic Drugs* in 1972. At one point Doctors Baker and Amini state:

> The main effect on the psychological functioning of the subject was a progressive disintegration. This is meant quite literally in that the subject apparently became less and less able to combine and integrate all the information available to him. As a consequence, a progressive narrowing of his field of awareness was observed. Past and future disappeared, and the subject became unable to correctly integrate information from his own body with that from the environment.
>
> Feelings that the extremities did not belong to the body, did not belong to the subject himself, were typical. . . Although the subject knew intellectually it was he who was speaking, his voice seemed to come from a distance as if someone were talking to him. . .
>
> The changes in perception came somewhat later than the disturbances in body image. These perceptual disturbances manifested themselves quite suddenly. . . .

In a study on the subjective effects of PCP it was found that in 1,008 of the cases, users experienced body image changes, estrangement, disorganization of thought (recent memory), drowsiness, and apathy; 78 percent of the users experienced feelings of inebriation; 67 percent of the users experienced negativism and hostility; 56 percent of the users experienced a hypnogogic state (a feeling of being far away); and 29 percent of the users experienced repetitive motor behavior or a parroting of questions.[27]

FIELD OBSERVATION OF PCP INTOXICATION

There are several obvious symptoms that a police officer will observe when coming into contact with a person under the influence of PCP. Some of these symptoms are also common to various stages of alcohol and barbiturate intoxication. These are the depressed abilities to walk and speak, redness of the eyes, flushing of the face, and sweating. With PCP intoxication, however, the officer should observe the "blank stare" appearance of the subject's eyes.

There are two field tests for PCP intoxication that can be performed by a police officer on the scene. When combined with the other physical symptoms of PCP intoxication already mentioned, these field tests provide enough probable cause for arrest for being under the influence.

Nystagmus: Have the subject keep his or eyes open with his head directed straight ahead. Hold an object in front of the subject's nose so that he can see it, then move the object to the subject's temporal area, directing him to follow it with his eyes only. Once the eyes are to the side, the police officer will be able to see that the eyeballs jerk uncontrollably from side to side. This test can also be performed for vertical nystagmus.

---

[27] Tennant, Forest Jr., M.D. *Research Studies in Phencyclidine (PCP)*. West Covina, CA: Veract, Inc., 1986.
"Phencyclidine: An Up-Date." National Institute on Drug Abuse. Monograph 64, 1986.

Hallucinogenic/Psychedelic Drugs

Pulse Rate: The police officer can take the subject's pulse manually. As noted previously, PCP generally increases the pulse rate, so the officer should not be surprised to find that the apparently "drowsy" subject has a pulse rate of over 100 beats per minute.

It should be noted that nystagmus is also present in some cases of alcohol and barbiturate intoxication. However, both of these drugs are depressants and subsequently would not be consistent with a high pulse rate. In addition, nystagmus in alcohol and barbiturate cases does not become evident until acute intoxication.

Recognition of PCP Intoxication

The most common observable signs of PCP intoxication include:

- Horizontal and vertical nystagmus
- Gait ataxia - muscle rigidity
- Blank stare appearance
- Non-communicative appearance

PCP has three general effects: anesthetic, stimulant, and hallucinogenic. Chronic users become tolerant to many of these effects. Tolerance to the following effects is rapidly developed: increase in pulse, blood pressure, and body temperature, nystagmus, hallucinations, and anesthetic properties. Due to the development of tolerance, the regular user of PCP may have few if any physical signs of drug use.

The diagnosis of "under the influence" of PCP means that there is evidence of PCP activity present. Such evidence could be provided by nystagmus, muscle rigidity, hallucinations, delusions, and PCP in the blood or urine. The diagnosis of "under the influence" is made by finding more than one item of evidence. The most important evidence to find is the presence of PCP in the blood or urine (and the absence of other drugs in the blood or urine). As mentioned, two or more of the following physical symptoms must also be present to give an officer probable cause to arrest for PCP influence:

1. The presence of nystagmus.
2. Presence of muscle rigidity or muscle relaxation to include droopy eyelids, slurred or slow speech, abnormal gait and nodding.
3. Disorientation—subject does not know person, time or place, or shows presence of amnesia.
4. Hallucinations.
5. Delusions such as thinking one is Jesus Christ.
6. Non-reactive pupils.

Remember that these items of evidence may be considered subjective; therefore, at least two observers are required to avoid criticisms of bias. Although there are other symptoms of PCP use, the increases in blood pressure, pulse, body temperature and reflex are too nonspecific to use as medico-legal evidence.

In sum, the field officer's complete evaluation of the PCP suspect should include the following:

1. Examine the eyes for nystagmus (vertical and horizontal), pupil size, and pupil reaction.
2. Is the speech slowed or slurred? Is the the subject unable to talk?
3. Smell the breath for the characteristic ether odor of PCP.
4. Observe gait for wide-stance.
5. Test arms for muscle rigidity.
6. Is the subject oriented as to person, time and place?
7. Is the subject seeing and hearing anything that may be a hallucination?
8. Is the subject having any obvious delusions?
9. Observe the subject for sedation by looking for droopy eyelids or general drowsiness.
10. Test the urine or blood for PCP and other drugs.

PCP can be easily detected in the blood or urine. It can be found in the blood 6 to 12 hours after last use. It can be found in the urine 24 to 48 hours after last use. If the suspect refuses a blood or urine test, this can be considered evidence of drug use. According to federal government regulations, refusal to give a urine sample in methadone programs is considered a positive or "dirty" urine.

Some other signs of PCP intoxication include:

— A fluctuating state of confusion or excitement

— Agitation or combativeness

— Aggressive or violent behavior

Duration of PCP Effects

The effects of PCP will vary greatly depending on the purity and amount of PCP used, the individual's metabolism, sex, age, mental state, psychological make-up, and tolerance.

After smoking phencyclidine, the onset of subjective effects is reported to occur within 1 to 5 minutes. The drug will peak or plateau in 15 to 30 minutes and the person will remain high for 4 to 6 hours. Generally, 24 to 48 hours are required until the person again feels completely "normal."

With chronic use, the time required to return to normal may be increased to several weeks or even years.

Clinical Observation of Emergency Room Cases

A typical street dose of 5 mg. produces a confusional state associated with a blank stare appearance. Horizontal and vertical nystagmus and gait ataxia are almost always present. Muscle rigidity may be present. Most individuals are alert and oriented within 5 hours of admission to the emergency room. However, some users remain confused for periods of 24 to 72 hours.

Larger doses, 20 mg. and greater, produce an unresponsive, immobile state where the eyes may remain open. Nystagmus, muscle rigidity and hypertension are common findings. With this dosage, it usually takes over 24 to 48 hours to recover.

Massive overdoses, exceeding 500 mg. of PCP, result in periods of coma from several hours to days. Seizures are also common with such large overdoses.

PCP will remain in an individual's system for a prolonged time period. The drug is stored in both fat and brain tissue. Consequently, the frequency of ingestion is of paramount importance.

Studies have been conducted on persons who have chronically used PCP three or more times a week for a period of at least six months.[28] These studies have shown that, after use of the drug is discontinued, users experienced lingering problems with speech, memory, concentration, and abstraction for several years. They also continued to experience periods of bizarre, violent or amnesic behavior (flashbacks).[29]

Summary of Signs and Symptoms of PCP Intoxication

— The PCP intoxicated individual shows signs of recent memory loss.

— The PCP user is often uncommunicative and stares blankly. The communication difficulty is seen with users attempting to talk in words, or fragments of words, instead of sentences.

— The user is unpredictable. There are fluctuating levels of consciousness from mite to action involving agitation, pacing, aggression, impulsiveness, and loss of control.

— The PCP user may have hallucinations that change rapidly from auditory to visual and visual to auditory.

— The PCP user sometimes shows facial grimacing or jaw clenching. This symptom is an important warning sign of unpredictable or violent biting.

— The PCP user has difficulty estimating time.

— The PCP user experiences changes in body image. He or she has difficulty accurately perceiving bodily experiences and sensations; he or she may experience floating in and out of the body. Users are occasionally found nude. They often overestimate body size, shape, and height. Frequently they believe themselves to be powerful, very large, invulnerable and endowed with unique or super physical or mental abilities.

---

[28] Tennant, Forest S. *Medico-Legal Identification of the Phencyclidine (PCP) User*. West Covina CA: Community Health Projects, Inc., 1983.

[29] Showalter, C. and W. Thornton. "Clinical Pharmacology of Phencyclidine. *American Journ. of Psychiatry*. 134:1234-1238, 1977.

— It is difficult to make meaningful interpersonal contact with the PCP user. "Talking down" is not effective with the non-communicative PCP user and may, in fact, agitate the user and endanger the officer.

— The PCP user appears to have long-term neuropsychological impairment.

— Muscle rigidity.

— Gait ataxia—difficulty in coordination. When asked to stand on one leg, the PCP user will often fall down.

CHEMICAL TESTING FOR PCP

There are some field test kits which allow the officer to perform a field examination of substances believed to be PCP. These tests function by color reaction. The suspected substance is placed in a vial and a particular color will appear if the substance is positive. Since PCP can be absorbed through the skin, officers should be careful when handling the evidence and performing such field tests. Never touch, taste, or smell PCP.

In addition to these direct tests of suspected substances, phencyclidine can also be identified in body tissues and fluids. Current techniques include thin layer chromatography, gas chromatography, gas chromatography/mass spectrometry and radio-immunoassay. Since the drug rapidly disappears from the blood and is excreted in significant amounts in the urine, urine is the preferred body fluid for sampling. Phencyclidine will appear in urine about one hour after it is used. PCP can also be detected in the blood and gastric content. The drug will usually be detected within 2 to 3 days after ingestion but can be detected for as long as 5 days.

The relatively long life of PCP in the body is due to both its solubility in lipids and its weak chemical base which allows the drug to readily ionize in the strong acid milieu of the stomach. One problem of detection is that PCP toxicity is sometimes mistaken for acute alcohol intoxication, and that persons are mistakenly placed in a drunk tank or jail cell, instead of being placed under treatment. Even while users are in treatment, there is no specific antidote for PCP intoxication.

Negative Urine Tests

As mentioned above, PCP will appear in the urine one hour after use. If you collect a urine sample before this hour the urine test for PCP may be negative.

Forty-eight hours after use, approximately 90 percent of PCP is eliminated from the body. Collecting a urine specimen after 48 hours may result in a negative test.

Also, when low dosages of PCP are used (below .25 μg./ml.) there may be too little PCP in the urine to detect its presence.

A negative test may result from a laboratory error.

How to Avoid Negative Urine Tests

Take more than one urine sample. Wait about one hour between collections. Check with the laboratory to see how they want the urine samples processed and labeled.

APPREHENSION AND CONTROL OF THE PHENCYCLIDINE USER

Departmental Policy: Since a person under the influence of phencyclidine may demonstrate psychotic behavior, departments should have specific established policies that set guidelines for contact with the phencyclidine abuser.

Detention vs. Booking: In all cases, a person who is detained for being under the influence of phencyclidine should be examined by a competent medical authority prior to being placed in a detention setting. An alternative to booking would be commitment under appropriate legal authority.

Safety: When dealing with a person under the influence of phencyclidine, precuations should be taken to ensure the safety of the officer, the public, and the user himself.

The officer handling a person under the influence of phencyclidine must remember that because of the anesthetic effects of phencyclidine, the person's pain threshold will be increased, rendering traditional police restraints ineffective. The officer should always request back-up, and when possible, wait for the user to become cooperative.

A person under the influence of phencyclidine can occasionally be talked down and may become cooperative, eliminating the need for physical confrontation by the officer. NEVERTHELESS, "TALKING DOWN" SHOULD ONLY BE ATTEMPTED IF A USER IS COMMUNICATIVE.

If physical confrontation does become *necessary* the most effective hold in dealing with a person under the influence of phencyclidine is the "carotid." The carotid is a control hold technique used to apprehend violent suspects. It can quickly render a suspect unconscious by application of pressure against the carotid arteries at the sides of the neck. When the hold is properly applied, it restricts or stops the flow of oxygenated blood to the brain, causing unconsciousness. This hold must be applied correctly to avoid serious injury to the suspect and to the officer. With appropriate backup (as many as eight officers) the best means of controlling the aggressive user is to hold him or her down by sheer body weight.

In all instances the "bar arm" must be avoided due to the possibility of the suspect suffering a broken neck. If the officer is unable to get backup, the "carotid" is the next best means of control. To reduce the possibility of respiratory failure, care must be used in applying weight to the chest.

If you have a PCP user who is communicative, ask the user the following questions to help you determine what the problem is:

1. What did you take?
2. Do you have any amount of the drug left?
3. Describe what you took (color, smell, taste).

4. How did you take it?
5. When did you take it?
6. Have you ever taken it before?
7. How do you feel?

Recently, several devices have been developed to restrain a person under the influence of PCP. One of these is the PCP net. Use of the Taser (50,000 volts) has also been found to be effective. Another effective restraining method employs a heavy, nylon cord strung around the ankles and attached to the handcuff chain. Minimally, the user should be handcuffed with his hands behind his back and his legs restrained. Remember that chemical mace does not work. The baton is also ineffective. In general, arrest control techniques that rely on pain compliance are ineffective. When transporting a PCP user place him or her face down on the floor in the back seat of the patrol vehicle. This tactic will minimize the possibility of injury due to the user falling off the back seat onto the floor. The PCP user should then be transported to a medical facility (usually a county hospital emergency room) for a medical clearance.

If You Encounter a Non-Communicative Person With a Blank Stare:

1. Call for back-up
2. Wait it out
3. Use a show of force—sit on the person (5 officers)
4. Use methods of restraint
   a. PCP net
   b. Carotid
   c. 6 pt. restraint—both arms, both legs, stomach and upper chest
   d. Leg restraint hooked to handcuffs
   e. Leg restraint with end out of door
   f. Taser gun

Remember that sensory stimulation (sight, hearing, feeling) can induce violent reactions in PCP users. Loud or aggressive questioning, a body search for weapons, lights flashed in the eyes or an attempt to handcuff the user may set-off explosive behavior. In summary, acts that tend to stimulate the senses (loud noises, flashing lights, etc.) may initiate violent reactions. On the other hand, conduct that produces calming, peaceful, quieting effects have been successful methods of control. The officer should not, however, relax his or her guard or vigilance. Do not turn your back on a PCP user. Do not touch a PCP user unless it is absolutely necessary. There is no easy or dependable method of controlling the always unpredictable PCP user.

Custody personnel should be aware of the potential problem when detaining a person under the influence of PCP. Persons under the influence of PCP often demonstrate homicidal and suicidal tendencies. While under the influence, the person may suffer respiratory depression, seizures, or coma.

ARREST REPORT AND EVIDENCE COLLECTION

The arrest report must include the specific objective symptoms of PCP intoxication which could be one or any combination of the following: muscle rigidity, nystagmus, hypertension, blank stare, non-communication, or impaired coordination. In addition to all of the elements of the crime, the report should include the result of a comprehensive interview with the arrestee regarding the quantity of PCP taken, the method(s) used, the source of supply, and the location of any PCP not recovered during the initial arrest. Any uncovered PCP or chemicals for making PCP represent an extreme danger to other persons.

In the process of collecting evidence, certain hazardous situations should be avoided. A "contact high" could result during activities from exposure to PCP in any of its forms by touching, inhaling, etc. The same contact hazards exist during transportation. In addition, there is danger from exposure to the volatile chemicals used in manufacturing PCP.

The extreme danger of transporting chemicals used to manufacture PCP necessitates that a court order be obtained to destroy all chemicals and containers except the quantity required for laboratory analysis and court presentation. Complete sets of sequential photographs are required to record the laboratory site, the location of all chemicals and equipment in the laboratory, and a complete inventory prior to destruction. In addition to the quantity of chemicals retained for the prosecution, limited amounts of all chemicals must be retained for use by the defense.

Limited amounts of all evidence must be preserved to satisfy the court requirements by both the defense and the prosecution. Consistent with the chain of evidence, chemicals should be stored in either air-tight or well ventilated areas where there can be limited or no contact or exposure to personnel.

In the process of booking, the officer should maintain the chain of evidence and book the property in accordance with departmental regulations. However, due to the hazards, no more material should be retained as evidence than is absolutely necessary for identification.

COURT PRESENTATION

The qualifications, experience and expertise of all expert witnesses should be documented for submission to the court. Methods for the documentation and verification of evidence include witnesses, videotape, chemical analyses, cassette tape or audio evidence, and urinalysis and/or blood toxicology.

ILLICIT MANUFACTURE OF PHENCYCLIDINE

Virtually the entire illicit supply of PCP is manufactured in clandestine laboratories. This synthesis process is not difficult and can be done by individuals who have only modest technical training. These laboratory operations vary in size and scope from a small quantity of chemicals and a few pieces of glassware to a large facility with the production capabilities of a commercial scale which include barrels of chemicals, sophisticated industrial equipment and major distribution networks. Although there is considerable diversity among the clandestine labs, most labs encountered by police have rudimentary equipment (facilities and are usually located in residential dwellings), are small in size and usually produce a few pounds per batch, and are dirty, usually containing byproducts and intermediaries from the chemical reactions which take place during the manufacturing process. Even though the size and production capability of the operations vary greatly, a small investment in a lab can yield enormous profit. An investment of $500 to $1,000 could yield the operator a $24,000 profit.

It is imperative that officers understand the inherent dangers surrounding any laboratory investigation. The chemicals used are often extremely toxic and may be highly volatile. For example, many laboratories contain cyanide and hydrochloric acid. When combined, these chemicals produce a lethal gas. When a fire erupts, some of the burning chemicals can produce extremely toxic fumes. The inhalation of these fumes or prolonged exposure to some chemicals can cause poisoning or death.

An additional danger from fire exists when dealing with chemicals. A spark or inadvertent chemical mixture can cause an explosion of fire. Phenyl magnesium bromide may explode with the addition of one drop of water. Ether will ignite with a spark.

The presence of illicit laboratories has created a hazard to citizens, police officers and fire department personnel. It has become almost commonplace for these laboratories to explode and burn, causing extensive property damage and personal injuries to bystanders. When basic guidelines are followed, an investigation can be effectively conducted with minimal risk to officers and the public. Short of life-saving measures, there is no valid reason for an officer to enter an illicit laboratory, unless accompanied by a criminologist or other qualified personnel to render the laboratory safe.

The process of manufacturing or cooking PCP produces a strong and offensive odor, which in turn may generate complaints from neighbors. Therefore, illicit laboratories are often discovered through a citizen's complaint or an officer's observation. Thorough interviews of complaining persons or other neighbors will usually provide cause to believe an illicit laboratory is in operation. During the interview, personnel should determine if certain indicators of an illicit laboratory are present.

PCP DEFENSES

It has come to the attention of authorities over the past few years that suspects involved in crimes such as homicide claim diminished capacity as a defense because they were under the influence of PCP at the time of the offense. This defense has proven satisfactory to the accused in several instances because it is not difficult to locate an "expert" who will testify that persons under the influence of PCP cannot be accountable for their actions while under the influence due to a loss of mental control. If a PCP user is encountered either in, or after, the commission of another crime, certain questions should be asked to refute the possible defense of diminished capacity. The user's awareness of these facts will support his or her presence of mind at this time.

When investigating a crime, the officer should immediately document the orientation of the suspect as to person, place, and time to clearly show the ability or inability of the individual to respond. Additionally, a biological specimen (i.e., blood and/or urine) should be obtained for further documentation and evidence. This procedure also applies to the ability of the suspect to voluntarily waive his or her *Miranda* rights.

Furthermore, PCP has been increasingly linked to murders—at least by lawyers hoping to ease penalties against their clients. The most celebrated local case occurred in August 1976, when Barry Braeseke and David Barker shot Braeseke's parents and grandfather in hopes of inheriting the family's wealth. In his confession, Braeseke blamed "crystal" for the crimes. "The idea (of murder) seemed neat to me because I was under the influence," he told sheriff's detectives.

His lawyer, James Crew, used that defense in Braeseke's trial, but the jury was not impressed. Braeseke and his accomplice were convicted of first degree murder. Both Crew and psychologist Lerner, who testified at the trial, believe that Braeseke would not have killed if he had not taken PCP.

Crew has the same opinion about another murder case he argued: the 1974 murder of 18-year-old Steve McQuinn. McQuinn was drowned by two friends, Dale Burdick and Michael Cortez, who decided during a session of PCP smoking that McQuinn was a police snitch. According to Cortez' court testimony, the pair took McQuinn to a flooded ditch in South Hayward and clumsily drowned him while McQuinn, apparently too stoned to resist, vainly called for help.

Crew, who defended Burdick, says this crime would never have happened without the presence of PCP intoxication: "They would have beaten him up, to teach him a lesson, but they never intended to kill him." Both youths pleaded guilty to second degree murder before trial.

WHAT IS A PCP TRIP REALLY LIKE?

The following is a reprint of material presented by the PROJECT DARE PCP unit, which has dealt extensively with persons under the influence of PCP. For the occasional user, a normal trip goes through three main stages:

Three to five minutes after smoking a PCP joint, the first effects are felt. The user will sit or lie down, because standing requires too much work. During this first "ozone" stage, which will last from 15 minutes to an hour and a half, depending on dosage and experience, the user will not feel like talking and speech will be slurred. He or she is "somewhere else" mentally. That somewhere else is different for each person. Some typical feelings a user has at this stage are a deadening of body sensation, a disinterest in what is going on in the environment, and sometimes feelings of being huge or tiny. But how the body feels is rarely the point for the user. The idea is to go off into the mental world where anything is possible.

The second "intimate" stage usually lasts from one to two hours and is very different from the first stage. Actually, the drug is now beginning to wear off, but the user does not perceive the situation this way. The smokers are feeling a real closeness to one another, a mental intimacy which sometimes seems to be telepathy. Each can tell the feelings of any of the others. Words and laughter come in waves of intensity. Now, too, it is easier to walk around and people may feel they are floating just above the floor. All powers of judgment are impaired. If someone suggests they all do something, the whole group could could engage in almost any activity, without regard for the consequences. At this point, if a trip is interrupted by someone who is angry, the easy-going, happy feelings can disappear suddenly and be replaced with hostile emotion, great strength, and violence.

The third "comedown" stage, which lasts from the end of the second stage until an hour or two later, is really an effect of the drug wearing off. Now users are generally more irritable and paranoid. They may become violent and/or demonstrate their ability to perform feats of strength and daring. The warm intimacy is gone, replaced by anger or resentment and a sense of isolation which is all the more devastating in contrast to their shared experience so short a time ago. Arguments or fights erupt. No one is happy anymore. Experienced users try to go home at this point and sleep it off to avoid trouble. The next day there is some leftover tiredness and fogginess of mind. The person may not feel "normal" for several days.

The daily or chronic user, as opposed to the occasional user, does not experience these three stages so sharply. He or she learns to maintain composure, or act as though the drug is not having a strong effect. The first stage may not be so incapacitating to this person. Gradually, over the weeks and months of using, it will take more and more PCP to create the high desired, and the joints will be smoked more frequently during the day so that the effects never really wear off.

This means that the user's power of judgment is constantly crippled. In addition, memory can become significantly impaired. For unexplained reasons, brain cells die and the mind is seriously affected with chronic PCP use. If regular use goes on long enough, serious mental handicaps develop, which do not go away after cessation of use. It may be several months or even years before the mind returns to normal and some people never seem to fully recover.

PCP AND HEROIN

Contrary to the downward pattern observed from 1979 to 1981, the availability and abuse of PCP has continued to increase in many major cities in the U.S. Concurrent with increasing PCP use has been the escalating abuse of PCP in combination with heroin.

Methods of administering PCP/heroin mixtures appear to vary by geographic region and ethnic background. Informal interviews conducted with treatment program staff and clients provided the following information:

— PCP/heroin combinations are known as "Sunshine" in the Washington, D.C., metropolitan area. Frequently, white users smoke PCP and inject heroin, while non-white users inject both PCP and heroin (either separately or in a pre-mixed powder).

— A new street drug known as "Black Dust" has appeared in certain minority sections of north Philadelphia. This combination, consisting of heroin, PCP, embalming fluid, and marijuana, is commonly smoked.

— A new street substance known as "the Boat" has surfaced in Washington, D.C., and minority sections of Prince George's County, Maryland. It resembles "Black Dust" and is now manufactured in the Washington, D.C. area, having first been discovered in Philadelphia.

— PCP/heroin injections are prevalent in Harlem, New York.

Hallucinogenic/Psychedelic Drugs

The complementary nature of PCP and heroin may be summarized as follows:

— Due to the anaesthetic and numbing effects of PCP, numerous heroin addicts have taken the drug as a method of self-detoxification to ease the pain of withdrawal.

— Informal discussions with ex-addicts indicated that heroin ameliorates the undesirable effects of PCP.

— PCP and heroin mixtures are often sold on the streets as high quality heroin, since a small amount of heroin mixed with 2 to 5 milligrams of PCP will yield a larger profit and boost a low purity heroin.

Because of the sophisticated techniques involved in detecting phencyclidine and the varying procedures employed by toxicologists in gathering information, the extent of heroin and PCP used in combination has been underestimated. Some counties conduct forensic analyses on a wider range of drugs than other counties. When drugs are detected, coroners also have difficulty deciding whether the death was by accident, suicide, homicide or natural causes, and to what degree (if any) a given drug contributed to that death.

Some facets of PCP's action within the body are not yet fully understood. In most hospital emergency room admissions, patients are not routinely tested for PCP. Levels of PCP in the blood of patients may be so low that it may not be picked up by any but the most sensitive analytical methods; the presence of PCP will certainly be missed by most screening tests. Levels in urine may be much higher, but PCP will be detected only if the urine is acidic.

One successful method of hair analysis to detect previous phencyclidine (PCP) use has been reported from California.[30] Researchers from a number of Los Angeles medical centers used the radio-immunoassay technique with hair specimens of 10 to 20 strands in newly admitted psychiatric patients. To establish reliability, verified non-users of PCP and volunteers admitting to frequent PCP use during at least the last six months were treated. No false positive or negative results were obtained. Hair analysis, in addition to traditional methods of PCP detection from blood and urine samples, was then obtained from 31 consecutively admitted psychiatric patients and 16 patients selected by the admitting psychiatrist. The 16 patients were selected for PCP testing on the basis of either prior history or present symptoms. Of these 47 patients, hair analysis detected 11 who had used PCP, while blood and urine analysis did not identify any positive samples. Although urine testing is more likely to identify PCP than blood testing, the researchers noted that eight patients refused to provide a urine sample. Four of these were identified as PCP users by hair analysis. In three patients, the

---

[30] Baumgartner, W. "Hair Analysis for Drugs of Abuse." *Journ. of Forensic Sciences.* 34:1433-1453, 1989. Rpt. in *The Narc Officer.* International Narcotics Enforcement Officers Association. Sept. 1990. pp. 14-16.

results of hair analysis helped establish a diagnosis of PCP intoxication. Despite these positive results of hair analysis, it is not exactly known how the rate of appearance and accumulation of PCP in hair changes with time or is influenced by hair growth. These variables are thought to correlate directly with the dose of PCP consumed. [31]

OTHER PSYCHOTOGENIC SUBSTANCES

TRYPTAMINE

Although it lacks any central activity of its own, many of the psychotogenic drugs are derivatives of tryptamine. Bufotenine, LSD, psilocybin, psilocin, DMT and DET, all belong to this general chemical class. Serotonin, the naturally occurring neurohormone in the central nervous system of humans, is also a tryptamine derivative (5 hydroxytryptamine). Tryptamine is readily obtainable from many sources and can be chemically modified to one of the potent hallucinogenic agents with very little difficulty.

DMT - DIMETHYLTRYPTAMINE

A synthetic derivative of tryptamine, DMT provides central effects similar to LSD but of shorter duration, including behaviorial excitability, visual distortions and hallucinations. Fifty to 60 mg. of DMT will produce an effect which lasts about a half hour. The drug is also derived from the powdered bark, seeds and leaves of various West Indian and South American plants.

DMT

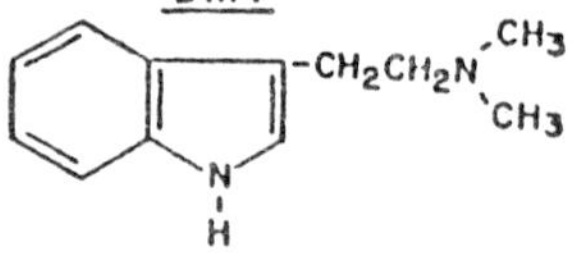

$-CH_2CH_2N(CH_3)_2$

N
H

BUFOTENINE - COHOBA

Some toads release hallucinogenic substances as well as toxins as part of their defense. The most commonly used toad for drug-taking purposes is the Colorado River Toad found in the Southwest U.S. and Mexico. It gives off a chemical called bufotenine. Shaking the toad and agitating it makes the animal release this chemical through the skin. The drug-taker then licks the chemical off the back of the toad. This chemical is in the same category of illegal drugs as LSD. Bufotenine is chemically known as the N'N'-dimethyl derivative of 5-hydroxytryptamine and its pharmacological actions are similar to this form of tryptamine.

BUFOTENINE

HO $-CH_2CH_2N(CH_3)_2$

N
H

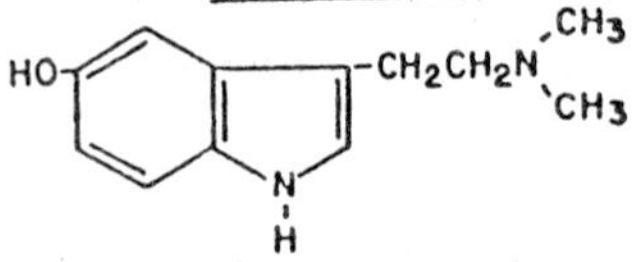

[31] Sramek, J.J. et al. "Hair Analysis for Detection of PCP in Newly Admitted Psychiatric Patients." *American Journal of Psychiatry*. 142:950-953, August 1985.

Hallucinogenic/Psychedelic Drugs

The origins of bufotenine have been isolated to the glands of toads and the seeds of the plant Piptadenia peregrina. South American Indians have long used these seeds to prepare a psychotropic snuff called "cohoba."

One other known method of use is intravenous injection. Intravenously, psychotic episodes and cardiovascular effects of short duration have occurred with the intensity being directly proportional to the dose of injection.

DET - DIMETHYLTRYPTAMINE

DET is a synthetic derivative of tryptamine similar in action to the chemically-related DMT.[32] In the United States, DET and DMT are manufactured in clandestine laboratories. Both drugs are usually smoked, although they can be injected. DET and DMT in powdered form are ineffective when taken orally. Nevertheless, these drugs do become absorbed through the mucous linings of the nose and throat. In the United States, DET and DMT are known as the "Businessman's LSD."

STP - 2, 5-DIMETHOXY-4-METHYLAMPHETAMINE

STP is chemically related to mescaline and amphetamine. Studies indicate that STP will produce hallucinogenic effects in doses greater than 3 mg. and mild euphoria in lower doses.[33] One report indicated a 2 mg. dose would produce a mild reaction lasting up to four hours, while 3.2 mg. would produce pronounced hallucinogenic effects lasting up to ten hours. Another study found that doses in excess of 5 mg. always produced marked hallucinogenic effects whose intensity and duration were related to the dose. Some reports claim that this drug could produce hallucinogenic reactions lasting up to 72 hours and could be intensified with the use of chlorpromazine. STP is 100 times more potent as LSD. Black market preparations of this drug are estimated to contain 10 mg. in each dosage unit.

The pharmacological effects of STP include pupillary dilation, increased pulse rate, increased systolic blood pressure, slight temperature increases, moderate euphoria, and slight perceptual distortion.

Toxic effects include nausea, sweating, paresthesia (prickling or itching sensation), and tremors. Perceptual changes include blurred vision, multiple images, vibration of objects, visual hallucinations, distorted shapes, enhancement of details, slowed passage of time, and increased perception of contrasts. According to reports from several hospitals, many persons who have used STP have suffered severe physical reactions as well.

Slang terms for STP include "serenity," "tranquillity," "peace," and "DOM."

MORNING GLORY SEEDS

Morning glory seeds have long been used as a psychotropic substance. These seeds were used extensively by South American civilizations

---

[32] Siegel, R.K. and M.E. Jarvik. "DMT Self-Administration." *Bulletin of the Psychonomic Society.* 16:117-120, 1980.

[33] Joffe, M. "Behavioral Effects of STP." Rpt. in R. Harris (ed.). *Drug Dependence.* Austin: University of Texas Press, 1970.

hundreds of years ago. Morning glory came into its own in the United States in the early 1960s when a series of scientific articles were published demonstrating the similarities between morning glory and LSD. The popular and "beat" press provided complete coverage; it would have been rare to find any individual who had not heard of the marvelous seeds.

Morning glory seeds contain lysergic acid amide, an alkaloidal derivative about one-tenth as potent as LSD. The seeds can be prepared as a tea or chewed to obtain the desired hallucinatory effect. Emesis, diarrhea, and dizziness are frequent accompanying reactions. Suicides have also been reported.

Morning Glory and Hawaiian Woodrose

In the 1960s, certain members of the common morning glory family were discovered to have psychedelic properties similar to those of LSD-25. Some of these plant seeds include "Heavenly Blue," "Pearly Gates," and their close relatives, the Hawaiian baby woodroses, Argyria nervosa and Ipomoea tuberosa. The psychoactive principles of these plants comprise several forms of lysergic acid amide, chiefly ergine (d-lysergic acid amide) and iso-ergine, 5 to 10 percent as strong as LSD. These are called "ergot-alkaloids," since they are identical to the psychotropic LSD-type alkaloids found in ergot fungus. It is estimated that 100 morning glory seeds, or four to eight Hawaiian baby woodrose seeds, are equivalent to 100 micrograms of LSD.

Although ergot-alkaloid producing morning glories grow in many parts of the world, their ritual use as drugs has been confined to Mexico and Central America. The most notable morning glories used for ritual purposes were the Aztec divine plant, ololiuqui (Rivea corymbosa) and the Mexican Indian drug, tlitiltzin or badoh negro, derived from Ipomoea violacea. These species of morning glory are cultivated in several ornamental varieties that include "Heavenly Blue," "Pearly Gates," and "Flying Saucer."

Modern use of these plants for their psychedelic properties began in the late 1950s and mid-1960s. In 1959 Dr. Albert Hoffman, the chemist who first synthesized LSD-25 from ergot fungus in 1942, isolated the lysergic acid amides in ololiuqui seeds. The psychoactive potential of Hawaiian baby woodrose was introduced to the public in 1965 in a scientific paper crediting these seeds with several times the potency of morning glory seeds.

Only the seeds of these plants are ingested. They are eaten whole, ground and eaten, or leached with water before drinking. Despite wide interest in the seeds, use has never been widespread and has declined in recent years. Woodrose seed use reached its zenith in the late 1960s and early 1970s; it was never extensive, but rather served as a substitute, albeit a poor one, for LSD when LSD was scarce and more desirable entheogens were unavailable.

The three primary liabilities of these hallucinogens are lack of potency, a rapid onset of tolerance, and the abdominal cramping that seems to inevitably accompany a psychedelic dose. The cramping, nausea and frequent diarrhea that accompany use of these seeds gave rise to a street belief that they either contained strychnine naturally, or were coated with poison by seed companies to discourage ingestion. The general feeling among users is that the trip is not worth the side effects.

Given the low potency of the seeds, physical distress is much more probable than psychological disruption. However, panic reactions and other psychedelic bad-trip symptoms may occur, especially in users who are unfamiliar with psychedelic effects. For adverse reactions, a talk-down similar to that used for LSD bad trips is effective. Be supportive and comforting. Remind the user that the drug's effects usually last less than six hours. Overdose victims should be taken to an emergency room or poison center.

Slang terms for morning glory include "Heavenly Blue," "Pearly Gates," "Flying Saucers," and "Elephant Creeper."

MDA (methylenedioxyamphetamine)

The Federal government has judged MDA to be a drug with high abuse potential and no redeeming therapeutic value. It is a Schedule I controlled substance on the list with heroin and LSD. There have been reports of death and serious injury from high doses of MDA, but the reported incidents have often been the result of an interaction of multiple drugs; occasionally the injuries or death were caused by other substances sold as MDA on the illicit market.

MDA has been on the street since 1967, when it first appeared in the Haight-Ashbury area of San Francisco, California. MDA and several of its close analogs, including MMDA and MDMA, are currently experiencing an upsurge in street popularity.

MDA is one of a family of drugs whose members are amphetamine analogs of the psychedelic drug, mescaline (methoxylated phenylethylamine). This group contains more than a thousand different but related chemical substances. Only a few dozen have been tested on human beings. A few hundred have been tested on animals. The known analogs include: MDA, MMDA, DOM, DOET, TMA, DMA and DMMDA. All of these are similar in chemical structure and effect. They differ mostly in dosage and duration of effect. For example, an average MDA dosage is 100 to 150 milligrams and its duration is eight to 12 hours. On the other hand, DOM (known on the street as STP), is potent at five milligrams and can last from 16 to more than 24 hours. With the latter, the effects of a high dose can last so long, ebbing and returning, that the user may think they will never end.

Although MDA and its analogs are synthetic, they are related to safrole, which is contained in oil of sassafras and oil of camphor; safrole is also the psychoactive agent in nutmeg and mace. The analogs are produced by modifying the major psychoactive components of nutmeg and mace into their amines.

MDA belongs to a category of drugs known as psychotomimetic amphetamines, which combine the stimulant effects of amphetamines and the psychedelic effects of drugs like mescaline. Large doses of MDA elevate heart rate and blood pressure, and can cause an irregular heartbeat. After high-dose MDA ingestion, there have been individual reports of cerebral aneurysm or stroke occurring as a consequence of the elevated blood pressure. In these cases, however, the victims have been predisposed to stroke because of previous cerebral aneurysm or congenital defect of the blood vessels in the brain. In women, MDA may activate latent infections or other problems of the genito-urinary tract.

With respect to MDA's psychological toxicity, some people can suffer panic reactions or "bad trips," as with other psychedelic drugs; some users mistake the increased heart rate for a heart attack, thus developing "cardiac anxiety," which increases the panic reaction.

Descriptions of MDA's psychological effects tend to sound like the fulfillment of a psychedelic user's fantasy. Users have reported the onset as a warm glow spreading through their bodies, followed by a sense of physical and mental well-being that gradually but steadily intensifies. Some users have described a sense of increased coordination and an ability to do things they could not ordinarily do. Unlike most stimulants, however, MDA does not increase motor activity; in fact, it suppresses motor coordination. Thus, consumers of MDA can sometimes sit in meditation, or do yoga and related activities, for long periods of time.

In their book, *Psychedelic Drugs Reconsidered,* researchers Grinspoon and Bakalar concluded that MDA produces feelings of aesthetic delight, empathy, serenity, joy, insight and self-awareness, without perceptual changes, loss of control or de-personalization. MDA also appears to eliminate anxiety and defensiveness. At one point, Grinspoon and Bakalar write: "The user actually feels himself to be a child, and relives childhood experiences in full immediacy, while simultaneously remaining aware of his present self and present reality."

MDA and MMDA showed great promise as an adjunct to psychotherapy in extensive research carried out in the late 1960s and early 1970s. In the mid-1970s, with MDA's inclusion as a Schedule I "narcotic," research on the methoxylated amphetamines came to a standstill.[34]

Several psychiatrists have reported that MDMA may "enhance emotion." and "feelings of empathy" and thus serve as an adjunct in psychotherapy.[35] Studies demonstrating that MDMA can be self-administered in non-human primates suggest that the drug may have high abuse potential in humans.[36] These reports are particularly disturbing as researchers have found that MDMA is a potent neurotoxin that appears to cause selective degeneration

---

[34] Barnes, D.M. "Ecstasy Returns to Schedule I." *Science.* 240:24, 1988.

[35] Greer, G. and R. Tolbert. "Subjective Reports of the Effects of MDMA in a Clinical Setting." *Journ. of Psychoactive Drugs.* 18:319-327, 1986.

[36] Bardsley, P.M. et al. "Self-Administration of MDMA by Rhesus Monkeys." *Drug and Alcohol Dependence.* 19:149-157, 1986.

Tomb, R.J. and R.R. Griffith. "Self-Administration of MDMA in the Baboon." *Psychopharmacology.* 91:268-272, 1987.

of brain serotonin neurons.[37] This effect of MDMA is comparable to that reported for its structural analog, MDA.[38]

It should be noted that, in the case of MDA, the synthetic substance is more benign than the natural one. Nutmeg and mace do have some psychoactive properties, but the after effects are dire enough to make these poor drugs of choice.

MDA can be toxic to certain individuals. Typical toxic symptoms are skin reactions, profuse sweating, and confusion. Some of the more serious cases resulted in aphasia and, in one case, death. This serious neurological toxicity is a result of elevated blood pressure and effects on the brain associated with higher doses.

If such problems develop, medical care is required; anti-hypertensive medication and neurological care may be necessary. Anxiety, panic or paranoid reactions can usually be handled by reassurance in a supportive environment. Occasionally, sedative medication such as Valium is recommended.

Anti-psychotic medication is not needed unless a prolonged psychotic reaction occurs. This usually happens only in individuals who have major underlying psychological problems prior to taking MDA. In these rare cases, prolonged psychiatric care may be needed.

Slang terms for MDA include the "Love Drug" and "Psychedelic Speed."

MDMA (3,4-methylenedioxymethamphetamine)

Effective on July 1, 1985 MDMA became a Schedule I drug under the Federal Control Substance Act.

3,4-methylenedioxymethamphetamine (MDMA) is a close structural analog of 3,4-methylenedioxyamphetamine (MDA) which is also in Schedule I of the CSA. Like MDA, MDMA is structurally related to amphetamine and methamphetamine (Schedule II), mescaline, STP, PMA, and TMA (Schedule I) in addition to other Schedule I hallucinogens. MDMA was first patented by E. Merck in Germany in 1914.

MDMA has no currently accepted medical use in the United States since the FDA has no investigational new drug (IND) or new drug applications (NDA) or approvals on file for this substance. There is no manufacturer of MDMA registered with the FDA. Several psychiatrists and therapists are using MDMA in their practices as an adjunct to psychotherapy without FDA approval. These individuals are either making MDMA themselves or obtaining it from chemists.

---

[37] Battaglia, G. et al. "MDMA-Induced Neurotoxicity: Degeneration and Recovery of Brain Serotonin Neurons." *Pharmacol. Biochem. Behav.* 29:269-274, 1988.

[38] Stone, D.M. et al. "The Effects of MDMA and MDA on the Monoaminergic Systems in the Rat Brain." *Eur. Journ. of Pharmacol.* 128:41-48, 1986.

Souza, E. and G. Battaglia. "Effects of MDMA and MDA on Brain Serotonin Neurons." Rpt. in *Pharmacology and Toxicology of Amphetamine and Related Designer Drugs.* NIDA Research Monograph Series 94, Rockville, MD, 1989. pp. 196-222.

Although chemically related, MDMA has never been proven to have the hallucinogenic properties that its analog MDA possesses nor the stimulating effect that is associated with methamphetamine usage. MDMA was first developed as an appetite suppressant by E. Merck and Company, but was never marketed. In the recent past it had been used by therapists in psychotherapy and marriage counseling because it was said to have few negative side effects; it eased psychic trauma and broke down barriers to communication between individuals. Normal therapeutic dosages range between 100 to 150 mg. with the onset of effects occurring 25 to 30 minutes after intake and lasting up to one hour.

MDMA is available in most sections of the country as evidenced by its identification in submissions of drug evidence to DEA, state/local, and anonymous testing laboratories. MDMA has been identified in drug submissions from 21 states ranging from New England to Florida, the South, Midwest, and the West Coast. Over 70,000 dosage units of MDMA have been analyzed by forensic laboratories since 1978. Since January 1984, anonymous testing laboratories in Florida and California have received more nationwide submissions of MDMA (29) than MDA (21).

MDMA is found in tablet, capsule, and powder form. The average dose is between 50 and 110 mg. Street prices currently range from $8 to $20 per dosage unit or $70 to $100 per gram. MDMA is sold as MDM, Ecstasy, XTC, ADAM, essence, cocaine, or MDA. A recent sample obtained in New York contained MDMA and PCP. Price quotations for MDMA are now included in *High Times* magazine, along with the prices of marijuana, LSD, cocaine, and hashish.

MDMA is synthesized in clandestine laboratories using methods and chemicals analogous to those used to produce MDA and methamphetamine. The DEA has seized five clandestine laboratories either producing or having the necessary chemicals to produce MDMA; three of the seizures have occurred since 1982.[39] These laboratories had the capacity to produce kilogram quantities of MDMA on a routine basis; over two kilograms of finished product were found at the laboratories.

The street sale and use of MDMA is promoted through the distribution of pamphlets and circulars entitled "Ecstasy, Everything Looks Wonderful When You're Young and on Drugs," "Flight Instructions for a Friend Using XTC," "Ecstasy, 21st Century Entheogen," "How to Prepare for an Ecstasy Experience," and "Reflections on the Nature & Use of XTC."

MMDA

MMDA is chemically known as 5-methoxy-3,4-methylenedioxy amphetamine and is obtained from nutmeg. Initial intoxication occurs at about one mg./kg. of body weight. Increased dosage merely prolongs the duration of the drug-induced episode. MMDA is approximately three times stronger than mescaline.

---

[39] Drug Enforcement Administration, Forensic Science Section. *Microgram*. Vol. XXV, No. 1, Jan. 1992.

BETEL NUT

More than 200 million people in the world chew a mixture of substances called betel nut. Although this substance is not illegal, it does present some potential heath complications.

What Is Betel Nut?

Betel nut is an ancient substance with notation in manuscripts dating back to before 600 A.D. It has been widely used in different parts of the Arab world; it was also an important aspect of the economy and social life in India, Malaysia, the Phillippines, and New Guinea. Betel nut was probably brought to Europe by Marco Polo in 1300 and was soon discovered to be an important commodity in the Western Pacific, since it was a source of taxation for the Dutch in the mid-1600s.

In western societies, there were numerous over-the-counter drug uses of betel nut and its ingredients. Probably the most interesting dates back to at least 1842 when the practice of including betel nut in toothpaste began in England. This substance was touted as an important way to prevent tooth decay, a claim that is probably accurate, although much larger doses than those found in toothpaste are required to be clinically effective. It was also said that this ingredient would help strengthen the tooth enamel and remove tartar, claims of questionable value. This drug and its component substances have also been used medically as a purgative and as a treatment for worm infestation in animals.

The major use is, of course, as a recreational drug. It is almost always consumed by chewing a mixture of ingredients called a quid. While the component substances differ in various regions of the world, all of the forms contain fresh chunks or dried powdered forms of the nut of the betel palm (Areca catechu), a plant growing between 18 and 27 feet high. Forms of the betel nut mixture used for children frequently contained only the husk of the nut, while the full strength form for adults included the nut itself.

The second ingredient of the quid is either a form of peppermint, mustard, or part of the shrub-like or climbing pepper plant vine (Piper betel). The latter is frequently consumed as either the leaf, bean, or the bark of the plant.

All forms of consumption of betel nut also require a third ingredient, slaked lime. This ingredient is usually produced from limestone or by burning sea shells or coral stones in the presence of water. This process produces calcium hydroxide, usually consumed as a white powder.

While all forms of recreationally used betel nut have some of these 3 components, other ingredients are frequently added. In India, tobacco is mixed with the quid. Some regions also incorporate spices, dyes, and some aromatic ingredients.

The combination of nut, mustard or vine, lime, and other ingredients creates an alkaline bitter-tasting mixture that is then chewed. The chewed paste generates large amounts of saliva and creates a red color that stains the teeth. Like tobacco chewers, betel nut consumers spit out the excess juices.

Patterns of Betel Nut Use

Consumption can occur in a variety of patterns. Some individuals chew from morning till night. Others use it as more of a social ceremony, not unlike the consumption of alcohol in western countries. In areas such as Paupa, New Guinea, betel nut mixtures are often offered before dinner as an "appetizer" or after dinner as a dessert.

Effects of Betel Nut Consumption

The major active ingredient in betel nut is arecoline, present in a concentration estimated to be 0.25 percent. The mixture also contains small amounts of pilocarpine and muscarine. These three ingredients are all natural plant products that act in the body in a manner similar to the normal brain neurotransmitter, acetylcholine. In the presence of calcium hydroxide, arecoline is also converted to another psychoactive substance, arecaidine.

Chewing produces immediate effects that in some ways resemble those of nicotine; however, the effects of betel nut are likely to continue for hours. These effects include euphoria, general arousal, and slight physical stimulation. The result is sometimes perceived as a decrease in tiredness and a blunting of irritability.

Although betel nut does not produce hallucinations, it does have acetylcholine-like actions in the brain. With respect to its neuro-chemical effects, betel nut can therefore be classified under the category of acetylcholine psychedelics. Compunds in this category are derived from plants such as jimpson-weed, thorn apple, and mushrooms. Like the compounds from other acetylcholine psychedelics, betel nuts in large doses can produce sweating, an increase in the production of saliva, an increase in breathing rate, and tearing of the eyes (lacrimation). The effects on the digestive tract include a decrease in appetite and, especially if the drug is taken on an empty stomach, diarrhea. All of these effects can be blocked by the anti-acetylcholine drug, atropine.

Dangers of Betel Nut Consumption

The acetylcholine-type drugs, especially muscarine, can be deadly when taken in high doses. In fact, muscarine is the active ingredient in some forms of lethal mushroom poisoning. It is unlikely, however, that the mixture of any of these plant products in betel nut preparations are potent enough to cause lethal overdoses.

The most prominent dangers associated with betel nut chewing are a combined effect of the active ingredients and the lime on the gums. The first and most frequently observed changes are white plaques in the mucosal lining of the mouth or on the tongue, called leukoplakia. This is a pre-cancerous lesion and often leads to a very aggressive and serious tumor, squamous cell carcinoma, that can subsequently invade the muscles and bone. It is estimated that the rate of developing this cancer among regular betel nut users might be as high as 7 percent. An additional area of high risk for potentially lethal cancers is the esophagus.

One other problem associated with betel nut chewing is a fiber formation (fibrosis) that occurs just beneath the gums. This is called oral submucous fibrosis, a problem estimated to be seen in mild forms in up to one-half of chronic betel nut chewers. This condition usually has a very slow onset; if use continues it is irreversible, untreatable, and likely to become progressively worse. The changes of this condition are observed within the mouth, but can also be seen in the back of the throat, or larynx. The major finding involves a stiffness of the mouth's lining, a condition that can become so severe that it interferes with the ability to eat. This health complication appears to result from changes in the elasticity of the mouth's tissues. Associated problems are a burning sensation in the mouth, ulcers, blisters, or dryness of the mouth's lining, and a decrease in the ability to taste.

There is little doubt that this substance can produce fairly intense *psychological dependence.* Individuals can develop a pattern of constant use, feeling unhappy and incomplete if they cannot get their betel nut. They are also likely to feel as if they cannot work properly without it, and can spend a great deal of time and money in order to obtain betel nut mixtures. It appears less likely that there is a prominent and identifiable form of physical withdrawal.

Betel nut consumption can also be viewed as a public health hazard. Since the saliva created by chewing is usually spit onto the streets, it is often considered a "public nuisance." This spitting is also felt to increase the spread of diseases such as tuberculosis, especially considering that widespread consumption of betel nut occurs in countries where these diseases are common.

Implications of Betel Nut Consumption for the United States

The DEA Lab in Chicago, Illinois recently received 3 pounds of a betel mixture. The chewable form consisted of the climbing pepper (piper betel) wrapped around or mixed with a whole betel nut (from the betel palm tree) and lime.

As immigration from the Western Pacific continues, U.S. law enforcement officers are likely to see increasing numbers of people who consume betel nuts. This phenomenon is especially likely to occur among individuals who come from the Phillippines, India, Sri Lanka, Malaysia, and Vietnam. The easiest way to identify a chronic user is by observing a red stain on the teeth.

REFERENCES:

Abraham, H.D. "Visual Phenomenology of the LSD Flashback." *Archives of General Psychiatry.* 40:884-889, 1983.

Abramson, H.A. "Lysergic Acid Diethylamide (LSD-25) as an Adjunct to Psychotherapy." *Journ. of Psychology.* 39:127, 1955.

Allen, R. and S. Young. "Phencyclidine: Induced Psychosis." *Am. Journ. of Psychiatry.* 135:1081-1083, 1978.

Alrozi, J. and K. Verebey. "MDMA Biological Disposition in Man: MDA is a Biotransformation Product." NIDA, Research Monograph Series 90, Rockville, MD, 1988.

Axelrod, J. et al. "The Distribution and Metabolism of Lysergic Acid Diethylamide." *Arch. Int. Pharmacol.* 120:292, 1959.

Bailey, D. "Phencyclidine Abuse." *Am. Journ of Clinical Pathology.* 72:795-799, 1979.

Bardsley, P.M. et al. "Self-Administration of MDMA by Rhesus Monkeys." *Drug and Alcohol Dependence.* 19:149-157, 1986.

Barnes, D.M. "Ecstasy Returns to Schedule I." *Science.* 240:24, 1988.

________. "New Data Intensify the Agony over Ecstasy." *Science.* 239:864-866, 1988.

Battaglia, G. et al. "MDMA-Induced Neurotoxicity: Degeneration and Recovery of Brain Serotonin Neurons." *Pharmacol. Biochem. Behav.* 29:269-274, 1988.

Baumgartner, W. "Hair Analysis for Drugs of Abuse." *Journ. of Forensic Sciences.* 34:1433-1453, 1989. Rpt. in *The Narc Officer.* International Narcotics Enforcement Officers Association. Sept. 1990. pp. 14-16.

Beecher, D., et al. "Betel nut chewing in the United States." *J. Indiana Dental Association.* 64:42-44, 1985.

________. *Clinical Toxicology.* Vol. 9, Issue 4, 1976.

________. *American Journal of Psychiatry.* 142:950-953, August 1985.

Block, W. "Pharmacological Aspects of Mescaline." M. Renkel and H.C. Denber (eds.). *Chemical Concepts of Psychosis.* New York: McDowell Obolensky, 1968.

Blum, Richard H. *Utopiates: The Use and Users of LSD-25.* New York: Atherton Press, 1964.

Burns, S. and S. Lerner. "Causes of Phencyclidine-Related Death." *Clinical Toxicology.* 12:463-481, 1978.

Cohen, Sidney. *The Beyond Within: The LSD Story.* New York: Athenum, 1964.

Cole, J.O., and M.M. Katz. "The Psychotomimetic Drugs." *JAMA.* 187:758-761, 1964.

De Bald, R. and R. Leaf. *LSD, Man, and Society.* Connecticut: Wesleyan University Press, 1968.

Drug Enforcement Administration, Forensic Science Section. *Microgram.* Vol. XXV, No. 1, Jan. 1992.

________. *Microgram.* Vol. XXV, No. 2, Feb. 1992.

________. *Microgram.* Vol. XXV, No.3, March 1992.

________. *Microgram.* Vol. XXV, No. 5, May 1992.

________. *Microgram.* Vol. XXV, No. 7, July 1992.

Fischer, R. "Sympathetic Excitation of Biological Chronometry." *Int. Journ. of Neuropsychiatry.* 2:116-121, 1966.

Fischer, R. et al. "Personality Traits: Dependent Performance Under Psilocybin." *Diseases of the Nervous System.* 31:91-101, 1970.

Giarman, N.J. and D. Freedman. "Biochemical Aspects of Actions of Psychotomimetic Drugs." *Pharmacological Review.* Vol. 17 (1):1-25, 1965.

Greer, G. and R. Tolbert. "Subjective Reports of the Effects of MDMA in a Clinical Setting." *Journ. of Psychoactive Drugs.* 18:319-327, 1986.

Grinspoon, L. and J. Bakalar. *Psychedelic Drugs Reconsidered.* New York: Basic Books, 1979.

Heim, R. et al. "Botanical and Chemical Characteristics of a Forensic Mushroom Specimen of the Genus Psilocybe." *Journ. of Forensic Science Society.* 6:192-210, 1966.

Huxley, Aldous. *The Doors of Perception: Heaven and Hell.* New York: Harper and Row, 1963.

Hallucinogenic/Psychedelic Drugs

Joffe, M. "Behavioral Effects of STP." Rpt. in R. Harris (ed.). *Drug Dependence.* Austin: University of Texas Press, 1970.

Johnson, K.M. "Neurochemical Pharmacology of Phencyclidine." R.C. Peterson and R. Stillman (eds.). *Phencyclidine Abuse: An Appraisal.* NIDA Report. Rockville, MD: 1978.

Kluver, H. *Mescal and Mechanisms of Hallucinations.* Chicago: University of Chicago Press, 1966.

LaBarre, W. *The Peyote Cult.* New York: Shocken Books, 1969.

Leonard, B.E. and S.R. Tonge. "Some Effects of an Hallucinogenic Drug (PCP) on Neurohumoral Substances." *Life Sciences.* 9:1141-1152, 1970.

Leuner H., and H. Holfeld. "Psychotherapy Under the Influence of Hallucinogens." *The Physicians Panorama.* 2:13, 1964.

Lindgren, J.E. et al. "The Chemical Identity of Hog—A New Hallucinogen." *American Journal of Pharmacy.* 141:86-90, 1969.

Ling and Buckman. "The Use of Lysergic Acid in Individual Psychotherapy." *Proc-Roy Soc. Med.* 53:927, 1960.

Masters, R. and J. Houston. *The Varieties of Psychedelic Experience.* New York: Holt, Rhinehardt, and Winston, 1966.

Metzner, R. et al. "The Relation of Expectation and Mood to Psilocybin Reactions." *Psychedelic Review.* 5:3-39, 1965.

National Institute on Drug Abuse. "Phencyclidine: An Up-Date." Monograph 64, 1986.

Pelner, L. "Peyote Cult, Mescaline Hallucinations, and Model Psychosis." *New York Journ. of Medicine.* 67:2833-2843, 1967.

PharmChem Laboratories. *PharmChem Newsletter.* Menlo Park, CA, July 1989.

Rainey, J.M., and M.K. Crowder. "Ketamine or Phencyclidine." *JAMA.* 230:824, 1974.

________. "Prevalence of Phencyclidine: Street Drug Preparations." *New England Journ. of Med.* Vol. 290 (8):466-467, 1974.

Reed, A. and A.W. Kene. "Phencyclidine (PCP): Another Illicit Drug." *Journ. of Psychedelic Drugs.* 5:8-12, 1972.

Rothlin, E. "Pharmacology of Lysergic Acid Diethylamide and Some Related Compounds." *J. Pharm and Pharmacol.* 9:569, 1957.

Roseman, B. *The Peyote Story.* Hollywood, CA: Wilshire Books, 1968.

Rosenberg, D.E. et al. "Observations on Direct and Cross-Tolerance with LSD and D-Amphetamine in Man." *Psychopharmacology.* 5:1, 1963.

Savage, C. "Lysergic Acid Diethylamide (LSD-25): A Clinical-Psychological Study." *American Journal of Psychiatry.* 1952.

Schmidt, C.A. "Neurotoxicity of the Psychedelic Amphetamine, Methylenedioxymethamphetamine." *Journ. of Pharmacology and Experimental Therapeutics.* 240:1-7, 1987.

Schullian, D.M. "Toothpastes containing betel nut from England of the 19th century." *Journal of History of Medicine.* 39:65-68, 1984.

Schultes, R.E. and A. Hoffman. *The Botany and Chemistry of the Hallucinogins.* Springfield, IL: Charles E. Thomas Pub., 1973.

Seedat, H.A., et al. *South African Medical Journal.* 74:568-571, 1988.

Shick, F., and D. Smith. "Analysis of the LSD Flashback." *Journal of Psychedelic Drugs*. Educational Off-Print Series. Vol. 3 No. 1, Sept. 1971.

Showalter, C. and W. Thornton. "Clinical Pharmacology of Phencyclidine. *American Journ. of Psychiatry*. 134:1234-1238, 1977.

Siegel, R.K. "The Natural History of Hallucinogens. B.L. Jacobs (ed.). *Hallucinogens: Neurochemical, Behavioral, and Clinical Perspectives*. New York: Raven Press, 1981.

_______. "MDMA: Non-Medical Use and Intoxication." *Journ. of Psychoactive Drugs*. 18:349-354, 1986.

Siegel, R.K. and M.E. Jarvik. "DMT Self-Administration." *Bulletin of the Psychonomic Society*. 16:117-120, 1980.

Silling, S.M., "LSD Flashbacks: An Overview of the Literature from Counselors." *American Mental Health Counselors Association Journal*. January, 1980. p. 39-49.

Souza, E. and G. Battaglia. "Effects of MDMA and MDA on Brain Serotonin Neurons." Rpt. in *Pharmacology and Toxicology of Amphetamine and Related Designer Drugs*. NIDA Research Monograph Series 94, Rockville, MD, 1989. pp. 196-222.

Sramek, J.J. et al. "Hair Analysis for Detection of PCP in Newly Admitted Psychiatric Patients." *American Journal of Psychiatry*. 142:950-953, August 1985.

Steiner, J.E. and F.G. Sulman. "Simultaneous Studies of Blood Sugar, Behavioral Changes and EEG on the Wake Rabbit after Administration of Psilocybin." *Arch. Int. Pharm.* 145:301-308, 1963.

Stone, D.M. et al. "The Effects of MDMA and MDA on the Monoaminergic Systems in the Rat Brain." *Eur. Journ. of Pharmacol.* 128:41-48, 1986.

Talonu, N.T. "Observations on betel nut use, habituation, addiction, and carcinogenesis." *Papua New Guinea Medical Journal*. 32:195-197, 1989.

Taufa, T. "Betel nut chewing and pregnancy." *Papua New Guinea Medical Journal*. 31:229-233, 1988.

Tennant, Forest Jr. *Research Studies in Phencyclidine (PCP)*. West Covina, CA: Veract, Inc., 1986.

Tennant, Forest S. *Medico-Legal Identification of the Phencyclidine (PCP) User.* West Covina CA: Community Health Projects, Inc., 1983.

Tomb, R.J. and R.R. Griffith. "Self-Administration of MDMA in the Baboon." *Psychopharmacology*. 91:268-272, 1987.

Ungerleider, T.J. *The Problems and Prospects of LSD*. Illinois: Charles C. Thomas, 1970.

Wasson, R.G. *Soma: Divine Mushroom of Immortality*. New York: Harcourt, 1968.

_______. "The Hallucinogenic Fungi of Mexico." *Botanical Museum Leaflet*. 19:137-162, 1961.

_______. "The Hallucinogenic Mushrooms of Mexico and Psilocybin: A Bibliography." *Botanical Museum Leaflet*. 20:25-73, 1963.

_______. "PCP (Phencyclidine): The New Delusionogen." *Educational Off-Print Series*. Madison Wisconsin: Stash Press, 1975.

_______. "Science and Medicine." *San Jose Mercury News*. 16 June, 1992.

CHAPTER XII

CANNABIS (MARIJUANA)

HISTORY

The first known textual reference to marijuana in India can be found in the *Atharva Veda,* which may date as far back as the second millennium B.C. Early references to cannabis also appear on certain cuneiform tablets unearthed in the Royal Library of Ashurbanipal, an Assyrian king. Ashurbanipal lived about 650 B.C.

In Asia, the use of cannabis can be traced to the Chinese text, *Herbal* (circa 1200 B.C.), in which the drug was described as a surgical anesthetic. Most likely, cannabis was used for other purposes as well. In 1090, Marco Polo returned from China with tales of a Persian religious cult that used hashish to induce visions of Paradise for cult members. The cult-leader, called the "Old Man of the Mountain," recruited men who were given the drug, subjected to ethereal pleasures and then sent on suicide missions of political murder. The promise of Paradise persuaded the recruits to commit the assigned crimes and assured their return. Although these recruited hit-men were called "hashishin" (etymological source of our word assassin), the legend has it that they were never permitted to use the drug during their acts of murder.

The ancient Greeks, on the other hand, used alcohol rather than marijuana as an intoxicant, but they traded with marijuana-eating and marijuana-inhaling peoples. Hence, some of the references to drugs in Homer may be to marijuana—including Homer's reference to the drug which Helen brought to Troy from Egyptian Thebes.

The date on which marijuana was introduced into western Europe is not known, but it must have been very early. An urn containing marijuana leaves and seeds, unearthed near Berlin, Germany, is believed to date from 500 B.C.

The first definite record of the marijuana plant in the New World dates from 1545 A.D., when the Spaniards introduced it into Chile. It has been suggested, however, that African slaves familiar with marijuana as an intoxicant and medicine brought the seeds with them to Brazil even earlier in the sixteenth century.

There is no record that the Pilgrims brought marijuana with them to Plymouth, but the Jamestown settlers did bring the plant to Virginia in 1611 and cultivated it for its fiber. Later, in 1629, marijuana was introduced into New England. From then until after the Civil War, the marijuana plant was a major crop in North America and played an important role in both colonial and national economic policy. In 1762, Virginia awarded bounties for hemp culture and manufacture; the state also imposed penalties upon those who did not produce it.

Three years later, in 1765, George Washington was growing hemp at Mount Vernon—presumably for its fiber, though it has been argued that Washington was also concerned with increasing the medicinal or intoxicating potency of his marijuana plants.

At various times in the nineteenth century large hemp plantations flourished in such states as Mississippi, Georgia, California, South Carolina, and Nebraska. Hemp was also grown on Staten Island, New York. However, the center of nineteenth-century production was in Kentucky, where hemp was introduced in 1775.

The major factors contributing to the decline of hemp cultivation in the United States were the invention of the cotton gin, other cotton and wool machinery, and competition from cheap imported hemp.

The decline in commercial production did not, however, mean that marijuana became scarce. As late as 1937, the American commercial crop was still estimated at 10,000 acres, much of it located in Wisconsin, Illinois, and Kentucky. At this time, four million pounds of marijuana seed were being used each year in bird feed. During World War II, commercial cultivation was greatly expanded at the behest of the United States Department of Agriculture, to meet the shortage of imported hemp for rope. Even decades after commercial cultivation had been discontinued, hemp could be found as a weed growing luxuriantly in abandoned fields and along road sides. Indeed, the plant spreads readily to different territories. In 1969, the total area of Nebraska's land infested with "weed" marijuana was estimated at 156,000 acres.[1]

EARLY RECREATIONAL USE OF MARIJUANA IN THE UNITED STATES

Marijuana was readily available in the United States through much of the nineteenth and early twentieth centuries; its effects were known; and it was somtimes used for recreational purposes. But use was at best limited, local, and temporary. Not until after 1920 did marijuana come into general use, and not until the 1960s did it become a popular drug.

Rather than a change in the drug itself or a change in human nature, it was a change in the law that stimulated the large-scale marketing of marijuana for recreational use in the United States. When the Eighteenth Amendment and the Volstead Act of 1920 raised the price of alcoholic beverages, made alcohol less convenient to secure, and made it inferior in quality, there sprang up a substantial commercial trade in marijuana for recreational use.

Evidence for such a trade comes from New York City, where marijuana "tea pads" were established in 1920. These "pads" resembled opium dens or speakeasies, except that the prices of marijuana were very low compared to the price of opium. A patron could get high on marijuana for a quarter in the marijuana pad, or for even less if the marijuana was purchased at the door

---

[1] National Commission on Marijuana and Drug Abuse. Raymond P. Shafer, Chairman. *Marijuana — A Signal of Misunderstandings.* New York: New American Library, 1972.

then taken away to smoke. It was said that most of the marijuana for these pads was harvested from supplies growing wild on Staten Island or in New Jersey and other nearby states. Domestic supplies were used because the marijuana and hashish imported from North Africa were more potent and were, therefore, more expensive. Much like the speakeasies of the time, these marijuana tea pads were tolerated by the city of New York. By the 1930s, there were said to be 500 of them in New York City alone.

MARIJUANA LAWS SINCE THE 1930s

Due to the legalization of weak beer in 1933 and the return of hard liquor the following year, the modest, localized popularity of marijuana during the Prohibition years may have declined some. The most important changes, however, resulted from legal intervention.

On January 1, 1932, the newly-established Federal Bureau of Narcotics, a unit in the Treasury Department, assumed responsibility for the enforcement of Federal anti-opiate and anti-cocaine laws. As these responsibilities were taken over from the Alcohol Unit of the Treasury Department, former Assistant Prohibition Commissioner Harry J. Anslinger took over as commissioner of narcotics. Commissioner Anslinger had no legal jurisdiction over marijuana, but his interest in it was intense. The Bureau's first annual report under his aegis warned that marijuana, dismissed as a minor problem by the Treasury one year earlier, had now come into wide and increasing abuse in many states. As a result of increasing abuse, the report also states that the Bureau of Narcotics had been endeavoring to impress on the various states the urgent need for vigorous enforcement of the local cannabis laws.

During his first year as commissioner of narcotics, Anslinger secured from the National Conference of Commissioners on Uniform Drug Laws the draft of a "Uniform Anti-Narcotics Act." This act was designed for adoption by state legislatures. The conference failed to include a ban on marijuana in the main text of this "model law," but it did supply to the states an "optional text" in addition to the basic act. Subsequently, state after state adapted the model legislation and began to enforce marijuana laws.

Later, Commissioner Anslinger continued to encourage states to adopt rigid marijuana laws. His 1935 report sent the following message to states:

> In the absence of Federal legislation on the subject, the States and cities should rightfully assume the responsibility for providing vigorous measures for the extinction of this lethal weed, and it is therefore hoped that all public-spirited citizens will earnestly enlist in the movement urged by the Treasury Department to adjure intensified enforcement of marijuana laws.[2]

By 1937, forty-six of the forty-eight states—as well as the District of Columbia—had laws against marijuana. Under most of these state laws, marijuana was subject to the same rigorous penalties applicable to morphine, heroin, and cocaine, although marijuana was often erroneously designated a narcotic.

---

[2] Smith, Roger. "U.S. Marijuana Legislation and the Creation of a Social Problem." *Journal of Psychedelic Drugs*. 2(1):93-99, 1968.

Commissioner Anslinger's drive for Federal as well as state anti-marijuana legislation shifted into high gear in 1937, when his superiors in the Treasury Department sent to Congress the draft of a bill that become the Marijuana Tax Act of 1937. Modeled on the Harrison Narcotic Act of 1914, the surface of this bill did not actually ban marijuana. It fully recognized the medicinal uses of the substance, specifying that physicians, dentists, veterinarians, and others could continue to prescribe cannabis if they paid a license fee of $1 per year; that druggists who dispensed the drug should pay a license fee of $15 a year; that growers of marijuana should pay $25 a year; and that importers, manufacturers, and compounders should pay $50 a year. At this time, only the nonmedicinal, untaxed possession or sale of marijuana was outlawed.

Since 1937, restrictive legislation on marijuana has increased in quantity and severity. Most state marijuana laws began to specify that marijuana penalties should be the same as heroin penalties. Thus, as heroin penalties were escalated through the decades, marijuana penalties were also increased. Moreover, the laws of nineteen states made no distinction between mere possession of one marijuana cigarette and the sale of large quantities of heroin. Under both Federal and state laws, as noted earlier, marijuana was designated a narcotic; therefore, marijuana was included in legislation against the "sale" of narcotics such as heroin.

Along with Federal heroin penalties, from time to time Congress escalated Federal marijuana penalties. In 1951, mandatory minimum sentences were fixed for all marijuana offenses and all but first-time offenders were rendered ineligible for suspended sentence or probation. In 1956, the mandatory minimum for a first-offense possession was fixed at two years (with a potential ten-year term). The mandatory minimum for a second-possession offense was fixed at five years (with a potential twenty-year term); second-possession offenders were also denied parole, probation, and suspended sentence. For sale offenses, the mandatory minimum was set at five years for a first offense and ten years for a second, while terms of twenty years for a first offense and forty for a second were possible. Likewise, parole, probation, and suspended sentence were banned for all sales offenses.

On a national scale, anti-marijuana propaganda kept pace with the continuing anti-marijuana legislation after 1939. In its legislation, the United States was vigorously anti-marijuana. Then, in 1970, Federal penalties for marijuana possession were reduced by the Comprehensive Drug Abuse Prevention and Control Act. When the Federal penalties for marijuana possession were reduced, many states followed suit. Since 1970 marijuana laws have been reduced to reflect a more enlightened view of marijuana use in the United States. While the legal trend has been to reduce penalties for possession of marijuana in small amounts, most state laws have retained controls against traffickers and dealers. At present, Federal and several state laws provide misdemeanor penalties for users or simple possessors. Some states are considering further reductions in penalties so that consumers will be charged with only a minor violation.

MARIJUANA USE IN THE UNITED STATES TODAY

Despite 50 years of prohibition against marijuana, recent figures indicate that marijuana is ranked among corn, wheat, and soybeans as one of the four major cash crops grown in the United States in terms of dollar-volume of sales. Some researchers claim that marijuana is the leading cash crop, but the clandestine (often in-door) farming caused by strict marijuana laws makes specific figures impossible to obtain. It is certain, however, that a tremendous amount of marijuana is grown in the United States.[3]

An even larger quantity of marijuana is grown abroad, in Mexico, Colombia, Panama, and Jamaica. This huge quantity of marijuana is then smuggled into the United States on planes, boats, cars, mules, and individuals who sneak across the international borders on foot. Added to the multi-billion-dollar crop grown domestically, imported or smuggled marijuana further contributes to what is, finally, an enormous quantity of marijuana trafficked throughout the United States.

Marijuana is one of the four most commonly used recreational drugs in the United States today; the other substances include ethyl alcohol (beer, wine, and liquor), nicotine (cigarettes, cigars, snuff, and other tobacco products), and caffeine (coffee, tea, and cola-based soft drinks).

Studies show that from 1969 to 1979 the total number of marijuana users increased steadily each year.[4] This total increase includes the number of persons who had ever used marijuana, those who had used it in the past month, and those who were daily users. From 1979 until 1985, however, the numbers in each category declined. For example, marijuana use peaked in 1979 when 11 percent of high school seniors reported using the drug daily or almost daily. This figure declined to 4.9 percent in 1985. Similar patterns have been found in other surveys of marijuana use in both the 1970s and the 1980s.

The reasons for these changes in attitude and behavior are unclear. It may be that knowledge of the health hazards associated with marijuana use has penetrated the using groups; it may also be that users have observed deleterious effects in their peers. The parents' movement (a "grass roots" effort by groups of parents to combat their children's drug use) may also have contributed to these developments. Some other possible factors include a shift to more socially conservative attitudes and the increased popularity of other illicit substances.

Despite the increasing popularity of other drugs such as heroin, in the 1990s, marijuana is still the most popular illegal drug. The pervasive use of marijuana may stem in part from the fact that it is a widely-known substance. One study has documented the tendency of marijuana users to turn others on to the drug, 25 percent within two years of first use, and 29 percent within five or more years of first use.[5] Another startling fact of this drug's popularity is that 66 million Americans have tried it at least once, many of them during its heyday in the 1960s and 1970s. Furthermore, the 1988 National Household Survey on Drug Abuse found that 6.6 million Americans

[3] "Increasing U.S. Pot Crop." *Register Guard.* Eugene, Oregon, January 8, 1985, p. 1A.

[4] Johnston, L.D., P.M. O'Malley, and J.G. Bachman. "Drug use among American high school students, college students, and other young adults." *National Trends Through 1985.* DHHS Pub. No. (ADM) 86-1450. Washington, D.C.: Supt. of Docs., U.S. Govt. Print. Off., 1986.

[5] Voss, H.L. and R.R. Clayton. *International Journal of Addictions.* 19:633-652, 1984.

used marijuana once a week or more, and 11.6 million had used it in the previous month.

This widespread usage has caused some states to increase the penalties in their legislation. Of the 11 states that de-criminalized marijuana possession for personal use during the 1970s, four have reversed course in recent years. For nearly 16 years, Alaska had the nation's most liberal marijuana law, one that gave adults the right to possess in their house less than 4 ounces. That law resulted from a 1975 state Supreme Court decision which said the health threat posed by marijuana was insufficient to warrant government intrusion on the privacy of Alaskans. In 1991, however, possession of a small amount of pot became a misdemeanor in Alaska—punishable by up to 90 days in jail and a $1,000 fine.

William J. Bennett, who resigned after 20 months as national drug control policy director, championed this more strict attitude toward marijuana use and campaigned for Alaska's increased legislation against the drug. Although Bennett told the Associated Press in 1990 that he believed marijuana was no more harmful than alcohol, he rejected legalization. He said: "The last thing I would want to do is recommend the wider use of a drug that makes young people stupid."

Maine, Ohio and Oregon have already tightened marijuana restrictions. Yet, in seven other states—California, Colorado, Minnesota, Mississippi, North Carolina, Nebraska and New York—marijuana arrest is still more akin to a traffic ticket than a criminal charge.

Recent Developments in the Classification of Marijuana

The removal of THC from Schedule I (no medical usefulness, high potential for abuse) to Schedule II (medical usefulness, high potential for abuse) is underway. A THC-containing product to be called Marinol will soon be available to treat the nausea and vomiting associated with cancer chemotherapy. Regardless of this recent development, all other trials of THC as a medicinal agent have not substantiated earlier impressions of its usefulness. Furthermore, THC's effectiveness as an anti-nauseant remains to be seen.

PHYSICAL CHARACTERISTICS OF MARIJUANA

The term "marijuana" commonly refers to the flowering tops and leaves of the plant Cannabis Sativa L. The leaves make identification of the plant very easy. Domestic marijuana leaves are usually green in color, containing a number of serrated leaflets that are 2 to 6 inches in length and pointed at both ends. The flowers of domestic marijuana plants consist of light yellowish-green clusters of oblong seeds.

On the other hand, the leaves of marijuana plants grown in other parts of the world sometimes have a different appearance. They can be brown or slightly red in color, with a number of short, fat leaflets with smooth edges. In any case, the whole cannabis plant, including the leaves and the flowers may attain a height of 20 feet. The term "marijuana" legally refers to:

1. All parts of the plant Cannabis Sativa L., whether growing or not;
2. The seeds of the plant;

3. The resin extracted from the plant (which is also legally referred to as "concentrated cannabis"—whether the resin is crude or purified); and
4. Every compound, manufacture, salt, derivative, mixture, or preparation of the plant, its seeds, or its resin.[6]

This definition from the California Controlled Substance Act (Section 11018 of the Health and Safety Code) does not include the mature stalks of the plant, the oil or cake made from the seeds of the plant, the fiber produced from the stalks, or any other compound, manufacture, salt, derivative, mixture, or preparation of the mature stalks (except the resin extracted therefrom). The definition also excludes the fiber, oil, or cake of the sterilized seed of the plant which is incapable of germination.

Dealers frequently include all parts of the cannabis plant (including the seeds, stems, and stalks) in the marijuana sold on the street. Not surprisingly, "street" marijuana has greatly increased in potency over the past years. Since THC is the active ingredient derived from the resin of cannabis, potency depends on the amount of THC concentrated in the marijuana. Confiscated cannabis in 1975 rarely exceeded 1 percent THC content. By 1987, samples as high as 5 to 15 percent THC content were common and Sinsemilla averaged 6.9 percent THC with some samples as high as 14 percent. Furthermore, "Hash Oil," a marijuana extract distilled from the cannabis leaves, was found to have a THC content of 10 to 40 percent.

FLOWERING TOP OF MARIJUANA PLANT

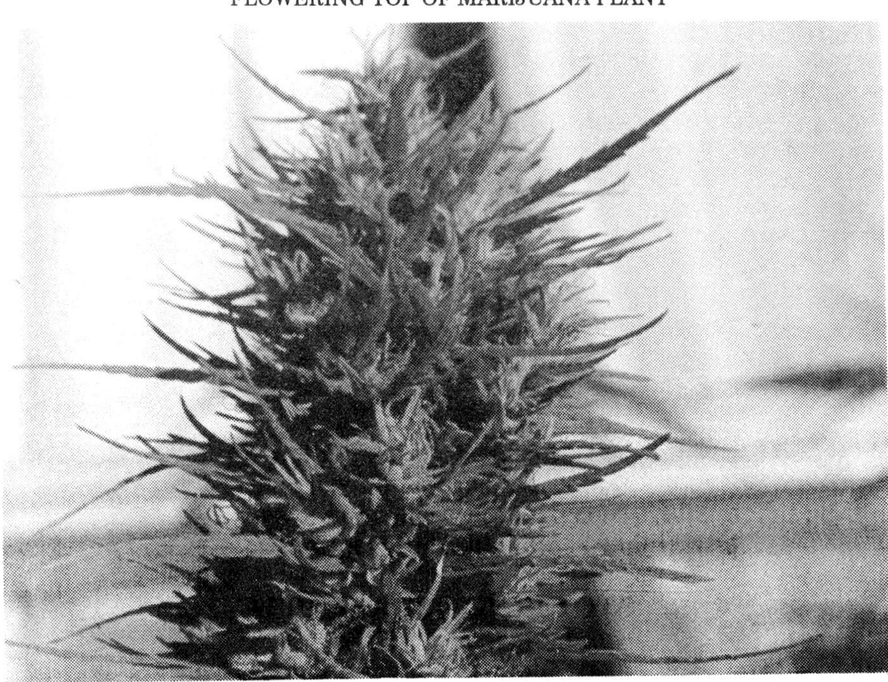

[6] Gould Publications. *Penal Code Handbook of California*. 1992.

The THC content, or potency, is effected by how the cannabis is grown, the amount of sunlight, how the marijuana is prepared, and how it is stored. For example, Sinsemilla is the cultivation of the female cannabis plant absent from the male cannabis plant.

CLASSIFICATIONS OF THC AND MARIJUANA

As mentioned above, the main psychoactive ingredient in the cannabis plant is Trans delta-9 THC (tetrahydrocannabinol). THC is a difficult substance to classify. At low to moderate doses, it is a mild sedative and hypnotic agent; its pharmacological effects resemble alcohol and the anti-anxiety substances (such as Librium and Valium). Unlike the sedatives/hypnotics, however, higher doses of THC may (in addition to sedation) produce psychological effects similar to a mild psychedelic experience. Also unlike the sedatives/hypnotics, higher doses of THC do not produce anesthesia, coma or death.

Marijuana has been classified as a narcotic, a psychedelic and a sedative/hypnotic. Because of the difficulty in correctly classifying the substance, it is often thought that a separate classification entitled "Cannabis" would be most appropriate.

VARIETIES OF CANNABIS

The several forms of the marijuana plant have been variously called "Cannabis Indica," "Cannabis Africana," "Cannabis Americana" and a variety of other names which represent the geographical regions in which the marijuana was grown. The hemp plant of India was once considered to be a distinct species but the most observant botanists, upon comparing it with a plant cultivated in the United States, have been unable to discover any specific difference. Therefore, "Cannabis Indica" is now regarded merely as a geographic variety. Likewise, the many other forms of marijuana are simply geographical varieties of the true species, Cannabis Sativa L.

The California Controlled Substance Act defines marijuana as all parts of the plant Cannabis Sativa L. Thus, only Cannabis Sativa L. is identified in the law. For this reason, many attempts are made to call each variety of the true species anything *but* Cannabis Sativa L. because any other species, if known or determined, would logically be exempted from California statutes. This is one such contention of the growers, sellers, and users of many of the hybrid forms of marijuana such as Sinsemilla.

However, a California Attorney General opinion stated that the true species of marijuana is Cannabis Sativa L. and all the other forms of cannabis are varieties from Cannabis Sativa L. They all contain THC and are all illegal under California law.

Colombian

Colombian marijuana is considerably more expensive than the Mexican-grown variety, but has an average range in THC percentage of 3 to 5 percent. Colombian replaced Mexican marijuana in the early 1970s as the most common commercial marijuana because of its reputation for superior quality. With massive increases in production, quality declined and now many users are interested in the more potent Sinsemilla. Today, Colombia grows many species of marijuana as well as Sinsemilla.

Cannabis (Marijuana)

Mexican

In the 1970s, there was much publicity about Mexican cannabis fields being sprayed with a herbicide called paraquat. Despite this bad press, Mexico is back in business supplying large amounts of marijuana to U.S. customers. Mexico is also growing Sinsemilla.

THAI STICKS

Thai or Thai Sticks

This variety of marijuana is grown in the country of Thailand or its neighboring countries Burma and Laos. These three countries are commonly known by drug traffickers as the "Golden Triangle." These countries grow tremendous amounts of both marijuana and opium and are considered major contributors to the world market. Regardless of which country actually grows the marijuana, it is all referred to as Thai marijuana in this country. The Thai growers cultivate and harvest their marijuana in near-perfect growing conditions. The fertile soil, the weather, and the general geographic factors are highly favorable to cultivation of marijuana. The THC content of Thai marijuana is comparatively high, ranging from 4 to 8 percent. The Thai method of cultivation is to grow marijuana to maturity, and allow the plants to bud and flower. They then harvest these "flowering tops" and separate them from the stalks and leaves of the plant. Even though the resin containing THC is found in all stalks and leaves of the marijuana plant, the highest concentration is always found in the flowering top. The Thai farmer then wraps these "tops" onto small bamboo shoots which are approximately 5 to 7 inches in length. The material which he or she uses to wrap the "tops" onto the shoots or sticks is the stringy material which can be peeled from the stalk of the plants. It is common for the growers or traffickers to wrap 15 to 20 individual Thai sticks into a bundle which weighs approximately one ounce. Again, these bundles are wrapped with the stringy material which is peeled from the stalk.

Sinsemilla

Sinsemilla is a Spanish word meaning "without seeds." This variety of marijuana is cultivated to eliminate seeds from the final product. It is believed that this method of cultivation is the same that is employed in the cultivation of Thailand or Hawaiian-grown marijuana. This process essentially involves isolating the female plants from the males to allow the female plants to mature without being pollinated. The theory, which has reportedly been tested successfully in many climates, is that the female plant puts at least 40 percent of her energy into the production of seeds once it has been pollinated by the male plant. If the female plant is isolated from the male, the energy of the female plant is channelled into the production of THC-laden resin, in an attempt to trap the pollen which has been denied as a result of the isolation process. The female marijuana plant attempts to reproduce so intensely that it will continue to produce resin until it is either pollinated or dead.

This is the practice of the Sinsemilla growers throughout California. The mountainous regions of Northern California provide the ideal climate, elevation, soil fertility and isolation necessary to the successful and prolific cultivation of marijuana. Specifically, the mountainous regions of Humboldt and Mendocino counties are popularly known as the birthplaces of Sinsemilla cultivation in this state.

The most significant change in marijuana cultivation since the introduction of Sinsemilla to California has been the importation of Cannabis Indica seeds. A good portion of California Sinsemilla is of the Indica type; it is a more desirous crop than Sativa because of the high THC and the resulting potency. However, due to a hybridization in California, many of the state's marijuana plants are now a mixture of Indica and Sativa. The hybrid tends to produce large plants with several large buds. It might also be noted that Indica plants mature in September and October.

At present, the market value of Sinsemilla marijuana in the United States is from $1,200 to $2,000 per pound. Due to the fact that the plants are allowed to grow a full season, from spring to fall, and the fact that they are grown under ideal geographical and climatic conditions, it is not unusual to net at least one pound of "tops" from each plant. A mere garden of 50 plants would then yield the grower somewhere around $50,000 to $100,000 for a single season's work. One might ask, "If there are no seeds, how does the plant reproduce?" It is said that one or two plants will produce enough seeds for next year's crop. The grower simply allows a few plants to grow in an area detached from the major crop, and from this small crop in which he allows both the male and female plants to grow, he can obtain the seeds for the next year's crop.

Quantitative analysis has been performed on a number of Sinsemilla samples and THC content has been found to be approximately the same as that of Thai-grown marijuana, ranging between 4 to 8 percent.

Maui Wowie and Kona Gold

These popular varieties of marijuana are grown in the Hawaiian Islands. Maui Wowie and Kona Gold are similar to both Thai and California's home-grown Sinsemilla; they contain approximately the same range of THC and are comparable in price. Some have said that the Hawaiian marijuana grown on the island of Maui (Maui Wowie) is especially popular and has become that island's chief resource.

Other Varieties

There are numerous other popular varieties of marijuana which are more costly than commercial, but generally less expensive than Sinsemilla, Thai, or the Hawaiian varieties. Some examples of these are: Guerrero (cultivated in the Mexican state of Guerrero); Oaxacan (pronounced Wa-hacon, and grown in the Mexican state of Oaxaca); Acapulco Gold (grown in the mountains surrounding the city of Acapulco, Mexico); and Panama (grown in the country of Panama). The name Panama Red refers to a reddish tint of the small hairs which grow around the flowering tops of certain plants. This phenomena occurs in certain hybrid varieties, as a result of cross-breeding. These kinds of plants have also been found growing in Southern California in the mountainous regions north of San Diego. The term "Red Hair" has also been applied to this variety of marijuana.

KENAF

Kenaf is an annual plant which grows from one to four meters in height. Kenaf's thick stalk and palmate leaves have three, five, or seven lobes which are somewhat serrated. From a distance, this plant looks very much like marijuana. However, upon closer examination, kenaf has some major differences. The most obvious of these are the large yellow flowers appearing at maturity.

Kenaf is grown in numerous states, particularly Louisiana. The plant is cultivated because its long stalks provide a fiber used to make burlap, rope, animal bedding, and packing material. It is also more profitable to grow than most farm crops. However, one of kenaf's two species may mislead some officers to believe that it is an illegal marijuana crop. The first species has leaves that look like a hibiscus plant, while the other, Hibiscus Cannabinus L., has an appearance similar to that of marijuana.

When kenaf leaves are dried and examined microscopically, however, there are no similarities to marijuana. The only hairs are unicellular types scattered on the veins in the leaves. The Duquenois-Levine test of this plant also proved to be negative, giving only a green color in both phases. Kenaf contains no THC.

The kenaf plant could cause confusion to law enforcement agencies due to its physical resemblance to marijuana when growing, especially prior to maturity (when it does not have large yellow flowers). Many people have mistaken it for marijuana. Awareness of the kenaf's existence and characteristics will help prevent costly and embarrassing mistakes.

HASHISH

Hashish, or "concentrated cannabis" as it is legally and medically known, is simply the concentrated resin which has been extracted from marijuana. A general range of THC content in hashish is 10 to 20 percent.

The chief producers of hashish are reported to be India, Afghanistan, Pakistan, Morocco, Mexico and the Caribbean regions. Hashish varies in color but is generally black, brown, or green; it may sometimes have a reddish tint. Hashish consists of the drug-rich resinous secretions of the cannabis plant, which are collected, dried, and then compressed into a variety of forms such as balls, cakes or cookie-like sheets.

Many users prefer hashish because it produces a quicker and more intense effect. Hashish is occasionally mixed into food preparations or boiled into a tea, but the most common method of use is smoking.

One way of collecting the resin is to rub the buds gently between the palms of the hands until a uniform coat of green resin forms from the fingertips to the wrists. This is scraped off with a knife, rubbed into long finger-wads, pressed flat in the palms and wadded up again until the texture is smooth and uniform.

Hashish can be obtained from any marijuana plant. The resin can be collected by contacting the leaf with leather and scraping the resin from the leather. Hashish, collected from the living plant by the use of leather, is considered the finest form.

Another method of gathering resin is obtained by threshing the cut plant. The hash falls from the dried plant in the form of dust and is collected on cloth. Likewise, a fourth method of collection is accomplished by pressing the cut (flowering) tops between coarse cloths to which the resins stick. Traders can tell whether hash has been obtained from the growing plant or from the cut, dried plant by the color of the substance.

The first quality hash is brown in color and becomes darker in aging. This quality of hash is generally sold in lumps or sticks and rarely exceeds one ounce per stick. The second quality (dried plant) has a brown-green or brown-grey color. It is sold in cloth bags and weighs one to three pounds.

Hash Oil

Sometimes called "Marijuana Oil" or "Honey Oil," hashish oil is legally considered "concentrated cannabis." This substance is an illicitly manufactured form of what was formerly known in the pharmaceutical and medical professions as Tincture or Extract of Cannabis, a lawful product once used for medicinal purposes. Although the medical preparations of Cannabis Sativa L. were restricted in this country in 1937, marijuana and hashish continued to flourish. Interestingly enough, hash oil all but disappeared until the early 1970s when it cropped up in the Orange County area of Southern California. It soon spread throughout the state and is, today, a much used and desired drug. In general, hash oil is about 3 to 4 times stronger than hashish and 30 to 40 times stronger than "commercial grade marijuana."

Hashish oil is produced by a process of repeated extraction of cannabis plant materials to yield a dark, viscous liquid. It varies in color, but can generally be found in amber, dark green, brown, or black. It has an average strength of between 20 to 60 percent THC, which makes it the closest thing to pure THC found on the street today. Although pure THC can be manufactured synthetically in a laboratory situation, the cost is prohibitive, the expertise is generally lacking and pure THC has an extremely short "shelf-life" requiring storage under nitrogen. These complications prevent pure THC from being found on the street.

Most users smoke hash oil by adding it to a marijuana cigarette or a commercial cigarette. Some users have reported taking hash oil by mouth, or by adding it to food preparations or liquids such as hot teas. Due to its consistency and the presence of solvents or other chemicals used in its extraction process, hash oil must be preserved in some airtight container and should be kept away from light and heat. The air, heat, and light will cause the oil to harden.

There are many ways to produce hashish oil, but the basic principle used by most clandestine operations is similar to that of percolating coffee. A basket filled with ground or chopped-up marijuana plant is suspended inside a large container, at the bottom of which is contained a solvent, such as alcohol, hexane, chloroform or petroleum ether. Copper tubing or similar material is arranged at the top through which cold water circulates. The solvent is heated and the vapors rise to the top where they condense, then fall into the basket of marijuana.

As the solvent seeps through the plant materials, the THC and other soluble chemicals are dissolved, and the solution drops back to the bottom of the container. Continued heating causes the process to occur over and over again. The solution becomes increasingly stronger until the plant material is exhausted of its THC. Sometimes new material is added and the same solvent reheated, yielding an even more potent solution.

The purity of the final product (i.e., the percentage content of THC) will depend on the degree of sophistication of the apparatus used, but it is presumed that with high vacuum distillation and further fractional distillation and use of chemical filters, the end product could approach 95 to 100 percent purity, as a clear liquid.

MARIJUANA PACKAGING

Marijuana will be packaged for street sale in a variety of different ways. The most common manner of packaging is to place the marijuana in a clear plastic sandwich bag which is then rolled up and taped, or simply tied at the open end. This is commonly referred to as a "bag" or "baggy" of marijuana. Pounds of marijuana are packaged in heavy plastic bags. Multi-pounds (kilos) are usually wrapped in heavy paper and shipped in large burlap bags.

You will frequently find marijuana in hand-rolled cigarettes. It might be sold in this form, but it is more often put into cigarettes by the user who has purchased a quantity of marijuana. The marijuana cigarette is shorter and thinner than a commercial cigarette, and the ends are crimped or twisted to prevent the contents from falling out.

There are several brands of rolling paper on the market. Some popular ones for marijuana smokers include "Zig-Zag" and "E-Z Widers." The paper may be yellow, white, or brown in color. Two papers are usually used to prevent any coarse material from piercing the paper.

METHODS OF MARIJUANA USE

Marijuana may be brewed as a tea for drinking or baked in cookies or brownies for eating. The most common method of use, however, is by smoking it in hand-rolled cigarettes, pipes, or water jars. Marijuana pipes are sometimes specially made pipes with relatively small bowls, or they might be improvised from regular tobacco pipes which are lined with aluminum foil to decrease the size of the bowl. Sometimes a Middle Eastern style "hookah" is used. A "hookah" is a large jar with water inside and a long tube through which the smoke is drawn. It may also be called a "water pipe." Smaller water pipes, commonly called "bongs," are also used because they are less bulky.

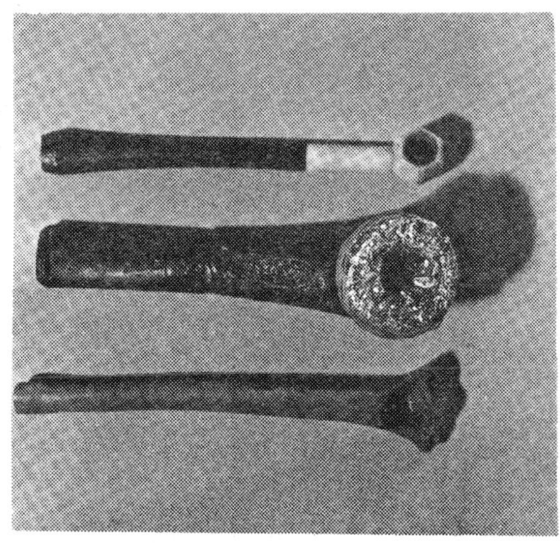

MAKESHIFT MARIJUANA PIPES

Generally, the marijuana cigarette is smoked completely. When the user gets down to the butt (known as the "roach") he or she may use a device called a "crutch" or "roach clip" to smoke the remaining amounts of marijuana. This device can be made from almost anything: tweezers, paperclips, hairpins, alligator clips, etc. A "roach clip" may be very simple or very ornamental. Many are put on necklaces or other jewelry items. These "roach clips" are not illegal to possess, but possession could be used to support a case for drug use.

Many cannabis users will smoke in an enclosed area (such as a vehicle with the windows rolled up) to prevent the smoke from escaping. When smoking marijuana, the user holds the smoke in his or her lungs as long as possible to maximize the drug effects. A non-smoking observer who is present in a location where there is a high concentration of marijuana smoke may also become affected, but to a lesser degree than those actually smoking. This is referred to as a "contact high," and is sometimes used as a defense or excuse by abusers when they are apprehended for drug influence.

Burning marijuana has a very distinct odor. It is easily recognized. It may be detected for a short time after smoking on the breath of the abuser, in the room or car where it was smoked, and on clothing.

A marijuana cigarette contains about 500 mg. of plant material. If the marijuana contains approximately 1 percent delta-9 tetrahydrocannabinol (THC), then 5 mg. of THC is available to the smoker. Half of the THC is destroyed by burning, 20 percent remains in the "roach," and 10 percent is lost in the sidestream smoke. This leaves about 20 percent or 1 mg. of THC in the mainstream smoke that is inhaled by the user. Of that amount, the brain does not receive more than its share by weight, or about 0.015 mg. Within the brain, the distribution of THC reveals higher concentrations in the frontal and visual cortex, the cerebellum, and the limbic system.

MARIJUANA AND HEALTH

Since 1967, the Federal government has spent approximately $50 million on marijuana research to support over a thousand research projects. Research supported by the National Institute on Drug Abuse (NIDA) includes investigations into the effects of marijuana on the heart and lungs; its effects on psychological, social, and physical development; its effects on pregnancy, as well as research into possible medical uses, including the treatment of glaucoma.

CHEMISTRY AND METABOLISM OF CANNABIS

Marijuana is quite complex, containing at least 421 individual compounds. When smoked, some of the chemicals are further transformed by burning (pyrolysis) into other compounds. A great deal of research has been done on the principal psychoactive ingredient in cannabis, delta-9 tetrahydrocannabinol (THC). However, THC is only one ingredient of the natural material.

The chemistry of marijuana smoke has commanded considerable attention in recent years. Some 150 compounds have been identified in the smoke itself. One of them, benzopyrene, known to be carcinogenic, is 70 percent more abundant in marijuana smoke than in tobacco smoke. There is also evidence that more "tar" is found in marijuana cigarettes than in high tar tobacco cigarettes.

A confirmation of these earlier findings was published in 1982. It was found that when marijuana and tobacco cigarettes were consumed under similar conditions, marijuana produced 38 mg. of tar, while 15 mg. were produced from a popular brand of high-tar cigarette. When marijuana was smoked as it usually is (i.e., deeply inhaled and unfiltered), then compared with a cigarette of equal weight smoked as tobacco typically is, the marijuana cigarette yielded 3.8 times as much tar as the tobacco cigarette suggesting that the health risk of one marijuana "joint" is much greater than that of smoking a modern high-tar tobacco cigarette.

These findings contribute to our current understanding of marijuana chemistry and metabolism. With respect to pregnancy, researchers have been able to demonstrate that marijuana constituents cross the placental barrier and, as a result, may affect fetal development. The presence of cannabinoids in the milk of the marijuana-using mother may also be transferred to the infant. Despite these possible dangers, research of marijuana's chemistry has also shown that one or more of the synthesized components of cannabis in its original or chemically-modified form may come to have therapeutic usefulness. Finally, our increased awareness of marijuana's chemical complexity and the ways in which components other than delta-9 THC modify the drug's effects may shed light on the common street belief that different types of marijuana have different effects not wholly related to their THC content.

MARIJUANA AND REPRODUCTION

It is now generally believed that the effects of cannabinoids on the hormones that modulate the reproductive process originate within the brain as a result of changes in neurotransmitters such as dopamine, norepinephrine, and serotonin. In monkeys, these amines alter the secretion of the gonadotropin releasing factor.[7] A principal site of action of THC is in the hypothalamus where production of the gonadotropin-releasing hormone is suppressed, which in turn inhibits secretion of the leutinizing hormone (LH), the follicle-stimulating hormone (FS), and prolactin in the pituitary.[8] These changes also induce decreases in the female sex hormones, estrogen and progesterone, interfering with ovulation and other hormone-related functions. When cannabis use is discontinued, however, these effects are reversible. After chronic administration of the drug, tolerance to the reproductive effects of THC is observed. Therefore, THC has its greatest effect upon the non-human primate's reproductive functioning when use is first initiated. The impact of marijuana or THC on human females requires further study.

Regular marijuana use during at least two developmental phases can be detrimental; during fetal development and during adolescence. The fetal risks will be discussed later. The endocrine events associated with puberty are strongly dependent upon a properly functioning hypothalamic-pituitary axis.

As indicated, many of the endocrine effects caused by the chronic treatment of animals with THC are reversible as tolerance to the drug develops. Still, many questions remain regarding the long-term consequences of use, for example, on sperm formation, psychosexual maturation, and sex organ function. Until these and other issues are resolved, marijuana consumption by adolescents or males with marginal fertility poses uncertain reproductive hazards.[9]

In laboratory animals, however, the administration of THC to male mice for five days has resulted in a reduction of sperm production and in an increase in abnormal sperm forms. In addition, testicular and seminal vesicle weights were decreased compared to the control group. These find-

---

[7] Tyrey, L. "Endocrine aspects of cannabinoid action in female subprimates: search for sites of action." In: Braude, M.C., and J.P. Ludford, eds. *Marijuana: Effects on the Endocrine and Reproductive Systems.* Research Monograph Series 44. DHHS Pub. No. (ADM)84-1278. Washington, D.C.: Supt. of Docs., U.S. Govt. Print. Off., 1984.

[8] Smith, C.G., and R.H. Ashe. "Acute, short term and chronic effects of marijuana on the female primate reproductive function." In: Braude, M.C., and J.P. Ludford, eds. *Marijuana: Effects on the Endocrine and Reproductive Systems.* NIDA Research Monograph Series 44. DHHS Pub. No. (ADM)84-1278. Washington, D.C.: Supt. of Docs., U.S. Govt. Print. Off., 1984, pp. 82-96.

[9] Harclerode, J. "Endocrine effects of marijuana in the male." In: Braude, M.C., and J.P. Ludford, eds. *Marijuana: Effects on the Endocrine and Reproductive Systems.* Research Monograph Series 44. DHHS Pub. No. (ADM) 84-1278. Washington, D.C.: Supt. of Docs., U.S. Govt. Print. Off., 1984, pp. 46-64.

ings are consistent with a decrease in gonadotropin-releasing hormones in the hypothalamus and subsequent decreases in LH and FSH as well as a reduction of testosterone (Harclerode 1984).

Effects Upon Fetal Development

In the 1980, the Secretary of Health, Education, and Welfare's annual report released some important information on "Marijuana and Health." Since then, additional information explaining the effects of marijuana on fetal development has been released.

Three studies have examined samples of sufficient size to adequately control for confounding effects.[10] One of these studied 1,690 mother/child pairs.[11] Marijuana in varying amounts was used by 234 mothers during pregnancy. Use was found to be associated with lower infant birth weight and length compared to non-users. Women who used marijuana less than three times a week delivered babies who were 139 grams lighter than those of the non-using group. Marijuana use was the strongest independent predictor of whether the infant would have congenital features compatible with the fetal alcohol syndrome (FAS). In fact, marijuana use was a better predictor of FAS symptoms than alcohol use.

A larger study sampled 7,301 births for abnormal infant characteristics.[12] This research showed that women who used marijuana during pregnancy were significantly more likely than non-users to deliver premature infants of low birth weight. The relationship of marijuana use to prenatal death did not achieve statistical significance, but was suggestive.

The largest study to date has sampled 17,316 women who gave birth at the Boston Hospital for Women.[13] A total of 12,718 were interviewed to determine the impact of marijuana and other risk factors on their newborn offspring. Of the ten independent variables analyzed (which included tobacco and alcohol), marijuana use was most likely to predict congenital malformations. Hingston et al. (1984) noted that tobacco and marijuana smoking, as well as alcohol and other drug abuse, frequently occur in the same women. Therefore, some of the adverse effects on fetal development attributed to maternal drinking or smoking may be due to an interaction with marijuana and other psychoactive substances. When a number of these toxic substances are consumed together, their toxic effects on the fetus may be cumulative.

Gross malformations in human infants due to prenatal exposure to cannabis have not yet been completely proven.

---

[10] See Hingston, R. et al. "Effects of maternal drinking and marijuana use on fetal growth and development." *Pediatrics*. 70:539, 1982.

[11] Hingston, R. et al. "Effects on fetal development of maternal marijuana use during pregnancy." In: D.J. Harvey, ed. *Marijuana 84: Proceedings of the Oxford Symposium on Marijuana*. Oxford: IRL Press, 1984.

[12] Gibson, G.T. et al. "Maternal alcohol, tobacco and cannabis consumption on the outcome of pregnancy." *Aust NZ Obstet Gynecol*. 23:16-19, 1983.

[13] Linn, S. et al. "The association of marijuana use with outcome of pregnancy." *Am J Public Health*. 73:1161-1164, 1983.

CHROMOSOME ABNORMALITIES

There is no new evidence in this area. While there were early reports of increases in chromosomal breaks and abnormalities in human cell cultures, more recent results have been inconclusive. Overall, there continues to be no convincing evidence that marijuana use causes clinically significant chromosome damage.

ALTERATIONS IN CELL METABOLISM

The implications of laboratory findings on the inhibition of DNA, RNA, and protein synthesis (all of which are related to cellular reproduction and metabolism) are still unknown.

IMMUNE STATUS

Although additional information regarding possible reductions in immune responsivity has become available since 1980, the evidence that marijuana smoking in humans decreases resistance to infection remains inconclusive. The question is of particular importance because THC is sometimes used to reduce nausea resulting from cancer chemotherapy. Since cancer chemotherapeutic chemicals are themselves severely immunosuppressive, any additional THC-induced immunosuppression would be very undesirable. It has been determined that THC does decrease host resistance to herpes simplex virus, type 2, in the guinea pig. This occurs in a dose-related fashion using amounts equivalent to human consumption levels.[14]

PULMONARY EFFECTS

Because marijuana is typically smoked, its possible adverse effects on the lung and pulmonary functions have long been of concern to researchers. It is noteworthy that one of the earliest attempts to assess the health and social implications of cannabis use, the "Report of the Indian Hemp Drugs Commission of 1893-94" includes observations about its pulmonary effects that are surprisingly similar to more contemporary observations. For example, this report mentions a possible value in the treatment of asthma because of the drug's pulmonary sedative qualities. However, it goes on to say that "long continued smoking . . . doubtless results in the deposition of finely divided carbonaceous matter in the lung tissues, and the presence of other irritating substances in the smoke ultimately causes local irritation of the bronchial mucous membrane, leading to increased secretion, and resulting in the condition which is described as chronic bronchitis in ganja smokers." [15]

Thus far, there is no direct evidence that smoking marijuana is correlated with lung cancer. The American experience with marijuana has been too brief for this to be a likely outcome. Nevertheless, there is good reason for concern about the possibility of pulmonary cancer resulting from extended use over several decades. Like tobacco smoke residuals or "tar," cannabis

---

[14] Cabral, G.A. et al. "9-Tetrahydrocannabinol decreases host resistance to herpes simplex virus type 2 vaginal infection in the guinea pig." In: D.J. Harvey, ed. *Marijuana 84: Proceedings of the Oxford Symposium on Cannabis.* Oxford: IRL Press, 1985.

[15] Indian Hemp Drugs Commission Report, 1894. Simla, India: Government Printing Office. 7 volumes.

Solomon, David, ed. *The Marijuana Papers.* New York, The New American Library, Signet Books, 1966, pp. 41-42.

residuals, when applied to the skin of experimental animals, have been shown to be tumor-producing. Analysis of marijuana smoke has also found evidence that it contains larger amounts of cancer-producing hydrocarbons. For example, benzopyrene, a known cancer-producing chemical found in tobacco smoke, has been reported to be 70 percent more abundant in marijuana smoke. Therefore, the carcinogenic effects of marijuana smoking are a potential health concern for chronic smokers.

Extensive pulmonary macrophage infiltration of the lung has been documented in animals and by biopsy in humans. One report describes autopsies of 13 known marijuana smokers who died suddenly from trauma.[16] This study indicates moderate to severe infiltration of the pulmonary alveolar spaces with pigmented macrophages leading to a fibrous tissue response and, finally, ulceration. The pigmentation was due to deeply inhaled marijuana smoke. Tobacco smokers of similar age (15 to 41) show little macrophage infiltration, and they do not develop the fibrosis and inflammatory changes until after many years of smoking. This suggests chronic obstructive pulmonary disease is a definite possibility in heavy users. One heavy marijuana smoker, 28 years old, had dyspnea on exertion due to alveoli being completely filled with macrophages.

From the total body of clinical and experimental evidence accumulated to date, it appears that daily use of marijuana leads to lung damage similar to that resulting from heavy cigarette smoking. Since marijuana users often smoke both tobacco and marijuana, the cumulative effects of the combination require additional study.

CARDIOVASCULAR EFFECTS

Marijuana significantly increases heart rate after smoking. There is evidence that in patients with already impaired heart function, use of marijuana may precipitate chest pain (angina pectoris) more rapidly and following less effort than tobacco cigarettes. Despite the limited evidence to date, heart patients and others who may have impaired cardiac function are at a higher risk of heart failure due to marijuana smoking.

BRAIN CHANGES

Brain wave changes from cannabis generally consist of an increase and deceleration of waves. This is consistent with the state of drowsiness induced by the drug. Although scalp electroencephalogram (EEG) records show minimal alterations, electrodes implanted in deep brain structures like the septum, a center for emotionality, obtain marked changes in electrical activity.[17]

The findings revealed by deep electrode recordings and by ultrastructural changes found in septal areas suggest that long-term, heavy use of marijuana or THC may produce microscopic changes. The possibility of

---

[16] Morris, R.R. "Human pulmonary histopathological changes from marijuana smoking." *J Forensic Sciences*. 30:345-349, 1985.

[17] Heath, R.A. et al. "Chronic marijuana smoking: its effect on function and structure of the primate brain." In: Nahas, G.G., and W.D.M. Patton, eds. *Marijuana: Biological Effects*. Oxford: Pergamon Press, 1979.

macroscopic changes in the form of cerebral atrophy remains open, and additional imaging studies must be done.

EFFECTS OF MARIJUANA ON INTELLECTUAL FUNCTIONING

A wide range of intellectual performance impairment due to marijuana intoxication is known. Cognitive tasks, such as digit symbol substitution, complex reaction time, recent memory, and serial subtractions are all performed more poorly when "high" as compared to performance during the sober state. Marijuana interferes with the transfer of information from immediate to long-term memory storage. Also, less demanding tasks, such as simple reaction time, do not appear to be affected by marijuana intoxication. A major unresolved question is whether long-term use produces irreversible effects.

MARIJUANA AND DRIVING

There is ample evidence supporting the belief that marijuana use at typical social levels impairs driving ability and related skills. Studies indicating impairment of driving skills include: laboratory assessment of driving-related skills, driver-simulator studies, test-course performance, and actual street-driver performance. As previously mentioned, another important study, conducted for the National Highway Traffic Safety Administration, researched information on drivers involved in fatal accidents.

One example of these findings may be cited from California. In a study conducted by the California State Department of Justice, it was determined that of the 1,800 blood samples taken from drivers arrested for driving while intoxicated, 16 percent were positive for marijuana. Where no alcohol was present in the blood sample (about 10 percent of the samples), the incidence of marijuana detected rose to 24 percent.[18] Additional studies of motorist impairment related to marijuana use are still being conducted.

For instance, in order to determine the role of alcohol and other drugs in fatal auto crashes, blood samples from deceased males between 15 and 34 years of age were obtained in four California counties. Driver responsibility for each fatal accident was determined. The blood was analyzed for 23 drugs or drug groups. The sample consisted of 440 drivers, slightly more than half killed in single vehicle accidents. In all, 88 percent of these drivers were considered responsible for the crash. Only 19 percent had no drugs present in their blood; 81 percent were found to have one or more drugs present.[19] Alcohol was detected in 70 percent of the drivers, cannabinoids in 37 percent, cocaine in 11 percent, diazepam and phencylidine in 4 percent, other drugs in 3 percent or less. Fifty-two percent of those who had alcohol present had blood-alcohol concentrations (BACs) of 0.1 to 0.19 percent, and 30 percent had BACs of 0.2 percent or more. THC or its acid metabolite were present in 0.2 to 50 ng./ml. concentrations in blood. THC was found alone in 12 percent of those studied; it was found in combination with alcohol in 81 percent, and with other drugs in 7 percent.

---

[18] California Narcotic Officers Association. *The California Narcotic Officer*. Winter, 1986.

[19] Williams, A.F. et al. "Drugs in fatally injured young male drivers." *Pharm Chem Newsletter*. 14:1-11, 1985.

Cannabis (Marijuana)

Although alcohol is the prime cause of automotive accidents, marijuana and cocaine are currently being found frequently enough to suggest that they are potentially significant contributors. It has been well-established that marijuana and alcohol have additive effects upon driving skills. Since marijuana metabolites were found in more than a third of the drivers, impairment due to marijuana may be contributing to the problem. One study demonstrated that blood levels of THC correlate with impaired performance for several hours after smoking on tasks that are related to driving performance.[20] Using a more complex task, it has also been determined that pilots are impaired for 24 hours following the smoking of one marijuana cigarette containing 19 mg. of THC.[21] Ten experienced pilots familiar with marijuana smoking were tested 1, 4, 10, and 24 hours after smoking. At each point, the test resulted in significant impairment of the ability to perform a landing maneuver. It might be noted, furthermore, that the 24-hour test occurred at a time that the pilots reported feeling alert and no longer under the influence of marijuana.

The parameter of impairment for the average driver under various dosages of marijuana cannot yet be adequately specified. Nevertheless, it is important to develop reliable standards to discourage potentially dangerous driving. At present, it is clear that driving while "high" presents a significant risk to highway safety and drivers should be alerted to these dangers.

MARIJUANA USE AND SEXUALITY

In a longitudinal study of white high school students, 61 percent of those who used marijuana and 41 percent of those who drank alcoholic beverages were sexually experienced compared to 4 percent among abstainers. Therefore, it may be concluded that heavy marijuana users have higher rates of sexual experience than do light marijuana users.[22] These differences are as likely to be explained on the basis of congruent lifestyle behaviors as on any sexually induced drug activity. A fairly common finding was that marijuana use is associated with adolescent depression and poor self-esteem, with the drug serving as a form of self-medication.

Another study has determined that marijuana use is associated with increased sexual activity in many individuals, which, in turn, appears to relate to their sensation-seeking lifestyle.[23] It might be said that many marijuana users take the drug to escape some unfavorable or unpleasant circumstance. It is common for adolescent marijuana users to openly provoke their parents with drug use or defy them in other ways. Defiance of school authorities is also common. Several users report that they "stone" themselves into unconsciousness or combine marijuana and alcohol to

---

[20] Barnett, G. et al. "Behavioral pharmacokinetics of marijuana." *Psychopharmacology.* 85:51-56, 1985.

[21] Yesavage, J.A. et al. "Carry-over effects of marijuana intoxication on aircraft pilot performance: a preliminary report." *Am J Psychiatry.* 42(11):1325-1329, 1985.

[22] Jessor, R., and S.L. Jessor. *Problem Behavior and Psychological Development: A Longitudinal Study.* New York: Academic Press, 1977.

[23] Abel, E.L. "Marijuana and sex: a critical survey." *Drug and Alcohol Dependence.* 8:1-22, 1981.

achieve this state. Adolescents repeatedly talk about using the drug to relax from tension and anger at home. Marijuana sometimes induces feelings of grandiosity that help adolescents deal with depression and poor self-esteem.

Combined with clinical studies, these patterns of use indicate that marijuana is often used as an escape, especially during adolescence, or is seen as a source of relief from coping with persistent difficulties.[24] However, marijuana keeps adolescents in a condition of troubled adaptation and reinforces their unwillingness to master their problems. As an escape, the drug helps them dismiss serious problems as unimportant ones. Through marijuana use, adolescents avoid choices and challenges associated with becoming an adult and planning for the future.

PSYCHOPATHOLOGICAL EFFECTS

There have been few new developments in research on the psychopathological effects of marijuana use. An acute panic anxiety reaction is the most common adverse psychological reaction to use, especially when unexpectedly strong material is consumed. A number of clinicians have cautioned against use of marijuana by those with a history of serious psychological problems or who have previously had drug-precipitated emotional disturbances (so-called bad trips). While more serious psychiatric problems such as cannabis-related psychosis have been reported in countries with a long tradition of use, such reactions do not appear common in the United States. Nonetheless, concern has been expressed that availability of much stronger varieties of cannabis may result in more serious problems than in the past.

CHRONIC MARIJUANA USE

The pure chronic marijuana user is hard to find. When a small group of such individuals are identified in outpatient treatment centers, they are either quite young, or turn out to be multiple drug users whose primary complaint relates to their marijuana usage.[25] Heavy marijuana users are typically either in a state of transition toward the use of other mind-altering substances, or are already multiple drug abusers who happen to believe that marijuana is producing the difficulties that require treatment. These concerns include panicky feelings, especially about changes in time sense, difficulties in sensing how other people are responding to the individual, or fears of losing control.

Performance decrements are another source of concern of some chronic marijuana smokers. Low energy levels, impaired school or job performance and loss of interest in other activities are mentioned in the high school senior and other surveys.

---

[24] Hendin, H. and A.P. Haas. "The adaptive significance of chronic marijuana for adolescents and adults." *Advances in Alcohol and Substance Abuse*. 4:99-115, 1985.

[25] Wish, E.D., and S. Deren. "Assessment of treatment services for marijuana users." *Progress Report to the NIDA*. 1985.

MARIJUANA AND PSYCHIATRIC ILLNESS

In a 1985 report on marijuana and psychiatric illness, researchers reexamined 97 regular marijuana users and 50 controls six to seven years after an original psychiatric evaluation.[26] The experimental group were not particularly heavy users—only 12 percent used the drug almost daily. High levels of depression and alcohol abuse were present in both groups at the time of both examinations. The only impressive difference was an increase in diagnosable antisocial personality disorder in the marijuana group from 6 percent in the initial evaluation to 21 percent in the follow-up. The figures for the control group were 0 percent initially which increased to 2 percent at follow-up. The researchers make no attempt to explain the difference or how it might be related to marijuana use.

MARIJUANA TOLERANCE AND DEPENDENCE

Tolerance to cannabis, i.e., a diminished response to a given repeated drug dose, is now well substantiated. Tolerance development was originally suspected because experienced overseas users were able to use large quantities of the drug that would have been toxic to United States users accustomed to smaller amounts of the drug. Carefully conducted studies with known doses of marijuana or THC leave little question that tolerance develops with prolonged use.

This is in some contrast with the original impression that users had a "reverse tolerance," i.e., a greater sensitivity to marijuana upon relatively low dose and infrequent use. Under those conditions, neophyte users may have become more aware of marijuana's subjective effects with repeated use partly as a result of social learning of what was to be expected from the experience and thus subjectively believed that its effects were enhanced.

Several more detailed reviews of tolerance development to the behavioral and physiological effects of marijuana in both animals and humans have been published.

The normal trend from tolerance to dependence does becomes complicated with respect to marijuana. The term "cannabis dependence" has often been used in an imprecise way with meanings ranging from a vague desire to continue use, if available, to the manifestation of physical withdrawal symptoms following its discontinuance. If "dependence" is defined as experiencing definite physical symptoms following withdrawal of the drug, there is now experimental evidence that such symptoms can occur at least under conditions of extremely heavy cannabis use. However, this amount of cannabis use is not typical of the social marijuana user in the U.S.

---

[26] Weller, R.A., and J.A. Halikas. "Marijuana use and psychiatric illness: a follow-up study." *American J Psychiatry* 142:848-850, 1985.

The changes noted after drug withdrawal under these experimental conditions include one or more of the following symptoms: irritability, restlessness, decreased appetite, sleep disturbance, sweating, tremor, nausea, vomiting, and diarrhea. Some of these symptoms were experienced in a similar research study by users who selected their own smoked marijuana doses. Such a "withdrawal syndrome" has thus far been reported clinically in only one formal research report.[27]

THERAPEUTIC EFFECTS OF CANNABIS

Marijuana has been used for thousands of years in medical and other clinical research. The ancient Chinese used marijuana in the treatment of a variety of ills. In the 18th century, this therapeutic use was introduced to England by the medical profession.

In 1839, W.B. O'Shaughnessy, M.D., an Englishman at the Medical College of Calcutta, reported treating rabies, epilepsy, tetanus and rheumatism with what he called "tincure of hemp." Its short-comings were its insolubility in water, instability in alcohol, and photolysis or degeneration in the presence of light.

Cannabis was readily available throughout the United States in the nineteenth and early twentieth centuries in the form of "Extractum Cannabis: Extract of Hemp." It was used as a sleep-inducing drug (hyponotic), an appetite enhancer, a pain reliever, and as an aphrodisiac.

Most of the cannabis preparations were marketed and used in liquid form, similar to the hashish oil illicitly available today. Much experimentation has been attempted in the treatment of a variety of illnesses, both physical and mental. Its use was gradually supplanted as more effective and predictable drugs, such as opiates, bromides, barbiturates and aspirin came into medical vogue.

In this country, some courts have sanctioned the use of marijuana under special conditions wherein medical experts testified that marijuana was the only drug which would be suitable treatment for their patients' conditions. Two such medical conditions have been glaucoma and nausea from chemotherapy. It has been stated by various medical authorities that the smoking of marijuana can relieve the glaucoma condition of some patients to a greater degree than the legal, more conventional medical preparations. Some medical authorities have also stated that the nausea condition commonly associated with chemotherapy can be relieved in some patients by smoking marijuana, and in many instances medical authorities have stated that there is no other medication capable of relieving this condition.

In further attempts to verify the medical usefulness of marijuana, California started a marijuana medical research program. This program

---

[27] Tennant, Forest. *Identifying the Marijuana User,* 1st ed. West Covina, California: Veract, Inc., June 1986, p. 39.

Teitel, B. "Observations on Marijuana Withdrawal." *American Journal of Psychiatry.* 134:587, 1977.

Vereby, K., M.S. Gold and J. Mule. "Laboratory Testing in the Diagnosis of Marijuana Intoxication and Withdrawal." *Psychiatric Annals.* 16:235-241, 1986.

resulted from Senate Bill 184. The bill took effect on January 1, 1980 and allows oncologists (qualified cancer specialists) to participate in a state-wide study of the effectiveness of marijuana (delta-9 THC) in relieving the nausea and vomiting associated with cancer chemotherapy or radiation treatment. The primary focus of SB 184 is on cancer chemotherapy. However, a pilot project on the effectiveness of marijuana in glaucoma treatment may be initiated (if medically appropriate) after the nausea and vomiting project is underway. Research projects concerning other therapeutic uses of marijuana could be sponsored by the researchers and approved by the research advising panel under existing statutes.

A variety of other clinical uses of marijuana have been suggested or experimentally employed. While marijuana's ability to dilate the lungs' air passages (bronchodilation) has been thought to have promise in treating asthmatics, the drug's lung-irritating properties seem to have offset this potential benefit.

Furthermore, the paradox that THC and marijuana have both convulsant and anti-convulsant properties has led to concern about the implications of marijuana use by epileptics and to speculation about its possible value in controlling seizures.

While there have been some clinical reports of marijuana reducing muscular spasticity in paraplegics and patients with multiple sclerosis, such work is still in an early stage, and a definite usefulness has not yet been found on a more systematic basis.

Still other applications of marijuana in the treatment of depression, pain, alcoholism, and drug dependence have been variously considered. Although these applications have not been adequately explored, there is little evidence that they are likely to prove useful at this time.

On March 10, 1992, the U.S. Public Health Service disclosed that it would not provide marijuana for medical purposes to any more patients suffering from AIDS, cancer, or glaucoma. The decision was made primarily because the Public Health Service feared that the smoked marijuana would be harmful to people with compromised immune systems.

Bill Grigg, Public Health Service spokesman, explained how scientists from the National Institute of Health had concluded that "existing evidence does not support recommending smoked marijuana as a treatment of choice for any of the medical conditions" of the patients who have recently applied for government supplied marijuana.

Previously the Public Health Service had approved 13 patients who were furnished marijuana from Federally-grown marijuana. The Food and Drug Administration had previously approved 28 patients to receive government supplied marijuana, but in view of the Public Health Service ruling, they will not receive any of the government-grown marijuana. The 13 will continue to obtain joints legally. As for the rest, the government says it will stop processing applications for legal marijuana until it finishes reviewing reports of its health benefits and dangers, including potential lung problems in AIDS patients and others with damaged immune systems.

"This is outrageous," says Randall, 44, the first person in the country to participate in the government program. "I will continue to see while other glaucoma patients go blind. Without marijuana," he says, "I would be walking around with a cane and a dog. Since I started smoking pot, my vision has not gotten any worse. I don't get the tri-colored haloes, the blurriness. We're not talking about subtle, discreet benefits; we're talking about overwhelming, immediate benefits."

Despite the apparent curative properties of marijuana, according to Mr. Grigg, marijuana could actually be dangerous to patients, especially to AIDS patients who are prone to pneumonia and other lung infections. Grigg cautions use because of substances in marijuana which may cause lung problems.

As to the claim that marijuana alleviates the painful condition caused by glaucoma—by relieving the pressure in the eye—Mr. Grigg said, "There simply isn't any evidence. . .that smoked marijuana would be any more useful or even as useful as what is available legally."

Despite the national ruling, 33 states (not including California) have already allowed physicians to prescribe marijuana for medical use. Those patients, along with the 13 already exempt, will remain able to use marijuana legally.

BENEFICIAL EFFECTS

In summary, doctors and patients say marijuana stops the nausea and vomiting associated with chemotherapy and illnesses such as AIDS, reduces eye pressure in glaucoma patients and eases muscle spasms common to such neurological conditions as multiple sclerosis. It stimulates the appetite, helping to curb the severe weight loss common to AIDS and cancer patients.

Due to these health benefits, the government will advocate the use of Marinol as an alternative to legal marijuana. Marinol is a pill containing a synthetic form of tetrahydrocannabinol (THC), marijuana's active ingredient. However, those with violent nausea say the pills do not work very well—if they can keep them down.

"I tried Marinol," says John Wilson of San Francisco, who has AIDS. "I went through five pills before I was able to keep one down. They are real expensive, about $6 or $8 a pill, and believe me, I was not able to reach into the toilet and try to get them back. When I did manage to keep one down, it took a long while to take effect, and only worked for about half a day. Two or three tokes on a joint helps me immediately."

Further support for the beneficial effects of marijuana comes from oncologist Ivan Silverberg of Davies Medical Center, a longtime proponent of the drug's medical use. Silverberg denounced the government's new ruling which prevents the legal distribution of Federally-grown marijuana:

> "A patient with cancer comes to me; I help them with drugs or chemotherapy, but the side effects can be awful. I know, from what my patients have told me over and over—marijuana really helps them. So what do I tell them? Go out and deal on a street corner? Don't they have enough problems already?"

Steep Prices

In addition, street marijuana is expensive—the asking price on the street is $300 to $500 an ounce. Most patients who would be using the drug therapeutically cannot afford those steep prices. "If you are dying, first and foremost, you are most likely impoverished," says Randall. "Or, you are a senior citizen with cancer who could never imagine going out and breaking the law."

In addition to the potential health hazards, the government has also said that marijuana use will lead to hard drugs; but this presumption has never been proven. Moreover, Federal legislators are ignoring the fact that marijuana sold on the street could be adulterated with other harmful substances.

According to Dr. Silverberg, marijuana is a curative substance similar to other therapeutic drugs. "I am not advocating legalizing marijuana," he says, "but we are dealing with human beings who are suffering. As a doctor, I am supposed to help relieve suffering. I can prescribe morphine, why not marijuana?"

Unless you already have a thriving cannabis garden in your back yard, growing your own is not a viable solution for most patients. "You're 60 years old, never smoked dope before, you're dying of cancer and you're going to spend 16 weeks watching your marijuana plants grow? I don't think so," says Randall. "You're a lucky duck if you find a friend who will give it to you. Medical care shouldn't depend on being a lucky duck. It should depend on a rational decision made by your physician, not a bunch of drug cops."

Those patients who have tried marijuana say they will continue to use it, despite the risks involved. Mary Gennoy, 40, of San Francisco, who has a bone disease and suffers from arthritis, says pot helps ease her muscle spasms and constant nausea. "I have a note from my doctor saying that marijuana is helpful for my symptoms," she says. She gets her supply from two or three people who sell her small quantities. "And I'm very fortunate to have some people who give me a little bit free every now and then. I don't want to get in trouble with the law, but I feel like I don't have any other alternative."

DOCTORS HIGH ON POT

For nearly 20 years, the government has resisted the appeals of cancer patients that marijuana be legalized for therapeutic purposes. Officials have said that the drug has "no currently accepted medical use."

Now the first published survey of cancer specialists on the issue indicates that many do believe that marijuana can lessen their patients' suffering. Policy analysts Mark A. R. Kleiman and Richard Doblin of Harvard's Kennedy School of Government anonymously surveyed 1,035 oncologists about marijuana's usefulness in controlling the nausea and vomiting many cancer patients experience during chemotherapy. Among the findings:

— 44 percent said they had recommended marijuana to at least one patient;

— 63 percent said marijuana was effective;

— 48 percent said they would prescribe it if it were legal.

One hundred and fifty-seven doctors also answered a question comparing marijuana with the synthetic THC tablets that can be prescribed legally. Seventy-seven percent of that group said they believed smoking marijuana was more effective than taking the THC tablets. Kleiman says that might be because smoking makes the drug take effect more quickly and because some patients with stomach problems have trouble absorbing the tablets.

Despite the study's results, it doesn't appear that the administration's policy is likely to change. A Drug Enforcement Administration spokesperson contends that marijuana's "potential for abuse" far outweighs any medical benefits it might have.

EFFECTS OF MARIJUANA IN COMBINATION WITH ALCOHOL

Since marijuana is so commonly used in combination with alcohol and other drugs, the combined effects of these drugs has potentially important implications. Given the extremely wide range of possible doses and interactions, it is not surprising that our present knowledge is still quite limited. This is true even of the most commonly used combination: alcohol and marijuana.

Animal studies of the behavioral effects of the alcohol-cannabis (or THC-alcohol) combination have generally found that the combined effect is greater than that of either alone. The limited human research to date is generally consistent with the results of animal research. Experiments at alcohol levels within the range commonly used by social drinkers showed that performance reductions from combined use are greater than those from the use of either alone. Such decrements have been detected in reasoning, manual dexterity and standing steadiness.

SUMMARY

Clinical observations from many parts of the world have long suggested that regular heavy use of cannabis may produce lung damage, impair reproductive and endocrine functions, cause long lasting disturbances of behavior and brain functions, and lower resistance to infection. What is not yet known is the frequency with which these health problems occur among cannabis users, the degree of use needed to produce them in humans, and the percentage of users at risk.

It is believed that people especially at risk with even moderate doses include anxious, depressed or unrecognized psychotic individuals, heavy users of other drugs, pregnant women, some epileptics, diabetics, individuals with marginal fertility and patients with chronic diseases of the heart, lungs or liver. In addition, as with any other psychoactive drug, adolescents who are undergoing rapid physiological and psychological development may be particularly susceptible to the development of a life-long pattern of use and to the health effects of long periods of cannabis intoxication.

The combination of the increasingly young age of current cannabis users, the greater frequency of use, and the greater potency of the smoked material completely change the situation that existed only a few years ago. Therefore, what was believed then may no longer apply now.

A new educational effort is needed to bring potential or actual users up to date. Just as the scare campaign of the Anslinger era was not based on evidence, so also the benign reputation of cannabis during the past decade also lacks a factual base. There are real areas of concern, some serious, that health professionals and the public should know about.

Most thoughtful members of all sides of the marijuana controversy would agree with the following statements:

1. Pregnant women should not use the drug.
2. Adolescents should be discouraged from use, especially heavy use.
3. People with heart problems may be further impaired by the heart-accelerating property of cannabis.
4. People with lung disease should not use the drug because of its irritant effects.
5. The infrequent use of marijuana (less than once a week) probably will not result in ill effects.
6. Continued work on the therapeutic potential of cannabis should proceed, especially in the control of nausea and vomiting and in open-angle glaucoma.

TREATMENT OF CANNABIS USE DISORDER

With more individuals seeking assistance in recent years because of higher potency marijuana and its more frequent use, it is becoming clear that the drug is capable of having adverse effects on physical and mental health.[28] The typical heavy marijuana user is also an excessive user of alcohol and other abused substances. Marijuana-related cognitive or behavioral difficulties are not attributed to marijuana initially. Only later in treatment does the adolescent client become aware of the role marijuana plays in his/her dysfunction. Older marijuana users are more likely to recognize a connection between their drug use and impairment of their various relationships or their inability to curtail their use of marijuana. Persuading the user to remain abstinent for two to three months may be therapeutic in itself because the individual often notices an emergence from mildly confused mentation, apathy, and loss of energy, whereas the entry into the state was imperceptible to him or her.

CONCLUSION

It appears that cannabis use in this country is evolving in new directions that will increase its potential for damage. To prevent the mental and physical consequences, high priority should be given to deterring children from becoming involved and over-involved. Legalization of the drug is not indicated in view of the recent research findings. De-criminalization of the possession of small amounts remains a tenable position. The harmfulness of making users of marijuana criminals is as serious as their occasional use. The unsatisfactory attempts to arrest and prosecute the large number of marijuana smokers also supports the de-criminalization statute.

---

[28] Jones, R.T. "Marijuana: health and treatment issues." *Psychiatric Clinics of North America.* 7:703-712, 1984.

HOW DOES MARIJUANA WORK IN THE BODY

The THC that is inhaled through marijuana smoking partially changes into two other compounds after it enters the human blood stream. These two compounds are chemically known as 11-hydroxy-9-tetrahydrocannabinol-9-carboxylic acid (C-THC).

THC is detectable in the human blood stream (plasma) for only about two hours. It produces euphoria and may cause visual, mental, and muscle (motor) impairment during this time period. OH-THC stays in the plasma four to six hours and may cause a small amount of euphoria. Depending on the amount smoked, C-THC may remain in the plasma for as long as three to six days. It causes no euphoria but may produce visual, mental and motor impairment. Consequently, users have no perception that they may be impaired.

SUMMARY OF MARIJUANA METABOLITES

Metabolite	Approximate Length of Time in Plasma	Causes Euphoria	Causes Visual, Mental and Motor Impairment
THC	2-3 hours	Yes	Yes
OH-THC	4-6 hours	Mild, if any	Yes
C-THC	3-6 days	No	Yes

C-THC stays in human plasma for so long because it is lipophilic or fat-soluble. It goes into fatty tissue and "sticks" until it is released back into the plasma. Because of the fat-solubility of C-THC, it can be found in the urine for many days after one has stopped smoking marijuana. C-THC has been found in urine for up to about 45 days in chronic or addicted marijuana users.

IDENTIFICATION OF ACUTE MARIJUANA INFLUENCE

ACUTE EFFECTS OF MARIJUANA

Marijuana has four basic effects, although all four may not exist in one person at the same time.

Stimulation:

Increase in Pulse Rate

Increase in Temperature

Increase in Blood Pressure

Decreased Attention Span

Sweating

Craving for Sweets

Mood Elevation

Poor Concentration

 md

Cannabis (Marijuana)

Sedation/Muscle Relaxation:

Droopy eyelids

Strabismus (non-convergence)

Slow or Non-reactive Pupil

Inability to Maintain Pupil Constriction

Giggly or Giddy

Visual-perception Disturbance

Poor Muscle Coordination

Mouth-Breather (dry lips/mouth)

Slow Gait

Poor Balance

Sleepy Appearance

Slow Speech

Anesthesia/Analgesia:

Pain Relief

Increased Hearing Threshold

Memory Loss

Time Distortion

Hallucinogenic/Psychedelic Effects (Usually only with high doses or combined with other drugs):

Hallucinations

Paranoia

Delusions

Marijuana is commonly used with alcohol (a sedative), cocaine (a stimulant), PCP, or other drugs which may potentiate some of its effects and reactions. Most of these effects last about 2 to 5 hours after smoking marijuana. Some effects, particularly vision, motor and mental effects may last for more than 24 hours, depending on the dosage taken.

Laboratory Findings and Degrees of Acute Influence

Only in the case of alcohol does the body fluid concentration reflect any predictable degree of impairment caused by acute influence. Most states use a blood-alcohol concentration of 100 mg./100 ml. or .10 mg. percent as the legal criteria for acute alcohol influence because this level is known to cause significant physical impairment in persons who are not tolerant to alcohol. At this time, it is not scientifically possible to determine the degree of acute influence or impairment by the concentration of other drugs of abuse present in blood or urine. Therefore, qualitative not quantitative urine and blood tests are the most appropriate to confirm a diagnosis of acute influence of marijuana, cocaine, heroine, amphetamines, and phencyclidine. It is also emphasized that the presence of abnormal physical signs, symptoms, and behaviors are the primary determinants of acute influence—not the laboratory test, which is only capable of confirmation.

Physical And Behavioral Signs Of Acute Influence

All psychoactive drugs, when high enough doses are consumed, will produce abnormal physical and behavioral signs in an individual who is not tolerant to the drug. Many of these signs are generic in that they are similar regardless of which drug, including marijuana, is taken. For example, a common misconception is that stimulants and sedatives cause very different acute physical and behavioral signs. Although there are some specific differences in the acute drug effects of stimulants and sedatives, both classes of drugs produce many identical symptoms. More importantly, low and high dosages of the same drug may produce different signs and symptoms. The degree of tolerance that a user may have will also influence symptoms. Persons in withdrawal from a stimulant, e.g., cocaine, may exhibit symptoms associated with the acute use of a sedative, e.g., heroin and vice versa.

Changes In Vital Signs With Acute Influence

Since marijuana has stimulant properties caused by its effects on norepinephrine, vital signs of marijuana users may show stimulatory effects:

PUPIL SIZE	Over 5.0 mm. in diameter
PULSE	Over 100 beats per minute *(Normal - 72 / minute)*
BLOOD PRESSURE	Systolic over 140 mm. Hg. *(Normal -120 mm. Hg.)*
RESPIRATORY RATE	Over 25 respirations per minute *(Normal - 20 / minute)*
TEMPERATURE	Over 100°F *(Normal 98.6° F)*

SPECIAL NOTE: If two of the above are present and there is marijuana derivative in plasma, urine, or saliva, acute marijuana influence should be considered to be present.

VISION EFFECTS WITH MARIJUANA

There is growing evidence that some abnormalities and possibly other neuro-muscular effects are present as long as marijuana's long-acting metabolite, C-THC, remains in the blood stream (plasma). Essentially, this means that marijuana may produce impairment and meet the criteria for acute influence for as long as three to six days after the last dose of marijuana. For example, a study was conducted at Stanford University in which ten licensed pilots were given a marijuana joint containing 19 mg. of THC. Twenty-four hours later they were tested on a flight simulator, and all made landing errors, including one pilot who missed the runway. Other examples of vision effects of marijuana include numerous drivers driving erratically who are routinely arrested by the California Highway Patrol. Upon examination they show eye findings of strabismus and slow or non-reactive pupils but claim to have not smoked marijuana for three to four days. Nonetheless, they show marijuana metabolite in their urine and no evidence of alcohol or other drug use.

Chronic marijuana users have been studied to correlate eye and other physical abnormalities with the presence of C-THC in plasma.[29] Although strabismus (non-convergence) and slow, or non-reactive pupils were not present in every user, they were found in some marijuana users three to six days after they claimed to have ceased use. The importance of this finding is that drug influence and impairment may remain for several days after marijuana was last used, even though the user has no feeling of euphoria or perception of impairment. The presence of strabismus and a non-reactive pupils can impair visual tracking ability which may produce accidents and injuries.

SUMMARY OF MARIJUANA'S EFFECTS ON THE EYES

Finding	How Often Present	Approximate Time May Last After Smoking
Redness	Frequent	4 to 6 hours
Dilated Pupil	Sometimes	2 to 4 hours
Non- or Slow-reacting Pupil	Frequent	1 to 3 days
Failure to Hold Constriction (Rebound Dilation)	Sometimes	4 to 6 hours
Strabismus (non-convergence)	Frequent	1 to 3 days
Droopy Eyelid	Frequent	2 to 4 hours
Failure to Estimate Distance	Frequent	4 to 6 hours

PHYSICAL EVALUATION/EXAMINATION OF A PERSON SUSPECTED OF ACUTE MARIJUANA INFLUENCE

Below is a list of physical evaluation procedures to be used when a person is suspected of acute marijuana influence. It is not necessary to do every procedure to make a correct medical and legal identification. Most of the following procedures can be performed by non-medical personnel:

1. Listen for speech rate.
2. Observe gait and balance.
3. Look for sleepy appearance, droopy eyelids, mouth breathing, dry lips, and green tongue.
4. Smell for odor of marijuana.
5. Assess responses for attention span, concentration, and giddiness.

---

[29] Tennant, Forest. *Identifying the Marijuana User,* 1st ed. West Covina, California: Veract, Inc., June 1986, pp. 17-23.

6. Assess depth perception by asking person to estimate a distance.
7. Examine eyes for droopy eyelid, pupil reaction, strabismus (non-convergence), and redness.
8. Determine muscle coordination and balance by finger-to-finger, finger-to-nose, step-test, and one leg balance count test (divided attention).
9. Take pulse, blood pressure, and respiratory rate.
10. Feel skin for sweating and tremor.
11. Note if hallucinations, delusions, or paranoia are present.
12. Instruct to give correct time, date, and place.
13. Observe for general physical and behavioral signs of acute drug influence.

IDENTIFICATION OF CHRONIC OR COVERT MARIJUANA USE

DIAGNOSIS OF CHRONIC MARIJUANA USE

There are two major criteria used in order to make a diagnosis of covert or chronic marijuana use when a person does not admit to use.

1) Presence of suggestive behaviors and signs.
2) Marijuana derivative in blood or urine.

The major problem of diagnosing chronic marijuana use is knowing when to suspect someone. When someone is suspected of chronic marijuana use, they can be confronted by telling them the signs and behaviors that make them appear suspicious. Once confronted, it may be appropriate for a physician, employer, parent, teacher, coach, etc., to ask for a urine test for definitive proof.

WHY MAKE A DIAGNOSIS OF CHRONIC OR COVERT MARIJUANA USE?

Chronic marijuana use has so many debilitating and negative consequences that it needs to be identified as early as possible in order to prevent its numerous medical complications and social problems.

In contrast to most other drug or alcohol abusers, marijuana users have a higher success rate in stopping and maintaining abstinence. Early identification and intervention usually produces good results. Consequently, the best way to help a chronic or covert marijuana user is to identify him or her as soon as possible.

WHEN TO SUSPECT CHRONIC OR COVERT MARIJUANA USE

Only a blood or urine test will definitively diagnose marijuana use. However, you should suspect chronic marijuana use if you observe a combination of some of marijuana's chronic effects. Some of these long-term effects can be scientifically attributed to the drug's ability to adversely alter the brain's norepinephrine or endorphin systems. In addition, chronic marijuana smoking causes irritation of the respiratory system, instability of glucose metabolism, and occasionally, abnormalities of sex hormones.

BASIC SIGNS AND BEHAVIOR ASSOCIATED WITH CHRONIC AND COVERT MARIJUANA USE

Frequent absences from school or work

Time distortion, including tardiness; unusual meal times

Frequent missed appointments

Constant use of eye drops (usually Visine)

Wears marijuana-leaf jewelry, insignia, or has clips to hold cigarettes.

Wear sunglasses indoors

Abnormal sleep pattern such as staying up after midnight or daytime sleeping

Repetitive forgetfulness or broken promises

Frequent accidents, injuries or traffic violations.

Loss of interest or motivation in job, school, or relationships

Deterioration of work or school performance

Careless hygiene and grooming habits

Recurrent respiratory infections

Poor pain and stress tolerance

Acne worsens

Sudden personality changes; person becomes dull, bland, or humorless

Binge eating of sweets and snacks between meals

Time Distortion With Marijuana

Chronic use of marijuana and many other stimulant drugs alters the brain chemistry so that normal time patterns are not maintained. For instance, the normal person tends to know when three meals per day should be eaten, when to go to sleep at night, take a 15-minute coffee break, or when to leave for school or work to arrive on time. A person whose internal time clock has been disturbed by chronic marijuana use will have distorted behaviors, including inability to keep appointments and meet time deadlines. Chronic users will also tend to stay up late at night or sleep during the day.

Motivational Disturbances

Marijuana may disrupt the endorphins and adrenaline-producing chemicals in the brain which motivate a person to carry out normal day-to-day activities. Lack of motivation exhibits itself in a number of rather typical ways. The most regular, daily motivations are particularly affected. These include the motivations to eating proper meals, to maintain normal hygiene, and to treat fellow human beings in a civil and decent manner. A chronic or covert marijuana user may be unable to maintain a sufficient level of motivation to carry out these routine daily functions.

Abnormal Self-Perception Of Job Or School Performance

Marijuana may markedly impair a person's job or school performance. For unknown reasons, however, the drug user may have little or no accurate perception of this impairment. The chronic user may insist that they are "doing fine" and that they do not deserve criticism in spite of failing grades or poor athletic or job performance. Unfortunately, the inability to accurately perceive one's performance may persist after drug use is discontinued.

Cigarette Smokers

Cigarette smoking is the single, biggest indicator that a person may be using illegal drugs. Approximately one-third of the adult population over age 18 years smoke cigarettes and of these, about 25 percent abuse drugs and/or alcohol. These figures may be higher for youth. The percentage of youth who are between 13 and 19 years of age, who smoke cigarettes and frequently use marijuana is nearly 50 percent. One reason youth who smoke cigarettes are likely candidates to use illegal drugs is because they are already knowledgeable about inhaling and are tolerant to the heat irritation produced by ordinary cigarettes. Physically and psychologically, it is a short step from cigarette smoking to marijuana or cocaine inhalation. Over 99 percent of heroin users smoke cigarettes; likewise, 90 percent of PCP and amphetamine users smoke cigarettes.

Craving For Sweets

Constant ingestion of sweets is a behavior that many chronic marijuana users exhibit. Marijuana releases norepinephrine from neurons which can reduce blood sugar and cause craving for sweets. Extremely poor dental hygiene is often observed in chronic marijuana users and this may be related to the constant ingestion of sweets.

BACKGROUND EVIDENCE FOR MARIJUANA ADDICTION

Marijuana addiction was described in the United States over 40 years ago.[30] In 1944, 35 "confirmed marijuana addicts" were admitted to a military hospital and developed withdrawal symptoms. Since this time, marijuana addiction has been reported in other countries. In addition, animals have demonstrated addiction to marijuana and there has been one carefully controlled trial where humans were given known quantities of THC; these humans developed withdrawal symptoms when marijuana was abruptly discontinued. Likewise, animals that are addicted to marijuana have demonstrated withdrawal symptoms when given naloxone. When naloxone precipitates withdrawal symptoms, it means that the addicting drug effects the body like an opioid (i.e., heroin, morphine, etc.). To complement these findings, another recent study in animals has demonstrated that THC will deplete endorphins in the nervous system. Furthermore, marijuana may also adversely affect the neurotransmitters norepinephrine and serotonin. Current evidence suggests that marijuana addiction exists, at least in part, as a result of depleted endorphin, norepinephrine, and possibly other neurotransmitters.

---

[30] National Commission on Marijuana and Drug Abuse. Raymond P. Shafer, Chairman. *Marijuana — A Signal of Misunderstandings.* New York: New American Library, 1972.

Cannabis (Marijuana)

Commonly Observed Marijuana Withdrawal Symptoms

The following symptoms have been reported by researchers studying the withdrawal effects of marijuana in animals and humans:

- Insomnia
- Nausea
- Anxiety
- Restlessness
- Irritability
- Chills
- Anorexia
- Cannabis craving
- Depression
- Mental confusion
- Yawning

BACKGROUND AND HISTORY OF MARIJUANA TESTING

Private industry has shown great interest in detecting the non-medical use of drugs during the very recent past. Since marijuana is the most frequently used illicit drug, it is of great interest to employers. In addition, the military services have pioneered mass urine screening for abused drugs because of their emphasis on alertness, the ability to make rapid decisions, and the need for unimpaired physical and mental functioning. More and more, large corporations are finding that accidents, breakage, absenteeism, theft, and poor productivity are associated with drug use—including marijuana use—in the workplace. Employers are testing urines (and less frequently blood) randomly, during pre-employment physical examinations, following accidents, and as a routine screening procedure for those who work in sensitive or public safety positions.

Acid metabolites of THC are found in the urine within an hour of smoking one "joint." They fall below the 20 ng./ml. level after about three days. However, chronic smokers whose fatty tissues are saturated with THC may continue to excrete detectable amounts for a month after last use.[31]

In addition to proper laboratory procedures and precise quality control, a supervised urine collection and a reliable chain of custody of the sample are necessary to provide accurate reports. A confirmatory test must also be performed after the positive screening test to assure that the positive result was definitely the acid metabolite of THC, 9-carboxy-THC. The possibility that a positive test was due to passive inhalation is kept at 20 ng./ml. or above. Due to the extended period of time during which urine tests for marijuana can remain positive, a positive result cannot prove use occurred at a specific time. A positive result simply indicates cannabis use at some point prior to testing which may have occurred hours or days earlier. While blood or sputum levels may eventually be correlated with intoxication, clearly defined criteria for impairment similar to those for alcohol do not yet exist.

Factors which can produce a false negative urine report for THC include: drinking large amounts of fluids; adding water, bleach, vinegar, detergent,

---

[31] Schwartz, R.H., and R.L. Hawks. "Laboratory detection of marijuana use." *JAMA*. 254:788-792, 1985.

or blood to the urine specimen; or substituting the urine of another person. These efforts to invalidate the test can be counteracted by appropriate measures. For example, determining the specific gravity of the urine will reveal whether it has been diluted; likewise, careful supervision of the process for obtaining specimens will discourage substitutions.[32]

RETENTION OF MARIJUANA IN PLASMA AND URINE

A great deal of publicity has been generated as to how long marijuana metabolites may remain detectable in plasma and urine due to the fact that it is fat-soluble. When smoked, marijuana metabolites enter the fat, lodge there, and then leak out over a period of time. It is important to point out that it is only the regular, chronic user who keeps marijuana in urine for more than a few days. The length of time that marijuana metabolites can be detected in plasma is much shorter than in urine because the drug's concentration in the urine is 100 to 1000 times more than the concentration found in plasma. Marijuana can be detected in urine much longer than in plasma due to the kidney's ability to concentrate drugs.

URINE RETENTION

Frequency of Use	Approximate Length of Time in Urine*
Once per week	2 - 20 days
Twice per week	5 - 30 days
	15 - 45 days

*Varies as to amount used and whether use is chronic or occasional.

PLASMA RETENTION

Metabolite	Approximate Time in Plasma*
THC	2 - 3 hours
OH-THC	4 - 6 hours
C-THC	3 - 6 days

*Varies as to amount used and whether use is chronic or an occasional.

SALIVA ANALYSIS

Saliva analysis for THC presence is possible because the marijuana smoke leaves THC residues in the mouth. If THC is found in saliva, it usually means that marijuana has been smoked within the previous one to three hours. However, this test cannot be relied upon for confirmatory diagnosis of marijuana use because the smoker can easily spit or wash the residue out of the oral cavity.

---

[32] *Ibid.*

MARIJUANA AND CRIME

During the past seventy-five years, several distinguished commissions have investigated evidence of the possible role of marijuana in criminal behavior. The different commissions reached strikingly similar conclusions: the behavioral effects of marijuana do not usually incite violent or sexual crimes; rather, the use of marijuana may reduce the possibility of aggression in most people. Recent laboratory and clinical studies support these conclusions and have demonstrated that while some individuals do commit crimes while under the influence of marijuana, most marijuana users tend to be under-represented in studies of assaultive offenders. This is especially true when a comparison is made with users of alcohol, barbiturates, and amphetamines. Some sub-groups of marijuana users do commit crimes against property, but non-pharmacological variables are probably more important influences on such behavior than the effects of the drug itself.[33] Thus, future research should analyze marijuana-crime interactions with the purpose of identifying and documenting these non-drug variables.

CANNABIS ERADICATION

The Drug Enforcement Administration started its cannabis eradication program in two states in 1981. Since then the program has progressed and developed into a 50-state operation with a budget of 3.63 million dollars. In 1985, the DEA conducted 21, one-week training seminars specializing in the detection and eradication of cannabis in the United States. A total of 931 Federal, state, and local officers attended these training seminars.

By the end of the 1985 growing season the DEA had discovered and eradicated approximately 39 million cannabis plants located in 40,000 fields, arrested 5,151 defendants, and seized 1,768 weapons.

As the program has developed, incidents of violence have greatly increased. During the 1985 Domestic Cannabis Eradication/Suppression Program, overt violence and the use of booby-trap devices associated with domestic cannabis cultivation were widespread with incidents reported in over 21 states. The range of sophistication and ingenuity exhibited by cannabis cultivators ranged from simple, innocuous, monofilament trip wires for alarms to explosive devices and firearm assaults which resulted in death. These booby-trap/protective devices were used as alarm deterrents against both the eradication efforts of law enforcement and the thefts of crops by "plot pirates."

The DEA has also seen a startling trend toward the use of dynamite, pipe bombs, and numerous other devices which had not been encountered to any great degree before the Domestic Cannabis Eradication/Suppression Program. In addition, marijuana traffickers are taking great pains to hide smaller fields in the edges of the forest or to intermingle the cannabis in

[33] National Commission on Marijuana and Drug Abuse. Raymond P. Sahfer, Chairman. *Marijuana — A Signal of Misunderstandings.* New York: New American Library, 1972. Chapter on "Marijuana and Public Safety," pp. 85-96.

________. *Drug Use in America: Problems in Perspective, Second Report.* Washington, D.C.: U.S. Gov't. Printing Office, 1973.

other crops such as corn. One of the newer trends in the last two years is to move cannabis plants indoors to greenhouse operations where they buy or rent multi-floor warehouses, old factories or even residences. In 1985, 951 greenhouse/indoor operations were seized.

In these locations, the traffickers are using artificial lighting and forced fertilization. It is obvious that the traffickers must grow fewer plants indoors. However, they are concentrating on perfecting the high potency variety called Sinsemilla, which has several times the THC content of normally cultivated cannabis.

Despite the move indoors, eradication efforts continue. On September 5, 1985, DEA Administrator John C. Lawn signed a Record of Decision with respect to the Environmental Impact Statement. The decision calls for the utilization of the full range of manual, mechanical, spot, and broadcast herbicidal methods to eradicate illegally cultivated cannabis on Federal lands. This position provides DEA and Federal land managers the operational flexibility to choose the most appropriate method of eradicating cannabis cultivation.

On September 6, 1985, the DEA conducted an herbicidal eradication project in the Mark Twain National Forest near Poplar Bluff, Missouri. Five separate 1⁄10 acre plots of cultivated cannabis were sprayed with the herbicide glyphosate from a backpack ground sprayer. Approximately 16,000 plants, ranging from ten to twelve feet in height were eradicated.

Later, on October 6, 1985, a six-acre cannabis plot in New Mexico, containing approximately 40,000 mature cannabis plants, was also eradicated by being sprayed with glyphosate. The plants had been cultivated and nurtured to assure a Sinsemilla crop. The spraying was done from a specially-equipped aircraft after an Environmental Assessment had been prepared by the DEA at the site. The site was on arid scrubland and measured about one mile long and 200 feet wide. This operation was the first aerial application of glyphosate after completion of the Environmental Impact Statement.

Indoor growers have also been apprehended. According to DEA statistics, nationwide seizures of indoor operations nearly doubled between 1984, when 649 facilities were seized in 22 states, and 1988, when authorities found 1,240 indoor operations in 41 states.

One advantage of indoor cultivation is that growers have developed new strains of marijuana that perform well under artificial lights and can produce buds in 90 days. The growers also have learned how to design facilities to minimize the chances of detection. In an indoor, pest-free, climate-controlled environment, skilled growers can produce four crops of marijuana buds a year.

"We have created this monster called 'the indoor grow' " remarked Charles Stowell, a DEA agent in Sacramento who coordinates anti-marijuana efforts in California. In this one state alone, authorities have seized several hundred indoor growing facilities each year for the past several years. California law enforcement first began running into highly sophisticated, large-scale indoor operations in the late 1980s. One of the largest indoor seizures in the nation occurred in June 1989, when 8,000 plants were founded in a barn on a farm near Sacramento.

Cannabis (Marijuana)

In 1990, drug enforcement authorities have dismantled what officials are describing as the largest and one of the most sophisticated indoor marijuana growing operations ever found in the United States. Local sheriffs' deputies and Drug Enforcement Administration agents seized five different facilities—two in Arizona and three in California—that are believed to have been planned and financed by the same ring of traffickers. The growing rooms were built underground, beneath structures designed to look like average family homes. More than 23,000 plants were growing at four of the sites when they were discovered. Officials estimated that the overall operation was capable of producing 46 tons of marijuana per year. That would represent more than half the total that authorities have seized so far this year in California, one of the major marijuana-producing states.

The five facilities in this recently discovered indoor growing operation were all located in remote desert areas. In one case, the location was on a gravel road miles away from the nearest highway. The underground growing chambers had thick concrete roofs to deter leakage of heat from dozens of powerful lamps, which otherwise could have been easily detected by infrared sensors on aircraft. The facilities were also equipped with wells, water tanks, and diesel generators, to keep down utility bills that otherwise would have drawn several thousand hours of electricity each month, compared with an average consumption of 900 kilowatt hours per month for a single-family home.

The production of marijuana at the facilities was highly automated. One of the facilities was hydroponic and had automatic timers to feed solution to the plants. Machines did some of the packaging. Thus, the entire operation could be run by two people from start to finish. The most elaborate of the facilities cost an estimated $1 million to build, officials said. Despite this high "overhead", the million-dollar facility was capable of producing a quantity and quality of marijuana worth nearly $25 million a year.

GLOSSARY OF CANNABIS SLANG TERMS

The following is a list of the slang expressions for the cannabis drugs covered in this chapter:

Marijuana . . . . grass, pot, weed, loco weed, tea, hay, Acapulco Gold, Mary Jane, J, 13, Colombian, Jamaican Red
Marijuana Cigarette . . . . joint, stick, reefer, number, roach (which refers to the butt of the cigarette)
Sinsemilla . . . . sin
Hashish . . . . hash, soles
Hashish Oil . . . . hash oil, honey oil

REFERENCES:

Abbot, S.R., Berg Jr., K.D. Loeffler, et al. "HPLC analysis of tetra-9-hydrocannabinol and metabolites in biological fluids." In: Venson J., ed., *Cannabinoid Analysis in Physiological Fluids.* ACS Symposium Series 98., ACS, Washington, D.C. pp. 115-36, 1979.

Abel, E.L. "Marijuana and sex: a critical survey." *Drug and Alcohol Dependence.* 8:1-22, 1981.

Barnett, G. et al. "Behavioral pharmacokinetics of marijuana." *Psychopharmacology.* 85:51-56, 1985.

Benusan, A.D. "Marijuana withdrawal symptoms." *Br Med J.* 3:112, 1971.

Black, D.L., A.G. Bruch, D.S. Isenschmid, et al. "Urine cannabinoid analysis: An integrated multi-method approach." *J Anal Toxicol.* 1:224-27, 1984.

Cabral, G.A. et al. "9-Tetrahydrocannabinol decreases host resistance to herpes simplex virus type 2 vaginal infection in the guinea pig." In: D.J. Harvey, ed. *Marijuana 84: Proceedings of the Oxford Symposium on Cannabis.* Oxford: IRL Press, 1985.

California Narcotic Officers Association. *The California Narcotic Officer.* Winter, 1986.

Chiang, C.N., and G. Barnett. "Marijuana effect and delta-9-tetrahydrocannabinol plasma level." *Clin Pharmacol Ther.* 36:254-258, 1984.

Coccheto, D.M., S.M. Owens, M. Perez-Reyes, et al. "Relationship between plasma delta-9-tetrahydrocannabinol concentration and pharmacologic effects in man." *Psychopharmacol.* 75:158-64, 1981.

Cohen, S. "Cannabis: Impact on motivation." *Drug Abuse & Alcoholism Newsletter.* Vol. X, Number 1, Vista Hill Foundation, January, 1981.

________. "Drugs in the workplace." *J Clin Psychiatry.* 45:4-8, 1984.

Dackis, C.A., A.L.C. Poltash, W. Annitto, et al. "Persistence of urine marijuana levels after supervised abstinence." *Am J Psychiatry.* 139:1196-1197, 1982.

Deneau, G.A., and S. Kaymakcalan. "Physiological and psychological dependence to synthetic delta-9-tetrahydrocannabinol (THC) in rhesus monkeys." *Pharmacologist.* 15:246, 1971.

Ellis, G.M., M.A. Marian, B.A. Judson, et al. "Excretion patterns of cannabinoid metabolites after last use in a group of chronic users." *Clin Pharmacol Ther.* 38:578, 1985.

El Sohly, MA, A.B. Jones, H.N. El Sohly, et al. "Analysis of the major metabolite of delta-9-tetrahydrocannabinol of urine. VI. Specificity of the assay with respect to indole carboxylic acids." *J Anal Toxicol.* 9:190-191, 1985.

Ferraro, D.P. "Acute effects of marijuana on human memory and cognition." *Marijuana: Research Findings.* Peterson, R.C., Ed., Washington, D.C.: US Government Printing Office, 1980.

Fletcher, S.M. "Screening for drugs by Emit." *J Forensic Sci.* 21:327-332, 1981.

Fraser, I.D. "Withdrawal symptoms in cannabis indica addicts." *Lancet.* II:747-748, 1949.

Frederick, D.L., J. Green, M.W. Fowler. "Comparison of six cannabinoid metabolite assays." *J. Anal Toxicol.* 9:116-120, 1985.

Freemon, F.R. "Effects of marijuana on sleeping states. *JAMA.* 220:1364-1365, 1972.

Cannabis (Marijuana)

Gibson, G.T. et al. "Maternal alcohol, tobacco and cannabis consumption on the outcome of pregnancy." *Aust NZ Obstet Gynecol.* 23:16-19, 1983.

Gorodetzky, C.W., E.J. Cone, and R.E. Johnson. "Validity of EMIT and RIA for detection in urine of marijuana cigarette smoking." *Pharmacologist.* 25:270, 1985.

Gould Publications. *Penal Code Handbook of California.* 1992.

Gupta, S., M.H. Gucco, and P. Cushman. "Impairment of rosette-forming T-lymphocytes in chronic marijuana smokers." *N Engl J Med.* 291:874-877, 1975.

Hansen, H.J., S.P. Caudil, and D.J. Boone. "Crisis in drug testing: Results of CDC blind study." *JAMA.* 253:2382-2387, 1985.

Hansteen, R.W., R.D. Miller, and L. Lonero. "Impairment of performance with low doses of marijuana." *Clin Pharmacol Ther.* 14:936-940, 1973.

Harclerode, J. "Endocrine effects of marijuana in the male." In: Braude, M.C., and J.P. Ludford, eds. *Marijuana: Effects on the Endocrine and Reproductive Systems.* Research Monograph Series 44. DHHS Pub. No. (ADM) 84-1278. Washington, D.C.: Supt. of Docs., U.S. Govt. Print. Off., 1984. 46-64.

Heath, R.A. et al. "Chronic marijuana smoking: its effect on function and structure of the primate brain." In: Nahas, G.G., and W.D.M. Patton, eds. *Marijuana: Biological Effects.* Oxford: Pergamon Press, 1979.

Hendin, H. and A.P. Haas. "The adaptive significance of chronic marijuana for adolescents and adults." *Advances in Alcohol and Substance Abuse.* 4:99-115, 1985.

Hingston, R. et al. "Effects of maternal drinking and marijuana use on fetal growth and development." *Pediatrics.* 70:539, 1982

________. "Effects on fetal development of maternal marijuana use during pregnancy." In: D.J. Harvey, ed. *Marijuana 84: Proceedings of the Oxford Symposium on Marijuana.* Oxford: IRL Press, 1984.

Hirschhorn, I.D., and J.A. Rosecrans. "Morphine and delta-9-tetrahydrocannabinol: Tolerance to the stimulus effects." *Psychopharmacology.* 36:245-253, 1974.

Hollister, L.E. "Cannabis and the development of tolerance." In: Nahas, C.G., and W.D.M. Paton, eds., *Advances in the Bioscience.* Vol. 22-25. "Marijuana: Biological Effects Analysis, Metabolism, Cellular Responses, Reproduction and Brain." Oxford: Pergamon Press 1979, p. 585-589.

Hollister, L.E., H.K. Gillespie, A. Olson, et al. "Do plasma concentrations of delta-9-tetrahydrocannabinol reflect the degree of intoxication." *J Clin Pharmacol.* 21:1715-1775, 1981.

Irving, J., B. Leeb, R.L. Foltz, et al. "Evaluation of immunoassays for cannabinoids in urine." *J Anal Toxicol.* 8:192-196, 1984.

Janowsky, D.S. "Marijuana effects on simulated flying ability." *AMJ Psychiatry.* 133:384-388, 1974.

Jessor, R., and S.L. Jessor. *Problem Behavior and Psychological Development: A Longitudinal Study.* New York: Academic Press, 1977.

Johnston, L.D., P.M. O'Malley, and J.G. Bachman. "Drug use among American high school students, college students, and other young adults." *National Trends Through 1985.* DHHS Pub. No. (ADM) 86-1450. Washington, D.C.: Supt. of Docs., U.S. Govt. Print. Off., 1986.

Jones, R.T. "Marijuana: health and treatment issues." *Psychiatric Clinics of North America.* 7:703-712, 1984.

Jones, R.T., N. Benowitz, and J. Bachman. "Clinical studies of cannabis tolerance and dependency." *Ann NY Acad Sci.* 282:221-239, 1976.

Kaymakacalan, S. "The addictive potential of cannabis." *Bull Narc.* 33:21-31, 1981.

Kaymakcalan, S., H. Ahyan, and F.C. Talunay. "Naloxone-induced or post-withdrawal abstinence signs in delta-9-tetrahydrocannabinol-tolerant rats." *Psychopharmacology.* 55:245-249, 1977.

Kim, J.H., and E. Cerceo. "Interference by NaCl with the EMIT method of analysis for drugs of abuse." *Clin Chem.* 22:2935-2936, 1976.

Knudsen, P., and T. Vilmar. "Cannabis and neuroliptic agents in schizophrenia." *Acta Pschiatr Scand.* 69:162-174, 1984.

Korgan, M.J., E. Newman, and N.J. Willson. "Detection of marijuana metabolite 11-nordelta-9-carboxylic acid in human urine by bonded phase absorption thin-layer chromatography." *J Chromotgr.* 306:441-445, 1984.

Koldony, R.C., W.H. Master, R.M. Koldner, et al. "Depression of plasma testosterone levels after chronic, intensive marijuana use." *N Engl J Med.* 290-875, 1972.

Law, B., P.A. Mason, A.C. Moffat, et al. "Passive inhalation of cannabis smoke." *J Pharm Pharmacol.* 36:578-581, 1984.

Lemberger, L., R.E. Crabtree, and H.M. Rowe. "11Hydroxy-delta-9-tetrahydrocannabinol: Pharmacology, disposition and metabolism of a major metabolite of marijuana in man." *Science.* 177:62-64, 1977.

Linn, S. et al. "The association of marijuana use with outcome of pregnancy." *Am J Public Health.* 73:1161-1164, 1983.

Manno, J.E., G.E. Kiplinger, S.E. Haine, et al. "Comparative effects of smoking marijuana or placebo on human motor or mental performance." *Clin Pharmacol Ther.* 11:808-812, 1970.

Marcotte, D.B. "Marijuana and mustism." *Am J Psychiatry.* 129:475-477, 1972.

Markionos, M., and A. Vakis. "Effects of acute cannabis use on urinary meurotransmitter metabolites and cyclic nucleotides in man." *Drug Alcohol Depend.* 14:175-178, 1984.

Mason, A.P., M. Perez-Reyes, and A.J. McBay. "Cannabinoid concentrations in plasma after passive inhalation of marijuana smoke." *J Anal Toxical.* 7:172-174, 1983.

Menhirota, S.S., et al. "Some psychological correlates of long-term heavy cannabis users." *Br J Psychiatry.* 132:482-486, 1978.

Michand, J.D., and D.W. Jones. "Thin-layer chromatography for broad spectrum drug detection." *Amer Laboratory.* 12:104-107, 1980.

Milman, D.H. "Marijuana psychoses." *JAMA.* 210:2397-2398, 1969.

Morgan, J.P. "Problems of mass urine screening for misused drugs." *J Psychoactive Drugs.* 16:305-316, 1984.

Morris, R.R. "Human pulmonary histopathological changes from marijuana smoking." *J Forensic Sciences.* 30:345-349, 1985.

Moskowitz, H., S. Sharma, and K. Zieman K. "The effect of marijuana on skills performance." *Proceedings of the 25th Conference of the American Association for Automotive Medicine.* San Francisco, 1981.

National Commission on Marijuana and Drug Abuse. Raymond P. Shafer, Chairman. *Marijuana — A Signal of Misunderstandings.* New York: New American Library, 1972.

_______. *Drug Use in America: Problems in Perspective, Second Report.* Washington, D.C.: U.S. Gov't. Printing Office, 1973.

O'Connor, J.E., and T.A. Rejent. "EMIT cannabinoid assay: Confirmation by RIA and GC/MS." *J Anal Toxical.* 5:168-173, 1981.

Perez-Reyes, M., S. DiGuiseppi, A.P. Mason, and K.H. Davis. "Passive inhalation of marijuana smoke and urinary excretion of cannabinoids." *Clin Pharmacol Ther.* 34:36-41, 1983.

Perez-Reyes, M., S. DiGuiseppi, K.H. Davis, et al. "Comparison of the effects of marijuana cigarettes of three different potencies." *Clin Pharmacol Ther.* 31:617-624, 1982.

Perez-Reyes M., S.M. Owens, and S. DiGuiseppi. "The clinical pharmacology and dynamics of marijuana cigarette smoking." *J Clin Pharmacol.* 21:201S-207S, 1981.

Pevick, J.S., D.R. Sasimeki, and F.A. Haertzen. "Abrupt withdrawal from therapeutically administered diazepam." *Arch Gen Psychiatry.* 55:995-998, 1978.

Schnoll, S.H., A.M. Daghestani. "Treatment of Marijuana Abuse." *Psychiat Annals.* 16:249-254, 1985.

Schwartz, R.H. "Frequent Marijuana Use in Adolescence: What are the signs, stages." *National Association of Secondary School Principals Bulletin.* 69:103-108, 1985.

Schwartz, R.H, and R.I. Hawks. "Laboratory detection of marijuana use." *JAMA.* 254:788-792, 1985.

Schwartz, R.H., G.F. Hayden, and M. Riddile. "Laboratory Detection of Marijuana Use: Experience With A Photometric Immunoassay to Measure Urinary Cannabinoids." *JAMA.* 139:1093-1096, 1985.

Smith, C.G., and R.H. Ashe. "Acute, short term and chronic effects of marijuana on the female primate reproductive function." In: Braude, M.C., and J.P. Ludford, eds. *Marijuana: Effects on the Endocrine and Reproductive Systems.* NIDA Research Monograph Series 44. DHHS Pub. No. (ADM)84-1278. Washington, D.C.: Supt. of Docs., U.S. Govt. Print. Off., 1984. pp. 82-96.

Smith, Roger. "U.S. Marijuana Legislation and the Creation of a Social Problem." *Journal of Psychedelic Drugs.* 2(1):93-99, 1968.

Solomon, David, ed. *The Marijuana Papers.* New York, The New American Library, Signet Books, 1966, pp. 41-42.

Sutheimer, C.A., K. Yarborough, B.R. Helper, et al. "Detection and confirmation of urinary cannabinoids." *J Anal Toxicol.* 9:152-160, 1985.

Swatck, R. "Marijuana use: Persistence and urinary elimination." *Journal of Substance Abuse Treatment.* 1:265-270, 1984.

Tashkin, D.P., J.R. Soars, R.S. Helper, et al. "Cannabis." *Ann Intern Med.* 89:539-549, 1978.

Taylor, D.A., and M.R. Fennessy. "Antagonist: precipitated withdrawal in rats after chronic delta-9-tetrahydrocannabinol treatment." *J Pharm Pharmacol.* 30:654-656.

Teitel, B. "Observations on Marijuana Withdrawal." *American Journal of Psychiatry.* 134:587, 1977.

Tennant, Forest. *Identifying the Marijuana User,* 1st ed. West Covina, California: Veract, Inc., June 1986.

Tyrey, L. "Endocrine aspects of cannabinoid action in female subprimates: search for sites of action." In: Braude, M.C., and J.P. Ludford, eds. *Marijuana: Effects on the Endocrine and Reproductive Systems.* Research Monograph Series 44. DHHS Pub. No. (ADM)84-1278. Washington, D.C.: Supt. of Docs., U.S. Govt. Print. Off., 1984.

Vereby, K., M.S. Gold and J. Mule. "Laboratory Testing in the Diagnosis of Marijuana Intoxication and Withdrawal." *Psychiatric Annals.* 16:235-241, 1986.

Voss, H.L. and R.R. Clayton. *International Journal of Addictions.* 19:633-652, 1984.

Weller, R.A., and J.A. Halikas. "Marijuana use and psychiatric illness: a follow-up study." *American J Psychiatry* 142:848-850, 1985.

Williams, A.F. et al. "Drugs in fatally injured young male drivers." *Pharm Chem Newsletter.* 14:1-11, 1985.

Wish, E.D., and S. Deren. "Assessment of treatment services for marijuana users." *Progress Report to the NIDA.* 1985.

Yesavage, J.A. et al. "Carry-over effects of marijuana intoxication on aircraft pilot performance: a preliminary report." *Am J Psychiatry.* 42(11):1325-1329, 1985.

________. "Increasing U.S. Pot Crop." *Register Guard.* Eugene, Oregon, January 8, 1985, p. 1A.

________. Indian Hemp Drugs Commission Report, 1894. Simla, India: Government Printing Office. 7 volumes.

________. "National Institute on Drug Abuse: Drug concentrations and driving impairment: Consensus panel." *JAMA.* 254:2018-2621, 1985.

A number of recent papers are worthy of further study. These include:

Adreasson, S. "Cannabis and schizophrenia." *Lancet.* II:1483-1486, 1987.

Mendhiratta, S.S., et al. "Cannabis and cognitive functions." *British Journal of Addicition.* 83:749-753, 1988.

Negrete, J.C. "What's happening to the cannabis debate?" *British Journal of Addicition.* 83:359-372, 1988.

Schuckit, *M. Drug and Alcohol Abuse.* 3rd ed., New York: Plenum Press, 1989.

Wu, T.C., et al. "Pulmonary hazards of smoking marijuana as compared with tobacco." *N.Engl. J. Med.* 318:347-351, 1988.

CHAPTER XIII

VOLATILE INHALANTS AND POISONOUS SUBSTANCES

INTRODUCTION

Volatile substances are chemicals that vaporize to a gaseous form at normal room temperatures. When inhaled they can intoxicate. Although the practice of inhaling volatile substances for mind-altering and recreational purposes is well over a hundred years old, today's sniffers consume a vast array of complex chemical compounds whose effects upon the human organism are poorly understood. While most of the volatile substances currently abused are commercial preparations that are generally safe when used as directed for their intended purpose, and often do not result in permanent injury even when they are abused, certain substances (such as the aerosols) have proven to be harmful or even fatal.

HISTORY OF INHALANT USE

The voluntary inhalation of toxic substances for the purpose of mood alteration is not a new phenomenon. In fact, the practice has endured for centuries. Its roots can be traced to the early Greek, Hebrew, and South American civilizations.

Abused volatile substances can be classified under three headings: anesthetics, solvents, and aerosols. Of these substances, anesthetics were the earliest to be abused. In the early 1800s, the anesthetics, nitrous oxide, ether, and chloroform were used as intoxicants. Medical applications in the fields of surgery and dentistry followed. The use of anesthetics for recreational purposes continued throughout the 19th century in Europe and America; in this century, recreational anesthetics re-emerged in the twenties and forties. Among the solvents, petrochemicals—primarily gasoline—were the most commonly abused. One of the primary articles published on the origin of gasoline sniffing in the United States appeared in 1934. The first known report of glue sniffing appeared 25 years later on August 2, 1959, in the *Denver Post.*

Although there were some isolated cases of inhalant use reported in the 1940s and 1950s, epidemiological interest in the use of inhalants did not become strong until the 1960s. Most cases from the 1940s through the 1960s were cases of "gasoline addiction." In the 1960s, many studies began to appear on the phenomenon of "glue sniffing." During the 1980s, the use of aerosols as a means of intoxication also became widespread.

Since the early sixties the practice of solvent sniffing has spread across a wide spectrum of commercial products that contain volatile substances in their preparation. Paint and lacquer thinners, nail polish remover, shoe polish, lighter fluid, and aerosol products such as spray paints, non-stick coating substances, shoe shine compounds, deodorants, hair sprays, and glass chillers are being sniffed for their intoxicating effects.

The use of inhalants continued to increase dramatically during the 1970s and 1980s. In fact, inhalant use has been reported not only in the United States, but also worldwide.

PREVALENCE OF INHALANT ABUSE

At the outset of the 1990s, school and public health officials estimated that at least seven million children between the ages of 5 and 17 had abused inhalants.

The startling fact is that the actual number of abusers could be much larger. A complete count of the number of inhalant abusers in this country is particularly hard to obtain for the following reasons: (1) inhalant abusers are only identified when brought to the attention of the authorities or while presenting themselves for treatment, (2) inhalant abuse often goes undetected when it is part of multiple drug abuse, (3) inhalant abuse will not be detected in standard urinalysis tests, (4) most studies are completed on student populations, thus excluding the dropout, working, and adult populations. Due to these problems in data collection, several drug abuse experts believe that the incidence of inhalant abuse is severely underestimated.

Reports on inhalant abuse vary from about 1 percent in some populations to 60 percent in others. In most national surveys, the percentage ranges from the low to high teens. Among reported inhalant abusers, early adolescent Hispanic males represent a large percentage. Yet, it is important to note that although the Hispanic population has been especially targeted by inhalant abuse research, the percentage of Anglo and African-American users has shown a steady increase.[1]

TYPES OF INHALANTS

ANESTHETIC AGENTS

Nitrous oxide or "laughing gas"—a colorless, slightly sweet-smelling gas—was first synthesized in 1772 by Joseph Priestly. It was not until 1799, however, that a chemist named Sir Humphrey Davy first inhaled it and experienced its unusual effects. He and several others became enthusiastically involved in experimentation with this "gas of paradise" after discovering that, under its influence, they felt exhilarated and euphoric. After these initial experiments, several mid-nineteenth century dentists became interested in the use of nitrous oxide as an anesthetic agent. By 1868, the gas was widely used as a pain killer. Nitrous oxide is still popular, not only as a dental anesthetic and analgesic, but sometimes as a social intoxicant as well.[2]

Another anesthetic agent, ether, was introduced to the medical world in the eighteenth century by Friedreich Hoffman. After its introduction, ether was then frequently prescribed in liquid form as a "soothing tonic" for a variety of ills. The first use of ether as a surgical anesthetic by a dentist in 1846 is often hailed as the birth of modern inhalation anesthesia. In addition

---

[1] Media Projects, Inc. "Inhalant Abuse: Kids in Danger/Adults in the Dark." Dallas, TX, p.4, 1990.
[2] For further information see *PharmChem Newsletter*. Vol.4, No.5.

to medical applications, ether drinking and sniffing for recreational purposes was quite popular in the nineteenth century; in fact, it was regarded as a harmless, cheap substitute for alcohol. Ether produced intoxicating effects similar to alcohol, was exempt from taxes, and did not cause hangovers. During Prohibition, when alcohol was unavailable, soft drinks were frequently "spiked" with ether. Numerous cases of ether habituation were reported during this time; users admitted inhaling as much as a pint a day over many years as a means to relieve anxiety, produce a sense of well-being, or induce sleep.

Like ether, chloroform is another highly volatile liquid that may be either ingested or inhaled. Chloroform was first produced in 1831, while in 1847 it was introduced as an anesthetic for women in childbirth. Recreational use began soon after its discovery; unfortunately, deaths from recreational overdose were not uncommon. Hence, chloroform never gained widespread popular acceptance as an intoxicant. Nonetheless, chloroform is an extremely versatile solvent; in addition to its many other uses, it appears as a common, though minor ingredient in many cough and cold preparations.

THE NITRITE INHALANTS (POPPERS)

In the era of Acquired Immune Deficiency Syndrome (AIDS), a discussion of nitrite inhalants is especially relevant. In the 1960s, clinicians began to note high rates of fatal infections and unusual tumors in homosexual men. A leading theory of this syndrome's origin was that the problems were caused by nitrite inhalants used by gay men in an attempt to enhance and prolong orgasm. While the deadly syndrome proved to be AIDS, there is some evidence that these substances may also contribute to immunologic problems, either exacerbating the syndromes associated with AIDS or causing additional problems on their own.

Amyl, Butyl, And Isobutyl Nitrite

These substances have had applications in medicine for years. One prominent action of nitrite inhalants is that they dilate blood vessels (they are vasodilators). Thus, these nitrite inhalants are often used in the treatment of angina (heart pain from exertion) and for diagnostic x-ray procedures where blood vessel size and flexibility are being evaluated. Some of these substances are also sold in adult sex stores under a variety of names including Rush, Kick, and Belt. The most potent form of the nitrite inhalants, amyl nitrite, is frequently prescribed for angina; however, it can be used "on the street" for the same reason as the other nitrites. These substances are generically called "poppers" because they are usually sold in small glass vials that are then broken or popped and sniffed when used.

Effects of Nitrite Inhalants

Inhalation of nitrite vapors in any form is usually associated with changes in psychological perceptions. First, these drugs produce a feeling of fullness in the head or a "rush," possibly caused by enlargement or dilation of cerebral blood vessels. Users also report a mild feeling of euphoria and a perception that time has slowed down; some users have mentioned an increase in sexual feelings or libido as well. These subjective effects usually last about a minute, but have been said to range in duration from five seconds or so to as long as a quarter-of-an-hour, depending upon the amount inhaled and the psychological state of the user.

Physical effects are also commonly observed with these inhalants. There is a general relaxation of both smooth muscles and the rectal sphincter. Increased heart rate is also a common effect. Research has not yet revealed whether the majority of homosexuals who use "poppers" take them in order to get the feelings of euphoria or if they are seeking some of the specific physiological effects. It may be a combination of the two.

Patterns Of Nitrite Inhalant Abuse

Many individuals experimenting with drugs, not just homosexuals, try inhalants. A recent survey estimated that 17 percent of 18 to 25 year olds have used these drugs. Those figures compare with 60 percent among homosexuals. The use pattern among gay men is estimated at approximately once per week, but as much as four times per week is not unusual. In another survey, 20 percent of the gay men surveyed had used some form of nitrite in the prior week.

The chances of a person having used a nitrite are determined through a number of variables. These drugs are more likely to be taken among urban individuals, men with a higher number of sexual partners, those who report having participated in group sex, and most likely among heavy-drinkers. In one survey, the age of first use occurred at 22 years (range of 16 to 24 years), with the peak incidence at approximately 25 years. Apparently, individuals who take nitrites have a strong preference for the amyl form, with 78 percent in one study having used amyl nitrite only. Consistent with the information listed above, the use of these drugs is frequently associated with sexual activity, although almost 60 percent of the individuals sampled report that they inhale the drug mostly during masturbation. Only about a quarter of the surveyed users have ever taken these inhalants independent of sexual activity. Approximately half inhale nitrites in conjunction with other drugs, especially marijuana and alcohol.[3]

Problems Associated With Nitrite Inhalants

The most disturbing data of nitrite inhalant abuse relates to the possibility (many would say the probability) that repeated heavy use of nitrites can impair immune functioning. There is evidence that in the presence of nitrites many white cells, especially the T-lymphocytes, may not function normally, and that there might be an additional suppression of natural killer-cell activity. There is also some laboratory evidence that in the presence of nitrites, certain normal body chemicals are converted into a carcinogenic substance, the nitrosamines. It is felt that this combination of events might contribute to a high risk for Kaposi Sarcoma among homosexuals, even among those who do not have AIDS. It has also been hypothesized that the concomitant use of nitrites with "unsafe" sexual activity might facilitate the transmission of the AIDS virus.

---

[3] Lange, W.R. et al. "Nitrite Inhalants: Patterns of Abuse in Baltimore and Washington, D.C." *American Journal of Drug and Alcohol Abuse.* 14:29-39, 1988.

A second medical difficulty associated with nitrite inhalants involves the respiratory system. When inhaled, these substances are irritating and can cause a bronchitis-like syndrome. In addition, in the presence of nitrites, the red blood cell component that is essential for carrying oxygen to the body cells, hemoglobin, can be converted to methemoglobin. This latter substance is not an efficient oxygen carrier and, thus, repeated use of inhalants might contribute to a lack of oxygen in the body and associated respiratory difficulties.

Of course, as is true with most substances, it is also possible to overdose or have a toxic reaction with inhalants. While these are rarely (if ever) lethal, they can disturb the body's normal functioning. This is likely to include nausea, vomiting, headache, and dizziness. Through their vasal dilation effects, these substances can also produce a significant drop in blood pressure. Moreover, some individuals develop allergies to nitrites which results in wheezing and itching.

One final psychological syndrome is worth describing. The use of nitrites among individuals with little prior exposure to these drugs can cause a state of psychological panic. This panic usually centers on fears that the feelings will not go away and that the person might not come out of the "high." A similar syndrome can be seen with naive users of marijuana and hallucinogens. All such panic reactions can usually be treated with reassurance and education, as the symptoms are likely to pass within minutes.

In response to some of the problems described above, especially the fear of compromising the body's immune functioning, it is possible that the use of inhalants in homosexual communities has decreased to some degree. In support of this contention is a series of surveys first evaluating homosexual men in the early 1980s and then reexamining them in 1986 with evidence of decreased intake patterns.[4]

OTHER VOLATILE SOLVENTS

When inhaled in sufficient quantity, all volatile hydrocarbons produce effects similar to alcohol intoxication. Almost all of these solvents have been misused by people seeking a cheap, easy high. Many factory workers who were continuously exposed to industrial solvents (prior to enactment of stringent health regulations) developed a strong attraction to the fumes and took to sniffing them deliberately. Gasoline, too, has its share of devotees, especially among children. Children were at the center of the highly publicized glue-sniffing craze of the 1960s, causing widespread alarm among concerned adults. The following chart shows some commonly abused commercial products and the solvents most often present:

[4] Lange, W.R. "Nitrite Inhalants: Promising and Discouraging News." *British Journal of Addiction.* 84:121-123, 1989.

Schuckit, M.A. *Drug and Alcohol Abuse: A Clinical Guide to Diagnosis and Treatment.* 3rd ed., New York: Plenum Press, 1989.

Product	Main Solvents
model cement, airplane glue	toluene, acetone, naphtha
rubber cement	benzene
fingernail polish remover	acetone, ethyl acetate
lighter fluid	kerosene, naphtha
cleaning fluid	carbon tetrachloride
spot remover	trichloromethane, trichloroethylene
gasoline	benzene compounds, maphthenes, other aromatics
aerosols	dichlorodifluoromethane (propellant 12) trichlorofluormethane, isobutane

Aerosols

These agents are liquid, solid, or gaseous products (or mixtures of the three) which are discharged by a propellant force of liquified and/or non-liquified compressed gas. Most aerosols contain three major components—propellants, solvents, and active ingredients—packaged under pressure in a disposable container. Commonly misused aerosol products include spray paints, insecticides, hair sprays, deodorants, glass chillers, and frying pan lubricants.

PHARMACOLOGY AND CHEMISTRY OF INHALANTS

With the exception of the anesthetics, the commonly inhaled volatile substances are complex chemical compounds. Their contents generally belong to chemical groups variously consisting of aromatic hydrocarbons, aliphatic hydrocarbons, aliphatic nitrites, fluorinated hydrocarbons, dechlorinated and trichlorinated hydrocarbons, alcohols, ketones, and esters. Substance sniffing results in an immediate and effective reaction in the body. The inhalation of volatile substances through the lungs carries the chemicals via the bloodstream directly to the brain. Thus, the effects of sniffing are felt almost instantaneously. The "high" can last anywhere from one to fifteen minutes.

The inhaled chemicals are carried by and stored in fatty substances known as lipids, which are also found in high concentrations in the brain and throughout the central nervous system (CNS). Since volatile substances are stored by lipophilic substances until they are eliminated from the body, a cumulative buildup may occur if new chemicals are absorbed before any stored residue is expelled. With repeated "huffing" or sniffing of inhalants, the body may not be able to dispose of these chemicals quickly enough, and a cumulative concentration in the brain and central nervous system can occur. The body disposes of volatile substances through exhalation and metabolism by the liver, with excretion in the urine.

The effects of inhalants on an individual will vary in accordance with body size and weight, and the amount of chemicals inhaled. Also, since inhalants may contain more than one of a number of toxic chemicals, the effects of multiple toxins on the body must be considered especially dangerous.

TOXICOLOGY OF INHALANTS

Although the toxic effects of sniffing most volatile substances are generally believed to be transient in nature, there are certain substances that present serious health hazards. Toxic effects of a transient nature include acute organic brain syndrome which is characterized by dizziness, loss of memory, inability to concentrate, confusion, and unsteady gait. Beyond this fairly common reaction to inhalants, toxicity problems become specifically related to different chemicals and combinations of chemicals.

Volatile substances commonly found in commercial products that may represent dangerous, toxic effects when inhaled include the fluorocarbons (aerosols), benzene, tetraethyl lead, carbon tetrachloride, and n-hexane.

The most prominent threat to health associated with inhalant abuse is the Sudden Sniffing Death (SSD) syndrome related to sniffing the fluorocarbons contained in aerosols. The SSD syndrome is caused when the fluorocarbons (particularly trichlorofluoromethane) sensitize the heart to the adrenal hormone epinephrine, which is in itself a strong cardiac stimulant. By potentiating the effect of epinephrine on the heart, wildly erratic heartbeat and increased pulse occur, resulting in heart failure and death.

The prevalence of SSD syndrome has been comfirmed by researchers at the U.S. Consumer Product Safety Commission; these researchers compiled accounts of over 300 deaths resulting from intentional inhalation of aerosol sprays. Their report states that "The hazard associated with aerosol containers that is most costly, in terms of loss of life, is intentional inhalation of aerosol spray vapors."

In addition to the aerosols, the substances benzene, carbon tetrachloride, and tetraethyl lead are among the most toxic. Benzene can cause death when inhaled in dense concentrations. The amount of benzene in gasoline is considered such a threat to health that the Occupational Safety and Health Administration gauges its standards for the amount of fumes gasoline workers may be exposed to on the percent of benzene contained in the gasoline. The danger of benzene is that it deteriorates the blood-forming elements of the body and is believed to cause chromosomal abnormalities and leukemia in humans. Like benzene, carbon tetrachloride can also cause death in high concentrations. In lower concentrations with prolonged exposure, carbon tetrachloride may cause permanent kidney and liver damage. Another volatile substance used as an additive in gasoline in tetraethyl lead. This substance may cause permanent injury to the brain and the central nervous system if inhaled in sufficient quantities.

Benzene, carbon tetrachloride, tetraethyl lead—and most likely the fluorocarbons—have been or will be in the near future banned for use in commercial applications. Except for their appearance in existing products still on the shelf, their toxic threat to inhalant abusers will soon be eliminated. In the case of the aerosols, however, it is not yet clear which chemical compounds will replace the fluorocarbons as propellants and whether or not the new substances will also induce the SSD syndrome.

Another widely used volatile solvent with adverse toxic effects is n-hexane. This solvent is frequently a component of model airplane cement. Excessive exposure to n-hexane through sniffing glue has been related to cases of nerve disorders resulting in either permanent damage and/or extended recovery periods.

The toxic effects of another common volatile solvent, toluene, are less clear than for n-hexane. Although it is generally believed that this widely abused substance is essentially harmless and any toxic effects are only transient in nature, there are documented cases which may indicate the contrary. These cases of chronic toluene sniffing presented bodily toxicities ranging from peripheral nerve damage to "permanent brain damage with diffuse cerebral atrophy."

According to Dr. Nancy Neff, an assistant professor of community medicine at the Baylor College of Medicine in Houston, individuals who regularly inhale the fumes of spray paint or similar chemical substances could also suffer permanent brain damage. "The primary physical effect of inhalant abuse is on the central nervous system (brain and spinal cord). It can cause organic brain syndrome, which is the diminished capacity to think, reason, remember, do calculations and abstract thinking," Dr. Neff says. Some spray paints and leather care products contain toluene which, when inhaled through the nose or mouth, is rapidly absorbed into the bloodstream and dissolves the fatty protective layer around nerves, thus causing them to wither and die. "Once a nerve is damaged, it is unable to regenerate and grow back. That's why I'm concerned that some of the neurological problems that we see may be permanent in these teen-age kids," says Dr. Neff.

In a four-year study of 97 teenage inhalant abusers as the Casa de Amigos Drug Treatment Program in Houston, Dr. Neff found that nearly half of them had evidence of long-term brain damage and physical deterioration. Simple neurologic tests, such as walking a straight line, touching the nose with a finger or maintaining balance while standing with eyes closed, were difficult for many of the inhalant abusers because of central nervous system damage.

In addition to brain damage, inhalant abusers may suffer nausea and vomiting, loss of appetite, ringing in the ears, a stuffy or runny nose, abdominal pain or cramps. More severe problems can include kidney damage, kidney stone formation, muscle weakness and paralysis. Female inhalant abusers who become pregnant face an increased risk of having a child with birth defects.

Moreover, serious personality problems may plague inhalant abusers. Previously stable teens can become violent and aggressive; feelings of anxiety, depression, and suicide are common. "Inhalant abuse, like many other forms of substance abuse, is probably a symptom rather than the problem itself," says Dr. Neff. "The kids get into it because they're unhappy, they're alienated from their families and other traditional support systems, they're bored and they're subject to peer pressure."[5]

---

[5] DeBorona, M. and D. Simpson. "Inhalant Users in Drug Abuse Prevention Programs." *American Journal of Drug and Alcohol Abuse.* 10:503-518, 1984.

Treatment of the medical complications of inhalant abuse and individual and family counseling are the most common methods of preventing further physical damage and continued misuse of the chemical substance.

DANGEROUS EFFECTS OF INHALANT ABUSE

The use of inhalants encompasses a wide variety of substances, thus producing numerous adverse physiological, psychological, and sociological effects. These effects are listed below.

Physiological

(short-term)	(long-term)
Severe headaches	Brain damage
Rashes around the nose and mouth	Liver damage
Weight loss	Kidney damage
Red eyes, glassy eyes	Central nervous system damage (manifested by palsy-like symptoms)
Menstrual disorders	
Irregular heartbeat	Sudden sniffing death syndrome (involves total heart failure)
Lack of appetite	
Frequent coughs/runny nose	
Upper respiratory problems	
Night sweats	
Shortness of breath	
Indigestion	
Constipation	
Acute poisoning	

Psychological

(short-term)	(long-term)
Mood swings	Inhalant psychosis
Acute depression	Schizophrenia
Passive-aggressive attitude	Severe psychopathology
Poor self-esteem	Hallucinations (continual)
Hallucinations (both aural & visual)	Lowered IQ
Paranoid delusions	
Memory loss	

Sociological/Behaviorial

(short-term)	**(long-term)**
Impairment in judgment	Violent, out-of-control behavior (In extreme cases, behavior has included assault and murder)
Anti-social behavior	
Low academic achievement	
Aggression	
Juvenile delinquency	

Withdrawal Symptoms

There is no physical addiction to these volatile substances. Therefore, the abuser will *not* suffer any withdrawal symptoms if deprived of the substance he or she has been abusing, as will the heroin or barbiturate abuser.

METHODS OF VOLATILE SUBTANCE ABUSE

The most common form of toluene abuse is by inhalation of the fumes. This may be done in various ways, but the most frequent method is to obtain a spray paint can that contains the substance. The paint is then sprayed onto a cloth material, usually a sock. The sock's toe area is generously coated with paint. The sock is then wrapped in a fashion so as not to have the paint come in contact with the skin. The sock is then placed to the nose and mouth area while the toluene fumes are inhaled into the body through a series of deep breaths. It might be noted here that silver and gold spray paints are rumored to contain higher contents of toluene.

Another popular method of inhaling volatile substances (like glue and cement) is to saturate the inside of a paper (or plastic) bag so the fumes can be contained at a concentrated level. The opened end of the bag is then placed over the mouth and the opening is sealed by holding the bag tightly to the cheeks. At this point the fumes are inhaled into the lungs, usually through one deep breath.

 md

Volatile Inhalants & Poisonous Substances

EARLY WARNING SIGNS OF INHALANT ABUSE

Many of the early signs and symptoms of inhalant abuse are similar to that of other forms of substance abuse:

Sudden change in choice of friends

Poor performance at school or work

Sloppy dress, sudden lack of personal hygiene

Lack of appetite, weight loss

Sudden mood settings, defensiveness

Withdrawal from family activities

The above signs by themselves do not indicate inhalant abuse, but parents, teachers, and health professionals should be aware of these signs when they are coupled with the following:

Chemical odors on the breath or clothing

Paint stains on clothing, fingertips, or around the nose or mouth

Runny nose and other cold-like symptoms

Red or glassy eyes

Rashes around the nose and mouth

Symptoms of Abuse

After inhalation, the toluene abuser will feel intoxicated and may appear to be drunk. The most visible objective symptoms are:

— Poor coordination

— Slurred speech

— Odor of the substance on the breath

— Excess nasal secretions

— Watering of the eyes

— Dilated (enlarged) pupils

— Sneezing and coughing

— Nausea and headache

While under the influence, the abuser will experience a feeling of euphoria, exaggerated well-being, vigor and high spirits. This may be accompanied or replaced with drowsiness and disordered perception. He or she may have hallucinations (seeing, hearing and experiencing things which are not there), double vision, and may even become unconscious.

INVESTIGATIONS OF VOLATILE SUBSTANCE ABUSE

The fumes of any inhaled substance may linger on for a long period of time after inhalation. In addition to recognizing the smell of volatile fumes, be sure to check the hands and facial area of suspected persons for tell-tale signs of paint. It is common for the paint to transfer onto the person's body when preparing and when ingesting the substance. If any skin areas have been exposed to the paint, they should be noted.

A check of the immediate area should also be made to attempt to locate the sock or other implements used in inhaling the substance. If this is found, a further check for the paint can or substance container should also be made.

A sobriety test of some sort should be administered to the subject when investigating the degree of intoxication. The symptoms noted previously should be documented, especially if the subject does have a strong odor of paint on his or her breath.

It is important to carefully secure any evidence obtained. If a sock or cloth material that is saturated with paint or some other substance is obtained, placement into a mason-type jar with a screw-on type lid is preferred. This will insure the freshness of the item for a later date in the event the matter goes to court. If no paint can is obtained, then this will further insure the quality of the evidence when it is sent to a crime lab for analysis. This last point is very important. The evidence, when obtained in the field, cannot be positively identified as containing toluene. A chemical test determining the chemical content is necessary. This is not possible in the field at this time, so analysis must be made at a lab. Also, this is the case when securing paint cans as evidence in the field. All paint cans or other substances that contain toluene are so noted on the label. As is most often the case, the subjects will remove the label in an attempt to conceal the fact that the substance does in fact contain toluene. If this does occur, a lab analysis is in order to definitely determine the chemical content of the substance.

REPEAT OFFENDERS

There are habitual offenders of inhalant abuse. The most plausible explanation one can offer is that the individual, when low on money, will return to the abuse of toluene as the need arises for a cheap high. That is precisely what "sniffing" paint or glue is: a very inexpensive form of getting intoxicated.

Another motivation for repeated inhalation is social pressure. The general consensus, according to Lynn Miller of the Santa Cruz County Probation Department, is that although the inhaling of toluene is not physically addictive, it is socially addictive when those in the surrounding environment are continually in quest of activities to occupy their time. Referring to inhalant abuse and its socially addictive capacity, Miller said: "It is a destructive effort to find an alternate way to occupy free time when the individuals are left unsupervised for any great lengths of time, which is the case with a large percentage of the youth in the community . . ."

THE SOCIOLOGY OF INHALANT USE

Early studies suggest that the social backgrounds of inhalant users are fairly homogeneous.[6] Latinos (Puerto Rican or Chicano, depending on the

[6] Cohen, S. "The Volatile Solvents." *Public Health Review*. 2(2):185-214, 1973.

 md

region) have often been reported to be overrepresented among samples of inhalant users, while blacks have been underrepresented.[7] In addition, studies have generally shown that the majority of sniffers come from low-income backgrounds.[8] However, there are samples—such as Bass' of 110 youths who died "sudden sniffing deaths"—which are primarily from suburban white middle-class homes.[9] Males have been reported to outnumber females as much as 10 to 1 (Cohen 1973). More recent samples of inhalant users suggest that they are well represented among all socio-economic levels.[10] There is anecdotal evidence suggesting that for many adolescent inhalant users sniffing is primarily a group activity.

The Causes of Inhalant Use

Implicit in most drug use research are assumptions about the causes of excessive drug use (even if "excessive" is seldom defined). Researchers have been remarkably consistent in assuming that the cause of excessive inhalant use lies in the disorganized existence of users, taking the form of either individual personality disruptions or massive familial disorganization, or both.[11]

Here again, a distinction between kinds of inhalant use may distinguish between different causes, for the question of what causes a certain kind of drug use varies widely with the relationship between person and drug (the most obvious example being the occasional social drinker versus the severe alcoholic).

Cohen (1973) suggests that some kind of emotional disruption, from whatever source, stands out as the common factor pushing individuals into persistent use of inhalants. The most disturbed individuals are more likely to remain heavily involved because they obtain the most relief from their anxiety, depression, or other negative feelings. Cohen further suggests that some of the variables which influence the choice of intoxicant for adolescents are (1) what the microculture is using, (2) availability of the agent, and (3) the secondary gains such as the "high."

The studies of drug use prevalence among young people in the United States today all indicate that inhalants are only one of a number of substances used by youths; thus, several studies indicate that inhalants are used concurrently with other drugs or are associated with greater drug experimentation.[12]

---

[7] Langrod, J. "Secondary drug use among heroin addicts." *International Journal of the Addictions*. 5:611735, 1970.

[8] Chapel, J.C. and D.W. Taylor. "Glue sniffing." *Missouri Medicine*. 65(4):288-292, 1968.

[9] Bass, M. "Sudden sniffing deaths." *Journal of the American Medical Association (AMA)*. 212:2075-2079, 1970.

[10] Dorman, M. "Inhalant abuse: a psychological research model." *National Institute on Drug Abuse: Third Technical Review on Inhalant Abuse*. Rockville, MD, 1976.

[11] For a comprehensive review of this trend, see Cohen, S. "The Volatile Solvents." *Public Health Review*. 2(2):185-214, 1973.

[12] D'Amada, C. et al. "Heroin addicts with a history of glue sniffing: A deviant group within a deviant group." *International Journal of the Addictions*. 12(2-3): 255-270, 1977. See also Schmidt, G.L. "A study of achievement motivation and frustration in glue sniffers." *Drug Forum*. 4(4):331-348, 1975.

The inhalation of certain commercial substances is potentially more dangerous both physically and psychologically than the use of marijuana or other drugs popular among youths.

However, to generate hypotheses about what "causes" inhalant use without considering the larger circumstances influencing the lives of adolescents and young adults (including drug use and abuse) can lead to oversimplification and a narrow view of the problem. A broader picture of the contexts of drug use can also provide opportunities for the emergence of innovative treatment and other alternatives.

The fact that inhalant use by adolescents has been reported in many areas of the world—in many subcultures of the United States, in Canada, Mexico, England, Sweden, Japan, Australia—should indicate that such substance use is part of a process that extends beyond the cities and towns of the United States (Cohen 1973). Many anthropologists would agree with the suggestion that it is a process tied to the universal problems of adolescents in finding their social and sexual identity.

Several reports offer suggestions about why inhalants might be the substance of choice among adolescents. The most obvious answer is the accessibility of the drugs. The range of commercial substances which will produce a high, including hallucinations, is vast. Many of them are household or workshop products. Particularly for children and adolescents this factor must be an important influence. The most commonly mentioned factor in interviews with adolescents is the hallucinations, often described as vivid, mystical, and as a center for group rituals and communication. In addition, users often mention feelings of power and invulnerability as positive factors. However, there are acute negative side effects described such as headaches, nausea, etc., and undoubtedly not all young people who experiment with inhalants respond favorably to them.

Why, then, if inhalants are so accessible and have such desirable "highs," are they not used by higher percentages of young adults and adolescents? An initial approach to this question offers two possible answers. The first is the widespread fear of the permanent physical and psychological effects of inhalants. User anecdotes suggest that such a fear is pervasive. The second possible explanation is the association of drugs with certain groups—social class, ethnic, or age groups—which tends to make them less desirable for use by members of other groups, especially if the using group is lower status. Within some drug-using subcultures, inhalant use may be seen as lower status because of its identification with younger adolescents.

These suggestions indicate a need for more research on the use of substances besides inhalants by those who report current inhalant use and by those reporting past inhalant use. More information is needed on the factors which motivate drug use. This research might be initiated with user interviews to document their attitudes toward different drugs. The research might be augmented then by a study of those youths in drug- and inhalant-using communities who have not become involved with inhalants.

POISONING INVESTIGATION

INTRODUCTION

The preliminary investigation of a poisoning can be of critical importance in saving the victim's life. An experienced investigator can detect several poisons. In order to administer the appropriate treatment, doctors will depend on the officer's ability to quickly locate and possibly identify the poison. Also, any available physical evidence must be carefully collected and identified. The evidence can indicate whether the poisoning is suicidal, homicidal, or accidental.

CLASSIFICATION OF POISONS

Solvents:

a. Ether
b. Acetone
c. Benzene
d. Carbon Disulfide
e. Carbon Tetrachloride

Inorganic Poisons:

a. Arsenic
b. Mercuric Chloride
c. Antimony Compounds
d. Lead Salts
e. Phosphorous

Organic Poisons:

a. Salicylate
b. Barbiturates
c. Narcotics
d. Strychnine
e. Nicotine

Gaseous Poisons:

a. Carbon Monoxide
b. Illuminating Gas
c. Hydrogen Sulfide
d. Sulfur Dioxide

INVESTIGATING THE SYMPTOMS OF POISONING

Symptoms of poisoning may include vomiting, abdominal pains, convulsions, coma, and delirium. Documentation of symptoms should include all information concerning the victim's actions immediately prior to death or unconsciousness. Information from friends, family, or bystanders may be helpful in determining the substance used.

In determining whether or not death or illness is due to poisoning, one must remember that the symptoms preceding the illness or death, as well as the external appearance of the body are of great importance. Many poisonings will produce some similar symptoms but when the outstanding symptom is one of those indicated below, there are definite poisons to look for first.

Symptoms Preceding Death

1. Convulsions — strychnine, nicotine
2. Delirium — atropine, hyoscyamine
3. Extreme drowsiness — opiates, hypnotics
4. Extreme rapidity of death — cyanide, strychnine, nicotine
5. Long delayed death — metals

6. Abdominal pains — metals, food poisoning
7. Diarrhea — metals, food poisoning
8. Vomiting — metals, food poisoning
9. Burning of the mouth — corrosives, mercury, arsenic

Poisoning May be Suspected If:

1. Nearby persons attempt to:
    a. Hurry embalming
    b. Hurry funeral
    c. Cremate body
    d. Falsify death certificate
2. There is sudden death of a healthy individual
3. Death apparently due to unknown causes

Preliminary Investigative Techniques Upon Arrival at the Scene

1. Summon medical aid, if necessary (i.e., paramedics, ambulance, etc.).
2. Locate, separate, and interview the witnesses.
3. Identify, control and separate the suspect(s), if present.
4. Follow the procedures for handling the source of poisoning, when located.
5. Try to ascertain the amount of poison ingested by the victim(s).
    a. If and when this information is determined, notify involved medical personnel immediately.
6. Determine the actions taken by the victim prior to becoming comatose or dead.
7. If the poison is present in the atmosphere and is posing a danger to others, immediately evacuate the area.
    a. Notify the fire department for a washdown and chemical neutralization, if necessary.
8. If the poison is criminally connected or there is suspicion of foul play:
    a. Use the basic preliminary investigative techniques.
    b. Do not overlook the possibility of latent prints.
    c. If the victim is in critical condition, accompany him or her to the medical facility in case a dying declaration is made.

Interviewing Victim/Witnesses

Questioning the Victim—If possible, question the victim. Prior permission should be obtained from the physician and his or her recommendations as to length of questioning should be followed. During the questioning, develop as much essential information as possible. Keep informed of the recovery progress of the victim and continue questioning as necessary.

Questioning and Investigating the Witnesses—Witnesses should be questioned to develop information regarding the poisoning and should be investigated to determine if they participated in the poisoning. Witnesses may include:

— Persons who witnessed the act of poisoning, or persons who have knowledge of a suspect's utterances or actions that would tend to establish a motive for the crime.

— Persons who have knowledge of the victim's consumption of food or drink within the period of time he or she probably received the poison.

— Persons who sold the victim or suspects drugs or medicines.

— Persons who have knowledge of the victim's movements prior to the time he or she was stricken, or persons familiar with the victim's habits, particularly:

a. Eating and drinking habits

b. Use of drugs and medicines

c. Attempts at self-medication

— Persons familiar with the victim's financial status, family background and social life.

Essential Information—By questioning witnesses and the victim, the investigator should try to obtain answers to the following questions:

— Where was the victim when the symptoms first appeared?

— What were the symptoms?

— Did someone intentionally give the victim poison? If so, who? What was the person's motive?

— Did the victim administer the poison himself or herself? If so, was the poisoning accidental or intentional? What was his or her reason?

— Had the victim ever contemplated suicide or attempted it before?

— Who summoned assistance? When? By what means?

— Prior to the appearance of the symptoms, what did the victim do? With whom did he or she associate?

— What did the victim eat or drink prior to the appearance of the symptoms? Where did this consumption take place?

— Did the victim request food and beverages, or was it offered to or urged upon him or her? Who prepared it? Who served it?

— Did the victim notice anything peculiar about the food or beverage? Did he or she regularly eat the food or beverage in question?

- Did the victim eat or drink anything after the symptoms first appeared? Was the victim in the habit of drinking any form of alcohol not intended for drinking purposes?
- Did the victim take any medicines prior to the appearance of the symptoms? Was this medicine prescribed by a doctor? Was the medicine given to the victim by someone other than a physician or a pharmacist? Where is the container in which the medicine was kept? Did the victim habitually take any kind of medicine? Was he or she addicted to any narcotic drug?
- Was the victim unhappy or depressed recently? Was he or she angry or jealous of anyone? Did the victim have money on his or her person prior to the symptoms? Is that money still in the victim's possession? What was the condition of his or her estate? Did he or she owe large sums?
- Who would inherit the victim's estate? Has the person lost money recently? Does victim handle money in his or her occupation?
- Did the victim have any recent difficulties with regard to his or her occupation or employment? Did anyone ever accuse the victim of misconduct or criminal actions?
- Was anyone jealous of the victim because of his or her position? Will anyone benefit from the victim's death through promotion? Did the victim recently receive any threatening letters or communications? How were they disposed of? Who sent them? If they were anonymous, who had a motive for sending them or possessed the information on which they were based?
- Did the victim write any letters recently? To whom? What was the subject matter of the letters?

Investigating the Victim's Activities—Investigation should be made of the activities of the victim during the period prior to the poisoning.

Ascertaining the Source of the Poison—Determining the source of the poison may furnish valuable investigative leads. Some possible sources that should not be overlooked are:

- Hospitals, dispensaries, laboratories, and pharmacies; offices, homes, and grocery stores. These may contain poisonous cleaning substances, rodent or insect poisons, and medicines that may be toxic if improperly used
- Depots, warehouses, storage areas, farms and similar places where rodent and insect poisons may be kept
- Filling stations, garages and other places where fuels with alcohol bases may be found
- Establishments where cleaning and solvent compounds containing poisons are kept or used
- Illicit narcotics channels
- Dealers in bad liquor

Volatile Inhalants & Poisonous Substances

The autopsy *may* disclose:

— The exact time of death

— The affected organ that directly caused the death

— The specific poison that caused the death

— The identification and analysis of the poison (may be performed by a toxicologist subsequent to the autopsy)

— The approximate time the poison was taken

— The food or beverage that contained the poison (this may not be possible if death is several days after the taking of the poison). The approximate time of death if the victim died before medical or public authorities could reach him or her.

— A disease or accident that may have caused death. Suicide victims will be surprised by the slowness of death and kill themselves by other means.

Collection of Physical Evidence

There are usually few witnesses to a poisoning; therefore, physical evidence is of vital importance. It is absolutely necessary that physical evidence be taken into custody in a legal manner, properly marked for identification, and safeguarded by a complete chain of custody covering every person who has such evidence in his possession from the time of the seizure until it is presented in court. In addition to the usual forms of physical evidence, the investigator or crime scene technician should obtain, when possible:

1. Remains of food and drink last taken
2. Drugs, medicines, narcotics, or chemicals in the home of the suspect and victim
3. Glasses, bottles, spoons, etc. from which the victim may have drunk
4. Vomit, urine, feces, etc.

In every suspected poisoning case, the officer should make an immediate search for the following:

1. The possible source(s) of the poison agent
2. The possible container(s) of the poison agent

Once the source of the poison agent is located, it should be isolated.

1. If the source is identified, notify concerned medical personnel immediately.
2. If the source is not identified, immediately have the suspected substance transported as quickly as possible to one of the following:
   a. Police crime laboratory
   b. Medical laboratory
   c. Emergency facility where victim is treated

Materials suspected as evidence should also be collected. These include:

1. All the contents of a medicine chest
2. Freshly used drinking glasses
3. Partially or fully emptied beverage bottles
4. Used spoons
5. Foods or beverages

All evidence should be photographed before being collected and identified.

All evidence to be analyzed at the laboratory should be:

1. Sealed in a clean glass container
2. Labeled to identify the evidence
3. Packaged in a suitable container to avoid breakage during transit to the laboratory
    a. If the evidence is not in a suitable container for shipment, it should be placed in a container provided by the investigator or evidence technician.

REFERENCES:

Bass, M. "Sudden sniffing deaths." *Journal of the American Medical Association (AMA).* 212:2075-2079, 1970.

Chapel, J.C. and D.W. Taylor. "Glue sniffing." *Missouri Medicine.* 65(4):288-292, 1968.

Cohen, S. "The Volatile Solvents." *Public Health Review.* 2(2):185-214, 1973.

D'Amada, C. et al. "Heroin addicts with a history of glue sniffing: A deviant group within a deviant group." *International Journal of the Addictions.* 12(2-3): 255-270, 1977.

DeBorona, M. and D. Simpson. "Inhalant Users in Drug Abuse Prevention Programs." *American Journal of Drug and Alcohol Abuse.* 10:503-518, 1984.

Dorman, M. "Inhalant abuse: a psychological research model." *National Institute on Drug Abuse: Third Technical Review on Inhalant Abuse.* Rockville, Md., 1976.

Gomage, J. and L. Zerkin. "The Deliberate Inhalation of Volatile Substances." National Clearinghouse on Drug Abuse Information 30, No.1, 1974, p.4.

Lange, W.R. "Nitrite Inhalants: Promising and Discouraging News." *British Journal of Addiction.* 84:121-123, 1989.

Lange, W.R. et al. "Nitrite Inhalants: Patterns of Abuse in Baltimore and Washington, D.C." *American Journal of Drug and Alcohol Abuse.* 14:29-39, 1988.

Langrod, J. "Secondary drug use among heroin addicts." *International Journal of the Addictions.* 5:611735, 1970.

Media Projects, Inc. "Inhalant Abuse: Kids in Danger/Adults in the Dark." Dallas, TX, p.4, 1990.

Schmidt, G.L. "A study of achievement motivation and frustration in glue sniffers." *Drug Forum.* 4(4):331-348, 1975.

Schuckit, M.A. *Drug and Alcohol Abuse: A Clinical Guide to Diagnosis and Treatment.* 3rd ed., New York: Plenum Press, 1989.

CHAPTER XIV

THE EVOLUTION OF DRUG LAW

INTRODUCTION

Throughout the history of chemical substance use, people have tried to regulate drugs by various laws or codes of conduct. Most laws have moral and sociological implications—for example, it is wrong to lose control of body and mind, to harm society, or to upset civilized codes of conduct. It is wrong to become unproductive, parasitic, or dependent on the community, or to be antisocial by stealing to obtain drugs, alcohol, etc. The enactment of laws depends on the prevalent moral and social codes and customs of the times. What may seem like a repressive law today may very well be changed over a period of time; strict laws may be replaced with light penalties or even be repealed. Again, these changes depend upon the desires of the people involved and the events that occur in any given historical era.

Over the years, the substances we call hallucinogens, depressants, narcotics, marijuana, coffee, tea, tobacco, and alcohol have all been subject to a wide range of controls, from none to rigid. Laws are often changed because so many people used a particular drug that it would have been impossible to enforce a ban, or because the government needed the tax revenue.

HISTORY OF DRUG LEGISLATION UP TO 1989

EARLY DRUG LAWS

The first significant piece of prohibitory legislation relating to drugs in the United States was an ordinance enacted in 1875 by the city of San Francisco prohibiting the operation of opium dens—commercial establishments in which the smoking of opium occurred. One western state after another followed San Francisco's lead and enacted legislation prohibiting opium smoking. In 1887, in response to U.S. obligations imposed by a Chinese-American treaty of commerce enacted in 1880, Congress prohibited the importation of smokeable opium by Chinese subjects. Despite these first legislative efforts, the incidence of drug use and addiction increased, as did societal concern and illegal drug smuggling.

Some related substance control legislation was later put into effect in 1906. The 1906 Food and Drug Act required manufacturers to disclose the contents of patent medicines directly on the manufacturing label. Although this disclosure law had the beneficial effect of substantially decreasing the use of proprietary or patent medicines containing opiates, other forms of opium use continued at alarming rates.

Although estimates concerning the number of drug addicts during the 50 years prior to the passage of more specific drug legislation (the Harrison Act) in 1914 are inherently suspect, the available information suggests that drug abuse during that period was a "major medico-social problem." In fact, by 1909, the United States was confronted with a significant and growing drug abuse dilemma. The increased opiate use and addiction in the United States subsequent to the Civil War has been attributed to several factors, including the indiscriminate use of morphine to treat battlefield casualties during the war. The increase in morphine addiction was so extensive that the phrase "army disease" was used to describe the drug use among ex-soldiers. The widespread administration of morphine by hypodermic syringe also contributed to overall increases in opiate abuse. Other circumstances exacerbating the situation during the period of 1865-1914 included the spread of opium smoking from Chinese immigrants to American citizens: opiate addicts tended to be middle-class and middle-aged women from rural areas or small towns. They took their morphine or opium orally and certainly were not regarded as criminal. Increases in opiate use were also caused by the manufacturing of opium and its derivatives in the American patent medicine industry. Beginning in 1898, this circumstance was particularly detrimental due to the marketing of heroin as a safe, powerful, and non-addictive substitute for the opium derivatives morphine and codeine.

It was said in 1928 that "no remedy was heralded so enthusiastically as was heroin." Indeed, some physicians even recommended heroin as a treatment for "chronic intoxication" resulting from the use of morphine and codeine. It was not until 1910 that the medical profession began to recognize the dangers of substituting heroin for other opium derivatives.

In 1908, the American Opium Commission investigated domestic opium use. In response to the results of this investigation, Congress passed "An Act to Prohibit the Importation and Use of Opium for Other Than Medicinal Purposes" in 1909. Among other things, this act permitted the importation of opium for medicinal purposes, but only to 12 ports of entry. However, it did not regulate domestic opium production and manufacture or the interstate shipment of opium products. Opium products were still available without a physician's prescription and were being marketed throughout the country by retail outlets and a growing mail order trade.

INTERNATIONAL AGREEMENTS

In 1909, the International Opium Commission met in Shanghai to discuss the possibilities of effecting international agreements aimed at restricting trade in narcotic drugs to the scientific and medical communities.

In Shanghai, the U.S. government took a position which has continued to be our hallmark in subsequent international discussions: pressing for more controls than other delegations were willing to support. At the 1909 Shanghai Convention, the U.S. delegation voted in favor of immediate opium prohibition as the ultimate goal in every country where opium is grown. Although the original purpose of the Shanghai Convention was to limit opium cultivation in the Orient, the Convention ended with a resolution advocating international opium control everywhere. Despite this resolution, the Shanghai Convention did not produce a treaty. A subsequent conference was necessary to make these resolutions binding.

The next significant international effort was held at The Hague in December 1911. When President Wilson signed the Harrison Narcotic Act on December 17, 1914, he said that this act was passed to fulfill our treaty obligations. The treaty obligations referred to by President Wilson were contained in the 25 articles set forth at The Hague Convention of 1912. In essence, the participants at The Hague Convention agreed that governments should control production, manufacture, and distribution of opium, certain opiates, and cocaine, both nationally and internationally.

It was further agreed that the control, manufacture, and distribution of opiate drugs would be limited to medical and legitimate uses only. The question of what constituted legitimate uses was a subject of debate and continues to be a subject of debate at all international conferences. Additionally, all nations which participated at The Hague Convention agreed to "examine the possibility of making possession of controlled drugs a crime." As a result, it was not surprising that President Wilson should characterize the Harrison Narcotic Act as a congressional statute passed in furtherance of an executive commitment.

Despite these agreements, The Hague Convention did not set up the proper machinery to enforce violations. Due to this inherent weakness, effective implementation of the treaty became impossible. Moreover, no mechanism was set up to monitor compliance with the treaty resolutions. In response to these weaknesses, the U.S. government quickly insisted upon the "limitation of production of opium," contending that unless production was limited, it would be virtually impossible to prevent smuggling.

In the early 1920s, the countries of Persia, Turkey, and Yugoslavia depended so heavily on opium as a commodity that abrupt cessation of production would have resulted in economic catastrophe. Because other nations failed to comply with the U.S. government's demands, we ultimately withdrew from the Convention.

At the Geneva Conference in 1924 and 1925, the U.S government again strongly recommended all nations participating in The Hague Convention to fulfill their obligations under that Convention. It was clear that our position, in part, stemmed from our inability to control our narcotics problems at home. Although the Harrison Narcotic Act had been in effect for almost 10 years and law enforcement had been given the clear responsibility for handling the entire narcotics addiction problem, our failures, at that point, were glaringly obvious. However, the U.S. continued to pursue an unalterable course of action by thrusting upon law enforcement the responsibility for controlling conduct which seemed, even at that time, to be impossible to control. Although our government had committed itself to a research program in order to explore the course of drug addiction, we failed to implement that commitment and continued to rely totally upon the police to resolve our drug addiction problems. The Harrison Narcotic Act failed to curtail addiction; thus, crimes related to addiction continued to multiply. Since legitimate sources of drugs were completely unavailable to addicts, users turned instead to buying smuggled drugs or to smuggling drugs themselves. Here again, the U.S. government failed to control the flow of smuggled drugs across American borders. The total prohibition approach which we advocated and attempted to implement had only appeared to be a simple and certain way to solve our domestic addiction problem.

EVENTS OF THE 1930s

The events which effected drug legislation in the 1930s were varied and, to some degree, inconsistent. From the old Narcotic Unit within the Treasury Department's Bureau of Prohibition, a new and expanded Federal enforcement agency was formed: The Bureau of Narcotics. Also situated within the Treasury Department, the Bureau was charged with the enforcement of the Harrison Act and other Federal laws pertaining to narcotics.

With regard to the enactment of criminal laws, there were two other important developments in the 1930s. The National Conference of Commissioners on Uniform State Laws promulgated the Uniform Narcotic Drug Act, a recommended model for the states, which was eventually adopted by every state in one form or another. At the state level, the Act criminalized the possession, use, and distribution of opiates and cocaine. These two classes of drugs were grouped together under the legal label of "narcotics." Although many states had enacted narcotic laws pre-dating even the Harrison Act, the element of uniformity among the states had been missing until the Uniform Act.

The United States Congress was also active in the creation of additional prohibitions. Acting upon the advice of the Bureau of Narcotics, Congress enacted the Marijuana Tax Act, placing cannabis under the same restrictions that were in effect for opiates and cocaine. Enforcement responsibilities were assigned to the Bureau.

The Bureau's articulated rationale for promoting the marijuana legislation was fear of the criminogenic effects of the drug. Harry J. Anslinger, the renowned Commissioner of the Bureau, cited numerous anecdotal case studies relating ingestion of cannabis and commission of violent and bizarre criminal acts. Although critics cited the obvious inaccuracies of Anslinger's claims, the lawmakers were sufficiently convinced of the possible dangers of "reefer madness" and passed the Act.

A number of theories abound in regard to the motives of Anslinger and Congress. Cynics charge that Anslinger merely wished to augment the size of his agency and chose re-definition of the Bureau's mission as the most convenient means. Others claim that passage of the Marijuana Tax Act was intended as an anti-Mexican measure aimed at discouraging immigration into the southwest. Adherents of this theory also hold that the opiate and cocaine laws were racially motivated (against Chinese and Blacks, respectively). Finally, some observers link the Marijuana Tax Act with the repeal of Prohibition (in 1933), the marijuana law serving as a replacement for the loss of Federal control over alcohol.

In response to the legacy of drug abuse that continued despite new laws, the U.S. government formally opened its first 'narcotics farm' at Lexington, Kentucky in 1935. This facility provided a psychiatrically-oriented inpatient setting for the treatment of opiate addicts. The second "narcotics farm" was opened at Fort Worth, Texas in 1938. Established as a result of a 1929 Congressional enactment, the Lexington and Fort Worth facilities offered treatment to specially assigned Federal prisoners and to voluntary admissions.

The primary impetus for creating these hospital facilities was to alleviate the overcrowding of addicts in Federal prisons. Federal prisons were ill-equipped to handle narcotics addicts as the post-Harrison Act addict inmates presented significant medical problems beyond the resources of conventional prisons. Thus, addict prisoners were permitted to serve their sentences at the Lexington and Fort Worth facilities. Fortunately, these inmates—in addition to the numerous voluntary admissions—served as ideal research subjects. Most of the early medical and behavioral knowledge of the addictive process was gained from the research at these hospitals.

THE 1940s

During the 1940s, America was preoccupied with the serious problems of war and post-war recovery. Consequently, little activity occurred with respect to control of psychoactive drugs. One of the few noteworthy actions was an amendment of the Uniform Narcotic Drug Act placing cannabis under its purview. The states thus followed the lead of the Federal government in criminalizing marijuana cultivation, possession, use, and distribution.

CHANGES IN THE 1950s

Major changes in drug law penalties occurred in the 1950s. First, in 1951, at the urging of Commissioner Anslinger and his Bureau of Narcotics, Congress passed the Boggs Act which imposed stiff mandatory minimum sentences upon narcotics offenders. Many states emulated this punishment and deterrence model, enacting more local versions of the Boggs Act. Only four years later, Federal narcotics penalties were again increased, fortifying its feature of a mandatory minimum sentence. Under the 1956 law, at the option of the jury, the death penalty could be imposed upon offenders convicted of sale of narcotics to a minor. The legislation also authorized the Bureau of Narcotics to conduct training programs for state and local enforcement personnel and to collect national statistics relating to narcotics patterns.

Analysts of the stiff penalty legislation in the 1950s are not in agreement with regard to their causes. Some of the often-cited causal factors include fear of widespread new narcotics usage, reaction to allegations of the Mafia's control over the narcotics trade, a general conservative drift in American politics, and effective law enforcement lobbying. One fact is clear, however: as a result of the statutes of this era, the United States had adopted one of the strictest narcotics control policies in the world. The lengthy and inflexible mandatory minimum sentence, later to be considered for more serious and violent crimes, had been specifically designed for the narcotics violator and exemplified the American commitment to a retributive-deterrent theory of addiction control.

THE 1960s

The decade of the 1960s was dominated by a spirit of experimentation. Lawmakers, executive officials, and the courts indicated a willingness to innovate and test new drug control policies. Much of the intellectual and political energy behind this movement stemmed from the joint American Bar Association/American Medical Association report on drug addiction released in 1961. The report, *Drug Addiction: Crime or Disease?*, criticized the popular law enforcement approach to addiction control and recommended a more balanced prevention policy. The report and the spirited debate evoked by its conclusions signaled a renewed socio-political interest in the medical treatment of drug abuse. A year after its publication, President Kennedy convened a White House Conference on Narcotics and Drug

Abuse. Rehabilitation rather than punishment of drug abusers emerged as the theme of that conference.

Taking the lead from the White House resolution on rehabilitation, the State of California enacted legislation in 1961 which authorized the involuntary civil commitment of narcotics addicts in need of treatment. New York passed a similar law in 1962, as did Congress in 1966. The civil commitment laws served both humanitarian and social control purposes. These statutes permitted long-term institutionalization of addicts, typically as an adjunct to the criminal process but sometimes as a diversionary substitution. Since then, however, poor treatment success, high operational costs, frequent civil libertarian criticism, and more attractive community alternatives led to de-emphasis of the civil commitment programs.

On the international scale, a major new multi-national agreement was formulated. In 1961, after nearly two decades of negotiation, the international community agreed on a new narcotics control compact. The Single Convention on Narcotic Drugs limited the production, manufacture, import, export, trade, distribution, use, and possession of opiate, coca leaf, and cannabis drugs to medical purposes only. The Single Convention replaced the earlier international agreements and the United States quickly approved the pact.

In 1962, the United States Supreme Court then re-entered the narcotics control arena with a landmark decision. In *Robinson v. California* (370 *U.S.* 660, 82 *S.Ct.* 1417, 8 *L.Ed.*2d 758, 1962), the Supreme Court ruled that a California misdemeanor provision prohibiting the condition or status of addiction was unconstitutional. The Court defined narcotics addiction as an involuntarily contracted disease not subject to the criminal law and urged states to adopt involuntary addict commitment laws based on the mental health model. The Court said it was cruel and unusual punishment, and therefore against the 8th Amendment of the Constitution, to arrest an addict for being an addict. Six years later, the *Powell v. Texas* decision (392 *U.S.* 514, 88 *S.Ct.* 2145, 20 *L.Ed.*2d 1254, 1968) narrowed the scope of the *Robinson* rule in refusing to invalidate public intoxication laws and explicitly disavowing some of the involuntary disease rhetoric of the *Robinson* decision. Yet, to this day, *Robinson v. California* remains a potential precedent for expanded judicial intrusion into drug control policies.

As noted earlier, the White House Conference on Narcotics and Drug Abuse supported a more balanced approach to addiction control. In 1966, Congress implemented the Conference recommendations and passed the Narcotic Addict Rehabilitation Act. This Act permitted Federal judges and prison officials to send narcotics addict probationers and inmates to the Lexington and Fort Worth treatment facilities as a condition of sentence. Release from the hospitals was followed by mandatory after-care supervision. The Act also permitted voluntary self-commitments by motivated addicts. As with the California and New York civil commitment programs, the Narcotic Addict Rehabilitation Act (NARA) program has been significantly restructured and de-emphasized in recent years.

New criminal laws regarding drugs also appeared in the 1960s. Depressant, stimulant, and hallucinogenic drugs were brought under Federal control for the first time with the passage of the Drug Abuse Control

Amendments of 1965. Possession, use, manufacture, and distribution of these substances were subjected to criminal control mechanisms. Nonetheless, the penalties established for violations involving these classes of drugs were less stringent than the comparable laws pertaining to narcotics.

Enactment of the Drug Abuse Control Amendments was a Congressional reaction to abundant evidence of rapidly increasing "soft" drug usage by American youth. Reports indicated that use of the specified drugs was pervasive, touching all strata of American society. Considering the extensive and varied nature of the abusing population, Congress opted for fairly mild actions, limiting possession for personal use to the misdemeanor level. Deterrence was intended, but Congress hoped to avoid criminalization and incarceration of such a large segment of the youthful population.

At the suggestion of the Federal government, and utilizing the model promulgated by the Food and Drug Administration, the states adopted uniform legislation regulating the possession, use, manufacture, and distribution of depressant, stimulant, and hallucinogenic drugs. Again, the penalties for violation of these laws were less stringent than the penalties for similar offenses involving narcotic drugs. Generically, these laws became known as "dangerous drug laws," while the earlier state legislation (covering opiates, cocaine, and marijuana) continued to be referred to as "narcotics laws."

The final event of the 1960s was an administrative action by the President. The two major Federal drug law enforcement agencies, the Bureau of Narcotics (Treasury Department) and the Bureau of Drug Abuse Control (Food and Drug Administration) were consolidated into a single agency, the Bureau of Narcotics and Dangerous Drugs (BNDD). Situated within the Justice Department, the new agency was assigned substantial responsibility for the enforcement of Federal drug laws. The reorganization was intended to centralize drug enforcement decision-making and to avoid the crippling jurisdictional disputes which had plagued prior Federal agencies.

The 1960s witnessed rapid and major changes in American drug control policies. Public attention was dramatically turned to the drug abuse phenomenon in the early part of the decade when public health and law enforcement officials announced the onset of a previously unparalleled epidemic of heroin use. The attendant rise in street crime and social decay aroused the American public to demand action. Reports of widespread drug use among the military in Vietnam then stimulated decisive Congressional action.

THE 1970s

In 1970, Congress passed the Comprehensive Drug Abuse Prevention and Control Act, popularly known as the Controlled Substances Act. The existing scattered Federal drug laws were repealed in favor of this unified act. All drugs subject to Federal regulation were entitled "controlled substances" and subjected to increasing levels of control on the basis of abuse potential and lack of therapeutic usefulness. The Act furnished the Attorney General and Secretary of Health, Education, and Welfare the flexibility to add new drugs to the "controlled substances" list, to modify the degree of regulation of drugs already classified, and to delete drugs from the list on the basis of new evidence pertaining to abuse capacity or medical usefulness. The formerly stringent, mandatory minimum penalties were substantially reduced while education, research, and rehabilitation projects were encouraged as adjuncts to enforcement. Modeled upon this Federal legislation, a state-level Uniform Controlled Substances Act was drafted later that year and has been adopted by over forty states.

Two other benchmark pieces of drug abuse legislation were enacted in 1972. As a direct response to the rising heroin epidemic and the impending return of the Vietnam Veterans, Congress and the President created the Special Action Office for Drug Abuse Prevention. The Office was mandated to coordinate and strengthen Federal drug abuse prevention efforts. Although the Special Action Office registered significant gains in achieving coordination of existing resources and in stimulating new programs, it was discontinued in June of 1975. The major functions of the Office were later resumed by the National Institute on Drug Abuse (NIDA) situated within the Department of Health, Education, and Welfare.

Simultaneous with the creation of the Special Action Office and its emphasis on improved treatment and rehabilitation, Congress created the Office of Drug Abuse Law Enforcement (ODALE) to develop a fortified approach to drug law enforcement. During its brief but spirited tenure, the Office focused its efforts upon high level intra-city trafficking with national and international enforcement responsibilities remaining under the jurisdiction of BNDD. Later, in 1973, some executive re-organization dismantled ODALE.

In the same year, at the request of the President and Congress, the United States State Department undertook a planned campaign to diminish Turkish opium production. Supported by an agreement of $35.7 million of aid from the U.S. as compensation for losses resulting from crop substitution, the Turkish government banned the cultivation of the poppy plant. Two years later, however, a newly formed Turkish government repealed the ban and permitted replanting of the opium poppy. Hence, the creation of BNDD in 1968 did not achieve its intended goal of centralizing and coordinating Federal drug law enforcement resources. Jurisdictional overlap and role confusion were not eliminated by that re-organization. As a result, the President ordered a new executive re-organization in 1973 to achieve the original objective of increased effectiveness.

By executive order, in 1973, the drug law enforcement resources of the Bureau of Narcotics and Dangerous Drugs, the Office of Drug Abuse Law Enforcement, the Bureau of Customs, and the Office of National Narcotics Intelligence were consolidated into a single Federal enforcement agency: the Drug Enforcement Administration (DEA). All of the functions performed by the predecessor agencies were integrated into the new umbrella agency.

Once established, the DEA played an increasingly crucial role in the coordination of Federal drug law enforcement; and during the 1970s a number of inter-agency efforts were launched. Among the coordination efforts undertaken by the DEA was the development of mechanisms to provide timely and accurate narcotics intelligence to drug law enforcement personnel at the Federal, State, and local levels.

One result of this DEA effort was an amendment to the 1970 Controlled Substances Act. Congress passed the Narcotic Addict Treatment Act of 1974 to require the annual registration of practitioners dispensing narcotic drugs, including methadone for maintenance or detoxification purposes. This legislation, which imposed standards for the legal dispensation of drugs, was deemed necessary because of the increased diversion of methadone for illegal sale and use.

That year also saw the passage of the Alcohol and Drug Abuse Education Act amendments. The Act placed greater emphasis on the need for prevention and early intervention programs, recognizing the crucial role of family, peer group, school, church, and other community institutions in influencing young people's behavior.

Enacting the 1974 Alcohol and Drug Abuse Education Act Amendments alerted Congress to the fact that most of the previously adopted Federal programs to reduce demand had been directed primarily at the person who was already in serious trouble with alcohol and/or drugs. The focus of the Drug Abuse Education Act of 1970 was significantly different in that it was directed toward those who had not yet experimented with drugs or those who had just begun to do so.

Five years later, the Drug Abuse Prevention, Treatment, and Rehabilitation Amendments of 1979 were enacted. The 1979 legislation authorized the NIDA's state formula grants, special grants, and contract programs for drug education and prevention to remain in effect through September 30, 1981. It did so because it found that the growing extent of drug abuse indicated an urgent need for prevention and intervention programs designed to reach the general population.

As a result of historical circumstances, the decade of the 1970s was an important one in the evolution of the Federal drug abuse effort. It began with a comprehensive restructuring of Federal laws relating to drugs and included a major reorganization of Federal drug law enforcement agencies in an effort to reduce inter-agency rivalries and to promote efficiency and leadership in the fight against drug trafficking. Equally important was the recognition that strategies to reduce the demand for drugs must be an essential component of the overall drug abuse policy and that the nation's drug abuse problem could not be regarded as a crisis susceptible to quick resolution. In addition, new laws were passed to respond to particular aspects of the drug problem, and new enforcement approaches were attempted in an effort to disrupt drug trafficking more effectively.

Unfortunately, some disagreements over certain fundamental issues remained unresolved at the end of the 1970s. Among these were the role of the Federal government in drug policy negotiations and the appropriate balance of strategies to reduce supply and demand. An even more disappointing fact of this decade was that, despite legislation, massive re-organizations, new enforcement techniques, and necessary attitudinal changes, the problems of drug abuse and trafficking continued on an increasingly widespread scale.

THE 1980s

On January 21, 1982, in a major policy shift, the FBI was given concurrent jurisdiction with the DEA for drug law enforcement and investigation. In addition, the Administrator of the DEA was required to report to the

Director of the FBI, who was given the responsibility of supervising general drug law enforcement efforts and policies.

In giving the FBI concurrent jurisdiction for enforcement of U.S. drug laws, the Attorney General followed the recommendation of a committee that he had established to study the need for increased coordination of the DEA and the FBI in the drug field. Although FBI expertise in organized crime and financial investigations would be available in drug enforcement work as a result of concurrent jurisdiction, the DEA would continue to function as a "single-mission narcotics enforcement agency" that would give the drug problem the kind of focus it needs.

Several other important legislative initiatives were adopted in the 1980s. For example, the Department of Defense Authorization Act of 1982 contained a provision entitled, "Military Cooperation With Civilian Law Enforcement Officials," which was intended to codify the practices of cooperation that had developed between military and civilian law enforcement authorities. The Act was also designed to improve the level of cooperation by delineating precisely that assistance which military commanders could provide and by permitting military personnel to operate military equipment that had been lent to civilian drug enforcement agencies. This legislation was deemed necessary for the following reasons:

> The rising tide of drugs being smuggled into the United States by land, sea, and air presents a grave threat to all Americans.
>
> * * *
>
> Only through the dedicated work of all of Federal, State, and local law enforcement agencies can we begin to stem this tide. In fighting this battle, it is important to maximize the degree of cooperation between the military and civilian law enforcement. At the same time, we must recognize the need to maintain the traditional balance of authority between civilians and the military.

The most important and innovative part of this legislation was Section 374, which permitted the Secretary of Defense to assign Department personnel to operate and maintain military equipment that had been made available to an agency with jurisdiction to enforce the Controlled Substances Act. This relatively simple change greatly increased the potential interdiction capability of Federal drug law enforcement agencies.

The year 1984 was a prolific one for legislation dealing with discrete areas in drug law enforcement. The Controlled Substance Registrant Protection Act of 1984 made it illegal, among other things, to steal any quantity of a controlled substance from a registrant. In addition, Congress passed the Aviation Drug-Trafficking Control Act, which among other things, requires the Administrator of the FAA to revoke the airman certificates and aircraft registrations of those convicted of violating any Federal or State law relating to controlled substances, except where the violations involved minor possession offenses.

Although the Controlled Substance Registrant Protection Act of 1984 and the Aviation Drug-Trafficking Control Act were necessary laws, by far the most important drug law enforcement measures passed in 1984 were contained in several provisions of the Comprehensive Crime Control Act of 1984. The Act included:

1. Bail Reform Act of 1984. This Act comprises many sections, but the most important and most controversial stipulated that when a person charged with an offense appears before a judicial officer, the judicial officer must order that, pending trial, the accused be either released on personal recognizance or upon execution of an unsecured appearance bond; released upon certain listed conditions; temporarily detained to permit exclusion or deportation if not a U.S. citizen or lawful permanent resident; temporarily detained to permit revocation of a prior conditional release; or detained.

2. Comprehensive Forfeiture Act of 1984. This legislation made extensive revisions to Federal, civil, and criminal forfeiture laws and procedures, which target the assets of racketeering and drug trafficking organizations. With respect to the Racketeer Influenced and Corrupt Organizations Act, the 1984 Comprehensive Forfeiture Act did several things, including confirming the Supreme Court's decision in *Russello v. United States*, 464 *U.S.* 16 (1983) that a defendant's ill-gotten profits from racketeering were forfeitable.

3. Controlled Substances Penalties Act of 1984. In essence, this legislation enhanced the penalties for violations of the Controlled Substances Act.

4. Dangerous Drug Diversion Control Act of 1984. This legislation represented the first major updating of the regulatory provisions of the Controlled Substances Act and the Controlled Substances Import and Export Act since their enactment in 1970.

5. Currency and Foreign Transactions Reporting Act Amendments. Without the means to launder money, thereby making cash generated by a criminal enterprise appear to come from a legitimate source, organized crime could not flourish as it now does. The 1984 amendments of the Currency and Foreign Transactions Reporting Act were designed to fine tune the active currency reporting laws in effect at that time.

As a whole, the Comprehensive Crime Control Act of 1984 was intended to, and did in fact, provide Federal law enforcement agents with better tools for combatting drug traffickers.

Controlled Substance Analog Enforcement Act of 1985

This Act was intended to help law enforcement curb the fabrication of drugs that are chemically similar but not identical to controlled substances (also known as drug analogs and designer drugs. The Act gives Federal drug enforcement agents authority to arrest analog manufacturers and dealers before the new substances are Federally controlled.

The Drug-Free American—October 1986

Some of the highlights of this Act include the following:

Grants to the states for prevention, treatment, and rehabilitation will represent the bulk of the demand reduction monies.

Treatment evaluation programs will be developed.

The Alcohol, Drug Abuse, and Mental Health Administration (ADAM-HA) will consolidate the prevention activities of the Drug Abuse and Alcohol Institutes under an Office of Drug Abuse Prevention which will include the clearinghouses of both Institutes to disseminate information on the health hazards of alcohol and drugs.

The desirability of health warning labels on beverage containers is to be studied.

The entertainment and media industries are requested to refrain from producing materials that in any way glamorize the use of illegal drugs and alcohol. In fact, they should develop materials that discourage drug and alcohol abuse.

A survey will be conducted by the National Academy of Sciences to study and report on the best available treatment for alcoholism.

A large-scale, school-based drug abuse education and prevention program will be funded. Curriculum development, teacher training, family participation and specially designed programs for high-risk youth and athletes are planned. Models to prevent youth and child drug use will be created with demonstration grants. The overall goal is drug-free schools.

The severe problem of drug and alcohol abuse, especially among Native American adolescents and adults, is approached through additional education, prevention, and treatment initiatives.

The Secretary of Labor will produce a study of the nature and effects of drugs in the workplace as well as a program to deal with them.

Additional funds will be appropriated for research.

Government employees and corporate supervisors will be educated and trained in identifying alcohol and drug abuse on the job. The Employee Assistance Program will be mandated. A study by the Institute of Medicine will examine the extent and adequacy of insurance coverage for substance abuse treatment.

A media commission on alcohol and drug abuse prevention is designed to study the public information programs already in existence. It will also coordinate the voluntary donation of resources from the media, sports, and business sectors. The de-glamorization of alcohol and drugs in the audiovisual media is re-emphasized.

Of the 1.7 billion dollars allocated by this Act, approximately 25 percent is appropriated for demand reduction activities. The remainder goes into interdiction, criminal justice, and other supply reduction operations.

The Anti-Drug Abuse Act of 1988 (P.L. 100-690, Sec. 5251)

At the outset, this Act states its purpose directly: "It is the declared policy of the United States Government to create a drug-free America by 1995". Some of the provisions of the law are as follows:

Drug users can lose public housing and a vast array of other Federal benefits.

Government contractors may lose contracts unless they provide for a drug-free workplace.

A high priority is placed on preventing AIDS by providing treatment for IV drug users. Whenever feasible, treatment on demand (within 7 days) is the goal.

The Act includes grants and contracts to establish employee assistance programs (EAPS).

A program of assistance to state and local narcotics control agencies has been set up through the Bureau of Justice Assistance in the Department of Justice.

There is a provision for developing a training program through the National Institute of Corrections that will assist in developing and improving rehabilitation programs for criminals convicted of drug-related crimes.

Regulation of Over-the-Counter (OTC) Look-Alike Products

In the early seventies, as amphetamines became increasingly difficult to obtain, street suppliers found it necessary to defraud their customers with phony products.

In the mid-seventies, the traffic in "phony amphetamines" became big business when the marketing operation turned to the "truck stop market." Business cards, catalogs, and local suppliers for these products sprang up all over.

The marketing venture in "phony amphetamines" was so successful that these entrepreneurs began looking for other markets. At first, their venture into advertising seemed restricted to handing out business cards and small cards containing pictures of their products. The suppliers seemed to concentrate their efforts on shopping centers, campuses, rock concerts, or other areas where young people might be found.

The success of this effort and the lack of any enforcement against it eventually lead to a nationwide phony amphetamine campaign with full-page color ads in magazines and newspapers.

Due to the success of phony amphetamines, reports of deaths and injuries to several young people increased. Finally, in the late seventies and early eighties, state and Federal authorities became alarmed and took action. The efforts of the Federal government were unusually strong, coordinated, and effective on the targeted distributors.

At about the same time, states reacted with a variety of legislative efforts. Most states enacted legislation to severely restrict trafficking in "counterfeit" controlled substances. In the majority of states, it became a criminal offense to possess, sell, manufacture, or advertise "counterfeit" controlled substances.

Drug Paraphernalia Act

Several states have enacted paraphernalia legislation. In the United States, there is an extensive industry dealing in the manufacture and sale of implements for preparing and using illicit drugs—primarily marijuana and cocaine. The products include "roach clips," water pipes, cocaine spoons, and sophisticated kits used to test or process these drugs. The annual sales of these products amount to several hundred million dollars.

The advertising, display, and open sales of these implements, usually in so-called "head shops" and often in conjunction with the sale of legitimate products promoted among adolescents, are an affront to the communities in which these shops exist because they appear to condone and even glamorize the use of illegal drugs. The attraction of such shops to minors is of particular concern to these communities.

As a result, interested community groups have begun to demand governmental action to deal with the drug paraphernalia industry. All levels of government have been contacted, and in response, a number of localities have passed ordinances. Many states have responded by prohibiting the sale of paraphernalia.

One setback to the regulation of paraphernalia distribution came on October 29, 1991. The U.S. District Court for the Southern District of New York held that the Federal Mail Order Drug Paraphernalia Control Act, which makes it a crime to use an interstate conveyance to sell drug paraphernalia or to offer drug paraphernalia for sale in interstate commerce, is unconstitutionally void for vagueness. The Achilles heel of the statute, 21 USC 857, is its definition of paraphernalia as objects that are "primarily intended or designed for use in" drug-related activities (*U.S. v. Schneiderman*, DC SNY, No. 90 Cr. 0656 (RWS), 10/29/91).

At the outset, the court rejected the notion—which some other courts have embraced—that the statute requires proof of some form of scienter (the defendant's knowledge of guilt). The court then held that the phrase "primarily intended or designed for use" makes the Act's parameters ambiguous and unclear. The court added that the U.S. Supreme Court's approval of a non-criminal ordinance prohibiting the unlicensed sale of objects "designed or marketed for use" with drugs, does not save the Federal statute (*Village of Hoffman Estates v. Flipside, Hoffman Estates Inc.*, 445 *U.S.* 489, 1982). The ambiguity of the statute's language, although acceptable in the context of the civil regulation at issue in Hoffman Estates, breeds arbitrary prosecutions and inconsistent results and is constitutionally intolerable in a criminal statue, the New York court said. The court stressed that the Act potentially covers a host of objects with permissible uses.

The Comprehensive Crime Control Act of 1989

Listed below are the four principles which provide the foundation of this anti-crime act:

- A primary purpose of government is to protect citizens and their property. Americans deserve to live in a society in which they are safe and feel secure.
- Those who commit violent criminal offenses should, and must, be held accountable for their actions.
- Our criminal justice system must have as its objective the swift and certain apprehension, prosecution, and incarceration of those who break the law.

— Success in accomplishing our criminal justice system goals require a sustained, cooperative effort by Federal, state and local law enforcement authorities.

The Comprehensive Crime Control Act of 1989 is a four-part act designed to strengthen current laws, enhance enforcement and apprehension of criminals, facilitate prosecutions, and expand Federal prison capacity. In 1989, it responded, in part, to the increasing need for restrictions against widespread drug trafficking.

Strengthening Current Laws

To ensure that those who commit violent criminal offenses are held fully accountable for their actions, it is essential to eliminate certain gaps in existing laws and to strengthen some current statutes.

Laws will be strengthened by enhancing penalties for firearms violations, restricting plea bargaining, enacting death penalty procedures, restricting imported weapons, preventing circumvention of imported laws, restricting gun clips and magazines, limiting access to weapons by criminals, and making drug testing a condition of parole/probation release.

Augmenting Enforcement

A primary purpose of government is to protect citizens and their property. This protection requires the sustained cooperative commitment of Federal, state and local law enforcement officials. Apprehending violent offenders requires increased enforcement personnel, improved cooperation among law enforcement authorities, and a cessation of evidence exclusion due to supposed legal technicalities.

This goal of increased protection is accomplished in the Comprehensive Crime Control Act of 1989 by providing additional ATF (Bureau of Alcohol, Tobacco and Firearms), U.S. Marshals, and FBI agents as well as developing coordinated task forces. In addition, the Act establishes a "good faith" exemption to the exclusionary rule regarding evidence.

Enhancing Prosecution

In order to assure that criminals are held accountable for their offenses, certainty of prosecution must accompany severity of punishment. Federal, state and local authorities must expand and coordinate their prosecutorial efforts.

This goal is accomplished in the Act by additional assistant U.S. Attorneys, Criminal Division Attorneys, additional housing for unsentenced prisoners, additional money to the courts to process criminals, and the reform of habeas corpus.

Expanding Prison Capacity

Prison overcrowding remains a national problem. The most acute problem is at the Federal level. At both the Federal and state levels, prison overcrowding continues to affect sentencing. At the state and local levels, overcrowding is often responsible for the early release of convicted criminals.

The goal of reducing prison overcrowding is accomplished in the Comprehensive Crime Control Act by expanding Federal prison facilities, converting unused Federal properties, deporting criminal aliens, encouraging state prison construction, and reviewing court-ordered prison cops.

DRUG LEGISLATION OF THE 1990s

THE OMNIBUS CRIME BILL OF 1990

The Omnibus Crime Bill of 1990 authorizes a doubling of Federal aid to local law enforcement (up to $900 million) for the purpose of achieving a Drug-Free America by 1995. The bill also doubles the number of FBI agents assigned to drug-related crime investigations and increases the number of DEA agents by 1000.

The 1990 anti-crime bill contains the following provisions:

Drugs: Adds 12 new chemicals to the list of precursor chemicals; enhances the penalties for offenses involving "ice," and strengthens the drug paraphernalia statute;

Asset Forfeiture: Improves the government's ability to dispose of real estate and other assets seized from drug traffickers;

Anabolic Steroids: Places anabolic steroids on Schedule III of the Controlled Substances Act and provides criminal penalties for the possession and distribution of these dangerous drugs (effective February 27, 1991);

Victims of Crime: Provides needed protection for abused children and other victims of crime;

Money Laundering: Makes essential improvements in the Federal money laundering statutes;

Firearms: Makes needed changes in several firearms statutes which had been requested by the DEA;

Child Pornography: Creates new recordkeeping provisions for those who produce sexually explicit materials and creates a new offense for those who possess pornographic depictions involving children; and

Savings and Loan: Provides tough penalties for addressing the savings and loan crisis.

The bill also authorizes a $20 million "rural drug initiative" to fund increased drug law enforcement efforts by local police and prosecutors in rural areas.

It includes a new provision to improve cooperation with foreign governments when prosecuting money laundering cases; likewise it closes the loophole that allows foreign money launderers to escape the reach of U.S. law.

The bill increases funding for DARE and other successful drug education programs. Finally, it extends the area of "drug-free zones" around public playgrounds.

Comprehensive Crime Control Act of 1991

In his message to Congress, President George Bush pointed out that the legislation contained in the Comprehensive Crime Control Act was "designed to address comprehensively the failures of the current criminal justice system." Bush warned that "There must be a clear understanding on the streets of America that anyone who threatens the lives of others will be accountable."

The President called for enactment of the legislation which would provide swift and certain apprehension, prosecution and incarceration, stressing that "too many times, in too many cases, criminals go free because the scales of justice are unfairly loaded against dedicated law enforcement officers."

The proposed legislation contained a broad spectrum of critically needed reforms to the criminal justice system, as well as new offenses and penalties for various acts of life-threatening criminal behavior. Key elements of the proposed bill include the following:

Restoration of the Federal Death Penalty by establishing constitutionally sound procedures and adequate standards for imposing Federal death penalties that are already on the books (including mail bombs and murder of Federal officials) and authorizing the death penalty for drug kingpins and for certain heinous acts such as terrorist murders of American nationals abroad, killing of hostages, and murder for hire.

Habeas Corpus Reform to stop the often frivolous and repetitive appeals that clog our criminal justice system, and in many cases effectively nullify state death penalties, by limiting the ability of Federal and state prisoners to file repetitive habeas corpus petitions.

Exclusionary Rule Reform to limit the release of violent criminals due to legal technicalities by permitting the use of evidence that has been seized by Federal or state law enforcement officials acting in "good faith," or by allowing as evidence a firearm seized from dangerous criminals by a Federal law enforcement officer. This proposal also includes a system for punishing Federal officers who violate Fourth amendment standards; furthermore, it provides for the compensation of victims who are unlawfully searched.

Increased Firearms Offenses and Penalties including a 10-year mandatory prison term for the use of semiautomatic firearms in a drug trafficking offense or violent felony, a 5-year mandatory sentence for possession of a firearm by dangerous felons, new offenses involving theft of firearms and smuggling firearms in furtherance of drug trafficking or violent crimes, and a general ban on gun clips and magazines that enable a firearm to fire more than 15 rounds without reloading.

In addition to the above proposals, the bill contains elements designed to curb terrorism, racial injustice, sexual violence and juvenile crime as well as to support appropriate drug testing as a condition of post-conviction release for Federal prisoners.

National Drug Control Strategy of 1991

The fundamental principal of the national strategy remains firm: to reduce drug use through a mix of supply and demand policies and programs. Like its predecessors, this strategy recognizes the key roles of Federal, state and local governments, the private sector, as well as communities and individuals across the nation. The strategy calls for applying pressure across all fronts of the drug war simultaneously, recognizing that prevention is the only answer in the long run, but that in the short run increased interdiction, international cooperation, and law enforcement efforts are necessary. The strategy also acknowledges the need for adequate medical treatment of those currently abusing drugs.

The National Drug Control Strategy declares that, as a nation, we must:

Establish meaningful and effective programs to prevent people from using drugs in the first place.

Provide effective treatment for those who need to and can benefit from it.

Hold users accountable for their actions and thereby deter others from using drugs.

Target and dismantle drug trafficking organizations.

Prosecute drug dealers and traffickers.

Punish those convicted of drug crimes.

Disrupt the flow of drugs, related chemicals, and drug money.

Engage other nations in efforts to reduce the growth, production, and distribution of drugs.

Support basic and applied research, medicine, and technology.

Improve our intelligence capabilities in order to attack drug trafficking organizations.

The National Drug Control Strategy established nine detailed goals and objectives. These goals were first set in the 1989 strategy as targets for 1991. As shown in the figures below, these objectives have been met.

* An 11 percent reduction in current overall drug use.
* A 13 percent reduction in current adolescent drug use.
* A 29 percent reduction in occasional cocaine use.
* A 23 percent reduction in frequent cocaine use.
* A significant re-shaping of student attitudes toward drug use.

The 1991 strategy follows the same format as previous strategies. In seven sections, The Criminal Justice System; Drug Treatment; Education, Community Action and the Workplace; International Initiatives; Border Interdiction and Security; A Research Agenda; and Intelligence and Information Management, the strategy presents a thorough discussion of issues, policies, and programs related to our national drug control activities. A broad review of Federal drug program management issues, budget proposals, high intensity drug trafficking areas, and recommended model state legislation are included as appendices.

For fiscal year 1991, the current government administration sought $11.7 billion in drug-related funding—a $5.3 billion (82 percent) increase since the beginning of the administration and a $1.1 billion (11 percent) increase over fiscal year 1991. Additional details on the National Drug Control Budget are available in the National Drug Control Strategy Budget Summary.

THE LATIN AMERICAN DRUG CONFERENCE OF 1992

On February 28, 1992, President Bush and six Latin American leaders ended a two-day conference on the drug problem with promises to broaden the War on Drugs. The President hosted the conference in San Antonio, Texas; it was attended by the Presidents of Colombia, Bolivia, Peru, Ecuador, and Mexico, as well as a delegation from Venezuela.

At a press conference, President Bush stated that the seven leaders "established an aggressive agenda for the rest of the century" for battling drugs.

The top 10 priorities of the drug-fighting strategy included:

— Reducing the demand for drugs.

— Continuing economic reforms, economic assistance, trade and investment.

— Improving eradication, interdiction, arms control, chemical controls, and asset seizure.

— Concentrating on judicial system reforms.

— Coordinating strategies to understand the needs of other countries.

— Helping Mexico and Colombia stop heroin production.

— Educating the media and public about progress in the War on Drugs.

— Remembering that our efforts transcend borders.

— Ensuring that the anti-drug effort conforms to democratic principles.

This was the second drug summit in which the President of the United States met with Latin American leaders to discuss means of counteracting international drug trafficking. The first was held in 1990 in Columbia where Bush met with the leaders of the Andean nations of Colombia, Bolivia, and Peru. The recent San Antonio conference added Mexico, Ecuador and Venezuela, which have seen increasing involvement in illegal drug trafficking as the Andean nations crack down.

Initiatives now include new legal efforts to curb money laundering, international control on the sale of chemicals used to manufacture cocaine, and missions to Canada, Japan and Europe to involve the rest of the industrial world in the anti-drug battle. The leaders of Mexico, Colombia and Venezuela—the more industrialized Latin American nations at the meeting—generally called for new measures to increase their countries' (legal) exports to the United States, thereby creating jobs and bolstering their economies.

The leaders of two less-developed South American nations, Peru and Ecuador, pressed the conference participants for outright grants to create new industries and agricultural markets in their countries; these would replace those industries and markets now consumed by the drug trade. Similarly, the Bolivian leader urged Bush to spur United States business investment in the Bolivian economy to create new jobs. In essence, the aim of all six was to provide new employment for thousands of peasants who now grow coca leaf or opium poppies or otherwise earn their livelihood in the drug trade.

At the conclusion of the conference, President Bush announced that the U.S. had given 12 UH-IH Huey helicopters, a total value of $20 million, to Mexico for interdiction efforts.

DRUG WAR COSTS

Federal money to fight drugs has doubled from $6.6 billion in fiscal year 1989 to a proposed $12.7 billion for 1993. Aid to Latin American countries for narcotic interdiction in 1991 totaled $20 million for Columbia, $15.7 million for Bolivia, $19 million for Peru, $1.5 million for Ecuador, $1 million for Venezuela, and $19.3 million for Mexico. In sum, the United States spends less than 5 percent of its $12.7 billion annual drug-control budget in Latin America. The bulk of the rest is spent on domestic drug-control efforts.

It might be noted here that proceeds from production and consumption of illicit drugs are more than $300 billion worldwide. Fortunately, these ill-gotten gains have been reduced in the 1990s. Among some recent achievements, Columbia seized a record 90 tons of cocaine in 1991. Bolivia cut coca cultivation from 50,300 hectares in 1990 to 47,900 in 1991. Furthermore, since 1900, Mexico has captured more than $1 billion in drug trafficking assets.

THE EFFECTIVENESS OF DRUG-CONTROL STRATEGIES

LIMITATIONS OF TACTICS AFFECTING SUPPLY

Traditionally, efforts to reduce the trafficking and abuse of illicit drugs in this country have been based on the theory that significant reductions of drug supplies would lead to equal reductions in drug-related problems. While this seems plausible, a review of the 75-year history of these efforts reveals that they have not reduced social, economic or criminal problems related to drugs. Despite continuing expressions of sincere determination, America's war on drugs seems nowhere near complete success. Now more than ever, drugs present problems of vast proportions.

This critique does not suggest that efforts to reduce supply—such as crop eradication, border interdiction, and prosecution—have failed. On the contrary, these efforts have achieved a measure of success. In 1983, for example, authorities estimated that approximately 10 percent of the drugs destined for illicit markets were interdicted. Crop eradication programs were significantly expanded in Colombia, where most of the world's cocaine is processed and nearly one-half of the marijuana consumed in the United States is grown. Moreover, indictments and convictions of some of the world's most notorious traffickers have been obtained in recent years.

Despite these efforts, however, American consumption of cocaine has continued. Cocaine, heroin, amphetamine, and methamphetamine-related deaths have increased. Likewise, cocaine, PCP, and methamphetamine-related emergency room visits have multiplied. In short, strategies to reduce supply are "working" by some standards, but only to a limited degree.

The effectiveness of these tactics is limited by several inherent factors. One is the fact that source country crop eradication or substitution efforts often fail in countries whose governments lack the resolve or power to effectuate these programs. The constantly changing patterns of drug trafficking compound the problem. Interdiction of drugs is extremely difficult because of the vastness of U.S. borders, the constantly changing nature of drug smuggling methods and routes, and the ease with which most drugs, particularly cocaine and heroin, are concealed. For example, five kilograms of heroin valued at more than one million dollars on the wholesale market, can fit into a shoebox. Furthermore, interdiction does not reach many of the most widely abused dangerous drugs, such as PCP and methamphetamine, which are produced in domestic clandestine laboratories. In view of these limited successes, it might be argued that the real problem lies in the overwhelming and continuing demand for illicit drugs among Americans. Millions of people want illicit drugs and are willing to violate the law, spend billions of dollars, and in many cases, risk their lives to obtain them.

SUPPLY VERSUS DEMAND

Although the supply of drugs and the demand for drugs have often been considered separate issues, by both the public and private sectors, they are in fact inseparable parts of a single problem. The success of supply efforts are related to commitments made to reduce the demand for drugs through drug abuse education, treatment, research, vigorous enforcement of drug abuse laws, and effective sentencing. Drug supply and demand operate in an interrelated and dynamic manner. The strategies employed to limit each should be jointly undertaken.

One Reason Why U.S. Drug Policy Fails
The Disparity in Federal Funds Devoted to Treatment and Enforcement[1]

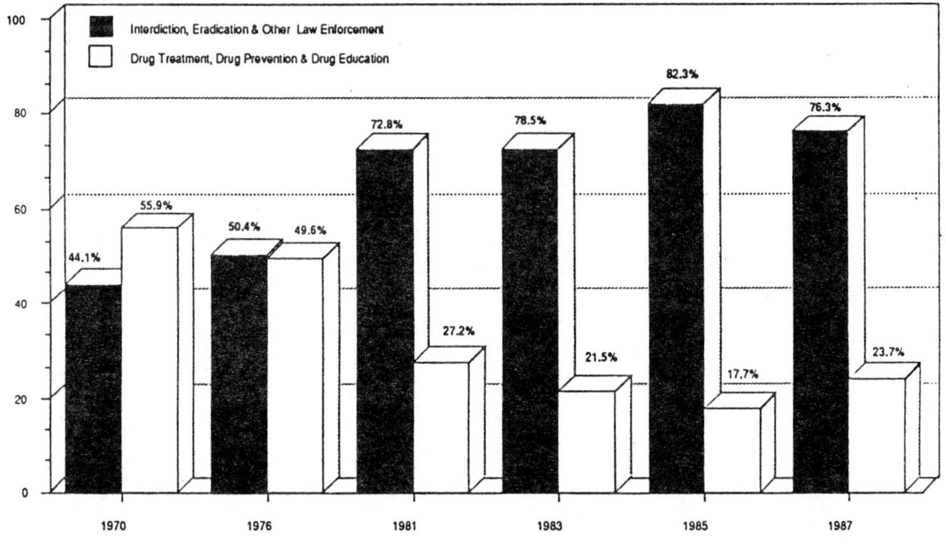

[1] U.S. General Accounting Office and U.S. Rep. Fortney "Pete" Stark.

The national fight against illicit drugs relies on two fundamental strategies: organized crime policy and drug abuse policy. Organized crime policy targets specific criminal groups and seeks to destroy those already in existence and prevent the emergence of new ones. This effort focuses on reducing supply. In contrast, drug abuse policy attempts to reduce drug use and its associated adverse effects. This effort is directed toward reducing the demand for drugs. Theoretically, organized crime policy and drug abuse policy can conflict. However, reducing the demand for drugs advances the goals of both organized crime policy and drug abuse policy. A significantly smaller drug market (which should result from a substantially reduced demand for drugs) would attack organized crime groups by limiting the huge profits currently available in drug trafficking. Simultaneously, this effort on the demand side of the equation should reduce the number of drug users, the goal of drug abuse policy.

TACTICS TO REDUCE DEMAND

More successful tactics to reduce demand may in the long-run decrease the need for current high levels of funding for approaches to reduce supply. A significant reduction in the demand for drugs as a complement to aggressive enforcement efforts is likely to make drug trafficking less lucrative for organized crime and thus prompt many organized crime groups to drop out of the drug business.

Skeptics have argued that past tactics to reduce demand have not been successful. However, the history of drug abuse prevention and treatment programs has been relatively short. It was not until the upsurge of drug use in the 1960s that these programs developed. Some early prevention approaches were ill-conceived. For example, they often presented information about drugs without persuasive arguments to deter their use, and other programs used exaggerated information.[2] Such programs have been criticized for unintentionally encouraging experimentation with drugs or squandering the credibility of anti-drug information.

The most recent and effective drug abuse education and prevention programs focus on the psychological and sociological factors that contribute to the onset of drug use.[3] Many of these programs are based on the anti-smoking campaigns of the 1970s and 1980s because it has been found that many of the same factors which lead to cigarette smoking also contribute to drug use. These efforts employ the "social pressures model" of drug prevention to teach adolescents how to resist peer and other social pressures to smoke cigarettes and to change attitudes about smoking. Today these efforts are considered a success. After reviewing several studies of anti-smoking campaigns, the Rand Corporation has concluded that these studies provide cumulative evidence that programs based on the social pressures model help reduce the smoking onset rate among adolescents.

---

[2] Polich J.M. et al. *Strategies for Controlling Adolescent Drug Use* 135. The Rand Corporation, Feb. 1984.

[3] Shore, Milton F. "Correlates and Concepts: Are We Chasing Our Tails?" *Etiology of Drug Abuse* 127, 128. NIDA Research Monograph 56, 1985.

Thus, drug education programs must be continually evaluated and improved to keep pace with changing drug abuse patterns. Prevention efforts targeted at adolescents and teenagers may significantly reduce the overall demand for drugs.

In a model program, the National Institute on Drug Abuse (NIDA) used the strategy of the anti-smoking campaigns of the late 1970s, which many feel were effective, to develop its "Just Say No" campaign against drug use. The "Just Say No" campaign recognizes and focuses on the impact of social pressure. NIDA seeks to show adolescents through a music video, television commercials, and other media that they can turn down drugs by simply saying "no" to those peers or dealers who attempt to coerce them into experimentation or frequent use.

While it is difficult to accurately measure the effectiveness of such anti-drug advertising, it is clear that the media can help shape attitudes. Just as beliefs about cigarette smoking have changed in recent years, so too can attitudes about drugs. In fact, many adolescents have endorsed the "Just Say No" campaign and organized youth groups of their own to help combat the prevalence of drugs in schools.

Furthermore, anti-drug advertising has an advantage over the anti-smoking campaigns: drug dealers cannot openly advertise their product. According to the New York advertising firm of Trout and Ries:

> Unlike cigarette manufacturers, drug producers and sellers cannot use advertising to promote a fashionable image for their drugs. Quite the opposite, the government can use advertising to make drugs less and less fashionable to use. Thus, if America runs true to form, advertising will dramatically reduce demand. When it's "out" in America, it doesn't sell.[4]

Any effort directed toward reducing the demand for drugs will require a long-term commitment; it takes time to change attitudes. This commitment must be made by Federal, state, and local governments as well as the private sector. Each sector must unequivocally reassert that any and all illicit drug use is unacceptable in light of the effects of drugs on individuals, families, communities, and governments. Only in this context can a war against drugs be effective in reducing both the supply of drugs and the demand for them.

DO DRUG LAWS WORK?

Penalties against drug use in the United States have escalated dramatically since crack began infiltrating the nation's cities about five years ago. During that time, Congress and nearly every legislature has overhauled drug laws to make them stronger, more consistent and, in a few cases, more creative.

Nonetheless, all signs suggest that the tougher laws have not been sufficient to prevent drug abuse from spreading; but there is little doubt that those who are caught are paying a higher price. While statistics on convic-

---

[4] Trout and Ries Advertising Agency. "A Way to Decrease the Demand for Drugs." Paper prepared for the President's Commission on Organized Crime. Oct. 1, 1985.

tions and sentencings for drug crimes are scarce, those in existence suggest that more people are going to prison for drug crimes than ever before.

In New York State, for instance, the number of people serving time for drug crimes has risen more than 400 percent during the past seven years. Federal drug convictions jumped 161 percent during the 1980s, and the percentage of Federal inmates serving time for drug crimes has more than doubled. Approximately half the inmates in Federal prisons today were convicted of drug crimes; moreover, by 1995, the Bureau of Prisons expects seven out of every 10 inmates to be a drug criminal. That figure is in addition to the high percentage of convicts who were "under the influence" of drugs when they committed non-drug crimes such as murder.

In contrast to these more recent drug-related arrests, drug laws in the 1970s appeared to be in remission. The recreational drug use that had become popular during the late 1960s had fostered a new sense of permissiveness in the following decade. In the 1970s, marijuana was decriminalized in some states, while laws against it went unenforced in other states. Strong laws against cocaine, heroin, and methamphetamines remained in place, but the judicial system was less eager than it once was to enforce them.

The appearance of crack, the highly addictive form of cocaine, ended that permissive trend. Crack appeared on the scene just as public concern over cocaine use seemed to be reaching a peak, and pushed concern into panic. Lawmakers responded with much tougher laws.

Although the goal of drug legislation in the 1980s was a drug-free America, the only certain result so far has been overcrowded prisons and overburdened courts. Yet, even critics acknowledge that courts have become less hospitable places for drug users and dealers.

The Federal government has been a leader in the crackdown, with Congress passing anti-drug bills in 1984, 1986, 1988, and 1989. The laws established mandatory prison terms and fixed sentences for drug offenders, taking much of the sentencing discretion from judges.

Similar laws have been passed by most states, and some have adopted more severe measures. During the past few years, virtually every state has raised the penalties for drug crimes that occur in or around schools. More than half have established stronger penalties for crack than for traditional powder cocaine. Furthermore, some states have extended the death penalty to include murders committed during drug transactions. In the most recent wave of legislation, about two-thirds of the states have enacted laws allowing the seizure of drug dealers' property.

Given that the drug problem continues to grow, it is difficult to prove the effectiveness of these laws. Some people believe the drug laws have not been effective. This ineffectiveness may be due, not to the strength of the laws, but to the application of them.

This hypothesis is explored by Jones, Shainberg, and Byer in their text, *Drugs and Alcohol* (1979). The authors point out that the number of known U.S. addicts reached a high of around 200,000 just before the first U.S. narcotic law was passed. More importantly, however, the authors explain how the addict population declined significantly as Federal narcotic agencies were set up to enforce these laws. Perhaps if more Federal funding were directed toward enforcement of drug laws, the laws themselves would, in essence, be more effective.

In addition to the need for increased enforcement, it might also strengthen drug laws to re-consider the rationale behind them. The common rationale for drug laws includes the following reasons: (1) drug use equals drug abuse, and drug laws that prohibit use automatically decrease abuse; and (2) by controlling or eliminating people's access to psychoactive drugs, drug dependence can be curtailed. While this rationale has been effective to some degree, a slightly different approach may better address the problem of addictive behavior that is associated with drug abuse and creates such a high demand for drugs.

In their text, *Drugs and Alcohol*, Jones, Shainberg and Byer also review the so-called "epidemiological" approach to the drug problem. In one passage, the authors summarize this approach as follows:

> Drug laws have been enacted to protect society. Legal controls such as quarantines, isolation, and penalties have always been necessary to stop the spread of various diseases and ailments. Since the best evidence supports the view that compulsive drug abuse is an indication of an emotional illness in an individual, society is justified in insisting on some type of regulation on the manufacture, distribution, and use of drugs. Such regulation can be viewed as part of preventive medicine.

Essentially, this approach holds that society must focus prevention efforts on target groups (such as young people) through education; society must also isolate contagious people (i.e., drug users and drug sellers) through jail sentences; and it must vigorously treat chronic drug users as if they were deathly ill. The armament in this public health battle include the police, who quarantine abusers and sellers via arrest; courts, which sentence users to jail and/or remand them to compulsory treatment centers; drug educators (prevention experts) who strive for complete abstinence from drugs in their students (inoculation via education); and drug therapists who attempt to cure drug abusers by modifying the user's self-perceptions, coping skills, and behavior through a myriad of intervention techniques.

Despite various rationales behind anti-drug legislation, many social critics believe that drug laws do not help in the battle to prevent drug abuse. Their arguments often diverge wildly from each other, but enough similarities exist to delineate four positions: (1) drug laws simply do not work, as evidenced by drug use statistics; (2) crime increases as a function of prohibitions; (3) true drug abuse (i.e., where measurable harm to the individual or society stems from inappropriate use of drugs) is not reduced by prohibition, but is perhaps even increased; and (4) laws that attempt to dictate morality or styles of living threaten civil liberties.

In addition to re-considering the rationales behind anti-drug legislation, it may also be productive to address the claim that drug laws are biased against certain ethnic groups and socio-economic classes.

ARE DRUG LAWS BIASED?

Although anti-drug legislation has had only limited success, the good news in the war against drugs is that the crack epidemic has peaked and even appears to be subsiding. The bad news is that black defendants convicted of selling and using crack cocaine are over-represented in Federal prisons.

The disproportionate number of blacks in prison may be due to the fact that crack cocaine users are treated differently than users of powder cocaine. Congress, responding to alarming reports about the highly addictive nature of crack and its association with gang violence, passed tough anti-crack laws in the 1980s. See 21 U.S.C. 841(b)(1)(A) as amended. The result of this legislation for sentencing purposes is that crack has 100 times the value of an equivalent amount of powder cocaine. In section 841 of 21 U.S.C., for example, it stipulates that being convicted of a drug offense involving 50 grams of crack will fetch the same 10-year minimum sentence as a conviction involving five kilograms of powder cocaine. Generally speaking, most of those convicted of crack-related drug offenses are black, while those convicted of using the powder form of cocaine are white. This disparity has caused some controversy over the possible biases of legislators and law enforcement officers.[5]

Exploring the possibilities of biased legislation, defense lawyers have raised the issue of racial disparity in several Federal circuits; however, they have had little success. Courts have consistently held that Congress could find a rational basis for treating the crack form of cocaine as a greater menace to society than other drugs.[6]

The Minnesota Supreme Court is perhaps the only state court to condemn the disparity in the treatment of crack and cocaine use in its state laws. In the case, *State of Minn. v. Russell* (1991) 477 NW2d 886, the court examined a year's worth of trial records and found that blacks comprised a 96.6 percent of those charged with crack possession, while whites made up 76.6 percent of those charged with possessing the powder form of the drug. The court suggested that this disparity should be further investigated.

On the other side of the debate, prosecutors emphasize that crack is treated differently because of its different effect on society. "The crisis of crack led Congress to react to what it perceived as an immediate and serious threat to the whole social fabric," says Joseph Russonello, former U.S. attorney for the Northern District of California and now a partner at Cooley, Godward, Castro, Juddleson & Tatum in San Francisco. He explains the disproportionate number of blacks convicted of crack-related crimes as follows: "The results you see are incidentally racially disparate. But as long as you have this perception that crack is a special and serious problem, law enforcement will continue to direct its focus and resources to those people who are most obviously in harm's way."

Others, however, have some slightly different opinions. In his article last year for *American Criminal Law Review,* Judge Gerald W. Heaney of the Eighth U.S. Circuit Court of Appeals wrote that African Americans, on

---

[5] For a discussion of this controversy, see Heaney. "The Reality of Guidelines: No End to Disparity." *28 Am Crim L Rev* 160, 1991.

[6] For court decisions, see *U.S. v. Hoyt* (9th Cir 1989) 879 *F.*2d 505, and *U.S. v. Thomas* (4th Cir 1990) 900 *F.*2d 505.

average, are sentenced to Federal prison terms that are 50 percent longer than terms given to whites and Latinos. Heaney said the harsher treatment of those convicted of crack use is one factor in the longer prison terms. Another factor, he said, is that local law enforcement officials divert "relatively minor offenses" into Federal court to take advantage of the longer sentences. Pointing out that "blacks are vastly overrepresented in arrest records for street crimes," Heaney added that many of the affected defendants are drawing mandatory extended sentences under Federal sentencing guidelines.

In the end, singling out crack as a greater social evil than other drugs may have little basis in fact. Dr. Darryl Inaba, director of the Haight-Ashbury Free Clinic drug program in San Francisco, says other drugs—such as methamphetamine and heroin—can be as lethal and as disruptive as crack. Methamphetamine use is increasing in white suburbia, Inaba says, and is also the drug preferred by runaway teens. Latinos tends to favor heroin and the animal tranquilizer PCP, he adds, while Asians tend to favor Quaaludes and crack. When talking about the drug of choice for different groups, Inaba frequently refers to a 1989 study conducted in Rockville, Maryland by the National Institute on Drug Abuse.[7] Whites were more likely to abuse drugs, the study concluded, followed by Latinos and Asians. In contrast, African Americans were least likely to abuse drugs among the various ethnic groups.

SHOULD DRUGS BE LEGALIZED?

INTRODUCTION

As discussed above, there are several arguments against the effectiveness of drug legislation. Some critics claim that the laws are ineffective because they are not adequately enforced; some argue that the rationale behind the laws themselves should be re-considered; still others argue that some drug legislation is biased. Furthermore, there are those who argue for the medical usefulness of some drugs such as marijuana. If marijuana were legalized, several physicians say they would prescribe it as a treatment for glaucoma. All of these arguments for re-conceiving anti-drug legislation raise the issue of legalizing drugs.

THE CASE FOR LEGALIZATION

There are several good points in the case for legalization of drugs. For example, as a society, we pay a high price for keeping drugs illegal. Once these drugs were declared illegal, millions (or perhaps billions) of dollars had to be invested through the Customs Service, police agencies, and (recently) the armed services in an attempt to stop the drugs from coming into the United States. These costs are still incurred today. Unfortunately, the effectiveness of this program of interdiction is difficult to evaluate because, in part, it is virtually impossible to have a free society and to stop all drug importation. In addition, many of the drugs can be produced within

---

[7] "Substance Abuse Among Blacks in the United States." National Institute on Drug Abuse CAP 34, 1989.

our national boundaries, making it almost impossible to determine whether interdiction has been effective at all or whether the costs have been justified. From this standpoint alone, it is worthwhile considering whether a change in social policy might save a great deal of money and allow us to abandon a program whose effectiveness is difficult to establish.

Second, as a consequence of the continued high usage rate of illegal drugs in our country, the relative lack of competition has allowed the drug underworld to set street values that allow for the accumulation of immense profits. This has given resources to an underworld that is becoming increasingly vicious and physically destructive, and has created profits that are then used to produce and underwrite other forms of crime. Thus, if an effective step can be taken to undercut the price of street cocaine or other drugs, there is the possibility that the underworld and its crimes could be curtailed.

Third, reflecting the high cost of these drugs, the user frequently resorts to crime in order to support his or her habit. Again, any steps that decrease the cost and increase the availability of illicit drugs might help law enforcement agencies to minimize burglaries, theft, and robberies by drug users.

Fourth, the production of street drugs offers the user no guarantees of quality control. Thus, individuals are likely to inject substances that are dangerous, are variable in quality, with resulting reactions to "fillers" as well as inadvertent overdoses. The latter occurs when individuals self-administer drugs of a quality that are higher than expected; thus, they inject greater concentrations of active ingredients than can be tolerated. The legalization of drugs would increase the probability that a user will get a more safe, standardized drug. Similarly, if along with legalization of drugs comes the supply of syringes and needles, it is possible that many severe medical complications such as HIV virus, hepatitis, abscesses, etc. can be minimized.

Finally, if drugs are legalized, they will be taxed. Especially if many people continue to use drugs (or the number of users increases), this step can be looked at as a potential revenue enhancer for the entire nation.

In summary, there are several logical arguments in favor of legalizing drugs. These include possible cost savings, a possible decrease in street crimes, an increase in the assurance to users of avoiding inadvertent overdoses and unwanted infections, as well as the possibility of an additional revenue source. However, despite the logic of these arguments, it is important to look closely at the potential price that society would pay for legalization.

THE CASE AGAINST LEGALIZATION

If the United States is to make a major change in its policy on drugs, it is important that the best data possible are used in order to project accurate consequences. On the issue of legalization, these center on the probability of increased use, the consequences likely to be associated with a higher prevalence of drug intake, and the costs likely to accrue from the continued need for enforcement against use by minors.

Increased Availability is Likely to Result in Increased Use

There is data from several sources indicating a high likelihood that if a drug is more available, more people will use it. With alcohol, there appears to be an increased prevalence of use with an increasing number of alcohol outlets as well as with decreasing cost. Similarly, fairly consistent (although indirect) data demonstrate that "epidemics" of such drugs as heroin and crack, along with associated medical problems including fatal overdoses, are likely to be seen when more street drugs are available, especially if they are available at a lower cost.

The ideal cost for any drug would be a balance between making the drug inexpensive enough so as to undercut the drug dealer while keeping the price high enough to discourage "heavy" use. According to one recent expert reporting on cocaine, however, the drug is so cheap to produce that it would cost as low as $2.00 or $4.00 per gram on the street. In such an instance, the cost of a "hit" of cocaine would be 40 cents to 80 cents—a price highly unlikely to do anything but encourage heavy regular use.

For Stimulants And Opiates Increased Use is Likely to Produce Several Problems

All drugs of abuse have dangers. However, the brain stimulants (such as cocaine and amphetamine) and opiates (such as heroin) are capable of producing a fairly rapid onset of tolerance and subsequent intense psychological and physical dependence. The intoxication associated with stimulants such as cocaine is very intense, likely to last less than one hour, and is usually followed by a period of sadness and lack of energy which is often subsequently relieved by another dose of the drug. Thus, the stimulants are highly reinforcing and are capable of producing an intense level of psychological dependence over a very short period of time. Similarly, tolerance and physical dependence develop very rapidly, with the latter resulting in physical and psychological symptoms likely to persist for months following heavy use.

Also, whether taken through an official "prescribed" dose or from the street, the acute effects of an intoxicating dose of cocaine can have severe physical consequences. At the very least these include an increase in heart rate and blood pressure, while at the other extreme they are capable of causing fatal heart-beating irregularities, life-threatening increases in body temperature, and severe convulsions.

Finally, in this brief review of problems likely to be observed with cocaine, it may be concluded that the stimulants produce severe states of emotional and psychiatric symptoms. With increasing doses, everyone is capable of developing a severely psychotic state (with hallucinations and paranoid delusions) that resemble schizophrenia. While this condition is likely to disappear within several days to several weeks, it is associated with chronic behavioral problems and can precipitate violence, including murder. Also, acute intoxication is likely to be associated with intense anxiety. Likewise, cessation of use (even after several days) is almost always accompanied by relatively intense levels of depression. Although it may continue at a decreasing level of intensity, the latter is likely to continue for many months.

In summary, while it is possible to project cost savings in interdiction and law enforcement, increased availability of these drugs is likely to result in increased use which will subsequently cause large costs in the treatment of physical and psychiatric difficulties.

Enforcement Costs Will Continue

Any "legalization" of drugs is likely to involve restrictions against the use of drugs by certain subgroups. Likely examples would be individuals under the age of 21 and, perhaps, men and women with psychiatric difficulties. Considering the fact that the age group with the greatest prevalence of experimentation with drugs includes individuals aged 20 and under, this would mean that a very large potential subgroup of users will still find that drugs are illegal for them. Therefore, an underworld of drug dealers will still exist and relatively high legal costs will remain due to the attempt to enforce the drug restrictions for this group.

Potential Problems With Legal Distribution

If drugs that are now illegal were to be legalized, who will distribute them? Will physician prescriptions be required? If so, many medical practitioners might be exceptionally reluctant to give out a drug with such dangers, raising the possibility that only the more unscrupulous individuals might choose to be involved in this "trade."

An alternative mode of distribution might be legal sales in government agencies. Perhaps, each state would develop a series of legal drug outlets with various ways of attempting to enforce the legal restrictions that remain. Once again, there will be costs of a bureaucracy, problems with enforcement, and legal difficulties if someone who buys a drug for "recreation" develops medical problems, or commits a crime while paranoid or otherwise impaired.

SUMMARY

As shown by the arguments briefly reviewed here, there are serious issues to be sorted out on both sides of the legalization controversy. When asking whether or not the war on drugs is succeeding, legalization may seem a feasible alternative. However, it is highly unlikely that all drugs will ever become legal for everyone. Some anti-drug legislation must remain in place. Thus, the issue of legalization might be best addressed through a careful review of the options for re-considering the legislation and rationales that already exist.

REFERENCES:

Brechner, E.M. "Drug Laws and Drug Law Enforcement: A Review and Evaluation Based on 111 years of Experience." *Drugs and Society.* 1:1-27. Fall 1986.

Burke, T. "The Issue of Legalizing Illicit Drugs." *The Narc Officer.* International Narcotic Enforcement Officers Association. Albany, NY: April 1990, p. 19.

Hamowy, R. *Dealing With Drugs: Consequences of Governmental Control.* Lexington, MA: D.C. Heath and Co., 1987.

Heaney, G.W. "The Reality of Guidelines: No End to Disparity." 28 *Am Crim L Rev 160,* 1991.

Jones, Shainberg, and Byer. *Drugs and Alcohol.* 1979.

Kaplan, J. "Taking drugs seriously." *Drugs and Society.* 3:187-208, 1989.

Kondracke, M.M. "Don't legalize drugs." *The New Republic.* 198:16-19, June 27, 1988.

Peterson, R. "Legalization: The Myth Exposed." *The Narc Officer.* International Narcotic Enforcement Officers Association. Albany, NY: December 1991, p. 27.

Polich J.M. et al. *Strategies for Controlling Adolescent Drug Use* 135. The Rand Corporation, Feb. 1984.

Shore, Milton F. "Correlates and Concepts: Are We Chasing Our Tails?" *Etiology of Drug Abuse* 127, 128. NIDA Research Monograph 56, 1985.

Sweet, R. "For Legalization of Illicit Drugs." Rpt. in *The Narc Officer.* International Narcotic Enforcement Officers Association. Albany, NY: May 1990, p. 12.

Trout and Ries Advertising Agency. "A Way to Decrease the Demand for Drugs." Paper prepared for the President's Commission on Organized Crime. Oct. 1, 1985.

U.S. Dept. of Justice. Bureau of Justice Statistics. "Federal Criminal Case Processing, 1980-1990." NCJ 136945, Sept. 1992.

________. Bureau of Justice Statistics. National Institute of Justice, Research in Action. NIJ Reports, SNI 202. "Controlling Drug Abuse and Crime: A Research Update by Mary Graham." March/April 1987.

________. Bureau of Justice Statistics. Office of Justice Programs. "Drugs and Crime Facts, 1991." NCJ 134371, Sept. 1992.

________. Bureau of Justice Statistics, Special Report. "Federal Sentencing in Transition, 1986-1990." June 1992.

________. Drug Enforcement Administration. "A Chronicle of Federal Drug Law Enforcement." Washington: December 1980.

________. National Institute of Justice. "Federal Drug Law Enforcement Review, 1981-1986." Rockville, MD: 1986.

Wilson, J.Q. "Against Legalization of Drugs." Rpt. in *The Narc Officer.* International Narcotic Enforcement Officers Association. Albany, NY: May 1990, p. 13.

________."Concise Argument Against Legalization of Drugs." Rpt. in *The Narc Officer.* International Narcotic Enforcement Officers Association. Albany, NY: June 1990, p. 61.

________. "Substance Abuse Among Blacks in the United States." National Institute of Drug Abuse CAP 34, 1989.

This page intentionally left blank.

CHAPTER XV

DRUG LAW ENFORCEMENT & INVESTIGATIONS

INTRODUCTION

The responsibility for enforcement of narcotic and drug laws is entrusted to law enforcement agencies at three government levels: local (including municipal and county), state, and Federal. Inevitably, the duties and responsibilities of these agencies will overlap to some degree.

Local Responsibility—Primary responsibility for enforcing narcotic law violations rest with local law enforcement agencies. The local agency is responsible for detection, arrest, and prosecution of persons who illegally use, sell, distribute, or manufacture dangerous drugs and narcotics within their community, regardless of the sophistication of the illicit operation.

Local agencies can be very effective in disrupting local illicit narcotic distribution patterns. They can diminish opportunities for dealers to develop new users. Moreover, local departments can furnish state and Federal agencies with information so that these agencies are better able to pursue large-scale operations.

In numerous parts of the country, local and state police agencies have pooled their specialized narcotic enforcement personnel and resources to establish multi-agency narcotic units entrusted with either the partial or whole responsibility of narcotic enforcement in their respective areas. Combined units of this type fill a void created by the inability of local police departments to devote the necessary resources to narcotic enforcement or their inability of these departments to pursue the enforcement of narcotic law outside the boundaries of their respective jurisdictions.

State Role—State narcotic enforcement units are responsible for providing local agencies, upon request, with the resources necessary to identify, investigate, and arrest narcotic traffickers. State narcotic units are also available to communities that need assistance with investigations that cross local jurisdictional lines or that require an undercover operation when local agencies cannot provide one. State law enforcement agencies also assist by providing local agencies with laboratory facilities for handling and processing narcotic evidence.

In areas where local enforcement units or general resources are absent, the state agencies assume primary responsibility for investigating narcotic cases. These state agencies also assume partial or whole responsibility for training local patrol officers and specialized narcotic investigators.

Federal Role—Federal enforcement agencies assume the primary responsibility for preventing illegal entry of drugs into the country and for providing assistance to local and state agencies whenever possible. The responsibilities of Federal agencies extends to the investigation of large-scale illegal operations involving more than one state. These Federal agencies also assist local agencies in identifying and eliminating large organizations which manufacture and sell drugs illegally; they provide drug intelligence data to both state and local agencies. Furthermore, Federal enforcement agencies are largely responsible for ensuring that drugs manufactured legally in this country do not appear on the illicit market. The Federal agencies supplement state enforcement efforts and operations which are weak or nonexistent. In such areas, the Federal government assumes some responsibility, consistent with Federal jurisdictional limits, for providing training, intelligence, and investigative assistance.

FIELD PROCEDURES FOR THE STREET COP

DRUG-RELATED CRIMES AND BEHAVIOR

Ninety percent of drug arrests in the United States are made by uniformed patrol officers. The arrests often result from observations made of suspicious or unlawful activities, or from calls for service (radio calls and citizen requests). The largest source of unlawful conduct observations are traffic violations.

What does all this mean? It means that the police officer should always be alert for drug-related behavior—whether on routine patrol, answering a radio call, processing an arrestee, or making a citizen contact. All of these activities can result in uncovering drug violations.

Additionally, there are some specific things a police officer should know about. The officer should know where addicts "hang out." Secondly, the officer should know how to recognize a drug addict.

Some crimes are very closely related to drug abuse and drug trafficking. Burglary, theft (such as shoplifting), some robberies, and forgery are the crimes most frequently committed by abusers who are supporting a heavy habit. Prostitution is a crime resorted to by many female addicts. You should keep these facts in mind while conducting preliminary investigations of these crimes. Also, when making arrests for these crimes, be alert for possible drug-related behavior by the arrestee. It is not uncommon for a shoplifting arrest to result in a drug-related booking.

One of the ways a police officer may come in contact with a drug abuser is when the officer finds drugs during a routine check or in the course of arrest for a totally unconnected offense. He or she may actually see a person taking drugs or find evidence of unusual behavior. The officer may also act in response to information from an informant.

Most investigations involving "buys" of drugs are made by an undercover officer or a reliable informant under immediate supervision. In most circumstances, the suspect is arrested and searched after the third or fourth sale, and the drugs found are seized as evidence. The charges lodged against the suspect will be for the illegal possession and sale of drugs.

The case will stand or fall on the testimony of the undercover officer and the officer who observed the transactions, as well as the lab analyst who examined the purchased drugs.

PROBABLE CAUSE TO ARREST IN DRUG CASES

Probable cause to arrest has been judicially defined as "such a state of facts as would lead any man of ordinary care and prudence, given the training and experience of a police officer, to believe and consciously entertain an honest and strong suspicion that a person is guilty of a crime."

A variation of this definition states: "The facts establishing reasonable cause to arrest must be sufficient to allow any prudent officer with similar experience and training to believe that a crime has occurred and that the suspect is responsible."

Probable Cause and/or Reasonable Cause

The terms probable cause and reasonable cause are nearly interchangeable. Yet, for the purposes of this chapter, probable cause will remain the standard term.

Knowledge of both what constitutes probable cause and the laws of arrest is an officer's best defense against possible criminal or civil action taken against him or her.

To have probable cause to arrest, a police officer need not be absolutely certain that someone is guilty of a crime. Typically, in situations that require action, you lack time for extensive investigation. You must act on the facts and circumstances as they appear to you at the time. Even if you have some doubt, you may still have probable cause to arrest.

Probable Cause: A Dependent Variable

Probable cause does not conform to one fixed definition. It is a versatile standard. In each case, it depends on the facts and circumstances as they were found to exist at that time. It is dependent on the person viewing the facts and the circumstances at the time.

To a certain extent, probable cause is in the eye of the beholder. An officer of greater experience than another may look at the same set of facts as the less experienced officer and come to a different conclusion. Likewise, the man or woman "of ordinary care and prudence" may fail to see probable cause in a situation that is obvious to the trained police officer. This is why case law allows the man or woman "of ordinary care and prudence" to be assumed in possession of the training and experience of the officer actually making the arrest.

If the validity of an arrest is later challenged, the courts will decide whether the officer making the arrest had probable cause to arrest at the time he or she acted. This standard alone—that of reasonable or probable cause—determines whether or not an arrest is valid.

It must be remembered that the standard of reasonable or probable cause is applied at the time of arrest, and not later. Reasonable or probable cause must exist prior to making an arrest. In making arrests, court interpretations of probable cause have become guidelines for officers to rely on, in addition to their own educated powers of observation and sound judgment.

Probable Cause: Two Aspects

— A lawful arrest is based on probable cause.

— Probable cause is based on facts sufficient to establish the following:

1. The officer has reason to believe that a crime has occurred; and that
2. The suspect is responsible.

In other words, the arresting officer must have probable cause to believe that a crime was committed, based on the establishment of the *corpus delicti*, or elements of the offense.

The arresting officer must have probable cause to believe that the person he or she is arresting is the perpetrator of the crime, or is a principal to the crime committed. The officer may not arrest on a hunch, a guess, or on a mere suspicion that the person is guilty. If the officer cannot reasonably conclude on the basis of facts and circumstances that guilt exists, there is no valid reason for arrest.

Facts are the essence of probable cause. An arrest based on insufficient fact is an unreasonable arrest. An arrest can never be justified by the notion that the courts will later declare the suspect not guilty if he or she is really innocent.

The highest law in this country, the U.S. Constitution, assures protection of the individual's freedom from unreasonable arrest and search (4th Amendment).

FACTORS ESTABLISHING PROBABLE CAUSE TO ARREST

What gives the officer probable cause to believe that a crime has occurred and that the suspect is responsible? It may be direct observation, coupled with his or her expertise, which is based on training and experience.

One day, officers driving down a residential street happened to look up at a first-floor apartment window, where they saw a marijuana plant. Their subsequent arrest of the tenant was based on the officers' observation of evidence in plain view. In this case, another factor also was present: the officers' knowledge of what a marijuana plant looks like.

Probable cause to believe may also rest on *information supplied by others*.

Consider this case: you receive information from an apartment manager that he suspects one of his tenants is dealing drugs. He states that people frequently visit the suspect's apartment, staying for only a short period of time. He has passed some of the people in the hallway and they seem high. He gives you several license numbers of cars that he took down from some of the people visiting the apartment. You run the numbers and they belong to people who are known drug users and dealers. You also find that the tenant has a past record for dealing narcotics. You go to the suspect's door and he attempts to run away. Do you have probable cause to believe the information supplied by the manager? When you locate the tenant, will you have probable cause to arrest him? Yes is the answer to both of these questions.

It should be remembered that not every bit of information from an informant will establish probable cause. In every instance you need to evaluate the reliability of the source. You must consider the informer's motivation in supplying the information and his ability to observe, interpret and report facts accurately.

Information you receive through official channels, i.e., your supervisor, a fellow officer, the police radio, can be assumed to be reliable. However, you should carefully consider the word of a witness or of a victim before accepting a statement as true. Under what circumstances might you doubt the statements of a witness? You doubt the statement when there is any possibility that the witness would have vindictive or other intentions which would raise a question in your mind as to the reliability of the information. Why might you doubt the story of a crime told by the victim? You might doubt it because the victim may be trying to protect his or her own interests, or the victim may have been injured emotionally and/or physically to an extent that his or her perceptions are unclear, or his ability to relate is impaired.

How can you attempt to resolve any doubts about a witness' statement? Proceed with further questioning. As you do so, ask yourself: "Could the witness have observed what he is telling me from where he was when the crime occurred? Was the witness in a condition, mentally and emotionally, to make an accurate observation? Was he or she a victim, or was he in some way involved as a co-principal?

Time and / or Place May Be Used to Establish Probable Cause—For example, you are in an area of the city where there have been frequent muggings, purse snatchings, and many complaints by merchants in the area that shoppers during the hours of 4 to 6 p.m. are particularly susceptible to these attacks. If you see a suspicious person loitering in this area between the hours of 4 to 6 p.m. with no apparent reason for being there, would you have probable cause to stop and talk to this individual and conduct a field interview? Yes.

Officer's senses (smell, hearing, observation)—The officer may also rely on senses, such as the sense of smell, for probable cause to arrest. For example: an officer stops a vehicle and asks the driver to roll down the window. The officer smells the odor of burning marijuana. In this case, the officer has probable cause to arrest for Section 23152 of the California Vehicle Code, driving under the influence of an alcoholic beverage or any drug.

Officer's training and experience—What appears to be innocent behavior by the average citizen may, in the eyes of a trained police officer warrant an investigation or even an arrest. For example: a suspect is negotiating a sale on a street corner; the officer, based on experience, suspects illegal activity and supports the conclusion when the suspect attempts to run from the officer and throw away the evidence.

Emergencies

Emergencies may also be a contributing factor for probable cause. Generally, an officer needs fewer facts to establish probable cause in an emergency situation. For instance, one in which you are endangered, or one in which a suspect is about to escape or destroy valuable evidence would be considered emergency situations. Factors such as flight are not ambiguous or neutral, but can be incriminating or guilt-laden facts, and can be used to establish probable cause.

For example, while on patrol you notice two people standing on the sidewalk. When they see your police vehicle they throw some small items to the ground and take off running. Do you have probable cause to investigate why the suspects are running? Yes.

Totality Of Circumstances

In the final analysis, the court will decide that you had probable cause to arrest only if the "total circumstances" gave you an honest and strong suspicion of a law violation. There are no magic formulas for deciding whether the circumstances "add up" to probable cause. One overwhelming fact may be sufficient by itself while a dozen "maybe's" could be insufficient. Also, one strong reason not to arrest may outweigh several weaker reasons for doing so. Finally, each case has its own set of circumstances; and while your past experience in similar cases may help you decide, you must still judge the present case on its own merits.

When establishing probable cause, the field officer might bear in mind the following court decision: "There is no mathematical formula to determine what specific facts constitute reasonable cause for an arrest; each case must be decided on the totality of facts and circumstances at the time an arrest is made" (*People v. Superior Court (Holquin)*, 72 *Cal.*3d 591, at 594).

The police officer can rely on the following information for probable cause to arrest in drug cases. Remember: just one piece of information may not justify probable cause to arrest.

Physical description—When an officer receives information from a police bulletin as to the description of a known narcotics violator, if he sees the person, he has probable cause to arrest. The defendant's physical appearance or condition in terms of drug use may also give the officers probable cause to arrest.

Failure to explain—This in and of itself is not probable cause to arrest. However, misleading statements can lead to probable cause. Probable cause for arrest might be justified when the suspect is confronted by the officers and he provides an implausible explanation for his presence near the scene of a crime, or attempts to mislead the officers.

Admissions—These occur when an officer overhears that the suspect is in the possession of drugs, and when the officer asks the suspect if he is under the influence, the suspect states that he is.

Reputation of the premises—The mere fact of a person on the premises where officers have reason to believe there is criminal activity in progress will not alone justify probable cause for arrest. There must be other evidence.

The reputation of the residence or place alone is not enough for probable cause to arrest. However, the actions of occupants—such as staying short periods of time and suddenly departing—does warrant at least an investigation. Arrest is justified if the officer witnesses furtive conduct on his or her approach to the scene.

Furtive conduct—This is conduct with which a person attempts to hide contraband, evidence of the crime, attempts to secrete or destroy evidence, or exhibits abnormal behavior at the approach of the officers.

A narcotics violator will often attempt to swallow the evidence; thus, movement toward the mouth might establish probable cause. If the person cannot swallow evidence, he might attempt to throw it away. A drug violator may be arrested after his attempt to hide or conceal the contraband.

Flight and attempts to escape—Even though mere flight at the approach of an officer is not of itself grounds for an arrest, the officer can investigate the reason for the flight. Here are some examples of such flight:

A. While conducting a pat-search, the defendant hits the officer in the stomach and attempts to flee.

B. Officer observes the defendant looking in his direction, saying "cops," then walking away.

C. Upon hearing officers announce their presence at the front door, the occupants of a residence flee through the back door.

PROBABLE CAUSE TO DETAIN

Prior to probable cause to arrest, the officer may obtain probable cause to detain. Furtive movements and unusual or suspicious conduct are examples of facts that may constitute probable cause to detain. The officer's right to detain is limited, but it increases in direct proportion to the number and severity of the facts unfolding before him or her. If the officer believes he may be dealing with a crime of violence, he is even less limited in his detention of a suspect. Generally speaking, a detention may continue as long as the investigation is in progress.

The test of sufficient probable cause to detain is outlined in *People v. Henze*, 253 *Cal.App.*2d 986. The requirements include:

A. A rational suspicion by the peace officer that some activity out of the ordinary is or has taken place.

B. Some evidence to connect the person under suspicion with the unusual activity.

C. Some suggestion that the activity is related to the crime.

The facts the officer needs to justify detention are similar to those he needs to justify arrest. But the officer may detain on a basis of facts that are not, or not yet, adequate for arrest. The courts have ruled that there may be strong reason to investigate in the absence of a legal basis for arrest.

The officer who is genuinely pursuing suspicious or unusual facts has the right to stop a pedestrian or a motorist. He or she may then frisk for safety (if circumstances permit); the officer may then question and detain, even when the officer has insufficient facts to justify a formal arrest. He can, however, detain and frisk only when this is justified. The officer can also ask a person to remain at the scene while he investigates further.

Detentions can only be temporary. If, as a result of his investigation, an officer does not establish probable cause to arrest, the officer must release the suspect. In such a case, the proper method of ending the detention would be to explain the reason for the detention. If a problem arises, such as a likelihood of a personnel complaint, summon a field supervisor to the scene.

FACTORS ESTABLISHING PROBABLE CAUSE TO DETAIN

Nighttime/High Crime Area

In recent years, California arrest and detention cases have placed less importance on some factors, such as "nighttime" or "high crime areas" (*Madrid*, 208 *Cal.App.*3d 822, 1989). It might be noted here that one frustrated judge said his entire city seemed like a high crime area these days. However, a police officer may still consider these factors, particularly if they are combined with additional specific facts. Furthermore, these factors are still given considerable weight by Federal case law (*Frederick B.*, 192 *Cal.App.*3d 79, 1987; *Holloway*, 176 *Cal.App.*3d 150, 1985). Below are some exemplary cases in which probable cause to detain on the basis of nighttime/high crime area is or is not justified.

> If you spot someone you don't recognize who is standing alone on a street corner in the business district at 4 a.m., your suspicion would be more reasonable in a small town than in Los Angeles. Even so, by itself, this fact probably wouldn't justify anything more than a "contact." However, if you add another factor or two, such as that the person has bulging pockets, runs away when he sees you, gives you a phony answer, and/or is holding a "scanner," then you probably would have enough "reasonable suspicion" to detain him for further investigation.

> An officer had made more than 200 arrests in and around a liquor store parking lot where drug transactions were continuously taking place. Nevertheless, it was illegal for the officer to detain three members of a group of men who were gathered there at 10:15 p.m., even though they ran away as he pulled in, because he had not seen or heard anything objectively suspicious (like a weapon or an exchange of merchandise). The factors of "nighttime" and "high crime area" were simply not enough by themselves. As for fleeing, the Supreme Court said, "The departure of defendant and others from an imminent intrusion cannot bootstrap an illegal detention into one that is legal" (*Aldridge*, 35 *Cal.*3d 473, 1984).

> At 6:40 p.m., officers on routine patrol in a high crime area saw a car parked in front of a house where numerous drug and alcohol-related arrests had occurred previously. Some of these activities had taken place just two weeks earlier. Two persons sitting in the car were talking to a male who was standing outside the vehicle, and who walked away abruptly upon noticing the approaching police car. This conduct was ruled an insufficient basis to detain (*Madrid*, 208 *Cal.App.*3d 822, 1989).

Hearsay

In *People v. Hale*, 262 *Cal.App.*2d 270, 1968, an undercover agent answered the telephone at the residence of the defendant. The caller identified himself as Tony and asked if Bill had "scored the stuff". The agent said yes and told him to come up. The court held that: "Arrival at a given location of a person bearing the same name as that given by the caller in a telephone conversation indicates that the caller and the person at the door are one and the same person." The arrest and search of "Tony" was therefore proper.

Race

Race is a factor which an officer may not consider at all unless it is part of a description of a specific suspect the officer is looking for. Below is a case in which an illegal detention was made on the basis of race.

 md

Drug Law Enforcement & Investigations

An officer observed one white male and several black males leaving a housing project populated by blacks. It was night, a high crime area, and in the past the officer had seen whites in that area at night only to buy drugs. The group dispersed as the officer approached. The Supreme Court said the detention of the white male was illegal. The reasons of race, time of night and type of neighborhood were too flimsy to connect the individual with crime (*Bower*, 24 *Cal.*3d 638, 1979; see also *Washington*, 192 *Cal.App.*3d 1120, 1987).

Drug Courier Profile

The legality of detentions based on a "drug courier profile," meaning noncriminal factors about an individual, such as coming from Miami, looking nervous, using cash, not having luggage, etc., has traditionally caused difficulty for the courts. Courts have ruled, generally, that such a "profile" will not automatically justify a detention because, by itself, it does not rise to the level of "reasonable suspicion."

Therefore, it has traditionally been safer to use "profile" information simply as a basis for further observations and investigation, or for the initiation of a voluntary consensual encounter, unless you have some additional information indicating ongoing criminal activity, such as evasion or the use of an alias.

Miranda Warnings

The general rule is that you do not have to give *Miranda* warnings to someone you have detained (1) on reasonable suspicion, (2) for a "site and release" offense (even though they may technically be under arrest), or (3) for investigative questioning at the scene of a crime (*McCarty*, 104 *S.Ct.* 3138, 1984.)

However, if your detention turns into an arrest because you use excessive force, extend the detention unreasonably long, or develop probable cause to arrest, then *Miranda* warnings would be required prior to questioning.

CASES OF PROBABLE CAUSE THAT RESULTED IN ARREST

PEOPLE v. HERRERA, 221 *Cal.*2d 8, 10, 12

In this case, after being qualified as a narcotics expert, the arresting officer testified that he observed what he considered to be hypodermic marks on the appellant's left wrist caused by the illegal use of narcotics. There were additional marks on the appellant's forearm. The officer then shone a light in the appellant's eyes and the pupils were pinpointed. This means that there was little or no reaction to light in the pupils and indicated, in the opinion of the officer, that the appellant was under the influence of narcotics at the time. The officer further testified that the appellant's speech was low and mumbled and at times. . ."he appeared almost to nod off or like he was about to go to sleep." The officer then said, "this would substantiate my earlier opinion that the defendant was under the influence of narcotics. The other two men had no marks on their arms and their eyes appeared normal. They were ultimately released from custody." Therefore, when the arresting officer, a Los Angeles policeman attached to the narcotics division and trained in that field, observed the marks on the appellant's arm, noted his pinpointed pupils, and saw his general somnolent condition, it was reasonable for him to conclude that the appellant was under the influence of narcotics and that an offense was being committed in his presence, for which an arrest could be made without a warrant. In summary, it should be noted that the officers detained all the suspects. As a result of the ensuing investigation, the officers established reasonable cause to arrest one suspect and released the other two. (See also, *People v. Di Blasi*, 198 *Cal.App.*2d 215, 220; *People v. Rogers*, 207 *Cal.App.*2d 254, 259 . . .; *People v. Newberry*, 204 *Cal.App.*2d 4, 8; *People v. Alcala*, 169 *Cal.App.*2d 468, 471.)

In *People v. Ferguson*, 214 *Cal.App.*2d 772, 776, the court held that the mere observation by officers of what they believe to be hypodermic marks, without more, is insufficient cause on which to base an arrest. But there were such additional factors which made the arrest reasonable.

The People, Plaintiff and Respondent, v. Walter Handy, Defendant and Appellant. In this case, the defendant had initially been arrested by two police officers who had noticed him late one evening while they were patrolling an area known for narcotics activity. He had apparently been engaged in a transaction of some kind, and when he realized that he was being observed by the police, he had ceased his conversation and rapidly put his hands into his pockets. The officers had then approached him and temporarily detained him for an interview. In the course of the detention, the arresting officer noticed that the defendant was sniffling and that his eyes were contracted. He was then arrested.

In another case in California, there was probable cause for the arrest of a person for violation of California Health and Safety Code Section 11550, which prohibits the use of narcotics and being under the influence of narcotics. The person had been observed by the arresting officers late at night, engaged in an apparent transaction of some kind in an area known for narcotics activity. In this area, the arresting officer, who had temporarily detained him for an interview, had observed that he was sniffling and that the pupils of his eyes were contracted. Furthermore, when the officers were about 40 to 50 feet from the corner they saw the defendant and another individual "standing approximately six inches to a foot away from each other." Their hands were between them "like shuffling or exchanging merchandise or objects."

The officers left the vehicle to conduct an investigation which was to consist of talking to the defendant and his companion. First, however, the suspects were asked to take their hands out of their pockets. Something was said to indicate to them that the officers wanted to talk to them. A pat-down of defendant's companion produced a small automatic pistol from his front pocket. Apparently, it was when Officer Long was ready to pat-down the defendant that he observed him sniffle, as if he had a cold. On further observation he saw that his eyes were contracted. The officer then looked at the defendant's arms and noticed hypodermic needle marks on the inside of the elbow, above the vein. All these observations indicated that the defendant was under the influence of an "opiate type drug." He was then arrested.

The jury declared: "Even if we disregard the rather unsatisfactory proof concerning the visibility of the needle marks without an intrusion into the defendant's privacy by having him roll up his sleeves, we believe that the sniffle and the contracted condition of his pupils—particularly the latter, when viewed against the entire background—supports the assumption that

 md

the defendant was then under the influence of a narcotic" (*People v. Moore*, 69 *Cal.*2d 674).

ARRESTS

DEFINITION

An arrest occurs when you take a person into custody. This means either that a police officer physically restrains the person or the person submits to the officer's authority (Cal.Pen.Code, § 835).

To be a valid arrest, the officer must take the person into custody "in a case and in the manner authorized by law" (Cal.Pen.Code, § 834).

WHO MAY ARREST

Under the proper circumstances, everyone has some authority to make an arrest. Furthermore, "citizen's" arrest is a poor label, since a person does not need to be a citizen to make a private arrest. Nonetheless, a peace officer has more authority to arrest than does a private person.

For a felony, a police officer may arrest a person (1) with a warrant (a private person may not) or (2) without a warrant if he has probable cause to believe the person committed a felony, regardless of whether or not it was committed in his presence.

For a misdemeanor, a police officer may arrest a person (1) with a warrant or (2) without a warrant if he has probable cause to believe the misdemeanor was committed in his presence (Cal.Pen.Code, § 836).

HOW TO ARREST

A police officer must either physically restrain the suspect or the suspect must submit to his authority. (Cal.Pen.Code, § 835.)

The police officer may use reasonable force to effect the arrest, overcome resistance, or prevent escape. (Cal.Pen.Code, §§ 835, 835a, 843.)

Normally, a police officer must tell the arrestee (1) he or she is under arrest (2) the reason for the arrest, and (3) the officer's authority (i.e., that you are a peace officer) (Cal.Pen.Code, § 841.)

MUST YOU ARREST?

An arrest initiates criminal proceedings against a person accused of a crime.

According to Section 836 of the California Penal Code, an officer "may make an arrest in obedience to a warrant, or may . . . without a warrant arrest a person:

1. Whenever he has reasonable cause to believe that the person to be arrested has committed a public offense in his presence.
2. When a person arrested has committed a felony, although not in his presence;
3. Whenever he has reasonable cause to believe that the person arrested has committed a felony, whether or not a felony has in fact been committed."

Note the wording of the Penal Code here: "the officer may arrest". The Penal Code does not dictate that the officer must arrest.

In a similar manner, a private person may arrest another person, but only when a crime in fact has been committed (Cal.Pen.Code, § 837). In other words, a peace officer, because of his or her professional training, is given greater discretion in determining probable cause than is a private citizen. With a few exceptions, the wording of the Penal Code is permissive. The laws of arrest are generally permissive. Even in the case of murder, the law is permissive. This gives the police latitude in their timing of an arrest, should there be good reason to postpone it. Especially in non-hazardous crimes such as petty theft, it is often wise to let a crime-in-progress continue to a point where criminal intent is easily proven, as long as the prolongation does not endanger life or property or allow a misdemeanor to become a felony.

However, departmental policies are usually less permissive than the Penal Code. A typical departmental policy would require that the officer take appropriate action promptly, especially in the case of a felony. The officer is expected to enforce the law. If he felt that he might arrest, or might not arrest—more or less at will—he would undoubtedly be destined for a brief career as a police officer.

When an officer contacts a person who appears to be a drug abuser, the circumstances may not always supply probable cause to arrest. In such cases, the officer should take the opportunity to refer the subject to an agency which may be able to help him with his problem. The same referrals can be used when an officer is approached by a concerned third party (a parent, a spouse, or a friend).

By removing a person who abuses narcotics from the community, incarceration accomplishes two objectives: it places the individual in an environment where he must withdraw from drugs and gives him an opportunity to receive treatment; at the same time, it eliminates the possibility (at least while he is incarcerated) that he might commit crimes in order to obtain money for drugs. The reason to enforce narcotic influence laws in this manner is to reduce crimes against property.

Since some individuals take it upon themselves to seek aid in reducing or overcoming their own need for drugs, officers should be familiar with the drug treatment programs in their area. Most departments have a list of referral agencies.

RECORDING PROBABLE CAUSE

When making an arrest, it is important that the officer remembers, or in the case of complicated circumstances, records the probable cause of his or her actions. The officer should remember or record why he knows or believes that a crime has been committed and why he knows or believes that the person he is arresting is guilty of the crime.

Probable cause facts become a part of the arrest report prepared by the officer. If the arrest is later questioned, the officer may wish he had kept better records. Probable cause is often based on many bits of information and observations that, after a lapse of time, will be difficult to recall accurately and describe and relate before a court.

SEARCHES DURING DETENTIONS (PAT-DOWNS OR FRISKS)

During a detention, a police officer has no power to conduct a general, full, exploratory search of the suspect.

However, he may conduct a search for contraband if the officer has probable cause to believe it is on the person—probably on the theory that his probable cause also provides a basis to arrest. In this case, the search is justified incident to that arrest, even though the search comes first (*Valdez*, 196 *Cal.App*.3d 799, 1987).

In another case, an officer who smelled PCP as he approached the suspect was entitled to search him for it (*Divito*, 152 *Cal.App*.3d 11, 1984).

The officer may also conduct a pat-down or limited weapons search of someone he or she has detained, but only of the suspect's outer clothing (*Terry*, 392 U.S. 1, 1968), and only if he has specific facts which make him feel in danger (*Hill*, 12 *Cal*.3d 731, 1974). "Standard procedure" isn't good enough; there must be further cause for the search (*Santos*, 154 *Cal.App*.3d 1178, 1984). For instance, the officer must reasonably fear that the person is armed or may be armed (*Orozco*, 114 *Cal.App*.3d 435, 1981), although the officer need not have positive proof before the search (*Wright*, 206 *Cal.App*.3d 1107, 1988; *Stephen L.*, 162 *Cal.App*.3d 257, 1984).

SEARCH AND SEIZURE DURING DETENTION

The officer may seize any weapons or other hard objects usable as a weapon which are discovered during a pat-down. Contraband or other clear evidence of crime may also be seized, as long as objective safety factors exist to justify the pat-search in the first place.

If a valid pat-down leads to discovery of a closed container, you may open it if you have a basis for thinking that it contains a weapon; this is because of the inherent "exigencies" involved in a weapon situation. However, if you discover a closed container which you do not think contains a weapon, but rather some kind of contraband (e.g., a cigarette pack which you think contains marijuana), you will need a warrant in order to legally open the container, unless the contents are clearly obvious by plain view, smell, or touch.

Plain View

An officer may also seize any weapons, contraband, or crime-related evidence which is in plain view or plain sight during a detention. This type of seizure is lawful because observing something in plain view is not considered a "search."

Here is another case of plain view seizure: during a traffic stop, a "neatly folded squared piece of paper" fell from the driver's wallet to the ground. The experienced officer recognized it as a likely bindle of cocaine or heroin. Therefore, it was proper to seize the bindle.

Abandonment

Similarly, if the suspect discards an object during a detention, it is generally proper to seize and examine it. However, if you are going to detain the suspect longer or arrest him because of a discarded object (for example, a bindle containing white powder which you think is cocaine), be sure you have the training or expertise to justify your suspicion.

Plain View Is Not A Search

In one case, officers made a traffic stop and saw, from outside the vehicle, marijuana debris on the floorboards. The observation provided probable cause to enter the passenger compartment, seize the evidence, and search for more. In another case, an officer smelled marijuana during a traffic stop. He lawfully entered the passenger compartment (because he had probable cause) and saw a concealed weapon. In this case, it was proper for the officer to seize the weapon.

Plain Smell

Just like "plain view," "plain smell" is also not considered a "search"; therefore, it too can provide probable cause for searching parts of cars and containers within cars. Below are some cases of plain smell which would or would not lead to probable cause for a search.

> An officer stopped Scott because the registration tag on his vehicle was not current. When Scott got out of this car, he was unsteady and had a blank stare. Scott told the officer that the officer could get the registration from the car. When the officer opened the door he smelled ether. As the officer's nose got closer to a box of Sherman cigarettes, his knowledge that Sherman cigarettes are often dipped in PCP gave the officer probable cause to open the box.

> An officer, while making a traffic stop, smelled the odor of marijuana coming from the passenger compartment. He properly searched the passenger compartment. However, because he found only evidence of "casual use" (i.e., some debris, perhaps a few "roaches," etc.) his search had to end there. Small amounts of marijuana do not provide probable cause to search the trunk.

> An officer made a traffic stop for speeding, then saw marijuana on the rear seat. While retrieving that marijuana, the officer smelled a further strong odor of unburned marijuana coming from the rear portion of the vehicle. That smell gave the officer probable cause to search behind the rear seat as well as in the trunk.

Undercover Entries

An officer may enter premises as part of an undercover operation if valid consent to enter is obtained from an occupant. The fact that you misrepresent your identity will not invalidate the consent (*Toubus*, 114 *Cal.App*.3d 378, 1981). Once inside, after the "buy" has taken place, you will then have probable cause to arrest and may do so without a warrant. Also consider the case below:

> An operator poses as a friend of a friend and asks to enter to buy narcotics. The suspect lets the operator in and makes a sale. The warrantless arrest which follows is valid because the consent to enter is valid. The courts see no trick or misrepresentation of purpose because the officer's stated or implied purpose was to make a buy, and with that understanding the suspect agreed to let him enter. In other words, you can misrepresent your identity, just not your purpose. The suspect takes his chances about who you really are.

This type of entry has been upheld even where there was enough probable cause to arrest prior to entry (*Evans*, 108 *Cal.App*.3d 193, 1980). Nevertheless, be careful not to abuse this procedure. Get a warrant unless you intend in good faith to continue the investigation after you are inside (e.g., by making a buy) and not just to arrest the suspect.

Reentries

Be alert to another problem area with undercover operations. It is alright for the operator, while still inside, to signal for reinforcements who then also enter to actually make the arrest (*Toubus*, 114 *Cal.App.*3d 378, 1981; *Cornejo*, 92 *Cal.App.*3d 637, 1979).

However, if the operator physically leaves the premises to get assistance, his subsequent reentry will probably be invalid, making the arrest invalid also.

In one case, acting on a tip, an undercover officer went to the defendant's house to try to sell him some "stolen" guns. He got the suspect's consent to enter, made the sale, then tried to signal for backup help. However, his transmitter was broken, so he stepped outside and was 15 feet from the residence when he signaled the others. The court said the warrantless (re)entry and arrest were unlawful. The original consent no longer applied and there were no exigent circumstances (*Garcia*, 139 *Cal.App.*3d Supp. 1, 1982).

ARRESTS IN HOMES: THE WARRANT REQUIREMENT

As a general rule, you must have an arrest warrant in order to arrest someone inside his or her home (*Ramey*, 16 *Cal.*3d 263, 1976; *Payton*, 445 *U.S.* 573, 1980). "Home" or "dwelling" can mean any place the suspect resides, such as his tent, motel room, boat, van, etc.

This same protection (the requirement of a warrant) also applies to those portions of a business or office which are not open to the general public.

The purpose behind this arrest warrant requirement (which also exists under Federal law) is the same as the purpose behind a search warrant. "A man's home is his castle," and police simply are not permitted inside without judicial authorization (the warrant), an emergency (exigent circumstances), or valid permission from the occupant (consent).

INVESTIGATION OF DRUG OFFENSES: CAR STOPS

A vehicle "stop" is an exertion of authority by an officer which is something less than a full arrest but more substantial than a simple "contact" or "consensual encounter." A detention occurs at the moment the officer turns on his red light or otherwise stops a vehicle to investigate a possible crime or to issue a traffic citation.

Note, however, that if an officer is dealing with a vehicle which is parked or already stopped for some other reason, it does not constitute a detention to walk up to the driver and ask (not demand) to see his or her driver's license or other identification (*Gonzales*, 164 *Cal.App.*3d 1194, 1985).

Reasonable Suspicion

A detention following a car stop is valid only if you have a "reasonable suspicion" that:

— something relating to a crime has just happened, is happening, or is about to happen; and

— the vehicle or the person in the vehicle you are about to detain is connected with that activity.

The officer's "reasonable suspicion" must be based on specific facts which he or she can articulate to a court. The court will then decide if the facts were enough to make the officer's suspicion reasonable. The officer cannot make valid detention based on a hunch, rumor, intuition, instinct, or curiosity.

The officer may also make a legal detention, vehicle or person, based on a "wanted flyer" or similar bulletin issued by some other jurisdiction and relating to a completed crime, as long as the other jurisdiction had a reasonable basis for issuing it, and the detention is not impermissibly intrusive (*Hensley*, 53 *U.S.L.Week* 4053, 1984).

Traffic Stops

Observation of a Vehicle Code violation will always provide a valid basis to detain.

If the officer has a "hunch" a vehicle or its occupants are involved in a felony, but does not have enough specific information to make a valid detention for the felony, the officer may make a traffic stop to see what he can see (assuming, of course, that a valid basis for the traffic stop exists).

However, the officer's actions must be consistent with the legal basis for the traffic stop if he expects the detention to hold up. Otherwise, the court may find that the officer made an illegal "pretext" stop (*Smith*, 803 *F.*2d 647, 11th Circ., 1986). In other words, the officer should follow through on the traffic ticket and not undertake any unrelated investigation, or prolong the detention, unless he discovers something suspicious or incriminating in the course of issuing the ticket.

The officer should always concentrate on the specific facts which create the suspicion. Remembering each of them, or listing them in his report, may well "save" a case.

If the traffic stop turns out not to be "routine" because the officer sees contraband (marijuana "roaches") or discovers something suspicious, (non-matching names and vehicle identification numbers), the stop has become an "investigative detention."

It is impossible to give a specific rule on how long the officer may properly detain someone on reasonable suspicion for non-traffic offenses. The permissible length is determined by considering the officer's purpose, diligence, and choice of investigative means (*Sharpe*, 53 *U.S.L.Week* 4346, 1985). Twenty minutes might be perfectly reasonable under one set of circumstances but not another.

Nevertheless, if the officer is not progressing in his attempt to obtain probable cause to arrest after a reasonable time of investigating, he should either:

let the detainee go (possibly after filling out a field interrogation card or otherwise ensuring that he can be found later); or

obtain the detainee's unequivocal consent to further detention.

Ordering Occupants Out

Pre-Proposition 8 in California case law indicates that to validly order someone to get out of a vehicle, you need something beyond a routine traffic stop on which to base concern for your safety, such as the driver was a suspect in a major felony, made a furtive movement, acted or talked in a hostile/dangerous manner, etc. (*Padilla*, 132 *Cal.App*.3d 555, 1982; *Faddler*, 132 *Cal.App*.3d 607, 1982). This is definitely still the law when it comes to passengers (*Maxwell*, 206 *Cal.App*.3d 1004, 1988).

When it comes to the driver, however, it is probably permissible to follow the Federal rule, which permits ordering out even during a routine traffic stop which has no additional factors of danger. All traffic stops, inherently, involve enough risk to justify the minimal additional intrusion of ordering a validly detained driver to get out of his or her vehicle (*Mimms*, 434 *U.S.* 106, 1977).

Besides, even if such an order turns out to be illegal under California law, any evidence which results from it is nevertheless admissible in court because of Proposition 8.[1]

Consent

As long as you have some basis for asking, it will always be proper to search any part of a car or anything in it if you first obtain a valid consent. However, there are problem areas within the "consent" exception which you must fully understand. These areas include:

— "voluntariness" (was the suspect coerced or pressured into giving consent?);

— "authority" (did you get consent from someone empowered to give it?); and

— "scope" (were any limitations placed on the consent?).

ALWAYS SEEK CONSENT TO SEARCH NO MATTER WHAT OTHER AUTHORITY YOU MAY HAVE FOR YOUR SEARCH. Consent can never hurt and it may validate an otherwise bad search.

Plain View

As mentioned earlier, "plain view" is not a "search." It is the observation of crime-related evidence from a place you have a lawful right to be (*Katz*, 389 *U.S.* 347, 1967).

A. Observation After Entry

If you are already lawfully within the vehicle, you may seize all crime-related evidence which you see. However, if you are not lawfully within the vehicle, it is illegal for you to seize any evidence. For instance:

1. An officer smells marijuana during a traffic stop. He lawfully enters the passenger compartment (because he has probable cause) and sees a concealed weapon. The officer may properly seize the weapon.

---

[1] The California Constitution allows for Independent State Grounds, or an expansion of rights above U.S. Constitution rights for those persons in California. Under Proposition 8, called the Victim's Bill of Rights, passed in 1982, no relevant evidence shall be excluded in a criminal proceeding unless it violates the U.S. Constitution. In other words, evidence seized in a manner that violates California Independent State Grounds will be admissible so long as the evidence is legally obtained as interpreted by the U.S. Supreme Court under the U.S. Constitution.

2. An officer stops a suspect on a traffic offense. The officer puts his head just inside the window and sees contraband. He may not legally seize the contraband because it was illegal for him to enter the vehicle before seeing the contraband.

Plain Smell

Just like "plain view," "plain smell" is also not a "search," and it too can provide probable cause for searching parts of cars and containers within cars (*Chavers*, 33 *Cal.*3d 462, 1983; *Weaver*, 143 *Cal.App.*3d 926, 1983).

Observation Before Entry

In a vehicle context (as opposed to homes), it generally makes very little difference that you observe the contraband or crime-related evidence from outside the vehicle before you enter it. Typically, you may still enter for the purpose of seizing it, at least when the car is occupied. This is because the area you can observe from outside (i.e., the passenger compartment) carries such a low expectation of privacy (*Brown*, 460 *U.S.* 730, 1983).

Using a Flashlight

The use of a flashlight, either from outside the car or after a lawful entry, changes nothing. You may use a flashlight to see anything which would have been visible during daylight hours (*Rogers*, 21 *Cal.*3d 542, 1978).

SEARCHES BASED ON PROBABLE CAUSE: THE "AUTOMOBILE EXCEPTION"

Parts of The Vehicle

Under both Federal and California case law, a police officer may conduct a warrantless search of any part of a car which he has lawfully stopped on the road as long as he has probable cause to believe the object he is looking for may be located in that portion of the car.

The key to understanding this "automobile exception" is realizing that it is based on "probable cause," and that "probable cause" here means exactly the same thing that it does in a search warrant context; namely, enough facts, knowledge, training, etc., to make it reasonable to believe that the object a police officer is looking for may be located in the place (portion of the car) he wants to search.

Plain view discovery of small amounts (personal use) of marijuana in the passenger compartment does not provide probable cause to search the trunk compartment (*Gregg*, 43 *Cal.App.*3d 137, 1974), but discovery of large amounts does (*Wimberly*, 16 *Cal.*3d 557, 1976).

Erratic driving, slurred speech, pinpointed pupils, and fresh puncture marks on the arm would provide probable cause to search the passenger compartment for narcotics (*Low*, 148 *Cal.App.*3d 89, 1983).

Motor Homes

In 1985, the United States Supreme Court made it clear that the "automobile exception" applies to motor homes as well. It ruled that when a motor home (here a Dodge/Midas Mini Motor Home) is (1) being used on the highways, or (2) capable of such use and is found stationary in a place not regularly used for residential purposes, the two justifications for the vehicle exception come into play. First, the vehicle is readily mobile, and second, there is a reduced expectation of privacy stemming from the pervasive regulation of vehicles capable of traveling on highways (*Carney*, 471 *U.S.* 386, 1985; *Ruggles*, 39 *Cal.*3d 1, 1985; *Black*, 173 *Cal.App.*3d 506, 1985).

This ruling means that you do not need a warrant to search a motor home which you stop on the highway, or which you find parked on the street or in a parking lot.

The same is true for a "van," which also falls within the "automobile exception" since it is even more like a passenger car than a motor home (*Chestnut*, 151 *Cal.App.*3d 721, 1983).

On the other hand, if the motor home is at a campground or other overnight facility, you should obtain a warrant, particularly if the vehicle is hooked up to outside facilities, especially plumbing.

Federal Rule On Searching The Passenger Compartment

The Federal "bright line" rule is relatively straightforward. When you make a custodial arrest of the occupant of a vehicle, you may search the passenger compartment of the vehicle, including the glove compartment, and including any containers you find, whether open or closed (*Belton*, 453 *U.S.* 454, 1981).

In other words, no matter what the arrest is for, as long as you are taking the driver or occupant into custody, you may search the passenger compartment and everything and anything in it. It makes no difference that the arrestee is already out of the car and is, as a practical matter, not able to reach inside anymore (*Lorenzo*, 867 *F.*2d 561, 9th Cir. 1989).

Note, however, that such a search is limited to the "passenger compartment" and may not include the vehicle's trunk.

SEARCHES INCIDENT TO ARREST

As defined earlier, an "arrest" occurs when a police officer takes someone into custody, either by the use of physical restraints or by the arrestee's submission to the officer's authority.

When the officer makes a custodial arrest of the driver or occupant of a vehicle, the law permits him to search the person and some portions of the vehicle incident to that arrest.

Note: "Cite and release" traffic offenses are not included here because, even though the driver is technically under arrest, he is not in custody. The law treats such situations as a "detention."

Searching Persons

The Federal rule for searching persons incident to a custodial arrest does not change just because the person is (or has just been) in a vehicle.

Briefly stated, the Federal rule allows a full body search, including any containers, incident to any kind of custodial arrest, from murder to outstanding traffic warrants (*Robinson*, 414 *U.S.* 218, 1973).

Stopping and Searching Vehicles

When making a car stop, the officer must keep the suspect under observation at all times. Watch the suspect's HANDS! All too often an officer will overlook a major law violation by being preoccupied with a "routine" car stop. While the officer is so engaged, the drug violator is busy throwing, or concealing contraband.

Once the decision has been made to arrest the suspect, search and handcuff the suspect IMMEDIATELY with his hands BEHIND HIM. Keep any recovered evidence out of the suspect's reach. How many times has this question been raised—"The suspect just ate the evidence. What do I do now?"

Request assistance as soon as conditions appear that additional help may be required. Whenever you can, make the car stop in an area where there is adequate light. Use the spotlight and headlights of the police vehicle to further illuminate the interior of the stopped vehicle. As you proceed with a routine stop, protect yourself. There has been an increasing number of attacks on police officers.

Conduct a thorough preliminary search. Check the obvious and not so obvious places of concealment such as trouser cuffs, inside of socks, inside of trouser waistband, items inside of other items such as a bindle of heroin inside a matchbook, fingernail clipper, or cigarette pack; and check inside the suspect's hand since drug users are very skilled at palming contraband until it can be thrown away or eaten. Keep in mind that weapons may be overlooked in a cursory pat search. Also, containers of narcotics are sometimes hidden in the body cavities such as the mouth, rectum, or vagina. For this reason, it is important to search the vehicle before the suspect is placed in custody and after the suspect is removed.

It might not be possible to conduct a thorough search of the body as you would like. Just remember that drug users will attempt to dispose of the evidence. When transporting the suspect, make sure to secure the suspect in the vehicle so no drugs can be disposed of.

SEARCH AND SEIZURE ON PREMISES

ABANDONMENT

A person who voluntarily abandons his or her property no longer retains any reasonable expectation of privacy in that property. Although it seldom occurs that entry into a home can be justified on an abandonment theory, it is possible.

More frequently, it is rented apartments or motel units which might be considered "abandoned" either because the rental term has expired and/or because it appears from all the circumstances that the tenant has permanently departed (*Ingram*, 122 *Cal.App*.3d 673, 1981).

PERSONAL PRIVACY

The United States Constitution guarantees everyone the right to be free from unreasonable governmental intrusion. This right is personal to every citizen. It can exist almost any time and any place as long as:

- — the individual has indicated that he personally expects privacy;
- — his expectation of privacy is objectively reasonable under the circumstances; and

— his expectation is one which society is prepared to recognize as legitimate (*Greenwood*, 108 *S.Ct.* 1625, 1988; *Ciraolo*, 476 *U.S.* 207, 1986; *Oliver*, 466 *U.S.* 170, 1984; *Edelbacher*, 47 *Cal.*3d 983, 1989; *Jacobsen*, 466 *U.S.* 109, 1989; *O'Connor*, 480 *U.S.* 709, 1987).

A person automatically has a reasonable expectation of privacy in his or her home. Of course, if he lives in a ground-floor apartment on a busy street and leaves his window shades wide open, he cannot reasonably expect his activities inside not to be observed.

Likewise, the owner of undeveloped land exhibits a greater expectation of privacy the more he attempts to keep the public out (by fences, signs, gates, etc.)

General Rule for Searching Premises

It is illegal for a police officer to physically enter into an area where a person has a "reasonable expectation of privacy" in order to conduct a search or for the purpose of seizing something, unless:

— the officer has a warrant; or

— there are exigent circumstances (an emergency); or

— the officer obtained a valid consent.

Garbage

Under the Federal law (the Fourth Amendment), the United States Supreme Court has made it very clear that there is no reasonable expectation of privacy in trash or garbage, even if it has been bagged and placed at curbside or otherwise outside the "curtilage" of the residence for pickup (*Greenwood*, 108 *S.Ct.* 1625, 1988). Therefore, it is lawful for an officer to conduct a search of garbage or trash for evidence.

Other Items

If a person leaves an object behind, or disclaims any knowledge of it or interest in it, he is waiving any reasonable expectation of privacy he might have had in the object. Under such circumstances, it is legal for you to search the item.

For instance, suspects were properly arrested inside a house where officers had reason to believe cocaine had just been delivered in a shoulder bag. The bag was discovered just inside the front door, but all the occupants/arrestees disclaimed ownership of, or any interest in, the shoulder bag. Therefore, it was legal for the officers to search it (*Mendoza*, 176 *Cal.App.*3d 1127, 1986).

Specific Situations of Privacy

The following is a discussion of specific situations and how they relate to both a person's expectation of privacy and an officer's legal jurisdiction.

1. **A Home**
   Everyone, of course, can reasonably expect privacy inside his own home, at least to the extent that no officer will enter unless the officer has a warrant, exigent circumstances exist, or consent has been obtained. On the other hand, a person can hardly claim he has

a reasonable expectation of privacy in areas around his home where the general public (mailmen, salesmen, visitors, etc.) would reasonably be permitted to go. For example, the garage of a condominium apartment, which is available to all tenants and readily accessible by members of the general public, would not receive Fourth Amendment protection (*Galen*, 163 *Cal.App.*3d 786, 1985).

2. **A Driveway**
It is normally proper for a police officer to view areas around the premises from someone's driveway (*Bradley*, 1 *Cal.*3d 80, 1969).

In one case, footprints in a front yard, on the driveway and the front porch—visible to any visitor approaching the front door—were in plain view (*Edelbacher*, 47 *Cal.*3d 983, 1989). In a similar case of "plain view" from the driveway, marijuana plants were visible 30-40 feet away (*Johnson*, 105 *Cal.App.*3d 884, 1980).

3. **The Front Yard**
A person normally has no reasonable expectation of privacy in the areas around the front of his home "where members of the public having business with the occupants" would naturally go. Two examples of this "front yard" rule are recounted below:

An officer missed a turnoff and ended up driving on a circular "loop" road which provided access to seven houses. When he turned into a driveway to ask Gray (who was outside) for directions, he noticed that Gray was carrying a trashbag filled with marijuana which protruded from the top of the bag. The officer arrested Gray and seized the marijuana. His observations were legal. Even though the road had some "no trespassing" signs, the officer was not there searching for contraband in an area where the desire for privacy was obvious. The "loop" was open, accessible, and frequently used by the residents. Turning around in the driveway was an act which could have been done by any one of the residents or their guests who regularly used the roadway, and Gray could have been seen from the roadway as well as his own driveway (*Gray*, 164 *Cal.App.*3d 445, 1985).

An officer went through an unlocked gate in a chain-link fence to talk to the occupant/suspect who was standing in the front yard about 75 feet from the gate. Up close, the officer could see the suspect was under the influence of an opiate. The court held that the suspect had no reasonable expectation of privacy in his front yard, despite the fence, because the fence was more for "discouraging dogs, children, handbill deliverymen and others from walking across the front lawn and flower beds," than it was for "excluding the public." However, the result would probably have been different if there had been a locked gate, a high solid fence blocking the front yard from view, a written notice to keep out or "beware of dog," or perhaps a doorbell at the front gate, warning that the visitor was unwelcome (*Mendoza*, 122 *Cal.App.*3d Supp. 12, 1981).

4. The Back Yard

Normally, a person has a higher reasonable expectation of privacy in his back yard than his front yard. This is because, by common sense and custom, members of the public are not normally invited into or expected to enter the back yard of an average residence. Therefore, a police officer may not normally enter the back yard to search or seize without a warrant, consent or exigent circumstances.

5. Windows

If a police officer is standing in an area where he has a lawful right to be, he may properly look through windows when the shades are sheer or not drawn. This is because anyone who leaves his shades open or who uses material which is easily seen through cannot reasonably expect privacy.

However, "peeking" through slits or under window or door shades is an improper "search." Anything an officer sees in such a "search" will usually be inadmissible in court (*Lorenzana*, 9 *Cal*.3d 626, 1973).

6. Fences and Walls

The general rule relating to the expectation of privacy created by the erection of walls and fences is that if, while standing in a lawful place, a police officer can see over or through the fence or wall (1) without extraordinary effort (e.g., without using a stepladder or standing on a car or cinderblock), or (2) without getting very close and "peeking," the viewing will normally not be considered a "search"; i.e., the person does not have a reasonable expectation of privacy in the area viewed. However, if the officer does need "extraordinary effort" to see through or over the fence or wall, then it is usually considered a warrantless search.

For example, an officer was told by an informant that Lovelace was growing marijuana. The officer went to the Lovelace residence and, while standing in the alley, looked through a small knothole in a six-foot-high wooden fence and saw marijuana growing. The officer then got a warrant and seized the marijuana (and other drugs in plain view). The evidence was suppressed because looking through the knothole was a warrantless "search." (*Lovelace*, 116 *Cal.App*.3d 541, 1981.)

7. Views from Neighboring Premises

A police officer may view the suspect's home or property from a neighbor's home or property if invited to do so, at least in situations where members of the public could also see the suspicious object. Below are two explanantory anecdotes.

Dillon's neighbor called the police and said that Dillon was growing marijuana in his back yard, which had a fence around it. An officer responded and viewed the marijuana from the neighbor's second-story window (40 feet away). The court ruled that this viewing was proper, but emphasized that "the view of the back yard was vulnerable to observation by any of the petitioner's neighbors, in essence, open to public view" (*Dillon*, 7 *Cal*.3d 305, 1972).

A suspect was growing marijuana in his back yard. The back yard was surrounded by a six-foot fence which was completely covered by ivy. Officers viewed the marijuana from the second-floor balcony of a nearby motel (with the consent of the motel owner or manager). The officer's observation is not considered a "search" under the Fourth Amendment because he could see and "recognize" the marijuana from a position which was generally accessible to the public.

8. **Open Fields**
"Open fields" are areas of land which are so open to public view that the owner or possessor is deemed to have "implicitly invited" the police to observe and seize his contraband.

Because of the lack of reasonable expectation of privacy in such areas, a warrantless entry into them does not violate the Fourth Amendment (*Lorenzana*, 9 *Cal.*3d 626, 1973).

Recent opinions by the United States Supreme Court (*Oliver*, 466 *U.S.* 170, 1984; *Dunn*, 480 *U.S.* 294, 1987) make it clear that the Fourth Amendment has no applicability to "open fields." "Open fields" means any outdoor real property outside the "curtilage" of the house or beyond the relatively small and usually well-defined area immediately around a residence to which the activity of the home-life extends. Furthermore, open fields do not have to be either "open" or real "fields" to qualify.

9. **Surveillance**
It is not a "search" for a police officer to conduct surveillance of private premises or to follow people who leave the premises, as long as the observations are made from a place the officer has a right to be (*Lorenzana*, 9 *Cal.*3d 626, 1973; *Thomas*, 112 *Cal.App.*3d 980, 1980; *Dunn*, 480 *U.S.* 294, 1987).

10. **Use of Binoculars**
Binoculars may be used to look onto premises or into a building if what is being viewed could be seen with the naked eye from a lawful position (such as the driveway). In other words, you may properly use binoculars to get a "better look."

11. **Federal Law on Overflights**
Federal law is clear that persons on the ground have no privacy from warrantless aerial observations made from aircraft flying in a physically nonintrusive manner in publicly navigable airspace, typically 1,000 feet or more above the ground (*Ciraolo*, 476 *U.S.* 207, 1986).

Such aerial observations are legal regardless of whether the flight (1) is part of a random, routine surveillance program or (2) is carried out to look at specific property in response to a tip.

Likewise, in the case of marijuana, it makes no difference where the marijuana is growing. From a lawful altitude, you may look not only into "open fields," but also into the "curtilage" of the residence, i.e., the yard or private area immediately surrounding a home (*Dunn*, 480 *U.S.* 294, 1987).

Although the observations in *Ciraolo* were made with the naked eye, the United States Supreme Court ruled in a companion case (*Dow Chemical*, 476 *U.S.* 227, 1986) that it is also legal to use aerial photography, including a camera which provides moderate enhancement. In both *Dow* and *Ciraolo,* however, the court warned that its opinion might well be different if the police used sophisticated "hi tech" equipment, not generally available to the public, which would reveal "intimate associations" below, i.e., activities not otherwise visible.

The court also warned that overflights which are too "physically intrusive" (i.e., too low, loud, frequent, prolonged, etc.) could make aerial observations illegal. Concerning elevation, this means you should conform to FAA rules and stay a minimum of 1,000 feet above ground level in "congested" areas and 500 feet in other, sparsely populated areas, when flying a fixed-wing aircraft. Federal law permits helicopters to legally fly as low as 400 feet (*Riley*, 109 *S.Ct.* 693, 1989).

Plain View

Under the general rule, when a police officer sees something in "plain view" (or plain sight) from a place he has a right to be, no "search" has taken place in any constitutional sense, because the person has no reasonable expectation of privacy as to items which are in plain view. A police officer may seize any object which is in plain view, as long as:

— he has a lawful right to be where the object is physically located; and

— there is probable cause to believe the object is crime-related.

Prior Lawful Intrusion

Before an officer may seize an object in plain view, he must lawfully be where the object is located. In the case of buildings, this means he must already legally be inside, i.e., he must have made a "prior lawful intrusion" (*Coolidge*, 403 *U.S.* 443, 1971).

WARRANTLESS ENTRY DUE TO EXIGENCY/EMERGENCY

You may enter premises without a warrant or consent if there are exigent circumstances. An exigency is an emergency situation requiring swift action to prevent any of the following:

— imminent danger to life

— serious damage to property

— imminent escape of a suspect

— the destruction of evidence (*Lucero*, 44 *Cal.*3d 1006, 1988; *Duncan*, 42 *Cal.*3d 91, 1986; *Wilson*, 865 *F.*2d 215, 9th Cir. 1989).

Often, the above-mentioned justifications for a warrantless entry or further search will overlap.

Protective Sweep

If a police officer is already lawfully inside or at a house and has some basis for believing there may be others inside who may pose a danger to him, he may undertake a "protective sweep"—a brief search (two or three minutes) to look for these other individuals (*Guidi*, 10 *Cal.*3d 1, 1973). In such an instance, the officer can only search areas where a person could possibly be hiding (not drawers, small cabinets, etc.).

If the officer sees crime-related evidence in plain view during such a search, he may seize it. It is normally better, however, to get a warrant for the evidence he saw and other similar evidence which may be on the premises.

Victim, Injured or Ill Person Inside

If there is reason to believe someone (victim or other person) inside a house may be injured or ill and in immediate need of help, the officer may enter the house without a warrant (*Hill*, 12 *Cal.*3d 731, 1974; *Roberts*, 47 *Cal.*2d 374, 1956—officers heard moaning inside dwelling).

Remember, however, that once a police officer is lawfully inside, he still may only search or do whatever is necessary to resolve the emergency, nothing more. The case summarized below illustrates this principle:

> Officers responded to a house where there had been reports of "screams." They knocked on the door and requested permission to enter and investigate. The man who answered the door appeared very nervous and ran back into the house toward a bedroom.
>
> Fearing for their own safety and that of a possible victim the officers followed the man and found weapons and contraband (narcotics) in the bedroom in plain view. After the defendant had been arrested and taken to the living room, one officer went back to the bedroom and looked around more closely. He found more narcotics in a cigar box. The court found the entry of the house proper. However, the search of the cigar box was invalid since it was not justified by either the emergency or by "plain view" (*Frazier*, 71 *Cal.App.*3d 690, 1977).

Suspected Child Abuse

Courts will go fairly far in finding an exigency and permitting a warrantless entry into premises to prevent possible child-abuse offenses.

Prevention of Serious Damage to Property

The warrantless entry of premises may be justified under the emergency exception to protect the property of the owner or occupant. If there is imminent likelihood of a fire, explosion, etc. (e.g., smell of gas or gasoline or PCP coming from a building), a warrantless entry is proper (*Stegman*, 164 *Cal.App.*3d 936, 1985).

Prevention of Suspect's Imminent Escape

It is proper to enter a residence without a warrant in order to prevent the escape of a suspect, especially if he is armed and dangerous or has just committed a violent felony (*Parrison*, 137 *Cal.App.*3d 529, 1982).

Prevention of Evidence Destruction

A police officer may enter premises without a warrant or consent when there is immediate danger of destruction of crime-related evidence, at least where a serious crime is involved (*Welsh*, 104 *S.Ct.* 2091, 1984). For example, warrantless entry of the residence of a suspected cop-killer—seconds after the shooting—was proper to prevent destruction of the evidence (*Parrison*, 137 *Cal.App.*3d 529, 1982). In another case, it was proper for the officer to enter a suspected felony drunk driver's residence 90 minutes after the offense in order to get a blood-alcohol sample (*Keltie*, 466 *U.S.* 740, 1984).

In addition to a serious offense, to prevail in court you must be able to prove that there was not enough time to get a warrant—possibly even a telephonic warrant (Cal.Pen.Code, Section 1528(b)). For example:

> An informant made a controlled buy of heroin from Ellers at Ellers' home and saw others doing the same thing. Afterwards, the officers met a mile away and spent 10 to 15 minutes planning the arrest. Then they returned, entered, and made a warrantless arrest. The evidence was suppressed. The court said the heavy traffic, without more evidence, did not justify immediate action, and that there was adequate time to get a warrant (*Ellers*, 108 *Cal.App.*3d 943, 1980).

Note: Once a police officer has a situation like this under control, it is normally better to secure the premises (from outside, when possible) and await the obtaining of a search warrant than it is to immediately seize the evidence you saw in plain view. (*Daughhetee*, 165 *Cal.App.*3d 574, 1985; *Larry A.*, 154 *Cal.App.*3d 929, 1984; compare *Segura*, 468 *U.S.* 796, 1984).

Warrantless Entry to Make an Arrest

A police officer may also enter a home without a warrant to arrest an armed or dangerous suspect he has been following in "hot pursuit."

Creating an Exigency

A police officer may not use exigent circumstances as an excuse for a warrantless entry if he has "created" the emergency by his own conduct. For instance:

> A reliable informant told officers that he had just seen contraband at Shuey's house, thereby giving probable cause to get a warrant. Instead, the officers went to Shuey's home, asked him about the contraband and requested consent to search. Shuey refused to talk or consent. The officers then secured the residence and got a search warrant. However, the evidence was suppressed because, although exigent circumstances existed to secure (Shuey would probably destroy the contraband), the officers had "created" the exigency themselves (*Shuey*, 30 *Cal.App.*3d 535, 1973).

> An anonymous tipster called officers and said that narcotics were being sold out of a certain apartment. An officer surveyed the apartment and saw many people come, stay a few minutes and then leave. One person left the apartment, drove erratically away and was stopped. Because the suspect had fresh marks on his arms, he was arrested. In a search incident to his arrest, the officers found a bag of "powdery substance." The officers then went to the door and knocked. When a person answered, the officers identified themselves and demanded entry. When the residents "began running," an officer "broke open the screen door." The officers then made arrests and seized evidence. The court ruled

that, even assuming probable cause existed, the officers should have gotten a warrant. In suppressing the evidence, the court stated, "To the extent that their actions created an emergency it was of the "do-it-yourself" variety condemned in *People v. Shuey*" (*Rodriguez*, 123 *Cal.App*.3d 269, 1981; *Larry A.*, 154 *Cal.App*.3d 929, 1984).

Clandestine Drug Labs

Will the discovery of a PCP "lab" justify a warrantless entry? In one case, the court viewed the smell of ether, and even of PCP, as just contraband. The court held that the plain smell of contraband without evidence of the element of imminent danger did not provide a sufficient basis for entering the premises without a search warrant (*Dickson*, 144 *Cal.App*.3d 1046, 1983; *Blackwell*, 147 *Cal.App*.3d 646, 1983). In another case, the officers' actions, including a five-hour delay, belied their concern about an imminent explosion (*Baird*, 168 *Cal.App*.3d 237, 1985).

In a similar situation, however, other courts have reached the opposite conclusion, probably because the officers acted with genuine concern (e.g., called the fire department, or evacuated neighboring houses) and gave testimony stressing the danger involved, i.e., the risk of explosion if ether fumes were to contact flame or other heat source (*Stegman*, 164 *Cal.App*.3d 936, 1985; *Patterson*, 94 *Cal.App*.3d 456, 1979; *Messina*, 165 *Cal.App*.3d 937, 1985; *Wilson*, 865 *F*.2d 215, 9th Cir. 1989).

The key is for the officer's actions to be consistent with his motive of preserving life or property (*Duncan*, 42 *Cal*.3d 91, 1986; *Osuna*, 187 *Cal.App*.3d 845, 1986).

Also, if you expect "exigent circumstances" to justify a warrantless entry, you will have to convince the court that it was reasonable to anticipate that an injury might have occurred before a search warrant, even a telephonic one, could have been obtained (*Blackwell*, 147 *Cal.App*.3d 646, 1983).

Once you have entered and controlled the situation, remember that if you leave, you will need a warrant to reenter and conduct a search (*Blackwell*, 147 *Cal.App*.3d 646, 1983) unless the emergency is still continuing (*Duncan*, 42 *Cal*.3d 91, 1986). For instance, if you were unable to turn off the furnace the first time, a subsequent warrantless reentry to do that task would still be justified (*Stegman*, 164 *Cal.App*.3d 936, 1985; *Abes*, 174 *Cal.App*.3d 796, 1985).

KNOCK AND NOTICE

The general purpose behind the "knock and notice" requirements is to protect the privacy of a person in his home and to minimize the possibility of a violent confrontation between police and private citizens which might occur if the police made sudden, surprise, unannounced entries. In particular, before a police officer enters (not *while* he enters) he or she must:

knock (or do something else which will alert the people inside to his presence);

identify himself as a police officer;

explain his purpose;

demand entry and then wait a reasonable period before entering.

Knock loudly on the door and then say in a loud voice, "Police Officers. Open up. We have a search warrant (or an arrest warrant) for X."

The "knock and notice" requirements are excused when facts make it reasonable for an officer to believe, in good faith, that compliance would:

result in increased danger to him;

result in the destruction of evidence;

frustrate the arrest by allowing a fleeing, dangerous suspect to escape.

However, a police officer cannot use generalizations or common knowledge in support of noncompliance. For example, it is not enough simply to believe that narcotics violators usually have guns and will use them on police, or that owners of guns will necessarily use them against approaching officers.

Instead, a police officer needs specific facts or reasons relating to the situation showing, for example, that a particular suspect on the premises is likely to shoot rather than submit peaceably to the entry. Below are two examples illustrating the "no knock" exception:

Officers serving a warrant had been told by a confidential, reliable informant that the informant had personally seen the suspect habitually answer the door with a gun in his hand. The court ruled that this was a sufficient reason for the officers to ignore the "knock and announce" requirements (*Dumas*, 9 *Cal*.3d 871, 1973).

The suspect's arrest record reflected a history of assaultive behavior, including a prior fight with a police officer because the suspect was carrying a gun. These facts were ruled enough to bring the officers within the "no knock" exception (*Henderson*, 58 *Cal.App*.3d 349, 1976).

Generally speaking, if exigent circumstances permit a police officer to enter the premises without a warrant, they will also excuse strict compliance with "knock and announce" requirements (*Escudero*, 23 *Cal*.3d 800, 1979; *Kizzee*, 94 *Cal.App*.3d 927, 1979). Nevertheless, it is good practice for a police officer to announce his or her identity and purpose whenever entering a residence.

When Compliance is Futile

A related exception excusing compliance with the "knock and announce" rule is when compliance would be "futile," i.e., when no purpose or reason to knock and announce exists because the occupant already knows your identity and purpose or has indicated that he is not going to cooperate (*Mack*, 155 *Cal.App*.3d 666, 1984). For example:

Officers went to a residence to investigate possible possession of marijuana in large quantities. As they approached, the occupant happened to come outside, yelling "Jesus, it's the cops." The occupant then ran into the garage, slamming the door behind him. In this case, it was proper for the officers to force entry into the garage without complying with "knock and notice" requirements (*Bigham*, 49 *Cal.App*.3d 73, 1973; see also *Mayer*, 188 *Cal.App*.3d 1101, 1987).

Ruse Entry

A police officer may use a false name or employ some other trick or ruse to obtain consent to enter if he already has a judicially authorized right to enter, e.g., a search warrant (*McCarter*, 117 *Cal.App*.3d 894, 1981).

SEEKING CONSENT TO ENTER

A POLICE OFFICER SHOULD ALWAYS ASK FOR CONSENT TO SEARCH EVEN WHEN HE HAS OTHER AUTHORITY FOR THE SEARCH. It can never hurt, and it may help a great deal, if other grounds (e.g., exigency or warrant) are ruled insufficient.

Consider the following scenario: officers serve a search warrant and find lots of evidence. Later, the warrant is ruled defective and all of the evidence is suppressed. A simple question asked politely and prior to showing the warrant to the "consenter" might (assuming consent was obtained) have saved all of the evidence.

Never show the warrant before asking consent. If you do and the warrant is later ruled defective, the consent will also be invalid.

Do Not Seek Consent Instead of a Warrant

Never attempt a consent search instead of obtaining a warrant. If a police officer has probable cause to search a house but tries to obtain consent rather than a warrant to search, he takes the great risk that the resident will refuse to allow the search. If the resident does, the officer may be sure that the evidence will be destroyed while he or she is obtaining the warrant.

Furthermore, courts have ruled that in such circumstances the officer may not secure or "freeze" the premises because he "created" the exigency (*Shuey*, 30 *Cal.App*.3d 535, 1973).

Therefore, if the officer has probable cause to search a residence (and no exigent circumstances exist), he should get a warrant first and then seek consent.

Indications of Consent

To be valid, a person's consent must be clear, specific and unequivocal. This clear, specific and unequivocal consent may be indicated in many ways by the consenter, i.e., "Yeah," "Go ahead," "Do what you want." Silence, of course, is not good enough, because every person has the right to remain silent, thereby refusing consent.

Although physical conduct, such as pointing or waving, can also constitute a valid "implied" consent, the wise officer will always get verbal (or better yet, written) consent when at all possible.

Misrepresenting Your Purpose

If a police office tells the consenter that he wants to enter for "X" purpose when his true purpose is to "search" (e.g.,look for narcotics, stolen property, etc.), any consent he obtains will be ruled involuntary. For instance:

> Undercover officers set up surveillance in an unoccupied apartment next door to a suspected dope dealer. One officer went to the suspect's door, knocked, and asked if he could come in to make a phone call. Once inside, the officer made the phone call, but also observed narcotics and elicited incriminating remarks from the suspect which were then used to obtain a search warrant. The court suppressed the evidence because the consent to enter was involuntary. The officer had misrepresented his purpose as being to use the phone, whereas his true purpose was to look for narcotics (*Lathrop*, 99 *Cal.App*.3d 967, 1979).

A refrigerator repairman observed marijuana in a home and phoned the police. An undercover officer went out to the house, knocked, and told the suspect that he wished to talk to the repairman. Inside, the officer confirmed the repairman's observations and then obtained a search warrant. The evidence was suppressed. The officer had misrepresented the real purpose behind his request to come inside (*Mesaris*, 14 *Cal.App*.3d 71, 1970).

Misrepresenting Your Identity (Undercover Operators)

If a police officer's true purpose (stated or implied) for entry is to further an investigation or complete an undercover deal (i.e., buy narcotics or stolen property, sell illegal weapons, etc.) and the consenter lets the officer in, his consent is valid. The fact that the officer misrepresents his name, job, or identification makes no difference.

However, if the real reason of the officer's entry is to search for evidence, then he has misrepresented his purpose and the evidence will be suppressed. Thus, misrepresentation of an officer's identity is, for undercover operators, permissible; while misrepresentation of an officer's purpose is impermissible.

KNOCK AND TALK

What do you do when you receive information that an individual is dealing drugs but you do not have probable cause to seek a search warrant, no informant to work the individual and surveillance is either impractical or fails to produce any useful information? The answer is the use of "knock and talk."

The method used is very simple. Under the circumstances described above go to the suspects' residence (or business or whatever place where the drug trafficking is occurring) and contact the suspect. Identify yourself as a police officer and tell him the purpose of your visit. Ask permission to enter the residence to talk about the problem. Once inside provide the suspect with the information that you have and ask him if he would like to respond to the allegations that he is dealing drugs. After the suspect either affirms or denies the allegations ask for permission to search the residence for controlled substances. Of course, if you find evidence to support an arrest, the suspect goes to jail.

Tom McCabe and Rich McGuffin of South Lake Tahoe Police Department first used this method in January 1986 that resulted in the suspect voluntarily surrendering almost one pound of cocaine and $23,000 in cash. Since then they have utilized this procedure about 60 times. We have experienced at least a 70 percent success rate in terms of consent to enter and search. With this method, officers have seized dope, money and assets.

Keep in mind that the purpose of the contact is to determine if the suspect is, in fact, trafficking in controlled substances. Normally the information in these cases comes from an anonymous source and most of the time the information is proven correct. However, in a few cases the informant gave false information as retribution for whatever reason. In those cases, the contact has served to remove suspicion from someone. Furthermore, in those cases where the informant gave false information, the "suspect" can usually tell who the informant is, giving us the opportunity to contact the informant and discourage future bogus calls to the police.

The element of surprise plays a significant role in the success of the "knock and talk" method. Suspects just don't expect the police to come to their house and confront them with the allegation that they are selling drugs. The contact should be low-keyed and polite. Always ask for the suspect's consent at every stage of the investigation.

Also bear in mind that there have been a percentage of cases where consent to search was denied. If you are asked to leave, then leave.

"Knock and talk" is a last resort procedure. If you have probable cause then get a search warrant. You cannot misrepresent your identity or purpose. You cannot coerce or trick. It is a straight up proposition and you must be prepared for that door to be slammed in your face. Nothing ventured, nothing gained. There is always tomorrow and at least the suspect will know you are there.

The suspect has the right to deny your request for consent to enter and search; he or she does not have to talk to you. Yet, each "knock and talk" will have its own set of circumstances and each will be judged on the facts of the individual case.

SEARCHES INCIDENT TO ARREST

When a person is arrested in a home or other building, a limited right exists to conduct a warrantless search not of the premises but of his person, as well as the area within his "immediate control" ("arm's length," "lunging distance") (*Chimel*, 395 *U.S.* 752, 1969).

It is impossible to state exactly how much area is covered by this exception. However, it is supposed to include any place from which the suspect might otherwise grab a weapon or destroy evidence.

As you can imagine, the area a police officer may properly search can get quite limited as the chances of the suspect having quick access to the area diminishes. Such limiting circumstances would exit if:

— the arrestee has already been handcuffed (particularly if his hands are behind his back);

— an officer is standing between the suspect and the place being searched;

— there are numerous officers and only one arrestee;

— the area to be searched is locked, closed, or otherwise difficult to get at or into; or

— there are no particularly dangerous circumstances surrounding the arrest or the arrestee.

A search incident to an arrest is permissible only if it takes place at the same place and at essentially the same time as the arrest, i.e., just before, during, or immediately afterward (*Chimel*, 395 *U.S.* 752, 1969).

Normally, any evidence a police officer finds by searching beyond the suspect's "immediate control" will be suppressed unless he sees it in "plain view" while he is still within the "immediate control" area.

Furthermore, it is improper for a police officer to try to expand or enlarge the "plain view" or the "immediate control" area by moving the suspect from room to room (*Eiseman*, 21 *Cal.App.*3d 342, 1971; *Sanderson*, 105 *Cal.App.*3d 264, 1980).

However, if the arrestee asks to go to another part of the premises (e.g., to get his billfold or shoes, to change clothes, to go the bathroom), it is perfectly legal for a police officer to accompany him for security reasons, and whatever you see in "plain view" while doing so may properly be seized (*Chrisman*, 455 *U.S.* 1, 1982).

SEARCH AND SEIZURE OF EVIDENCE ON A SUSPECT'S BODY

Occasionally an officer must obtain evidence from a suspect's body (e.g., hair samples). Evidence obtained from certain parts of a suspect's body may be seized without a warrant; evidence seized from other parts may be seized only with a warrant.

When Evidence May be Seized Without a Warrant

Normally, if there is no "bodily intrusion" (entry of the suspect's body) or only slight bodily intrusion to seize the evidence (blood sample taken in medically approved manner), the courts have ruled that no warrant is necessary. For example:

> Officers searched Lara's jail cell and found a syringe. An officer then told Lara to strip and open his mouth. When Lara opened it a little, the officer saw a yellow balloon. The officer then put his left land on Lara's chest and his right hand behind his head, thereby forcing Lara's chin against his chest making it more difficult for Lara to swallow. Lara was told repeatedly to spit the balloon. Lara, however, tried to swallow the balloon. The officer then reached inside Lara's mouth and warned him, "If you bite my finger, I'm going to bust your head open." The court ruled that the balloon of heroin was admissible evidence because the method used to seize it was reasonable (*Lara*, 108 *Cal.App.*3d 237, 1980).

Choking a suspect to keep him from swallowing contraband may be excessive. If an officer must choke, he must be sure that:

> he has probable cause to believe the evidence to be swallowed is contraband and that it may be life-threatening if swallowed; and
>
> he must note in his report that the ingestion of the drug could have resulted in serious injury.

Can the officer have a physician pump the stomach of the suspect to recover narcotics? No, this is conduct that "shocks the conscience" of the court. This procedure is possible only to save the life of the suspect.

Can the officer take photographs, fingerprints, palmprints and obtain handwriting from the suspect? Yes, and the officer need not advise per *Miranda*.

Can the officer request the suspect to speak for voice identification? Yes, the suspect has no constitutional right to refuse to speak for purposes of voice identification.

Can the officer force a urine sample? No, the suspect is obligated to provide a urine sample and has no legal right to refuse, but the officer cannot force a urine sample.

When A Warrant Should Be Obtained

Normally a warrant is required to "enter" a person's body to seize evidence unless there are extreme exigent circumstances justifying the entry (*Rochin*, 342 *U.S.* 165, 1952—pumping Rochin's stomach to recover crime-related evidence was held unconstitutional).

The questions a court must answer in determining whether the warrant for an intrusion is permissible include the following:

was there probable cause?

would the method used normally work?

how serious was the offense?

how important was the evidence?

was there an alternative to the intrusion?

how unsafe, uncomfortable, and undignified was the intrusion? (*Scott*, 21 *Cal.*3d 284, 1978.)

Note: If possible, always contact a district attorney before attempting to obtain evidence from within a suspect's body.

POSSESSION OF A CONTROLLED SUBSTANCE

In short, a person cannot legally possess a controlled substance unless the substance was obtained upon the written prescription of a physician, dentist, podiatrist or veterinarian licensed to practice in the state.

When does a person have possession? How do you prove that a person has possession of a substance? To support a conviction of possession, it must be proven that the defendant had knowledge of the presence of the drug, that the drug was in his or her immediate possession and control, and that there was a usable quantity of the drug. However, actual physical possession is not required to be proven, so long as constructive possession is established. Because the element of knowledge is seldom susceptible of direct proof, knowledge is proven by evidence of acts, declarations, or conduct of the defendant from which it may be fairly inferred that he or she knew of the drug's existence in the place where it was found. Therefore, knowledge may be proven by the defendant's physical demeanor or appearance, drug debris on the person, drug paraphernalia, prior arrests, associates, literature, notes, and ledgers.

Where narcotics are found on the premises under the control of the defendant, this fact, in and of itself, gives rise to an inference of knowledge and possession by him which may be sufficient to sustain a conviction for unlawful possession, as long as there are no other facts and circumstances which might leave in the mind of the jury reasonable doubt as to his guilt. Whether there is possession and whether there is knowledge are both questions of fact to be determined by the jury or court.

Based on this rule of constructive possession, several court cases have discussed the fact of knowledge. For instance, in *People v. Traylor*, 23 *Cal.*3d 323, 333, testimony was elicited from the officer, consisting of the officer's opinion that the defendant was a user of narcotics at the time of his arrest. With the addition of this opinion, the entire testimony became directly relevant to the culpability of the defendant as to one element of the crime charged. Thus, an essential element of the crime of narcotics possession is knowledge of the narcotic character of the article possessed (see *People v. Winston*, 46 *Cal.*2d 151, 161, 1956). For establishing the fact of this knowledge, it is admissible to cite evidence of prior narcotics use—such as the presence of needle marks.

Remember that knowledge required for having possession is both knowledge that the substance is in one's presence and knowledge that the substance is a narcotic drug. Can one be inferred from the other? If the suspect knows the substance is in his possession, can it be presumed he knows what the substance is? Most courts accept the proposition that knowledge can be presumed where the defendant is in actual possession of the drug. Actual possession is when the drug is on your person, in your hand—when you have actual control over it.

Yet, when the drug is not in the actual possession of the defendant, possession can still be proven. The test for constructive possession (not actually in possession of the drug) is whether or not the defendant exercised dominion and control over the drug. In other words, the drug may not be in the actual possession of the defendant but within his reach, or in a place where he is storing it—in his car, lunch box, locker, desk, etc.—and where it is available to him for future use. According to *United States v. Salinas-Salinas*, 555 *F.*2d 470, 473 (5th Cir. 1979): "Constructive possession may be proved by ownership, dominion or control over the contraband itself, or dominion or control over the premises or vehicle in which the contraband was concealed." Thus, constructive possession can be established through the suspect's control over the drug, even if it is not directly on his or her person. "In essence, constructive possession is the ability to reduce an object to actual possession" (*United States v. Martinez*, 588 *F.*2d 495, 498 (5th Cir. 1979).

However, a person's mere association with drug users who possess illegal drugs is not constructive possession. Nonetheless, if the individual is in close proximity to a location in which drugs may be found, this proximity could be considered constructive possession provided the circumstances clearly show that the defendant had dominion or control over the drugs. According to *United States v. Jones*, U.S. Court of Appeals, 764 *F.*2d 885 (1985) "proximity may, under certain circumstances, amount to constructive possession." In this case, the court went on to say that "possession of a narcotic drug may be either actual or constructive. . . Constructive possession may be shown through direct or circumstantial evidence of dominion and control over the contraband. . . , and may be found to exist where the evidence supports a finding that the person charged with possession was knowingly in a position, or had the right to exercise dominion or control over the drug."

In yet another case, *United States v. Disla*, 805 *F.*2d 1340 (9th Cir. 1986), the court stated that constructive possession is a common sense notion that an individual "may possess a controlled substance even though the substance is not on his person at the time of arrest." The court further defined constructive possession as follows: "Constructive possession may be demonstrated by direct or circumstantial evidence that the defendant had the power to dispose of the drug . . . or the ability to produce the drug . . ., or that the defendant had the exclusive control or dominion over property on which contraband narcotics are found." The most important question is whether "the evidence establishes a sufficient connection between the defendant and the contraband to support the inference that the defendant exercised a dominion and control over the substance . . . Mere proximity to the drug, mere presence on the property where it is located, or mere association, without more, with the person who does control the drug or the property on which it is found, is insufficient to support a finding of possession." On the other hand, as the court points out, "It would be odd if a dealer could not be guilty of possession, merely because he had the resources to hire a flunky to have custody of the drugs."

Thus, constructive possession can be proved by dominion over the contraband. Evidence for dominion could even take the form of a key owned by the defendant. If it can be proven that the defendant possesses a key which opens the suitcase, locker, vehicle, or desk where drugs are found, then constructive possession may be established.

In addition, two or more defendants may possess a drug. This is called a "joint venture." Showing joint possession may be proved by constructive possession. In *Commonwealth of Pennsylvania v. Kitchener,* 351 *Pa.Super.* 631 *A.*2d 941 (1986), the court stated that "possession of an illegal substance need not be exclusive; two or more can possess the same drug at the same time." (quoting *Commonwealth of Pennsylvania v. Macolino*, 503 *Pa.* 201 (1983)). The court in *Kitchner* said, "The drugs were found in a dwelling where defendant and her boyfriend were the sole adult residents, (and in specific locations) which would be particularly within the access and knowledge of the residents," finding that, "it was reasonable for the fact finder to conclude that defendant knowingly or intentionally possessed the controlled substance." (See also *United States v. Valentin*, 589 *F.*2d 1069 (9th Cir. 1979.)

Usability

In addition to the fact of knowledge, analysis of the contraband is another essential element of any prosecution for violation of narcotics laws. Most of this analysis is straightforward, yet occassionally an issue of usability arises at the time of filing or trial. Of the many issues confronting the drug analyst, usable quantity is undoubtedly the thorniest. The issue of usability is really more legal than scientific. Over the years, courts have struggled with the idea that to sustain a conviction of possession of a controlled substance, the quantity of the substance must be "sufficient for use."

When is a given amount of cocaine a non-usable "trace," and insufficient for use? As a chemist, the analyst can rather easily extract microgram quantities of cocaine from an otherwise "empty" paper bindle. It is important to ask, "Is it reasonable to expect a drug user to manipulate quantities this small?"

With regard to usable quantity, different drugs will have different cutoffs. Marijuana would have to be present in quantities much greater than cocaine or heroin, for example. Another consideration is the method of packaging. Here again the analyst is asked to form an expert (although subjective) opinion. The method of packaging must be evident as an attempt to conserve the substance, as opposed to waste material. Of course, persons intent on recovering trace amounts of drugs could do so even from paper currency withdrawn from a bank. The operative question is, "What is reasonable?" A very large plastic bag which at one time held a kilogram of cocaine might now have only a thin film of cocaine dust clinging to it. A determined individual could perhaps recover a small bindle of cocaine from that same bag. But this "imaginary" bindle was not submitted for analysis, rather the bag was, and it is up to the analyst to decide if that amount is to be considered "usable." It may be suggested to the prosecutor that, "If the amount of residue had been collected and placed in a bindle, it would be usable."

Dosage form must also be considered. A tablet or capsule is by definition a usable quantity.

Fortunately, the issue of physiologic effect is not relevant to the question of usability, despite many attorney's attempts to make it so. Case law is generally in agreement that the state does ". . . not have to prove that the contraband possessed had a potential of producing a narcotic effect."

Another "red herring" frequently encountered is the "percent purity" argument. "Suppose," one is often asked, "that only a tiny speck of the drug was necessary to know what portion of the powder is a controlled substance." It is sufficient in most instances simply to show that there was sufficient powder to manipulate, that the tests for the drug were positive, and that the drug was packaged in an apparent attempt to conserve it.

Likewise, where a chemist found that the contents of some balloons contained heroin, the evidence was sufficient to show that the heroin was in a usable quantity even though the chemist did not perform a quantitative analysis and was unable to provide the percentage of heroin contained in the total volume of substance from the balloons.[2]

Possession of a Controlled Substance for Sale

In possession for sale and actual sales cases, knowledge of the narcotic nature of the substance is usually easier to prove. A defendant's heroin habit may be the motive to sell heroin or to possess heroin with the intent to sell. It is common knowledge that users often deal to support their own habit.

For example, in *People v. Perez*, 42 *Cal.*3d 470, a defendant sold heroin to an undercover officer. One week later, a search warrant was served on the defendant's house, where an outfit and a quantity of heroin were seized. The court allowed evidence of track marks on the defendant's arms to show MOTIVE to sell as well as KNOWLEDGE of heroin.

The elements of simple possession also apply to possession for sales cases—with two exemptions. Possession for sales involve an element of intent and a quantity and/or purity of the substance that would indicate more than personal use. In this respect, many courts have held that a conviction of possession for sales may be based upon evidence as to the quantity of the drug possessed.

One of the most important elements in possession for sale is quantity; large quantities (more than personal use) strongly suggest possession for sale. Thus, the following court cases have established the defendants' possession for sale (intent to distribute) based on the evidence of quantity: *United States v. Vergara*, 687 *F.*2d 57, 62 (5th Cir. 1982) (five ounces of heroin, valued at $8,500); *United States v. Edwards*, 602 *F.*2d 458, 470 (1st Cir. 1979) (200 grams of heroin); *United States v. DeLeon*, 641 *F.*2d 330, 335 (5th Cir. 1981) (294 grams of cocaine); *United States v. Echols*, 477 *F.*2d 37, 40 (8th Cir. 1973) (199.73 grams of cocaine); *United States v. Mather*, 465 *F.*2d 1035, 1037- 38 (5th Cir. 1972) (197.75 grams of cocaine); *United States v. Muckenthaler*, 584 *F.*2d 240, 247 (8th Cir. 1987) (147.09 grams of cocaine);

[2] *People v. Piper*, 19 *Cal.App.*3d. 248. *People v. Pohle*, 20 *Cal.App.*3d 78. California Jury Instruction Code (CALJIC), Part 12, 5th ed., 1988.

United States v. Love, 599 *F*.2d 107, 109 (5th Cir. 1979) (26 pounds of marijuana).

How do you prove the person intended to sell the drug? Intent may be indicated by observation of the suspect's movements, his associates, and the location of the two. Intent may also be shown by the way the drugs are packaged or by the possession of paraphernalia such as scales, cutting agents, paper bindles, penny balloons, or notebooks with names of customers. If at all possible to obtain, a statement by the defendant saying he intended to sell the drug is sure evidence.

In contrast to large quantities, possession of small quantities of a controlled substance usually indicates personal use rather than intent to distribute. For instance, *United States v. Washington*, 586 *F*.2d 1147, 1153 (7th Cir. 1978) (possession of 1.43 grams of cocaine) held that "proof of possession of a small amount of a controlled substance, standing alone, is an insufficient basis from which an intent to distribute may be inferred." However, possession of a small concentrated amount of a drug that can be adulterated, "cut," to make a larger amount to sell can be considered possession for sale. Purity levels are also important in considering whether or not possession is for sale.

In addition to quantity, however, there are other factors that would support possession for sale in most circumstances. For instance, *United States v. Staten*, 581 *F*.2d 878, 866 (D.C. Cir. 1978) held that "intent to distribute may be inferred from possession of drug-packaging paraphernalia." Likewise, other courts have found that weighing scales, possession of significant quantities of glassine bags, foil packets, vials, etc. have supported possession for sale. In *United States v. Franklin*, 728 *F*.2d 994, 999 (8th Cir. 1984), the court found that possession of substances to cut or dilute a controlled substance would lead to an inference (circumstantial evidence) that the controlled substance is not for personal use.

Alongside paraphernalia, large amounts of money may also suggest possession for sale provided that a connection between the money and the drugs can be established. In other words, the money must have come from the sale of the drugs. (See e.g., *United States v. Tramunti*, 513 *F*.2d 1087, 1105 (2d Cir. 1975); likewise in *United States v. Marszalkowski*, 669 *F*.2d 655, 662 (5th Cir. 1982), possession of 38.2 grams of 84 percent pure cocaine along with cutting substance, a large amount of cash, and a weapon amounted to an intent to distribute.)

Furthermore, it is known that drug dealers protect themselves from "rip-offs." The possession of a firearm, along with the drug, can be considered evidence of intent to distribute. (See, *United States v. Moses*, 360 *F.Supp.* 301, 303 (W.D. Pa. 1973)—possession of a weapon and heroin sustained an inference of an intent to distribute; and *Marszalkowski, supra*, 669 *F*.2d at 662, in which the weapon was evidence contributing to the inference of intent to distribute.)

In possession for sale cases, a slightly different form of evidence may be that of addiction to the drug. While *United States v. Ramirez-Rodriguez*, 552 *F*.2d 883 (9th Cir. 1977) stated that "a finding of addiction may support an inference that a larger quantity of the drug may be kept for personal use," the fact that the defendant is addicted to the drug may also support the inference that the defendant needed to sell the drug to support his or her addiction. This inference is especially true of the defendant who is in possession of a drug other than the drug to which he or she is addicted.

These different factors establishing constructive possession and possession for sale are easier to determine with experience. Once you become an expert witness (that is, qualified by the court as an expert in narcotics), you will be permitted to testify about controlled substances and drug activities that are not within the common knowledge of the average lay person. Many courts will allow you to testify about the processing, packaging, and characteristics of controlled substances, their street value, how they are used, the amount used, and what distinguishes a possession from possession for sale case.

Transportation of a Controlled Substance

In the California Health and Safety Code, legislation on transportation of a drug can be found in the same section as sales of a drug. An essential element of the offense of transportation is the defendant's knowledge of both the presence of the drug and its narcotic character. The suspect must also have actual or constructive control over the substance.

Transportation is commonly proved by the circumstance of possession, even though possession is not an essential element of a transportation offense. Someone may transport drugs even though he or she is in the exclusive possession of another. For example, where the suspect was shown to have aided and abetted his passengers in carrying, conveying or concealing drugs in their possession, he can be charged with transportation. Thus, to prove transportation, it is not necessary to prove that the drugs were intended for sale or distribution.

In cases of the offense of being present where certain controlled substances are being used, there is a principle that in one's own residence or automobile one may have the responsibility to prevent the illicit use of the drug since the owner has some control over the premises or vehicle. An analogous principle should apply in cases of transportation. Regardless of purpose or intent, the driver or owner of an automobile has the responsibility to prevent the conveyance of contraband by himself or his passengers at least while the vehicle is under his dominion or control. Given this principle, proof of the knowledge of the character and presence of the drug combined with control over the vehicle is sufficient evidence to establish guilt without further proof of an actual purpose to transport the drug for sale or distribution.

Selling a Controlled Substance

The legislation for selling drugs is similar to that for such acts as furnishing, administering, giving away, importing and transporting. Selling is defined as the act of exchanging drugs for money. The elements necessary to establish selling of a controlled substance include knowledge, dominion and control, usable quantity, and intent. Two of the most frequent ways to enforce this legislation are 1) for the police officer to purchase the drugs himself, or 2) for the police officer to use an informant—who is under his immediate and direct supervision—to purchase the drugs.

Being Present Where Controlled Substances are Unlawfully Being Used

It is unlawful to visit or to be in any room or place where narcotics, mescaline, peyote, THC, cocaine, etc., are being unlawfully smoked or used with knowledge that such activity is occurring. The words "with knowledge that such activity is occurring" were added by the California Legislature in 1956 after two court of appeal decisions had held the previous provisions unconstitutional. Many suspects arrested for the offense will claim that they did not know about the drug activity. Knowledge is an important element to prove in this offense. The fact that the person was present and drugs were there would not constitute sufficient evidence to infer knowledge of its use on the premises.

If one purchases a ticket and enters a motion picture theater where one has every right to remain and midway through the film one views a person in the theater using cocaine, must one leave immediately for fear of prosecution or force the person to stop using the drug? No. Yet in one's own residence or automobile, one has the responsibility to prevent the use of narcotics. The elements necessary to establish this crime are knowledge, the person's physical presence in the location where the substance is being used, and usable quantity.

LOCATION, COLLECTION, AND PRESERVATION OF EVIDENCE

Locating Evidence

A police officer will be faced with many situations requiring him to conduct a lawful search for drugs or evidence of drug abuse.

Where does an officer locate evidence? The answer is simple, but the method is very complicated. You may find drugs and evidence of drug abuse ANYWHERE. Therefore, you should never overlook any place when conducting a search. Look in any location that is capable of containing physical evidence, whether it is on a person, in cars, in houses, etc. Drug abusers will hide (or "stash") their contraband in places you wouldn't usually think about.

On a person, you might look:

Under collars, lapels, cuffs and any folds of material in clothing.

In the backs of watches, lockets or other jewelry.

Behind belts or belt buckles.

Inside any pockets.

Inside packages of cigarettes, or even inside the cigarettes themselves.

Inside any body cavities.

BUT DON'T STOP THERE!

Inside a vehicle, you might look:

In ashtrays or similar receptacles.

Under the dashboard for secreted items or containers, like a hide-a-key box attached to some metal part.

Behind sun visors, under seats, under floor mats, etc.

BUT DON'T STOP THERE!

Inside houses, you might look:

In vents, electrical sockets, outlets, and similar receptacles.

Under sinks and toilets, or inside toilet tanks or lids for items that might be taped down.

For false bottoms in furniture or similar objects.

Inside objects like cookie jars, sugar bowls, etc.

BUT DON'T STOP THERE!

Use a little common sense; it is always your best guide. The drug abuser has put some thought into hiding his or her "stash," and the officer will have to put some effort into finding it! Often the hiding places are so obscure, only a dope dog will find the evidence. If your department has a dog, it is well worth using the dog for searches.

Collection and Preservation of Evidence

Successful evidence collection is the mark of the competent law enforcement officer. As every officer knows, evidence can be overwhelmingly persuasive to the police in charge of a case, but if it is inadmissible in court, the evidence is meaningless.

What is evidence? Evidence is anything which may be used in court as proof of a point in question. It may be found by the investigator at the crime scene or by one coming to or from the crime scene. It can include things understood and things not understood by the investigators. The important factor, from the officer's point of view, is that it be properly collected, properly preserved and, when necessary, subjected to evaluation and identification by an expert. Corroboration, preferably by another officer, is of paramount importance.

To ensure a systematic and thorough search, it is best to assign only one officer to direct the collection of evidence in a given case.

Areas of search should be exchanged to avoid overlooking facts. When evidence is discovered, the searcher should not attempt to move it. He should make sure that others see the evidence in sight, that photographs are taken, and that notes are made on its location. Frequently, drugs are stashed in several different hiding places, so it is important not to abandon the search after the first discovery. The officer should note any evidence that will prove that the suspected violator actually possessed the drug. Care should be taken to protect evidence so that it can be processed for latent fingerprints or foreign materials on the container that can identify the evidence with the suspect.

The investigating officer's responsibility does not end with the discovery of evidence. Evidence must be handled in such a way that its admissibility in court is not jeopardized.

Evidence is admissible in court only when a direct chain of custody can be established from the moment of discovery until the evidence is introduced in court. Every person handling the evidence is introduced in court. Every person handling the evidence is a link in the chain and must be known and available to the court in case the chain of custody is challenged.

Several steps must be taken to ensure the completeness and security of the chain of custody. The first is establishing the location of the evidence upon discovery. This can be done with photographs, sketches, and the observations of several officers.

When the evidence permits, permanent markings for future identification should be used. The name of the investigating officer, case number, date, time and location are normally sufficient. A complete inventory of the evidence should also be maintained. If evidence leaves the officer's possession, receipts should be obtained and preserved. (They form part of the chain of custody).

Even if it is not going to be shipped or mailed, evidence should always be kept in a tamper-proof container. If "lock-seal" envelopes are not available, sealing wax is an acceptable substitute. If the evidence must be mailed to a laboratory for analysis, it should be carefully wrapped and addressed correctly and completely (including return address). On the outside of the wrapper, print the instruction, "EVIDENCE—TO BE OPENED BY AUTHORIZED PERSONNEL ONLY." Evidence should be sent only by registered mail or Railway Express, and a return receipt should be requested.

Evidence should be stored only in a special evidence area or in a property safe until presented in court. If evidence is kept in a locker or file drawer, it may be lost or damaged and may prove inadmissible.

The officer's overall responsibility may be summed up with two points:

1. Make a legal, systematic, and thorough search for evidence.
2. Handle and preserve the evidence to maintain an accurate and direct chain of custody that can be established easily in court.

Ten Points to Remember in the Collection and Preservation of Drug Evidence:

1. Before evidence is recovered by the finding officer, he should have the location witnessed by another officer.
2. All evidence should be marked with the initials of the finder and the date. These markings should be on the item of evidence itself whenever possible. If this is not practical for reasons of size, shape, contamination, etc., then the container in which the evidence is found or stored should be marked.
3. Evidence should be marked with a writing instrument that will not rub off. Most ball point or felt tip pens are not suitable. The purchase of a "permanent" type marking pen can save you needless hours of embarrassment on the witness stand trying to locate initials that have been rubbed off.
4. Evidence received from a citizen should be initialed and dated by the citizen prior to being received by the officer who in turn adds his initials prior to booking the evidence.
5. In cases where many items of evidence have been seized and must be marked for inventory, it is helpful to note the location of the find on the evidence tag. For example, glove compartment of vehicle, right front seat of vehicle, etc.
6. Collection of blood and/or urine samples should be taken from those who are suspected of being under the influence of a narcotic or dangerous drug, those who are being charged with "use," or specified cases where this type of evidence may be crucial to show knowledge on the part of the suspect.
7. Do not tie knots, staple, glue or otherwise make the evidence bags or containers semi-impregnable once you have placed the evidence in them. The follow up officer or perhaps you will have to untie or remove all of the encumbrances. All that is required is that the evidence be tagged for identification and placed in a secure locker.
8. Maintain the integrity of the evidence by not contaminating evidence obtained from one source with that of another. For example, marijuana found on the person of a suspect should not be mixed with marijuana found in another location.

9. Handle evidence carefully in order to preserve fingerprints.
10. Maintain the chain of custody.

PROCESSING NARCOTIC/DRUG ARRESTEES

There are several different procedures for processing a narcotic/drug arrestee. We will consider each one separately.

Booking Approval - When a suspect (adult or juvenile) has been arrested for a drug violation which requires booking, you should transport him or her to the area of narcotic investigators for an interview and booking advice. Depending upon your department, procedures for booking could be different.

Preliminary Chemical Test - When contraband is involved in the drug arrest, the officer is sometimes required to complete a preliminary chemical test on the suspected drug. The type of testing equipment varies with the type of drug involved. Instructions for completing the test are usually listed on the testing equipment.

Remember - Never Taste Any Suspected Drug or Narcotic!

Obtaining Urine Samples - When an arrestee displays objective symptoms of being under the influence, a urine sample should be obtained and booked. The officer must include in the arrest report: the time the sample was obtained and the name and serial number of the officer who obtained the sample.

Photographing Hype Marks - When "hype marks" (the marks made by numerous injections—also called "tracks") are present on an adult arrestee, they should be photographed. For males and females this will generally be done at the booking location.

Booking the Arrestee - Generally, adult males being booked for a narcotic or drug felony are booked into the jail. Adult females being booked for a narcotic or drug felony are booked at a women's detention facility or other facility designated by your department. Information regarding detention for a juvenile arrestee may be obtained from your department.

Required Medical Treatment - The procedures for obtaining medical treatment for drug arrestees are the same as with any other arrestee, with one exception: a juvenile who is under the influence of drugs or narcotics and is to be detained MUST be examined by a doctor or county hospital to determine whether the juvenile should receive additional medical attention at a juvenile hall. If a juvenile is to be released to a parent or guardian, a chemical test should be administered, if at all possible, before the release. However, if immediate treatment appears necessary, the juvenile shall be taken for medical treatment regardless of whether the juvenile is to be detained.

One additional comment is necessary here: the officer should closely observe any narcotic arrestee for the possibility of an overdose. (See "Crisis Intervention for Drug Abusers" in the Appendix to this volume.) There are several reasons for this. Drug users are often unaware of the potency of drugs on the "black market." Also, users frequently try to destroy the evidence by swallowing the drugs, and you might not even realize that they have done so. The arrestee may appear to be O.K. when you first contact him or her, but after a little while, he or she may begin to show increasing signs of drug overdose. Be alert; if the arrestee is showing any signs of overdose, immediately transport him or her to a hospital.

Booking Evidence - As mentioned above, the "chain of custody" for drugs seized as evidence is very critical. It must remain unbroken. This means that the status of the evidence must be accounted for, from the time it was found, until it leaves the officer's custody. The officer must account for:

Who found it.

When and where it was found.

Who marked it.

Who transported it.

Who booked it.

Where it was booked.

It is very important to have only one officer involved in the collecting and processing of evidence. This will simplify the process required in court for establishing the "continuity" of the evidence. If "continuity" cannot be established, the evidence can be held inadmissible and the case may be lost.

Report Writing

The successful prosecution of a narcotics case depends upon the quality of the initial offense report. The police report must contain in chronological sequence who, when, where, what and why. For example:

> On July 1, 1989 at 10:00 p.m., Officer Smith and Jones were east bound on Main Street approaching Almaden Avenue. Officer Smith was driving the marked police vehicle and Officer Jones was the passenger. At the intersection of Main and Almaden, a blue 1980 Chevrolet, 4-door, license #XYZ 123 was observed traveling north bound on Main Street at a high rate of speed. The vehicle was pursued and clocked at 60 mph (posted speed 35 mph), and subsequently stopped at First Street under a nearby street light.
>
> As Officer Smith approached the vehicle from the driver's side, he observed the driver, later identified as Mr. John Brown, lean forward as if to be reaching under the front seat.
>
> Officer Jones approaching the vehicle from the passenger side observed the passenger, later identified as Mr. Jim Black, throw an object, appearing to be a small colored object, out of the passenger's side window.
>
> The driver, Mr. Brown, and the passenger, Mr. Black, were asked for their identification by the respective officers. When the suspects were producing their identification, Officer Smith observed two rolled penny balloons in plain view on the floorboard of the vehicle.
>
> Both suspects were removed from the vehicle, searched and handcuffed. Officer Jones retrieved the objects thrown by Mr. Black and identified the objects as two penny balloons, filled with some powder.
>
> Both suspects were placed under arrest for violation of 11350 H & S, and were advised of their constitutional rights by Officer Smith.
>
> The interior of the vehicle was examined by Officer Smith and no further contraband was found.
>
> The vehicle was registered to Mr. Brown and was towed to Big M storage lot at 111 South, 10th Street.
>
> The suspects were transported to the detective bureau by Officers' Smith and Jones. The evidence seized remained in the custody of the receiving officers and was later booked into narcotic locker #33.

> Both suspects were stripped and searched by Officer Smith prior to being photographed and interrogated by Detective Keith. Both suspects gave a recorded statement admitting to the offense charged — See supplementary report by Detective Keith. Both suspects were booked by Officers' Smith and Jones on 11350 H & S, possession of heroin—date July 1, 1989.
>
> Report Officer:
>
> J. Smith, Badge 101
> S. Jones, Badge 329

While it is not possible to cover every eventuality, the example above serves to point out some basic rules about report writing:

1. Write your report as the event occurred in the case. Unless a continuity of thought can be established as to what happened and in what order, the report is of negligible value.
2. Whenever possible, keep specific events separated by using new paragraphs. This not only makes the report easier to read, but emphasizes specific action taken.
3. Careful attention to detail is a critical part of the report. Specific information as to the exact location of evidence, when it was found, who advised suspects of their rights, who searched the suspects, etc., are points that are sure to be brought up during a trial—a trial that may come too far in the future to depend on memory.

After your arrest, interview, and completed 11550 report, you must decide if you are going to book the suspect or release the suspect with a citation to appear in court after you have obtained a urine sample. Ask yourself the question, "Is the addict capable of caring for his safety or the safety of others?" If the addict cannot care for himself, then he must be booked on these charges, while the 11550 H & S is booked separately. In many jurisdictions, the only time an addict is booked into jail for an 11550 H & S charge is when he or she refuses to give a urine sample or when the addict is under the influence to such an extent that he cannot take care of himself or he is in need of medical attention.

The Drug Abuser In Confinement

All drug suspects should be stripped searched prior to leaving them alone. Also it is important that the officer be sure of himself before taking a drug from a suspect. This is particularly true if the suspect is being jailed. In many instances, the drug could be vital to the suspect's health. Arrangements should always be made to continue essential medication while the suspect is in jail. Yet, special precautions are necessary for jailed drug abusers. To the drug abuser (particularly the narcotic addict), the most important thing in the world is his need for drugs, and he will go to tremendous lengths to satisfy his craving. Anything sent to him from "outside" must be inspected. Contact with visitors must be closely supervised. The drug abuser must not be given "trusty" status. Once the drug abuser establishes a source of supply, he may spread drugs throughout the confinement area.

Following the arrest of a person known to be or suspected of abusing drugs, a "skin search" is necessary. Drug abusers often place their supplies in body openings or swallow them via balloons for later recovery. The drug abuser is generally skillful at concealing his supplies, and it is important to prevent the smuggling of drugs into your confinement area.

Testifying In Court

The arresting officer is often a non-expert witness. If you are not yet qualified as an expert witness in narcotics cases, the only way to obtain this qualification is for you to acquire knowledge through narcotics training and education and to develop your skills through experience (arrests).

Whether you are an expert or non-expert witness in narcotics cases, before going to court to testify, be sure to read your police report. If it is a heroin influence case, clearly state the defendant's symptoms and the reasons for arresting the defendant under 11550 H & S. While you are developing your expertise, it is a good idea to keep track of the narcotics schools or classes you have completed, your experience in narcotics arrests, drug books you have read, etc. In Appendix B, there is a form entitled Summary of Narcotics Expertise. Use this form to record your expertise.

INFORMANTS

BACKGROUND

Informants have gained a bad reputation. Most of the lay public has a stereotypical image of informants. The stereotype is usually of a "snitch," or criminal informant. However, that stereotypical image is in many cases a mistake, since informants range from undercover police officers to dope addicts, including "citizen informants," who act openly in aid of law enforcement, with no motive in informing except to rid the neighborhood of undesirables. This type of "citizen informant" often includes crime victims. Thus, an informant could be a fellow officer, a crime victim, a criminal suspect, or a police dispatcher. In essence, an informant is anyone who gives second-hand information to be used in court for obtaining a search warrant, or anything else. Information from an informant is regarded as hearsay when used in court.

THE EVOLUTION OF RELIABILITY

The subject of informants has recently undergone a significant change. In 1983, the U.S. Supreme Court changed the entire law regarding informants in the now-famous case of *Illinois v. Gates*.

To understand the *Gates* case, one must understand the law which preceded it. For years, the *Aguilar-Spinelli* rule stated the law on informants. There were two "prongs" to this rule, both of which had to be satisfied in order to obtain a search warrant, arrest warrant, etc., based on the informer's information.

After the *Gates* case, however, even though the same two factors are still considered by the courts under the totality of the circumstances, the two prongs are not strictly mandatory. In effect, the court said in the *Gates* case: "We're going to keep the *Aguilar-Spinelli* rule as a guide, but we're going to relax the rules to allow for common sense."

The *Aguilar-Spinelli* 2-Prong Test

The two prongs of this test are as follows: an informant must be RELIABLE, and must speak from PERSONAL KNOWLEDGE.

PRONG ONE: RELIABILITY

The following people are considered inherently reliable:

— Law enforcement officers, by virtue of their profession. This kind of information is sometimes called "official channels."

— "Citizen" informants. There is a presumption that anyone who, with no ulterior motive, acts openly in aid of law enforcement is reliable and therefore needs no corroboration. The informant's name, address, etc. must be obtained, since, if it is not, the informer will be classified as an "anonymous" informant, and will require corroboration.

With citizen informants, make sure the citizen knows what he or she is reporting. For example, a person calls you and tells you that there is a narcotics party going on next door. Can you get a search warrant based on his information? Yes, but there will be questions from the defense, regarding the informer's knowledge of dope, and his experience to testify that what he saw was marijuana, cocaine, etc. If this was the first and only time he or she ever saw drugs being abused, chances are that the court will throw out the evidence.

The officer must make sure the informant is really a citizen informant before using him or her for probable cause on a search warrant. If the officer merely believes that the person with whom he is dealing is a citizen informer, and uses him on an affidavit without checking, the evidence obtained by such a search will be excluded, even if the informer turns out to be a legitimate citizen informant. It is assumed that citizen informants, since they have nothing to gain from lying, will tell the truth. It is just the opposite with criminals, who inform to stay out of jail, or to get better treatment by police.

In order to use a criminal suspect as an informant, you must make the criminal informant "reliable." There are two ways of doing this:

1. **Show the court that the informant has given accurate information in the past.** The mere fact that a criminal informant gave accurate information to police on even one occasion is enough. The information provided by such an unreliable informant need not result in a conviction, or even an arrest, so long as the informant gave information, and that information turned out to be correct.

2. **Use corroboration.** Any type of corroboration will do. Two or more untested informants may corroborate each other, so long as there was no collusion prior to such corroboration.

3. **Skelton affidavit.** For this reliability test, you bring an informant in front of a judge and have the judge examine him. If the judge determines that the informant is telling the truth, he may issue a search warrant based solely upon the informant's statement (*Skelton v. Superior Court,* 1 *Cal.*3d 144, 1969).

PRONG TWO: PERSONAL KNOWLEDGE

Under the *Aguilar-Spinelli* rule, it is not sufficient to prove only that your informant is reliable. What if the information were third- or fourth-hand? The informant must also speak from personal knowledge. Think about the consequences of the officer's not being required to speak from personal knowledge.

Example: Officer X is testifying about information received from a C/I (confidential, reliable informant). He testifies that, "My C/I informed me that there was a narcotics party in progress at 312 Elm Street." This is good information, and will, assuming that the C/I is reliable, provide probable cause—but if and only if the officer knows how the C/I got the information. To verify the informant's personal knowledge, it is always best to say to the C/I, "And how do you know this information is correct?"

Example (from personal experience): I received word that one of my snitches wanted to see me. I was working in the Mission Beach area of San Diego. When we met, he was in a hurry, but told me that a large amount of narcotics was now being sold at an address he gave me. I recognized the address as one I suspected of selling dope. I thanked the C/I profusely, and called for a "telephonic" search warrant. After relaying my information to the DA, I felt very good about the warrant I was about to get, and was already wondering how long it would be until I got my department commendation, when the DA asked me that giant mankiller of a question "How does your informant know the information you just gave me is correct?"

In essence, the DA's question was: "Could this be second-hand information, or third-hand, or eighth-hand?" There was no way that the judge could tell from the conclusionary language used. In effect, the statement was double-hearsay; that is, hearsay on hearsay. Multiple-level hearsay is admissible only if you are able to find an exception for each level.

The lesson to be learned here is not to use conclusionary language. If, in the above example, I had asked the informer how he knew that dope was being sold from that address, and he told me that he himself was in the house an hour ago, and had seen sales himself, then the personal knowledge prong of the two-prong informant test would have been fulfilled.

However, in *Illinois v. Gates,* the Supreme Court abandoned the two-prong *Aguilar-Spinelli* test.

Illinois v. Gates: Its Impact on the Subject of Informers

For years, and with good reason, prosecutors felt that the old *Aguilar-Spinelli* rules were cumbersome and overly technical. Finally, the U.S. Supreme Court granted *certiorari*, and subsequently ruled that the *Aguilar-Spinelli* test violated the due process clause.

In *Gates*, the Supreme Court adopted a less demanding standard for determining whether an informer's tip establishes a probable cause for the issuance of a warrant. The new test was received with mixed emotions in the law enforcement community. On the one hand, the new standard made a police officer's job much easier. On the other, however, the new guidelines were more vague and were subject to varying interpretations by lower courts.

The new ruling on informant reliability stipulates that a court must review the *totality of the circumstances*. Some facts of the *Gates* case may help to establish the rationale behind this ruling.

Illinois v. Gates, 462 *U.S.* 213 (1983). One day, the police department of Bloomington, Illinois received an anonymous letter. The letter explained that Brad and Susan Gates, who lived in the same area as the scrivener, made their living by selling narcotics. The letter went on to describe exactly how the Gateses obtained the narcotics. It detailed how Brad would drive and Susan would fly to Florida on a certain day of the week where they would meet with a distributor who sold them the dope. The letter even gave an exact description of the car in which they would drive back to Bloomington. Moreover, the letter explained that when the Gateses pulled their car in the garage on that one day of the week, it would always contain about $200,000 worth of narcotics.

Needless to say, this informant's letter was very incriminating for the Gateses. However, consider the legal implications of what happened (or didn't happen) at the end of the letter. There was no signature, no return address, nothing. The letter could not meet either prong of the *Aguilar-Spinelli* rule, since there was no indication that the writer was reliable; nor was there any indication of personal knowledge.

With the help of the DEA, Bloomington Police checked out the contents of the letter. They followed the Gateses as they went to Florida; the couple did everything that the letter said they would do. As they arrived back home, the police served a search warrant on their car and home, finding the narcotics described in the letter.

The Gateses appealed, arguing that neither prong of the two-prong test had been satisfied; whereas, case law under *Aguilar-Spinelli* held that both prongs must be satisfied.

The U.S. Supreme Court, in upholding the warrant, stated that the old *Aguilar-Spinelli* rule was too rigid and inflexible; the court then adopted a more reasonable "totality of the circumstances" test. This test holds that the relative weight of each prong (reliability and personal knowledge) should be measured only against the totality of the circumstances such that the "whole picture" would convince a reasonable and prudent person.

Although the *Aguilar-Spinelli* rule is no longer in effect as a rule of law, it must be kept in mind, since even under the more relaxed standards of *Illinois v. Gates,* both prongs are still relevant (*People v. Love*, 168 *Cal.*3d 104, 1985).

OTHER PROPER USES OF INFORMANTS

Unknown, Untested Informants

Unknown, untested informants cannot be used to develop probable cause, at least not without further evidence. Nevertheless, any corroboration at all may supply probable cause, and the corroboration need not amount to probable cause itself (*People v. Lissauer*, 169 *Cal.*3d 413, 1985).

Two Untested Informants May Corroborate

Probable cause for arrest, search warrant, etc., may be attained through two or more untested informants as long as each informant is a separate, unrelated source (*Clifton v. Superior Court*, 7 *Cal.*3d 245 (1970); *People v. Ballassey*, 30 *Cal.*3d 614, 1973).

Spontaneous Statements by Unknown Persons

A spontaneous statement, made by an unknown person to aid police, is reliable, and does give probable cause (*People v. Galosco*, 85 *Cal.*3d 456, 1978).

Statements Against Penal Interest

If an informant gives information against his or her own penal interest when implicating the suspect, then that statement alone may be used to develop probable cause even though the informant is not otherwise known to be reliable (*U.S. v. Harris*, 403 *U.S.* 573 (1971); *People v. Hall*, 42 *Cal.*3d 817 1974).

EXAMPLE: A and B commit a robbery/rape/murder. The next day, A calls B's girlfriend and tells her the story.

Note: This is not a situation where boyfriend tells girlfriend about a crime he has committed. If it were, then the second-hand confession would be admissible as a confession.

Here, however, the law presumes that when a person makes a statement against his own penal interest to a third party, it must be true, otherwise why would he make the statement? (*People v. Campa*, 36 *Cal.*3d 870 1984).

Disclosure of Confidential Informants

The 6th Amendment to the United States Constitution guarantees every criminal defendant the right to "be confronted with the witnesses against him; [and] to have compulsory process for obtaining witnesses in his favor . . . ."

The Federal Government and most states have enacted statutes, based on the common law we inherited from England, which gives law enforcement a privilege to refuse to disclose the identity of a person who has furnished information on criminal activity. One of the policies underlying this privilege is to encourage persons to communicate their knowledge of criminal acts to law enforcement without fear of reprisal (see *McCray v. Illinois*, 386 *U.S.* 300, 308, 309).

The privilege is limited, however. When there is a conflict between the defendant's 6th Amendment rights and the government's privilege, the privilege must yield (see *Roviaro v. United States*, 353 *U.S.* 53, 59; *People v. Borunda*, 11 *Cal.*3d 523, 527).

The Legal Test to Determine Disclosure

Almost all motions to discover the identity of an informant are in cases in which a search warrant was issued, based primarily on information from an informant. The test used to determine whether the informant's identity should be revealed is stated as follows: The informant is discoverable if the informant could give evidence material to the issue of guilt. If the informant only supplied probable cause, (i.e., simply points the finger of suspicion towards a person who has violated the law) the informant is not discoverable (see *People v. Borunda*, 11 *Cal.*3d 523, 527; *People v. McShann*, 50 *Cal.*2d 802, 808).

Since the rules of evidence require that witnesses, except experts, have personal knowledge of the matter they are asked to give testimony on, the legal test for disclosure can be correctly restated as follows: if the informant was percipient to an element of the crime or to a possible defense of the crime, and therefore potentially helpful to the defense, the informant is discoverable. If the informant was only percipient to those factors relied on for probable cause, then the informant is not discoverable.

The Defense Evidence to Support The Motion to Disclose

The defense has the burden of demonstrating "a reasonable possibility that the informer could give evidence on the issue of guilt that might result in the defendant's exoneration. This rule of evidence is founded on the principle that nondisclosure in this situation would result in a denial of a fair trial to a defendant" (see *People v. Garcia*, 67 *Cal.*2d 830, 839-840; *People v. Tolliver*, 53 *Cal.App.*3d 1036, 1943). The defense may be able to demonstrate this possibility by calling an officer to the stand, by relying on statements in the affidavit, or most likely, by calling the defendant or someone closely associated with the defense to the stand (*Garcia* at 839, fn.10; *Tolliver* at 1044).

In this case, the witness will be asked questions concerning the person identified as the suspect in the affidavit. The witness will also be asked questions relevant to a defense such as entrapment, coercion, or planted evidence by the informant (see *People v. Fried*, 214 *Cal.App.*3d 1309, 1312). The defense argument will be: "The informant will be able to testify that the person identified as the seller, or possessor of drugs in the affidavit, was not this defendant. The informant will testify that the defendant was not even at the place on the dates mentioned in the affidavit." Or, "the defendant did have the drugs on the date of the alleged offense, but only because the informant begged him to do it as a favor for the following reason: the informant . . . would be killed . . . lose face with his friends who were invited to a special party . . . tell the defendant's wife that the defendant was unfaithful . . ." (use your imagination here).

The Government's Evidence For Non-Disclosure

The investigator must be aware of the elements to the crimes which may be charged against the defendant as well as the defenses to those charges. The best definitions can be found in the Jury Instruction books. The investigator has to develop evidence at the time of the investigation and execution of the warrant which will disprove any predictable defenses. At a minimum, the investigator should monitor, when possible, the informant's activities. The investigator, while searching for drugs (evidence of the crime), must also be looking for evidence which proves that the defendant didn't just happen to be in the wrong place at the wrong time. List evidence on the warrant, then try to find the evidence which proves that the defendant does occupy the place and is or was committing crimes there. Be prepared to prove that it was not possible for some other person to have been committing the crimes you are accusing the defendant of.

The In-Camera Hearing

If the prosecution is unable to convince the court that the informant is not material to an issue of guilt in the open court proceeding, and if you are claiming the privilege, then the prosecution is entitled to an in-camera hearing. This hearing is conducted outside the presence of the defendant and defendant's attorney. The record of this proceeding is sealed.

You must be prepared to offer "competent" evidence which refutes the defense claim as to why the informant is material to an issue of guilt. In many cases, the informant will be the only competent witness who can give testimony (see *People v. Lee*, 164 *Cal.App*.3d 830, 836). Therefore, make sure the informant will be available to testify at the in-camera hearing, or be able to produce other witnesses, (even yourself) who could give evidence which proves the informant could not assist the defense (see *People v. Alderrou*, 191 *Cal.App*.3d 1074, 1081; *People v. Fried*, 214 *Cal.App*.3d 1309, 1313-1314).

Sanction For Non-Disclosure

All the charges on which the "undisclosed" informant may be material to an issue of guilt must be DISMISSED! (*Eleazar v. Superior Court*, 1 *Cal*.3d 847, 851.)

ENTRAPMENT

DEFINITION OF THE ENTRAPMENT DEFENSE

Most legal defenses to criminal charges are what might be characterized as "true defenses." That is, they are circumstances which the law recognizes as *negating* guilt, rather than *excusing* it—for example, self-defense, defense of others, necessity, accident and misfortune, and insanity.

Other defense theories fall into a category of "technical defenses"; these are defenses which are created at law on public policy grounds which have nothing to do with the guilt or innocence of an accused, but simply represent the legislative or judicial view of procedural standards for criminal proceedings. This category includes, for example, the defenses based on double jeopardy, statutes of limitations, and lack of independent proof or corpus for a confessed crime. A defendant who asserts a "technical defense" is not necessarily claiming to be innocent of the charges—he or she is merely saying that some procedural irregularity prevents conviction on the charges, even though he or she may actually be guilty.

The entrapment defense falls into this latter category. A defendant who was improperly motivated by police to commit a crime is still morally guilty of the crime—he committed every element of the offense, and he has no "true defense" to negate his guilt. But the courts have decided that police conduct falling below a certain standard may be asserted—even by a guilty defendant—as a "technical defense" to his conviction.

RATIONALE BEHIND THE ENTRAPMENT DEFENSE

In California, the reasoning for permitting a defense of entrapment is set out in a series of decisions:

> California has recognized the defense of entrapment for reasons substantially similar to those which caused the courts to adopt the rule that

> evidence obtained in violation of constitutional guaranties is not admissible. . . the court refuses to enable officers of the law to consummate illegal or unjust schemes designed to foster rather than prevent and detect crime.
>
> Although there is an instinctive sympathy for the originally well-intended defendant who is seduced into crime by persuasion and artifice, such a defendant is just as guilty where his seducer is a police officer as he would be if he were persuaded by a hardened criminal accomplice. Entrapment is a defense not because the defendant is innocent but because . . . "it is less evil that some criminals should escape than that the government should play an ignoble part" (*People v. Benford*, 53 *Cal.*2d 1, 9, 1959).
>
> In essence, the courts have concluded that recognition of the defense of entrapment is crucial to the fair administration of justice. . . The function of enforcement officials is to investigate, not instigate, crime; to discover, not to promote, crime (*Patty v. BME*, 9 *Cal.*3d 356, 364, 1973).

When the California State Supreme Court reexamined the entrapment doctrine in two 1979 decisions, it referred frequently to passages from other opinions indicating that the justification for permitting an entrapment defense was the necessity to "deter police misconduct":

> ". . . courts must be closed to the trial of a crime instigated by the government's own agents" . . . because . . . deterrence of impermissible law enforcement activity [is] the proper rationale for the entrapment defense. . .
>
> The courts refuse to convict an entrapped defendant. . . because, even if his guilt be admitted, the methods employed on behalf of the Government to bring about conviction cannot be countenanced.
>
> . . . In *People v. Benford*, this court unanimously embraced the public policy/deterrence rationale. . . (*People v. Barraza*, 23 *Cal.*3d 675, 686-688, 1979).
>
> . . . the test of entrapment we adopt herein is designed primarily to deter impermissible police conduct. . . . *Barraza*, fn. 5.
>
> We recently reviewed the entrapment doctrine in *People v. Barraza* and emphasized the deterrent purpose of the rule. . . .Such an approach focuses on the methods used by the government to apprehend criminals and does not permit a defendant to be convicted when police conduct "falls below an acceptable standard for the fair and honorable administration of justice." (*People v. McIntyre*, 23 *Cal.*3d 742, 745, 1979).

STANDARDS OF POLICE CONDUCT

What standard did the court believe should apply to police participation in a criminal scheme? The California State Supreme Court decided the following:

> . . . we hold that the proper test of entrapment is the following: was the conduct of the law enforcement agent likely to induce a normally law-abiding person to commit the offense? . . . it is impermissible for the police or their agents to pressure the suspect by overbearing conduct

> such as badgering, cajoling, importuning, or other affirmative acts likely to induce a normally law-abiding person to commit the crime (*Barraza* at 689-690).

As a guideline for measuring whether police conduct in any particular case violated this standard, the court announced two principles to be applied, and gave examples of each:

> First, if the actions of the law enforcement agent would generate in a normally law-abiding person a *motive* for the crime *other than* ordinary criminal intent, entrapment will be established. An example of such conduct would be an appeal by the police that would induce such a person to commit the act because of *friendship* or *sympathy*, instead of a desire for personal gain or other typical criminal purpose.
>
> Second, affirmative police conduct that would make commission of the crime *unusually attractive* to a normally law-abiding person will likewise constitute entrapment. Such conduct would include, for example, a guarantee that the act is *not illegal* or the offense will go *undetected*, an offer of *exorbitant consideration*, or any similar enticement (*Barraza* at 690, emphasis added).

SUSPECT'S PREDISPOSITION

Under the Federal law, the suspect's predisposition to commit the kind of offense in question is a proper subject of jury focus in deciding whether or not the suspect was entrapped. The argument for this doctrine is that a person who was ready and willing to commit the crime—as shown by his or her criminal record of similar offenses—needs little encouragement and has no cause to complain when his criminal inclinations lead him into a police trap (see *Sorrells v. U.S.*, 287 *U.S.* 435; *Hampton v. U.S.*, 425 *U.S.* 484, 1976).

In adopting a test which focuses on the inducement activities of the *police*, the California Supreme Court in *Barraza* declared that the "character of the suspect, his predisposition to commit the offense, and his subjective intent are irrelevant." A defense of entrapment cannot be overcome, therefore, by offering to show that the defendant is a "known dealer," a "known fence," or a "known prostitute." Such evidence is *not admissible* on the entrapment issue (and is not affected by Proposition 8, which changed only the rules of admissibility of *relevant* evidence, but did not re-define what is relevant).

PERMISSIBLE POLICE CONDUCT

Even though the *Barraza* court was obviously concerned about criminal prosecutions involving police participation, the justices recognized that some kinds of crimes could never be detected or prosecuted without undercover police activity. The court approved police deception which does not violate its standard:

> Official conduct that does no more than offer [an] opportunity to the suspect—for example, a decoy program—is therefore permissible (*Barraza* at 690).
>
> There will be no entrapment. . . when the official conduct is found to have gone no further than necessary to assure the suspect that he is not being "set up." The police remain free to take reasonable, though restrained, steps to gain the confidence of suspects. A contrary rule

 md

would unduly hamper law enforcement; indeed, in the case of many of the so-called "victimless" crimes, it would tend to limit convictions to only the most gullible offenders (*Barraza* fn. 4).

Although the suspect's historical predisposition to criminality is irrelevant, the court said that in considering whether police conduct violated the entrapment standard, relevant circumstances could include the following:

> . . . the transaction preceding the offense, the suspect's response to the inducements of the officer, the gravity of the crime, and the difficulty of detecting instances of its commission (*Barraza* at 690).

ORIGIN OF INTENT

Before *Barraza*, a highly-relevant factor in the entrapment defense was the origin of the intent to consummate the subject crime: if the government "implanted the criminal design in the mind of the defendant," entrapment would come into play; if the defendant first suggested the crime, this would expose his criminal predisposition and negate any entrapment defense. (Police officers trained in the pre-*Barraza* era were routinely advised that if the police were the first to suggest to someone that he do something which would make him subject to arrest, the entrapment defense would prevent conviction.)

One consequence of California's rejection of the so-called "origin of intent" test of entrapment is that as long as the "normally law-abiding person" standard is observed, police *can* be the first to suggest a criminal enterprise without being guilty of entrapment. The *Barraza* test changes the emphasis from *whether* police conceived the idea of the crime to *how* police induced the suspect to go through with it:

> . . .*we are not concerned with who first* conceived or who willingly, or reluctantly, acquiesced in a criminal project. What we do care about is how much and what manner of persuasion, pressure, and cajoling are brought to bear by law enforcement officials to induce persons to commit crimes (*Barraza* at 688, emphasis added).

For example, where undercover agents originated the idea that defendants sell cocaine to an undercover officer, the defendants tried to base an entrapment defense on the fact that police made the first suggestion. However, the Appellate Court rejected this effort:

> The defendant also urges that the jurors should have been instructed that a law-abiding person is any person who does not generate or originate the intent to commit the crime. . . Such a test, however, runs counter to the Supreme Court's explicit determination that *the sequence is not relevant* (*People v. Kelley*, 158 *Cal.*3d 1085, 1096, 1984, emphasis added).

Likewise, where agents obtained prescriptions for controlled drugs from a medical doctor by simply requesting them, without any complaints of medical condition, the fact that the idea originated with the government did not mean the doctor had been entrapped:

> Certainly, the agents lied to Douglass. But *Barraza* does not prevent government agents from lying. . . .Here, the agents' conduct simply

> provided Douglass the opportunity to engage in unprofessional conduct for the ordinary criminal motive of pecuniary gain. . . . Accordingly, there is no evidence the agents entrapped Douglass (*Douglass v. BMQA*, 141 *Cal.*3d 645, 656, 1983).

USE OF CIVILIAN AGENTS

In those cases where an informant or other civilian agent is used against the suspect, the basic rules of agency apply: the agent is also forbidden to use improper or excessive means to induce the suspect to commit a crime, and if he or she does so under the direction of law enforcement officials, the defense of entrapment will arise. In fact, even if the agent is unaware that the person prompting him to influence another's actions is a police office, the defense still applies:

> . . . manipulation of third party by law enforcement officers to procure the commission of a criminal offense by another renders the third party a government agent for purposes of the entrapment defense, even though the third party remains unaware of the law enforcement object (*People v. McIntyre*, 23 *Cal.*3d 742, 748, 1979).

Notice, however, that since entrapment is a "technical defense" and guilty defendants do not have any absolute right to assert it, the defense—like the exclusionary rules—is only to be invoked where its application may serve its purpose: to deter police misconduct. Logically, therefore, when police properly instruct an agent to observe the judicial rules on entrapment and the agent *independently* violates the standard by using improper motivations, there has been *no* police misconduct; there is nothing to deter; and so the entrapment defense should not apply.

To help prevent civilian agents from unwittingly laying the groundwork for an entrapment defense, *and* to aid the prosecutor in arguing to the court that no deterrable police misconduct occurred (and therefore no entrapment instruction should be given to the jury), law enforcement agencies should require civilian agents to *read* and sign an advice form. (Undercover and uniformed officers should also be aware of this information, of course.)

Hopefully, agents will adhere to these guidelines and avoid entrapping a suspect. And if an overzealous agent violates the standards, the prosecutor can offer the information form as evidence that the agent was acting outside the scope of his or her agency, and that no deterrable police misconduct was present (although the prosecution does not have the burden of proving the absence of entrapment—*In re Foss*, 10 *Cal.*3d 910, 932-932—it is still necessary to rebut defenses which might prevent a conviction).

ENTRAPMENT vs. SOLICITATION

By coincidence, crimes of solicitation (such as prostitution, lewd conduct, subornation of perjury, soliciting murder, and offers to sell weapons or narcotics) are often the crimes where undercover or decoy operations are necessary for enforcement, and thus the defense of entrapment is most likely to be asserted. Unfortunately, this coincidence has created a tendency for some people to blur the distinction between entrapment and solicitation. The result is a confusion under which defendants often cry "Entrapment!" when what they really mean is that they did not commit the *solicitation* element of the crime.

For example, it is illegal to solicit anyone to engage in lewd conduct in public. If an undercover officer or agent approaches a suspect in a public toilet and asks the suspect to join him in a lewd act there and the suspect agrees, he has *not* been *entrapped*, because no undue influence was used. A normally law-abiding person would not have agreed to the act. However, it was not the *suspect* who did the soliciting in this example, but the *officer*. The suspect's proper defense is that *he* did not commit an essential element of the offense (solicitation).

The distinction, is simple, but it somehow frequently confounds police officers, attorneys and judges alike. *Entrapment* occurs when improper or excessive inducement is used; *solicitation* crimes require that the suspect do the soliciting. (But note that crimes committed by either soliciting, *agreeing to* or *engaging in* proscribed behavior can be committed by the suspect even if the officer is the first to suggest the act—e.g., PC 647(a), PC 647(b)—and as long as no undue pressures are used, no entrapment defense holds.)

Testing For Entrapment

The test for the defense of entrapment focuses entirely on the conduct of the officers. The central question can be formulated as follows: Was your conduct likely to cause a normally law-abiding citizen to commit the crime? (*Barraza*, 23 *Cal.*3d 675, 1979). Other relevant questions would include: Did you appeal to friendship or sympathy? Did you offer extraordinary profit?

The most common situations where the entrapment defense is asserted is, of course, where an officer or his agent buys contraband from the suspect (*McIntire*, 23 *Cal.*3d 742, 1973). Entrapment can be asserted, however, in any situation where officers do substantially more than just provide an opportunity for the suspect to commit a crime.

Usually, suspects who assert the entrapment defense at trial are without other alternative defenses, e.g., misidentification. If a suspect is questioned before he retains a lawyer, he will seldom assert the defense of entrapment. No matter how strong the evidence is against him, the suspect will almost always claim misidentification or some other defense which can be easily rebutted at trial. Once the suspect has asserted a "bad" defense in his statement to police, he has committed himself to that defense at trial.

DRUGS AND EVIDENCE IN COURT

Prosecution must prove two points:

1. The controlled substance is illegal—done by a chemist who analyzed the evidence.
2. Chain of custody—The prosecution must be able to prove that the same drugs in court are the drug seized at the time of arrest or purchased from the suspect at the time in question.

Dope Lawyers

Lawyers who specialize in controlled substance cases are called "dope lawyers." They are key players in the legal system. According to attorneys and judges familiar with the craft, being a dope lawyer requires a different set of skills than those required of an attorney who represents defendants accused of other crimes.

Even though many dope lawyers are skilled trial attorneys, the skill of presenting a case to a jury is not the most important. The reason for this is that very few cases go to trial, and when a case does go to trial, the police have overwhelming evidence and a solid case.

The dope lawyer is most skilled in keeping evidence away from the jury. This involves skill in pre-trial motions aimed at getting evidence that has been seized thrown out of court on the grounds that the police misbehaved in obtaining it. Success in a "search and seizure motion" means that since there is no evidence, there is no crime.

If the dope lawyer fails in pre-trial motions, then plea-negotiation is important. For example, the job is to get a charge of sales of cocaine reduced to simple possession.

QUALIFICATION AS A NARCOTICS EXPERT

To qualify an officer as an expert witness, the District Attorney will most often ask the officer the following questions:

1. Occupation, assignment, years of experience
2. Training
3. Courses, books, studies
4. Ever observed person under influence of narcotics? How many? Circumstances?
5. Ever observed injections of narcotics by hypodermic needle? Where? Where on the person? By whom?
6. Were the injections administered by physicians or persons acting under their direction? Have you noticed what traces, scars or scabs are left or form later, if any?
7. What have you observed about injections that are self-administered by narcotic users?
8. How long does it take a scab to form?
9. How long does it remain?
10. What size are those scabs? What is their appearance?
11. Did you interview the defendant? Where? When?
12. Did you examine the defendant's arms? What did you observe?
13. Please tell the court and jury what you recall of the details of defendant's arms.
14. Based upon your training and experience in hospitals and with physicians, together with your training and experience as a police officer, your observation of persons who use narcotics, their appearance, and the marks, scars and scabs upon such persons and further based upon your examination of the defendant's arms, and the

appearance, number of location of the marks, scars and scabs on the defendant's arms, do you have an opinion as to the cause of those scars and scabs? Answer: Yes.

15. Based upon the nature of these marks, do you have an opinion as to whether they were administered by a physician or one under his direction or were they the result of a self-administered injection? Answer: self-administered.

16. Now, based upon the number, the location and the nature of those marks, do you have an opinion as to what was injected? Answer: Yes, a narcotic.

After answering the questions put by the deputy district attorney, the defense counsel has the right to take the investigating officer on voir dire, the right to inquire in greater detail regarding the experience, schooling or any other endeavor claimed by the officer as establishing his knowledge of the subject.

Remember, a witness is confined to testimony involving only those things coming in contact with one or more of his five senses. This is not the case with an expert witness who is expressing an opinion on a particular subject. Acceptance of his opinion is dependent upon his ability to express himself fully and understandably, particularly to a jury.

Expert Testimony

A person is qualified to testify as an expert if he has special knowledge, skill, experience, training, or education sufficient to qualify him as an expert on the subject to which his testimony relates.

Duly qualified experts may give their opinions on questions in controversy at a trial. To assist you in deciding such questions, you may consider the opinion with the reasons given for it, if any, by the expert who gives the opinion. You may also consider the qualifications and credibility of the expert.

In resolving any conflict that may exist in the testimony of expert witnesses, you should weigh the opinion of one expert against that of another. In doing this, you should consider the relative qualifications and credibility of the expert witnesses, as well as the reasons for each opinion and the facts and other matters upon which it was based.

You are not bound to accept any expert opinion as conclusive, but should give to it the weight to which you find it to be entitled. You may disregard any such problem if you find it to be unreasonable.

CONTACT WITH NEWS REPORTERS

Many reporters for newspapers, radio, and television know little about amphetamines, barbiturates, tranquilizers, phencyclidine and narcotic drugs. Because of this, and because reporters often are under the pressure of deadlines, they frequently rely on the police for information. By informing yourself about these drugs and giving news reporters accurate information about situations involving drugs, the officer can do much to assure that the public will receive accurate news reports. The officer will also want to make sure that he is conducting himself within the regulations, if any, set up by his own department.

News reporters will usually appreciate anything the police can do to provide factual information about drugs. Performing a service of this kind enhances the reputation of law enforcement with the press and also serves to build public confidence in the police. Providing the press with accurate information is also important because inaccurate or exaggerated news reports can lead to embarrassment or other difficulties for law enforcement officers.

Here are some points an officer should remember when dealing with news reporters:

— You should confine your remarks to information about which you are positive. For example, you should never speculate about the identity of confiscated tablets or capsules.

— You should be careful in the use of slang expressions for amphetamines, barbiturates and other types of drugs. Although many people have heard about whites, downers, chiva, etc., few know the specific references for these terms.

REFERENCES:

Holtz, Larry E. *Contemporary Criminal Procedure.* Gould Publications, 1992.

CHAPTER XVI

UNDERCOVER NARCOTICS AND CLANDESTINE LAB INVESTIGATIONS

INTRODUCTION

Any careful approach to the overall drug problem must consider two main factors. First is the detection, arrest, prosecution, and incarceration of the drug traffickers, thus slowing the supply side of the pendulum. Second is the seizure of quantities of illicit drugs; supplies to make, process, and distribute the drugs; and any assets of the trafficker including vehicles, planes, boats, cash, bonds, and real estate. These seizures enormously inconvenience the traffickers and further weaken the supply side. Faced with possible incarceration for an extended period of time—and the loss of assets—the drug trafficker will become more cautious about those to whom he sells. Likewise, the clandestine meeting places will become much more hidden and difficult to locate or access by law enforcement or the drug buyer.

ESTABLISHING AN UNDERCOVER INVESTIGATION

There are many steps involved in initiating a narcotics investigation; these include receipt and verification of information as well as planning the operation of the investigation. Since information is received from a multitude of sources, a determination must be made as to the value and validity of the information received and the credibility of the source supplying the information. Narcotics units routinely receive information regarding illegal drug activity from anonymous telephone callers. If the information is of any value or substance, the unit may begin an investigation or write an Intelligence Information Report. Talking on the telephone to the anonymous caller helps the narcotics investigator to establish the validity of the information and to determine whether or not the caller has genuine first-hand knowledge of the information that he or she is giving. A large percentage of law enforcement agencies utilize a telephone recording device to receive these anonymous tips. This telephone number and recording device may be called secret witness, crime stoppers, TIP (turn in a pusher), or any other name to catch the attention of the public. With some agencies, a cash reward is offered for information; the caller is given an identification number to claim the cash reward. Regardless of whether a reward is offered, the anonymous caller is a valuable asset to any narcotics unit.

Another equally important source of information to a narcotics unit is the informant. The informant is often more reliable and the information the informant gives is generally easier to verify than that of the anonymous caller. The informant is generally a person who is actually involved in some facet of the particular crime being investigated. In the area of narcotics informants, the informant is almost always either a user or seller. Because of this fact, the informant can often introduce the undercover narcotics agent to a source of illicit drugs.

 md

Once the determination has been made that the information received is of some merit and warrants an investigation, it is assigned to a narcotics agent for follow-up. Ideally, a narcotics agent would, through an introduction, infiltrate some level of an illicit drug distribution system. When an informant is available for assistance in a particular drug investigation, the infiltration is often easier and more successfully completed.

An overall objective must be established in each undercover narcotics investigation. Starting with an overview and synopsis of what is known about the current "target" operation, the narcotics agent can determine the most effective method of gaining access. There must be a well-defined plan to successfully complete a detailed undercover operation. Haphazard investigations could ultimately result in serious injury to or death of the narcotics agent, or the loss of a case in court.

Although undercover operations are crucial to the successful enforcement of drug laws, not all law enforcement officers are able to perform in an undercover capacity. Intricate and grueling mental work is involved. The requirements of the undercover officer vary with each investigation. Often the undercover agent is forced to assume the role of a drug dealer or drug user, and may be offered illicit drugs for personal consumption or use.

It should be noted that undercover operations may take place in virtually any facet of police investigations. However, undercover work is most generally associated with narcotics investigations. Narcotics agents must be fast on their feet and able to adapt to any situation. To preserve his undercover identity, the narcotics agent must be able to perform the roles of the drug dealer and buyer both physically (in appearance) and mentally. Most law enforcement officers find it unnatural to be involved in criminal activity. For the narcotics agent, this must become second nature. Due to the undercover officer's "participation" in criminal activity, it should be stressed that undercover narcotics agents must be dedicated, above all, to the enforcement of the law; they must maintain the highest integrity. The ultimate goals are the reduction of illicit drug trafficking, the apprehension of the perpetrators, and the conviction and incarceration of all parties involved in the manufacture, production, and distribution of illicit drugs.

THE UNDERCOVER OPERATION

Before an undercover operation can be established, there must be some sort of objective and a "target." The term "target" refers to an individual or group targeted by a law enforcement officer/agency for apprehension. Once the target has been chosen, the investigators can decide the best way to accomplish the objective. The objectives are generally 1) an arrest with as large an amount of illicit drugs as possible; 2) the seizure of as many assets of the perpetrator as can be legally seized including cash, automobiles, planes, boats, homes, businesses, jewelry, stocks, and bonds; and 3) the incarceration of the perpetrator for as long as is legally possible. Even under ideal circumstances, all of these objectives are seldom obtained unless an extensive long-term operation is run on the target. Most municipal, county, and state narcotics bureaus do not have the manpower or budget to single-handedly allow for this type of operation. Therefore, when a long-term extensive operation can be run, two or more agencies frequently combine efforts. By combining efforts, the agencies can reduce the number of agents used, the cash outlay, and the manhours invested. With a variety of officers and expertise, combined efforts may also lead to greater success in the undercover operation.

One requirement of multi-agency involvement is the distribution of assets seized during the investigation. Generally the distribution is determined by the each agency's level of involvement. The greater the involvement, the greater the amount of seized assets which go to that agency.

Another consideration of multi-agency involvement is that, depending on the particular target, the operation may require assistance from the Drug Enforcement Administration of the United States Department of Justice (DEA). If the only assistance rendered by the DEA is the furnishing of money or assets to purchase illegal drugs, then the amount of seized property disbursed to the DEA is generally minimal. If the DEA or the Federal Bureau of Investigation (FBI) is used as a means of asset condemnation, there is generally a percentage charge for administrative work performed to condemn the assets.

BUY OPERATIONS

"Unlike most criminal offenses, the sale of narcotics usually occurs between two individuals neither of whom could realistically be classified as a victim."[1] Even though the above statement may be considered true, many administrators take it to heart in the most literal sense. The illegal sale of drugs is often called a victimless crime. True enough, the actual sale does not produce a victim as would an assault, robbery, or burglary. In reality, however, the sale may produce a multitude of victims. The drug addict will ultimately resort to other crimes to obtain the money necessary to finance his or her habit. Traffickers will combat one another for control of drug markets. Because of these facts, the illegal sale of drugs cannot truly be a victimless crime. In fact, the mere transaction of one sale has resulted from or results in a multitude of victims. Richard M. Smith, the Editor-In-Chief of *Newsweek* magazine, aptly summarized the chain reaction of drug trafficking when he wrote: "An epidemic is abroad in America, as pervasive and as dangerous in its way as the plagues of medieval times."[2]

Until very recently, the actual sale of illicit drugs took place in only the most private places. As a result, the law enforcement officer is often forced to go undercover to penetrate and hopefully make undercover buys which generally result in arrest. The private location for illicit drug sales is usually a location well-known to the dealer. Depending on the amount of a particular drug to be sold, the dealer may have counter-surveillance set up in an attempt to detect any law enforcement officers in the area of the sale. For this reason, the undercover buy becomes an even greater tool of law enforcement.

The ultimate goal of any undercover operation is the arrest of the drug dealer. As mentioned, this task will almost always be accomplished from an

[1] U.S. Dept. of Justice, Drug Enforcement Administration. *Narcotics Investigators Manual.* p. 99.

[2] Smith, Richard M. "The Drug Crisis." *Newsweek.* June 16, 1986, p. 15.

undercover buy. Accordingly, one of the most common ways for an undercover investigation to get initiated is through an informant. Informants are an invaluable asset to narcotics agents, and because of their knowledge of and involvement in the particular crowd of people being investigated, they become the safest means of leading an undercover officer to a target.

After initial introductions are made and the undercover officer has begun to gain the confidence of the target, then the buys are set up. In the safest method of undercover operation, the buy is made by undercover agents and arrest warrants are obtained and executed at a later time. Thus, a buy is made but no arrest is effected at the time of the buy. The number of buys made will be determined by several variables. The first, and administratively speaking, most important consideration is the amount of money allocated for drug buys. Depending on the size of the law enforcement agency, the money allocated for undercover narcotics operations could be dramatically limited. Since the illicit drug sale is viewed as a victimless crime by many police administrators, funds to support undercover operations are often very limited.

The next consideration is where the undercover buys will lead and how many buys will be made from a particular target. Depending upon the dealer who is being sought, there may be few or several buys made from one particular source. Assuming there are unlimited funds, if a source or target can be used to move up to a high-level dealer, several buys may be made.

After all the buys have been made on a particular operation, the arrest warrants will be obtained. The ensuing arrest—or round-up—is often a large operation with multiple suspects to be apprehended. Since drug dealers are generally transient in nature, undercover agents involved in the buy should always know where to locate and arrest the suspect.

BUY/BUST OPERATIONS

Another form of undercover work is what is known as the "buy/bust" operation. As the term implies, the buy/bust operation utilizes an undercover officer to buy an illicit drug and, immediately thereafter, the seller is arrested for the drug sale.

With most agencies, the buy/bust is used for large buys where large amounts of money are needed to complete the transaction. Due to these large amounts of money, the investigating agency is often concerned about the possibility of a "rip-off" (rip-off referring to the actual robbery of the undercover agent by the drug dealer). Therefore, agencies prefer to utilize as many cover agents (support personnel or backup agents) as possible to assist in the bust part of the buy/bust operation.

Another major concern and reason for doing a buy/bust operation is the safety of the undercover agent. If there is a threat caused by the individual being targeted or if there is not enough information known about the target, a buy/bust is the best method to use for the safety of the undercover agent. After all, the safety of the undercover agent is tantamount to everything else and should be the first consideration. If the target is a major distributor for a particular region, the necessity for a buy/bust becomes imperative. Major drug dealers continue to mount serious and violent attacks on undercover drug agents, thus requiring the efficiency of the buy/bust.

Undercover Narcotics & Lab Investigations

The usual scenario for a typical police agency buy/bust operation is as follows:

1. The undercover agent either sets up the transaction personally or the deal is set up by a third party. This third party is generally an informant, but could be an associate of the target who is indirectly involved.
2. After the deal is set up and the quantity and price are negotiated, the location and time are set. This is the most critical consideration. The undercover agent must make the location of the deal a location that can be adequately covered by support and back-up personnel.
3. Prior to meeting the target, a predetermined bust signal is established to notify the cover team that the deal has taken place and the arrest should be effected. The cover team will know the deal has transpired, because either the undercover agent, the room, or both are equipped with audio surveillance equipment. This allows the cover team to monitor and record the conversation between the undercover agent and the target.
4. After the bust signal is given, the cover team will rapidly move in to make the arrests. For the safety of the undercover agent, and sometimes to protect his or her identity, the undercover agent is generally arrested at this point also. Since a greater number of drug dealers are armed with some type of weapon, the arrest must take place rapidly to minimize any risk to the agent.

REVERSE STING OPERATIONS

Another type of undercover operation is the "reverse sting." This controversial operation, in which an undercover police officer sells narcotics to a suspected user, is technically illegal. Yet, a California state appeals court has ruled that this sort of operation is still a proper tactic in the war against drugs.

In *People v. Wesley*, three judges on a 2nd District Court of Appeals panel unanimously ruled that law enforcement's sale of drugs is valid and officers are immune from prosecution—even though the sales violate state health and safety codes. Prosecutors said *Wesley* is a case of first impression in the state. "It is a crime, but he [the undercover officer] is immune from prosecution if possession or sale occurs while investigating narcotics violations in the performance of his official duties," the panel said.

The ruling also validated the use of contraband by police; it was deemed lawful for police officers to employ drugs confiscated in previous cases for the purpose of catching other criminals. The *Wesley* case involved a Pasadena policeman posing as a street corner drug dealer, selling rock cocaine. One of his "customers" was Christopher Wesley, who allegedly approached the officer and said "I need a dime," street jargon for a ten-dollar rock of cocaine. Seconds after the exchange, two other undercover officers moved in to make an arrest (according to the panel's opinion). Wesley quickly threw down the rock, but police retrieved it.

At a preliminary hearing, public defenders moved to strike the charges, accusing the police of "outrageous conduct for selling illicit drugs." Superior

Court Judge Gilbert C. Alston granted the motion. He ruled the sting operation was "fatally flawed," because the defendant did not have "uncontested possession" of the rock, and there was no competent testimony that the rock in question was actually cocaine.

However, the appeals court panel said the weight of evidence made it clear that Wesley had the rock in his possession, however briefly for his own use, and that he threw it down as he was about to be arrested. Likewise, even though it was not conclusively established that the rock was genuine cocaine, the appellate panel said it was sufficient that the undercover officer said, in his opinion, it was rock cocaine. "Evidence that will justify a prosecutor need not be sufficient to support a conviction," wrote Justice Mildred Lilly. Justices Earl Johnson Jr. and Norville Frederick Woods Jr. concurred.

The bulk of the appeals court opinion dealt with the legality of the "reverse sting." Deputy Public Defender Elizabeth Warner-Sterkenburg argued that the police were breaking at least two state laws by redistributing illegal narcotics on the street. Warner-Sterkenburg cited the State Supreme Court's ruling in *People v. Backus*, 23 *Cal.*3d 360, which held that police officers who supply contraband drugs to informers are guilty of a crime.

"The police can lawfully arrest anyone for soliciting a purchase of narcotics. But that's only a misdemeanor," she argued. "So, in order to make a felony arrest (possession of cocaine), police are breaking the law by dispensing drugs on the streets." The appeals panel disagreed. It said that the "sting" appeared to stay within the rules. The undercover officer made no effort to solicit a sale, but merely nodded when Wesley solicited the sale.

As for the sale of contraband, the panel said police upheld the spirit of the law, which is to insure that confiscated drugs stay off the streets. "The cocaine was simply used as bait," the panel noted. "It was intended to be, and was retrieved by the officers after it served its purpose."

After winning the case, L.A. Deputy District Attorney Martha Bellinger said, "We're pleased because we now have a published decision that supports these kinds of operations." Bellinger argued the case on appeal for the county. She also cited a similar ruling which upheld the legality of "reverse stings" (*People v. Williams*, 216 *Cal.App.*3d 331). "These sting operations are not the answer to our drug problem, but they are effective in cleaning out problem neighborhoods," added Bellinger.[3]

UNDERCOVER NEGOTIATING

An important variable in the success of any undercover operation is the negotiating skill of the undercover officer. Good undercover narcotics officers must possess a variety of interpersonal skills and talents. They must be able to put forward their own agenda, as contained in their operational plan, and maintain their position in spite of the stress and pressure placed on them by the very nature of their undercover role. They cannot allow themselves

---

[3] *PORAC Law Enforcement News*. Official publication of the Peace Officers Research Association of California. Vol. 24, No. 2, February 1992.

to be unduly influenced by the assertive and manipulative personalities of the suspects with whom they are interacting.

It is vital that their assertive personalities be supported by a well-developed understanding of the principles of effective negotiating. Very often, undercover narcotics officers approach their assignments with little more experience in negotiating than what they learned in the course of purchasing a major appliance. They often approach the negotiations of an undercover drug transaction as if they were a series of hurdles to be surmounted: the quicker the better. They tend to see each issue under negotiations as if it were a stumbling block to be avoided, rather than the vehicle that will eventually deliver them safely to their destination.

For the undercover narcotics officer, good negotiating skills are basic survival skills. For this reason, law enforcement agencies must not only develop training programs that will teach the elements of effective negotiating, but they must also tailor such training for the specific tasks required in undercover narcotics work.

In the case of the undercover narcotics officer, the innocent party is the agent himself, and while the threats may not be as direct, they are nonetheless real. The activities being negotiated are criminal in nature and generally involve relatively large amounts of money and highly valued contraband. The underlying premise, whether stated or implied, is that any failure on the part of the undercover officer to act in good (criminal) faith will be met with maximum retaliation on the part of the target. Furthermore, it can be presumed that any vulnerability or perceived weakness on the part of the undercover officer will also result in his victimization by the person with whom he is negotiating. This victimization will take the form of either some type of a "burn" (fraudulent deception during a transaction) or a straight "rip-off" or robbery. Because of the prevalence of weapons utilized in the drug trade, both of these forms of victimization can easily result in death or injury to the undercover officer. The officer is literally negotiating for his own life, and he is usually alone with his adversary at the time the undercover officer is really attempting to set his adversary up for eventual capture. While he endeavors to gain his opponent's trust and draw him into what seems to be a beneficial agreement, the officer is actually trying to lure his subject into a position that will eventually result in the neutralization of the adversary.

Undercover narcotics officers can benefit enormously from an analytical review of the negotiating process, and can do much to improve their skills by studying the methods employed by other successful police negotiators.

The Elements Of Negotiation

In his bestseller, *You Can Negotiate Anything,* Herb Cohen identifies three variables that are critical to the successful outcome of any negotiation. These variables are information, time, and power. In a conventional narcotics transaction, the undercover officer begins with considerable information about his adversary. He knows that the drug trafficker is selling a contraband product that has no legal or legitimate market. The trafficker may have many potential customers for his product, but his market is limited to criminals, whom he can never totally trust. Furthermore, the undercover officer knows that the trafficker is driven by greed, tempered by concerns for self-preservation. In many instances, these two needs are compounded by substance abuse, resulting in both an extreme need for money and extreme paranoia.

Specific investigation of the target will add to the body of information available to the undercover officer prior to actually engaging in negotiations. The focus of this investigative research should center on the target's specific needs. What does he need from his negotiation? What are his short-term or immediate needs, and what might his long-term or ultimate needs be?

Undercover officers often presume that the suspect desires only financial benefit from any illicit transaction. However, this is never entirely the case. Even in those instances where the transaction being negotiated is a relatively small, street level purchase, the suspect couples his need for money with his need for security. He will generally conduct all such street-level transactions in a location of his own choosing—most likely a location over which he has a good degree of control.

The undercover officer may be able to get the dealer to compromise his security (i.e., control of location) if he can change the focus of the negotiation from a consideration of immediate needs to one of long-term needs. This might be accomplished by suggesting that the current transaction is nothing more than a "sample" in the eyes of the undercover officer. Therefore, the officer should direct his negotiations toward issues such as consistent quality, and ease and security of future transactions. The locations of future transactions are part of this consideration. By focusing on the future, the undercover officer can create a rationale for expressing concern over the location and circumstances of all transactions, including the current one. By appealing to what Cohen would call "the power of precedent," the undercover officer can insist that all major transactions such as this are conducted in a location of mutual agreement—typically a neutral location. Since this rather small transaction is really part of an ongoing series of larger transactions, then it is only right that it be conducted in a manner and location similar to those future transactions.

The second variable, time, is a major part of every undercover drug transaction. The traffickers consider themselves to be under severe time constraints by virtue of the fact that the longer they are in possession of contraband, the greater the chance of being discovered by either the authorities or criminal adversaries. In either case, the trafficker remains vulnerable and will therefore choose to limit the time of his actual possession of drugs. He is likely to have his greatest quantity of illicit drugs at one time and, over time, he will reduce his inventory of drugs while increasing his capital. Because both of these commodities are of great value to the dealer, he will develop a strategy for protecting them. This strategy is his survival plan and it will usually be directed against the undercover officer.

Cohen points out that, in any negotiation, there is a tendency for each party to perceive the other as being under fewer organizational pressures, time constraints, and restrictive deadlines. The effective undercover officer will attempt to emphasize and draw attention to those time constraints that favor his goals rather than those of the dealer. For instance, the undercover officer might carry with him an airline ticket envelope that is casually made apparent to the dealer while the officer explains that he is leaving town and thus has only a limited period of time in which to complete the transaction.

By creating a time constraint, the officer is forcing the dealer into a schedule of the officer's choosing. Since this schedule is imaginary, the officer can change it or not, depending on what suits him, rather than becoming caught up in the dealer's schedule. The airline ticket envelope serves to reinforce the time constraint through the power of legitimacy; that is, printed words (in this case the envelope) carry an authenticity of their own.

In addition to these imagined time constraints, there is often real pressure on the undercover officer to rush or push the negotiations along. This pressure, arising from management or from fellow officers who are supporting the undercover officer by providing covering surveillance, may be articulated directly in terms of "time limits." The skilled negotiator will recognize that pushing for a deal before gaining his opponent's trust will only foster doubt and suspicion. Since the dealer really doesn't know the undercover officer well, his criminal survival instinct will cause him to suspect that the undercover officer might be out to hurt him—and might even be a police officer.

Nothing builds trust better than the passage of time. Experienced undercover officers are in almost unanimous agreement that nothing will instill greater trust in a trafficker than shutting a negotiation down and walking away. Therefore, it may be best to put off the transaction if it appears that the dealer is suspicious.

Negotiating an illegal drug transaction is similar to other high-stakes buyer/seller negotiations. The undercover officer will always improve his chances for success if he creates competition for his side of the equation. If he is conducting a conventional drug buy, he must let the dealer know that he has other possible sources of supply who are competing for his business. Obviously, it should not be represented as a "perfect" deal, since it would make no sense to negotiate with the target suspect in that case. On the other hand, the undercover officer must never express total satisfaction with the offer and the conditions being put forth by the suspect. By always maintaining a sufficient level of dissatisfaction, the undercover officer creates negotiating leverage, to be strategically applied under the conditions most conducive to his own safety and survival.

An example of the proper use of this negotiation ploy would have the undercover officer suggest to the target that there is another possible dealer from whom he can purchase a similar quantity and quality of drugs, and that the final price might even be slightly better. However, the competition has stipulated other conditions that are totally unacceptable. Naturally, the suspect will want to know what the conditions are, since his potential customer finds them so unacceptable that he might be willing to change suppliers, or even pay a slightly higher price.

When the suspect conducts this rudimentary market research (and he will), he will discover that the undercover officer is unwilling to take his money, by himself, into a location that favors the dealer. The officer might even describe a particular problem, such as a "rip-off" that grew out of an earlier episode in which he naively agreed to such conditions, only to regret it later.

By informing the suspect indirectly about his needs in regard to the ultimate location and circumstances of the deal being considered, the officer has also suggested his limits in a non-threatening, non-confrontational manner. The dealer may then choose to make concessions in regard to these issues in an effort to finalize the deal. He certainly won't suggest the same set of conditions that have already been rejected.

The skilled undercover negotiator will use the suspect's failure to contest the location and conditions of the actual deal as an agreement to meet his own requirements. Naturally, the suspect will always pressure the officer to make last-minute changes in his favor. It is at this time that the officer will assertively exercise his leverage. He will insist that it is too late to make changes, emphatically reminding the suspect that they had already reached an agreement concerning these very points, and that any last-minute changes on the suspect's part are totally unacceptable. The undercover negotiator will then point out that if he is required to make these concessions, he would be better off doing business with his original source, where the price was better.

By making it clear that the suspect has created a problem that may cost him the sale, and by clearly demonstrating a willingness to walk away from the deal as it stands, the undercover officer will force the suspect to decide between his need for money and his need to control the location and conditions of the transaction. Most drug dealers will choose the money. If he does, the undercover officer will be able to manipulate the location and conditions of the actual transaction—whether it is a straight purchase or a "buy/bust"—using sound tactical planning to ensure his own safety and survival. If, on the other hand, the dealer refuses to comply with the conditions as negotiated, the negotiator must exercise his ultimate survival strategy by shutting the deal down and walking away.

It is not unusual for undercover officers who have not been properly trained in successful negotiation strategies to succumb to the pressure of completing a drug transaction under the conditions preferred by the suspect. However, any concessions to the last-minute changes demanded by the suspect, typically concerning the "flashing" of buy money, the locations and condition of the actual transaction, and the timing or sequence of the events of the transaction, will directly affect the tactical safety of the undercover officer.

To be a successful undercover narcotics officer, confident negotiation skills are vital. No matter what the product, no matter what the price, the undercover negotiator is really dealing for his or her life.

SURVEILLANCE

TARGET AND OBJECTIVES

In addition to undercover buy operations, surveillance may also play an important role in the eventual arrest of a drug trafficker or user. For instance, you may need to enact a process of surveillance in order to obtain information to warrant a legal search. In any case, the target of a surveillance is a person or group of people, a vehicle, or a place (house, open field, etc.). The objectives of a surveillance are to obtain information concerning the activities and identities of individuals, to obtain evidence of a crime, and to protect undercover officers. A surveillance may also meet the following objectives:

- To locate persons by watching their hangouts and associates.
- To check the reliability of informants.
- To locate hidden property or contraband.
- To obtain probable cause for search warrants.
- To prevent an act or catch a suspect in the commission of an act or crime.
- To obtain information for later use in interrogating.
- To develop leads and information received from others.
- To know the whereabouts of an individual at all times.
- To obtain admissible legal evidence for court.

CATEGORIES OF SURVEILLANCE

To meet these objectives, there are several different categories of surveillance. These categories and their particular goals are listed below.

Intelligence-Seeking Surveillance

- Learning everything you can about an activity or crime.
- Learning the suspect's source of supply (SOS).
- Identifying the suspect's couriers.
- Identifying the suspect's co-conspirators.
- Identifying the suspect's distributors.

Pre-Purchase Surveillance

- To gather intelligence to assist the U/C (undercover agent), who will attempt to purchase from the suspect.
- To identify associates of the suspect and their relationship or association.
- Attempt to determine the source of supply (SOS).
- Identify the suspect's couriers or distributors.
- Identify any counter-surveillance.

Cover Surveillance

- Primarily used for the protection of the U/C officer.
- To corroborate the U/C officer's testimony.
  a. Corroborate times and locations.
  b. Corroborate the transaction.
- Identify approaches to and escape routes from buy location.
- Determine the amount of force and manpower which will be necessary to assist the U/C officer.

Post-Purchase Surveillance

— To identify where the money goes after the sale.

— To identify other customers of the seller.

— To keep suspect under surveillance in case the U/C was sold "bunk."

— To identify suspect's residence, vehicles, associates, or source of supply (SOS).

— To obtain intelligence for future search warrants, buy-bust operation planning, and execution of search warrants.

— Planning of future meetings.

— Identify any counter-surveillance the suspect may have.

PREPARATION AND EQUIPMENT

Personnel

— Surveillance officers should be of ordinary appearance.

— Avoid anything which will attract attention.

— Make assignments based on factors such as race, appearance, ability to blend into the area or neighborhood.

— Must have the ability to act natural under any circumstances.

— Must have a high degree of alertness and resourcefulness.

— Must have good powers of observations and memory (events, description, contracts, or times of occurrences).

Pre-Surveillance Preparation

— Gather information and compile a file relating to the suspect's activities and criminal history.

— Get intelligence on the suspect's working and neighborhood environments as well as all vehicles involved or associated.

— Obtain detailed descriptions and photos of suspects, including, if possible, their habits and normal routines.

— Obtain identities and descriptions of known or suspected contracts or associates and the scope and extent of criminal activities of the suspect involved.

— Become familiar with the neighborhood or area where the operation will take place.

Equipment

— Props of certain dress or vehicles should blend into the area or neighborhood.

— Carry with you cameras, binoculars, telescopes, recording equipment, body wires, monitoring equipment.

— If assigned to fixed surveillance, think about personal needs and carry money and change.

— Carry clothes and personal hygiene items in the vehicle in cases of an extended long-term surveillance.

— Surveillance vehicles should fit the setting in which they are to be used.

— Vehicles should be occupied by two officers (one to drive, the other to handle the radio and take notes).

— Be prepared for emergencies:

a. Search kits.

b. Raid equipment.

c. Food/beverages.

Carry such items as jackets, caps or glasses to change your appearance, if necessary.

PLANNING THE SURVEILLANCE ASSIGNMENTS

When planning a surveillance there are various assignments to make. Assign an officer in charge. If necessary, designate who will be involved in a stationary surveillance or foot surveillance. Coordinate a point car and assure rotation of the car if it is an extended surveillance. Assign arrest teams and an officer who will obtain search warrants; assign search teams and officers who will process in-custody suspects; and above all advise your supervisor and the watch commander of the surveillance's jurisdiction.

It is also very important to conduct a formal briefing to update the officers involved in a surveillance. Have a tactical plan, briefing sheets, and maps of the area. Distribute to all officers photos of the suspects, descriptions of the vehicles, license plate numbers, addresses of residence, and informants; most importantly, identify the undercover officer. Clearly explain the objectives of the surveillance, outline under what circumstances you want arrests to be made and under what circumstances you want the surveillance discontinued. Plan a debriefing after the surveillance is discontinued. Plan a debriefing after the surveillance to compare notes and put observations in chronological order and critique the operation for the success of future operations.

TYPES OF SURVEILLANCE

Foot Surveillance

One-man foot surveillance is extremely difficult and should be avoided. Two-man foot surveillance gives greater flexibility. Three-man foot surveillance, or the ABC method, is considered the best method. "A" is to the rear of the suspect, a reasonable distance behind the suspect. "B" is behind "A," at more distance than that between "A" and the suspect. "B's" responsibility is to keep "A" in sight. "C" is across the street from the suspect and slightly to the rear. "C's" responsibility is to keep both the suspect and "A" in sight.

Frequent changes between A,B, and C should be made. The most common mistake in foot surveillance by new agents/officers is too much distance between himself and the suspect. Also, make sure that you carry your handheld radio at all times during a foot surveillance.

Vehicle Surveillance

The appearance of your vehicle must fit into the environment of the area under surveillance. There should be two officers per vehicle: one can operate the radio and take notes, while the other is available for foot surveillance. For the officer operating the vehicle, driving skill and knowledge of the area are very important. Officers should also anticipate being stopped by the police, especially in other jurisdictions.

Use good judgment when violating any traffic laws (be sure the suspect does not see you). To protect yourself from discovery, have surveillance vehicles equipped with shut-off switches for the headlights, tail lights and brake lights. In addition, you should designate a point vehicle and rotate it frequently. Ensure that the point vehicle and its relief inform everyone when they are changing positions. The point vehicle must ensure that the relief vehicle is in position before pulling off or continuing straight.

Maintain strict radio procedures. The lead car should be the only one calling the surveillance (location/direction). Other units should only talk on the radio if absolutely necessary. While on the radio, the point vehicle should provide frequent locations, direction, approximate speed and number of the lane traveled. If the area is unfamiliar to the officers involved, provide landmarks such as businesses, schools, and service stations over the radio. While tracking the suspect, avoid giving directions such as "the suspect turned right" or "the suspect turned left." Use the directions east, west, north, and south to prevent confusion.

Two-vehicle surveillances should be avoided; you either lose the vehicle or the suspect will identify you. Only the lead vehicle should be in close proximity to the suspect. When following the suspect also keep in mind that, for surveillance, left turns are more difficult than right turns. A good rule of thumb is as follows: when the suspect turns, the lead vehicle should proceed straight; but make sure another vehicle is in position to take your place.

There are some situations during surveillance that require the lead vehicle to remain behind the suspect, in spite of the lead vehicle's best judgment that it needs to relinquish its position. In this situation, the lead vehicle should never become so anxious that they remove themselves before the number two vehicle can take the lead. Leading surveillance can also be used if the suspect's route of travel is known.

When following the suspect in a vehicle, care must be taken at intersections, especially if the suspect goes through a yellow or red light (in this case, a paralleled vehicle can assist). For this reason, an aircraft is very useful. Aircraft may also assist surveillance in sparsely populated areas, areas with very little traffic, or areas with congested traffic. Another aid is electronic surveillance; electronic devices may be used for different types of surveillance to prevent detection by the suspect.

In the event that the suspect on foot should board a bus, taxicab, or other form of transportation, a combination of foot and vehicle surveillance may be the most efficient.

Stationary Surveillance

Stationary surveillance frequently involves a great deal of manpower and long hours during the day and night. Therefore, a stationary surveillance van is frequently used.

The primary consideration in a stationary surveillance is whether the observation position affords the necessary vantage point to observe significant activity without being detected. Also, entry and exit points for stationary surveillance must be located so as to avoid attracting attention. Careless actions by the officers may end the surveillance and leave those involved with a feeling of being burned.

Technical Equipment:

- Binoculars.
- Radios/extra batteries.
- Infra-red scope.
- Electronically amplified night scope.
- Florescent markers and ultra-violet lights.
- Small flashlight/penlights.
- Cameras.
- TV and movie camera.

Personal Equipment (extended surveillance):

- Porta-Potty or some type of container.
- Changes of clothing.
- Food and beverage.
- Hygiene items.
- Writing utensils.
- Safety equipment and raid gear.

Surveillance Log:

- Surveillance log should be constantly maintained.
- Notations should be made on events as they occur.
- Include all observations, even though they may appear insignificant at the time.
- Include descriptions of subjects, vehicles and activity; date, time, and place of occurrence.
- Include weather conditions, distance between observation point and the activity.
- Surveillance notes should be as accurate and complete as possible.
- Indicate who made the observations on the log.

THE USE OF SURVEILLANCE EQUIPMENT

Before any surveillance operation always survey and preview the location prior to the surveillance operation. Drive a cold vehicle into the area and survey the location. Walk the area on foot and see what the area is like. Look at the surveillance location from different angles and see what pit-falls you observe from each angle. Determine the objectives for the operation, i.e., to identify vehicles or persons, etc.

When trying to identify vehicles, you can do this from a greater distance than when trying to identify faces. The overall distance should be determined by what type of equipment you are using. The best video camera for this type of operation is the Canon L-1 HI-8 mm.; the second best is the Sony EXC-10-PAC 8mm.

The period of surveillance should be determined by how hot the area is. Keep a keen look-out for how people react to your surveillance vehicle or location. In any given neighborhood location, do not do more than two days of surveillance in a row. Locals will very quickly identify your location and cause problems. The overall decision of surveillance duration may be further determined by how well you and your vehicle fit into the neighborhood. Thus, business or corporate environments are a lot easier since there is a lot more traffic in those locations and you should not to be too concerned with local neighbors identifying or dismantling your operation.

AVOIDING DETECTION BY THE LOCALS OR THE SUSPECT

Surveillance officers must fit into the location. If this requirement is not met, officers will stand out as not belonging there. In addition, watch out for little children. Children are very perceptive; they know what vehicles and people belong in a neighborhood and what vehicles and people do not. Be aware of the area in which you park. Children will stop and even ask what you are doing; so take precautions.

If using a van or fixed sight location, be very careful when you change shifts or when exiting or entering from the surveillance van. The best way to change shifts is to have a person drive the vehicle into the area and walk away from the van. Likewise, while you are in the surveillance van or away from it, do not leave the case file out in the open, on the seat of the car where people can walk up and read the information. Keep all case material and surveillance equipment hidden; you may simply keep these under a jacket or a towel.

Another way to blow the cover on your operation real fast is through radio transmissions. Use covert radio equipment whenever available. Furthermore, do not throw anything—even cigarette butts—outside the vehicle. Never leave anything behind. Never make yourself conspicuous.

NARCOTICS RAID PLANNING

Once suveillance has confirmed preliminary information, it may be possible to enact a narcotics raid. Planning narcotics raids has proved to be one of the most challenging and dangerous responsibilities of law enforcement agencies. At the top of the priority list for law enforcement are concern for officer safety and the need to ensure that no innocent parties are injured. Furthermore, we live in an increasingly litigious society; no agency or its officers wish to suffer from a liability suit due to errors in planning for tactical raid operations.

Most raid planning will revolve around containment, locating personnel properly, eliminating confusion and maximizing observation of the suspect building. These principles are best applied by doing the following in a methodical manner:

When planning raids, always use a raid-planning checklist. This checklist will help to clarify the details of a dynamic entry; swift, confident, and complete room clearance; efficient apprehension of the suspects; and proper seizure of the evidence.

To facilitate and support planning strategies, surveillance should be conducted. The objective of surveillance is to evaluate procedures which will be used to initiate tactical raid operations. Surveillance is gathered so officers can become familiar with the suspects and can learn more about the type of crime committed, criminal patterns, etc.

In the planning process, tactical scouting reports can be authenticated, positions of cover evaluated, and access routes for convoying can be verified. Likewise, emergency medical personnel can be notified to the possibility of a medical rescue operation.

Planning will also necessitate a series of briefings conducted to explain all the phases of operation. This stage of planning will include the following members: Raid Operations Commander, Raid Team Personnel, representatives of appropriate divisions/units such as intelligence, patrol, and emergency services unit (SWAT), and legal representatives where necessary.

The briefing will encompass reviewing the planned approach to the location, personnel assignments (coordinated deployment), positioning of personnel for entry, entry technique, room clearance, suspect and bystander control, communications, and evidence management. In addition, an equipment check will be completed during one of the raid briefings to ensure proper and functional equipment is available. If an informant is being used, appropriate briefing information will be disseminated, as would be the case when using an undercover/covert police officer.

Often, narcotics raids uncover hazardous materials, as well as clandestine narcotics laboratory setups which may vary from rudimentary to extremely sophisticated. Therefore, safety procedures for hazardous materials protocol will also be reviewed at a briefing. A representative of the fire service may be invited to attend a selected briefing with appropriate safety recommendations.

The following checklist provides information on the development of a raid management plan.

- ☐ Records information (See I.)
- ☐ Identify incident location and approach procedure. (See II.)
- ☐ Review approach to location (See III.)
- ☐ Evaluate interior hazards (See IV.)
- ☐ Establish perimeters, pedestrian evacuation control.
- ☐ Cordon area and isolate from pedestrian and vehicular traffic. Identify those approved to enter area.
- ☐ Evacuate citizens and interview them.
- ☐ Provide officers stationed on perimeter with suspect photographs.

Notify:

- ☐ Watch Commander and Senior
- ☐ Executive Personnel
- ☐ Communications Division —Select tactical frequency
- ☐ Area/Division Commanding Officer
- ☐ Fire Department/Medical Services
- ☐ Mutual Aid Agencies
- ☐ Public Information Representative

- ☐ Establish alternate routes for citizen traffic.
- ☐ Acquire appropriate maps (Grid. Telephone)
- ☐ Determine probable location of suspect
- ☐ Personnel assignments
- ☐ Evidence management
- ☐ Minimize suspect control area (Kill zone)
- ☐ Determine type and range of suspect's weapons.
- ☐ Select tactical frequency to be utilized; advise communications and responding units.
- ☐ Check all equipment before initiating.
- ☐ Determine access routes and advise concerned units.
- ☐ Be prepared to initiate Officer/Victim Rescue Plan
- ☐ Designate Command Post Location and O.I.C. and Asst. O.I.C.
- ☐ All personnel report to C.P. or police staging area prior to deploying.
- ☐ All personnel are adequately briefed regarding problem, assignment and unit designation.
- ☐ All personnel have communications capability.
- ☐ Procedures for activating Emergency Services Team
- ☐ Maintain incident log for Protracted operations.
- ☐ Review "Hostage Negotiations" procedures.

I. RECORDS INFORMATION

Warrant #
Issuing Court:
Date Issued:
Address of Seizure:

II. DESCRIPTIVE INFORMATION ON LOCATION

a. Number of rooms, floors, attached and adjacent buildings, doors, cellar/attic, color, construction of building, i.e. brick, stucco.

b. Sketch of outside — location of abutting streets, driveways, outbuildings, doors, fences, shrubbery, etc. obscuring view from inside, exterior lighting on property/on street, etc.

c. Sketch of interior — indicating locations of rooms, doors, closets, stairways, large furniture.

III. EXTERIOR AND APPROACH INFORMATION

(Note answer: NONE, UNKNOWN, or describe details for items 1-8)

1. Gate locks (type: padlock/built-in)
2. Height of fences (type: wood, chain-link)
3. Alarms (type: motion, foil, trip wire, etc.)
4. Lookouts/dogs (location)
5. Motor vehicles likely to be on premises (reg. Nos. and description).
6. Exterior Doors (Type: wood, screen, metal, hollow-core).
   a. Location of doors
   b. Swing of doors (In-Right, In-Left, Out-Right, Out-Left, Sliding)
7. Door locks (Type: dead-bolt, chair, doorknob)
8. Presence of glass in door or one-way viewer.

IV. INTERIOR HAZARDS

1. If drug raid — type of operation (stash house, lab etc.)
2. Type of controlled substance(s) alleged to be on premises.
3. Location of contraband/evidence.
4. Chemicals, explosives, inflammables likely to be on premises.
5. Location of any structural defects/hazards.
6. Type and probable location of any weapons.
7. Dogs (describe: size, noisy and/or aggressive, etc.).
8. Persons likely to be on premises.
9. Note: Elderly, young children, and ill-disabled persons, hostages.
10. Alleged perpetrators (names, identifiable descriptions, reputations for violence, photographs).

ENTRY

ALTERNATIVES TO A FORCED ENTRY

Alternatives to a forced entry should always be considered. One of these alternatives is the "Soft Knocks" approach. Simply knock on the door courteously and state your purpose. Despite its calmness, sound safety principals must be used with this method. Another alternative is the "Ruse Entry." Using this method, the officer poses as a delivery man or salesman. Ruse entries must have immediate back-up available and the ruse man must be able to keep calm and play out the role effectively.

FORCED ENTRY: USE OF THE RAM

Often, however, a forced entry is unavoidable—especially when serving a search warrant at a fortified crack house. A forced entry consists of forcefully entering the premises and taking the suspect away from the location. Although it can be time-consuming, this method works well if you have both the time and the personnel.

Forced entry is often achieved through the use of a battering ram. As long as search warrants are served and dope dealers refuse entry, it will be important to know how to use a ram properly. Several narcotics agents have had bad experiences trying to enter a door that appears to have been welded shut. As long as the most serious setback from such a delayed entry is only some flushed dope, the matter is not so grave. Concern should lie with the possibility of an officer being injured because a dealer had the time to arm himself due to a delayed entry. To avoid such consequences, effective use of the ram can be broken down into five areas. These include: mental preparation, foot position, using your entire body, where to strike the door, and getting out of the way.

Mental Preparation/Focus

One of the most important members on the entry team is the person with the ram. If you can't open the door, your team's entry will be delayed. Anyone who has rammed a door knows that standing in front of a door with a holstered gun is an unpleasant thought. It's very natural to start backing for cover as your ram is halfway to its target. This, however, can cause the ram to fall short of making a solid, strong hit. A weak or glancing blow is often the result. This forces you to return to the same undesirable spot with a crook inside who has had 3 to 5 more seconds to destroy evidence or plan an assault.

The proper technique is to focus not only on striking the door, but on striking through the door. You should envision the ram landing through the door. This mental preparation of the outcome will force you to stick around until after the mission is accomplished.

Foot Position/Balance

When preparing to strike the door, your feet should be positioned at shoulders width. Depending upon the length of your arms, your exact distance from the door will vary. Nevertheless, you don't want to be at a distance that causes the ram to land lazily on the door. If you find yourself lunging at the door just to make contact, you are too far away from it. At the same time, you don't want to be so close that you can't extend your arms completely. Take a few minutes, in a non-hostile environment, to find the right position.

Using Your Entire Body

Anyone involved in sports knows that the strongest person is not always the one who hits the ball farther or delivers the hardest serve. Likewise, brute strength alone will not knock down a door; yet, the speed generated by the ram will. If your ram hasn't reached top speed at the point it reaches the door, you're cheating yourself. If it reaches top speed before it strikes the door, you are also cheating yourself.

The top speed of the ram is directly proportional to your body position, particularly your lower body. Velocity generated by a solid stance and a twisting torso is delivered right into your upper body and arms as they carry the ram into the strike zone. The importance of the lower body in generating velocity cannot be emphasized enough: imagine throwing an object from a kneeling position, thus eliminating the input from your lower body. Obviously, the velocity would be significantly decreased from such an inadequate position.

Where to Strike the Door

A battering ram can be lost through the middle of a door. Although everyone agrees that the deadbolt should be your target, it is still not uncommon to see such center-door or doorframe strikes. In most cases, the misplaced strike results from a lack of concentration at the moment of impact. After all, it's only a matter of inches between a successful strike and a lost ram through the middle of a door. Take care to ensure an accurate strike directly on the deadbolt.

Getting Out Of The Way

By using the preceding tips, you will have better success in getting most doors to open. Yet, once the door is down, many officers will make the error of wanting to be the first through the door. While this may be noble, it is extremely dangerous. An armed suspect will have little difficulty in shooting at an unarmed cop who is trying to hide behind a ram as cover. You will also make it difficult for fellow officers to return fire if you are between them and the suspect.

The proper move is a sidestep away from the threshold; discard your ram and take the wall as cover. As your team enters, you can safely unholster your gun and then enter the residence behind them.

FORCED ENTRY CONSIDERATIONS

If you do use a forced entry method, several considerations should be kept in mind. First, avoid parking in front of the location. If anyone has to be parked in front of the location it should be a marked patrol unit. Second, provide cover for both the containment team and the entry team while approaching the location. Allow sufficient time for the containment team to get into position prior to any entry. Third, all diversions, such as breaking windows, should be done away from the point of entry with the exception of gun-porting a window next to the door to cover the entry team. Finally, all precautions should be taken to avoid possible cross-fires between entry personnel and containment personnel.

Door Breaching Techniques

When using a forced entry method, opening the doorway is the first and most important step. Team members should be provided with cover as they breach the door. Personnel with entry equipment should use the door jambs for cover as they work on the door. Furthermore, as the door is opened those personnel with the equipment should back away, secure their breaching gear, and then prepare to enter. Gloves and eye protection should be worn to avoid injury during the breach. If using a door pick on a metal door, try to pry the frame away using body weight and not arm strength.

Doorway Entry Techniques

At least two team members may use the cover of the door jamb to bracket the doorway. It might be noted that most residential doors open in. Strive to always have a team member at the hinge side of the door. This will facilitate a maximum view of the room when the door opens. When the door is finally opened, entry personnel should delay entering until the room is scanned for potential threats. Some further techniques of entry are detailed below:

1. "Quick Peek"
   a. Look before you leap!
   b. Allows you to gather intelligence before committing.
   c. Works best when close to walls and when kneeling.
2. "Roll Out"
   a. Same principle as the quick peek but uses more room and allows more mobility.
   b. Works best in hallways or while moving.
3. "Button-Hook"
   a. Wrapping around the door frame after you have quick peeked, moving slightly into the room to avoid being backlit or to allow room for the next team member.
4. "Cross Method"
   a. Simply crossing the doorway to the other side after quick peeking.

The above techniques should always be used with another team member covering while the one is moving. Proceeding at an even, controlled pace will allow you to move as a team while taking in as much as you can. During this process you should continually evaluate your movements. Keeping track of other members and yourself may prevent the "conga line" effect, which occurs when there is no organization or plan for movement. As a result of haphazard and inefficient entry, this effect endangers team members.

Remember that stairways and hallways can be dangerous areas due to the lack of cover opportunities. You should maximize your efforts here by employing two team members on each side of the stairs or hall. This will facilitate two different viewing areas and provide immediate back-up and firepower. This rule of thumb also reduces the possibility of a one-on-one confrontation.

Post-Entry Considerations

After entering any room or hallway using the quick peek or roll out to gather intelligence, assess any major threat areas. Important considerations include darkened areas where you can be seen but you cannot see (such as closets) and partially closed doors to rooms.

Once the danger areas have been assessed and the situation is under control, place the suspect out of view, walk through the entry and debrief. Prior to leaving the entry, draw a floor plan and diagram of the location and save it for future use. If the suspect is cooperative, ask him or her what happened during the entry and what their thoughts were.

THE ROCK HOUSE OR CRACK HOUSE

One place that frequently requires forced entry is the "rock house." The "rock house," also known as a "crack house," is a specially fortified building used by drug traffickers as a headquarters, a distribution center, a warehouse, or a consumption area. The purpose of fortification is to delay entry time by police officers serving warrants, allowing enough time to dispose of the evidence down a drain or by some other disposal method. Fortified houses are not only used by crack dealers. They are in use by distributors of several other drugs, such as "meth."

Although drug dealers do not usually make special efforts to kill police officers (because they prefer to maintain low profiles), there have been enough instances of police officers killed in drug raids to justify strong precautions. A dealer trapped in his rock house may fight out of desperation; he may also use gunfire to delay entry by arresting officers.

Furthermore, a rock house is likely to have more than one occupant who is street-wise, tough, and unwilling to give up easily. Occupants are usually prepared for a raid by a competitor, and will have taken many defensive measures to slow down or stop anyone trying to get in. Some have well-rehearsed plans. For instance, one member will flush evidence down the drain whenever anyone gives the alarm, such as the shouted warning: "COPS!"

ROCK HOUSE DEFENSES

Rock house occupants use a variety of defensive measures, including walls, fences, weapons, and combat tactics. Some are just obstacles and are not lethal. Others, however, are extremely dangerous, and many defenses are unseen from the street because occupants want to keep a low profile. Officers planning a warrant service on a rock house's external appearance may be easily deceived. In addition to "outer" defenses, rock house occupants frequently use weapons. Although drug dealers' arsenals may contain high-capacity semi-automatic and full-automatic weapons, most defensive measures use weapons which are perfectly legal and easily obtainable.

Barriers

At the edge of the rock house property is usually a fence. A major tactical reason for a fence instead of a wall is that it prevents entry while allowing a good view of anyone approaching. There may be barbed wire at the top of the fence. There may even be broken glass placed on a top of a slump block fence. Nearly always, the gate of the fence is locked—sometimes with a chain and padlock for extra security.

The outer fence, with its dogs and booby-traps, keeps casual visitors off the property, thus avoiding inadvertent tripping of the alarms. It also helps provide early warning. The most important purpose, however, is to slow down an intruder. Therefore, even beyond the fence, doors and windows will be barred. Instead of wood hollow-core doors, there will be steel ones to resist both kicks and battering rams. Occupants may have gone to the trouble of installing steel bars set into wall brackets to further reinforce the door. There could be a wrought iron outer gate to protect the inner door. Glass windows may have been replaced with a polycarbonate material to prevent shattering. A panel of 3⁄8″ Lexan will stop a .38 Special bullet. More powerful bullets will penetrate this type of Lexan, but there won't be any danger from flying glass. Although Lexan is very expensive, drug wholesalers can afford it. Most importantly, Lexan panes are commonly available and perfectly legal to buy. In addition to these fortified windows, walls will probably be of block or cement construction. If not, there will most likely be reinforcements of sandbags or concrete inside the walls.

Alarms

Almost all commercially available alarm systems are suitable for a rock house. A special type of alarm system that is cheap and extremely reliable is the trip-wire connected to an alarm box. A fine, hair-thin wire follows the entire perimeter just inside the fence. Anyone breaking this wire will alert the occupants. There may be other wires to catch anyone who misses breaking the perimeter wire. This second type of alarm is battery-powered, a common model operating from four D-cells. It is a favorite among drug traffickers because it is portable, can be deployed anywhere, and is immune to power outages. Anyone encountering any sort of trip-wire has to be very careful, since it may set off a bomb instead of a mere alarm.

Dogs

Another type of rock house defense is a guard dog. A keen-eared and excitable family mutt who barks when anyone approaches is a simple and fairly reliable alarm. Some rock houses make use of specially bred and trained dogs, such as Shepherds and Rotweilers, to bark and to attack anyone who enters without authorization.

Booby-Traps

Booby-traps are surprisingly cheap and easy to install. They can stop or delay an entry, and impede a search. They may be almost anywhere, depending on the intent and sophistication of the occupant. Literature and manuals on booby-trap designs are widely available in bookstores, on newsstands, and by mail-order. Most manuals have diagrams to help uneducated readers build very lethal weapons.

Indoor Defenses

The inside of a rock house will be as heavily protected as the grounds. To prevent an intruder's viewing the inside, windows are likely to have curtains or shutters. Interior walls may also be reinforced, for additional protection in case intruders breach the door. Steel plates and sandbags provide mini-bunkers for local defense.

The layout of the house will be designed for defense. There is always more than one room, and often four or more. The "safe room" will be without any outside walls or windows. This will also have reinforced walls and a stout door, to delay anyone trying to enter. A toilet or sink will serve for flushing narcotics down the drain. A stove, fireplace, or paper shredder is usually present for destroying documentary evidence.

It should be noted that the safe room may have an escape tunnel. This might lead to a nearby garage where an escape vehicle is waiting, but in urban areas a better plan is to have the tunnel lead to a sewer, storm drain, or other underground conduit which already exists and which can take escapers miles away from the scene. The tunnel may also lead to a house in the next street, from which the escapers can emerge without attracting attention.

Defense Tactics

Hard-core drug wholesalers are not stupid, and many have had military experience. Others have studied military science at a training camp or trained themselves informally. They are likely to understand the basics of cover and concealment, and they understand S.W.A.T. operations through the media and reports from other lawbreakers. The media, showing explosive entries and officers repelling from helicopters, tend to exaggerate the facts. This alarms rock house occupants and probably results in more solid and thorough preparations than they would have taken otherwise. The occupants will most likely have gas masks, commonly available for only a few dollars on the surplus market. Since body armor is also commonly available, there is a good chance that the defenders will have some.

Because it is practically impossible to approach the premises undetected, defenders will be prepared. Unless they are tactically ignorant, they will have put the lights out, relying upon outside light to silhouette any intruders. Officers should remember that the interior of a building with obstructed windows can be very dark, even in daylight.

Defenders may also anticipate that police will cut the power. For nighttime, battery-powered external lights are commonly available in hardware outlets. Flashlights can provide the little interior lighting needed. Defenders will probably have enough tactical savvy to know that showing a light can draw fire.

Weapons used may include handguns, shotguns, and even full-automatic weapons in some cases. Because the suspects do not need to conceal these weapons on the person, they can easily chose shoulder weapons. Suspects are not likely to be concerned about stray shots injuring innocent parties, because they don't worry about lawsuits; thus, they will be more willing than police officers to open fire.

Since the interior will be set up for defense, not social calls, remember that furniture is likely to be just inside the doors and windows—to cause injury to anyone trying to dive into the room. Any entry team stopped by these obstacles provides stationary targets for the defenders. Trip-wires or marbles on the floor also slow up an advance. Additionally, spiked boards are quick and easy to deploy inside a doorway.

The occupant will probably know that an elementary precaution against tear gas, stun grenades, and gasoline bombs is to avoid defending a room from inside. This precaution also protects against cross-fire; thus, the defenders are unlikely to be in a room which has windows or doors leading to the outside. Officers who get inside are likely to find no targets in the same room. However, there may be loop-holes in the walls, or defenders may fire through a doorway.

Another nasty prospect is the defender's use of tear gas or a gasoline bomb to cover his or her escape. Throwing a grenade or bomb into the outer room will delay officers long enough to allow escape down a tunnel. Officers must be aware that although "flak jackets" and ballistic vests will stop some fragments, they don't protect against gasoline bombs.

Due to these significant risks, the best choice in coping with fortified premises is avoiding entry altogether.

Arrests

One alternative to entry is luring the occupants outside. Persuading them to emerge, using the "pizza man" and other subterfuges to bring the suspects away from their premises can avoid casualties. Isolating a suspect from his companions also reduces the chances of violent resistance.

Search Warrants

If you must enter a rock house to serve a search warrant be extremely careful. Because of booby-traps and the extensive precautions necessary when approaching rock houses, no search can be quick. Still, the best time for serving a search warrant is when the premises are unoccupied. With luck, it may be possible to find all occupants gone for a long enough time to send in a search team and set up a perimeter to detain any returning occupants. When caught outside their fortified premises, the occupants are unlikely to resist; but if they do, they won't have the defensive advantages of the rock house.

Assaults

If it becomes necessary to hold a full-scale assault, it is best to prepare carefully: try to nullify the defender's advantages. The basic preparation is to have accurate information about the defense. This information is often available only from an informant or undercover agent. If possible, officers should make themselves aware of all the rock houses within their jurisdiction, and collect as much information about them as possible. Technical surveillance techniques, exchanging information with other agencies, and probing suspects for additional information all help fill in the picture. Developing this preliminary information can save lives at the time of an entry.

PREPARING FOR COURT

Once an arrest has been made on a target, through either a forced entry, a search warrant or through an undercover operation, the court preparation must begin. A detailed and often lengthy case file is assembled on the target for presentation to the prosecuting attorney. This enables the prosecutor to know what took place from the initial meeting until the arrest. It also gives the prosecuting attorney an idea of any offers or deals to be made with the defendant for the defendant's assistance—or the defendant's plea of guilty. Many times a defendant will plead guilty either as charged or to a lesser included offense after finding out the key witness in the case is an undercover agent.

Handwriting Evidence In Drug Cases

In a drug case, the question of who wrote the drug records is often important to answer when establishing the legal elements of control or knowledge. In the prosecution phase, these and other elements must be established, sometimes by no other means than documentary evidence.

For example, drug prosecutors can satisfy the elements of control, knowledge and sale when the written documents are connected to an individual. The "resident" documents, such as rent receipts, leases, and drivers' licenses can establish the element of dominion and control by showing that a particular person resided at the drug location. There have also been cases whereby the drug records in one location were connected to another location by indented impressions, photocopier identification, and extraneous marks. Whatever role documents play in a drug case, certain methods of collecting handwritten evidence from the suspects will ensure greater success in connecting the suspect to the contraband.

With all document evidence, the best results come from cases where writing samples were collected early in the investigation and under the same conditions in which the questioned documents were written. For example, when the drug ledger consists of handprinted columns of dates, names and numbers on a 3″ x 4″ piece of lined paper—written in pencil—then the officer should obtain writing samples of handprinted columns of dates, names and numbers on a 3″ x 4″ piece of lined paper written in pencil, as well as some samples in ballpoint pen.

Of course, in the real world nothing is as easy as following simple rules and getting great results. Document evidence in drug cases is no exception. There are a few factors that can impede good results if the narcotics officer is caught unaware. First of all, drug busts are inherently dangerous. Therefore, a quick and efficient method of collecting documents and writing samples from the suspects must be created and followed.

Secondly, people involved with drug activity frequently do not have such written documentation ready at hand. Such documents might include bank accounts, job applications, and credit applications. However, these normal business records are crucially important in establishing the suspect's normal writing habits. Without them, it is difficult to establish whether or not the requested samples truly represent the normal writing habits of the suspect. Requested exemplars are far too often affected by nervousness or attempts to alter or change the writing. Therefore, all requested samples should be accompanied by some normal course of business record.

Third, many drug offenders learned to write under a different national system. A characteristic that appears to be unique or unusual to us is really quite common in a foreign system. This fact is important in evaluating handwriting for identification. A class characteristic which is common to many people is not as valuable for identification purposes as one which is unique to an individual.

Fourth, a drug bust may involve numerous suspects and only a couple of them will be associated with the record keeping. To make it even more complicated, there are numerous documents, and often more than one writer on a page. A narcotics officer in the heat of a seizure will not have time to study all the records to determine which are incriminating and who in the crowd is responsible. Therefore, samples must be obtained from all suspects and in a manner that is not too unwieldy.

Obtaining these writing samples brings us to the fifth and final factor: uncooperative suspects. Suspects may not want to give writing samples, claiming Fifth Amendment rights. However, there are no such rights in obtaining handwriting samples.

The best way to overcome these five obstacles is first to know about them. Different situations will dictate to the narcotics officer how to handle them. In addition, there are a few tips that have served officers in the past. These tips are explained below.

Make up a generic exemplar form that contains the usual drug record information. This form will be much better than the traditional handwriting exemplar card that most police departments have on hand since that card was designed for check-forgery cases. Your generic exemplar form should be used in conjunction with the samples that duplicate the format of a particular drug record.

Exhibit 1 is an example of a form that not only contains some letter and number combinations found in drug records but when folded in half, conceals the fact that the suspect is filling out a handwriting exemplar. The top portion of the form was designed to cause the suspect to concentrate on the content of the information, rather than the act of writing.

Have pages of steno pads, notebooks, address books, accounting books, and note pads on hand. These are the usual source of paper used for most drug records; they will give you a ready supply for duplicating the paper size and format of the drug record that is found at the scene.

When taking the samples, dictate the information in whole phrases in a normal speaking pace, pausing at the end for the writer to finish before continuing with the next phrase. This pace will cause the writer to think about the context of the message, rather than the act of writing, which only gives the writer time to think about the normal way he makes the forms and how he can alter them to avoid identification.

Get enough samples that repeat the letters, words and figures at least four times. For example, if the drug record is one page of writing, get four pages of samples. If, on the other hand, the record is made up of numerous pages, chances are that the letters, words and figures are repeated throughout the pages, therefore one sample of each page should be sufficient.

Have the suspect fill out the booking sheets. Again, the suspect has to think about the information rather than concentrate on the act of writing, and it is another writing sample usually taken at a different time and under different conditions. If the booking sheets are incomplete, illegible, or if your department has a policy that only the officer or booking personnel does this task, then a second set of booking sheets can be filled out simultaneously or afterward.

Exhibit 1

NAME		PHONE NUMBER	DATE
ADDRESS	CITY	STATE	ZIP CODE
DATE OF BIRTH	PLACE OF BIRTH	DRIVER LICENSE	
OCCUPATION	EMPLOYER	PHONE NUMBER	
IN CASE OF ILLNESS NOTIFY:		PHONE NUMBER	RELATIONSHIP
ADDRESS	CITY	STATE	ZIP CODE

Signature ______________________________ Date ____________

The above is a sample of my handwriting using my ☐ right ☐ left hand.

Witnessed by: ______________________________

FOLD HERE

JANUARY 28, 1976	JOSEPH S. FRANCK	$6,000.00
APRIL 30, 1988	MICKEY MOUSE AND DONALD DUCK PRODUCTIONS	$2,000.00
NOVEMBER 4, 1981	ROBERT S. THOMPSON	$50,000.00
DECEMBER 6, 1985	IGLESIA N. CRUZ CO.	$9,473.00
FEBRUARY 18, 1972	CATHERINE LINDA YUMA	$2,000.00
MARCH 11, 1986	GEORGE HOWARD WHITE, INC.	$937.45
SEPTEMBER 16, 1985	RINGO'S SALSA BAR	$7,456.00
JULY 22, 1983	MIGUEL ARTURO VALENTINO	$37.98
OCTOBER 16, 1987	E.B. PENNY, LTD.	$5,640.00
AUGUST 15, 1982	PAUL T. AND HARRY N. KANE	$12,450.00

Undercover Narcotics & Lab Investigations

Obtain a copy of the driver's license applications when requesting a soundex copy of the driver's license. There are samples of writing other than the signature on the driver's license application.

When submitting the document evidence to the document laboratory, place the known documents in one package and the questioned documents in another. Avoid writing on documents that are placed on top of drug records, because the indented impressions you make may obscure indented impressions made by the suspect. If the drug records are going to be processed for fingerprints, always submit them to the document laboratory first and advise the examiner to take precautions.

Only submit the "smoking gun" documents. Select the pages that make the best connection between the suspect and the contraband. Every scrap of paper and ledger is not necessary in most cases. It will only bog down or overwhelm the document laboratory.

These tips have made many successful identifications in drug cases. The main thing is to remember to duplicate the conditions of the questioned material. That's easy when you have the drug record and know what the test is and what kind of paper and writing implement was used. When you haven't had time to go through all the material before taking samples of writing, then use your generic form. This sample can be used as a gauge for subsequent samples which were taken after the suspect had time to think about how incriminating his writing may be.

Sometimes, the best efforts still fall short of full identification of a suspect. However, a probable or even possible conclusion from a document examiner can and has worked in the prosecution's favor when the supporting reason for the conclusion is that the known samples do not sufficiently represent all the normal writing habits of the suspect. This shows objectivity and care on the examiner's part, and uncooperativeness on the defendant's part, implying guilt.

The Legal Use Of Dogs In Narcotics Cases

Another tool that officers may use to assist their arrest and prosecution of narcotics trafficers is the drug detection dog. Due to their highly developed olfactory sense, dogs have become common "equipment" used in narcotics investigations. However, since drug detection dogs are extremely effective, traffickers have attempted to thwart their efforts by packaging drugs with moth balls and garlic; traffickers have even gone so far as to put out contracts on the lives of certain detection dogs. Nonetheless, drug detection dogs have been successful; and the courts have recognized their value when they are well-trained and properly employed.

 md

In any narcotics investigation, law enforcement officers must be careful to use detection dogs within the boundaries set by the courts. Those boundaries can be summarized as follows:

> If the dog is used to sniff an area where the defendant has an extremely high expectation of privacy, then a warrant based on probable cause or an exception to the warrant requirement is a prerequisite;
>
> If the sniff is to occur in an area of reduced expectation of privacy, then a mere showing of reasonable suspicion is all that is required; and
>
> If the dog is used to sniff an item located in a public place or a place controlled by a third party, then no search will occur and Fourth Amendment proscriptions regarding searches need not be a concern.

Although other constitutional considerations may arise, such as the level of suspicion needed to seize luggage from a traveler or the amount of time an item may be detained prior to conducting a sniff test, law enforcement officers can help ensure the legality of the dog sniff itself by staying within these boundaries. For further information regarding particular circumstances, see the following court cases: on the use of dogs in public places, *United States v. Place*, 103 *S.Ct.* 2637 (1983); on the use of dogs in third party controlled areas, *United States v. Lovell*, 849 *F.*2d 910 (5th Cir. 1988); on the use of dogs in private residences, *United States v. Thomas,* 757 *F.*2d 1359 (2d Cir. 1985); and on the use of dogs in motor vehicles, *United States v. Whitehead,* 849 *F.*2d 849 (4th Cir. 1988).

SEARCH WARRANTS & TACTICS

WHY WARRANTS ARE PREFERABLE

Another legal consideration for law enforcement officers is the proper use of search warrants. The most important thing to realize is that a search made without a warrant is unlawful unless it falls within at least one recognized—and narrowly drawn—exception to the warrant requirement. This is the gist of the Fourth Amendment. In the courtroom, the burden of proof is on the prosecution to prove a warrantless search was lawful. The converse is also true—and herein lies a tremendous advantage accorded to warrant users: a search carried out pursuant to a search warrant is presumed lawful, and the burden of proof is on the defendant to prove it unlawful. The corollary to this rule will be explained later, but it basically adds up to the fact that a defendant has virtually no chance of successfully attacking even a marginally strong warrant as long as it was obtained and executed in good faith and is based upon a truthful affidavit. When there is no warrant, however, you may spend hours in court trying to explain that the defendant consented to the search of his home and that the consent was free, voluntary and knowing, notwithstanding the fact that he was surrounded by armed officers, was cuffed, speaks only marginal English, and signed the consent form only after the search was conducted because you didn't have a consent form handy at the scene.

If the defense does attack the warrant, it will be in a proceeding wherein the judge simply reads the warrant and determines its validity, and 99 percent of these warrants will be upheld, either because the warrant is supported by ample probable cause, or even if it isn't, the search will be saved under the holding of *United States v. Leon*—the "good faith" rule.

In essence, the *Leon* case ruled that even if the warrant is quashed for lack of probable cause, the remedy is not to suppress the evidence obtained during the search—as long as the officer conducted the search in good faith reliance on the validity of the warrant. The only exceptions are, (1) lies in the affidavit (or reckless mistakes or omissions), (2) a non-neutral signing judge who has wholly abandoned his or her judicial function, (3) a warrant so lacking in probable cause that no reasonable officer could have believed the warrant was good, or (4) the warrant is facially defective in that it totally fails to describe the places to be searched or items to be seized. As you can see by these exceptions, it is very difficult for a defendant to win a motion to quash.

OBTAINING A SEARCH WARRANT

To illustrate some of the circumstances under which a warrant may be obtained, let's assume that an informant with a very good history of reliability tells you that Josephine Smith is dealing ounces from her 1990 Honda, California license COKE4U. The informant also gives you Smith's home address on Main Street, and tells you that she has been in the house within the past week and has seen cash and about one pound of coke there. You run Smith and find that she has a five year old coke conviction, but is not currently on probation or parole and thus has no search conditions. You decide you'd like to search the car and house. A short surveillance of the house reveals little. You follow Smith away from the house, however, and see her make what you feel are deliveries from the car referred to by the informant. The informant is very valuable to you and has given information to you in the past which has allowed you to seize a lot of dope and prosecute several individuals, including some associates of Smith. What do you do at this point?

Well, you could catch Ms. Smith in her car and do an auto search under *United States v. Ross*, which would be fully lawful. Then, you could obtain a consent for the house, depending upon what you did or didn't find in the car. Or, you could search the car under *Ross* and get a warrant for the house. Lastly, you could simply obtain a warrant for both the car and house. All are viable options.

Another very helpful tactic used by experienced officers and prosecutors is to structure the prosecution along the same lines as the facts set forth in your search warrant affidavit. For instance, there was a case against seven Colombian coke dealers caught with 1,000 pounds and $600,000. The search warrant involved weeks of detailed surveillance coupled with several expert opinions about such things as stash houses, mail drops, the lack of any visible employment by the suspects notwithstanding their rather upscale lifestyle, car switches, brief meetings in public places, beeper calls, cellular phones and the other things usually involved in such cases. The warrant was quite lengthy and was in effect, the blueprint for the jury trial.

Seventy-five percent of the trial in this case consisted of the narcotics agent explaining to the jury how a major narcotics organization operates, explaining beepers, cellular phones, car switches, etc., and then explaining how the defendant's conduct fit within that framework. The narcotics agent also offered the jury his expert opinions regarding various matters in controversy. Since the affidavit already existed well before the trial and, in fact, existed even before the defendants were arrested, the defense could in no way argue that the testimony had been tailored for the trial. Furthermore, since the cocaine, money, beepers and all other items sought by the warrant were in fact owned by the traffickers, the facts and opinions contained within the affidavit became self-fulfilling prophecies in a sense. The prediction of criminality in the warrant, coupled with its eventual and obvious uncovering at the time of arrest, became very compelling evidence at trial. The case basically tried itself from the plan laid out in the affidavit, and all that was needed on top was a correlation and presentation of the additional evidence found at various locations (bogus leases, phone records, pay-owes, etc.).

In summary, the concept to be gleaned from this case involves the dual use of facts, both as probable cause for the arrests and searches, and as substantive evidence of guilt given to the jury.

WARRANTS WILL SAVE TIME LATER

It takes a couple of hours to write a warrant and two minutes to get a consent. It is true, on occasion you may spend more time in the field if you issue a warrant than if you don't. But if you have ever spent three days on the witness stand testifying about a series of warrantless arrests, searches and "securing" of residences, while six dope lawyers systematically seek to destroy you, I'll bet you would opt for the extra couple of hours in the field. Also, your increased chance of losing when you forego a warrant means that all of the time spent during your investigation and all of the prosecutor's time, as well as the judge's time are risked unnecessarily. The extra time you spend obtaining a warrant will pay off in better searches, more wins at trial, less court time for you, and less risk that the time you do spend is wasted by having your evidence suppressed.

Also, the typical warrant does not take that much time to prepare. The affidavit accompanying most warrants is under 10 pages, with some as short as two or three pages. You can shorten matters substantially by having your expertise pre-printed and updated periodically for use as the first pages of your affidavit. Also, get a copy of the D.A. Search Warrant Manual if you don't already have one; keep it, some blank warrants, and some pre-printed expertise pages with you in your car. You should also learn to do telephonic and oral warrants.

MOST JUDGES DO NOT LIKE TO SUPPRESS EVIDENCE

Most judges, contrary to some popular wisdom, aren't really thrilled with setting an obviously guilty party free because the evidence must be suppressed. In fact, most judges frown upon this result. Believe it or not, the officer has much more control over this than does the judge. A judge simply cannot suppress evidence seized pursuant to a warrant without a darned good reason, or the appellate court will simply reverse. But a judge faced with a warrantless search or seizure that is weak can do you in, simply by making a credibility call against you. And no court of appeal can do a thing about it.

Furthermore, when an officer proceeds via warrant, he or she is reinforcing the image of police officers as professionals, concerned with making strong cases and conducting legal searches, and dispelling the image that some judges may hold of narcotics officers as cowboys who search first and come up with the bad taillight later. Obtaining a warrant from a judge also gives you the opportunity to interact with the judge on a one-on-one basis, usually outside of the courtroom. This is valuable to both the officer and the judge. Some bench officers, believe it or not, are not ex-prosecutors, and may have little empathy for or understanding of how the police operate. Some judges may have never socialized with police officers before becoming judges, and may even feel intimidated or threatened by them. Likewise, many officers who would never think of speaking to a judge unless absolutely necessary, perhaps viewing the judge as an enemy just looking for a way to free dangerous defendants. However, the cooperation of judge and police officer will only result in enhanced communication and a smoother trial.

Another reason for obtaining a search warrant is issue of civil liability. Let's assume you conduct a search of a suspect's home and come up dry; then this suspect decides to sue you. Would you rather go into the civil trial holding a document signed by a judge that ordered you to conduct the search in question (remember, a search warrant is an order in writing to conduct a particular search and seizure), or would you rather argue to the jury that the suspect consented to the search, although he and his eight family members claim you kicked the door and never mentioned consent?

SERVING THE NARCOTICS SEARCH WARRANT

There are several kinds of search warrants. Their use may range from looking for evidence in cases of theft, narcotics, and explosives, or even murder. I would like to focus on the small-time dealer or dealer/user who is close to the bottom rung of the narcotics ladder. This person is extremely dangerous not only because he is usually a multi-time ex-con, but also because he cannot afford another arrest. In this case, and several others, serving a search warrant can be one of the most dangerous duties an officer encounters in his or her career.

To obtain a warrant, as discussed above, a "buy" is usually made by an undercover officer, special employee, or confidential and reliable informant. Right after the buy is made, an interview with the buyer may help to procure some necessary information which includes: description of suspect, layout of interior of house, weapons, where the narcotics are kept, and how many people live or stay in the house. It would also be helpful to get some details on such questions as how are the doors secured? With deadbolts? Are there boobie traps? etc.

Decisions

After the warrant is written and signed by a magistrate, you should decide when to serve the warrant. For legal reasons, it should be served as soon as possible after the magistrate signs it; but in most cases the warrant does not have to be served immediately. The more time between the "buy" and the serving of the warrant, the more likely the informant's identity can be concealed.

You should also decide to serve the warrant in either the daytime or nighttime. There are many reasons to justify either time, but nighttime usually offers more concealment for the raiding party when approaching the house. On the other hand, early daylight offers the opportunity to catch the occupant of the house at home, hopefully, with his stash. The decision also depends on other factors, such as when the dealer gets resupplied and if you want to get more players and users in the house when you hit it.

Warrant Serving Strategy—Seven People

5 front/2 rear. A game plan should be made up as to how many people are going to be used and how they will be assigned. There should be at least two uniformed officers utilized in serving the warrant; one positioned at the front door and one at the rear door. A good idea is to have a third person (detective) in the rear yard with the uniformed officer. They should each be placed diagonally away from the door, strategically out of the line of fire. Their main purpose is to prevent escape. Hopefully, if one of the dealer/users tries to escape, they can verbally stop him from exiting the rear door.

When serving the "average" search warrant, five persons should be used on the entry. The "knock and announce" should be made by the affiant, team leader or other person knowledgeable in the legalities of making a lawful entry. This person, along with all other non-uniformed personnel, should be dressed so that there could be no mistake that they are police officers. A good idea would be to wear an outer garment that is marked "POLICE" and to attach a badge to this outer garment. Have all participants wear bulletproof vests.

The person who knocks on the door should have the warrant in his hand and show it to the person opening the door. The entry in most narcotics cases should be done very quickly in order to prevent the destruction of evidence and to prevent officer injury; it must also be done legally. Therefore, the person who knocks on the door (known as the "knocker") has an extremely important position. If the "knocker" hears retreating footsteps or if the occupant refuses admittance, then forced entry should be made. The knocker must announce his purpose and authority and demand entry (in most cases) prior to forcing entry.

If forced entry is needed, the "doorkey" person will then, hopefully, open the door with one swing of the sledgehammer or ram. The first swing should hit the deadbolt lock mechanism and open the door. Upon entry, the first person through the house should be the uniformed officer. This officer should have his gun drawn in case firepower is needed. Before opening any other interior doors, this officer should also "knock and announce." When the interior situation is stabilized, he or she should be the one to open the rear door after loudly announcing "Police, I am opening the rear door."

The "doorkey" person should be the second one through the house. He or she should assist the uniformed officer in situations where a person needs to be controlled or arrested and firepower is not needed. He or she is also responsible for forced entry if an interior door needs to be taken down.

The third and fourth persons through the house should be a team of shooters: the third person in case of a firefight situation and the fourth, a fighter, in case of a physical confrontation. This teamwork situation should help cut down on accidental discharges but should not preclude the "fighter" from pulling and using his or her weapon if necessary.

If a ruse is used to gain entry, such as an officer dressed as a deliveryman, letter carrier, etc., this person should take on the same responsibilities as the "knocker." The "knocker's" responsibility is to allow no one to exit the front door and to prevent non-police personnel from entering the house.

This initial game plan should be set up without the need for radio transmissions. Many drug dealers monitor police channels, so it behooves the search warrant team to use hand signals, unless they are using scramblers or in the case of an emergency situation.

If shots are fired within the house, the officers in the rear should maintain their position. They should not subject the other officers to a cross-fire situation but instead maintain "cover" and listen for further communications. If a firefight ensues, the Team Sergeant (who may be the 2nd, 3rd, or 4th team member) should radio via walkie for reinforcements. Depending on the situation, the Sergeant should generally call for setting up a double perimeter and command post. He or she should also determine if there is a need for a Special Response or S.W.A.T. Team.

The Search

The search should be made carefully and systematically. For best results, every room and everything should be searched twice (by two different people). There is no limit on where and how to search. Narcotics may be found anywhere from plain view to hidden in walls, toilets, wall sockets, safes, vacuum packed cans, furniture, body cavities, etc.

If your courts allow it, the best scenario would be to have each individual officer locate or spot the contraband and then have one officer be designated as the finder. The finder systematically "finds" all the contraband and books it as evidence, which makes both accountability and courtroom testifying easier.

SEARCHES FOR NARCOTICS TRAFFICKING IN THE WORKPLACE

Another situation in which an undercover officer may be required to do a search or a surveillance is in the corporate or industrial workplace. Increasingly, narcotics have been trafficked by workers at their place of employment. The prevalance of this phenomenon and the role of the undercover agent are discussed in the report below.[4]

UNDERCOVER INVESTIGATORS: A NEW EMPLOYER DRUG WAR TOOL

Concerns about drug abuse in the workplace have led some employers to hire investigative services to place undercover agents in their work forces, according to representatives of private investigative agencies.

Ron Janick, vice president of investigative services for CPP/Pinkerton, headquartered in Van Nuys, Calif., said he has observed a 40 percent increase during the past six months in the number of employers requesting undercover investigations into suspected drug abuse.

Increasingly, employees are complaining to management — often anonymously — that other employees are working under the influence of drugs or selling drugs in the workplace, Janick said. Employees are concerned about their safety, he said,

---

[4] *International Drug Report.* International Narcotic Enforcement Officers Association. Albany, N.Y. January 1990, p. 7.

citing a recent example in which an employee who allegedly was using drugs had an accident while operating a forklift truck.

Spouses and relatives also sometimes tell employers about an employee's use of drugs on the job, according to Edward P. DeLise, a vice president with Investigations Corporation of America, based in Atlanta, Ga.

It is not always co-workers or family members who clue the employer that there is a drug problem. Employers sometimes observe behavior or other circumstances that leads them to believe there is a problem. Absenteeism, inventory shrinkage, increased workers' compensation claims, and diminished product or service quality are all potential signals of a drug problem, according to the investigators.

While absenteeism can be a signal of employee drug abuse, some employees involved in selling drugs have very good attendance records, according to DeLise. "Oddly enough, dealers are usually at work every day because that's where their connections are," he noted.

Theft in the workplace and drug abuse very often go hand in hand, according to Bobby Newman of Acta Investigations Inc., in Houston. Newman estimated that in some workplaces, employee involvement in the use or delivery of drugs runs from 10 to 30 percent of the workplace. He cited one instance where 100 employees out of a workforce of 150 were involved in narcotics use or transactions.

Corporate investigators say their clientele represents a broad range of U.S. workplaces, from banks to hospitals, schools to factories.

Surveillance: 'Preventive Medicine'

Although many employers request undercover investigations to target what they see as a specific problem, others use the investigations more as "preventive medicine." A Pinkerton advertisement suggests that undercover investigations can be "regularly used by sophisticated management as a precautionary measure—much like a surprise audit or annual physical checkup—to verify that operations are actually being conducted in accordance with the management's expectations and understanding."

Most operatives are placed in entry-level or secretarial positions, but they can be placed almost anywhere, the investigators said.

The fewer people who know about an undercover investigation, the better, investigators agree, noting that a human resource official is often one of the people appraised of the operation.

Pinkerton investigators usually suggest that a high-level human resource or personnel official be aware of the investigations, as these people often have to deal with the outcome, Janick said.

DeLise of ICA estimated that 80 to 85 percent of the time, a human resource official is aware of undercover operations conducted by his firm. A personnel official's cooperation often is needed to "get our operative in" to the work site, he said.

Secrecy is Key to Investigation

DeLise said if more than three people from a company are aware of an undercover investigation into suspected drug abuse, he will not take the case "because it can be dangerous." He added that he doesn't use agents from the local area for this reason and because when the operation is over, he wants to get them out.

Most investigations range from one to four months, but some can take up to a year. Investigators agree that it can take time for the undercover operative to be accepted by co-workers.

The investigators said they bring the police in as soon as there is evidence of narcotics activity. It is particularly important to notify law enforcement officials in order to preserve the "chain of custody" of the evidence, DeLise said. In addition, since his investigators are often from out of town it is important that the police know of their presence so there is no confusion as to their role in the drug activity.

Worker discipline resulting from undercover operations usually sticks, according to the investigators. There is seldom a problem because the investigators often back up their observations with video or film, Newman said.

Although direct observation of workplace activity by management and supervisors is well accepted in employment law, new technology—especially electronic and video surveillance equipment—has raised fear among employees of privacy invasions, an employment attorney told a recent conference on employee surveillance.

The entry of new technology into the workplace sets up a clash between the employer's need to supervise its employees and the privacy rights of the employees, said Morton Orenstein of the San Francisco law firm of Schacter, Kristoff, Ross, Sprague & Curiale.

California and some other states have privacy guarantees in their state constitutions that could affect the ability of employers in those states to use various forms of workplace surveillance, he said.

THE INVESTIGATION OF CLANDESTINE LABORATORIES

There are several natural drugs (not illicitly manufactured) found on the street. The most popular ones are marijuana, psilocybin, and peyote. However, most of the drugs that police officers see on the street are clandestinely manufactured. Morphine is converted to heroin. PCP and LSD are synthetic and chemically manufactured. Based on the process required to manufacture any particular drug, there are different types of laboratories. Some basic manufacturing processes are described below.

1. Extraction: the raw plant material is changed into a finished product by the use of chemical solvents. The chemical structure of the drug is not altered. Examples include: cannabis to hashish, hashish to hashish oil, opium to morphine.

2. Conversion: a raw or unrefined drug product is changed into a finished or refined drug. Here the chemical structure is changed. Examples: morphine to heroin (diacetylmorphine), cocaine base to cocaine hydrocholride, cocaine hydrochloride to crack cocaine.

3. Synthesis: a combination of proper raw materials in required portions results in a finished drug product through chemical reaction. Examples: chemicals to phencyclidine, LSD, etc.

4. "Tableting": The machine processing of the final drug product into a dosage form (tablet).

Where Are The Labs?

In 1986, a total of 509 clandestine labs were seized in the U.S. by the Drug Enforcement Administration—a 150 percent increase since 1982, when 197 labs were seized. During these raids, agents confiscated more than

1,000 firearms. Many of the labs also contained explosives and were protected with booby traps.[5]

The largest cocaine processing facility ever seized was a laboratory complex in Colombia; it was seized in March 1984. The complex was discovered through the investigation of a shipment of 76 barrels of ether purchased by Colombian traffickers in the U.S. A total of over 10,000 barrels of chemicals were later seized at that lab.[6]

Within the United States, the largest clandestine laboratory was raided in Blenheim, NY on April 20, 1992. The following article explains the magnitude and scope of this laboratory seizure.[7]

NATION'S LARGEST CLANDESTINE LABORATORY RAIDED

What authorities described as one of the nation's largest clandestine laboratories producing the "love drug" Ecstasy was shut down Tuesday, April 20, 1992, when police swooped into a booby-trapped Schoharie County cabin and arrested two people.

NY State Police and Federal Drug Enforcement Agency investigators said they found enough chemicals on the secluded property off Blenheim Road to manufacture 50 pounds of Ecstasy, a banned drug also known as MDMA, or methyldioxmethamphetamine.

Unceremoniously roused from bed at 8 a.m. by the police raiding party were Gary Treistman, 38, of 462 W. 58th St. in New York City and an 18-year-old woman described by police as his girlfriend, Onya Sheckley, whose address was not available.

Both were charged with Federal offenses of illegal manufacture of a controlled substance and possession of a controlled drug with the intent to distribute. The two were ordered held without bail when they were arraigned in Albany before U.S. Magistrate Ralph W. Smith.

State Police Capt. Jeff Hines of the Troop G Bureau of Criminal Investigation said Treistmann had placed a gasoline explosive device near the lab to destroy the chemicals in the event that police approached it. Hines said police also found motion-sensing "electric eyes," video surveillance gear, and traps set up around the lab to warn Treistman of police or intruders. Kevin Whaley, agent in charge of the Albany DEA office, called the Blenhiem lab "one of the most prominent in the nation."

Hines said the lab was the largest Ecstasy lab ever found in the northeastern U.S. The discovery of the lab, police said, again points up the fact that drug producers in remote areas of upstate New York can find ideal locations for setting up clandestine factories. Over the past seven years, police have found major cocaine-processing plants in Minden, Montgomery County, the Otsego County community of Fly Creek, and Danube, outside Little Falls in Herkimer County.

Ecstasy has gained limited popularity on college campuses and in night clubs, with wide-eyed users saying it produces a sense of alertness and pleasure, and it

---

[5] Lazlo, Anna T. "Clandestine Drug Laboratories: Confronting a Growing National Crisis." *The National Sheriff.* August-September 1989, pp. 9-44.

[6] U.S. Department of Justice, Office of the Attorney General. "Drug Trafficking: A Report to the President of the United States." Washington, D.C., August 3, 1989.

[7] *International Drug Report.* International Narcotic Enforcement Officers Association. Albany, NY. Vol. 33, No. 6, ISS 0148-4648, June 1992.

heightens sexuality. Researchers have expressed concern that the drug, first synthesized as an appetite suppressant 70 years ago, can cause serious, even permanent, damage to the brain.

According to a report by former state Division of Substance Abuse Services researcher William Hopkins, "Ecstasy is regarded by many as a white person's drug."

Officials said Tuesday the drug is particularly popular among some "Deadheads," followers of the Grateful Dead rock band.

Hines said the Ecstasy from Blenheim was to be distributed in New York City and in Europe. When asked if Treistman had ties to any criminal organizations, the captain said investigators were still delving into his background.

The probe that led to Tuesday's raid began a month earlier after three people were arrested in Cayuga County on drug charges, one of them for the sale of Esctasy, said Cayuga County District Attorney James Bargason and an investigator in his office, Richard Middleton.

Police have kept a close watch on the Blenheim property, owned by Treistman, for the past several weeks.

"The place was a pigsty," said State Police Lt. Ronald Tritto, noting the "sophisticated" consumers of Ecstasy might retch if they realized the drug was produced under such highly unsanitary conditions.

Treistman and Sheckley offered no resistance when police rolled into the property in 4-wheel drive vehicles Tuesday, though investigators said they found a rifle, handgun and a small quantity of heroin there.

Police kept the property off limits to the press and the public for several hours after the raid, saying some of the chemicals were highly volatile. A team of DEA chemists was brought to the property to ensure that the chemicals were stabilized.

The chemicals included toulene acetone, isosafrole, peroxide, alcohol and formaldehyde. A single kilogram of Ecstasy, approximately 2.2 pounds, sells for about $20,000, Hines said.

With increasing seizures such as the one reported above, it has become apparent that clandestine laboratories are more and more prevalent among drug traffickers. The two most common types of labs are phencyclidine (PCP) and methamphetamine (Speed) labs. Laboratories vary in sophistication. Some are expensively equipped and some consist of makeshift equipment such as plastic buckets, plastic barrels, and broom and mop handles. These laboratories can present a danger to the responding police officer in terms of the suspects therein and the inherent dangers posed by the improper manufacture of drugs. There are chemicals present that are highly toxic and highly explosive so the officer must exercise extreme caution. Since police officers are usually first on the scene, the officer must have a basic knowledge of how to go about handling a suspected clandestine laboratory.

Recognition of Clandestine Laboratories

Clandestine laboratories are not restricted to any particular geographical area. They may be found in a single family dwelling, an apartment complex, or in a remote area. The labs are usually detected by the strong odor of chemicals emanating from the site. When an informant calls the police or fire department, it is usually because of the odor of ether and other strong odors.

The following are the most common indicators of an illicit drug laboratory:

1. Usually, because of the danger of fire and the presence of toxic fumes, no one will actually live at the location. The laboratory operator will only periodically visit the location.
2. The doors and windows will be somewhat sealed in an attempt to conceal the strong odor.
3. The operator may, depending on the location, install large ventilation fans to disperse the fumes.
4. 55-gallon steel drums will be delivered to the location by a chemical company or common carrier.
5. Inordinate amounts of ice will be delivered to the location. (Ice is required for the cooling process during "cooking.")
6. A strong, distinctive odor of ether may be noticeable. If questioned, the operator will frequently indicate the odor is from a legal activity of plastic manufacturing or photograph developing.
7. The location will be sparsely furnished.
8. The neighbors notice that the operator appears to exit the location solely to get fresh air or to have a smoke.
9. The neighbor or a friend may have been inside and observed the laboratory in operation.
10. The operator may dump chemicals in the yard, causing destruction of plant life.

Upon responding to a suspected lab, a uniformed field officer should make contact with the informant and gain as much information as possible regarding the occupants of the building. The officer can then make a visual inspection of the location, looking for signs that a clandestine laboratory is in operation. One of the signs is chemical odors being ventilated from the building by fans, blowers, and other types of ventilating equipment. The officer should look for empty chemical containers around the building or in the trash.

Upon locating a suspected laboratory site, the field officer will generally back off and call for assistance while maintaining surveillance of the site. A narcotics unit should be called to the scene. If the officer feels there is an immediate danger to people in the surrounding area, he can call for the fire department and begin to evacuate persons from the area. He may also want to block off access roads to the area. The Uniform Fire Code allows fire departments to enter any structure if a hazard exists and authorizes police officers to assist fire departments in any function. The *Patterson* decision, 94 *Cal.App.*3d 456, 1979, states that a residence, in its entirety, can be an extreme explosion hazard because petroleum ether creates a very volatile fume when improperly ventilated.

Search and Seizure

All investigative discoveries should be included in the affidavit. These might include persons ordering chemicals under false names; chemical odors around the suspected laboratory site; officer's observations from within the lab site; expert opinion; and the evasive movements of the suspect.

When effecting entry without a warrant due to exigent circumstances, the fire department and a criminalist should always be notified immediately. As soon as the laboratory has been rendered safe, the search should be stopped and a warrant obtained.

SAFETY RULES OF THE CLANDESTINE LABORATORY FOR POLICE, FIREFIGHTERS AND PUBLIC

Safety rules of the clandestine laboratory include the following:

1. Secure adjoining houses or apartments; evacuate surrounding area as necessary.
2. Have ambulance standing by, if necessary.
3. Have fire equipment standing by. After suspects are secure, move fire equipment into area.
4. Turn off gas and electricity at the outside source to the building.
5. Use gas probe to determine fire potential.
6. All personnel entering the lab should wear self-contained breathing apparatus.
7. A trained criminalist should always accompany investigators.
8. The criminalist should be responsible for shutting down the operations and the indication of possible dangerous chemicals.
9. Make sure the clandestine laboratory is well ventilated by opening doors and windows. Mechanical ventilation equipment should only be used outside the location.
10. Do not turn on lights to the location until it is well ventilated.
11. Do not smoke at the scene.
12. Do not allow acid and cyanide to be mixed or come together. This mixture is used in the gas chamber and is lethal.
13. Do not remove any flasks or containers from ice baths.
14. Photograph only with electronic flash.
15. Wash thoroughly after leaving the scene.
16. Curiosity seekers or unauthorized persons can only result in contamination of the scene and possible injury.

Safety

If you can, avoid entering a laboratory. If you have to enter a suspected laboratory site, the officer must remember that he is dealing with highly toxic and volatile chemicals. If there is a strong odor of ether, he must know that an explosion may result from a spark or flame. The officer should never turn on or off any electrical switch or appliance in the lab area. The fire department should stand by, and entry to the lab should be made with a qualified chemist. The building should be immediately ventilated to eliminate the danger of explosion. The officer must avoid accidentally mixing any chemicals present. Hydrochloric acid and sodium cyanide are commonly found at PCP lab sites and, when combined, they form cyanide gas. Cyanide gas is a very deadly substance.

Search Warrant

Usually, a search warrant will be obtained by the narcotics officers. The affidavit must allege facts sufficient to establish probable cause. A case decision, *United States v. Tate*, 1982, established that the odor of ether, alone, is not sufficiently distinctive to identify the manufacturing of PCP. The Court said that there are other legitimate reasons for the use of ether, which is not illegal to possess; therefore, in the absence of other circumstances, the odor of ether alone does not constitute sufficient probable cause. If officers cannot establish an immediate danger to allow entry to the premises under fire code sections, they may have to set up a surveillance to establish further circumstances to obtain a search warrant.

Chemicals Found at Clandestine Laboratories

There are certain chemicals that must be present to manufacture PCP or methamphetamine; these are called precursors. The necessary precursors for manufacturing methamphetamines are methylamine and phenyl-2-propanone. Other chemicals may be used in various combinations. Below is a list of the chemicals commonly used in PCP and Amphetamine labs.

PCP LABS

1. Piperidine
2. Cyclohexanone
3. Bromobenzene
4. Petroleum ether
5. Anhydrous ether
6. Magnesium turnings
7. Sodium bisulfite
8. Sodium cyanide
9. Iodine
10. Hydrochloric acid
11. Ammonium hydroxide

AMPHETAMINE LABS

1. Methylamine
2. Phenyl-2-propanone
3. Petroleum ether
4. Aluminum foil
5. Hydrochloric acid
6. Acetone
7. Palladium
8. Benzyl chloride
9. Ephedrine
10. Phosphorus

Alternative Method For Crank Synthesis

The recent seizure of a methamphetamine laboratory in Redding, California has revealed a synthesis method to produce phenyl-2-propanone (P-2-P) that has not been widely used in the past. This new method seems to be on its way to becoming more prevalent in clandestine lab activity.

The method is known as the "Nitrostyrene Route" and utilizes the uncontrolled precursors nitroethance and benzaldehyde. This reaction is quite simple and is analogous to the manufacture of phencyclidine in that it involves a two-stage reaction. The first stage is the synthesis of an intermediate called 1-phenyl-2-nitropropene. This is accomplished by way of refluxing the precursors listed above in a round-bottom flask with a solvent and catalyst. The reaction takes approximately 8 hours if using heat; or the chemicals can be simply set in a dark place at room temperature for 1 to 2 weeks. The trade off is time vs. heat. The resultant product (1-phenyl-2-nitropropene) is a yellowish crystal that has an indefinite shelf life.

The second stage involves the suspension of the intermediate in water in a reaction flask, adding again a catalyst and a reagent. The solution is heated and hydrochloric acid is added slowly over a period of hours, converting the intermediate to P-2-P. This process is known as hydrolysis (decomposition in which a compound is split into other compounds by taking up the elements of water).

There are several dangers associated with this reaction: nitroethance can be explosive and is an irritant to the eyes and mucous membranes; the acid, of course, is corrosive; the solvents are flammable; and one of the catalysts is a mucous membrane irritant.

One the advantages of the "Nitrostyrene Route" is that this reaction does not have the nasty odor associated with the old phenylacetic acid route. The odor associated with this reaction is consistent with Maraschino cherries, which is quite pleasant comparatively. The down side to this process, for the user, is the fact that P-2-P crank is less reactant in the body due to the (dl) form of the methamphetamine rather that the (d) form, which is produced from ephedrine crank. Due to the availability of the precursors involved in this manufacturing method, the process may become more prevalent.

Collecting Laboratory Evidence

Regardless of the type of lab you encounter, the process of collecting evidence is extremely important. All chemicals, apparatus, and the laboratory site should be photographed before collected as evidence; likewise, printable surfaces should be fingerprinted before collected as evidence. In addition, the criminalist should make a complete inventory of all chemicals at the location. The following evidence should be collected:

1. Samples of the precursor chemicals (liquid and solids).
2. Samples of intermediate compounds.
3. Samples of finished products.
4. Samples of all remaining chemicals.
5. Formulas and books, etc., to verify that illicit products were being manufactured.
6. Laboratory equipment.

Disposal

When the investigation of a clandestine laboratory is concluded, the problem of disposing of the chemicals and equipment remains. After the chemist takes samples of the various chemicals found at the lab, a toxic waste disposal company, under contract with the city or county, will package the items in metal containers for disposal.

However, there are still other health and environmental concerns generated by illicit manufacturing at clandestine labs. For instance, the indiscriminate disposal of hazardous waste by outlaw laboratory operators may lead to contamination of surrounding water sources, soil, and air, as well as the building and its fixtures.

Due to manifold health dangers, more comprehensive cleanup actions at laboratory sites—in addition to the immediate or planned removal of bulk chemicals and contaminated materials—are necessary to prevent harm to public health and to the environment. Factoring into this cleanup question are such pressures as a growing environmental awareness in the public and regulations forwarded by the U.S. Environmental Protections Agency (USEPA) and the Occupational Safety and Health Administration (OSHA). This complex rat's nest of issues has impacted law enforcement officers by requiring specialized medical training and the use of protective raid garments by any personnel involved in clandestine drug laboratory seizures. In addition, the Federal government has mandated a more comprehensive cleanup program.

Federal Cleanup Measures

On November 18, 1988, Congress enacted the Anti-Drug Abuse Act of 1988, Public Law 100-690. With respect to chemical cleanup issues, section 2405 of this act mandated the Drug Enforcement Administration (DEA) and the U.S. Environmental Protection Agency (USEPA) to form a joint Federal Task Force to formulate, establish, and implement a program for the cleanup and disposal of hazardous waste produced by illegal drug laboratories. The law also required the Task Force to develop and disseminate guidelines to law enforcement agencies that are responsible for the enforcement of drug laws. The law further stipulates that after the final guidelines are published and disseminated, the Attorney General shall make grants to and enter into contracts with state and local governments. These governments must agree to comply with the guidelines and the contracts will be made for demonstrations projects to clean up and safely dispose of substances associated with illegal drug laboratories—especially those substances which may present a danger to public health and the environment. The proposed guidelines are now available for review by state and local agencies and any other interested parties.

These proposed guidelines have integrated the experience of DEA Special Agents and Forensic Chemists and USEPA Emergency Response Technicians, including various guidance documents developed by USEPA for cleaning up hazardous waste sites and various health and safety programs established by the DEA, USEPA, and OSHA.

The guidelines suggest that state and local law enforcement and environmental and health agencies implement a comprehensive approach to clandestine laboratory cleanup. The guidelines also outline measures which can be taken to reduce the hazards associated with clandestine drug laboratories and provide information on relevant and applicable hazardous waste statutes and regulations, such as the Resource Conservation and Recovery Act (RCRA), which may apply to cleanup activities at clandestine drug laboratories.

The guidelines contain information on chemicals commonly found at drug laboratory sites, DEA clandestine laboratory safety certification programs, and personnel medical requirements for participation in the clandestine drug laboratory program. The guidelines also include sample forms such as contamination reports, uniform hazardous waste manifests for transporting hazardous waste, and additional information that may be used to develop state or local clandestine drug laboratory cleanup programs.

Requests for copies of the guidelines should be addressed to: Drug Enforcement Administration, Office of Forensic Sciences, Hazardous Waste Disposal Unit (AFSH), Washington, D.C. 20537.

Summary

As a result of increasing clandestine manufacturing, the major illicit drug trafficker and manufacturer of the late 1980s and 1990s is far different from his counterparts of the 1960s and 1970s. Today's drug trafficker is much more clever, greedy, ruthless, violent, and dangerous. Drug trafficking and the illegal manufacturing of narcotics and dangerous drugs has become a multi-million dollar business. Stakes are high. A trafficker could invest 2 to 5 million dollars in a deal and make a profit of 25 million dollars.

When Congress passed the Racketeer Influence Corrupt Organization (RICO) and Continuing Criminal Enterprises (CCE) statutes, the stakes in the war on drugs rose even higher. Drug traffickers have taken severe steps to protect their assets from law enforcement and from each other. With asset forfeiture, traffickers have become acutely aware that if they get arrested by narcotics agents, then they stand to lose much of what they have.

Many narcotics agents have been killed. Even juvenile drug dealers have become more violent nationwide. Thus, a well-educated and well-trained officer will be best prepared to deal with the changing drug world.

POLICE WORK AND AIDS

INTRODUCTION

The first cases of AIDS (Acquired Immunodeficiency Syndrome) were diagnosed in 1981. No one knows how many people are HIV (Human Immunodeficiency Virus) positive or how many have the full-blown AIDS disease. Nonetheless, one in twenty-five people in San Francisco, California is now infected with the HIV virus that causes AIDS. The international numbers are estimated to be in the millions. Much of the attention given to AIDS has assumed that it is a disease that primarily affects IV drug users and homosexuals. This is no longer true. AIDS is most commonly transmitted through heterosexual contact—sexual intercourse between man and woman—and this is its main method of transmission throughout the world.

THE CHANGING FACE OF AIDS

As the AIDS epidemic approaches its second decade, Americans are hearing less about it, so they may assume that the worst is over. However, both the number of new patients infected with HIV (the virus that causes the AIDS disease) and the number of full-blown cases of the disease are expected to continue rising sharply for at least the next few years in the U.S. and worldwide. This is true even though there is at least one drug, AZT, that may slow the progression of the HIV infection. It is even true considering the medications available to treat certain opportunistic diseases to which people with AIDS are susceptible. The Center for Disease Control (CDC) estimates that a million Americans are infected with HIV, most of them with no symptoms and no knowledge that they are carriers. Another 7 to 9 million people around the world are also infected, according to estimates by the World Health Organization (WHO). As of the end of 1990, more than 150,000

Americans have been diagnosed with AIDS, and two-thirds of them have died. The CDC estimates that by the end of 1993 there will have been between 390,000 and 480,000 Americans diagnosed with AIDS and between 285,000 and 340,000 deaths from the disease.

"The disease is becoming a generalized fact of American life, rather than the burden of well-defined risk groups," according to the National Research Council. In particular, heterosexual transmission (not via intravenous drug needles) is on the rise: though it still accounts for a relatively small percentage of cases in the U.S., such heterosexual transmission is the predominate mode of spread in most countries. Among American heterosexuals, sexual partners of IV drug users and people with multiple partners remain at greater risk. Here are some additional facts:

By the year 2000, there will be 25 to 30 million people infected with HIV internationally, according to projections by WHO.

AIDS is rising sharply among American women, especially poor African-Americans and Latinos. The death rate from AIDS among women aged 15 to 44 quadrupled between 1985 and 1988 and has undoubtedly continued to rise. By the year 2000, the number of new cases among women worldwide will begin to equal the number of newly diagnosed men, according to WHO estimates.

As of 1990, about 700,000 infected infants had been born worldwide. Approximately 10 million infected infants will have been born by the year 2000, according to WHO. And there will be millions of uninfected orphans whose parents died from AIDS. About 6,000 infected American women gave birth in 1989 alone (and one-third of those babies born to HIV-positive mothers in the U.S. become infected).

AIDS is not just a disease of young people. Those over 50 account for about 10 percent of all cases in this country. AIDS-related symptoms are more likely to be misdiagnosed among these older people because doctors may assume that they are not at risk for the disease.

Some people complain that too much money is being spent on AIDS research and care, pointing out that many more people die from heart disease and cancer. While more money should indeed by spent on research into heart disease and cancer, AIDS remains a priority because it is contagious and is one of the leading causes of death among young people. Moreover, the comparison between these diseases is not valid, since AIDS research is starting from scratch, whereas much of the basic research into heart disease and cancer has been continuing for decades. Furthermore, the information scientists are gaining from their studies into AIDS has important implications for research involving cancer and other diseases.

Researchers have discovered that it takes 12 to 15 weeks to develop the HIV antibody. During that time the only symptom might be a minor case of the flu which might go away. You will at that point be an infected carrier of the HIV virus, but may not be sick. People are highly infectious at this time. It may take several months or several years, but gradually you will have a reduced natural immunity and then you will start getting generalized symptoms which include swollen glands, night sweats, fevers, and weight loss. Then toward the end of the disease or when the disease is diagnosed, you will develop a progressive neurological disorder. Eventually, you will die; it is only a matter of how long your immune system can last, how much treatment you get, and how you are treated. This is true because the more illnesses you get, the less likely are your chances of longevity and survival.

The virus lives in very small amounts of saliva. If somebody was to bite you but not break the skin it is fairly clear that you would not get the disease; it would be very rare. But if the person had blood in their mouth mixed in with the saliva and broke the skin of the individual, there would be a distinct possibility of transmission. This scenario happened in New Jersey when a prisoner bit a corrections officer and the prisoner was sentenced for attempted murder. The case is now under appeal.

As for "safe" bodily fluids, tears may be considered among them. Also, urine is not of concern but if the person was kicked in the groin or received a seat belt injury in a motor vehicle accident there could be particles of blood in the urine, so infection control would be very prudent for this body fluid. For feces, the same holds true. Feces by itself does not harbor the virus as we know it today, but then again we do not know exactly what is going on in the individual's system, whether the person has hemorrhoids, bleeding somewhere in the body or has something causing blood in the feces. Furthermore, hepatitis lives in all these body fluids.

Hepatitis throughout the United States each year infects 12,000 hospital care workers of which 200 hundred die. Thus, there is a sustained risk in being unprotected and also getting involved with other people's bodily fluids. Whether it be AIDS, hepatitis or whatever, precaution is the key word. The virus is transmitted by these four other body fluids: blood, semen, vaginal secretions, and breast milk. A woman could deliver a baby HIV free, but later on during breast feeding, the baby could pick up the virus from breast milk. Any body fluid that is in the body, be it cerebral spinal fluid, cinoval fluid, or the fluid around the heart, is also a highly contaminated fluid if the person is HIV positive. So again, the rule of thumb is anytime you are doing anything with any individual and there are any body fluids, take full precautions.

Among the common AIDS-related illnesses is a type of skin cancer which is mostly found in gay males. Keep your eyes open for any signs of this illness. Also, pneumonia is common in AIDS patients. This is usually the illness that takes the patient out; the patient may have several bouts or she might have one bout which becomes fatal. Furthermore, tuberculosis is coming back in the United States in epidemic proportions and is directly related to cases of AIDS—especially in New Jersey. Another possible illness is a yeast infection in the mouth, thrush, or trachea. This will not be life-threatening but it is very uncomfortable for the person with the disease and also a sign that they have cancer on the roof of the mouth and need extensive dental treatment.

The chronic symptoms of the AIDS disease are swollen glands in three places: under the neck, under the arm pits, and in the groin. The patient will also experience unexplained weight loss—called a "slim disease" in many parts of the world. There will be chronic and persistent fever and diarrhea for a month or more, resulting in the huge amount of body fluids lost. The most important symptoms for the field officer to remember are fatigue, night sweats, and yeast infections in the mouth and throat. If you were to arrest a person with dementia you may think that he or she is under the influence of alcohol or drugs. The person may not be able to understand you if you are giving commands such as "turn around and put your hands behind your head". The person may not understand why you are hand cuffing them; they might be agitated; they may experience memory loss. Remember that AIDS is a neurological impairment; therefore, it should be distinguished from intoxication or chemical impairment. Try to make this distinction when you are following arrest procedures. The disease is mainly a sexually transmitted disease whether it be between male and female, male and male, or female and female.

If, as a police officer, you are called to deliver a child or to assist in delivery, remember that the amnionic fluids and the fluids on the baby from the placenta may be infected with the HIV virus. You would not want to get this in your eyes, in your face—especially near your nose where there are a lot of surface blood vessels—in your mouth, or on unprotected skin that may have a small cut. Also exercise precautions with food—especially around prisoners. There was an incident in New Jersey where a prisoner bled into an officer's coffee while the officer left the room and the officer came back and drank the coffee; the prisoner then said he gave the officer AIDS. Of course, the heat of the coffee killed the AIDS virus because the AIDS virus is very fragile and it dies from heat immediately. But still the officer went through a so-called "health period" until he was to find out the individual did not have the disease. Thus, you should be wary of food stuff around prisoners and eat where you believe your food will be free from contamination. Despite these precautions, when dealing with prisoners or responding to calls, treat everybody the same regardless of their sex, race, social, or economic status. There should be no difference because you don't know who has the disease and who doesn't.

It might be noted here that one other concern among officers is for their K-9 dogs. It may be thought that K-9 dogs can get AIDS from biting someone with the disease. However, animals cannot get human AIDS and cannot transmit it to one another or to human beings.

INFECTION CONTROL PROCEDURES

Given the many concerns of interpersonal activity and the spread of AIDS, the Center for Disease Control (CDC) has promulgated guidelines for the prevention of HIV transmission in the workplace. These guidelines are relevant to police officers and narcotic officers. Police officers should follow these control procedures.

- — avoid needle sticks and other sharp instrument injuries;
- — hypodermic needles should be placed in an impervious bag, tagged and marked for evidence;
- — use a mask when administering rescue breathing or CPR;
- — wear gloves when contact with blood or body fluids is likely;
- — use disposable shoe coverings if considerable blood contamination is encountered;
- — keep all cuts and open wounds covered with clean bandages;

- — avoid smoking, eating, drinking, nailbiting, and all hand-to-mouth, hand-to-nose, and hand-to-eye actions while working in areas contaminated with blood or bodily fluids;
- — wash hands thoroughly with soap and water after removing gloves and after any contact with blood or bodily fluids;
- — clean up any spills of blood or bodily fluids thoroughly and promptly, using a 1:10 household bleach dilution;
- — clean all possible contaminated surfaces and areas with a 1:10 household bleach dilution; and
- — place all possibly contaminated clothing and other items in clearly identified impervious plastic bags.

SEARCHES AND EVIDENCE HANDLING

Although the risk of HIV infection from being cut or punctured by contaiminated needles or other sharp instruments appears to be very low, many criminal justice personnel are concerned about such incidents. Cuts, needlesticks, and puncture wounds might be sustained by officers while searching suspects, motor vehicles, or cells, or while handling evidence in a variety of settings. There is particular concern regarding searches of areas where sharp objects may be hidden from view—such as pockets and spaces beneath car seats. The following precautionary measures will help to minimize the risk of infection:

- — whenever possible, ask suspects to empty their own pockets;
- — whenever possible, use longhandled mirrors to search hidden areas;
- — if it is necessary to search manually, always wear protective gloves and feel very slowly and carefully;
- — use puncture-proof containers to store sharp instruments and clearly marked plastic bags to store other possibly contaminated items; and
- — use tape—never metal staples—when packaging evidence.

Rubber gloves are currently the only type of gloves suitable for conducting searches. Although they can provide some protection against sharp instruments, rubber gloves are not, however, puncture-proof. Moreover, there is a direct tradeoff between levels of protection and manipulability. In other words, the thicker the gloves, the more protection they provide, but the less effective they are in locating objects. Agencies should select the thickness of glove which provides the best balance of protection and search efficiency.

ORANGE COUNTY PROGRAM

With regard to the issue of puncture wounds and bodily fluids received by police officers, a program has been developed by Orange County, California that originally came from San Francisco and is also being used in New Jersey. In some cases of receiving wounds or fluids, it is known that the person has AIDS. Yet, in other cases—such as an abrupt physical confrontation—the person takes off and is unidentified. In these cases, because of confidentiality laws in some states, you cannot get the suspect tested for AIDS. In response to these cases, the Orange County program has been established; it offers the police officer the drug AZT or Retrovau for 40 days. In this 40 day period, the AIDS virus will not replicate and the person will be so-called "free" of the disease. This treatment is, essentially, chemotherapy. It should also be noted that the AZT is fully experimental even though it has been accepted by the FDA for treatment of people with AIDS. It causes a lot of side effects such as anemia, upset stomach, and nausea; but, luckily, officers who undertake this treament will only experience these effects for 40 days.

Given the lethality of AIDS, exposure to HIV or AIDS produces great mental stress for the officer and his or her family. It affects the officer's career and family directly. Thus, it might be reminded that the illness caused by AZT is very small in comparison to the mental stress and possible infection of the AIDS virus.

Since a cure for AIDS is not likely to be developed for some time, police officers must take utmost precaution when they are in the field or on the street. It is important for an officer to understand the basics of infection control—putting barriers between your skin and someone else's as well as washing thoroughly. To protect ourselves, we have to go back to the basics and practice infection control at all times—especially since we are among the public on a regular basis.

REFERENCES:

Bigbee, David. "The Collection and Handling of Evidence Infected with Human Disease Causing Organisms." *FBI Law Enforcement Bulletin.* July 1987.

Blair, Monte, Director. "AIDS Education for Emergency Workers Project." American Red Cross, Sacramento Area Chapter.

Chubin, Dale E. and Vincent J. O'Connor. "State of Alaska Canine Unit Report." Rptd. in *The Narc Officer.* New York, April 1989, p. 41.

Cohen, Herb. *You Can Negotiate Anything.*

Garcia, Juan. "America's Best Friend." Rptd. in *The Narc Officer.* New York, April 1989, pp. 37-39.

Gruetter, Robert. "U.S. Customs Service Canine Enforcement Program." Rptd. in *The Narc Officer.* New York, April 1989, pp. 31-33.

Hammett, Theodore M. "AIDS and the Law Enforcement Officer: Concerns and Policy Responses." National Institute of Justice, 1987.

________. "Precautionary Measures and Protective Equipment: Developing a Reasonable Response." National Institute of Justice. *AIDS Bulletin.* U.S. Department of Justice, February 1988. NCJ 108619.

Hicks, Jerry. "In War on Drugs, It's Winston by a Nose." Rptd. in *Narcotic Officer,* publication of the California Narcotic Officers Association, Santa Clarita, CA, 1988, pp. 91-97.

International Narcotic Enforcement Officers Association. *International Drug Report.* Vol. 33, No. 6, ISS 0148-4648, June 1992.

________. "Undercover Investigators: A New Employer Drug War Tool." *International Drug Report.* January 1990.

Jarlais, Don Des. "AIDS and Intravenous Drug Use." National Institute of Justice *AIDS Bulletin*. U.S. Department of Justice, February 1988, NCJ 108620.

Lazlo, Anna T. "Clandestine Drug Laboratories: Confronting a Growing National Crisis." *The National Sheriff.* August-September 1989, pp. 9-44.

Lewis, Arthur B. "Canada Customs Detector Dog Services." Rptd. in *The Narc Officer.* New York, April 1989, p. 23.

National Institute on Drug Abuse. "AIDS and the Law Enforcement Officer." November-December 1987, NCJ 107541.

Peace Officers Research Association of California. *PORAC Law Enforcement News*. Vol. 24, No. 2, February 1992.

Rochan, G. "Canada Customs Drug Interdiction Program." Rptd. in *The Narc Officer.* New York, April 1989, pp. 25-29.

Smith, Richard M. "The Drug Crisis." *Newsweek*, June 16, 1986, p. 15.

U.S. Department of Health and Human Services, Public Health Service, Center for Disease Control. "Guidelines for Prevention of Transmission of Human Immunodeficiency Virus and Hepatitis B Virus to Health-care and Public Safety Workers: A Response to P.L. 100-670, The Health Omnibus Program Extension Act of 1988." Atlanta, GA, February 1989.

U.S. Department of Justice, Drug Enforcement Administration. *Narcotic Investigators Manual*. p. 99.

________. National Institute of Justice, Research in Action. "Help You Respond to the AIDS Challenge." August 1988.

________. National Institute of Justice. "AIDS Training and Education in Criminal Justice Agencies." *AIDS Bulletin*, 1987.

________. National Institute of Justice. "Risk of Infection With the AIDS Virus Through Exposures to Blood." *AIDS Bulletin*, October 1987.

________. Office of the Attorney General. "Drug Trafficking: A Report to the President of the United States." Washington, D.C., August 3, 1989.

For more information about AIDS:

The U.S. Public Health Service operates the National AIDS Hotline 24 hours a day, 7 days a week. Call 1-800-342-AIDS.

This page intentionally left blank.

CHAPTER XVII

DRUG TRAFFICKING, TERRORISM AND ORGANIZED CRIME

PATTERNS OF ORGANIZED CRIME

There is no single drug problem; rather, there are several separate drug problems, each interacting with and affecting the others. Similarly, there is no single pattern in the structure and operation of drug trafficking organizations. These organizations vary widely in size, sophistication, area of operation, clientele, and product. They have differing degrees of vertical and horizontal integration, differing propensities to violence, and differing patterns of interaction with other organizations.

On the other hand, drug trafficking organizations share the obvious characteristic that they are all engaged in some way in illicit activity; therefore, they do not have access to and are not subject to the normal channels of production, distribution, sales, finance, taxation, regulation, and contract enforcement that mold and shape both the playing field and the players in the legitimate world of commerce. However, these "businesses" are subject to the same economic laws of supply and demand, the same need for efficiency in operation, and the same need for a set of rules by which to operate as are other business operations.

Thus, drug traffickers must operate outside of the normal financial and legal structures of commerce while simultaneously remaining subject to all the market and social pressures which that structure normally accommodates and ameliorates. Understanding this dichotomy is one of the keys to understanding the nature of drug trafficking organizations. They must re-create the structures of the legitimate world of commerce—which they do with astonishing fidelity—yet they are skewed by the constraints and imperatives of the illicit nature of their activities.

On the one hand, large, well-established drug trafficking organizations may have a board of directors, a CEO, and a bureaucracy that are disciplined and whose functions and benefits mirror those of executives and middle-level management in a modern corporation, complete with expenses accounts, bonuses, and even "company" cars. On the other hand, the normal commercial concept of contracts, in which disputes are adjudicated by an impartial judiciary and restitution is almost always of a financial nature, is twisted into a system where the rule of law is replaced by the threat of violence and retribution. The very word "contract" is often used by drug trafficking organizations as a synonym for "death sentence."

Although there is no single type of organizational structure that serves to define major drug trafficking organizations, there are a few well-defined patterns. There are the major international, vertically integrated trafficking groups, best exemplified by the Colombian cartels. There are also groups such as the outlaw motorcycle gangs, which operate domestically and tend to have smaller, less sophisticated operations: lines of supply are shorter, bank accounts are fewer, and the quantities of drugs transported are not as great. Then there are city-based drug operations such as the California street gangs, which have even less sophisticated organizational structures at the management end, but which have extensive sales networks of low-level operatives, many of whom work directly on the street and who are primarily involved in local distribution and the retail sale aspect of trafficking.

A feature common to many of the largest organizations is an ability to tap alternative sources of supply and to adapt readily to changing conditions. Thus, the Colombian cartels can buy their coca leaf or paste in Peru, Bolivia, Ecuador, or in Colombia itself. When Turkish authorities clamped down on the illicit cultivation of opium-producing poppies, drug organizations shifted productions to the Golden Triangle region of Southeast Asia and to the mountainous regions on both sides of the Afganistan-Pakistan border. This flexibility enables the major traffickers to regroup and to redirect a part of their operations without disrupting the whole.

In certain ways, the Colombian cartels are on the cutting edge of international technology. They are capable of operating easily across international borders, and the fluidity of their structures results in the ability to form joint ventures and transient limited partnership arrangements among themselves and with other groups for specific goals.

The broader organizations, like large legitimate businesses, have grown so large because they are good at what they do. They usually do not make careless errors; they do not take unnecessary risks. Moreover, their leaders are well aware of the advantages of insulating themselves and the upper echelons of their organizations from those who actually carry out the risk-taking activities involved in the enterprise.

The predilection for dealing in cash and for getting that cash into the legitimate economy so that it can be translated into legitimate goods and services is a characteristic that pervades the organized drug trafficking world—whatever the size, area of operation, or structure of the organization. This propensity creates problems for drug traffickers, problems that become increasingly hard to deal with as the organization grows. The need to "launder" large amounts of "dirty" money is the Achilles heel of most large drug trafficking organizations.

There is so much cash involved in large, illicit drug trafficking operations that tracking the proceeds of such activities is often a more fruitful investigative endeavor than tracking the underlying criminal activities. Their ill-gotten wealth is the one part of their activity from which even the most cautious of drug kingpins will probably not isolate themselves. It is often through the tracking of their attempts to "launder" cash that the highest-level operatives in these organizations are identified and brought to final justice. In fact, monetary operations are such an overriding concern of drug trafficking organizations that an entire section of this chapter is devoted to exploring the mechanisms attendant to this aspect of the drug trafficking world.

PRINCIPAL DRUG TRAFFICKING ORGANIZATIONS

COLOMBIAN DRUG CARTELS

The Colombian drug cartels are prime examples of the large, international, vertically-integrated trafficking groups. The major elements of this type of organization are present in the Colombian cartels. They are structured in what can be characterized as an onion-like layering of organizational power, with kingpins at the center, directing operations but insulated by layer upon layer of protective subordinate operatives, until one reaches the outside layer, the skin of the organization. Here are found the individuals who deal directly with the production, supply, and sale of the illicit product: the growers, the smugglers, the small-time distributors, and the street pushers. Nurturing and tending this structure are the providers of services: the accountants, the chemists, the lawyers, the paid politicians, and the corrupt customs officials who help to support the organization and who gain sustenance from it while never fully comprehending its entire scope or true nature. Here, the operatives' services are blindly given and easily replaced.

There are four principal cartels operating out of Colombia. The two largest, the Medellin and the Cali cartels, most closely approximate the model sketched above. These cartels are named after, respectively, Colombia's second and third largest cities, in which they are based. Between them they control approximately 70 percent of the cocaine processed in Colombia and supply 80 percent of the cocaine distributed in the United States. These cartels act as true cartels in the classic sense that they attempt, through collusion, to set prices and to eliminate any effective competition.

The Colombian cartels not only attempt to limit competition by making agreements to divide market segments, they also use wealth and force to corrupt and intimidate those government officials and law enforcement agencies charged with the tasks of shutting down their operations and bringing their members to justice. In Colombia, these coercive tactics have been widely used. When public officials cannot be bought, they are subjected to threats of violence. If this does not work, they are often assassinated. This intimidation is not restricted to government personnel. Business and community leaders, journalists, and anyone else who might pose a threat to their operations are subject to either the lure of corruption or the threat of violence.

Evidently, these tactics have been successful in Colombia, where the cartels are becoming more accepted and their employees, among the more well-paid in the society, are vesting themselves with the trappings of middle-class life. Cartel chiefs control most of the modern office buildings in the city of Medellin and many of the retail establishments in the El Poblado section, where most of them live.

The Medellin cartel is generally thought to be the strongest of the Colombian cartels. It was formed in the early 1980s by four major Colombian traffickers: Jorge Luis Ochoa-Vasquez, Pablo Emilio Escobar-Gaviria, Jose Gonzalo Rodriguez-Gacha, and Carlos Enrique Lehder-Rivas. Part of the impetus for the formation of this organization was the need to combat kidnapping gangs who had targeted the families of wealthy Colombian drug traffickers and businessmen.

Today, the Medellin cartel's operations are directed by Pablo Emilio Escobar-Gaviria, his cousin Gustavo de Jesus Gaviria-Rivero, and by Jorge Luis Ochoa-Vasquez and Jose Gonzalo Rodriguez-Gacha. Among the cartels, the Medellin cartel has the most sophisticated organization. There are close ties to Colombian business interests and strong "home-office" control over overseas operations. Regular fax transmission links are maintained, and managers are sent, on a rotating basis, to supervise operations in the United States.

Jose Rodriquez, who operates out of the city of Pacho, about 80 miles from Medellin, has emerged as, perhaps, the most powerful of the Medellin cartel leaders. This development was, no doubt, facilitated by the apprehension and eventual conviction, in June 1988, of one of the cartels' other founders, Carlos Ledher. He was convicted of charges brought in the Middle District of Florida and sentenced to life imprisonment with no chance of parole.

Jose Rodriguez's organization differs slightly from those of his colleagues in the Medellin cartel. He maintains direct supervision of his transportation and distribution networks. He has representatives in south Florida and southern California who are in charge of receiving, inventory control, accounts receivable, and general organizational support. Unlike the representatives of the Pablo Escobar group, who work on commission, Rodriguez's U.S. representatives work on straight salary. They work regular business hours, wear suits and ties, and are instructed to keep a low profile.

Of the three other major Colombian organizations, the Cali cartel, begun in the late 1970s and early 1980s, comes closest to rivaling the Medellin cartel in wealth and influence. The Cali cartel works outs of the Colombian cities of Cali and Buenaventura and once worked closely with the Medellin cartel, dividing up trading areas and engaging in joint operations. This close working relationship has deteriorated to the point where, since 1988, the Medellin and Cali cartels have been engaged in a vicious trade war with one another, as well as with other cocaine trafficking organizations. For instance, a tacit agreement of 10 years standing, giving the bulk of the New York City cocaine trafficking distribution to the Cali cartel, was breached, as tons of cocaine were shipped directly into that market by the Medellin organization. In other areas, such as Miami, which has always been considered an open trading area, the two organizations have jockeyed violently for a more prominent position. The Cali cartel has recently formed alliances with the North Atlantic Coast cartel and, within the United States, is moving beyond its traditional bases in New York, Miami, and Los Angeles.

In contrast, the Bogota cartel has kept a much lower profile than the two major cartels described above. This organization seems to have been adept at buying police protection in Colombia. Originally a smuggling organization dealing in a wide variety of contraband, it entered the drug trafficking world through contacts with American criminal organizations—notably those connected with Miami—and Caribbean associates of the notorious Meyer Lansky group. By networking, leaders of the Bogota cartel have taken pains to become well-connected politically in Colombia. They have used their wealth to buy land and have set up processing plants near growing areas in eastern Colombia in an attempt to become more vertically integrated.

The North Atlantic Coast cartel is the smallest and least cohesive of the four major Colombian trafficking organizations. It is based mainly, as its name suggests, in Colombia's coastal cities—notably Cartagena, Barranquilla, Santa Marta, and Rio Hacha. Like the Bogota cartel, it was originally a smuggling organization. It graduated from marijuana to cocaine when it began providing fixed-fee shipping services to the Medellin and Bogota cartels. Operations were established in Miami, Jacksonville, Gainesville, Atlanta, New York, Boston, Los Angeles, and San Diego to support the cartels' efforts. Today, a major portion of the North Atlantic Coast cartel's activity is centered around providing smuggling and money laundering services for the other cartels.

All of these cartel operations working in the United States have been characterized by a propensity for violence that has not been seen in the American underworld since the bootleg days of Prohibition in the 1920s and early 1930s. As in their home bases in Colombia, the cartels have attempted to use their wealth and powers of intimidation as leverage to corrupt and intimidate American law enforcement personnel, public officials, and members of the financial and business community whose cooperation or complicity would expedite the illicit activities of the cartels. Likewise, the cartels have not been loath to back up their threats of violence with action. They have murdered informers and government witnesses, put out "contracts" on law enforcement personnel, and engaged in violent wars for "territory," which have produced record homicide rates in American cities from Washington, D.C. to San Diego, California.

By corrupting public officials in such places as the Bahamas, the Turks and Caicos Islands, and Panama, the cartels have been able, over the years, to develop a network of "safe haven" transshipment points. Using these points as stopover and staging areas, the Colombians found it relatively easy to transport drugs into the Southern District of Florida, sometimes using island hopping to disguise their activities and sometimes simply blending into the steady stream of legitimate traffic between the Florida coast and points south.

In the most notorious case of third country complicity in the Colombian drug traffic into the United States, Panamanian strongman Manuel Antonio Noriega was indicted for accepting payoffs from the Medellin cartel. It is alleged that Noriega provided services to the cartel that ran from protecting a cocaine laboratory that the cartel was building in Panama, to arranging for the transshipment of intermediate chemicals needed to process cocaine, to permitting the laundering of millions of dollars through Panamanian banks.

Over the past decade, the cartels have found first the Southern District of Florida, and then the Central and Southern Districts of California, to be ideal areas in which to center their U.S. operations. These regions of the United States contain a combination of large metropolitan areas and close-by, relatively isolated rural areas with convenient landing strips. They also have long, hard-to-patrol coastlines or border areas, large transportation hubs, populations containing large numbers of transients and immigrants, a well-developed system of international banking and financial institutions, and access to sophisticated communications systems. This combination of elements has proven extremely advantageous to the cartels' operations.

In the early 1980s, for example, Florida became the point at which all cocaine trafficking roads converged. It became the cocaine capital of the United States. Miami, although a market for some of these drugs, was and is primarily a transshipment point to all areas of the United States. It also remains a banking center through which flow huge amounts of cash derived from illicit drug sales.

In the mid-1980s, as law enforcement pressure on drug traffic in south Florida grew, the cartels began to shift their transshipments through Mexico. From there, drugs could easily be transported across the border into California. Los Angeles and San Diego began to rival Miami as centers for distributing cocaine and for laundering the proceeds.

As this brief discussion indicates, the operations of the Colombian cartels, from the fields of coca cultivation in South America to the final sale of crack cocaine on a street corner in Des Moines or a schoolyard in Hartford, represent a massive production, distribution, and sales effort carried out over thousands of miles, using the nationals of various countries, the resources of several separate, coordinated organizations, and the expertise of hundreds of specialists in all aspects of drug trafficking.

This broad network allows trafficking activities to be widespread throughout the United States. The Colombian organizations operate in almost all sectors of the country, with many large urban areas serving as battlegrounds for drug wars between operatives of rival factions. Yet, even though their activities are concentrated in urban areas, they have spread to rural areas as well.

New York City has long been a central point of Colombian-dominated cocaine trafficking. This activity has been shown to extend to the Northern District of New York, to towns such as Minden, Flycreek, Fallsburgh, Coxsackie, Newburg, and Little Falls, where cocaine processing plants have been shut down by authorities. The processing plant in Minden was, purportedly, the largest in existence in North America. All of these factories had been run by a joint venture of the Medellin and Cali cartels. Furthermore, individuals tied directly to the Colombian cartels have been convicted in Minnesota in cases involving the transport of drugs through networks based in New York. Even in Massachusetts, a Colombian-controlled organization, the Triple X group, was operated out of Framingham by a Colombian national. This organization had a client list of hundreds and kept meticulous accountings of its activities. It was run like a business, with workers in the organization receiving "company benefits" such as regular vacations.[1]

As would be expected, the widespread success of Colombian cartels in the United States has led to massive needs for money laundering services. Thus, the Medellin cartel has affiliated itself with two groups in the State of Connecticut that provide them with money laundering services for their cocaine operations in New York City, Newark, Miami, Detroit, Chicago, Los Angeles, and San Francisco.

---

[1]International Narcotic Enforcement Officers Association. *International Drug Report.* Albany, N.Y. Vol. 33, No. 6, ISS 0148-4648, June 1992.

LA COSA NOSTRA AND THE SICILIAN MAFIA

La Cosa Nostra (LCN), literally "Our Thing," was founded in the 1930s. It was an out-growth of the consolidation that occurred during a period of warfare among Italian immigrant gangs operating in the ghettos created by a flood of over two million Italian immigrants in the early years of the century. The gangs were originally formed by the small number of immigrant criminals who belonged to the three major southern Italian secret societies—the Sicilian Mafia, the Neapolitan Camorra, and the Calabrian N'Drangheta. LCN soon emerged as the preeminent American criminal empire, distinct from its Italian antecedents.

Today, the organization descendant from the original LCN consists of families that constitute formally recognized power structures within the organization. There are 25 known families, which among them have over 2,000 members and several times that many associates. The families are largely independent, local organizations joined together in a confederation that acknowledges the authority of a commission consisting of the heads of the most powerful LCN families.

Each family is led by a boss, who is supported by a principal underboss. Consiglieres or counselors, usually with significant contacts outside of the family, provide advice and mediate disputes but have no line of authority. Soldiers, the lowest-level family members, are organized into groups led by a caporegime (capo), or street boss. The structure of the various families is remarkably similar and has remained stable since LCN's early years.

Until the mid-1960s, LCN was run, on a day-to-day basis, by upper- and middle-level managers in the prime of life. Today, the seasoned upper- and middle-management level of this structure has been devastated by the government's continuous attack on LCN. The membership losses caused by this attack, and the resulting convictions, have presented LCN with a number of problems, including leadership vacancies and, as a result, operational difficulties. Within many families, a number of leaders at the caporegime level and above were simultaneously removed. This forced sudden promotions from lower, less experienced ranks, which, in turn, has led to a new breed of soldier who is greedier, who enjoys the high profile eschewed by the older capos, and who is less disciplined and more prone to violence. Because of their youth, the new middle-level leaders do not have the old, established lines of communication within the family or with other LCN families. Also, they are more willing to become involved in drug trafficking.[2]

From the outset, certain families have had prohibitions against drug trafficking. LCN has a tradition of not unnecessarily attracting the attention of law enforcement agencies, and older members were aware that drug trafficking would elicit a strong response from the law enforcement community. Older members also had a traditional distaste for drugs, which were considered a scourge and not a desirable LCN activity. A ban prohibiting

---

[2] President's Commission on Organized Crime. Report to the President and the Attorney General. "America's Habit: Drug Abuse, Drug Trafficking and Organized Crime." Washington, D.C.: U.S. Government Printing Office. March 1986.

involvement of LCN members in drug trafficking was allegedly ratified by the major LCN figures at a famous Apalachin, New York, conclave on November 14, 1957.

Despite this ban and the sentiment against involvement in drug trafficking among the older capos, individual LCN members have had a history of involvement with the importation and high-volume distribution of heroin from Southwest and Southeast Asia. Individuals found to be involved in drug violations have come from at least 19 of the 25 known families, despite official LCN opprobrium of drug trafficking.

A recent survey of LCN-related intelligence from the Boston FBI files indicates that, notwithstanding the family rule against involvement in drug activities, approximately 50 percent of New England LCN members have had some form of involvement in illegal drug trafficking or personal drug abuse. Observance of the prohibition is not widespread and is not enforced by the family hierarchy. Individual members and capos cannot resist the lucrative drug profits. The potential for tremendous wealth, when coupled with the changing LCN membership, has given rise to a new and potentially more violent role for the LCN in drug trafficking operations.

The most obvious drug trafficking partner for LCN is the Sicilian Mafia, which is independently active in the United States. Both groups associate and criminally interact in a number of areas of mutual interest. The Sicilian Mafia is primarily involved in international heroin trafficking and is associated with LCN in several locales, including Buffalo, Boston, New Jersey, Chicago, and Detroit.

In New York, the Sicilian Mafia conspired with LCN to import and distribute almost 4,000 pounds of heroin, and untold amounts of cocaine, over a 10-year period, realizing a 60-million-dollar profit. This famous case, popularly known as the "Pizza Connection" because many of the participants owned pizza parlors, resulted in the imprisonment of over 15 LCN/Sicilian Mafia kingpins for 20- to 45-year sentences.

Current estimates indicate that LCN and the Sicilian Mafia together are responsible for a significant portion of the total volume of heroin brought into the United States annually. Additionally, it has recently been reported that, with the assistance of LCN family members, the Sicilian Mafia is exchanging heroin for cocaine, as South American cocaine moves through the United States to Europe and heroin moves from the Middle East through Italy to the United States.

This middleman role in cocaine distribution has resulted in ties between individual LCN members and the Medellin cartel. These ad hoc relationships developed on the basis of a common desire to expand both their markets and their product lines. The relationships are generally initiated through introductions by mutual criminal associates. These relationships are rather tentative at first, but once trust has been established, extensive interaction results.

As LCN family members are involved in a broad array of criminal activities, it is realistic to expect them to further develop the avenues and methodologies to profit from the drug trade. They will not initiate direct confrontation with the Colombian or other major drug cartels. They are not in a position to, nor would they want to go head to head with the Colombians. They are, however, prepared to coexist and cooperate with the Colombian cartels and other drug-specific groups and organizations, as they have done for many years with the motorcycle gangs in the distribution of methamphetamine.

Although LCN maintains specific working relationships with certain other organized crime groups in order to fulfill its racketeering objectives, it is developing ties to South American drug trafficking cartels. The Gambino, Bufalino, and Bonanno families have strong ties to Colombian and Cuban drug cartels in the greater Miami area, providing these families with drugs for distribution in the United States. Individual LCN members work with Asian and Latin American organized crime groups and cartels that manufacture and smuggle narcotics. They also collaborate with ethnic street gangs and outlaw motorcycle gangs involved in high-risk, low-level distribution and street sales. Thus, the changing character of LCN membership and the potential profits to be realized continue to increase LCN's role in drug trafficking.

ASIAN ORGANIZED CRIME GROUPS

Within the past five years, Asian gangs have become a major force in the illicit drug market in the United States. Asian gangs, primarily of Chinese origin, are operating on both coasts and have become significant players in the international drug trafficking scene. As with some other ethnic groups, Chinese Organized Crime (COC) leaders in this country have used their ties with overseas criminal organizations to assure a regular supply of whatever commodity they wish to distribute—whether the commodity is Chinese video cassettes, prostitutes, or heroin.

Since the mid-1960s, three events have had an impact on the growth of Asian organized crime in this country: the liberalization of quotas for Asian immigrants in 1965; the abatement of the Vietnam War; and the agreement between the United Kingdom and the People's Republic of China under which Hong Kong will revert to the latter in 1997, after more than 150 years of colonial rule.

These events wrought profound changes within Asian American society. The first two transformed conservative, insular communities, while the third may have lead some of the most dangerous Hong Kong criminals to move their operations here. The Immigration and Naturalization Act of 1965 repealed restrictions on Asian immigration dating from the Chinese Exclusion Act of 1882. With the influx of immigrants from Southeast Asia, as the war in Vietnam drew to a close, the Asian American population increased dramatically. Between 1960 and 1980, the total number of Asian Americans grew from 878,000 to 3.5 million. By 1980, 91 percent of Vietnamese Americans, 66 percent of Filipino Americans, and 63 percent of Chinese Americans—but only 28 percent of Japanese Americans—had been born overseas. By then, Asian Americans had become the largest ethnic group among all immigrants in the United States.[3]

---

[3]U.S. Department of Justice. "Drug Trafficking: A Report to the President of the United States, Compiled by the United States Attorneys and the Attorney General of the United States." Washington, D.C. August 3, 1989, p. 24.

The increased immigration opened up the limited, rather circumscribed world of the older criminal groups. The new immigrants tended to be young; they knew little English and, like some immigrants before them, they were likely to see criminal organizations as the quickest road to advancement. In attempts to protect themselves from attacks by American-born Chinese, Chinese immigrant youth formed street gangs. Among the first were the Wah Ching in San Francisco and the Ghost Shadows in New York.

Including the street gangs, there are two primary classifications of Chinese Organized Crime groups operating in the United States today: American COC, and Triads. Hong Kong serves as the primary base of operations for the Triads. It is estimated that there are as many as 100,000 Triad members belonging to more than 50 Triads in Hong Kong. The major Triads are organized in five primary groups, the Wo Group and 14K being the largest. In Taiwan, the United Bamboo Gang boasts 1,200 members, and the Four Seasons Gang is 3,000 members strong.

The United Bamboo Gang has spread far beyond Taiwan in the 28 years since its founding. Today, the United Bamboo Gang has approximately 15,000 members worldwide. Charges filed in Houston and New York allege that Houston resident Chen Chih-Ye was the kingpin for United Bamboo in the United States. In that role he is alleged to have planned the murder of a California journalist, Henry Liu; conspired to import 660 pounds of heroin from Thailand to New York; and led Las Vegas gambling operations, protection schemes, and various gun and marijuana trafficking enterprises.

Traditionally, Triads have had rigid, hierarchical structures. At the apex of the organization is the Triad leader, the Shan Chu. Below the Shan Chu is the Deputy. Below the Deputy are two positions of comparable rank, the Heung Chu, the ceremonial officials, and the Sing Fung, who handles recruiting. They are joined by other senior Triad officials. Below this level are a number of "Red Poles," the enforcers and hit-men who have direct control of some operational Triad groups. At the same level as the Red Poles are a "White Paper Fan," the general administrative official, and a "Straw Sandal," who handles liaisons between and among the Triads and other groups. Ordinary members, or soldiers, comprise the remainder of the organization.

Currently, most Triads lack the traditional organizational structure. More are run by a chairman, who is usually a "Red Pole." There is also a governing central committee of six to nine members. A "White Paper Fan," as a member of the central committee, is usually the treasurer.

In its traditional origin, Chinese organized crime is similar to LCN. Like LCN, Chinese organized crime grew out of much older secret or fraternal societies which have evolved into criminal groups. The Triads originated in China during the 17th century to oppose the ruling Manchu dynasty. The organization then moved from political purposes into a variety of rackets. In the late 19th century, the Tongs (Chinese fraternal organizations) began as perfectly legitimate mutual aid societies for immigrants brought to the United States as contract railroad laborers. Today, while most American Tongs still serve legitimate business purposes, several are closely tied to organized crime.

Parallels between Chinese criminal organizations and the traditional LCN go even deeper than their historic connection to protective and fraternal societies. Both the Chinese groups and LCN place an unusually strong emphasis on family and group loyalty. They both practice retribution against those who reveal secrets to outsiders; their organizational structures are characterized by the same type of fragmentation into subgroups controlled by powerful leaders; and they have the same independence from their parent overseas organizations. Both the Chinese gangs and LCN practice the use of extortion and the corruption of public officials to promote their activities, and both gained their initial power and eminence through exploitation of large populations of non-English-speaking, innocent immigrants. Finally, both the Chinese groups and LCN have historically been involved in a broad range of criminal activities of which drug trafficking is but one part.

A much greater threat than that of the Triads is presented by the sophisticated criminal organizations that have evolved from the street gangs, for example, the Wah Ching, which is the most developed of such organizations on the West Coast. The Wah Ching's organization, with 600 to 700 members, 200 of whom are "hard-core," is extremely loose-knit and fluid. It has a central leader who is supported by four deputies under his normal control. Various deputies employ groups of Viet Ching (ethnic Chinese from Vietnam) to serve as enforcers under the direction of their lieutenants. It is believed that the Wah Ching are affiliated with the Sun Yee On Triad in Hong Kong.

In New York City, on the other hand, the street gangs are affiliated with the Tongs. The Tongs have a complex organizational structure. The organization includes co-presidents, executive officers, and a wide assortment of designated administrators and coordinators. This complex system allows for affiliations with various street gangs. For instance, the Flying Dragons Gang is affiliated with the Hip Sing Tong; the Ghost Shadows Gang is attached to the On Leong Tong; and the Tung On Gang and the Tung On Tong are both headed by the same person.

In Boston, the COC activity is dominated by the Ping On Gang, which is believed to have about 200 active members. However, the current internal functioning and degree of cohesiveness in this gang are matters of conjecture.

Since these gangs have grown, Chinese Organized Crime has expanded from Chinese gambling, extortion, pornography, and entertainment to include large-scale, international narcotics trafficking. While Chinese criminal organizations do not approach the scale of the Colombian cartels, the scope of their operations is impressive. Working with Asian nationals, Chinese American criminals are the largest importers of heroin from Southeast Asia, virtually all of it originating in the Golden Triangle at the juncture of Burma, Thailand, and Laos. The February 1989 seizure of more than 800 pounds of processed heroin in New York's Chinatown reveals the magnitude of this traffic.

Other reports from numerous areas on the East Coast underscore the growing prominence of Asian trafficking activities. Operation Bamboo Dragon in the District of Columbia (discussed later in this chapter) resulted in the arrest of 20 Asians in both the United States and Hong Kong for heroin trafficking. The Royal Hong Kong Police Narcotics Bureau described the operation as one of the most significant drug cases ever made there.

Likewise, in New York City, Chinese organizations are the dominant force in heroin trafficking, capable of smuggling loads of 10 to 50 kilograms into the city on a regular basis. In New Jersey, Chinese groups have become a major force in the importation and distribution of heroin at the highest levels. Chinese and other Southeast Asian trafficking organizations are also heavily involved in heroin trafficking in Massachusetts. In October 1988, Customs agents in Boston seized 180 pounds of heroin, the largest such seizure in New England history. The heroin had been carefully concealed in a piece of Chinese restaurant equipment—a bean sprout washer.[4]

Like the heroin seized in Boston, most of the heroin that originates in the Golden Triangle is shipped to the West Coast of the United States via Hong Kong and such secondary transit as Singapore, Seoul, Tokyo, and Taipei. The destination is New York; from there, about half the heroin moves to other East Coast cities. Thus, Chinese criminal organizations operate mainly as shippers and wholesalers: they buy the raw product; process it; arrange for its transshipment; and, finally, turn it over to retailers. From what is known, Chinese traffickers also work through other groups, especially LCN, who distribute the product to the ultimate user.

Although the Hong Kong Triads are involved in drug trafficking, their role cannot be categorized easily. Some of the ethnic Chinese who smuggle heroin out of the Golden Triangle, and others who ship it to New York, are not affiliated with the Triads. Traffickers may be entrepreneurs who work with organizational crime groups on specific ventures, while in other cases drug trafficking is simply a means of transferring assets from Hong Kong to the United States.

To some extent, the magnitude of Chinese drug trafficking is reflected in the amount of money flowing out of Hong Kong to U.S. banks, especially those on the West Coast. However, much of this money simply represents assets that Chinese business people want to transfer to a safe haven before Hong Kong reverts to the People's Republic of China. By merely measuring the volume of foreign money entering the United States, we fail to distinguish between legitimate asset transfers and the laundering of drug money. The important point is that there is a huge and growing inflow of money from Hong Kong, primarily to banks in San Francisco, Los Angeles, and New York. This provides a wide stream in which laundered drug money inconspicuously flows. Some of these funds flow into large American commercial banks, with the rest going into some 100 Chinese-owned and operated banks. Most of these are small and cater exclusively to a Chinese American clientele; at some banks, tellers are assigned to service one or two accounts exclusively.

Traffickers in Hong Kong, Taipei, and Singapore can send funds by wire transfer or letters of credit to banks in southern California, knowing that such transfers trigger no reporting requirements. Where such electronic

---

[4]*Ibid.*, p. 26.

transfers are impracticable, drug dealers can use Smurfs (see section on Money Laundering) to make several daily deposits under the $10,000 reporting limit. As with other regions, these transfers of drug money lead to huge surpluses at regional Federal Reserve banks. As of May 1989, the Los Angeles branch of the Federal Reserve had accumulated surpluses of approximately $4 billion.[5]

Compared to Colombian drug profits, more Asian-based drug money is invested in real estate than in personal property. An investigation centered in the Northern District of California positively identified one drug asset-related real estate empire. Numerous Hong Kong corporations, such as Dragonet, Ltd., and Tradewise Far East, Ltd., were found to be conducting no business in the United States other than holding title to real estate. In three instances, expensive properties held by these corporations had major drug dealers as residents. Subsequent grand jury investigations resulted in extensive seizures, numerous indictments, and, predictably, several fugitive warrants. Criminal organizations based in Asia are also investing heavily in shopping centers, apartment complexes, and office buildings. The result has been to drive up real estate prices, especially in those areas with large Asian American populations. Chinese American criminals, on the other hand, prefer investing in businesses where most transactions are based on cash: nightclubs, restaurants, travel agencies, and jewelry stores. The advantage of owning such businesses is that, besides serving as fronts for criminal activities, they are ideal for co-mingling legal and illegal funds in a way that avoids detection.

There is much that law enforcement organizations have to learn about Asian organized crime; only recently have they begun to give the problem the attention it deserves. The lack of agents with the background to infiltrate the Asian criminal organizations means that much about their operations remains unclear. It is clear, however, that the larger gangs—the Wah Ching on the West Coast, several New York gangs dominated by Tongs, and the Boston Ping On Gang—are powerful and sophisticated criminal organizations.

JAMAICAN POSSES

Approximately 40 Jamaican organized crime gangs, known as posses, operate in the United States, Canada, Great Britain, and the Caribbean. The combined membership of these gangs is conservatively estimated to number over 10,000, the majority of them convicted felons, illegal aliens, or both. Many of the mid- to high-level positions in the posse organizations are held by individuals who began their criminal careers in Jamaica and who are fugitives from justice there. The low-level positions in the posses are often filled by Americans, recruited primarily from black urban areas. Generally, these gangs grew out of specific geographic and political affiliations in Jamaica, but have long since become exclusively profit-oriented drug trafficking organizations.

---

[5] *Ibid.*, p. 27

The Jamaican posses, which began as marijuana traffickers, have been active in the United States since about 1984, but have only recently been recognized as a major drug trafficking force. They are, perhaps, the ultimate example of stepping up to dealing lethal drugs, most notably crack cocaine. Almost all posses have connections in New York and Miami, which have large Jamaican populations.

The Jamaicans' operations are structured in a distinctive manner. For example, even more than the Colombians, the posses are vertically integrated in the U.S. The operators are involved in the United States as importers, wholesalers, local distributors, retailers, and even money launderers. By excluding the middleman, the posses can substantially raise their profit margins, to the point where one posse controlling 50 crack houses can make $9 million a month.

They normally purchase cocaine from Colombians or Cubans in Jamaica, the Bahamas, southern California, or southern Florida—usually in small quantities of four or five kilos. Also, recent investigations show that Jamaican criminal groups are establishing new drug shipment routes distinct from Miami, the traditional entry point.

There are indications that Jamaicans have been entering the United States by wading across the Rio Grande into Texas and that these groups may be linked to Colombian drug suppliers arrested in the Houston area. In one instance, 15 Haitian and Jamaican aliens had arranged to be smuggled from Belize to Juarez, Mexico; from there, they would enter the United States with the help of a Jamaican involved in drug trafficking.

Distribution of the drugs is directed by key posse members at "controlling points." Drugs, drug paraphernalia, and weapons are stored at "stash houses," which supply the street-level distribution points known as "crack houses," "gate houses," or "dope houses." Those at the controlling points are responsible for re-supplying the street-level distribution points, usually located in apartments or rented houses.

Crack houses operated by Jamaican posses are often sophisticated distribution operations. They are shuttered from outside view, often with blackened windows. They have extensive defensive mechanisms in place, ranging from specially constructed entrance barricades composed by two-by-fours (known as "New York Stops") to lookouts using walkie-talkies to warn of police raids. Armed guards or "managers," located at the crack houses, also keep intruders or law enforcement personnel from entering. Some Jamaican posses have reportedly told their guards to shoot any law enforcement officer who raids their crack house. The Northern District of Texas reports that in many cases a gun is held to a customer's head until the drug transaction is completed, in case the customer is found to be a troublemaker, an informant, or an undercover agent. In addition, the "houses" are usually equipped with secret hiding places for drugs and have ladders or other emergency exit routes. To frustrate police attempts at identifying trafficking locations, the crack house's site is often changed.

However, the posses do not restrict their operations to crack houses. In some cases, even more temporary quarters will do. Posse members in Columbus, Ohio; Frederick, Maryland; and Wilmington, North Carolina set up retail distribution networks in economy motels, usually located near interstate highways. It is believed that these operations were a form of market testing; where the market proved lucrative, the Jamaicans subsequently leased rental properties for use as crack houses.

Unlike most drug organizations, Jamaican posses often do their own money laundering. They have used Western Union for wire transfers of money, purchased legitimate businesses (restaurants, auto repairs, record shops) as fronts, and bought real estate for quick resale. In one such case, investigators found that a doctor at the University of Mississippi Medical Center had conspired with a Jamaican dentist to launder money through a Panamanian front company that made false loans to the Jamaican.[6]

There are further indications that Jamaican organized crime is developing working relationships with West Coast street gangs, traditional organized crime, and Colombian narcotics cartels. The exact nature of the relationships among the posses and West Coast street gangs remains unclear. It is known that Jamaican drug dealers are operating in "the Jungle," a small area in Southwest Los Angeles known for drug activity and drug-related violence, and that the Los Angeles gangs known as the Crips are moving into crack distribution markets in Kansas City, Cleveland, and Dallas, where Jamaican criminal organizations are also operating. It is also known that Jamaican criminals have had long-standing relations with Colombians, as the former buys cocaine directly from the latter.

While informants have revealed the existence and operating locations of a few specific posses, the posses usually impose a code of silence on their members. A Jamaican criminal, when arrested, will rarely discuss his posse and will even deny that such bands exist. Of the posses identified thus far, the largest and most violent are the Shower and Spangler posses. Drug wars between the Spanglers and rival gangs have led to between 350 and 525 murders during the last five years, and the posses as a whole have accounted for at least 1,000 murders in the United States since 1985. In general, these and other posses have demonstrated a willingness to turn to violence and torture at the slightest provocation, which is unusual even among drug traffickers. Victims in some homicides were apparently shot in the ankles, knees, and hips before being shot in the head. It also appears that other victims were subjected to scalding hot water before being murdered and dismembered.[7]

The posses' violence is directed at anyone who they feel is in their way: members of their group, rival groups, individuals who interfere with their drug territories, wives, girlfriends, and even children. Even witnesses who have been interviewed by the police—but gave no evidence—have been subsequently murdered. From the perspective of the posse, this has the advantage of intimidating a whole neighborhood and discouraging anyone from cooperating with the police.

The willingness of posse members to engage police in shootouts while resisting arrest makes them even more dangerous. They have not hesitated to issue contracts on the lives of police and Federal agents who they feel are

[6] *Ibid.*, p. 28.
[7] *Ibid.*, pp. 29-30.

disrupting their business, even to the point of offering a $25,000 "award" in Virginia to anyone who killed a police officer.[8] Jamaican criminals have attempted to entrap police by identifying their telephone and beeper numbers and luring them to staged shootouts.

From the time they enter the United States illegally to the point where they launder their drug profits, members of Jamaican organized crime are adept at throwing law enforcement officials off their track. This can involve anything from substituting photos or names on valid passports to forging Social Security cards, birth certificates and INS "green cards." In the course of breaking up a fraudulent document ring in Kingston, Jamaican police discovered electronic typewriters similar to those used by the Jamaican and U.S. Governments, as well as a variety of forged documents for each of the localities that Jamaican criminals wished to penetrate. In another case, an investigation in Pennsylvania exposed a veteran of the State Police who had been selling blank driver's license applications to members of the Shower posse, who then entered any name or date of birth that they wished.[9]

Equipped with multiple identities and adept at all types of identification and passport fraud, Jamaican posse members are extremely mobile; they are world travelers. In one case the same passport was used by 15 different posse members, using the same name but with a different picture each time. Posse members are able to travel freely between the United States, Mexico, and Commonwealth countries such as Canada. This mobility is a distinct advantage when law enforcement personnel are often bound by the constraints of territorial and jurisdictional boundaries.

Although Jamaican organized crime is concentrated in metropolitan areas, it is starting to move outward. The experience of the Northern District of West Virginia is a case in point. After Jamaicans arrived in the Martinsburg area in the early 1980s as migrant workers to pick fruit at harvest time, many stayed on to peddle cocaine and crack. After a 1986 raid in which authorities closed down the Martinsburg operation, much of the street action moved to Charles Town, 16 miles away. In the spring of 1988, Federal, State and local enforcement officers conducted a raid and made a series of arrests of suspected street-level crack dealers in Charles Town. What they found was a well-run operation, in which dealers were selling cocaine in gram quantities at the street level, with the crack running at a purity of 90 percent or better. These dealers received their supplies from couriers shuttling between Jamaican gangs in Miami, New York, and Washington, D.C.

Crack began appearing in Roanoke, Virginia (population 90,000), in the second half of 1988. The abundance of crack there today is directly attributable to an influx of Jamaican nationals. The 25 to 40 Jamaican nationals residing in Roanoke have been identified as being associated with the Jamaican Shower posse in New York City. They purchase guns in Virginia and exchange them for crack from New York.[10]

---

[8]*Ibid.*, pp. 29-30.
[9]*Ibid.*, pp. 29-30.
[10]*Ibid.*, p. 30.

The posses' mobility, their large networks of distributors and couriers, and their persistent use of aliases compel enforcement agents to use innovative techniques in investigating them. Among these techniques are the review of Western Union wire transfers, telephone toll analyses, and the tracing of firearms recovered from Jamaican criminals. An increasingly useful information source is the Federal Bureau of Prisons. The Bureau has computerized listings on the approximately 800 Jamaican criminals who have passed through the Federal prison system, about a quarter of whom are still in custody. The violent nature of Jamaican posses and the threat they pose to security have led the Bureau of Prisons to attempt to set up a data base tracking links between Jamaican inmates and specific posses.

In December of 1987, the Jamaican Parliament ratified a treaty that broadened the category of offenders found in Jamaica who could be returned to the United States. Under the terms of the treaty, Jamaica must extradite fugitives wanted in the United States for any offense that would also be a crime in Jamaica. The treaty also covers fugitives wanted in the United States for conspiring to traffic in narcotics, a charge not extraditable before the treaty was ratified. The new treaty and the legislation that implements it also permit the extradition of offenders wanted for offenses involving the unlawful possession or use of firearms, another crime not formerly covered.

OUTLAW MOTORCYCLE GANGS

Outlaw motorcycle gangs were first thrust upon the American culture in the 1950s, when they were portrayed romantically in a number of Hollywood films. They again achieved notoriety in the early 1970s, when members of the Hell's Angels were hired to provide "security" for the Rolling Stones at an Altamont, California rock concert that degenerated into a deadly riot.

Like the films their activities inspired, the outlaw motorcycle gangs were originally created in California. Also like these movies, the gangs have achieved national "distribution." They no longer spend their days on the road terrorizing small California towns and their nights swilling beer and working on their "hogs." Today, they are highly structured, often national, drug trafficking organizations that control most of the amphetamine manufacture and distribution in the United States. These motorcycle gangs have also developed working relationships with a number of other drug trafficking organizations.

The Hell's Angels is the oldest, largest, and best known of the outlaw motorcycle gangs. It was founded in 1950 in Fontana, California. Throughout the 1950s and 1960s other gangs were formed. These gangs were generally structured into chapters, with a "mother" chapter and a number of subsidiary chapters. The formative years were ones of rapid growth in which gangs came and went, were absorbed and consolidated, and in which various forms of illegal activities were practiced. Even today, the gangs pursue a wide gamut of illegal activities: prostitution, burglary, rape, assault, murder, contract killings, and more sophisticated activities such as illegal banking, loan sharking, and financing of drug deals. It was not until the mid-1960s that the motorcycle gangs began to specialize in drug trafficking and to take on the highly disciplined structure that now characterizes them.

The organizational structure of the major outlaw motorcycle gangs has evolved from the "chapter" model described above to a structure resembling that of La Cosa Nostra (LCN). The national officers correspond to LCN commission members; chapter presidents perform the roles of LCN bosses; vice presidents act as underbosses; and road captains and sergeant-at-arms are the gang equivalents of caporegimes. Like LCN, these gangs operate legitimate businesses that function as fronts and/or as money laundering operations. In some parts of the United States the bikers actually work with LCN in arrangements in which the bikes control methamphetamine distribution through various LCN outlets.

There are at least 500 outlaw motorcycle gangs currently operating in the United States. The four most important are the Hell's Angels, the Outlaws, the Pagans, and the Bandidos. These four gangs are national in scope and have a long record of drug trafficking.

The Hell's Angels got its start in drug trafficking in the mid-1960s, with local distribution of LSD in the San Francisco area. From this beginning, the Angels expanded into extensive trafficking in cocaine, PCP, marijuana, and methamphetamine. By the early 1970s, the Angels had moved into the clandestine manufacture of methamphetamine, an activity in which the gang is both highly skilled and highly influential. As a result of these activities, the Hell's Angels gang has grown to become the wealthiest and most powerful of the outlaw gangs. With between 500 and 600 members nationwide, the Angels' "Mother Chapter" is based in Oakland, California, with chapter president Sonny Barger the organization's national leader. The New York City chapter President is Sandy Alexander.

Another motorcycle gang, the Outlaws, was founded in Chicago in 1959 and later absorbed the Canadian "Satan's Choice" gang in 1977. This merger created the largest motorcycle gang in the United States and Canada, with approximately 1,200 to 1,500 members. It has 31 chapters, six of which are in Canada.

Yet another gang, the Pagans, was established in Prince George's County, Maryland, outside of Washington, D.C., in 1959. Located primarily in the Northeast, with their largest chapter in the Philadelphia area, the Pagans have structured their organization somewhat differently than the other national gangs. Instead of a geographically fixed mother chapter, a "Mother Club," composed of 13 to 18 chapter presidents, directs the Pagans' organization. There are 700 to 800 members in 44 chapters located between New York and Florida. In addition to developing a national network of drug dealers, firearms traffickers, and murderers, the Pagans appear to have ties to organized crime, particularly LCN.

Finally, the youngest of the four major criminal motorcycle gangs, the Bandidos, was established in Houston in 1966. In the 1970s, the gang expanded and eventually established chapters as far away as South Dakota and Washington State. Now, the Bandidos have approximately 500 members and a network of 2,000 associates.

Each of the major gangs specializes in some particular aspect of the drug trade. For example, the Bandidos are heavily involved in methamphetamine manufacturing, distribution, and sales. The Pagans dominate the PCP and methamphetamine trade in the Northeast, while the Outlaws, through their

Florida chapters, which may be involved with Cuban and Colombian suppliers, are engaged in cocaine trafficking. The Outlaws also traffic in a bogus form of "Valium," manufactured in illegal Canadian laboratories and distributed from a base in Chicago.

As their structures have become more sophisticated and their activities more widespread, the bikers have developed more sophisticated ways of defending themselves and their activities. The tire chain and the rumble have been replaced by more streamlined methods. The Bandidos and the Outlaws carry tape recorders to record conversations with any law enforcement officers who might confront them. They attempt to get the officers to make statements that will contaminate any case brought against them and record the conversations for later use by their lawyers. The major gangs have begun to exchange computerized information on law enforcement officers and their informants. They have also been known to place operatives in court houses, prisons, and police stations, to gather intelligence on law enforcement operations and planning.

As for their "home base," gang clubhouses vary in location and layout. They may be located on farms, in the center city, or in residential areas. While the clubhouses are used for business meetings, partying, and working on motorcycles, they must also be tightly secured against unexpected police raids or attacks by rival gangs. Some gangs place their houses under 24-hour guard, with steel-reinforced doors and standard chain-link fences topped with barbed wire as a perimeter defense. In many cases, the house itself is also protected by concrete cinderblock walls with built-in gun ports. Guard dogs often roam in the area between the fences.

Inside the clubhouses, other security measures are taken, including wooden or steel shutters that close from the inside, exterior walls fitted with sheets of armor plating, and electronic security equipment, including tracking devices, closed-circuit TV cameras, and telephone eavesdropping units. Even this is not enough to satisfy some gangs' security concerns; some have actually planted poisonous snakes in dresser drawers, kitchen cabinets, or boxes, ready to strike out at whoever rummages in their hiding place.

Therefore, the major outlaw motorcycle gangs are extremely difficult to infiltrate. Also, like Jamaican criminals, gang members go to considerable lengths to conceal their identities, using special "street names" in their everyday dealings. By forcing candidates to engage in bizarre rituals or commit major crimes, thus binding them to membership for life, and by playing on their fears of certain reprisal if they cooperate with the authorities, the gangs have largely succeeded both in screening out undercover agents and in tightening their grip on members' loyalty. Members are almost never allowed to leave a major biker gang alive.

However, law enforcement officials have had some success in "turning" members who fear that their days within the gang are numbered. They have also exploited intra- and inter-gang rivalries to gain information on gang activities. Law enforcement pressure on the West Coast has succeeded in causing the Hell's Angels to set up methamphetamine manufacturing businesses in other areas such as western Missouri. However, much more must be done before the goal of breaking up these gangs can be achieved.

It is not only the four major outlaw motorcycle gangs that are involved in drug trafficking operations. There are a number of local and regional motorcycle groups that are deeply involved in drug trafficking in their areas. These gangs often work closely with each other and with the major gangs to produce and distribute drugs. For example, members of the "Grim Reapers" motorcycle gang operated as a network of drug dealers in the Galesburg/Peoria, Illinois area. Reportedly, they were responsible for 80 percent of the cocaine trafficked in the Galesburg area and for a majority of the cocaine distributed around Peoria. One chapter of the gang also distributed methamphetamine in both areas. They received their cocaine from gang members located in California and Florida. The methamphetamine was manufactured by two members of the Bandido motorcycle gang in Texas and by members of the Satan Brothers gang in Oklahoma. In western Tennessee, outlaw motorcycle gangs involved in methamphetamine and other drug trafficking, besides the local chapter of the Hell's Angels, include the Outlaws, the Saints, the Iron Horsemen, and the Road Barons. Operating in the Middle District of Alabama are the Devil's Disciples, the Ghost Riders, the Peacemakers, the Rattlers, and the Iron Cross.[11]

CALIFORNIA STREET GANGS

In addition to spawning the outlaw motorcycle gang phenomenon, California is home to one of the most dangerous and menacing developments in drug trafficking: the large-scale organized street gang. These gangs first appeared in Los Angeles in the late 1960s. Their activities have escalated from the instigation of neighborhood violence to large-scale drug trafficking throughout the United States.

Although there are many smaller independent gangs and minor organized gang groups in the Los Angeles area, the most successful and dangerous California street gangs are divided into two major organizations, the Crips and the Bloods. Each of these organizations is composed of numerous smaller gangs called "sets." It is estimated that there are approximately 190 Crips sets and 65 Bloods sets. Law enforcement officials believe that these approximately 250 sets have a combined membership of nearly 25,000.

These sets are generally geographically based. Some derive their names from local street names: "Five-Deuce Hoover Crips" (52nd and Hoover Streets) or "110 Main Street Gangster Crips" (110th and Main Streets), while others have descriptive names of arcane derivations—"Rollin 60 Crips," "Blood Stone Villains," and "Neighborhood Bloods."

The sets are structured along lines of seniority and function. They have caste-like subdivision within each set, notably (1) original gang members (O.G.); (2) gangsters, the hard-core members, whose ages range from 16 to 22; (3) baby gangsters, who are between nine and 12; and (4) in some gangs, tiny gangsters, who are even younger. While some age groups go to the late 20s and early 30s, the most violent and active members are those between 14 and 18, many of them "wantabees" who want to prove themselves in order

---

[11] *Ibid.*, p. 33.

to be accepted by other gang members and who are precisely the ones most useful as soldiers in gang activities.

The Crips and the Bloods organizations are primarily involved in PCP and crack cocaine trafficking. They have developed clandestine laboratories for drug manufacture in the Los Angeles area and have become adept at seeking out secluded areas where their manufacturing activities will be undetected. They have also developed supply sources for the constituent chemicals needed to fuel their production activities.

Since the advent of crack cocaine, the manufacture and distribution networks in the Los Angeles area have expanded tremendously. Crack is increasingly the drug of choice for the majority of users there. The usual arrangement is for an O.G. or former gang member to establish relations with Colombian or Mexican suppliers of powder cocaine HCl. The O.G. is at the head of the local distribution network and receives the cocaine either on consignment or with an up-front payment. First, he turns over multi-kilogram quantities of cocaine HCl for processing into crack, or rock cocaine. The newly produced crack is then given out in multi-ounce quantities by the supplier to street distributors, to be sold to the end user. The street distributors typically carry only small amounts, concealing the rest in convenient locations from which they can quickly replenish their stock.

California street gang sellers use a number of techniques for distributing crack. Sometimes they employ "spotters" to direct customers to where the street distributor is waiting, or they may sell to drivers of passing cars. Another approach is to make the sale from heavily fortified "rock houses," to which the customer has only limited access. The customer may have to wait outside until the transaction is completed—with the seller out of sight—or the customer may be admitted only as far as a caged area in the front end of the house. However, crack dealers are moving away from rock houses toward street sales and sales from motel rooms. In the latter case, dealers will usually pay in cash, rent multiple rooms, and use pagers and cellular phones to contact suppliers and purchasers of controlled substances.

The Los Angeles gangs are radiating out from the areas where they originated—up the West Coast as far as Seattle and Vancouver, into the heartland as far as Denver, Kansas City, and Chicago, and even to cities on the East Coast. Police in all these cities report that Los Angeles gangs are establishing branch operations to sell crack, sometimes in competition with other gangs who consider the cities their territory. This is the case, for instance, with the Samoan gangs in the San Francisco Bay area. In Baltimore, local law enforcement agencies have identified a trend, as Los Angeles gangs send cocaine HCl by way of their own gang members, "wantabees," or by way of local drug dealers looking for a purer or cheaper supply. Following the arrest of two Crips in Maryland and the Eastern District of Virginia, authorities began a special Organized Crime Drug Enforcement Task Force project to determine the extent of infiltration of the area by Los Angeles street gangs.

Kansas City, Missouri is another metropolitan area to which the Bloods and the Crips have migrated and established themselves. They were identified in Kansas City in the summer of 1987. They had sent representatives there to exploit the cocaine distribution market which, at the time, had a gap due to the successful neutralization of Jamaican drug factions. The gangs have generally taken up residence in the outlying areas of Kansas City but have targeted the inner city for cocaine distribution. Initially, the gangs were readily identifiable by their dress, language, and habits, but they now tend to avoid such dead giveaways to prevent unwanted attention from law enforcement.

After reviewing the situation in Kansas City, the Middle District of Tennessee feels it too is experiencing an expansion of Los Angeles drug gang activity. It is known for sure that a drug distribution network affiliated with street gangs has been operating in Nashville for about a year. The network stretches from Los Angeles to Nashville and involves at least 50 individuals. In response, the Metropolitan Nashville Police Department has increased its street gang unit from 6 to 50 fifty officers.

In Colorado, the Denver Police Department has documented 700 members of the Bloods and the Crips in the Denver area and reports that recruitment remains active there. Similarly, the migration of the Bloods and the Crips to the Seattle-Tacoma area was rated the "number one" news story of 1988 by readers of the *Seattle Times.* The Bloods even made it to Sioux Falls, South Dakota (population 100,000), where they were identified as the suppliers of a recently raided crack house.

One of the most frightening aspects of the California street gangs is their willingness to direct their violence at each other, at the police, at members of the public—at anyone who stands in the way of their operations. What makes this violence especially threatening is the amount of firepower at their disposal. Where the gangs once had to make do with zip guns, small-caliber revolvers, and sawed-off shotguns, they now have the wherewithal to acquire semi-automatic rifles and large-caliber handguns. In parts of Los Angeles, the weapon of choice is the AK-47 with a 30-round clip—a large-caliber (7.62 mm.) weapon that dramatically increases the chances of inflicting deadly injury. With so much firepower, gang-related homicides in the Los Angeles area have risen steadily.

Given the violent, elusive, and migratory habits of these street gangs, they are very difficult to investigate. The lack of audit trails, the high mobility of the principal drug dealers, and the relative absence of a formal organization have hindered attempts to infiltrate the gangs. However, as law enforcement agencies begin to understand the gangs better, they are learning to spot their weaknesses. For instance, many gang leaders outside the Los Angeles area will often return to Los Angeles for long periods, leaving their organizations more or less to fend for themselves. Additionally, when Los Angeles gangs try to move into new geographical areas, law enforcement officials can sometimes count on information from local dealers who resent being cut out of their own territories. Experience had led agencies to develop strategies for dealing with the gangs, such as using Federal drug statutes (which tend to be more stringent than state statutes) to prosecute drug traffickers; to develop profiles of gang members dealing in drugs; and to build up case files of the gangs themselves.

OTHER DOMESTIC TRAFFICKING ORGANIZATIONS

In addition to California street gangs, several traditional criminal organizations specializing in drug trafficking are known to be active in urban areas across the country. These organizations and their activities are well-documented in cities such as Detroit, Chicago, St. Louis, and East St. Louis, Illinois. The bosses, or kingpins of these operations supervise their highly structured and disciplined organizations which are composed, for the most part, of extremely violent career criminals. In some cases, the bosses retain control even if they have been convicted and are serving time.

The kingpin oversees the major distributors in his area as well as a body of "enforcers" who are often heavily armed with automatic weapons and explosives. These urban organizations seek to monopolize their segment of the drug trade in their area and routinely murder rival traffickers. They are also noted for using violence against witnesses; more recently, they have even been prone to attacking law enforcement officers and prosecutors.

The drug sources on which these urban trafficking organizations rely are often Mexican and South American nationals. The profit margins are unusually high in most of the cities where these urban trafficking organizations operate due to a combination of low supply and difficulty in transportation to the area. This high profitability becomes a great incentive to maintain control of trafficking territories and increases the propensity of these organizations for violent confrontation with rival groups.

Because of their relative stability and long-term involvement in their communities, many of these organizations have infiltrated the legitimate power structure of the jurisdiction and have formed close ties with city officials and local law enforcement personnel. These relationships often allow the urban trafficking organization to gather intelligence on law enforcement operations in their area, thus decreasing their vulnerability to prosecution.

An example of such an organization is the Alex Beverly group in Chicago. In operation for over 15 years, it was the city's largest black drug organization. The 100-member gang has been connected with a dozen drug-related homicides. Alex Beverly was convicted for conducting a Continuing Criminal Enterprise (CCE) and is now serving 40 years, with no possibility of parole.[12]

On a smaller scale, there are some regional or even local, domestically based trafficking organizations which operate in areas throughout the United States. In some instances, these organizations are customers of the larger organizations. In other instances, the smaller organizations provide the larger ones with their local infrastructure and are hired by the large organizations to provide specific services or perform specific functions in the drug trafficking chain of operations. These local organizations are often drawn into overt conflict with larger organizations when their geographical or operational sphere of influence is invaded.

Thus, Los Angeles is not alone among major cities in spawning drug trafficking street gangs. Although none are as active or as far-reaching in their activities as are the Bloods and the Crips, one other active drug

---

[12]*Ibid.*, p. 36.

trafficking street gang is the "Miami Boys," an organized crack trafficking gang from Florida whose activities have spread to the Atlanta area.

The "Miami Boys" handle the importation of crack into the Atlanta area, supervise young street dealers (most in their middle teens, but some as young as 10 to 12 years old), and handle crack trafficking revenues, which are wired daily to gang leaders in Florida. The "Miami Boys" are reported to be partial to the techniques of intimidating young welfare mothers into allowing the use of their apartments as rented "crack" distribution points. The welfare mothers are paid a going rate of $100 a day; in return they acquiesce to the use of their domiciles for the storing of drugs and as money collection points.

Farther north, Minneapolis-St. Paul is supplied with crack not only by the Crips and the Bloods from Los Angeles, but also by the Vice Lords and El-Rukins from Chicago. It has been estimated that 60 percent of the crack cocaine distributed in Cleveland, Toledo, and Akron is controlled by a combination of Los Angeles and Detroit based street gangs.

However, not all drug traffickers are members of large urban criminal organizations or motorcycle gangs. In the Western District of Washington, the prosecution of a cocaine distributor and several of his customers—business people and professionals—demonstrated the "yuppie" cocaine connection. The distributor was recorded as telling customers not to worry about being caught because "the police are after the black, inner-city dealers and not such people as us."

There are several high-level drug traffickers who do not fit the stereotypical profile of an inner city criminal. In Columbus, Ohio the profile of the highest-level cocaine dealer is that of a middle-aged white residing in one of the city's more affluent suburbs. In Colorado, cocaine trafficking groups are composed primarily of upper middle-class individuals of Caucasian or Hispanic background. Moreover, a 1986 investigation in Lawrence, Kansas discovered that 19 prominent community citizens, including the executive Secretary to the Chancellor of the University of Kansas and a former Deputy Attorney General for the state of Kansas, were arrested and convicted on state and Federal cocaine charges. Needless to say, the community was shocked that such respectable, high-level citizens were involved in drug trafficking.

Another "yuppie" connection was discovered in Pennsylvania. The Air America Organization in the Middle District of Pennsylvania was a consortium of airline pilots who brought 9½ tons of cocaine into the United States, one of the largest quantities of cocaine ever smuggled by a single organization. In addition, tens of millions of dollars in cash were smuggled out of the country, directly to Colombia, by these pilots, who were paid $1 million per successful flight.

The individuals and informal organizations that fit these non-traditional patterns are differentiated by the circumstances of their origins and the surroundings in which they operate. Yet, both young urban professionals and rural or small-town locals may sometimes turn to selling drugs, either as a sideline or as a full-time occupation. In some instances, the operation of a drug trafficking enterprise is just a variation on criminal activities that predate any connection to drugs. In parts of the rural Southeast, some families who once produced moonshine or engaged in local criminal activities now cultivate marijuana or traffic in cocaine. The isolation of the rural areas in which these people operate creates ideal circumstances for drug-drops, as well as for marijuana cultivation. Many of these individuals start out trafficking in small quantities of cocaine and move on to working in clandestine rural drug laboratories.

A similar situation exists in the Northern District of West Virginia. In this state, drug trafficking is engaged in by several indigenous organizations whose members have been entrenched in the district for a number of years and who have extensive records of criminal activity.

Likewise, in the Northern District of Georgia a portion of the total drug traffic is attributed to a plethora of "southern style" career criminals, regionally referred to as the "Dixie Mafia." One of the district's most significant methamphetamine investigations targeted several "Dixie Mafia" defendants. The investigation determined that these established career criminals, who had well-documented records as marijuana and cocaine traffickers, were receiving monthly shipments of between 50 and 72 pounds of methamphetamine from a clandestine laboratory in Washington State.[13]

On the other hand, the young professionals or "yuppies" who become involved in the drug trade bring a different background and perspective to their illicit activities. Many of those who went through college and graduate school experimenting with drugs either never gave them up or began using them again when the increased income and pressures of professional life made drugs both available and seemingly attractive. As stockbrokers, doctors, lawyers, and participants in other high-stress professions, some developed dependencies on an occasional snort of cocaine or on some other drug-related experience. Occasionally, these people are confronted with incentives and opportunities to become full time-traffickers, especially those professionals with access to essential chemicals or prescription drugs which can be diverted. In many instances, however, the yuppie drug dealer is driven by the same forces which motivate his professional life: greed and the desire to get rich quick.

The different perspectives and lifestyles of both the rural, blue-collar workers and young professionals engaged in selling drugs carry over into their trafficking operations. The rural traffickers usually live and operate in smaller, more stable communities and draw their partners in crime from family and friends. Young professionals form more collegial relationships, often engaging in short-term operations with old college friends or sympathetic office workers who are drawn together by an initial common interest in obtaining illicit drugs. For example, a case in Montgomery County, Virginia involved the arrest of 17 individuals for dealing in cocaine, marijuana, and other drugs. The group, whose customers included students at Virginia Tech, consisted of a number of the sons of prominent political figures in the area. The sons recruited people with whom they had gone to

---

[13] *Ibid.*, p. 37.

school and people whose other interests and backgrounds made them comfortable in forming a "business" relationship.

Rural organizations, on the other hand, tend to be structured more like traditional criminal organizations than are the yuppie groups, whose members usually do not consider themselves to be career criminals and whose idea of an acceptable relationship tends more toward the contractual and the communal rather than the hierarchical. Joint ventures are popular in yuppie trafficking organizations. Whereas the rural organizations seem to be more stable, with each person assuming a more or less permanent place in the trafficking hierarchy, yuppie groups are more ephemeral and more likely to be organized along the lines of the specific expertise that each member of the organization brings to an operation. Typically, yuppie organizations are established around short-term goals, while rural traffickers are more adaptable and more likely to be in for the long haul. It is not uncommon for these organizations to move their operations to a nearby town or urban center and proceed to transform into a full-fledged hierarchical trafficking organization.

TRAFFICKING BY FOREIGN NATIONALS

The influx of immigrants, the changing immigration laws and patterns of the last few decades, and the increased mobility of residents in drug producing countries, have led to a great increase in the drug trafficking operations of foreign nationals in the United States. This new activity has in no way been restricted to the Colombian cartels, the Jamaican posses, and the Asian gangs cited above. Many less well-known trafficking organizations operate throughout the United States. The area of operation of any individual group of foreign nationals may be limited to a single locality or may encompass parts of several different states. In some instances, the traffickers operate through contacts with their fellow countrymen residing in drug import areas such as Miami and Los Angeles/San Diego, while also remaining in contact with nationals in their home countries. Distribution and/or importation is sometimes arranged through one of the larger trafficking organizations, such as the Colombians or the Jamaicans.

Mexican nationals represent one of the oldest groups of foreign nationals engaged in drug trafficking in the United States. They have been operating in the United States for years, especially in the Southwest and Far West. They traffic mainly in heroin and marijuana; however, trafficking in cocaine is also common, and over the past few years Mexico has become an increasingly important conduit for South American cocaine. A number of factors have combined to stimulate this activity: a long, hard-to-patrol border with the United States; an extensive rural Mexican countryside, with many mountainous areas, ideal for cultivating, processing, and manufacturing illicit drugs; a tradition of corruption in elements of the Mexican government and law enforcement agencies; and the growing drug market in the United States over the past decade.

Within the whole group of Mexican nationals, there are a number of different, often competing, Mexican organizations. These include the so-called "Mexican Mafia," with roots in Mexican "prison gangs"; loosely knit cartels, primarily specializing in one or more illicit substances; and smaller, less integrated trafficking groups of a less stable nature.

Drug Trafficking, Terrorism & Organized Crime

Reports indicate that the structures of Mexican drug trafficking organizations are much more family-oriented than those of other large-scale trafficking groups. A Mexican trafficking operation is often vertically integrated, using family members for each stage of the operation. For example, the Central District of California reports that the Sanchez-Carranza organization relies upon family relatives living in mountainous areas of Durango, Mexico to cultivate its opium poppy fields. These family members send the crop to other family members in Mexico, who process it into heroin. The heroin is then smuggled into the United States by couriers, many of whom are family members, and delivered to yet another set of family members who live in the United States. The families in the United States oversee the heroin's distribution throughout California and the neighboring states of Washington, Idaho, Arizona, and Nevada. Some Mexican groups take the process a step further and employ family members in direct sales on the streets of U.S. cities.

However, not all foreign nationals have penetrated the U.S. market to the extent that Mexicans have. In some cases, foreign nationals have found that they can engage in U.S. drug trafficking from "on the boat," without having to really "enter" the country. Pakistani nationals, members of the crews of boats docking at Baltimore harbor, have been reported to be engaging in heroin trafficking from their ships. They call at the Baltimore port every 4 to 6 weeks, usually in the middle or latter part of their itinerary. Their points of sale include most of Baltimore's inner-city heroin distribution organizations.

Other groups do get "off the boat" and spread to various parts of the country, blending in with legitimate refugees and immigrants and setting up their trafficking organizations in places where law enforcement may not expect to find them. For example, in Wichita, Kansas, two organizations of Dominican Republic nationals are engaged in separate but overlapping cocaine trafficking operations. Furthermore, the principal heroin distribution groups in Rhode Island are also composed of Dominican Republic nationals. Unlike many of the foreign nationals operating as traffickers in the United States, the Dominicans in Rhode Island, who form the country's third largest Dominican population after New York City's and Miami's, are reported to be interested in permanent residence. The more prevalent pattern is for nationals to be transitory residents, intent on returning to their country of origin and usually sending back home a large portion their illicit proceeds.

Another group of foreign nationals is operating out of Delaware. Haitian traffickers have become one of the primary sources of crack cocaine in southern Delaware. This network grew out of the influx of migratory Haitian workers seeking employment in Delaware's agricultural and poultry industries. Members of the trafficking network in Delaware have connections with a Haitian community located in Ft. Pierce, Florida. This information was discovered because one of the traffickers prosecuted in Delaware was buying automobiles with the proceeds of his trafficking, sending them to Ft. Pierce, and having them shipped to Haiti, where he intended to open a taxi business.

As the Delaware case suggests, a foreign national may engage in drug trafficking operations independently, relying on connections with his fellow countrymen for supply and distribution. Yet, these traffickers can be just as dangerous as those with formal organizational ties. In the Southern District of Alabama, for example, a black Haitian male moved into an economically depressed housing project and began recruiting local street dealers. Considered unwanted competition by some local dealers, he showed his propensity for violence when confronted. In one instance, he shot a man in the back of the head in an attempt to execute him; miraculously, the victim survived.

Other groups of foreign nationals also exist. Nigerian heroin smugglers have utilized the London to New York commercial airline route as their main avenue of access. The couriers are recruited in Nigeria, usually from among those with legitimate reasons for travel to the United States. These "mules" bring the heroin into the United States for transport by automobile to its ultimate point of distribution. The Nigerian smugglers, even though not always professionals, have been loathe to cooperate with authorities against their source of supply, making it hard to develop a clear picture of the detailed structure of this heroin operation.

Moreover, organizations of Cuban nationals are reported to be involved in cocaine trafficking operations in the Western District of Wisconsin. Such organizations were first uncovered in the wake of their developments, in the early 1980s, and include many criminal refugees who arrived in this country during the Mariel boat-lift. These Cuban organizations are often traditional families in which the parents, brothers, and sisters operate different aspects of the narcotics trafficking business. In Wisconsin, as a result of their ties with other criminal refugees in Florida, these organizations developed a pipeline for bringing large quantities of cocaine into the state. Again, investigations of this operation have been hampered by its familial nature, as defendants have been reluctant to testify against family members.

Other groups of foreign nationals are involved in drug trafficking in Cedar Rapids, Iowa. In less than three years, there have been two major international heroin smuggling cases involving foreign nationals in this area. The more recent case involved the arrest of a Lebanese individual who had smuggled several kilos of heroin and hashish from Lebanon on various occasions. Earlier, in 1985, over 20 individuals were prosecuted for involvement in a Nepalese smuggling operation.[14]

While most of these groups of foreign nationals do not represent a threat as great as that of the larger groups, they are cause for concern. They are highly mobile and difficult for law enforcement agencies to track and prosecute. They provide a local distribution network for the major importers and distributors in areas where these organizations have no local network in place. And, most disturbingly, they have the potential for developing organizations that could rival those of the Colombians and the Jamaicans, should the circumstances of supply, distribution, and organizational ability conspire to catapult one of them to prominence. For these reasons, it is necessary to maintain our constant attention to the activities of these trafficking organizations. It is also necessary to be vigilant in identifying

---

[14] *Ibid.*, p. 39-40.

any new or expanded areas of activity. This is an especially difficult task given the constantly shifting patterns of social, economic, and geographic status that characterize most populations of foreign nationals residing in the United States.

DRUG TRAFFICKING, TERRORISM, AND INSURGENCY

Several established drug trafficking organizations in various regions of the world coexist and cooperate with political insurgent groups and terrorists. Mark S. Steinitz, who served in the Drug Enforcement Agency's Office of Intelligence from 1979 to 1983, defines terrorism and insurgency as follows:

> The terms terrorism and insurgency are used to describe two forms of systematic, low-level political violence conducted by militant subnational groups. The difference between the two is difficult to define precisely. The terrorist, however, has little hope of inflicting a significant military defeat on an opponent regime and relies almost exclusively on the psychological impact of violence. His targets are chosen for their symbolic value and are often civilians. The terrorist avoids set battles with security forces, has no standing force in the field, rarely wears distinguishing insignia during operations, and shows little interest or ability in occupying a significant portion of territory. Although relying at times on the psychological impact of violence, the insurgent seeks primarily to affect political behavior through the material impact of violence and selects targets for the instrumental value. The insurgent is willing to engage security forces at least on the small unity level, wears some type of uniform, has a permanent force in the field and generally controls territory, at least in the latter stages of struggle.[15]

While drug traffickers are not—by the above definition—terrorists or insurgents, they rely heavily on terrorist tactics to obtain limited political objectives. The use of threats, violence, assassination, and kidnapping by trafficking organizations to prevent vigorous enforcement of drug laws can only be categorized as terroristic in nature.

The use of terrorist tactics is most evident among traffickers in Colombia, Peru, and Mexico. In Colombia, much of the violence is caused by the extradition of reputed Colombian drug traffickers to the United States for trial. In Peru, drug-related violence has been increasing since 1983. A series of violent attacks by traffickers on police units and eradication workers in that area led to the November 1984 torture and murder of 19 members of a Untied States-financed coca-eradication team. Less than one year later, these violent attacks also included the brutal murder of 17 United States-financed eradicators by about 50 traffickers armed with submachine guns.

In Mexico, trafficking violence culminated in the kidnapping, torture, and murder of DEA Agent Enrique Camerena and a Mexican pilot. Camerena's abduction occurred shortly after Mexican police, alerted by DEA, raided the largest marijuana plantation ever discovered in that country and seized an estimated 8,500 tons of the illicit substance. The trafficking-related violence in Mexico escalated further in November 1985, when 17 police officers and

---

[15] Steinitz, Mark S. "Insurgents, Terrorists, and the Drug Trade." *The Washington Quarterly*. Fall 1985, pp. 141-153.

other members of an anti-drug team working in southern Mexico were lured into an ambush, tortured, and killed by a large group of drug traffickers armed with automatic weapons.

As these incidents indicate, the spread of drug trafficking across the world has greatly expanded the role of terrorists and insurgents since the early 1970s. It should be kept in mind that the links between terrorist/insurgent groups and traffickers are most substantial in drug source countries, such as Colombia, Peru, Burma, and Thailand.

CORRUPTION

In conjunction with increasing terrorism, the expanded drug-related involvement of high-level professionals and government employees has made corruption an international problem, a blight on the character and operations of criminal justice systems throughout the world. In many cases, forms of corruption in the justice system are no more than manifestations of greater societal problems, including dishonesty and payoffs in the political, government, and business sectors. It is particularly troubling when the agents of society responsible for maintaining justice give way to greed and temptation.

The problem is compounded by what has come to be a common practice of situational ethics, in which justice agencies overlook criminal activity and corruption in an effort to make larger gains. It took some time before the United States made a decision to indict Panama's strongman, General Manuel Noriega. Meanwhile he salted away millions of dollars. U.S. Justice Department officials who handled the case were well aware of Noriega's activities prior to taking action. Such was also the case of former Philippine President Ferdinand Marcos, whose reputation for corruption was well known.

A little closer to home in the United States, police corruption appears to be on the upswing after a decade of relative decline. In spite of Federal investigations and prosecutions, cases of judges and court officials caught with their hands in the till have become more commonplace. Even the reputation of the Federal Bureau of Investigation was tarnished when an agent was accused of selling secrets to the former Soviet Union.

Astonishingly, one out of every ten officers in the Miami Police Department has been involved in drug-related corruption, according to *Law Enforcement News*.[16] This figure was given to *LEN* by Miami Chief of Police Clarence Dickson, who heads the 1,000-member department. To date, about 59 Miami police officers have been suspended or dismissed from the department on suspicion of wrongdoing. Some of the charges are of serious crimes such as shooting drug dealers for drugs and/or cash.

The discoveries of corruption are the result of a two-year investigation by Federal and local agencies. According to *LEN,* corruption has resulted from "the pervasive influence of drug trafficking in the Miami area, the too-rapid

---

[16] _______. *Law Enforcement News*. John Jay College of Criminal Justice, New York City. December 8, 1990.

expansion of the Miami Police Department during the early 1980s, and inadequate background checks conducted on police applicants at that time."

Outside of the United States, in the former Soviet Union, several high ranking officials have been accused of corruption; and, in unusual moves, their transgressions have been reported by the press. The head of Moscow's Police Investigations Department was dismissed for corruption and an amoral private life.

Throughout the world, there are such reports of official misconduct. In China, cultural modernization has brought a level of corruption that has startled the authorities. In Hong Kong, official corruption has become so widespread that a special unit, the Independent Commission Against Corruption (ICAC) has been established and given extraordinary powers. This commission is credited with major reforms and accomplishments.

Based on the reports of the past decade, it would appear that two major forms of influence have come to exert pressure on the criminal justice systems of the world. The first is "influence peddling," which usually results in officials overlooking a criminal act for a fee. The second is the widespread acceptance of illegal drugs coupled with large amounts of money used to entice the officials in power.

In fact, illicit drugs have become so pervasive as a part of the economy that, according to a recent United Nations publication: "Because of the far-reaching consequences of the drug trade, the integrity and stability of governments may be threatened. This wide range of illegal activities presents an equally wide range of vulnerability to law enforcement action."[17]

Will corruption among officials who inhabit the halls of justice and represent the forces of law cause those very bastions of social order to crumble? There does not appear to be complete consensus among those who are responsible for managing this problem; yet, as these scrupulous officials relate more and more personal experiences with cases in their own cities or countries, it becomes a matter of increasing concern.

REFERENCES:

California Council on Criminal Justice. *State Task Force on Gangs and Drugs, Final Report.* Sacramento, CA, January 1989.

________. *State Task Force on Youth Gang Violence, Final Report.* Sacramento, CA, January 1986.

Drug Enforcement Administration. "Special Report: Worldwide Cocaine Trafficking Trends, 1985." Washington, D.C., pp.4-9

Drug Interdiction Symposium before the President's Commission on Organized Crime. Testimony of A. Barry Seal. October 7, 1985.

---

[17] ________. "Combating Drug Abuse and Related Crime." United Nations Publications, 2 United Nations Plaza, N.Y., E.84-III. N.1-88-7621-825-4.

Ehrenfeld, Rachel. "Narco-Terrorism and the Cuban Connection." *The Narc Officer.* INEOA, Albany N.Y., November 1988.

Galvan, Brad A. "Gang Involved Narcotic Transactions." *The California Narcotic Officer.* CNOA Vol. 9, No. 1, January 1992, pp. 12-13.

House Committee on Rules and Administration. Hearings to Create a Select Committee on Narcotics Abuse and Control. 196th Congress, 2nd Session, 1980.

International Narcotic Enforcement Officers Association. *International Drug Report.* Albany, N.Y., Vol. 33, No. 6., ISS 0148-4648, June 1992.

President's Commission on Organized Crime. Hearing IV: Organized Crime and Cocaine Trafficking. November 1984.

_______. Report to the President and the Attorney General. "America's Habit: Drug Abuse, Drug Trafficking and Organized Crime." Washington, D.C.: U.S. Government Printing Office. March 1986.

Senate Committee on Foreign Relations and Senate Committee on the Judiciary. Hearings on The Relationship of Drug Trafficking and Terrorism, 1985.

Steinitz, Mark S. "Insurgents, Terrorists, and the Drug Trade." *The Washington Quarterly.* Fall 1985, pp. 141-153.

U.S. Department of Justice. "Drug Trafficking: A Report to the President of the United States, Compiled by the United States Attorneys and the Attorney General of the United States." Washington, D.C., August 3, 1989.

_______. *Law Enforcement News.* John Jay College of Criminal Justice, New York City. December 8, 1990.

_______. "Combating Drug Abuse and Related Crime." United Nations Publications, 2 United Nations Plaza, N.Y., E.84-III. N.1-88-7621-825-4.

CHAPTER XVIII

DRUG TREATMENT AND REHABILITATION

INTRODUCTION

In the 1962 landmark case of *Robinson v. California,* the United States Supreme Court established as a matter of law that drug addiction itself is an illness and not a crime; therefore, a person cannot be punished for the mere status of being a drug addict.

Neither *Robinson* nor any Federal or state Supreme Court ruling since that time has accepted the view that a criminal offender lacks the capacity to form the criminal intent (*mens rea*) to commit a crime because he or she, at the time of committing the illegal act, is under the influence of drugs. Hence, while the status of being a drug addict is not itself a crime, the sale of or knowing possession of illegal drugs by the addict, or the commission of drug-related crimes such as larceny to finance drug habits, continue to be punishable as crimes. Subsequent to *Robinson*, the Federal government, with many of the states following suit, re-organized its drug laws in 1970 into a uniform Controlled Substances Act.

Furthermore, by holding that the states could not only require an addict to submit to treatment through a noncriminal avenue, but could also impose subsequent criminal penalties for failure to comply with this legal requirement, *Robinson* caused the drug treatment community and the criminal justice system to devise procedures for channeling drug-addicted criminal defendants into treatment.

Consequently, drug abuse treatment has become a significant industry in the United States. In 1982, there were more than 3,000 treatment facilities, accounting for over $500 million in expenditures. Much of this effort was supported by Federal, state, and local governments (63 percent). Over the past few years, however, Federal support for treatment has declined. Yet, treatment still consumes a portion of total drug control expenditures.

Despite increased activity in the field of treatment, there is little consensus among practitioners about the best methods for treating drug abuse, or even the nature of the problem to be treated. Treatment programs vary widely, depending on whether the patient's drug abuse is ascribed to biological malfunctions, personality disorders, personal relationships, or other factors.

WHAT IS TREATMENT?

Many intervention programs could be classified as either treatment or prevention. Whether an intervention is called drug abuse treatment or drug abuse prevention depends less on the actual mode of intervention than on the perceived degree of involvement in the drug by the person being treated. Less drug-involved people receive preventive measures while more drug-involved people receive treatment. Often the distinction between treatment and prevention is made from the frequency of use and/or the problems (dysfunctions) caused by excessive use. Generally, treatment is given to individuals who use drugs frequently, who take large amounts, and who experience significant dysfunctions or adverse effects as a result. Treatment is given to the addicted—to those who cannot say no, who have lost control, who are compulsive in behavior, and who continue to use drugs in spite of adverse consequences.

TREATMENT IN THE UNITED STATES

For all the ambiguity about what constitutes drug treatment, it is a major activity in the United States, involving government at all levels, private charitable organizations, private for-profit organizations, individual health care professionals, and concerned lay people. This multiplicity of service providers actually prevents knowledge of the extent of drug treatment. For example, if the child of a well-paid and well-insured lawyer obtains individual psychotherapy because cocaine use has caused a drop in high school grades, neither the treatment nor the money expended on it is likely to be incorporated into any statistical description of the extent of drug treatment.

Drug treatment in the United States was traditionally oriented toward opiates, while the popular image of drug treatment still focuses on heroin addiction. Indeed, the vast majority of treatment research and evaluation has dealt with heroin addiction and heroin treatment centers. However, this emphasis is changing as attention turns toward abusers of multiple substances (polydrug users), as other drugs such as cocaine and PCP become more heavily abused, and as the relationship between alcohol and drug use is studied. Treatment for marijuana use has also become a more frequently researched topic, but efforts have concentrated on epidemiology and prevention.

MODES OF TREATMENT

There are four generally recognized modalities of treatment programs. These are detoxification (DT), methadone maintenance (MM), therapeutic communities (TC), and drug-free (almost always outpatient) treatment (DF). Each of these modalities has several variations within it.

Detoxification (DT)

DT is a medical treatment intended to terminate current drug use via a safe withdrawal procedure. It largely involves supervised abstinence from the substance, with such medical and psychological support as necessary while the person goes through the trials of physical withdrawal. As such, DT is strictly physiological in orientation, and does not address the patient's psychosocial or economic well-being; these latter are deferred to post-DT treatment, if any. The early treatment programs at Federal hospitals in Lexington, Kentucky and Fort Worth, Texas were stereotypical examples of detoxification institutions, spawning the popular detox image. However, these were institutionalized treatment programs enmeshed within the criminal justice system; presently, over two-thirds of DT is done on an outpatient basis. Although many different drug programs have detoxification as the initial step in an overall treatment plan, a modality is classified as DT only if detoxification is the principal or only treatment provided.

Drug Treatment and Rehabilitation

Methadone Maintenance (MM)

MM is a treatment in which a synthetic opiate is administered to an addict as a substitute for the opiate of abuse, typically heroin. Although the client remains dependent on the substitute, there are several clear advantages to the change of opiate:

- The synthetic does not produce the intense "highs" or other sensations of the original drug of abuse.
- It blocks the effects of any other opiates taken during treatment, thus eliminating some motivations to continue those drugs.
- It is administered orally instead of by injection.
- It is longer-acting, therefore requiring fewer administrations than the typical opiate of abuse.

The underlying idea is that MM frees the client from the pressures of obtaining illegal heroin, from the dangers of injection, and from the emotional rollercoaster that most opiates produce. Even though addicted to a substance, the addict can muster the effort required to gain social stability. Since its development in New York City by Dr. Vincent P. Dole and Dr. Marie Nyswander, it has become one of the most widely accepted of the treatment modalities for opiate addiction. It should be noted that MM is appropriate only for opiate addiction, and not for the treatment of abuse of other drugs such as cocaine, hallucinogens, or marijuana.

The synthetic originally used in MM treatment was methadone, hence the name now generically applied to substance substitution treatment. Recently, however, methadone has been supplemented by new substances that serve the same function but offer additional advantages. For example, LAAM (L-acetylmethadol) is quite similar to methadone in form and effects, but is longer-acting, thus requiring fewer administrations. Presently, any drug-substitution treatment of this form is known as MM. In a typical MM treatment, the addict comes to a clinic regularly (e.g., daily for methadone, or three times a week for LAAM) for administration of methadone and an inspection (typically urinalysis) to ensure that other drugs are not being used. Virtually all MM programs serve addicts on this type of outpatient basis.

Many clinics provide long-term MM programs in keeping with a philosophical view of addiction as a long-term chronic condition. The original MM model offered chronic maintenance, with little or no psychosocial intervention. A second model, now more popular than the first, offers both psychosocial interventions and plans to taper off and withdraw all drug maintenance.

Therapeutic Communities (TC)

A TC is a residential treatment center in which the drug user lives, sheltered from the pressures of the outside world and from drugs, and in which he can learn to lead a new, drug-free life. The goal of TCs is to re-socialize the drug abuser by creating a structured, isolated mutual help environment in which the individual can develop and learn to function as a mature participant.

TCs developed during the 1960s in part as a reaction against the authoritarian treatment structure of the DT approach. The original TC was Synanon; other communities, such as Daytop Village, Phoenix House, Pathways, CAPS (Combined Addicts and Professional Services), have achieved some reputation for success. Most TCs are largely staffed by ex-addicts. Some even view professional providers of drug abuse treatment with disdain, although professionals have had critical roles in the establishment of successful TCs. The original TC approach sharply restricted the personal freedom of people undergoing treatment and emphasized public self-criticism, criticism by others, and severe sanctions for violations of the community rules and norms. This practice has waned over time, with many present TCs replacing confrontational criticism with more supportive strategies.

Although originally used almost exclusively by heroin addicts, TCs have come to be a modality for pill takers, alcoholics, cocaine users, marijuana users, and even people who wish to change their food-taking habits. Many present-day TCs report large populations of polydrug users. Moreover, TCs have been founded to serve specialized communities such as blacks, women, youth, and born-again Christians who suffer from drug abuse.

Drug-Free (Outpatient) Programs (DF)

DF is a generic term for all of the remaining modalities of treatment, which are non-institutional, non-residential, and do not provide alternative drugs. Over 50 percent of all treatment is in this category, as is virtually all of the treatment of non-opiate drug abuse. Among the more commonly used techniques, especially with youthful drug abusers, are:

> *Crisis intervention centers*. These are locations where users in distress can turn for help. They include walk-in centers, 24-hour telephone hot lines, "crash pads" for emergency living arrangements, and referral centers. They deal with overdoses, help during "bad trips," and other short-term services. As with TCs, crisis intervention centers are largely staffed by non-professionals with whom the addicts can identify.
>
> *Psychotherapy and counseling*. Talking with abusers is the most common form of treatment, and occurs in every modality. As a primary mode of treatment, psychotherapy tries to help the individual behave in healthy ways.

Additionally, many different types of therapeutic intervention have been attempted under DF. Among these are behavior therapies (both reinforcement and aversive), biofeedback, and hypnotherapy. In reinforcement behavior therapy, the addict is placed in a controlled environment where drug-related stimuli are presented to him, and is rewarded or punished depending on his response to the stimuli, so that the addict learns appropriate (drug-rejecting) responses. In aversive behavior therapy, the addict is presented with drug-related stimuli concomitantly with a noxious condition (such as being induced to be nauseous or receiving mild electric shocks), such that the drug-related stimuli become associated with the noxiousness and produce avoidance reactions (via conditioning). In biofeedback, addicts are presented with information based on electronic monitoring of biological processes (such as blood pressure, heart rate, or various brainwaves), and learn to maintain levels of these processes that are consistent with drug avoiding behaviors. Hypnotherapy uses post-hypnotic suggestion in conjunction with behavior therapy techniques to reduce the psychological craving for drugs.

Summary

The four modalities of DT, MM, TC, and DF treatment are outgrowths of different theoretical orientations towards drug abuse. DT and MM are largely based on theories of biological malfunctions, and treat the abuser as having chemical dependencies in need of correction. TCs, on the other hand, are founded on theories of interpersonal problems and treat the abuser as needing re-socialization. DF treatment is based on theories of personality or interpersonal difficulties; if the problem is viewed as one of self, the treatment becomes individualized. In some cases, group psychotherapy may be used as opposed to family or other systems-based therapies.

DOES TREATMENT WORK?

The effectiveness of current drug abuse treatment methods has been variously interpreted. Some people find that no general evaluation can be made; some find no evidence that treatment does any good at all; some do not discuss empirical evaluation; and some claim that treatment programs have been effective.

It might be said that the field of drug treatment is in the stage that its cousin, psychotherapy, was in 20 years ago. Each of a variety of treatment approaches claims for itself at least some degree of success. Scientific evidence on the effectiveness of drug abuse treatment is limited. Most of the systematic evaluations contain design defects such as inadequate outcome measures, absence of appropriate control groups, or lack of randomized assignment to treatments. Nevertheless, the weight of the available evidence suggests that certain forms of treatment—methadone maintenance, drug-free therapy, and residential "therapeutic communities"—work better than no treatment at all. "Detoxification-only" treatment, which consists largely of custodial care during withdrawal, appears to have some benefits as well.

Research on drug treatment effectiveness also indicates that the longer an addict remains in treatment, the better the prognosis. "Graduates" have better outcomes than dropouts. Although it may be true that addicts benefit from greater amounts of treatment, we cannot rule out the alternate explanation of a "selection effect"; that is to say, more successful addicts may elect to remain in treatment. This election, rather than the treatment itself, may be the cause of better prognoses for addicts in long-term treatment.

According to a national survey in 1988, methadone programs had significantly more clients who ended treatment because they returned to continued use, they failed to pay or they died. Two important outcomes are as follows: (1) only 26 percent of methadone clients were reported to have ended treatment because they met their treatment goals, as opposed to 51 percent in drug-free programs; and (2) approximately 50 percent of methadone clients had a post-treatment plan established for them compared with 75 percent in drug-free programs.[1] In any event, dropout rates are still high.

Another critical issue related to effectiveness is the availability of treatment for adolescents. Many observers advocate "early intervention" with young people, before their drug abuse has become severe, but such intervention has not been empirically evaluated. A second approach, family therapy, treats the family as well as the patient, viewing the family relationships as the cause of the young person's drug abuse. Family therapy has received favorable evaluation as a treatment for other psychiatric disorders, and has proved effective in one well-designed randomized trial with adult heroin users. However, it has not been tested with adolescent non-opiate abusers, and its potentially high costs must be weighed against its benefits.

NARCOTICS TREATMENT IN ENGLAND

Serious considerations of the British approach to the treatment of heroin addiction have often been clouded by misinformation about the system, which ranges from the assertion that narcotics are legal in England to the belief that the British approach is identical to the American treatment policy. Neither statement is completely true. Although an addict in Great Britain can, through the proper channels, legally obtain heroin or morphine, narcotics are not legal. As in the United States, there has been increasing emphasis on switching the addicts to methadone maintenance and/or eventually encouraging them to undergo withdrawal. The history of British narcotics treatment policy may be divided into three major periods.

First Period: The Rolleston Committee (1924)

In 1924, the British Minister of Health appointed a group of distinguished physicians to consider the possibility that the practice of administering heroin to addicts might have been a violation of legal statures. This committee, headed by Sir H. D. Rolleston, published a report in 1926 which concluded:

> . . . morphine or heroin may properly be administered to addicts in the following circumstances, namely a) where patients are under treatment by the gradual withdrawal method with a view to cure, b) where it has been demonstrated that after a prolonged attempt at cure that the use of the drug cannot be safely discontinued entirely, on account of the severity of the withdrawal symptoms

[1] National Institute on Drug Abuse. "Outpatient Drug Abuse Treatment Services, 1988: Results of a National Survey." NIDA Research Monograph Series. *Improving Drug Abuse Treatment.* Rockville, MD, DHHS Pub. No. (ADM) 91-1754, 1991, pp. 63-92.

Select Committe on Narcotics Abuse and Control. "Methadone Maintenance: Some Treatment Programs are not Effective; Greater Federal Oversight Needed." GAO testimony by Mark V. Nadal, Associate Director, National and Public Health Issues, March 23, 1990.

> produced, and c) where it has been similarly demonstrated that the patient, while capable of leading a useful and relatively normal life when a certain minimum dose is regularly administered, becomes incapable of this when the drug is entirely discontinued.[2]

It should be noted here that this early decision of the Rolleston Committee has set the tone for subsequent British narcotics legislation.

Until the early 1960s, the number of known narcotics addicts in England remained insignificant; the total number of all known narcotic addicts averaged under 500 for any year between 1924 and 1960. In addition, almost all of these were not "street" addicts, but "therapeutic" addicts, i.e., initially addicted in the course of medical treatment.[3]

In pre-World War II years, addicts were overrepresented among professional people, such as doctors and nurses; they were more often female than male and were usually middle-aged. The majority of these addictions were of therapeutic origin. Exemplifying the concept of the "stabilized addict," these British individuals were able to live useful and relatively normal lives with small, regular daily doses of narcotic drugs obtainable on prescription.

The 1950s, however, marked a change in this pattern of narcotics use. The addicts during these later years tended to be younger and predominantly male. They congregated in groups in the music clubs of London. Throughout the 1950s, the medical profession in Great Britain jealously guarded its prerogative to prescribe heroin to addicts.

Second Period: Convening of the First Brain Committee (1958)

In 1958, a committee was appointed under the chairmanship of Lord Brain to review the advice of the Rolleston Committee. The committee met to consider whether new methods of treating heroin addiction rendered the Rolleston recommendations obsolete and to decide if the increasing popularity of synthetic analgesics, such as pethidine and methadone, should come under stricter control or review. Their final report, published in 1960, recommended no major changes in British drug policy and reaffirmed the doctor's prerogative to prescribe narcotic drugs, including heroin. This decision was based on the belief that there had been no major increase in the number of new addicts per year.

Beginning in 1960, the British began to see an increase in the number of new known addicts, although this number has still remained small: in 1959, there were 454 known addicts; in 1960, 437; in 1961, 470; in 1962, 532; in 1963, 635; and in 1969, 2,881. By 1975, this figure had dropped to 1,954.

By 1983, however, heroin addiction increased to 5,850 addicts. This was an increase of 1,750 addicts from 1982—a 42 percent increase. Many more of the new addicts were under 20 years old and seizures of heroin by police and customs officials doubled to more than six times the annual average of

---

[2] May, Edgar. "Narcotics Addiction and Control in Great Britian." *Dealing with Drug Abuse: A Report to the Ford Foundation.* The Drug Abuse Survey Projects. New York: Praeger Publisher, 1972, p. 351.

[3] National Institute on Drug Abuse. Report Series 13, No. 2. See also "The British Narcotics System." U.S. Department of Health and Human Services, April 1978.

the 1970s. The addicts tended to be multiple drug users using cocaine as well as heroin.

Third Period: Convening of the Second Brain Committee (1964)

In 1964, the Interdepartmental Committee reconvened to consider whether, in the light of recent experience, the advice they gave in 1961 in relation to the prescribing of addictive drugs by doctors needed revising; and if it did, the Committee was to make recommendations. Reports from the Home Office indicated that, although both organized trafficking in dangerous drugs and illicit importation of drugs remained at insignificant levels, there was now evidence of increasing heroin abuse, fed mainly by the activities of a few doctors whose overprescribing had created a surplus.

For example, in 1962, one million tablets of heroin (one-sixth grain each) were prescribed; 600,000 of these came from one doctor in London.

In 1965, the Committee recommended a complete revision of the British approach to drug abuse treatment. The proposed controls more closely approximated the concept of a formal system than anything that had existed previously. Their conclusions were five-fold: (1) specific centers should be organized to treat addiction problems; (2) only licensed doctors should be authorized to prescribe heroin and cocaine to addicts for the purpose of treating their addictions—in practice, these licenses are issued on a selective basis to doctors working in the field of drug addiction; (3) a formal system for the notification of addicts should be established; (4) doctors at the centers should be given advice in cases where addiction was in question; (5) doctors at the centers should be given the power, in certain circumstances, to detain addicts in inpatient facilities without the addicts' consent. By the spring of 1968, all but the last recommendation were passed into law.

Operation of the British System After 1968

In the spring of 1968, seventeen clinics had been set up to provide both inpatient and outpatient facilities for the treatment of narcotics addiction. A patient who did not wish to undergo withdrawal treatment could be maintained on a minimum dosage of heroin with the understanding that the staff of the clinic would work to win his or her confidence and trust so that he or she might be eventually convinced to undergo withdrawal.

The Advisory Committee on Drug Dependence, established approximately at the same time that the clinics were being set up, published a report emphasizing that outpatient clinics should not be "regarded as mere prescribing units without any positive objective. Outpatient clinics are also rehabilitation clinics. Their object should be to encourage the addict to accept hospital admission for withdrawal and to make use of the opportunity which prescribing gives to build a constructive relationship with the patient."[4]

In 1969, the clinics were attended by approximately 1,300 patients a month. These patients attended the clinics every week and picked up daily

---

[4] "The Rehabilitation of Drug Addicts." The Advisory Committee on Drug Dependence. London: Her Majesty's Stationery Office, 1968.

prescriptions at local pharmacies. Efforts were made to spread prescriptions around town in order to avoid the problems that had existed earlier, when groups of addicts "hung around" specific pharmacies. Urine tests indicated that most patients used the drugs prescribed as well as other substances, primarily amphetamines and barbiturates. More recently, many of the licensed physicians in the treatment clinics have shifted from prescribing heroin to methadone, because the latter is a longer acting drug and is available in sterile solution suitable for use in intravenous injections.

Current Policies and Patterns of Drug Abuse in Britain

Patterns of drug abuse in Great Britain are changing. After 1968, there was a rapid increase in amphetamine and barbiturate misuse. When the prescription of heroin and cocaine was restricted, a few doctors irresponsibly switched their addicts to methamphetamine. Finally, a voluntary agreement was made between the pharmaceutical manufacturers and the Ministry of Health, whereby supplies of methamphetamine were restricted to hospital pharmacies; thus, a potential epidemic was averted. Currently, a number of methadone addicts who had no previous experience with heroin have been coming to the clinics as new patients. This suggests that a limited amount of the methadone prescribed by registered practitioners has been diverted to the black market. This may be due to the fact that the prescription of methadone has always been open to any registered physician.

Furthermore, methadone is replacing heroin as the drug of choice for maintenance therapy, even though the policy on prescribing drugs for the treatment of narcotics addiction has remained unchanged: it is still a clinical decision as to which drug to prescribe. Nonetheless, methadone—either orally or intravenously—is being prescribed much more frequently.

Since 1971, the British policy has been to treat the individual opiate addict as a medical patient rather than as a criminal. Furthermore, once the U.S. made treatment widely available in the 1970s and once the U.S. began to use methadone, the differences between the British and American approaches diminished greatly.

As with the U.S. system, there has been considerable confusion over the success of the British system in curtailing the rising tide of individuals becoming addicted to heroin. In order for a narcotics addict in Britain to be accepted for treatment at one of the 35 narcotics addict treatment centers (15 in London and 20 in the Provinces), the physician in charge must be satisfied clinically that the addict is dependent on narcotic drugs and that he or she will be treated for his or her addiction. There is no regulation that there must be a 2-year history of addiction, as there is in the U.S.

As suggested ealier, the heroin legally produced in Britain is only available in one dosage form, a tablet of 10 mg. (1/6 of a grain). The availability of this tablet dosage form led to a new trend in Britain from 1970 onwards: new addicts entering treatment were offered methadone instead of heroin, as methadone was available in sterile injectable dosage form.

By providing legally-produced heroin, it has been said that the British system has curtailed drug-related crime. However, arguments that the British system has been successful in undercutting the black market and destroying the incentive for organized crime seem to have been premature.

Today, the price of illegal heroin on the streets of London is about the same as the price on the streets of New York City. In light of this, it might be more accurate to say that the British pattern of narcotics control and licensed distribution served successfully to maintain pre- and post-war generations of therapeutic addicts. At that time, Great Britain did not have the street addict problem that has always characterized the American heroin experience. But, since the 1960s, addiction has been spreading to the streets and, as a result, stricter controls—like those in place in the United States—are necessary.

Summary

The history of the British narcotics system is fraught with controversy. For years, debate has raged over whether or not the British drug program actually constitutes a system. Some say that a system can be just as much a loosely gathered set of regulations and customs as it can be a tightly structured organization of laws. Others insist that it has only been in recent years, when policies have been coordinated, that we can justifiably speak of a "British system." On the part of Americans, there has been much misunderstanding about what the British program intends to do and how it strives to reach its objectives.

TREATMENT RESEARCH

RESEARCH ON TREATMENT EFFECTIVENESS

In the past, research on the treatment of substance abuse has been concentrated on the management of narcotics addiction; however, the recent rise in cocaine addiction in the United States has prompted a great deal of activity in new areas. The increased awareness of drug abuse in the workplace has also spurred the development of innovative programs for early detection and treatment of workers before drugs have caused the loss of their jobs. Moreover, the diversification of treatment approaches has led to increased attention to the complex interactions of drug-use behavior and social functioning, family problems, and occupational difficulties. Thus, effectiveness of any treatment may be influenced by specific variables such as availability of family support for the patient and more general factors such as the local economy and levels of unemployment. There is increasing recognition that substance abuse is a multifaceted syndrome rather than a straightforward medical problem requiring medical treatment. Substance abusers have been found to be a heterogeneous group who cannot be classified simply on the basis of their preferred drug. These issues are critical to research on treatment effectiveness because they call into question any simple measure of how severe the condition was before treatment and how much improvement there has been after treatment.

Different Treatments for Different Types of Patients

As with other chronic diseases such as arthritis, it is best to speak of remissions and improvement rather than "cures" in treating substance abusers. Research has shown that substance abuse treatment is associated with significant changes in drug use, employment, crime, and psychosocial adjustment; but until recently there had been no indication that any particular type of treatment was any better or worse than any other form of treatment. Considering the major conceptual and practical differences between such treatments as methadone maintenance and drug-free therapeutic communities, it was puzzling that there had been no demonstration of outcome differences among these major forms of treatment.

Similarly, there had long been recognition of wide differences among substance abuse patients in demographics, patterns of drug use, employment skills, crime backgrounds, etc. However, there was very little evidence that this variability was associated with differences in treatment outcome across the different modalities, or even within a particular modality. There was, of course, general indication that those patients who entered treatment with more severe problems (particularly crime problems) had poorer outcomes, but there was little evidence that certain types of patients might be matched to specific kinds of treatments as a means of increasing the overall effectiveness and efficiency of a treatment system.

The Addiction Severity Index (ASI) (McLellan et al. 1980, 1983, 1985), was designed on the premise that addiction to either alcohol or street drugs must be considered in the full context of those additional treatment problems that may have contributed to and/or resulted from the chemical abuse. The objective of the ASI was to produce a "problem severity profile" of every patient through an analysis of seven areas commonly affected in alcohol- or other drug-abusing patients. These areas include medical condition, employment, alcohol and drug use, legal status, family relations, and psychiatric condition.

This ASI instrument was used in a four-year study in 1982 of six programs treating alcohol/drug addicts, in an inpatient and outpatient program, and again in a series of studies in 1986 (McLellan et al.). Based on the findings of these studies, it was concluded that substance abuse treatments do have specific and predictable effects on particular patient subgroups; these subgroups can be easily and reliably identified at the time of admission so that they may be assigned to the most appropriate and cost-effective treatments.

ADVANCES IN SPECIFIC TREATMENT MODALITIES

Since substance abusers suffer from such a complex of medical and social problems, it is not surprising that multiple treatments are often used in the same patient. Researchers usually try to isolate each element of treatment in order to study it scientifically. In practice, however, several treatment approaches are typically used simultaneously or sequentially. For purposes of discussion, various categories of treatments will be listed although there is a good deal of overlap. For example, specific types of behavior therapy or psychotherapy could be used either in patients on methadone maintenance or in drug-free therapeutic communities.

Detoxification

Most treatment programs begin with detoxification. This simply means withdrawing the drug upon which the person is dependent. The withdrawal symptoms usually consist of the opposite effects from those produced by the drug. Cocaine, for example, produces euphoria and increased energy; however, cocaine-dependent persons usually become tired and depressed during withdrawal. Detoxification from sedatives can be life-threatening because of seizures and cardiac effects, but medical treatment with prescribed sedatives in decreasing amounts is usually successful.

Detoxification from opioids—while less dangerous—is still quite uncomfortable without medical help. Detoxification from short-acting opioids takes seven to ten days, but subtle symptoms can continue for months. Protracted withdrawal symptoms can be a significant problem, especially for those trying to withdraw from such a long-acting opioid as methadone.

A significant development in recent years (Gold et al. 1980) is the use of the anti-hypertensive drug clonidine to treat the symptoms of opioid withdrawal. Clonidine is not an opiate-like drug, but it relieves many of the symptoms of opioid withdrawal, particularly those which involve physical symptoms of autonomic nervous system hyperactivity. Since clonidine is not an addicting drug, it can be given in medical settings where amelioration of withdrawal symptoms by prescription opiate is not desirable. Interestingly, clonidine may relieve the symptoms of nicotine withdrawal in smokers attempting to quit (Glassman et al. 1984). This suggests that there may be a common neural pathway involved in the production of withdrawal symptoms among several classes of addicting drugs.

Detoxification is also the first step in the treatment of cocaine-dependent persons. Often this step is quite difficult because the patient has a tremendous craving to resume the use of cocaine, and the presence of severe depressive symptoms makes participation in an overall rehabilitation program limited. However, the antidepressant drug desipramine has been reported to decrease cocaine craving on a long-term basis (Gawin and Kleber 1984, 1985).

It has also been theorized that cocaine-dependent patients suffer from a dopamine depletion syndrome and thus the dopamine receptor stimulant bromocriptine has been tried to relieve withdrawal symptoms. (Dackis and Gold 1986). Early results suggest some positive results, but much more research is needed to confirm the utility of this treatment.

While detoxification has generally been viewed only as the first step in a long-term treatment program, there is some evidence that some addicts benefit from detoxification by itself (Newman 1979). Detoxification programs provide a humane means of reducing drug dependency, an opportunity to break the cycle of addiction, and a chance to enter longer term treatment.

Prevention Of Relapse

After detoxification, patients are encouraged to enter a long-term treatment program to prevent their returning to drug dependence and to give them time to reconstruct their lives. Recently, a new drug that aids in preventing relapse to opioid dependence was approved by the Food and Drug Administration. The new drug is called naltrexone (Trexan), and it is one of a class of compounds known as opiate antagonists. It is not an opiate itself, and it is not addicting. The main effect of this antagonist is to occupy opiate receptors and prevent opiate drugs from exerting any effect.

This new drug, naltrexone, is not a treatment by itself, but it has been shown to be effective within the context of a comprehensive rehabilitation program for prevention of relapse to opioid use. After detoxification, the patient can be given naltrexone as infrequently as two to three times per week. This medication will provide protection from re-addiction should the person impulsively take a dose of an opioid. The action of any opiate or opioid will be blocked resulting in no euphoria or reward. Unlike the alcoholic receiving disulfiram (Antabuse), there is no unpleasant reaction should the naltrexone-treated patient take an opioid. There is only a feeling that he has wasted his money because the effects of the heroin or other opiate have been neutralized.

Naltrexone is the product of many years of both NIDA-funded research and pharmaceutical industry investigations in pursuit of the "perfect antagonist." Naltrexone fits this description in many ways since it is effective against all opioids, is not itself addictive, is relatively long acting, and has few side effects. Unfortunately, such a drug appeals only to highly motivated patients who sincerely wish to give up experiencing opiate-induced euphoria. This describes only a minority of street addicts. Despite this limitation, naltrexone has become the treatment drug of choice in many centers for physicians, nurses, and white collar workers with opioid-dependence problems. In particular, physicians constantly exposed to the temptation of a return to opiate use seem to benefit from this new treatment aid.

Behavioral Approaches

Several behaviorally based treatments have been studied recently. One of the most promising is known as "contingency contracting" (Crowley 1984; Dolan et al. 1985; McCarthy and Borders 1985). This treatment involves setting up an explicit contract between the patient and therapist requiring specific behaviors from each.

Contingency contracting can be combined with other treatments such as detoxification, psychotherapy, therapeutic community, opiate antagonist, or methadone maintenance. It is then possible to analyze the relationship between treatments and determine what motivates a given patient. Contracts may include both rewards and punishments. Research has shown that external motivation imposed by a therapist or even a judge or probation officer can provide an important stimulus for the patient in early treatment. Eventually, the patient tends to incorporate the goals of treatment into his or her own value system and the new constructive behaviors become rewarding in themselves.

Extinction Of Conditioned Responses

Research dating back many years has shown that drugs of all types produce powerful conditioned responses. This means that the reliable pharmacological effects produced by drugs become associated with the environment or the situation in which the drugs were used. Even long after a person has stopped using drugs, the environmental stimuli may trigger a drug-like or a drug withdrawal-like response. Often these responses consist only of craving the drug, but sometimes strong physiological responses are evoked such as nausea, tearing, or sweating. These can occur when the former addict returns to his home or when he sees former friends using drugs. Of course, such reactions can lead to resumption of drug use and re-addiction. There is evidence that such conditioned reactions play a role in relapse to cocaine and opioid use and to the resumption of smoking.

Recently new treatment research has been aimed at extinguishing these responses in the hopes that this will aid the patient to remain drug-free

(Childress et al. 1985, 1987). The treatment consists of gradually exposing the patient to drug-related stimuli. These begin with mental images of the drug-using environment, progressing to images of the situations surrounding drug use. If the patient becomes anxious or develops withdrawal symptoms, he or she is taught to relax and deal with these feelings without resorting to drug use. Over several weeks, the program progresses to video tapes of drug-procuring and drug-using behaviors. Finally the patient is given bags of heroin (or cocaine) to use for a mock drug-preparation ritual. The patient's responses are measured both by recording physiological responses using a polygraph and by obtaining the patient's subjective response to the procedure.

This new treatment is imbedded within a standard treatment program. The patients have first been detoxified and have received drug-free treatment in a therapeutic community. The results so far show that the extinction treatment procedures can reduce or even eliminate the conditioned responses to drug-related stimuli. The current research question is whether this extinction results in an improved ability to remain drug-free at long-term follow-up.

Methadone Maintenance

For opioid (heroin) addicts, methadone has had a tremendously positive impact since its introduction in the 1960s. Patients who have been unable to completely stop heroin and detoxify or those who relapse shortly after detoxification can be easily transferred to a maintenance dose of oral methadone. Methadone prevents opiate withdrawal symptoms for 24 to 36 hours, and in proper doses it does not produce sedation or euphoria. Urine test results show that patients on methadone reduce or eliminate their use of street drugs. The best results have been achieved by those programs which utilize contingency management along with methadone.

Methadone is well accepted by most patients, and it enables them to turn their attention to social and occupational rehabilitation. Studies have shown that 65 to 85 percent of patients remain in methadone treatment for 12 months or more and during this time there is a dramatic reduction in crimes committed and an increase in gainful employment. Some patients remain on methadone for many years and it enables them to function well and in many cases make significant contributions to society. In response to possible negative effects, studies of long-term cases have failed to find evidence of toxic effects from long-term methadone ingestion (Kreek 1983).

Of course, most programs have as their stated goal achieving a drug-free state. But this is not practical for those patients who do not wish to stop methadone maintenance. Success rates for stopping methadone and remaining drug-free are reasonably good when both patient and therapist feel that the patient has made sufficient progress such that he or she is now ready to stop. Stimmel (1979) studied such a patient group and found that 57 percent were still drug-free at an average follow-up period of 31 months. Such patients, however, constitute a minority of those admitted to methadone programs.

Drug Treatment and Rehabilitation

Residential Treatment

The primary residential treatment model is the therapeutic community (TC). As mentioned above, TCs emphasize a self-help approach, frequently using former addicts as counselors, administrators, and role models. The atmosphere in the programs is highly structured, especially for newer members. Clients progress through the program in clearly delineated stages. Each successive stage usually carries more personal freedom and responsibility. Group counseling or therapy sessions, which are usually confrontational in nature—stressing openness and honesty—are a cornerstone of the TC approach to treatment.

TC treatment involves stays within the program usually measured in months; however, drop-out rates are fairly high. In seven programs surveyed by DeLeon and Schwartz (1984), retention rates for a 12 month treatment stay ranged from 4 to 21 percent. In follow-up evaluations (DeLeon et al. 1982; Simpson and Sells 1982), improvements in drug use, employment, criminality, and psychological well-being were noted both for the program graduates and for the dropouts. In general, studies (not corrected for presence or severity of psychiatric disorders) indicate that those patients who remain in TCs longer experience more successful and lasting treatment.

Outpatient Drug-Free Treatment

The outpatient drug-free modality subsumes a wide variety of approaches to treatment. In large surveys of treatment, this is the most popular modality accounting for nearly half (48 percent) of all patients in treatment. Programs vary widely from drop-in "rap" centers to highly structured programs mostly providing counseling or psychotherapy as the treatment mainstay. Simpson and Sells (1982) reported improvements in the opioid abusers who received treatment in outpatient drug-free programs. Daily opioid use declined from 100 percent pretreatment to 44 percent at the end of the first year and 28 percent in the third year. Arrests also showed a significant decline and employment increased after treatment. However, because individuals entering outpatient drug-free treatment have not been adequately described on a variety of severity variables, the significance of the above findings is not yet clear.

THE POLICE CAN PLAY AN IMPORTANT ROLE IN TREATMENT

To understand the underlying dynamics of drug-related crime, the police need to understand that not all addicts are the same. There are two kinds of drug addicts who commit crimes: the addict-criminal resorts to crime to pay for drugs; the criminal-addict uses drugs as part of a broader pattern of criminal behavior.

The importance of the distinction is that the opportunities for law enforcement to make an impact differ dramatically, depending on the kind of addict that officers are dealing with. With the addict-criminal, if you treat the addiction, the person usually stops committing any crimes; without the drugs, the addict-criminal would not be involved with crime. With the criminal-addict, the original criminal activity usually persists even after drug treatment.

The police have a unique opportunity to use the threat of jail as a way to goad the addict-criminal into a recovery program. It makes sense for law enforcement officers to target these individuals for special attention, because once they are treated, the chances are good that they will not create problems for the police or the community in the future. Identifying the addict-criminal is difficult. But community policing, which puts officers in closer contact with members of a community, may assist in identifying those for whom treatment offers the best hope of living within the law.

Dealing with the criminal-addict is much more difficult, since these individuals often continue to be problems in the community, even if their addiction is under control. Likewise, incarceration is less of a stigma, so the threat of jail may not induce them to seek treatment.

FUTURE DIRECTIONS

Thus far, most treatment programs have not been based on good empirical evidence about program effectiveness. Despite the problems, however, several general conclusions with regard to treatment may be drawn. Given proper treatment, the prognosis for youth might be better than that for adults. Differences between youthful and adult abusers are generally those differences that predict treatment success. The qualification is important, because we do not yet know what constitutes a good treatment for either youth or adults.

This uncertainty underscores the need for more carefully conducted treatment research, especially in the face of the great numbers of adolescent drug abusers who do require some treatment. There are practical problems in random assignment of clients to treatment, constructing adequate and appropriate control groups, and having well-defined, meaningful outcome measures. Nonetheless, better and more standardized evaluation of adolescent treatment facilities is required to ascertain which, if any, of them are effective, and what factors lead to effectiveness. As theoretical concepts of drug abuse lead to implications for treatment, these treatments should be tested.

All of this research is expensive, and it does not provide direct treatment. But the alternative is to continue spending money on treatment programs without knowing whether they are doing any good. It may be that the only treatments that are effective are complex and expensive, in which case careful decisions must be made as to whether and when to implement them. But if any treatment proves effective, then at least a door is opened for consideration of less costly versions that may be as effective. Therefore, at least for the present, treatment research should be as widespread as possible.

Summary

Treatment for drug abuse is a multifaceted phenomenon; its variances depend upon the applied definition of drug abuse and the treatment practitioner's theoretical view of its etiology. Many different services, ranging from chemotherapy and psychotherapy, to social assistance and residential care are provided under the name of drug treatment. Often there is no coherence to the collection of services provided, and even less frequently is the treatment protocol tailored to the needs of the individual client.

Despite a lack of over-arching organization, drug treatment facilities may be generally classified into one of four types: detoxification, methadone maintenance, therapeutic communities, and (mostly outpatient) drug-free programs. Most of the treatment in the first three types of programs has been for opiate abuse. Of all youth in treatment, however, 79 percent are in drug-free programs, with most of the remainder in some form of therapeutic community.

The scientific evidence on the efficacy of treatment is scant; virtually all of the reported studies suffer from one or more serious defects in design. Nonetheless, several conclusions may be drawn. A study of long-term treatment effects showed that methadone maintenance, therapeutic communities, and drug-free treatments were all superior to no treatment and to detoxification unaccompanied by other services. For non-opiate clients (a category into which most adolescents would fall) drug-free programs were the treatment of choice.

The longer a client remains in treatment, the more likely the treatment will be successful. However, the reasons why this is so are not well-established. At present, it seems just as reasonable to assume that people who stay in treatment do so because of their own predisposition to improve as it is to assume that staying longer increases the likelihood of improvement because of the treatment method. In any event, a major problem with all drug treatment programs is the high dropout rate; any research leading to greater client retention would increase overall program effectiveness.

The research on program control over clients and behavior modification techniques is inconclusive: there is so little research, and its results are so mixed, that one cannot currently recommend how to structure a program or when to use behavior modification techniques.

With respect to treatment specifically aimed at adolescents, the research evidence is scarcely better than that for treatment in general. Programs for early intervention treatment, although popular, have not been proven effective by scientific standards. Family therapy, which is an increasingly popular form of treatment for adolescents, has been shown effective in some contexts, but because of its particular problems of implementation, this method needs better scientific support before it could be broadly recommended as a treatment of choice.

REFERENCES:

Childress, A.R. et al. "Behavioral therapies for substance abuse." *Int J Addict.* 20(687):947-969, 1985.

________. "Development of a procedure for assessing and extinguishing conditioned opiate withdrawal-like responses." *Problems of Drug Dependence.* NIDA Research Monograph Series. 1987.

Crowley, T. "Contingency contracting treatment of drug-abusing physicians, nurses, and dentists." Grabowski, J. et al., eds. *Behavioral Intervention Techniques in Drug Abuse Treatment.* NIDA Research Monograph 46. DHHS Pub. No. (ADM) 84-1284. Washington, D.C.: Supt. of Docs., U.S. Govt. Print. Off., 1984, pp. 68-83.

Dackis, C.A. and M.S. Gold. "Bromocriptine as treatment of cocaine abuse." *Lancet.* 8438:1151-1152, 1985.

DeLeon, G. and S. Schwartz. "Therapeutic communities: 'What are the retention rates?' " *Am J Drug and Alcohol Abuse.* 10(2):267-284, 1984.

DeLeon, G. et al. "The therapeutic community: Success and improvement rates 5 years after treatment." *Int J Addict.* 17(4):703-747, 1982.

Dolan, M.P. et al. "Contracting for treatment termination to reduce illicit drug use among methadone maintenance treatment failures." *J of Consult and Clin Psychol.* 53:549-551, 1985.

Dole, V.P. "Methadone Maintenance Treatment of 25,000 Heroin Addicts." *Journal of the American Medical Association.* Vol. 215:1131-1134, 1971.

Dole, V.P. and M. Nyswander. "A Medical Treatment for Heroin Addiction." *Journal of the American Medical Association.* Vol. 193:646-650, 1965.

________. "Rehabilitation of Heroin Addicts After Blockade with Methadone." *New York State Journal of Medicine.* Vol. 66: 2011-2017, 1966.

Dole, V.P., M. Nyswander and A. Werner. "Successful Treatment of 750 Criminal Addicts." *Journal of the American Medical Association.* Vol. 206:2708-2711, 1968.

Gawin, F.H. and H.D. Kleber. "Abstinence symptomatology and psychiatric diagnosis in cocaine abusers. Clinical observations." *Arch Gen Psych.* 43(2):107-113, 1986.

Glassman, A. et al. "Cigarette craving, smoking withdrawal and clonidine." *Science* 226. pp. 864-866, 1984.

Gold, M.S. et al. "Opiate withdrawal using clonidine." *Journel of the American Medical Association.* 243:343-346, 1980.

Judson, Horace. *Heroin Addiction: What Americans Can Learn from the English Experience.* New York: Vintage Books, 1975.

Kreek, M.J. "Health consequences associated with the use of methadone." In: Cooper, J.R et al., eds. *Research on the Treatment of Narcotic Addiction: State of the Art.* NIDA Treatment Research Monograph Series. DHHS Pub. No. (ADM)83-1291. Washington, D.C.: Supt. Of Docs., U.S. Govt. Print. Off., 1983, pp. 456-494.

May, Edgar. "Narcotics Addiction and Control in Great Britian." *Dealing with Drug Abuse: A Report to the Ford Foundation.* The Drug Abuse Survey Projects. New York: Praeger Publisher, 1972, p. 351.

McCarthy, J.J., and O.T. Borders. "Limit setting on drug abuse in methadone maintenance patients." *Am J Psychia.* 142:12, 1985.

McLellan, A.T. et al. "Increased effectiveness of substance abuse treatment: A prospective study of patient-treatment 'matching.' " *J Nerv Ment Dis.* 171(10):597-605, 1983.

________. "Is substance abuse treatment effective? Five different perspectives." *Journel of the American Medical Association.* 247:1423-1428, 1982.

________. "New data from the Addiction Severity Index: Reliability and validity in three centers." *J Nerv Ment Dis.* 173:412-423, 1985.

National Institute on Drug Abuse. "Outpatient Drug Abuse Treatment Services, 1988: Results of a National Survey." NIDA Research Monograph Series. *Improving Drug Abuse Treatment.* Rockville, MD, DHHS Pub. No. (ADM) 91-1754, 1991, pp. 63-92.

________. Report Series 13, No. 2.

Newman, R.G. and W.B. Whitehill. "Double-blind comparison of methadone and placebo maintenance treatments of narcotic addicts in Hong Kong." *Lancet.* (8141):485-488, 1979.

Drug Treatment and Rehabilitation

Select Committe on Narcotics Abuse and Control. "Methadone Maintenance: Some Treatment Programs are not Effective; Greater Federal Oversight Needed." GAO testimony by Mark V. Nadal, Associate Director, National and Public Health Issues, March 23, 1990.

Simpson, D.D. and S.B. Sells. "Effectiveness of treatment for drug abuse: An overview of the DARP Research Program." *Advances in Alcohol and Substance Abuse.* 2(1):7-29, 1982.

Stimmel, B. et al. "Ability to remain abstinent after methadone detoxification." *JAMA.* 237:1216-1220, 1979.

U.S. Department of Health and Human Services. "The British Narcotics System." April 1978.

________. "The Rehabilitation of Drug Addicts." The Advisory Committee on Drug Dependence. London: Her Majesty's Stationery Office, 1968.

This page intentionally left blank.

CHAPTER XIX

DRUG PREVENTION AND EDUCATION

INTRODUCTION

Concern about drug use and abuse is not new to our society and our time. For centuries, communities have addressed drug issues in a variety of ways, most commonly through legislation and education. The degree of interest in preventing drug use and related problems, however, has depended on the nature and level of the perceived problems, the political climate, agenda-setting by the media, and pressure from interested groups.

While the first half of the 20th century was marked by extensive efforts against drug use (the temperance movement of the first two decades and the campaigns against marijuana and heroin in the 1930s), concerted efforts to reduce youthful drug use did not arise until the late 1960s. By then it had become clear that drug use was widespread and growing among young people from all segments of society. In 1970, President Nixon called for preventive drug education at all levels of schooling from kindergarten through the 12th grade; subsequently, Federal expenditures for drug prevention programs rose dramatically.

The reasons why people use illicit drugs, however, are complex; these reasons result not only from the legality or illegality of the drugs, but also from familial, societal, and cultural factors. It has become increasingly obvious that law enforcement can be but one part of any government's program to reduce drug use. Law enforcement must by supplemented by educational programs to inform people about the properties of various drugs and the risks associated with their use. These programs include public school drug education courses, mass media and other advertising campaigns, and grassroots programs (for example, the "Just Say No" movement).

Although the public may perceive that substantial resources have been allocated to drug use prevention through education and public information campaigns, the amounts spent on these efforts are small compared with those spent by agencies that enforce drug laws. This results from a historical emphasis on solving drug problems by reducing supply rather than demand.

FEDERAL STRATEGY

The current Federal strategy for the prevention of drug abuse involves a comprehensive approach to reducing the availability of illicit drugs and reducing the adverse effects of drug abuse on the individual and society.

The five major elements of the strategy include the following:

- International Cooperation
- Drug Law Enforcement
- Education and Prevention

— Detoxification and Treatment

— Research

In the areas of education and prevention, the Federal strategy is a comprehensive, long-term campaign to discourage drug and alcohol use among school-age children (youth under the age of 18) and to reduce the demand for illicit drugs in all age groups.

Education:
The goal is to educate the parents of school-age children about drugs and how to recognize and deal with drug abuse in their homes, schools, and communities.

Prevention:
The goal is to reduce the level of drug use among all Americans, but especially among school-age children, for they are the future of our country.

CONTROL OF DRUG ABUSE THROUGH EDUCATION

Many attempts have been made to control the use and abuse of drugs (including alcohol and tobacco) through education. Society's readiness to seek educational solutions for social ills reflects the value it attaches to education per se, and its commitment to the notion of education based upon rational argument and experience.

Educational strategies and programs to combat drug abuse differ in many regards, including the drugs and groups the programs target, their content and objectives, the media, settings, and processes they use, and their effectiveness. Drug abuse education is neither a simple nor a single concept; it refers, rather, to a collection of laws, policies, programs, and actions designed to influence the use of drugs.

Today, there are thousands of drug prevention and education programs in schools and communities across the United States, but comparatively fewer Federal dollars for financing them. Whether funded privately or publicly, however, most are based on one or more of four prevention models.

The Information Model

The information model constituted the dominant prevention mode for many years. It assumes that adolescents use drugs because they lack information about their negative effects and therefore have neutral or even positive attitudes toward trying them. This model sees providing information about drugs—their properties, their methods of use, and their consequences—as the solution. Such information is expected to produce less positive attitudes toward drugs. Those attitudes should, in turn, inhibit drug use.

Several states require drug education in the schools, but the specific content and amount of time devoted to the subject are usually left up to the school district, or even the individual school. Instruction therefore varies widely from one school to another, and examples of programs based on the information approach may vary from two pages in a school textbook to a highly structured, multiple-session health curriculum with audiovisual materials.

Drug Prevention and Education

Typically, these programs provide information about the physical and psychological effects of specific drugs, their pharmacology, and the legal implications of using illicit drugs. Most school-based information programs are presented by teachers using a didactic delivery style; some use outside experts such as a doctor, nurse, or narcotics officer, and some provide for class discussion. While the questionable "scare" tactics of early drug-education programs have largely been abandoned in favor of a more balanced presentation of the facts, the emphasis is usually on the harmful consequences of drugs, particularly the long-term effects of continued and heavy use. The content frequently goes beyond a "just the facts" approach to include an exhortation not to use drugs.

The Individual Deficiency Model

The individual deficiency model emerged as an important approach in the early 1970s. This model assumes that the problem lies within the child—that children use drugs to compensate for a lack of self-esteem, or because they lack adequate tools for making rational decisions. Programs based on this model seek to provide general skills that will enhance the youngster's self-esteem or decision-making skills. They also frequently seek to encourage a school or home climate that emphasizes each child's special qualities and individual value.

The Social Pressures Model

The social pressures model is the most recent approach to drug prevention. This approach emphasizes the external influences that push adolescents toward drug use, particularly the subtle pressures of the media and the actual behavior and attitudes of key people in the adolescent's life; adults who drink, smoke, or use pills and, most importantly, friends and other peers who use drugs. The social pressures model also recognizes the special vulnerability of adolescents who are in a transitional status between childhood and adulthood: their general desire to appear grown up and to emulate what they perceive to be adult behavior. Accordingly, social pressures programs seek to provide adolescents with specific skills and support for saying "no."

The Alternatives Model

Closely related to both the individual deficiency and the social pressures approaches, the alternatives model assumes that adolescents may start using drugs for a variety of reasons, including both internal and external pressures, but emphasizes providing alternative activities to keep them busy and productive as the solution.

Current Trends

The current trend is to include a variety of components designed to influence knowledge, feeling, skills, and behavior. This multiplicity of program elements includes attempts to develop or enhance general interpersonal and coping skills, and specific skills related to drug use, such as assertiveness and refusal to use drugs.

WHAT IS PREVENTION?

Prevention programs aim at the reduction, delay, or prevention of drug use before it has become habitual or clearly dysfunctional. On the other hand, treatment programs seek to reduce or eliminate drug use among people for whom it has become so dominant that it interferes with their lives. Thus, the major distinction among interventions aimed at potential or actual users is between prevention and treatment.

The association between level of drug involvement and type of intervention provides a context for relating categories of prevention to the successive stages of drug use through which an adolescent might pass over time. Figure 1 depicts four such stages based on frequency of use: (1) non-use, or never having tried the specific drug at issue; (2) experimental or episodic use; (3) social or recreational use; (4) regular or frequent use; and (5) heavy use.

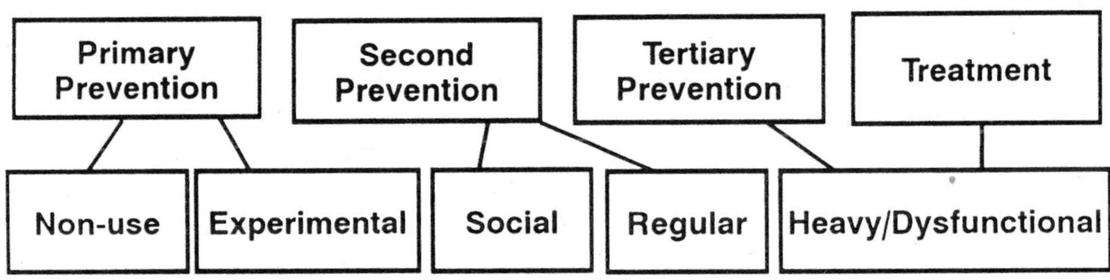

Fig. 1—Types of intervention associated with drug use stages

Within these schemes, primary prevention is focused on the early stages—trying to keep young people from ever starting at all; or, if they have experimented already, trying to keep them from shifting into regular use. Secondary and tertiary prevention programs seek to prevent regular users from getting into serious trouble, e.g., from becoming habitual users who are psychologically or physically dependent on the drug or mired in other maladaptive behavior such as frequent school absenteeism or delinquent activities. Secondary prevention programs target youths who have not yet exhibited ill effects from drug use, but who are identified as "at risk" of becoming problem users. Tertiary prevention programs focus on groups that have already manifested some problems resulting from or associated with drug use (absenteeism, learning difficulties, delinquency, health problems, etc.), but have not yet become psychologically or physically dependent upon the drug. Both secondary and tertiary prevention programs serve specific target populations that have had prior drug experiences. The dividing line between tertiary prevention and treatment is indistinct, though treatment programs typically focus on people whose drug use is more habitual, extensive, or clearly dysfunctional.

DRUG ABUSE ETIOLOGY AND PREVENTION/EDUCATION RESEARCH

Understanding the factors associated with becoming a drug abuser and, ultimately, understanding the mechanisms of drug abuse etiology is fundamental to effective prevention. Our knowledge of the psychosocial and biological factors that play a role in smoking, alcohol, and other drug abuse continues to be limited, although it has grown significantly in the last decade. While experimentation with tobacco, alcohol, and other psychoactive substances is common in adolescence, certain risk factors are more common in children and adolescents who become heavily involved in smoking and substance abuse than in others who do not. These risk factors have been comprehensively studied in research funded by the NIDA (Hawkins et al. 1985). As with the risk factors for heart disease and other illnesses, these are characteristics that have been found to be associated with a greater-than-average chance of developing the problem. Individuals with one or more of these risk factors do not, of course, invariably become substance abusers. A brief review of the known risk factors, however, will provide a useful backdrop for discussing the basis of effective prevention strategies.

Family Factors

1. A family history of alcoholism: Research has established a link between drinking problems in the family and adolescents or young adults abusing alcohol or other drugs. For example, the presence of an alcoholic family member approximately doubles the risk that a male child will later abuse alcohol or drugs.
2. A family history of criminality or antisocial behavior: Children from families in which other close family members have a criminal history are more likely to abuse alcohol and other drugs than children whose relatives have not been involved in such antisocial behavior.
3. Problems of parental direction or discipline: Unclear and/or inconsistent parental rules for behavior; inconsistent parental reactions to their children's behavior; unusual permissiveness; lax supervision of children's behavior or, conversely, excessively severe discipline, and constant criticism and an absence of parental praise or approval have all been found to be associated with higher rates of drug abuse among children.
4. Parental drug use or parental attitudes approving use are also associated with children later becoming drug abusers. Parents serve as models for their children's behavior in many ways. Children whose parents smoke, drink, or abuse drugs are more likely to do so than those children whose parents abstain from these activities. Parents who express favorable attitudes or approval of alcohol or other drug abuse also increase their children's likelihood of abusing these substances.

Peer Factors

Children whose friends (or brothers and sisters) use drugs are much more likely to use them than those whose peers do not. Not only is having friends who are drug users a strong predictor of drug use, there is also sufficient evidence to estimate that most initiation into drug use occurs through friends rather than strangers.

Achievement, School Commitment, and Social Alienation

1. Children who fail in school in their mid to late elementary school years are more likely to become adolescent drug abusers than those who do not. Children who fail in school for whatever reason—boredom, lack of ability, a mismatch with an unskilled teacher—are more likely to experiment with drugs earlier and to become regular users than those who do not.

2. Adolescents who are not interested in school and academic achievement are more likely to use drugs than those who are. Use of drugs, such as cocaine, other stimulants, or hallucinogens, is significantly less common among college-bound teenagers than among those who are not interested in their own education.

3. Children who feel alienated, strongly rebellious, and at odds with the dominant social values are at higher risk of abusing drugs than those with strong bonds to their family, their school, and to other conventional institutions.

4. Antisocial behavior during early adolescence, including school misbehavior, a low sense of social responsibility, fighting, and other types of aggression, have been found to be more common among drug abusers.

Age of First Use

The earlier the child begins to drink or use other drugs the greater the likelihood of later developing drug problems. Using drugs before age 15 greatly increases the risk of later drug use.

While the factors described are clearly associated with greater drug involvement, the reasons for this are often unclear. Vulnerability probably involves both psychosocial and biological elements. Having friends who are drug users or a parent who is alcoholic may provide a "model" for use, but other neurophysiological factors such as the drug being unusually reinforcing for the individual in relieving depression, anxiety, or producing euphoria may be decisive. For example, it is now well-established that children of alcoholics have a greater vulnerability to becoming alcoholics—even when raised by adoptive parents who are not alcoholic.[1]

Furthermore, experimentation with one psychoactive substance has, on the average, a predictable relationship to the later use of other psychoactive drugs. Use typically begins with alcohol and tobacco; in contemporary American culture, use of these substances then "progresses" to marijuana use.[2] Some individuals may go on to use sedatives, stimulants, and psychedelics. Still fewer (in the general population) will go on to use opiates such as heroin. While alcohol and tobacco are often described as "gateway" drugs in the sense that their use usually (but not invariably) precedes the use of other drugs, the progression need not imply that some property of these substances "causes" later use of the other drugs. The more common—easily available — psychoactive substances may be used first simply because they are so readily obtainable. Thus, a shift in availability may alter this order of progression. Early use may also occur partly because those who are most tempted to use psychoactive substances are those who have an earlier sense of need in themselves that these substances can potentially satisfy.

---

[1] Bohmen, M. "Some genetic aspects of alcoholism and criminality." *Arch Gen Psychiat* 35:269-276, 1978.

[2] Kandel, D., ed. *Longitudinal Research on Drug Use: Empirical Findings and Methodological Issues.* Washington, D.C.: Hemisphere (Halsted-Wiley), 1978, pp. 3-38.

TRADITIONAL PREVENTION APPROACHES

Considering the difficulty and cost of treating individuals with substance abuse problems, the prospect of developing effective substance abuse prevention programs has long held a great deal of appeal. Until recently, the standard prevention approach has involved either the presentation of factual information concerning the dangers of substance use or what is sometimes referred to as "affective" education. Informational tobacco, alcohol, and drug education programs are based largely on the assumption that increased knowledge about these substances and their hazards will effectively deter potential users (Goodstadt 1978). In other words, this type of prevention strategy is based on the belief that if students are fully aware of the dangers of tobacco, alcohol, or drug use they will make rational decisions not to use them. Fear arousal messages are frequently used by such programs to frighten individuals into not smoking, drinking, or using other drugs. Such programs have been conducted by teachers and other school personnel as well as by outsiders such as physicians, the police, and ex-addicts.

A second type of substance abuse prevention involves "affective" or "humanistic" education. These programs are generally designed to enhance self-esteem, to encourage responsible decision-making and to enrich the personal and social development of students (Swisher 1979). Affective education approaches are based on the following assumptions: (1) substance abuse programs should aim to develop prevention-oriented decision-making concerning the use of legal or illicit drugs; (2) such decisions should result in fewer negative consequences for the individual; and (3) the most effective way of achieving these goals is by increasing self-esteem, interpersonal skills, and participation in alternatives to substance use. Consistent with these assumptions, prevention programs of this type attempt to increase self-understanding and acceptance through values clarification and decision-making; to improve interpersonal relations through communication training, peer counseling, assertiveness training, etc.; and to increase students' abilities to meet their needs through conventional social institutions. This material is generally taught through class discussion and a variety of experiential classroom activities.

Although programs utilizing information dissemination/fear-arousal approaches as well as those emphasizing affective education have proliferated for at least a decade and a half, the available evidence suggests that neither approach is effective (Schaps 1981). A great many programs have been able to show an increase in knowledge of the negative consequences of substance use; some have also shown an impact on students' attitudes. However, few programs have been successful in changing actual substance use. Due to this ineffectiveness, the challenge in prevention has been to demonstrate that there are approaches which can change substance use behavior—to show that substance abuse prevention can "work."

PSYCHOSOCIAL PREVENTION APPROACHES

Substantial progress has been made during the past five years in new areas of prevention, and there is growing evidence supporting the effectiveness of some new approaches. Thus far, these techniques have been primarily used in preventing cigarette smoking, but the efficacy of this type of prevention beyond one or two years has not yet been proven. Researchers have focused on preventing adolescent cigarette smoking for several reasons. First, cigarette smoking is a major risk factor for such chronic diseases as coronary heart disease, cancer, and emphysema. It is widely recognized as the single-most important preventable cause of death and disability in the United States today.

Second, cigarette smoking is the most widespread drug dependence in our society. Moreover, cigarette smoking occurs toward the very beginning of the developmental progression of substance use (Kandel 1985). There have been some preliminary reports that the prevention programs initially developed to deter adolescent cigarette smoking may also deter the use of other substances, notably alcohol and marijuana (Shaffer 1983).

The substance prevention approaches which focus primary attention on the psychosocial factors involved in substance use and initiation show promise of increased effectiveness. Reviews of these programs not only highlight the evolution of the newer "psychosocial" approaches to substance abuse prevention over the past seven or eight years, but also describe the greater sophistication and increased methodological rigor of this research compared to earlier prevention research. These approaches fall into two general categories: (1) programs that focus on social influences believed to promote substance use and (2) broader life/coping skills and training approaches designed to enhance personal and social competence.

Social Influence Approaches

The development of smoking prevention strategies focusing on social influences promoting use is based on the fact that peer and family influences have been consistently demonstrated to play important roles in beginning to smoke. Although not yet established empirically, media influences may also play an important role in influencing adolescents to begin smoking. In general, the social influence approach to smoking prevention involves (1) making students aware of those social pressures to smoke to which they are likely to be exposed, (2) teaching specific coping skills (e.g., refusal skills) with which to resist these pressures, and (3) correcting misperceptions of social norms regarding smoking (e.g., making students aware that, in fact, most adults and adolescent do not smoke).

Most of the research that has been done with the social influence approach has been based on the pioneering work of Richard Evans and his colleagues at the University of Houston (Evans 1976, 1978). An underlying assumption of this approach is that students can be effectively "inoculated" against social influences to smoke by gradually exposing them to progressively more intense pro-smoking social influences. In addition, Evans' films provide students with specific tactics for resisting these pro-smoking influences. This approach, therefore, is based on the idea that students' resistance to group social pressures to smoke can be increased by making them: (1) more aware of those pressures and (2) helping them develop effective counter-arguments.

Other investigators have elaborated on this model, placing more emphasis on actually training students to deal with both peer and media pressures to smoke. These intervention strategies go beyond the basic psychological inoculation model developed by Evans and place greater emphasis on social learning theory (Bandura 1977). Two distinctive features of these expanded approaches are (1) the use of peer leaders (either older or the same age) to deliver some or all of the program and (2) the use of role playing and social reinforcement techniques to teach students specific skills for resisting group pressure to smoke. Some studies have also included a public commitment component in which students are encouraged to avow they will not smoke in the future.

Most research studies on the social influence approach have been targeted at junior high school students, with the intervention generally beginning in the seventh grade. Some studies have included students as young as fifth and sixth graders, while others have been aimed at high school students. All of the studies (over a dozen) have found reductions in smoking onset among students who have participated in the experimental programs when compared to those in the control group. As might be expected, these reductions are usually greatest shortly after the program is concluded (i.e., within a few weeks of completion) and tend to diminish over time.

Overall, the studies completed thus far have generally reported significant reductions in the proportion of individuals who begin to smoke following participation in the new programs compared to those who have not. Effects on individuals who are at an especially high risk of becoming smokers have not generally been studied using these techniques.

Although the social influence approach has been primarily evaluated in terms of its impact on cigarette smoking, there is limited evidence that it may sometimes reduce alcohol and marijuana use as well. Nonetheless, no firm conclusions can be drawn concerning the components that are most or least important, concerning who is most effective in conducting the programs, or concerning the age at which the programs should be presented to students.

Personal and Social Skills Training Approaches

Research has also been conducted on the efficacy of broader-based substance abuse prevention programs. In addition to including many of the components of social influence approaches, these programs emphasize acquiring more general personal and social skills. Their theoretical roots are largely based in social learning and problem behavior theories. From this perspective, substance abuse is a socially learned, purposive, and functional behavior that results from an interplay of social, environmental, and personal factors. Substance use behavior, like other behavior, is learned through modeling and reinforcement.

The modeling and reinforcement process occurs in several ways. Some individuals seek out others who smoke, drink, use drugs, or who are interested in doing so as an alternative means of achieving some desired goal. Adolescents who are doing poorly academically or socially and have no other basis for distinction, may begin to use drugs as a substitute means of enhancing their self-esteem or social status. Similarly, using tobacco, alcohol, and other drugs may be a way of coping with tension or anxiety, particularly social anxiety. Others may begin smoking, drinking, or using other drugs after repeatedly observing parents, siblings, or other esteemed role models doing so; they may also begin as a result of persuasive appeals by peers or advertisers. The extent to which individuals are susceptible to these influences may be related to their personal characteristics. For example, individuals with low self-esteem, low self-confidence, and those lacking a sense of personal autonomy appear most likely to succumb to social influences. Based on this principle, some researchers (Botvin, 1982; Hawkins, 1986) have hypothesized that susceptibility to substance abuse may be decreased by using broader-based intervention approaches that help develop personal characteristics associated with a low susceptibility to substance abuse.

Researchers in such states as New York, Tennessee, and Washington have studied the effectiveness of personal and social skills training for substance abuse prevention. The research has shown that, as is true of the social influences approach, the content and structure of this training varies widely. While some programs contain material similar to that in social influences programs, others do not. Generally, the more broad-based programs emphasize two or more of the following:

1. Developing general problem-solving and decision-making skills (e.g., "brainstorming," systematic decision-making);
2. Developing cognitive skills for resisting a range of interpersonal and media influences (e.g., identifying persuasive advertising appeals and how they work, developing personal counter-arguments to these appeals);
3. Increasing self-control and self-esteem (e.g., self-instructional techniques, self-reinforcement, goal setting);
4. Learning non-drug coping strategies for anxiety and tension reduction (e.g., relaxation techniques, cognitive coping skills);
5. Enhancing interpersonal skills (e.g., the ability to initiate social interaction, conversational techniques); and
6. Assertiveness training (improving the ability to make requests, how to say "no," expressing feelings and opinions more effectively).

These abilities are taught through instruction, demonstration, feedback, reinforcement, behavioral rehearsal (practice in class), and more extended practice is encouraged by the use of "homework" assignments. The underlying objective is to teach general life/coping skills with a broad range of applications rather than approaches that are situation- or problem-specific. However, these programs also emphasize applying these general skills in substance abuse-related situations (e.g., using assertion abilities to resist pressures to smoke or use other drugs).

Virtually all of the studies published to date have reported significant behavioral effects in the form of sharply reduced numbers of initially non-smoking participants who became smokers in the experimental group compared to the control group on a short-term basis (under one year).

Reductions range from less than half as many becoming smokers in the year following training to 75 percent fewer students in the experimental group becoming smokers at least over the short run.[3]

Transferring Smoking Prevention Concepts to Drug Prevention

Can concepts used in cigarette smoking prevention be transferred to other drug prevention programs? While the prognosis appears favorable, there are reasonable arguments on both sides. On the positive side, we know that many of the factors that precipitate smoking also apply to marijuana, the most commonly used illicit drug among adolescents. The primary factors associated with smoking onset include the influence of friends and parents; attitudes and beliefs about smoking; rebelliousness and independence; low academic performance and motivation; and prior manifestation of problem behavior. Each of these factors plays a role in adolescent experimentation with other drugs.

On the other hand, it can be argued that anti-smoking programs are effective because the general social climate has changed so radically over the past twenty years. As compared with 20 or 30 years ago, today most people (both adults and adolescents) do not smoke; the great majority believe it is harmful to their health, and increasing numbers not only disapprove of smoking but feel much freer to ask others to refrain from smoking in their presence. One might argue that these are only preconditions for an effective anti-smoking program, and that these preconditions do not exist for other drugs. However, recent data provide evidence that beliefs about marijuana and cigarettes, at least, are converging.

The Unanswered Questions

Although research on the newer prevention approaches is encouraging, particularly when contrasted with the evidence that earlier approaches were uniformly ineffective, fundamental questions remain unanswered. Perhaps the most basic is just why some individuals, by their biology or psychosocial development, are more predisposed to substance abuse than others. As the outline of risk factors indicates, there is evidence that both kinds of factors play a role, but neither is sufficiently well-understood to provide the foundation for more precisely focused prevention that exists in other areas of public health.

More Questions To Address

Users or nonusers? For any program, there are several possible target audiences and corresponding objectives. The typical classroom, for example, is composed of a variety of subgroups representing a wide range of motivations and experiences with respect to drug use. The typical program may include any of these objectives, depending on the target groups:

---

[3] Dentz, Mary Ann. "Prevention of Adolescent Substance Abuse Through Social Skill Development." NIDA Research Monograph Series. *Preventing Adolescent Drug Abuse: Intervention Strategies*. Rockville, MD, 1985, pp. 195- 225.

McAlister, Alfred. "Social-Psychological Approaches." NIDA Research Monograph Series. *Preventing Adolescent Drug Abuse: Intervention Strategies*. Rockville, MD, 1985, pp. 36-50.

— For committed users, to prevent or delay the onset of drug use.

— For former users, to reinforce the decision to quit drug use.

— For nonproblem drug users, to examine their drug use and, as a minimum, to keep their current use from escalating to problem levels.

— For problem users, to reduce drug use or effect a change in patterns of use.

It is important to realize that most young people and adults do not use drugs other than alcohol, most do not abuse drugs, and many drug users abandon drugs after a short period of experimentation.

Should a program direct its efforts toward youths or adults? It is reasonable to give special attention to educating young people about drugs; they are at higher risk and more accessible. Young people are more easily influenced than adults, and it is easy to reach them through schools and the media. Early patterns of thought and behavior will remain with them and guide their later behavior, and they are the principal resource for society's future.

There are, however, good reasons for giving attention to adults. Adults are more likely to abuse certain categories of drugs, especially the legal drugs, and some are particularly at risk: young adults who drink and the elderly who use medications, for example. Moreover, adults are important role models for younger members of society, in their positions as parents, teachers, youth leaders, public figures, and celebrities. Finally, adults are society's decision-makers: they set the norms and pass the laws.

Peers or parents? Recent emphasis on the influence of peers in stimulating adolescent drug use does a disservice to both adolescents and their parents. First, the portrayal of overwhelming, one-way peer pressure minimizes the active role of adolescents in selecting the peer groups to which they respond best. It also ignores the influence of individuals on other group members and fails to consider the importance of positive peer norms in regulating behavior.

Second, the attention given to peer pressure detracts from the importance of parental influence. Although responsiveness to peers increases during adolescence, parental influence still continues to be felt. Children's use of alcohol and tobacco is influenced more by parental use of these substances than by peer use. Parental attitudes toward illegal drugs also have an impact on children's illegal drug use, even though peers' attitudes drug are a powerful influence.

Knowledge, attitudes, or behavior? Since the onset of drug prevention programs, educators have faced a dilemma concerning the relationship between what people know, what they feel, and what they do. More significant questions explore the connections between the changes in knowledge and attitudes and changes in behavior. Research and program experience have demonstrated that changes in significant behavior, such as drug use, do not readily follow from modifications in knowledge and feeling. Educators now have greater appreciation for the complex nature of human behavior and for the need to take situational, social, and individual factors into account when attempting to change behavior. These new insights suggest that drug education programs should contain a variety of informational, affective, and behavioral objectives.

Informational objectives may include raising levels of awareness about the nature and effects of drugs, the role of drugs in society, appropriate ways of using drugs, alternatives to drug use, and sources of help for drug-related problems.

Affective objectives may be equally diverse, focusing on feelings, attitudes, and values regarding drugs, drug use, abuse, and addiction, as well as feelings about those people who use or abuse drugs. More ambitious objectives might include, among others, a concern for improving people's self-concepts.

Behavioral objectives may include a range of different aims.

— Abstaining totally from drugs.

— Retarding the onset of drug use.

— Reducing drug consumption.

— Promoting responsible use.

— Modifying the situations in which drugs are used (e.g., separating drinking from driving).

— Identifying problem drug use early.

— Helping those with drug problems.

— Improving social skills associated with communication and assertiveness; improving personal skills in decision-making, coping, stress management.

— Modifying lifestyles.

— Promoting alternatives to drug use.

— Supporting prevention efforts.

Abstinence or responsible use? One policy issue with which educators constantly struggle is whether to encourage complete abstinence from drug use or to encourage responsible use. Some people believe that responsible use of drugs is not an acceptable objective for education programs, especially for the young; but this position ignores some of the realities of drug use. First, use of alcohol and medications with parental supervision is usually neither harmful nor illegal. Second, it is unrealistic to talk to illegal drug users as if they do not, and would not, use drugs. Efforts to prevent drug abuse by reducing the most risky forms of drug use (for example, drinking and driving) need not condone illegal drug use. Third, it may be unrealistic to counsel immediate abstinence for chronic drug users; more responsible use of an illegal drug may be an appropriate intermediate objective for such a population.

How Can We Make Drug Education More Effective?

Plan. Effective planning begins with an identification of needs, both those that are perceived to exist in a community and those that actually exist.

Careful planning helps in specifying goals and objectives. Decisions regarding program content and processes should be based on a thorough understanding of the drug problems and an appreciation of the dynamics of individual and social change.

Take account of previous history. Too often, educators operate as if people had no previous history; yet from their earliest years, people are constantly exposed to drug-related messages and behavior. From these they acquire knowledge, form attitudes, and develop their own behavioral tendencies. Most important in this regard is the influence of parents, siblings, peers, and the public media.

Acknowledge the positive reinforcements of drug use. Drug use consequences are not all negative; if they were, nobody would continue to use drugs. Moderate use of some drugs offers physical, psychological, and social benefits for some people. Drug education programs that do not take into account this important aspect of the decision to start or continue using drugs diminish their credibility and effectiveness.

Establish links between the educational setting and the rest of the student's experience. Students will be exposed to powerful influences when they leave the classroom. By integrating drug education into other curriculum areas (for example, English, mathematics, science), and by implementing schoolwide drug use policies for both students and teachers, educators can create a school environment that reinforces the positive efforts of the classroom and minimizes competing negative forces of students' social environments. The idea is for the desired behavior, skills, and attitudes to be rehearsed in the supportive environment of the school's educational program. And finally, the efforts of the school require reinforcement from students' homes and from their communities.

Implement programs. Educational programs lose effectiveness if information about them is not appropriately disseminated. The mere availability of programs does not ensure their use. Programs and supporting materials must reach the decision-makers and those who will implement the programs, and the latter must be adequately trained in all aspects of the program.

Allocate resources. Communities devote less attention and fewer resources to drug education than to law enforcement and drug abuse treatment programs. Within schools, drug education programs suffer from minimal allocations of curriculum time, poor staff training, and negligible teacher and student accountability.

Evaluate. It is clear that not all approaches are equally effective for all target audiences or for all drugs. Without evaluation, little progress can be made in identifying which forms of drug education are effective in preventing and reducing drug-related problems. In addition, careful research can clarify the reasons why some educational programs are effective and others are not.

Significant Trends In Prevention

It is important that other possible school- and community-based prevention alternatives be explored that may contribute to changed attitudes toward substance abuse by youth and the larger community. Programs in which youth themselves take the initiative to discourage substance abuse may be an important deterrent. Students Against Drunk Driving (SADD) is an example. The family substance abuse prevention tactics, which have been advocated by the "parents' movement," is also an example of a community program organized by parents themselves to reduce the drug problem.

Another very visible effort by a parents' group has been carried out by MADD (Mothers Against Drunk Driving). Again, the impact on substance abuse is not easily measured, but may be important both directly by inhibiting irresponsible behavior and indirectly by making the community more aware of the hazards of substance abuse.

A number of professional associations in medicine, psychology, social work, education, and other areas concerned with young people have also begun to play greater leadership roles by developing their members' professional skills concerning substance abuse and encouraging them to be more active in prevention, early detection, and treatment of abusers. The burgeoning efforts of these groups will undoubtedly contribute to a "critical mass" that seems likely to substantially reduce the acceptability of smoking, alcohol, and other drug abuse throughout American society.

Finally, the recent national interest is drug testing to prevent drug use and abuse in the workplace is assisting in the prevention of drug abuse.

Summary

The most optimistic conclusions are related to prevention—not because past drug prevention programs have proven eminently successful (which they have not) but because we can see why past approaches have failed; they were grounded in outmoded assumptions of why adolescents begin using psychoactive substances. In contrast, there is encouraging evidence supporting the success of new smoking prevention programs, which are based on a more up-to-date model of adolescent behavior.

Recent longitudinal studies have tracked the process by which adolescents start using drugs. It usually starts in a group setting, among their peers or relatives—social influences are the main influences on adolescent drug-taking. Secondly, young people have a strong desire to appear "grown up" and independent. If drug use is defined as an adult activity and adolescents see older youth or adults taking drugs, they are more likely to imitate that behavior in an attempt to claim a mature status. Third, young people are present-oriented. They are much more concerned with their life at school, their current social milieu, and their acceptance within the adolescent social group than with the long-term risks of their actions. Thus, warnings about future disease are likely to fall on deaf ears.

Most drug use prevention programs do not focus on social factors. The majority of past "drug education" was based on an information-oriented approach: it provided facts about the pharmacology and effects of drugs, often as a lecture by a teacher, physician, police officer, or former drug user. Such programs assume that children use drugs because they are ignorant of the dangers. Unfortunately, there is a wealth of evidence suggesting that mere knowledge of the facts does not affect behavior directly, particularly if social influences contradict the facts. In addition, many previous education efforts were marred by exaggerations or "scare tactics," which today's sophisticated youth easily detect and discount.

Programs in "affective education" have been the other main approach in the past. These programs, including values clarification, skill development, and efforts to increase self-esteem, have been popular in the past decade but they have not been proven effective by any scientific evaluation. The model for such programs holds that adolescents start using drugs because they lack some essential trait or ability, such as self-esteem, interpersonal skill, or the capacity to translate values into rational decisions. Such traits are valuable, but there is no credible evidence that improving them reduces drug use. Indeed, the best-implemented example of such a program, which also contained a well-designed evaluation, showed virtually no effects on drug use.

In contrast, there are several successful new programs based on a social influence model of adolescent behavior, all aimed at preventing cigarette smoking among junior high school students. These programs begin by identifying the messages and arguments in favor of smoking—messages that come explicitly or implicitly from peers, adults, and the media. They show adolescents how to counter those arguments, thus providing an "inoculation" against future pro-smoking influences. Then they teach students effective but socially acceptable methods of resisting pressure to smoke: how to "say no" gracefully. The reasons for wanting to "say no" are illustrated by the short-term effects of smoking, such as bad breath, discolored teeth, and increased carbon monoxide in the blood, rather than by long-term health effects that seem uncertain and far in the future to most young people. These themes are developed by group discussion in a 7th- or 8th-grade classroom, sometimes led by an older peer such as a high school student. Such programs have been successful in preventing adolescent cigarette smoking, reducing the number of smokers by one-third to two-thirds in a number of independent studies.

Furthermore, in the NIDA Report on Drug Use Among American High School Seniors, 1975-1990, regarding attitudes and beliefs about drugs and their harmfulness, two-thirds (68%) of the seniors studied judged that regular use of cigarettes (one or more packs a day) entails a great risk of harm to the user. In addition, 78% of the seniors judged that regular use of marijuana involves a significant health risk.[4] Thus, a healthy base of skepticism already exists among adolescents about the wisdom of using such harmful substances.

REFERENCES:

Bandura, A. *Social Learning Theory.* Englewood Cliffs, NJ: Prentice Hall, 1977.

Bohmen, M. "Some genetic aspects of alcoholism and criminality." *Arch Gen Psychiat* 35:269-276, 1978.

---

[4] National Institute on Drug Abuse. "Drug Use Among American High School Seniors, College Students, and Young Adults, 1975-1990." Vol.I "High School Seniors." Rockville, MD, DHHS Pub. No. (ADM) 91-1813, 1991.

Drug Prevention and Education

Botvin, B.J. "Broadening the focus of smoking prevention strategies." Coates, T. et al, eds. *Promoting Adolescent Health: A Dialogue on Research and Practice.* New York: Academic Press, 1982.

Dentz, Mary Ann. "Prevention of Adolescent Substance Abuse Through Social Skill Development." NIDA Research Monograph Series. *Preventing Adolescent Drug Abuse: Intervention Strategies.* Rockville, MD, 1985, pp. 195-225.

Evans, R.I. "Smoking in children: Developing a social psychological strategy of deterrence." *Preventive Medicine* 5:122-127, 1976.

Evans, R.I. et al. "Deterring the onset of smoking in children; Knowledge of immediate physiological effects and coping with peer pressure, media pressure, and parent modeling." *J of Applied Social Psychology* 8:126-135, 1978.

Goodstadt, M.S. "Alcohol and drug education." *Health Education Monographs* 6(3):263-279, 1978.

Hawkins, J.D. et al. "Childhood predictors of adolescent substance abuse: towards an empirically grounded theory." *J of Children in Contemporary Society* 18(1 and 2):1-65, 1986.

________. "Childhood Predictors and Prevention of Adolescent Substance Abuse." Jones, C.L. et al, eds. *Etiology of Drug Abuse: Implications for Prevention.* NIDA Research Monograph No. 56. DHHS Pub. No. (ADM)85-1335. Washington, D.C.: Supt. of Docs., U.S. Govt. Print. Off., 1985, pp. 75-126.

Kandel, D., ed. *Longitudinal Research on Drug Use: Empirical Findings and Methodological Issues.* Washington, D.C.: Hemisphere (Halsted-Wiley), 1978, pp. 3-38.

Kandel, D.B. and K. Yamaguchi. "Developmental patterns of the use of legal, illegal and medically prescribed psychotropic drugs from adolescence to young adulthood." Jones, C.L. et al, eds. *Etiology of Drug Abuse: Implications for Prevention.* NIDA Research Monograph No. 56. DHHS Pub. No. (ADM)85-1335. Washington, D.C.: Supt. of Docs., U.S. Govt. Print. Off., 1985, pp. 193-235.

McAlister, Alfred. "Social-Psychological Approaches." NIDA Research Monograph Series. *Preventing Adolescent Drug Abuse: Intervention Strategies.* Rockville, MD, 1985, pp. 36-50.

National Institute on Drug Abuse. "Drug Use Among American High School Seniors, College Students, and Young Adults, 1975-1990." Vol.I "High School Seniors." Rockville, MD, DHHS Pub. No. (ADM) 91-1813, 1991.

Schaps, E. et al. "A review of 127 drug abuse prevention program evaluations." *J of Drug Issues, Inc.* Winter: 17-43, 1981.

Shaffer, H. et al. "The primary prevention of smoking onset: An inoculation approach." *Journal of Psychoactive Drugs* 15(3):177-184, 1983.

Swisher, J.D. "Prevention issues." Dupont, R.I. et al., eds. *Handbook on Drug Abuse.* National Institute on Drug Abuse, Washington, D.C.: Supt. of Docs., U.S. Govt. Print. Off., 1979. pp. 423-435.

This page intentionally left blank.

CHAPTER XX

EFFECTIVENESS OF DRUG CONTROL ACTIVITIES AND CONCLUSIONS

It seems wrong—by some accounts, even evil—for drug traffickers to supply drugs to users, and it seems unjust that drug traffickers grow rich and powerful on their ill-gotten gains while regular users are often poor. These simple intuitions establish two quite different perspectives for looking at drug trafficking.

Drug trafficking as drug supply. From the perspective of drug control policy, the worst thing about drug traffickers is that they supply drugs. Too many drugs reach illicit users in the United States. The objective of drug trafficking policies should be to minimize the supply capacity of the distribution systems so that the smallest possible volume of drugs reaches users.

Drug trafficking as organized crime. Some criminal organizations engaged in drug trafficking grow rich and powerful. This situation, in turn, undermines citizens' confidence in their government. When drug trafficking is viewed as an organized crime problem, the objective of control efforts is to arrest and punish rich traffickers and to prevent new groups from arising.

To a degree, these perspectives and objectives are congruent. For instance, a principal means for minimizing the flow of drugs to the United States is to immobilize major trafficking organizations. In some circumstances, however, these objectives diverge. Aggressive law enforcement efforts directed at marginal trafficking organizations might well reduce the overall supply of drugs to illicit markets. But these efforts, by eliminating marginal traffickers, may increase the wealth and power of the drug trafficking organizations that remain by allowing them to gain effective control over the market.

ALTERNATIVE APPROACHES

Choices between approaches for dealing with drug trafficking will depend on which aspects of the trafficking problem are deemed most important and on the costs and efficacy of particular policies.

Legalization

The most radical approach to dealing with drug trafficking is to legalize drugs. Yet, legalization can mean many different things. At one extreme, it can mean complete elimination of any legal restrictions on the production, distribution, possession, or use of any drug. On the other hand, it can mean allowing limited uses of some particular drugs, producing the drugs only under government auspices, distributing them through tightly regulated distribution systems, and punishing with severe criminal penalties any production or use outside the authorized system.

The goal of legalizing drugs is to bring them under effective legal control. If it were legal to produce and distribute drugs, legitimate businessmen would enter the business. There would be less need for violence and corruption since the industry would have access to the courts. And, instead of absorbing tax dollars as targets of expensive enforcement efforts, the drug sellers might begin to pay taxes. So, legalization might well solve the organized crime aspects of the drug trafficking problem.

Furthermore, drug use under legalization might not be as destructive to users and to society as it is under the current prohibition: drugs would be less expensive, more pure, and more conveniently available. However, by relaxing opposition to drug use, and by making drugs more freely available, legalization might fuel a significant increase in the level of drug use. It is not unreasonable to assume that the number of people who become chronic, intensive users would increase substantially. It is this risk, as well as a widespread perception that drug use is simply wrong, that stops outright legalization.

An alternative is to choose a system more restrictive than outright legalization but one that still leaves room for legitimate uses of some drugs. Arguably, such a policy would produce some of the potential benefits of legalization without accelerating growth in the level of drug use. The difficulty is that wherever the boundary between the legitimate and illicit use of drugs is drawn, an illicit market will develop just outside the boundary. Indeed, if the boundary is more restrictive, the resulting black market will be larger and more controlled by "organized crime."

At present, the existing drug laws in the United States establish a regulatory rather than a prohibitionist regime. While most uses of heroin and marijuana are illegal, some research uses of these drugs are authorized under the current laws, and there is discussion of the possible use of these drugs for medical purposes such as the treatment of terminal cancer patients. Likewise, cocaine is legal for use as a medical drug. Moreover, barbiturates, amphetamines, and tranquilizers are legalized for a variety of medical purposes and distributed through licensed pharmacists and physicians.

However, the fact that there are some legal uses of these drugs has not eliminated illicit trafficking. For marijuana, heroin, and cocaine, the restrictions are so sharp relative to the current demand for the drugs that virtually the entire distribution system remains illicit and depends on drug trafficking. For amphetamines, barbiturates, and tranquilizers, the restrictions are fewer, so a larger portion of the demand is met from illicit distribution. Distribution of these drugs takes the form of diversion from legitimate channels rather than wholly illicit production and distribution.

Source Country Crop Control

A second approach to dealing with drug trafficking is to try to eliminate the raw materials that are used to produce the drugs. For heroin, cocaine, and marijuana, this means controlling opium, coca leaf, and marijuana crops in countries such as Turkey, Afghanistan, Thailand, Bolivia, Columbia, Peru, Mexico, and Jamaica. For marijuana, illicit domestic production is also important.

Efforts to control these foreign crops generally take one of two forms. Governments either try to induce farmers to stop producing the crops for illicit markets or attempts are made to destroy those crops that can be located. Sometimes the inducement takes the form of subsidies for growing other crops. Other times foreign crops are bought and burned before they reach illicit channels. Eradication may also be accomplished by airborne chemical spraying (which has the advantage of being controlled by a relatively small number of people, and the disadvantage of doing a great deal of collateral damage to legitimate crops), or by ground-level destruction of crops through cutting and digging (which has the disadvantage of relying on large numbers of people and of being quite visible well in advance of the operations).

In general, these efforts suffer from two major difficulties. First, there seems to be no shortage of locations in which the crops may be grown. If Turkey stops growing opium poppies, Mexico, Afghanistan, and Southeast Asia can eventually take up the slack. If Colombia stops growing coca, Peru can replace it. If Mexico eliminated marijuana production, the hills of California would be even more densely filled with marijuana plants than they are now.

The second problem is that foreign governments cannot always be relied on to vigorously enforce crop control policies. Sometimes the difficulty is that the crops lie in parts of the country that are not under effective governmental control. Other times the problem is inefficiency or corruption in the agencies that are managing the programs. In the worst cases, the crops are sufficiently important to the domestic economy (or the personal well-being of high government officials) that the government prefers not to act at all.

When foreign governments are reluctant to cooperate, the United States government must balance its interest in advancing its drug policy objectives against other foreign policy objectives. One perplexing problem is posed by governments that acquiesce to drug trafficking but are important to the United States as regional bulwarks against communist expansion. In these countries, the U.S. government may feel required to overlook drug trafficking in order to maintain the other government's anti-communist activities.

These observations do not imply that crop control policies can never be effective. In the early 1970s, more effective control of opium poppies in Turkey produced a 2- to 3-year reduction in the supply of heroin to the East Coast of the U.S.; it also produced an observable reduction in the rate at which new users were becoming addicted.

These observations do indicate, however, that crop control programs cannot be counted on as long-term solutions: they will take place sporadically and unpredictably. This suggests that an effective way to manage our crop control efforts is to position ourselves in foreign countries to notice and exploit opportunities when they arise, but not to rely on this approach as our major initiative for controlling drug trafficking.

Interdiction

Interdiction efforts aimed at stopping illicit drugs at the border are compelling. If we cannot rely on foreign countries to help us with our drug problem, we will do it ourselves by establishing defenses at the border. The fact that government agencies have special powers to search at the border should also make it easier to find illicit drugs there. Forces of the U.S. Customs Agency and the U.S. Immigration and Naturalization Service inspect people and goods passing through official "ports of entry," and they patrol between "ports of entry" to ensure that no one can cross the border without facing inspection. The Coast Guard, the military, and civilian aviation authorities all have capabilities that allow the government to detect who is crossing the border and to prevent illegal crossings.

There are, however, two problems with interdiction. One is the sheer size of the inspection task. More than 12,000 miles of international boundary must be patrolled. Over 420 billion tons of goods, and more than 270 million people, cross these boundaries each year, yet the quantities of drugs are small—a few hundred tons of marijuana and less than 20 tons of heroin or cocaine. Moreover, the heroin and cocaine arrive in shipments of less than a hundred pounds.

That the volume of heroin and cocaine imported is much less than the volume of marijuana points to the second problem with interdiction. It is a strategy that is more successful with marijuana than with heroin or cocaine. Marijuana's bulkiness makes it more vulnerable to interdiction efforts. This situation is unfortunate because, in the eyes of many, marijuana presents fewer problems than heroin and cocaine. Moreover, marijuana can be grown easily in the United States. If foreign supplies are kept out, the supply system can adjust by growing more marijuana domestically.

That seems to be what has happened. Current estimates indicate that interdiction efforts are successful in seizing about a third of the marijuana destined for the United States. Yet, except for a few local areas, the impact on the price and availability of the drug has been minimal. To make matters worse, the current domestically-grown marijuana is more potent than the imported marijuana.

High-Level Enforcement

A fourth attack on illicit trafficking is directed at the organizations responsible for producing, importing, and distributing drugs. The basic aim is to immobilize or destroy the trafficking networks.

In the past, enforcement agencies have tended to view this problem as "getting to Mr. Big"—the individual kingpin who, it was assumed, controlled an organization's capacity to distribute drugs. If that person could be arrested, prosecuted, and imprisoned, the network would fall apart.

More recently, the law enforcement community has become less certain that this strategy can succeed. Even when "Mr. Big" is in prison, he can continue to manage the distribution of drugs. Moreover, the organizations seem less dependent on single individuals than enforcement officials once assumed. Indeed, the whole drug distribution system is less centralized than was once assumed. Relatively small and impermanent organizations—freelance entrepreneurs—supply a large proportion of illicit drugs.

To deal with this decentralization, enforcement aims have shifted from stopping individual dealers to destroying whole networks. Federal investigators have been granted special powers to seize drug dealers' assets, including boats, cars, planes, houses, bank accounts, and cash.

The main problem with attacking illicit trafficking organizations is that it is enormously expensive. Convincing evidence can be produced only through sustained efforts to recruit informants, establish electronic surveillance, and insinuate undercover agents. It is difficult for prosecutions to succeed because of the complexity of conspiracy laws and the particularly intrusive investigative methods that must be used to gather evidence.

Street-Level Enforcement

A fifth line of attack is to go after street-level dealers through the use of physical surveillance or "buy and bust" operations. In the recent past, this approach has been de-emphasized. It seemed to have no impact on the overall supply because dealers who were arrested were jailed only intermittently and when they were, they were easily replaced. At best, drug dealing was driven off the street temporarily, or to a different street. Many hours were spent to produce small, transient results, and these operations seemed to invite abuses of authority and corruption. As a result, many police were removed from street-level enforcement.

Recently, police have renewed street-level enforcement efforts, but they have altered their objectives. To the extent that street-level enforcement increases the "hassle" associated with using drugs, it can make a contribution to the objective of reducing drug use. If drugs, already expensive, can be made inconvenient to purchase, some non-addicted users may be persuaded to abandon drugs. Street-level enforcement can also encourage criminally active drug users to reduce their consumption, or draw them into treatment programs. It can contribute to the objective of immobilizing major traffickers by identifying defendants who can provide information about major trafficking networks. Ultimately, it can contribute to the quality of life in neighborhoods by returning the streets to community control.

These rationales give street-level enforcement some plausibility. What gives it real force is that it seems to work. For example, Operation Pressure Point, carried out on the Lower East Side of Manhattan, reduced robberies by 40 percent and burglaries by 27 percent.

There have also been some important failures. An operation in Lawrence, Massachusetts, modeled after the Lynn program, failed to produce any important effect on levels of crime or drug use in that community. The reasons seem to be that the effort was too small relative to the size of the opposing trafficking networks, and that the effort was focused on cocaine rather than heroin. Similarly, an operation in Philadelphia failed to produce anything other than angry citizens and a stern rebuke by the courts because it was carried out without any consultation with the community, and without any regard for evidentiary standards.

Subsequent discussions of these results among academics and practitioners have produced several guidelines for successful street-level enforcement. First, the scale of the enforcement effort should be in some sense proportionate to the effective size of the trafficking network. Second, police should carry out the operation after obtaining widespread community support, and with scrupulous attention to the niceties of search and seizure. Otherwise, the operation will lack the legitimacy necessary to sustain continued support. Third, it is important to complement the street-level enforcement effort with other investments, not only in the criminal justice system, but also in the treatment system. Otherwise the opportunities created by street-level enforcement will not be fully realized.

LAW ENFORCEMENT

U.S. policy has always relied heavily on law enforcement to control the illicit drug market. When considering enforcement, the most fundamental point is that the supply of drugs can never be completely eliminated. Most of the illegal drug supply originates overseas, in regions where drug crops are the farmers' most profitable products. The central governments in these regions are often weak, and some are not sympathetic with U.S. concerns. Perhaps the most important consideration here is that most illicit drugs are exported by several source countries; when one source is shut down, other producers fill the vacuum. Accordingly, past efforts to reduce drug crops have had little lasting effect on the U.S. market, and we cannot expect more in the foreseeable future.

Nor is it likely that supply can be much reduced by stopping drugs "at the border." Although the Federal government has greatly expanded its interdiction efforts, most drug shipments still get through and prices have not risen. Moreover, doubling interdiction would probably have little effect on retail prices. The key reason is that a drug's import cost is only a small fraction of its retail price. The price for a given quantity rises very steeply as it passes down the chain from producer to consumer. Hence, intervening at the top levels of the market can exert very limited effect on the final price. Other factors also work against interdiction, such as the smuggler's ability to adapt to enforcement pressure, and his or her capacity to recruit large numbers of foreign boat crewmembers at low wages.

Even within the U.S. borders, there are poor prospects for increasing pressure against retail drug dealers. Local police make many arrests, but retailers number probably over half a million. Therefore, only a small fraction are arrested, and an ever smaller proportion are imprisoned—by our estimates, far less than 1 percent. With state prisons currently overcrowded and local courts backlogged, it is not feasible to raise those risks significantly. Even if it were feasible to arrest and incarcerate many more, the effect would be only a small price increase. The trade has simply become so vast that any reasonable increase in police pressure could deliver only a small impact on a very large market.

Undercover investigations of high-level dealers may offer better prospects, but even here the costs would be great and the results uncertain. Most of the innovative techniques that law enforcement agencies have developed can be evaded by dealer adaptations. Perhaps Federal agencies could incarcerate more high-level dealers if their investigative budgets were greatly increased. However, such investigations are time-consuming and expensive. More intense law enforcement is not likely to substantially affect either the availability or the retail price of drugs in this country.

This is not to imply that enforcement against drug traffickers should be abandoned. Past enforcement has certainly increased the price of drugs beyond what it otherwise would have been. In addition, enforcement may make it more difficult for novices to find dealers.

TREATMENT

Another facet of the drug abuse problem involves treatment. Treatment of drug abuse is an extensive and multifaceted industry in the United States, accounting for over $500 million in annual expenditures. Originally, Federal authorities conceived of treatment and law enforcement as complementary methods of containing the heroin problem; law enforcement would deter addicts and dry up drug supplies, so users would be forced into treatment centers where they could be withdrawn for the drug. Thus, treatment was, and still is, largely oriented toward heroin users.

A critical issue is the relative effectiveness of the various treatment approaches. For instance, many observers recommend "early intervention" with young people, before their drug abuse has become severe. Another promising approach, family therapy, is based on the premise that drug abuse often originates in family dysfunctions; accordingly, the therapy brings the family together into treatment in an attempt to resolve the underlying problem. However, even though family therapy has achieved demonstrated positive effects in a randomized experiment with young adult heroin users, it has not been systematically tested with adolescent drug abusers, and the costs could be quite high.

Some evidence suggests that it should be possible to develop effective treatment for drug abusers. First, evaluation studies indicate that certain forms of treatment—drug free-therapy, methadone maintenance, and residential "therapeutic communities"—work better than no treatment at all. Second, the longer a patient remains in treatment, the better are his or her chances of improvement; and patients who complete treatment have better outcomes than those who drop out. Although we cannot say with certainty whether this means that patients would benefit from longer treatment (because dropouts could differ from graduates in other ways), the relationship lends some credence to the belief that treatment, in general, produces positive effects.

PREVENTION

It has become increasingly obvious that prevention programs offer brighter prospects for reducing adolescent drug use than any other method. There is now a considerable base of knowledge about how young people begin using drugs, plus some experimental evidence suggesting that prevention programs can keep adolescents from starting to smoke cigarettes. Preventing a phenomenon can best be done with a clear understanding of the processes that cause it. In the case of drug use, there is now abundant research supporting the hypothesis that the primary cause of initial drug use is social influence. Most people first begin using drugs because their friends do. This carries several implications for prevention programs. First, such programs, should be designed to help individuals learn effective methods of resisting social pressure. Second, the programs should try to reinforce and solidify social norms against drug use. Third, the most effective appeals are likely to come from other adolescents, rather than from teachers, parents, or adult authorities.

Peer influence, of course, interacts with the individual's beliefs and orientations. Two aspects of adolescents' orientations are particularly important: (1) their desire to appear mature; and (2) their orientation toward the present rather than the future. Adolescents are vulnerable to pro-drug appeals because they wish to appear mature and free of the restrictions of childhood. Smoking, drinking, and using illicit drugs are all methods of demonstrating a new-found independence. Furthermore, young people are not likely to be deterred by warnings about adverse effects far in the future; most adolescents are much more concerned about their immediate circumstances, friendships, and activities than about future health problems. Therefore, prevention programs need to counteract the belief that drug use shows maturity, and to indict drugs for their short-term rather than long-term consequences.

The effectiveness of such an approach is illustrated by the contrast between older anti-drug programs and the newer anti-smoking programs. In the past, many prevention efforts assumed that drug use resulted directly from the user's lack of information or from their personal problems such as a lack of self-esteem. Early drug education programs based on these concepts produced disappointing results.

The more recent anti-smoking programs, based on a social influence model of initial use, have accumulated a more positive record. Such programs help children identify the pressures to smoke, particularly peer influences, and arm them with arguments against smoking. To tap into the adolescent's present orientation, these programs base their counterarguments on the immediate undesirable effects of smoking, especially those that harm one's appearance. And to counter the claim that smoking represents maturity, they often use nonsmoking older peers who can testify that smoking does not confer independence or adult status. These programs have been tested in several locations and evaluated by independent research teams, and they have generally shown significant effects in preventing cigarette smoking.

In this respect, national survey data suggest that for most drugs, prevention programs can be appropriately targeted at junior high school students. Even programs in elementary school on health, nutrition, drug use, abuse, and addiction may help promote a healthy lifestyle among students nearing adolescence. According to the National Household Survey on Drug Abuse, the average age of first use of cigarettes was 14.9 years.[1] Furthermore, the study found that cigarettes were, on the average, used first before alcohol or illicit drugs. It appears that a great majority of drug use can be prevented with strong, positive prevention programs aimed at elementary and especially junior high school students. These programs can take advantage of the anti-drug social norms that exist in a group of non-users.

Unfortunately, these arguments do not hold for alcohol. Alcohol is so common in American society that a substantial number of 7th grade students have already become regular users. Moreover, unlike cigarette smoking and illicit drug use, adults' use of alcohol is broadly accepted, and a "primary" prevention program suggesting that young people never start drinking is likely to be ineffective.

---

[1] National Institute on Drug Abuse. "The National Household Survey on Drug Abuse: Main Findings, 1990." DHHS Pub. No. (ADM) 91-1788, 1991, p. 26.

But there is a reasonable chance of adapting the anti-smoking model to other drugs. Marijuana is likely to be the best immediate target. Adolescent beliefs about marijuana and cigarettes have recently been converging; in 1991, about equal proportions of high school seniors believed that regular marijuana use and regular cigarette smoking posed great risks of harm.[2] Furthermore, longitudinal studies of adolescents have shown that drug use develops in a series of successive stages, beginning with use of alcohol or cigarettes; some of those users subsequently go on to marijuana, and some of the latter then proceed to other illicit drugs.[3] This offers hope that a program starting early and targeting marijuana and cigarettes may not only prevent use of those substances, but may also "spill over" to prevent use of later-stage illicit drugs.

Today, the scientific evidence is in favor of prevention approaches over the others. It seems, therefore, that prevention should receive greater credence in the future, and that a higher priority should be placed on developing and testing prevention methods that may ultimately reduce the demand for drugs. Thus, more appropriations for drug abuse should be directed toward prevention efforts.

CONCLUSIONS

Drug abuse is fundamentally a social problem which cannot be solved by the government alone. Federal and state governments can support drug abuse prevention and treatment programs, conduct research, enforce drug laws, and provide leadership in the fight against drug abuse and drug trafficking. However, not until public and individual attitudes change will illicit drugs and the organized criminal groups that traffic in them be eliminated. Individuals need not accept drug use in their midst. There is no "right" to use drugs. Government efforts to combat drug trafficking and drug abuse are a vital effort, but they are ultimately only a holding action, while consensus continues to build among individuals concerning the utter unacceptability of drug use.

Despite this growing consensus, a profound disparity exists between principle and practice. Popular entertainment and advertising, sometimes subtle, sometimes not, regularly reflects and even promotes the view that the use of illicit drugs is glamorous, exciting, and sophisticated, or at least harmless and amusing.

The illusion that drug use is glamorous is regularly, if somewhat indirectly, reinforced by revelations that drug use is commonplace among celebrities in the sports and entertainment worlds. In August 1985, for example, the

[2] National Institute on Drug Abuse. "Drug Use Among American High School Seniors, College Students and Young Adults, 1975-1990." Vol. I, "High School Seniors." DHHS Pub. No. (ADM) 91-1813, 1991.

[3] Clausen, J. "Longitudinal Studies on Drug Use in the High School: Substantive and Theoretical Issues." In Kendel, D. ed., *Longitudinal Research on Drug Use.* Washington, D.C.: Hemisphere Publishing Corp., 1978.

DuPont, R.L. *Getting Tough on Gateway Drugs: A Guide for the Family.* Washington, D.C.: American Psychiatric Press, Inc., 1984.

New York Times reported cocaine's alleged use by players on virtually every baseball team in the major leagues, prompting the Commissioner of Baseball to declare drug use the "number one" problem facing the game.[4] Drug-related controversy in major league baseball was then followed by a similar situation in professional football, reaching all the way to the National Football Leagues's championship contest.[5]

It is even possible to find purportedly responsible groups urging not only recognition but acceptance of drug use as a feature of daily life. An article in the January/February 1984 issue of *Social Work*, the journal of the National Association of Social Workers, prescribes the following for adolescent marijuana use: "Use should be moderate . . . no more than four to five joints per week seems advisable."[6]

Such acceptance of drug use may be shared by many who resign themselves to the fact that drug abuse is inevitable. However, such a view reflects a failure of will on the part of the American public. American society may view drug use in the abstract as wrong, and many people agree that heroin addicts who commit additional crimes to support their drug habits should be jailed. Yet, many people react with ambivalence to the drug use in their midst. Even while the U.S. government spends almost a billion and one-half dollars on drug law enforcement, threatens to cut off foreign aid to drug producing countries, and extradites and imprisons foreign nationals on drug trafficking charges, we appear to lack the same degree of resolve to hold this country's drug users, as well as those who directly or indirectly promote drug use, accountable for their actions and their consequences.

While attitudes are ultimately an individual matter, actions need not be. It is in combination with others that private citizens have been most effective in combatting drug abuse. Private sector initiatives to combat drug use include: The National Coalition for Prevention of Drug and Alcohol Abuse, comprised of 35 private sector organizations representing 15 million members, which seeks to expand drug abuse prevention activities. Member organizations include the American Medical Association, the International Association of Lions Clubs, the National Parent/Teacher Association, and others. Furthermore, the National Football League works with the International Association of Chiefs of Police, the Drug Enforcement Administration and the High School Athletic Coaches Association to carry anti-drug messages to 5.5 million student athletes across the country; the Newman Center, a private foundation in Los Angeles, California, offers technical assistance about drugs to the entertainment industry for its portrayals of drug use and provides awards to television writers, producers, and directors who present the best shows about drug use; McNeil Pharmaceutical company sponsors "Pharmacists Against Drug Abuse," a nationwide campaign in which local pharmacists are the focal points in the community for information about drugs; and the National Broadcasting Company sponsored the "Don't Be A Dope" drug abuse awareness campaign, which was aired in 1983 and 1984.

---

[4] *N.Y. Times*. Aug. 19, 1985: A1.

[5] "It's a Crime." *Washington Post*. January 30, 1986: A24.

[6] Smith, T.E. "Reviewing Adolescent Marijuana Abuse." *Social Work*. Jan./Feb. 1984: 17, 19.

Effectiveness of Drug Control and Conclusions

As discussed above, athletes, entertainers, manufacturers, advertisers, and the media can promote drug use by their individual examples or by favorable portrayals of drug use. However, these elements of society also have the power to shape different public attitudes about drug use by presenting the truth about drugs. The media and entertainment industries should carefully review their portrayals of drug use and its consequences to ensure their accuracy.

Efforts to combat drug abuse can also be successful in the workplace. Many businesses across the country have Employee Assistance Programs (EAP's), which seek to prevent drug abuse at the worksite, offering treatment and referrals. In addition, many businesses now test employees or prospective employees for drug use. According to a survey of 180 Fortune 500 companies, two-thirds refuse to hire job applicants who fail such tests, 25 percent fire employees, and 41 percent require treatment for employees who fail.[7] Drug testing protects businesses because they lose billions of dollars each year in reduced productivity as a result of drug use among employees and the public. Drug testing in certain "critical positions," such as in the transportation industry, law enforcement, and education is particularly important. For instance, on January 27, 1986 the U.S. Supreme Court vacated a stay thus allowing drug testing in certain instances for more than 200,000 railroad workers and job applicants for those positions.[8] Mandatory drug testing in the Navy has reportedly reduced the drug abuse rate from 48 percent to three percent in two years.[9] Also, the Federal Aviation Administration has approved a plan requiring this country's 14,000 air traffic controllers to submit to annual drug tests.[10] The *New York Times* and *Chicago Tribune* have required drug testing of new employees for years. Finally, the Baltimore Orioles are the first professional baseball team to institute voluntary drug testing.

In addition to efforts in the workplace to combat drug abuse, health professionals—physicians, nurses, psychologists, and social workers—can help identify and treat drug users. Health professionals should be thoroughly trained before identifying and counseling drug abusers. However, formal training in the diagnosis and treatment of drug abuse is currently limited.

On a final note, it should be re-emphasized that decisions to use or not to use drugs are ultimately derived from values that are best inculcated and reinforced in families, churches, civic organizations, schools, and local communities. The efforts of organizations which seek to help families prevent drug use, such as the National Federation of Parents for Drug-Free Youth, are essential to the fight against drug use and drug trafficking. Relying on the task force approach which law enforcement officials have used successfully, parents, churches, schools, civic organizations, and business associa-

---

[7] Dunivant, Noel and Associates. Survey rpt. in "Firms Screen Workers." *USA Today*. Nov. 6, 1985: 1B.

[8] *Dole v. Railway Labor Executives Association.*

[9] *Washington Times*. Dec. 2, 1985: 1D.

[10] "Many Employers Test Workers For Drug Use." *Washington Post*. Feb. 2, 1986: A14.

tions should form community task forces in every community across the country to provide a unified front against drugs.

REFERENCES:

Clausen, J. "Longitudinal Studies on Drug Use in the High School: Substantive and Theoretical Issues." In Kendel, D. ed., *Longitudinal Research on Drug Use.* Washington, D.C.: Hemisphere Publishing Corp., 1978.

Dunivant, Noel and Associates. Survey rpt. in "Firms Screen Workers." *USA Today.* Nov. 6, 1985: 1B.

DuPont, R.L. *Getting Tough on Gateway Drugs: A Guide for the Family.* Washington, D.C.: American Psychiatric Press, Inc., 1984.

National Institute on Drug Abuse. "Drug Use Among American High School Seniors, College Students and Young Adults, 1975-1990." Vol. I, "High School Seniors." DHHS Pub. No. (ADM) 91-1813, 1991.

________. "The National Household Survey on Drug Abuse: Main Findings, 1990." DHHS Pub. No. (ADM) 91-1788, 1991, p. 26.

Smith, T.E. "Reviewing Adolescent Marijuana Abuse." *Social Work.* Jan./Feb. 1984: 17, 19.

APPENDIX A

CRISIS INTERVENTION FOR DRUG ABUSERS

HEROIN (NARCOTIC) OVERDOSE

Principal Manifestations

1. Coma.
2. Respiratory depression.
3. Flaccid muscles (tongue may fall back to occlude airway).

When you encounter someone who has overdosed on a narcotic, remember that a narcotic overdose causes severe respiratory depression. Emergency treatment should be sought immediately. With opiates, first aid is a must since you only have 3 to 5 minutes at most. Without oxygen exchange, the brain begins to deteriorate.

Principles of Emergency Treatment

Follow A, B, and C. Don't do B until A is working, and don't do C until A and B are working.

A. AIRWAY

— Place addict on his or her back with the head positioned so that the airway is not cut off. Tilt the head back.

— Check mouth for mucus, blood, broken teeth, etc.

— Maintain open airway.

B. BREATH

— Apply mouth to mouth resuscitation properly. Begin with 4 quick breaths, then 12 breaths per minute.

C. CARDIOVASCULAR

— Check pulse - carotid.

— If no pulse, start CPR.

BARBITURATE AND SEDATIVES/HYPNOTICS OVERDOSE

With sedatives/hypnotics the emergency is the same as with a heroin overdose: establish a clear airway. You should never give a semiconscious person fluids; nor should you induce vomiting.

Principal Manifestations of Acute Barbiturate Withdrawal

1. Convulsions and preconvulsive symptoms.

Emergency Treatment

— Open airway.

— Support breathing.

— Assess cardiovascular system.

— In all cases take the victim to a hospital. Barbiturate withdrawal is much longer and more physically dangerous than heroin withdrawal.

AMPHETAMINE OVERDOSE

Principal Manifestations

1. Irritability.
2. Hyperactivity.
3. Suspiciousness.
4. Possible violence.
5. Paranoia.

In suspected amphetemine overdoses, be careful. Try to come across to the person as non-threatening. Make no sudden moves, no threatening gestures. Don't touch the person. Toxic psychosis from amphetamines results from continuing use (3 to 5 days). It is characterized by vivid hallucinations, both visual and auditory, and paranoia. This happens 36 to 40 hours after taking large amounts of the drug. Toxic psychosis demands hospitalization. While fatal overdoses are rare, death by convulsions may occur. The signs are semiconsciousness, extremely high pulse, hyperventilation, and cold and clammy skin.

Emergency Treatment

— Reassurance, under constant observation, in quiet surroundings.

— Do not touch the person.

— Seek professional medical treatment.

ACUTE PHASES OF PCP INTOXICATION

Principal Manifestations

1. Blank stare—very spaced out, may not respond to questions.
2. Ataxia—loss of limb coordination.
3. Catatonic appearance—rigid, fixed body posture.
4. Nystagmus—jerky eye movements.
5. Agitated and/or paranoid appearance—the presence of systematized delusions.
6. Unpredictability.
7. Violent behavior.
8. Combative aggression—fright or loss of control.

Emergency Treatment

— All approaches to the individual should be made slowly and calmly and only after clear identification is made.

— Request back-up—five officers minimum.

— Control user's actions—cumulative body weight—carotid restraint.

— Transport to emergency room.

— Reduce external stimulation.

— Remember that the user is unpredictable.

PSYCHEDELIC/HALLUCINOGENIC OVERDOSE

Principal Manifestations

1. Irritability.
2. Apprehension.
3. Suspiciousness.
4. Possible violence.
5. Panic.

Emergency Treatment

— Create a calm, reassuring environment.

— The "Talkdown."

a. The patient needs help to fully experience and complete his or her trip—this may take as many as eight hours.

b. Talk the patient down by reassuring him that he is in a safe place, is with sympathetic people, and can manage his own trip.

— Upon initial contact treat the person as you would an amphetamine user. Get help from the person-crisis intervention center; seek medical treatment, etc.

APPENDIX B

Summary of Narcotics Expertise

Name ______________________________

Rank ______________________________

Department or Agency ______________________________

Bureau/Division/Special Assignment Assigned to: ______________

Years Employed as a Peace Officer ______________________

Years in Present Assignment ______________________

Education: A. Formal

High School Graduate: Yes __________ No __________

Number of College Units Completed ______________

Degree ______________________ Major __________

Graduate Units ________ Degree ________ Major __________

Units in Police Related Field ______________

B. Training

1. In-Service Training Schools - Narcotics
   List Hours and Dates Completed

   ____

   ____

   ____

   ____

2. Specific College Courses Completed in Narcotics

   ____

   ____

   ____

   ____

3. Specialized Out-Service Narcotics Training, i.e.,
   a. DOJ 80-Hour Narcotics Investigation School
   b. 80-Hour DEA Basic Drug Law Enforcement School
   c. 24-Hour Narcotics Enforcement and Case Development - Los Angeles State
   d. 40-Hour Narcotics Addiction and Drug Influence - OCSO List All Books

Appendix B

List all books read on Narcotics and Narcotics Investigations:

____

____

____

List all Technical Journals and Articles Read Relating Specifically to Narcotics:

____

____

____

Experience In Drug Investigation: (Update Monthly) ________________

____

	Hall	Heroin	Marij	Amphets	Barb	Coke
No. of Drug Purchases Made						
No. of Posses. Cases Worked						
No. of Drug Possess./Sale Cases Worked						
No. of Times Affiant of Search Warrants						
No. of Times Supervised Informant Purchases						

No. of Times Testified as an Expert in the Following Categories:

	Hall	Heroin	Marij	Amphets	Barb	Coke
Possession						
Possession/Sale						
Sale						
Under the Influence						

What Courts have you Testified as an Expert In?

Municipal ____________________________

Superior Court ____________________________

County ____________________________

APPENDIX C

SLANG TERMS FAVORED BY ILLICIT DRUG USERS AND DEALERS

During each chapter discussion, there were several slang terms given for the different types of drugs. There are many other slang terms related to drug abuse that may be heard on the street. The following is a partial list of drug-related slang terms:

Acid Head .... One who uses LSD
Amped .... High on stimulants, usually amphetamines
Bag .... $10 to $25 worth of heroin
Baggy .... A quantity of marijuana in a plastic bag
Balloon .... A small amount of heroin, sold in a toy balloon or condom
Bindle .... A small packet of narcotics
Blow a Stick (or Joint) .... To smoke marijuana
Blow your Mind .... To get high on a hallucinogenic drug
Bummer, Bum trip, Bad trip .... Bad hallucinogenic drug experience
Burned .... User has received phony or very weak drugs
Cap .... A capsule of drugs
Carry, Carrying ..... To be in possession of drugs
Chip, chipping ...... An occasional narcotic user who takes small doses
Clean .... Not in possession of drugs, or having withdrawn from drug use
Crash .... A stupor caused by an overdose of drugs
Cut .... To dilute a drug with some other substance
Deal .... To sell drugs
Dealer .... Someone who sells drugs
Dime Bag .... A $10 purchase of drugs (usually heroin)
Dirty .... To be in possession of drugs
Drop .... To swallow drugs
Dry up .... To inject drugs
Dump, Flash .... To vomit after taking drugs
Fix .... To inject narcotics
Flipped out .... Crazy
Guide .... A babysitter for an abuser of hallucinogens during an experience
Head .... An addict
Heat .... The police or a narcotics officer
High .... Being under the influence of drugs
Hit .... Taking a drag of marijuana cigarette
Holding .... Having drugs in possession
Hooked .... Addicted to drugs
Hot Shot .... A fatal dosage of narcotics
Keister Plant .... Drugs which are hidden in the rectum
Kick (the habit) ..... Abandon a drug habit

Kilo	2.2 pounds, a common quantity of marijuana and narcotics for sale
Lid	1 oz. of marijuana
Light up	To smoke marijuana
Loaded	Being very high (under the influence) on drugs
Looking	Wishing to purchase drugs
Mainline	To inject drugs directly into the vein
Mainliner	A person who injects drugs directly into the vein
Make a Buy, Make a Meet	To purchase drugs
Matchbox	½ oz. of marijuana
Mule	A person who sells or transports for a regular peddler
Narc	A narcotics officer
Needle Man	An addict
Nickel Bag	$5 purchase of drugs
On the Nod	To get sleepy from heroin or depressants
O.D.	To overdose on drugs
Pad	A user's residence
Paper	A bindle of heroin
Plant	A location where drugs are concealed
Pop, Skin Popper	An injection just under the skin
Pothead	A marijuana user
Psychedelic	A mind-altering hallucinogenic experience
Push	To sell drugs
Pusher	A person who sells drugs
Rat	An informer
Rush, Flash	A strong, pleasurable feeling following a drug injection
Score	To purchase drugs
Shoot up	To inject drugs
Shooting Gallery	A place where narcotic addicts inject heroin
Snowbird	A cocaine user
Spaced Out	Out of touch with reality
Speed Freak	A chronic user of methamphetamine
Spike	A hypodermic needle (with syringe) used to inject drugs
Spoon	About 2 grams of heroin
Stash	A personal supply of drugs
Stepped on	A drug that has been diluted (same as "cut")
Stoned	Being under the influence of drugs
Stoolie	An informer
Strung Out	Being addicted; in bad physical shape due to drug habit
Swing Man	A drug supplier
Toke, Toke up	To smoke marijuana
Trip, Tripping	Being under the influence of a hallucinogenic drug
Turn on	To take a drug, or introduce someone else to drugs
User	Someone who takes drugs, or is an addict
Wasted	Being under the influence of drugs
Weed Head	A regular marijuana user
Wiped Out	To have lost consciousness from abusing drugs

Works . . . . Drug injecting equipment
Zonked, Zonked Out . Really "loaded" or overdosed on drugs

Read over this list again because you should become very familiar with these terms. You will need to know what is really being said on the street when you hear terms like "I'm looking for my swing man," or "Let's go score a lid and start toking."

Slang Term Practice Exercises
Translate the slang terms into official terminology.

A narc is questioning Sam:

Narc: You dealing Sam?

Sam: I ain't even carrying. I'm clean, man!

Narc: Where's your stash?

Sam: Hey, I'm telling you, I've kicked it, man.

Narc: How come we caught you with a spike?

Sam: Some needle man gave it to me to hold for him. No law against that, is there?

Narc: That's the least of your worries, Sam. Freddie says he almost got a hot shot from you yesterday.

Sam: Freddie's stupid. If he O.D.'s, that's his problem.

Narc: Get off it, Sam. You're loaded right now! We'll see how smart you are when you crash.

A pusher is talking to an addict named Harry:

Harry: I'm looking for a score.

Pusher: You don't need to look any farther, man.

Harry: Are you holding?

Pusher: I got it by the bag, and I got it by the bindle.

Harry: I only chip, man, so I'll score a bindle.

Pusher: You got the works?

Harry: Ya, I'm all ready to fix—just let me have the stuff.

Al is hooked. He's looking for his dealer, so he can buy a spoon of smack. The dealer has just received a kilo of the stuff, and has cut it and packaged it into dime bags and balloons. Al finds him and scores. He goes to his pad and gets his kit. Because Al is a mainliner, he cooks up his stuff, ties off, and fixes. Al feels the rush, and before long, he's on the nod. He starts thinking about how he got where he is. He remembers how he used to drop reds and blow a joint once in a while. Then, a user started him on shit, and he soon went from chipping to being totally strung out. Now, he wonders if he will ever be able to clean up.

INDEX

All references are to page numbers.

 md

md

Index

 md

 md

md

 md

 md

 md

Index

 md

 md

 md

 md

 md

 md

 md

 md

Index

 md

This page intentionally left blank.

MCC UMBREIT LIBRARY
103276